BUKHARIN

and the Bolshevik Revolution

BUKHARIN
and the
Bolshevik Revolution

A Political Biography
1888–1938

STEPHEN F. COHEN

VINTAGE BOOKS

A Division of Random House
New York

FIRST VINTAGE BOOKS EDITION, January 1975

Copyright © 1971, 1973 by Stephen F. Cohen

Library of Congress Cataloging in Publication Data

Cohen, Stephen F
    Bukharin and the Bolshevik Revolution: a political biography, 1888–1938.
      Bibliography: p.
      1. Bukharin, Nikolai Ivanovich, 1888–1938.
    2. Russia—Politics and government—1917–1936.
    3. Russia—Economic policy—1917–1918.   I. Title.
[DK268.B76C63 1975]   947.084'092'4 [B]   74-7047
ISBN 0–394–71261–7

Grateful acknowledgment is made to the following for permission to reprint previously published material:

The New York Times: For an excerpt from an article by Harold Denny, March 14, 1938. © 1938 by The New York Times Company. Reprinted by permission.

Political Science Quarterly: For permission to reprint "Marxist Theory and Bolshevik Policy: The Case of Bukharin's Historical Materialism," by Stephen F. Cohen, *Political Science Quarterly*, 85 (March 1970), 40–60.

To the Memory of My Father,

Marvin S. Cohen

We soon find how different were the antecedents and the capacities of the men whom the Revolution attracted and used; how many currents flowed into its flood; and how impossible it is to include all its aspects or ideas within the scope of an epigram, or the terms of a definition.

—J. M. THOMPSON, *Leaders of the French Revolution*

The history of the party is the history of our life.

—AN OLD BOLSHEVIK WHO SURVIVED,

1965

This book originated under the auspices and with the support of the Research Institute on Communist Affairs, Columbia University.

CONTENTS

PREFACE

THIS IS A BOOK about the Bolshevik revolution and about one of its most important and representative figures, Nikolai Ivanovich Bukharin.

First and foremost, the book is a political and, because Bukharin was a man of ideas, a Marxist thinker, an intellectual biography. The need for a full-scale study of Bukharin is obvious, since for more than two decades his career was central to the turbulent history of the Bolshevik Party and Soviet Russia. Yet, because his role as a founding father has been maligned by official Soviet historiography, he is sometimes remembered only as the author of several once-famous Communist handbooks and as the chief defendant and victim of the Moscow purge trials of 1938. Often obscured is Bukharin's eminence as a ranking member of Lenin's original revolutionary leadership and of the ruling party's Politburo until 1929, as the editor of *Pravda* and for almost a decade the official theorist of Soviet communism, and as the head of the Communist International from 1926 to 1929. His role in Soviet politics after Lenin's death was especially important, as co-leader with Stalin of the party between 1925 and 1928, and as the main architect of its moderate domestic policies which pursued an evolutionary road to economic modernization and socialism; as leader of the anti-Stalin opposition during the fateful events of 1928–9; and, even in defeat, as the symbol of Bolshevik resistance to the rise of Stalinism in the 1930's. Nor are Bukharin and Bukharinism without contemporary significance in the Communist world, where his ideas concerning a more consensual society and humane socialism have experienced a remarkable revival since Stalin's death.

The other purpose of this book has been to study Bukharin as a way of reexamining the Bolshevik revolution and the formative decades in Soviet history. I have been guided in this by the venerable assumption that by focusing upon an important part, the whole can be made clearer and more understandable. Except in Chapter IV (which departs from chronology to discuss Bukharin's famous work on Marxist social theory, *Historical Materialism*), I have tried to present and interpret Bukharin's politics and ideas in the larger context of Bolshevik party politics and Soviet history. I hope that whatever shortcomings this approach may impose upon the book as formal biography will be compensated for by the new insights it may yield.

Indeed, a full study of Bukharin based on Russian materials[1] becomes "revisionist" in specific as well as more general ways. In addition to his own central role, Bukharin was a prolific (and often official) commentator on the events of his time. As one historian has observed: "There is virtually no aspect of the first twenty years of the Soviet experience which can be explored without recourse to Bukharin's views on the subject."[2] Thus, reexamining the history of the Bolshevik revolution through the prism of Bukharin promises to broaden our knowledge, and at times revise our understanding, of major episodes, from the shaping of Bolshevik radicalism on the eve of revolution, the nature of party politics and policy disputes during the crucial decade of the 1920's, to the murky political history of the Soviet 1930's, which culminated in Stalin's great purge and the destruction of the old Bolshevik Party.

I do not wish to be misunderstood nor to obscure what should be emphasized. This book relies heavily upon, indeed could not have been written without, the work of those scholars whose pioneering writings inform these pages and are cited regularly in the notes. I wish only to say that in telling the story of Bukharin, I have tried also to illuminate the larger events and developments about which our knowledge remains elliptical.

More generally, I regard this book as a contribution to the ongoing effort by various scholars to revise the customary interpretation which views the Bolshevik revolution after Lenin chiefly in terms of a Stalin-Trotsky rivalry. Much of what follows will suggest that by the mid-twenties Bukharin, what he represented, and his allies were more important in Bolshevik politics and thinking than Trotsky or Trotskyism. It will suggest, in short, that the view of Trotsky "as the representative figure of pre-Stalinist communism and the precursor of post-Stalinist communism" is a serious misconception.[3] This issue relates in turn to the prevailing view that Stalinism was the logical, irresistible outcome of the Bolshevik revolution, an assumption now being contested by a growing number of Soviet and Western writers, myself among them.

All biographers ought to resist overstating the importance of their subject. I may have failed, but if I have I hope that the evidence presented here is nonetheless sufficient to show that the Bolshevik party was far more diverse in character than is often imagined, and the outcome of the revolution considerably less predetermined. To persuade the general reader of that, and to encourage other scholars to reconsider questions that have seemed to many to be settled, would be contribution enough.

This said, the reader should know also that this book must sometimes be incomplete and tentative in its presentation and judgments. While Bukharin's career and thinking up to 1928–29 are substantially matters of public record, accessible in Western libraries, his last years, like the traumatic political history of which they were a part, remain considerably more obscure. After his political defeat in 1929, little that was reliable appeared about Bukharin in Soviet publications; and for twenty years after his arrest in 1937, he could be mentioned only as an "enemy of the people."

Although the easing of Soviet historical censorship since Stalin's death in 1953 has produced much valuable information about the pre-Stalinist period, Bukharin himself still remains an officially proscribed and distorted subject. Even after (to borrow from Trotsky's biographer) "the huge load of calumny and oblivion" imposed by two decades of Stalinist invective is scraped away, important aspects of Bukharin's life and times are still unclear, and the process of reconstructing them, as other writers have observed, is sometimes akin to paleontology. In particular, we know very little about the private lives and thoughts of Bukharin and other old Bolsheviks, partly because of their common reticence about such matters and partly because of their collective fate under Stalin. Suffice it to point out that of all the Soviet founding fathers, including Lenin, only Trotsky has left us a real autobiography and uncensored private papers.

Even a book which gathers everything now available about Bukharin, as I believe this one does, cannot, therefore, lay claim to being "definitive." When Soviet scholars are eventually able to study and write freely about their revolutionary founders and their formative history, the account in this book will presumably be supplemented, and some of its judgments revised.

*　　*　　*

Whatever that is good in a book covering a large and complex period and touching upon many subjects always reflects the generous help of friends and colleagues. I wish to acknowledge and express deep gratitude here to the many people who have assisted me during the seven years I worked on this study. Whatever remains that is wrongheaded is there despite, not because of, their assistance.

My greatest debt is to Robert C. Tucker, who for more than a decade has been my teacher, friend, and colleague. He introduced me to Soviet politics, taught me to be scholarly and critical-minded, and he has repeatedly taken time from his own work to comment critically on this manuscript. Without his inspiration and encouragement, it would not have been written.

Four other fellow scholars have read all, or large parts, of the manuscript: George Enteen, Alexander Erlich, Loren Graham, and John N. Hazard. Each has advised and corrected me in many ways, and whenever necessary tolerated my stubborn inability to change my mind or to do better. Robert Conquest, Zdenek David, A. G. Löwy, Sidney Heitman, the late Boris I. Nicolaevsky, and Robert M. Slusser regularly answered my questions and generously shared their great knowledge with me.

I owe special thanks to my friend William Markle, who miraculously reproduced from decrepit publications several of the photographs which appear here, and to my editors, Angus Cameron and Ed Victor, who guided me in ways too numerous to list. In addition, the following people have helped me research and prepare the manuscript over the years: Priscilla Bua, Marvin Deckoff, Lorna Giese, Margot Granitsas, Birgitta Ingemanson, Norman Moscowitz, Thomas Robertson, Anthony Trenga, and Carl Walter.

The preparation of this book has also been assisted by the financial support of several institutions. The Research Institute on Communist Affairs of Columbia University enabled me to develop what began as a doctoral thesis into a larger, full-scale study. I am deeply grateful to that community of scholars and to its Director, Zbigniew Brzezinski, for early and sustained support. I have received and appreciated additional grants to continue my work from the following institutions: the American Council of Learned Societies; the Center of International Studies of Princeton University; and the Council on International and Regional Studies and Committee on Research in the Humanities and Social Sciences, both of Princeton University. I also wish to thank the Russian Institute of Columbia University and its Director, Marshall D. Shulman, for allowing me to participate in its intellectual life over the years, and the Houghton Library of Harvard University for permission to use materials in the Trotsky Archives.

Parts of this book appeared earlier in the journals *Soviet Studies* and *Political Science Quarterly*, and in the collection *Revolution and Politics in Russia: Essays in Memory of B. I. Nicolaevsky*, edited by Alexander and Janet Rabinowitch (Bloomington: Indiana University Press, 1972). I gratefully acknowledge the editors' permission to incorporate those sections here.

Finally, I owe deep gratitude but also something more to Lynn, Andrew, and Alexandra, who have put up with Bukharin and without me for far too long. To them I owe and hereby give a heartfelt apology.

New York City   S.F.C.
December 1972

Note on Transliteration

THERE IS no entirely happy solution to the problem of transliterating Russian names and words into English. I have followed the familiar Library of Congress system, but with two exceptions. First, I have dropped the Russian soft sign, represented in English by an apostrophe, from names and words appearing in the text—thus, *Sokolnikov*, not *Sokol'nikov*—while retaining the sign in all bibliographical references. Second, wherever there is a customary English usage, I have allowed it to prevail: thus, *Trotsky* rather than *Trotskii*, and *Krupskaya* rather than *Krupskaia*—but, *Tomskii* and *Piatikov*.

One highly characteristic feature of Soviet revolutionary writing was the emphatic polemical style of political discourse, which in print frequently took the form of italics. All italics in materials quoted in this book appear in the original.

BUKHARIN

and the Bolshevik Revolution

CHAPTER I

The Making of
an Old Bolshevik

*He who seeks the salvation of the soul, of his own and
of others, should not seek it along the avenue of politics,
for the quite different tasks of politics can only be
solved by violence.*

—MAX WEBER

*I contend that a thinking, cultured person cannot
stand outside politics.*

—BUKHARIN

GREAT EVENTS GIVE RISE to enduring myths. In 1917, their rivals
having acted irresolutely, incompetently, or not at all, the Bolsheviks (later known as Communists) reached out and with stunning
ease took charge of the Russian revolution. From the audacity of
this act, played out against the indecision of other politicians, sprang
the legend that the Bolshevik leadership, unlike that of other political parties, was a united, homogeneous, singleminded group of men
and women. Although untrue, the myth lived on among students of
the revolution for many years.[1]

Apart from the leadership's own repeated insistence, especially
during moments of stormy internal discord, that the party had once
been characterized by "a single psychology and a single ideology," [2]
it is unclear why the legend had currency. The pre-1917 history of
Bolshevism—itself a product of factionalism within the Russian
Marxist or social democratic movement—related endless disputes
over fundamental issues, particularly between Lenin and his fellow
leaders. Even the decision to take power was a perfect example of
party disunity, bitterly opposed and briefly disavowed by many of

Lenin's oldest associates, including his chief lieutenants, Grigorii Zinoviev and Lev Kamenev. Nor did events after 1917 suggest an underlying unanimity on basic principles. From the rise of a powerful opposition to Lenin's domestic and foreign policies in early 1918 through the wide-ranging programmatic controversies of the Soviet twenties, the pattern of Bolshevik disunity continued and intensified, interrupted only by brief interludes of unity imposed by the desire to survive. As one Soviet historian later remarked, the party's leadership politics between 1917 and 1930 was "a thirteen-year factional struggle." [3]

After two decades of intra-party warfare and Stalin's fratricidal blood purges of the thirties, the myth of a monolithic Bolshevik leadership finally gave way to another, only partially more accurate myth. This argued that the movement had been characterized from the beginning by a fundamental duality—that two opposing currents had co-existed within the party. On one side were the Bolshevik "Westerners," the party intelligentsia, who had lived abroad before 1917, assimilating Western political and cultural traditions, and who represented Bolshevism's link with European socialism and its internationalist impulse. On the other side, it is said, were the party's "natives," Bolsheviks who had remained in Russia and operated the underground organization before the revolution. Skilled in organizational politics rather than ideas, pragmatic and little concerned with traditional socialist values, the "natives" are seen as representing Bolshevism's nationalist tendency and the embryo of the post-1917 party bureaucracy, the *apparatchiki*.

Bolshevik politics after 1917, the argument continues, may be viewed in terms of this duality.[4] During the first years of Bolshevik rule, the Westernized intellectuals dominated the party leadership, but were defeated and ousted in the late twenties by the "natives," the party bureaucrats led and personified by Stalin. Because this concept of a bifurcated movement suggests one source of future party disunity, namely, the conflict between internationalist and nationalist currents, it is closer to reality than the original myth. However, it fails by suggesting that among the Western-oriented intellectuals there was a fundamental identity of outlook.

The opposite was true. On the eve of the revolution, the party's "Westerners" included many types of Bolsheviks and almost as many understandings of Bolshevism. Indeed, it was largely their disagreements that generated the substantive political controversies of the first post-revolutionary decade. In addition to their diverse personalities and intellectual backgrounds, they were a heterogeneous group reflecting, among other things, the multi-national character of the pre-revolutionary Russian empire, as well as the generational split between fathers and sons already present within the "old Bolshevik" movement itself. These and other divisive factors were to play a conspicuous role in party disputes after 1917.

Most important, the original Bolshevik leaders—the intelligentsia—were not, as is often assumed, united by their common adherence to Marxism.[5] Due partly to the richness of Marx's thought, his followers have rarely agreed on its interpretation or political application. Bolsheviks were no exception. Though Russian Bolshevism was only one small current of European Marxism before 1917, it included rival intellectual schools and political tendencies of its own. Some Bolsheviks had been influenced by other European Marxisms, some by non-Marxist ideas, some by Russian populism or anarchism. In part, of course, their subsequent political disagreements derived from the unexpected victory in backward, agrarian Russia of a Marxist party whose revolutionary doctrines related to mature industrial societies. But even those Marxist propositions that were commonly accepted—the efficacy of economic planning, for example—soon generated bitter controversy.[6] In short, behind the facade of professed political and organizational unity known as "democratic centralism," there was no consensual Bolshevik philosophy or political ideology in 1917, or for several years thereafter. Rather, "party members exhibited a remarkable variety of views: the differences ranged from those of emphasis to serious conflicts of outlook." [7]

Unlike the legend, then, Bolshevism came to power and for several years remained a diverse movement led by dissimilar men and women who had followed various roads to the October revolution. The party was less an ideological or even organizational monolith than *"a negotiated federation between groups, groupings, factions, and 'tendencies,'"* [8] though this its leaders sternly denied. Such federation is true of political parties generally, and probably also describes the leadership of all major revolutions. We begin, therefore, as did a historian of the French revolution, by being aware of "how different were the antecedents and the capacities of the men whom the Revolution attracted and used; how many currents of thought flowed into its flood; and how impossible it is to include all its aspects or ideas within the scope of an epigram, or the terms of a definition." [9]

*   *   *

Nikolai Ivanovich Bukharin was born in Moscow on September 27 (October 9, new style), 1888,* the second son of Ivan Gavrilovich and Liubov Ivanovna Bukharin. We know nothing of the lives of his brothers, Vladimir and Petr; they are mentioned only once in the history of revolutionary Russia, in a police dossier prepared on Nikolai. Little more is known about Bukharin's mother, the former Liubov Ismailova. Like his father, she was a Moscow primary school teacher in the 1880's. In a brief autobiographical essay written in 1925, Bukharin remembered her as "a very sensible woman of rare honesty and diligence, who doted on her children" and who was puzzled by but tolerated the occasionally bizarre antics of her middle son. On discovering that he no longer shared the family's orthodox religion, the young Nikolai wondered: "Am I not the Antichrist?" Since "the mother of the Antichrist had to be a prostitute, I interrogated my mother," who was "embarrassed and could in no way understand how I could ask such questions." [10]

Ivan Gavrilovich appears to have been the model father of a Russian revolutionary—a man of traditional leanings, orthodox in religion, and conservative, or possibly liberal when that became fashionable, in politics. A graduate of Moscow University and a mathematician by training, he remained a Moscow schoolteacher until about 1893, when he obtained a position as tax inspector and moved the family to the distant province of Bessarabia. (Except for a brief stay in 1918, when Petrograd was the revolutionary capital, these four years in Bessarabia were the only time during Bukharin's life in Russia when he lived voluntarily outside Moscow. He was a Muscovite, a fact that later acquired political importance.)

The family's fortunes become obscure at this point. Ivan Gavrilovich having relinquished or lost his post, the Bukharins returned to Moscow in 1897. Two years of unemployment followed, during which the family was in "great need." In his autobiography, Bukharin says nothing more about his father's fortunes, though one learns elsewhere that by 1911 Ivan Gavrilovich had bettered himself considerably, having acquired the official title of provincial councillor,[11] a position fixed at rank seven on the fourteen-rank system governing the czarist civil service and which bestowed personal (not hereditary) nobility on the holder. It is unlikely that Bukharin was embarrassed by his father's subsequent success. Like Marx and Engels, few Bolshevik leaders were of working-class

---

* Until the changeover in 1918, Russia's calendar was twelve days behind the Gregorian Calendar in the nineteenth century and thirteen behind in the twentieth. Unless otherwise noted, Russian dates prior to 1918 are given here according to the old calendar.

origins. Bukharin in particular had no cause for embarrassment. The careers of his father and Lenin's father were strikingly similar: both were university graduates (not a common achievement in nineteenth-century Russia) and mathematicians; both began as schoolteachers and later made their way up through the civil bureaucracy. In this respect, Lenin's father was even more successful, attaining rank four and thus hereditary nobility.[12]

However divergent their political views, Bukharin always regarded his father, who was still alive in the 1930's, with love and admiration.[13] A genuinely cultured man, Ivan Gavrilovich devoted himself to the boy's education, and was partly responsible for his becoming the most intellectual and broadly educated of the Bolshevik political leaders. His parents, Bukharin wrote, educated him "in the usual spirit of the intelligentsia: at four and a half years, I could already read and write." In addition, three lifelong interests originated under his father's influence. One was natural history, the "passion of my childhood." [14] Visitors to Soviet Russia would later report that no gift pleased Bukharin more than a rare addition to his collection of birds and butterflies. His lepidopteral knowledge was sufficient to impress Ivan Pavlov, another amateur enthusiast; and tales of his private menagerie, which in the twenties filled a summer cottage and overflowed into the Kremlin cellar, became legendary.[15] His father also fostered in him an enduring interest in world literature, the background of Bukharin's prominence as a Bolshevik literary critic, and in art. The latter preoccupation grew into another "passion," and before discovering that "one life could not be divided between two such exacting gods as art and revolution," Bukharin considered becoming a painter. After 1917, this ambition found a lesser outlet in political caricatures, which foreign Communists counted among their prized possessions.[16]

These early years of "unsystematic" learning and reading "positively everything" formed an essential part of Bukharin's education. Many Bolshevik leaders were members of the intelligentsia, but few were truly intellectuals, seekers in the world of ideas. Most entered revolutionary politics at an early age with limited formal education, and even those who went on to a university were soon swept into the student movement, usually to the detriment of their studies (as would be the case with Bukharin). As a result, while politically articulate and ideologically sophisticated, their horizons and interests often did not extend beyond the limits of prevailing socialist doctrine. When Bukharin joined the party at seventeen, he had already acquired the intellectual curiosity and background, including a knowledge of foreign languages, that were to work against the likelihood of his viewing Bolshevism, or even the larger body of Marxist thought, as a closed system. He became the most versatile of the Bolshevik theorists, and throughout his adult life the political leader most familiar with and influenced by contemporary, non-Marxist ideas.

Bukharin's intellectual dissidence also seems to have originated early in life. While his assertion that he had developed "an ironic attitude toward religion" before his fifth birthday may be taken with some skepticism, the family's hard times after returning to Moscow apparently did affect him deeply. He began to look upon contemporary urban life "not without some contempt." During his primary school years, he underwent a "spiritual crisis"—a standard event in the life of a fledgling Russian intellectual—and "broke decisively with religion." If this troubled Bukharin's orthodox parents, they were probably consoled by his academic success. In 1900 or 1901, having completed primary school with the highest marks, he entered one of Moscow's best gymnasiums. The curriculum, a classical humanities program designed to prepare the schoolboy for the university, was demanding and of high quality. He again compiled an outstanding record, "not exerting any effort." [17]

It was in the gymnasium that Bukharin, like many others of his generation, first encountered political radicalism. The Russian gymnasium, with its emphasis on the classics, sought to inculcate a reverence for traditional society. Instead, it often served as a way station on the road to revolutionary politics, the school's rigid discipline apparently provoking widespread defiance of authority. In the lower grades, student dissidence took innocuous forms—surreptitious smoking, gambling, cribbing, and defacing lavatory walls. But by the time Bukharin entered the upper grades, on the eve of the 1905 revolution, student dissent had become more sophisticated. He became a member of a radical student group that organized discussion circles and circulated illegal literature. His initial political leaning was "quite harmless," being influenced by the nineteenth-century thinker Dmitrii Pisarev, whose association with nihilism and glorification of a "critically thinking" revolutionary élite had perpetuated his appeal among Russian youth. By the autumn of 1904, however, Bukharin and his fellow students had "passed through the stage of *Pisarevshchina*" and on to ideas more appropriate to the times.[18]

Russia's disastrous war with Japan in 1904–5 had exposed dramatically the profound backwardness and crippling injustices of czarist society. Social unrest and open protest, on the rise since

1900, deepened and spread. The peasantry (over 80 per cent of the population), resentful about its semi-feudal burdens and hungering for land, turned increasingly to sporadic acts of violence against landlords and their great estates; the small but growing industrial proletariat tested its strength in successive waves of strikes; and in the cities, educated political opposition of all shades grew more vocal and daring. The forces of approaching revolution were also felt in the gymnasium, where the oppositionist ideologies of nineteenth-century Russia yielded to the updated populism of the Socialist Revolutionary Party and the Marxism of the Social Democratic Labor Party, itself already split into two rival wings—the radical Bolsheviks, headed by Lenin, and the more moderate Mensheviks. Symptomatic of the student mood, constitutional liberalism, despite its considerable success in the larger political arena, found few sympathizers in the gymnasium. Bukharin and his friends invited the well-known Marxist professor Mikhail Pokrovskii to speak to their circle, and were impressed by his passionate anti-liberalism and "proletarian Jacobinism." [19]

By 1905, at sixteen, Bukharin was already a leading member of the illegal student movement associated with the social democrats.[20] Characteristically, he was first attracted to the Marxist movement less by its political stance than by the "unusual logical harmony" of Marxist social theory. Socialist Revolutionary theories, on the other hand, "seemed to me to be some kind of pap." [21] His political commitment, however, developed quickly during the turbulent events of 1905.

From "Bloody Sunday" in January, when czarist troops fired into an unarmed crowd bearing a petition of grievances, until the crushing of the Moscow insurrection in December, Russia witnessed an epidemic of political agitation and opposition. Throughout the year, the voice of the autocracy's opponents, repressed for decades, made itself heard unceasingly; and with each passing month it grew more radical. By summer, the influence of liberal opposition to czarism was on the wane, and the revolutionary parties, particularly the social democrats in Moscow, moved into the foreground.[22] "The workers and the student youth literally seethed," Bukharin wrote thirty years later. "Meetings, demonstrations, and strikes multiplied. The crowds moved through the streets . . . and everywhere 'The Workers' Marseillaise' rang out: 'Arise, revolt, toiling masses!' " [23] Czarism survived this revolutionary prelude to 1917. But in defeat, the Russian Marxist movement acquired new symbols and fresh affirmation of its faith. The Moscow and St.

Petersburg Soviets, the Moscow general strike, and the December barricades seemed to prove at last that European Marxism and the Western insurrectionary model were applicable to peasant Russia.

The feverish disorders of that year drew Bukharin and a generation of like-minded schoolboys out of the gymnasium and into the arena of serious revolutionary politics. The center of their activity was Moscow University, the revolutionary "meeting hall" of 1905 and the scene of "exciting events." In its lecture rooms, emptied of classes by student strikes, schoolboys sat day and night alongside university students, workers, and professional revolutionaries, watching "speeches made, resolutions adopted, decisions taken." The writer Ilya Ehrenburg, Bukharin's schoolboy friend and comrade, recalled: "We sang the 'Marseillaise.' . . . Huge hats inscribed 'Your contribution means arms for us' were passed from hand to hand." Their participation was not merely vicarious. Social democratic propaganda was conducted largely by young students.[24]

Although he did not formally join the party until the following year, the events of 1905 "completed" Bukharin as a "revolutionary Marxist-Bolshevik." [25] Once in contact with the social democratic movement, he was drawn directly to its militant Bolshevik faction. Moscow was one of the few cities where the Bolsheviks were stronger than their Menshevik rivals, and where they controlled most of the party committees. Their success in attracting a popular following in 1905 was remarkable. The Bolshevik appeal to a schoolboy may have been as simple as Ehrenburg suggests: he "understood that the Mensheviks were moderates, more like my father." [26] Whatever the reason, Bolshevism made dramatic gains among Bukharin's contemporaries; he was only the most famous of a generation of future party leaders recruited during the revolutionary events surrounding 1905. (Of 171 delegates responding to a questionnaire circulated at the party congress in July–August 1917, 58 had joined Bolshevik organizations between 1904 and 1906, and 23, the largest single group, in 1905. The average delegate age was twenty-nine—the seventeen-year-old schoolboy of 1905.[27]) In Bukharin and his contemporaries, the party acquired its second generation of leaders, a group, particularly the Muscovites, distinguished by generational associations, loyalties, and, as would be evident in 1917–18, a strong sense of political identity and confidence.

The last spasms of the failed revolution passed in 1906, and Russia settled down to test the short-lived, quasi-constitutional concessions of a reluctant czar. For Bukharin and his friends, it meant a year of political transition and decision, as Ehrenburg explains: "There were no more meetings at the University, nor demonstrations, nor barricades. That year I joined the Bolshevik organization, and soon it was good-bye to my schooldays." [28] Older than Ehrenburg and already graduated from the gymnasium, Bukharin also joined a Bolshevik organization in the second half of 1906.[29] At seventeen, he thus became what Lenin called a professional revolutionary, protected in his illegal activities by the party and working mainly as a Bolshevik organizer and propagandist during the next four years. Bukharin's presence among underground Bolshevik committeemen and organizers—the "natives"—suggests that they were not so clearly distinguishable from the party *intelligents*, of whom he was to be a leading example, nor as grim and humorless as is imagined. Ehrenburg later wrote: "We talked about party matters, but we used to joke and laugh as well . . . what good jokes Nikolai Ivanovich used to make, how bold and bright was our early youth." [30]

Bukharin's initial party assignment was as a propagandist in Moscow's Zamoskvoreche district. Most of his activities, now sufficiently prominent to bring him to the attention of the czarist political police (the Okhrana), involved the student movement of which he was a product. In the autumn of 1906, he and Grigorii Sokolnikov, another young Muscovite and later an important Soviet leader, united the Moscow youth groups into an all-city organization, and in 1907 they convened a national congress of social democratic student groups. The congress identified with the program and tactics of the Bolsheviks, and formed what was intended to be a permanent national organization, which dissolved the following year due to police harassment and the transfer of its leaders to other party work. (After 1917, the party's youth organization, the Komsomol, traced its ancestry back to the 1907 Moscow congress; Bukharin, then the Politburo's specialist on Komsomol affairs, was a personal link with its pre-revolutionary past.)[31] By 1907, Bukharin was also involved in industrial politics, he and Ehrenburg leading (or merely taking part in, the record is unclear) a strike at a large wallpaper factory.[32]

A professional revolutionary could supplement his occupation. Amidst his illegal activities, Bukharin also prepared for his university entrance examinations, entering Moscow University in the fall of 1907. Although he remained formally enrolled in the economics division of the juridical faculty until his administrative exile in 1910, he apparently spent little time in the classroom and even less pursuing an academic program.[33] Full-time party work and occasional appearances as a student at the university were wholly compatible.

The autocracy, having reconsidered its constitutional concessions, was now reverting to open repression, and Moscow University was again becoming a center of protest. Shortly after his admission, Bukharin and N. Osinskii (the alias of Valerian Obolenskii), another young Bolshevik, organized the university's first mass student rally since 1906.[34] His chief purpose in the university, however, appears to have been what he called "theoretical raids." Along with other Bolshevik students, Bukharin would appear at seminars to deliver Marxist critiques of "some venerable, liberal professor." [35]

The fact that political rather than academic affairs dominated Bukharin's time and energy was evidenced by his meteoric rise in the Moscow organization. In 1908, two years after joining the party, he was co-opted onto its city executive organ, the Moscow Committee, and made chief organizer in the large and important Zamoskvoreche district. His seat on the Moscow Committee was ratified by election in early 1909, which made Bukharin at twenty a ranking Bolshevik leader in Russia's largest city.[36] It also assured that the police would not leave him at liberty much longer. During a raid on the Moscow Committee in May 1909, Bukharin was arrested for the first time. Though released a few months later, the detention signaled the end of his uninhibited revolutionary activities; he was rearrested in the fall and again released, this time on security pending trial.[37]

His arrest was only a small episode in the downward turn in social democratic fortunes throughout Russia. The membership of the whole Social Democratic Labor Party, perhaps as high as 100,000 in 1907, had fallen to less than 10,000 in two years. No more than five or six Bolshevik committees were still operating in Russia, and the Moscow organization could boast only 150 members at the end of 1909.[38] Illegal work had become impractical, and some social democrats ("liquidators," as they were called) advocated disbanding the underground party machinery altogether. Bukharin strongly opposed "liquidationism," but he, too, found it necessary to turn to legal undertakings after his second release from prison. He worked in Marxist schools and political clubs and on a trade union newspaper until the autumn of 1910, when he went into hiding, presumably to avoid being rearrested for the forthcoming trial of the Moscow social democrats. He eluded the police until the end of the year, when the Okhrana, aided by informers in the party, rounded up the remaining Moscow leaders, including Bukharin, and virtually destroyed the remnants of the city organization.[39]

The circumstances leading to Bukharin's capture were later to influence his relations with Lenin. The party had been plagued by double agents for several years, a situation which attained ludicrous proportions in the Moscow organization where in 1910 no less than four of its leaders were Okhrana spies. Bukharin's final arrest, following a series of earlier incidents, convinced him that Roman Malinovskii, a high-ranking Moscow Bolshevik who had known his whereabouts, was a police spy.[40] This suspicion, which Lenin steadfastly refused to consider seriously, became an abiding source of friction between Bukharin and Lenin from their first meeting in 1912 until 1917, when Malinovskii's guilt was finally established by police archives. That Bukharin would be irked by Lenin's unwillingness to believe the charge was understandable. Betrayal by Malinovskii ended his pre-1917 career in Russia. Confined in Moscow's Butyrka and Sushchevka prisons for over six months, in June 1911 he was exiled to Onega in the remote province of Arkhangelsk. Believing that he would soon be transferred to a penal colony, he disappeared from Onega on August 30, 1911. He appeared next in Hanover, Germany, and did not return to Russia until 1917.[41]

When Bukharin left Russia in 1911 to take up the life of a wandering émigré, he was twenty-three, a five-year veteran of underground party committees and a rising Moscow Bolshevik whose revolutionary commitment had been tested in factories, streets, and prisons. The familiar appearance and personality of the later Bukharin were already evident in his casual dress and life style. He was a short (just over 5 feet), slightly built man with a boyish face and blue-gray eyes highlighted by prominent forehead, red hair, and thin beard. A woman who met him in émigré circles in Vienna in 1913 recalled that "Bukharin stood out . . . through a quality of his own. There was in his appearance something of a saint, rather than a rebel or thinker. . . . His open face with the huge forehead and clear shining eyes was in its quiet sincerity sometimes almost ageless." Attractive to women, easy with children, comfortable with workers as well as intellectuals, he was a "sympathetic person" even to political opponents. The youthful enthusiasm, conviviality, and puckish humor that later distinguished him as the "Benjamin" of the Bolshevik oligarchy, the "favorite of the whole party," had already impressed his acquaintances. They spoke of him as kind, gentle, expansive, and zestful.[42]

Less evident in the fragmentary record of Bukharin's early career are foretokens that he would become both a political maverick (and thus oppositionist) among Lenin's close associates, and, according to Lenin, Bolshevism's "biggest theoretician." Of his party politics before emigration, Bukharin later wrote: "I was always an orthodox Bolshevik . . . neither a 'recallist' nor a 'conciliator.' . . ." [43] In the two major factional disputes inside the Bolshevik Party * during these years—between Lenin and the left-wing "recallists" who opposed Bolshevik participation in the czarist parliament (the Duma), and Lenin and the right-wing "conciliators" who favored reconciliation and reunification with the Mensheviks—Bukharin stood with Lenin against both "deviations." His lack of sympathy for opponents of participation in the Duma is particularly significant, since they were strong in the radically oriented Moscow party. If nothing else, his "orthodoxy" belies the impression that Bukharin began his party career as a member of the uncompromising Bolshevik Left.

Hints that he would become the party's major theorist were more apparent. He had already begun to study, however "unsystematically," the main subjects of his mature theoretical work—economics, philosophy, and sociology. He is known to have published at least one article between 1906 and 1910, a critical review of a book by a Menshevik economist, and to have drafted an article on the revisionist economist Mikhail Tugan-Baranovskii, subsequently published in Germany in 1913. Theoretical economics, it is clear, had already become his specialty. [44] But the surest foreshadowing of the later Bukharin—if evidence presented by his admiring disciple Dmitrii Maretskii is reliable—was his early interest in contemporary, non-Marxist social theories. European thought after Marx, as Maretskii observed, had been largely ignored by "the previous generation of revolutionary Russian Marxists." [45] Bukharin's lifelong interest in it set him apart as a thinker from the older Bolsheviks, including Lenin.

His appreciation of new intellectual currents probably underlay his single "deviation" prior to emigration, "a certain heretical inclination toward the empirio-critics" represented in Russia by the Marxist philosopher Aleksandr Bogdanov. [46] Bogdanov, a high-ranking Bolshevik leader, had undertaken an ambitious attempt to formulate a philosophical synthesis of Marxism and the empiriocriticism of Mach and Avenarius. The result was a three-volume treatise, *Empiriomonism,* published between 1904 and 1908. Although Bogdanov's far-reaching revisions of Marx immediately set

---

* Until 1918, formally a wing of the Russian Social Democratic Labor Party. In 1918 the Bolshevik Party changed its name to the All-Russian Communist Party (Bolsheviks). It later became the All-Union Communist Party (Bolsheviks) and in 1952 the Communist Party of the Soviet Union.

off a heated ideological controversy in Marxist circles, Lenin stood aside from the debate for five years, apparently not wishing to jeopardize his political collaboration with the philosopher. By 1908, however, Bogdanov had emerged as the political leader of the Bolshevik Left (including the "recallists"), a development which brought an angry Lenin into the ideological campaign against him. The following year Bogdanov and the Left broke formally with Lenin's political leadership, and Lenin published his *Materialism and Empiriocriticism*, a relentless assault on Bogdanov's "reactionary philosophy." [47]

Bukharin followed the bitter philosophical controversy from Moscow (Lenin and Bogdanov were in exile in Europe). That he leaned toward Bogdanov was not surprising. *Materialism and Empiriocriticism*, its vaunted status in Soviet philosophy notwithstanding, was one of Lenin's least impressive efforts, while Bogdanov's writings, however questionable in their fidelity to Marx, constituted an exciting reinvestigation and adaptation of Marxist theory. Bukharin's later work, particularly *Historical Materialism* (1921), showed Bogdanov's enduring influence on his intellectual development. Bukharin was not, however, Bogdanov's disciple, as his party enemies were later to argue. He did not accept the older theorist's philosophical arguments, but rather admired and was influenced by his capacity for creative innovation within the framework of Marxist ideas. Theirs was a similarity of intellectual temperament. Like the mature Bukharin, Bogdanov was a "seeking Marxist," refusing to regard Marxism as a closed, immutable system and regularly alert both to its inadequacies and to the accomplishments of rival doctrines. Lenin, suspicious of Bogdanov's theoretical innovations and enraged by his political opposition, insisted that the two were somehow related and condemned him as unworthy in every respect. Bukharin, on the other hand, while sharing none of Bogdanov's political views, continued to respect him as a thinker. When the philosopher died in 1928, after almost twenty years outside the party, Bukharin published a moving tribute to this man who had "played an enormous role in the development of our party and in the development of social thought in Russia." [48] From their contrary estimations of Bogdanov was to come yet another source of friction between Bukharin and Lenin.

But neither his early philosophical leanings nor his factional politics influenced Bukharin's subsequent career as much as the fact that he was a Moscow Bolshevik and member of the impressive generation of future party leaders who came to Bolshevism as a result of 1905. The young Muscovites with whom he began his career—among them Osinskii, Vladimir Mikhailovich Smirnov, Sokolnikov, Grigorii Lomov, V. N. Iakovleva and her younger brother Nikolai, Grigorii Usievich, and Dmitrii Bogolepov [49]—and his continuing association with the Moscow party generally were to figure prominently in his political biography, from his rise to the inner Bolshevik council in 1917 and his leadership of the Left Communists in 1918, to his position as head of the Bolshevik Right in the 1920's. His personal friends among the Moscow generation of 1905 became his political allies in the intra-party struggles of 1917–18. The ties that made them a special group inside the party were personal as well as political. Included in their circle from 1906 to 1910, for example, was the young Bolshevik publicist and future Soviet historian Nikolai Lukin, whose sister, Nadezhda Mikhailovna Lukina, Bukharin married sometime between 1911 and 1913.[50]

His pre-emigration friendship with two young Muscovites, Osinskii and Smirnov, was to be particularly important. Like Bukharin, they came from a middle-class background, attended a Moscow gymnasium, were drawn into radical politics in 1905, joined the Bolsheviks in the aftermath (in 1907), and then entered Moscow University. They met Bukharin in 1909 in his role as a Bolshevik organizer of student groups (he was the senior political member of the threesome from the outset). They were first identified as a trio at the university, as student Bolshevik ideologists and leaders of the theoretical "raids." What drew Bukharin, Osinskii, and Smirnov (as well as the other young Muscovites generally) together was their youth, shared experiences, and mutual passion for Marxist theory (all three were economists). Together they rose in the Moscow party organization, studied Marxism, defended their ideas against rival parties, and, in the case of Bukharin and Osinskii, went to prison in 1910.[51] Above all, they shared a sense of generational identity in the party: compared to a "veteran" Bolshevik of thirty, they at first considered themselves to be "boys," [52] a deferential attitude that did not last very long. Bukharin's emigration temporarily disbanded the trio. But it regrouped in 1917 when he, Osinskii, and Smirnov came together in Moscow to challenge older party leaders unsympathetic to Lenin's radical course, and then again in 1918, when they challenged Lenin himself.

It was in emigration that Bukharin emerged as a major figure in the Bolshevik Party. Though already known to Lenin and the leadership abroad when he left Russia in 1911, he was identified mainly as a local committeeman with special responsibility for the student movement.[53] By the time he returned six years later, he was an acknowledged party leader, an established theorist who had contributed greatly to the development of Bolshevism as a separate and distinct ideological variety of European Marxism, and, insofar as the appellation had any meaning, one of Lenin's "close comrades-in-arms." In addition, emigration made him one of those Bolsheviks who were, by experience and in outlook, internationalists. For six years, he lived and worked among social democrats in Germany, Austria, Switzerland, Sweden, Norway, Denmark, and the United States. He became a familiar figure among Western socialists as well as anti-socialists: to his Russian arrests were added short prison stays in Europe and Scandinavia. (The Swedish police, falsely it seems, charged him with conspiring to blow up bridges.)[54]

At the same time, Bukharin's literary career began in earnest. Freed from the daily rigors of underground work in Russia, he immediately set out to complete his education. He familiarized himself with Western languages (by 1917 he read German, French, and English, speaking the first two well) and with recent theoretical literature. European and later American libraries provided what he called the "fixed capital" of his major theoretical work.[55] While he would later see these years abroad in terms of flawed ideas and political innocence, they constituted a formative and remarkably productive period in his career. A regular contributor to Marxist periodicals, he published several articles of enduring value on theoretical economics, completed the manuscripts of two books, *The Economic Theory of the Leisure Class* and *Imperialism and World Economy*, pioneered arguments that became a constituent part of Bolshevik ideology, and articulated concepts and interests central to his thinking for the rest of his life.[56] By 1917, his reputation as a Bolshevik theorist was second only to Lenin's; and in the minds of some, he had no peer.

Emigration also brought him into personal contact with Lenin for the first time, initiating one of the stormiest, sometimes most touching relationships in Bolshevik history. He saw Lenin infrequently between 1912 and 1917, and was rarely close, geographically or politically, to the small coterie of émigré Bolsheviks around the leader. Their relations were almost always strained, due partly to Lenin's intransigence and suspicion of ideological innovation, and partly to Bukharin's independence, a trait emphasized even by his initial destination on leaving Russia. Postponing the customary pilgrimage to Lenin, then living in Cracow, he went directly to Hanover. Germany, the country of Marx and of the largest social democratic party in the world, held a strong attraction for Bolshevik intellectuals of Bukharin's generation.[57] He stayed almost a year, during which he established contact with the Bolshevik Central Committee abroad. In September 1912, he represented the party at the German Social Democratic Congress in Chemnitz, after which, having decided to move to Vienna, he traveled to Cracow (under the name of Orlov) to meet Lenin.[58]

It could not have been an auspicious beginning. They had "quite a long talk," in which Malinovskii undoubtedly figured prominently. The police agent had now risen to the Central Committee, having become head of the Bolshevik delegation in the Duma and the ranking party leader inside Russia. Other Bolsheviks (as well as Mensheviks) had repeatedly warned Lenin about him; but the accumulating reports only provoked his anger against Malinovskii's detractors. Each time, including the occasion when he received Bukharin's evidence, he paid no heed. This stubbornness must have shaken Bukharin's faith in Lenin's judgment and reinforced his opposition later when programmatic and ideological questions divided them.[59] Nor did Lenin quickly forgive Bukharin's willingness to believe the worst about his trusted lieutenant. Attacking Bukharin's theoretical views in 1916, he charged that in addition to having succumbed to "semi-anarchistic ideas," Bukharin was "credulous toward gossip," a clear reference to the Malinovskii affair.[60]

Nonetheless, their first meeting was not a disaster. Bukharin came to Lenin as an admiring follower and departed, or so he remembered thirteen years later, with his "perspectives broadened, new worlds discovered." Despite Lenin's "obsession" about Malinovskii and their disagreements in emigration, Bukharin's personal affection for the leader endured.[61] Lenin, in turn, was prepared to overlook temporarily Bukharin's addiction to "rumors." Czarist reaction and the defection of the Bogdanovists had thinned the ranks of his supporters; a promising young follower was to be welcomed. He invited Bukharin to contribute to the party's theoretical journal Prosveshchenie (Enlightenment), help solicit funds and materials for its newspaper Pravda, and participate in speech-writing and strategy sessions for the Duma Bolsheviks. Bukharin accepted, remaining in Cracow for several weeks before taking up residence in Vienna in late 1912. No serious disagreements troubled their relationship during the following two years. Pleased by Bukharin's articles and his energetic work on behalf of the party, Lenin paid him the honor of a visit in Vienna in June 1913.[62]

It seems clear in retrospect that this rare two-year period of harmony in their political relations derived largely from the fact that Bukharin was engaged in the least controversial project of his theoretical career. He had moved to Vienna to begin "a systematic criticism of the theoretical economics of the new bourgeoisie," that is, of the growing body of work by non-Marxists and Marxists alike which had appeared over the past thirty years challenging Marx's basic economic theories. Bukharin particularly wanted to confront Marx's academic critics and take up the defense of orthodox Marxist theory: while "the correctness of Marx's conception is borne out by the facts, its acceptance among official scholars is not only not advancing, but even declining." [63]

He chose as his first target Marx's most influential critic, the Austrian school of economics headed by Eugen von Böhm-Bawerk, Karl Menger, and Frederick von Wieser. Attacking Marx at his most vulnerable point, the labor theory of value, and arguing their own theory of marginal utility (according to which value is determined not by the amount of labor incorporated in a product, but by its utility to individual buyers), the Austrians had challenged Marx's fundamental analysis of capitalist economics. The labor theory of value underlay Marx's understanding of capitalist profit and accumulation, and, above all, his contention that he, unlike previous socialists, had demonstrated capitalism's exploitative nature scientifically rather than morally. The considerable success of Austrian marginalism in the early 1900's, particularly Böhm-Bawerk's *Karl Marx and the Close of His System* (1896), drew Bukharin, like a holy avenger, to the University of Vienna, where he attended the lectures of Böhm-Bawerk and Wieser. [64] His theoretical writings of 1912–14—a series of articles and a book—were devoted to the defense of orthodox Marxist theory against the Austrian school and other Western and Russian "bourgeois" critics. [65]

The Economic Theory of the Leisure Class, Bukharin's attack on Austrian marginalism and his first book, was completed in the autumn of 1914. While drawing heavily on earlier critiques of marginalism, his contribution was to combine the existing "methodological criticism" with a "sociological criticism." The first approach had already been undertaken, most notably by the Austrian Marxist Rudolf Hilferding, and Bukharin did little more than restate fundamental Marxist propositions about the study of political economy and society generally: "The methodological difference between Karl Marx and Böhm-Bawerk may be summarized . . . as follows: objectivism-subjectivism, a historical standpoint—an unhistorical standpoint, the point of view of production—the point of view of consumption." To this he added a sociological analysis. Marginalism, he argued, was "the ideology of the bourgeois who has already been eliminated from the process of production"—the rentier. Brought to the fore during the evolution from industrial to monopoly capitalism, the rentiers constituted a parasitic and super-fluous group within the bourgeoisie—"its representatives often do not even cut their own coupons"—whose decisive economic inter-est lay in "the sphere of consumption," a social bias reflected in the marginalist ideology with its emphasis on individual, consumer preferences.[66]

Unlike much of his subsequent work, Bukharin's Vienna writ-ings were squarely in the mainstream of orthodox European Marx-ism. Any Marxist, Bolshevik or otherwise, who wished to preserve the labor theory of value could agree that *The Economic Theory of the Leisure Class* provided "a very valuable extension and deep-ening of . . . older Marxist criticism of Böhm-Bawerk." [67] Because it successfully combined two approaches to prove that marginalism was "a marginal theory of the marginal bourgeoisie," it became on its publication in 1919 a popular item in Marxist literature. Widely translated, it gave Bolshevism one of its few critical successes capa-ble of standing alongside Western defenses of orthodox Marxist economics. In Soviet Russia, it inevitably became the definitive statement on the Austrian school, a basic textbook in educational institutions where it was said that no one could treat the subject "without repeating the arguments of Comrade Bukharin." [68]

Apart from establishing Bukharin as a Marxist economist, the book's real importance was as the first stage of a lifelong project which he later envisaged as a multi-volume exposition and defense of Marxism's influence on contemporary thought. Though practi-cal politics prevented him from working on it regularly, this proj-ect, parts of which were published in the twenties and thirties, ensured that he would continue to follow closely new develop-ments in Western thought, particularly those which represented a direct challenge to Marxism as social science or revolutionary doc-trine.[69] From the late nineteenth century onward, many influential social theorists had in one way or another been responding to Marx's formidable intellectual legacy. Bukharin believed that their rival theories were to be answered with "logical criticism" rather than invective. Given his commitment to ideas, it was natural that he would be influenced, however obliquely, by these thinkers. For, while sharing the Marxist assumption that all theorizing reflects a class bias, he also presumed that non-Marxist theory "may and does discharge a socially useful work," and that "with a sufficiently critical attitude, it is possible to obtain from such performances abundant material for making one's own conclusions." [70] The impact of Marx's critics on Bukharin, unlike most Bolsheviks, was to be considerable. After 1917, for example, he became sharply aware of the implications of the élite theories of Pareto and Michels, and of the theories of bureaucracy by Max Weber, whom he regarded as the outstanding non-Marxist theorist, for the emerging Soviet order.[71]

Bukharin's Vienna period also brought him into contact with the most accomplished theoretical school of European Marxism, Austro-Marxism. Vienna was the home of Otto Bauer and Rudolf Hilferding, whose writings on monopoly capitalism and imperialism were the highest achievements of latter-day Marxism.[72] Austro-Marxism, particularly Hilferding's *Finance Capital: The Newest Phase in the Development of Capitalism,* was to have a lasting influence on Bukharin. Immediately, the discussion of monopoly capitalism and imperialism that he encountered in Vienna contributed to his decision in 1915 to turn from his research on bourgeois economic theory—he had been planning a volume on Anglo-American marginalism—to the nature of neo-capitalism itself. Even after 1917, when Bolsheviks contemptuously dismissed Austro-Marxists as "reformists," Bukharin retained a grudging admiration for their theoretical achievements, an intellectual sympathy not shared by many Bolsheviks, including Lenin.[73]

As Bukharin's stay in Vienna drew to a close in the summer of 1914, there were still no disagreements (apart from the Malinovskii affair which flared up again in May) between him and Lenin, who continued to approve and publish his articles.[74] Even the issue that was soon to divide them bitterly, the national question, had not yet generated friction. Lenin had paid increasing attention to the subject since 1912, and by 1914 had decided on a party slogan advocating the right of self-determination, a position seemingly in conflict with the internationalism of radical Marxism. But if Bukharin had misgivings in Vienna, they were not apparent. In January 1913, a Georgian Bolshevik, Iosif Stalin, came to Vienna on Lenin's instructions to prepare a programmatic article on "Marxism and the National Question." Bukharin assisted Stalin (who knew no Western languages), a collaboration producing no recorded disagreements between them or Lenin, who approved the final product. Indeed, as late as April 1914, Bukharin was drafting a speech on the nationalities question for the Duma Bolsheviks, an assignment presumably entrusted to him by Lenin.[75] His stay in Vienna ended with the coming of the First World War. He was arrested in

August in a roundup of aliens. A few days later, after the intervention of Austrian social democrats, he was deported to Switzerland, where he took up residence in Lausanne.[76]

The war profoundly altered the history of Bolshevism. In the end, of course, it brought down the czarist autocracy and laid the foundations for the party's victory in October 1917. More immediately, it alienated the anti-war Bolsheviks, irrevocably perhaps, from the loose agglomeration of social democratic parties known as the Second International, the overwhelming majority of which voted to support their respective governments in the approaching holocaust. As the sentimental proletarian internationalism that had given socialists a sense of community fell before the separate nationalisms of war, the idea of a Third International, still four years away, was born. For Bolsheviks like Bukharin, who had thought of themselves as European social democrats and adherents of the advanced Marxisms of Germany and Austria, the "betrayal" of the social democrats was "the greatest tragedy of our lives." [77] It made even the most Western-oriented among them, such as Bukharin, more sectarian in their outlook and less inclined to look beyond Russian Bolshevism for ideological or political guidance.

War also set the stage for Bukharin's long history of selective opposition to Lenin. Emigré Bolsheviks began gathering in Switzerland to decide the party's position and tactics in regard to the war (communication between the party sections abroad having broken down after the outbreak of hostilities). Lenin arrived in Bern in September, and scheduled a conference for early 1915. Bukharin, meanwhile, remained in Lausanne working on the Anglo-American economists and beginning a study of imperialism.[78] In late 1914, he became friendly with three young Bolsheviks living in the nearby village of Baugy: Nikolai Krylenko, Elena Rozmirovich, and her husband Aleksandr Troianovskii. He had known Troianovskii well in Vienna, but it was with the first two that he found himself in sympathy on a variety of political issues. The three decided to publish and edit a new party newspaper, Zvezda (The Star). Lenin learned of their plan from another source in January 1915 and reacted angrily.[79]

Why he did so is not fully clear. His professed objection was that scarce party funds should not be diverted to a new publication, but he also accused the Baugy group (as Bukharin, Krylenko, and Rozmirovich were known in early 1915) of launching a rival, oppositionist organ.[80] The charge was without basis, at least in regard to Bukharin, who as late as January still expressed "full principled solidarity" with Lenin. Explaining that Zvezda was conceived "not *as an opposition* ... but as a *supplement*," he asked Lenin: "What can you have against another party newspaper which in the very first editorial states that it stands on the viewpoint of the Central Organ?" [81] If the Baugy three shared a grievance against the leader, it concerned Malinovskii (Rozmirovich was also convinced of his guilt and had been rudely rebuffed by Lenin); there is no evidence that they had any oppositionist motives as yet. Rather, Lenin was reacting in a manner that characterized his relations with Bukharin and exacerbated their genuine disagreements for the next two years: he objected to any independent undertaking, whether organizational, theoretical, or political, on the part of young Bolsheviks, especially Bukharin.[82]

Substantive, though not irreconcilable, disagreements first appeared at the Bern conference in February and March, where Bukharin strongly dissented from four of Lenin's proposals relating to the war and the party's program. First, he opposed Lenin's appeal to the European petty bourgeoisie, arguing that in a revolutionary situation the small proprietor would inevitably support the capitalist order against the proletariat. Bukharin's disinterest in the petty bourgeoisie, peasant or otherwise, as an independent revolutionary force or potential ally remained constant until after 1917, when he placed just such an alliance at the center of his understanding of socialist revolution. Second, in a set of theses submitted to the conference, he criticized Lenin's emphasis on minimum democratic demands instead of specifically socialist ones. Third, he, Krylenko, and Rozmirovich supported Lenin's call to transform the "imperialist war into a civil war," but objected to his exclusion of peace slogans appealing to broader anti-war sentiment, and to his labeling Russia's defeat a "lesser evil"—they preferred to damn all belligerents equally. Finally, while endorsing Lenin's call for a new socialist international, the Baugy trio argued that it should include all anti-war social democrats, including left-wing Mensheviks around Lev Trotsky, whom Lenin was ostracizing. Bukharin and his friends simply wanted the new organization to be as broad as possible.[83]

Contrary to later Soviet and Western versions, Bukharin's opposition to Lenin at Bern was neither total nor ultra-leftist.[84] On the issues of peace slogans (which Lenin himself was to employ skillfully in 1917) and the composition of the proposed international, he, Krylenko, and Rozmirovich took a position less extreme in effect than Lenin's. As for Bukharin's theses, which no one else endorsed (he was very disappointed), they did not constitute a blanket rejection of the party's minimum program. He qualified his advocacy of socialist demands by adding that because "the *matur-*

ing of a socialist revolution is a more or less lengthy historic process, the proletariat by no means repudiates the struggle for partial reforms. . . ." And later in the conference, when Lenin had to defend crucial points in the party's minimum program against other dissidents, Bukharin supported him. The outcome of the conference showed that their differences involved emphasis rather than principle. A commission composed of Lenin, his erstwhile lieutenant Zinoviev, and Bukharin was appointed to reconcile the different points of view. Though, according to one participant, it required two days of "heated disputes . . . with Comrade Bukharin," the final resolution was adopted unanimously.[85]

This does not mean that the conflicts before and during Bern were inconsequential. Bukharin's independent posture in the *Zvezda* incident (resolved when the Baugy group reluctantly agreed to abandon the venture)[86] and at the conference itself, as well as the intrusion of the Malinovskii affair into other political questions, foreshadowed the bitter controversies that shortly followed. Moreover, it was at Bern that Bukharin began his association with Iurii Piatakov, another young Bolshevik who had just arrived from Russia and who became his closest friend in emigration.[87] Piatakov was an outspoken adherent of Rosa Luxemburg's thinking on the national question, which maintained that in the era of modern imperialism, when the world was being transformed into a single economic unit, national boundaries and appeals to nationalism were obsolete—a prognosis directly contrary to Lenin's new thinking on self-determination. Though the issue seems not to have arisen at Bern, Bukharin had already begun his own study of imperialism which led him to a position similar to Piatakov's. By late 1915, he, Piatakov, and the latter's wife, Evgeniia Bosh, were in fierce opposition to Lenin on the issue.

When the conference ended in March, however, Bukharin and Lenin parted amicably. They did not meet again until mid-1917. Bukharin returned to Swiss libraries and his study of contemporary capitalist developments. Correspondence between the two men resumed, revealing neither hurt feelings nor conflicting viewpoints. Lenin was in a conciliatory mood; at one point he even asked Bukharin to move to Bern to help edit the party's central organ.[88] In the spring of 1915, Piatakov and Bosh obtained some funds and proposed a new theoretical journal to be called *Kommunist*. In contrast to his reaction to *Zvezda*, Lenin agreed; an editorial board of himself, Zinoviev, Piatakov, Bosh, and Bukharin was formed.[89] Harmony seemingly restored, Bukharin decided (with Lenin's approval and perhaps at his urging) to move to Sweden, a key link in the Bolshevik underground route between Russia and Europe and a stronghold of radical Scandinavian social democrats, whose views on the war were close to the Bolsheviks'. In July 1915, under the improbable name of Moshe Dolgolevskii and in the company of Piatakov and Bosh, he journeyed through France and England (where he was arrested and detained briefly in Newcastle) to Stockholm.[90] There he settled to finish his book *Imperialism and World Economy* (completed in the autumn of 1915 but not published in full until 1918) and to begin a reinterpretation of the Marxist theory of the state—two works that contributed to a new Bolshevik ideology and represent his major achievements during emigration.

In the interconnected body of ideas that may properly be termed "Bukharinist," *Imperialism and World Economy*, rather than his earlier book on marginalism, was the opening statement and one of the most important. For the first time, Bukharin set out concepts and themes that, in one form or another, would be present in his thinking about international and Soviet affairs for the next twenty years. The small book included theoretical understandings that were to influence his politics as leader of both the Left and Right Bolsheviks. *Imperialism and World Economy* was another kind of landmark as well: it was the first systematic theoretical explanation of imperialism by a Bolshevik. Its completion predated Lenin's more famous *Imperialism, the Highest Stage of Capitalism* by several months, and Lenin borrowed freely from it.[91]

The book's originality lay less in its separate ideas than in the way in which Bukharin employed and extended existing Marxist insights into the nature of modern capitalism. The profound changes in capitalism since Marx's death, its enormous growth at home and the expansionist policies of the leading capitalist nations abroad, had been studied and debated by Marxists for more than a decade. Most agreed that at best Marx had only hinted at these developments and that latter-day capitalism was distressingly unlike the classical free enterprise system analyzed in *Capital*. A sizable body of literature adapting Marx's theories and prognoses to the reality of contemporary capitalism already existed by 1915. Bukharin, as he readily acknowledged, drew upon much of it; but his starting point and essential inspiration was Hilferding's *Finance Capital*, published in 1910 and immediately recognized as a seminal work in Marxist thought.[92]

Hilferding's achievement here was to relate the rise of imperi-

alism to the far-reaching structural changes within national capitalist systems, that is, to the transformation of laissez-faire capitalism
into monopoly capitalism. Extending Marx's analysis of the concentration and centralization of capital, he described the rapid
proliferation of combining forms of ownership and control, particularly trusts and cartels, which had to an unprecedented degree
devoured and supplanted smaller units. Hilferding paid special attention to the new role of the banks in the monopolization process,
pointing out that the concentration of capital had been accompanied and spurred on by the concentration and centralization of
the banking system. The modern bank, he observed, had emerged
as an owner of a large part of the capital employed by industry.
To accommodate this phenomenon, Hilferding introduced a new
analytical concept—finance capital: *"bank capital—that is, capital
in monetary form—which has in this way been transformed into
industrial capital, I call finance capital."* [93] Mature capitalism was
for him finance capitalism, a unique system, he went on to demon-
strate in great detail, distinguished from the laissez-faire model by
its powerful organizing tendencies. As finance capital permeated
the entire national economy and large combines became predominant, planned regulation gradually eliminated the economic anarchy
that had previously derived from the unfettered competition of
smaller units. National capitalism was increasingly becoming a
regulated economic system, or in the term closely associated with
Hilferding, "organized capitalism."

Finance Capital, in other words, was concerned mainly with
the national structure of neo-capitalism. Hilferding's theory of imperialism was little more than a by-product of this central analysis.[94]
Having monopolized the home market and erected high protective
tariffs against foreign competition, monopoly capitalism was led to
expansionist policies in its pursuit of higher profits: in colonies it
acquired raw materials and, above all, new markets for capital ex-
ports. In Hilferding's analysis, imperialism was the economically
logical foreign policy of finance capitalism. He indicated briefly
how similarly motivated capitalist powers competed for colonial
markets in the way individual enterprises had once competed on
the home market, a development which explained the increasing
militarization of modern capitalism and the growing belligerence
(he was writing well before the war) in international relations.

Bukharin took over Hilferding's theory of imperialism, but
with the intention of updating and, in significant respects, radicalizing it.[95] He, too, defined imperialism as "the policy of finance capitalism." Unlike Hilferding, however, he insisted that "finance

capital cannot pursue any policy other than an imperialist one . . .", and that therefore "imperialism is not only a system most intimately connected with modern capitalism, it is also the most essential element of the latter." More dogmatically than Hilferding, Bukharin formulated imperialism as an inevitable "historic category," one which must appear at a specific stage (the last) in capitalist development. Colonies providing raw materials and markets for surplus commodities and capital were essential to the very economic existence of monopoly capitalism: imperialism "upholds the structure of finance capitalism." With this argument, Bukharin was contesting the prevailing social democratic view that imperialist policies, while deplorable, were not an indispensable feature of capitalism.[96]

The definition of imperialism as an organic, inevitable manifestation of monopoly capitalism brought Bukharin, as it had Hilferding, to the question of war. But here, too, he differed from Hilferding in his certainty that, in the imperialist age, wars were inevitable. Bukharin regarded as "fantasy" the supposition, widespread among social democrats, that imperialist nations could coexist without war, that a further stage of capitalist development might witness the peaceable organization of the world economy ("ultra-imperialism," as Kautsky suggested). In the early period of colonialization, imperialist powers had aggrandized themselves with minimal conflict, through "the seizure of free lands." Noncolonized areas no longer remained, however; the necessity for "a fundamental redivision" had come. Competition among imperialist nations had reached its most acute form, armed struggle; desperate for new markets, they turned against each other with "fire and sword," the weak to be colonized by the strong.

The point of Bukharin's argument, of course, was that the First World War was neither a historical mishap nor a solitary conflagration; it was the first in an epochal series of "unavoidable" imperialist wars. But, he concluded, while the age of imperialism brought the horrors of war, it also revealed the final intensification of capitalism's fatal contradictions, and thus "the ripeness of the objective conditions" for socialist revolution.[97] Insofar as Bukharin's overall argument differed meaningfully from Hilferding's, it was in the way he translated the latter's insights into a sequential, and inevitable, historical equation: monopoly capitalism → imperialism → war → proletarian revolution.

If this scheme is familiar, it is because it reappeared (with some significant differences) in Lenin's *Imperialism* and became the orthodox Bolshevik interpretation of modern imperialism. The theory of imperialism, however (and even less of colonialism), formed only a part of Bukharin's book. For like Hilferding, but to a large extent unlike Lenin, he was deeply interested in the substructure of imperialism: national capitalism.[98] And it was in the course of updating and extending Hilferding's findings in this area that he formulated his theory of state capitalism, a concept about which he and Lenin were to argue for many years.

According to Bukharin, the monopolization and trustification of the capitalist economy had proceeded dramatically since Hilferding's writing. The elimination or subordination of weak competitors and intermediate forms of ownership, coupled with the relentless organizing energies of finance capital, had virtually transformed "the entire 'national' economy into a combined enterprise with an organizational connection between all the branches of production." Bukharin occasionally implied that this was still only a tendency, but more often he posited it as an accomplished fact: "Every one of the capitalistically advanced 'national economies' has turned into some kind of a 'national' trust." This contention was not present in Hilferding's analysis. Because trustification had come to involve a merging of industrial and bank interests with state power itself, he termed it a "state capitalist trust," and the system "state capitalism." While noting that mobilization for war had been largely responsible for the state's extensive intervention in the economy, he insisted that it was a permanent development: "the future belongs to economic forms that are close to state capitalism." [99]

The most striking feature of modern capitalism was for Bukharin the new interventionist role of the state. As the term "state capitalism" was meant to indicate, the state had ceased to be merely the political instrument of the ruling class (or classes), the disinterested adjudicator of laissez-faire economic competition between groups of the bourgeoisie. Instead it had become, through the agency of finance capital, a direct organizer and owner in the economy, "a very large shareholder in the state capitalist trust" and its "highest and all-embracing organizational culmination." The "colossal, almost monstrous, power" [100] of the new bourgeois state so impressed Bukharin that on finishing *Imperialism and World Economy* he immediately began a long article entitled "Toward a Theory of the Imperialist State." Completed by July 1916, it was in effect a sequel to his book.[101] In it, he elaborated on his theory of imperialism and state capitalism, and set out a radical reinterpretation of the Marxist view of the state.

He began by "rescuing" Marx and Engels's original understanding of the state. It was necessary to reiterate these "old truths," he explained, because revisionist social democrats, intent on collaborating with and reforming the bourgeois state, had forgotten or consciously expunged them from Marxism. They had betrayed Marx's essential proposition: "The state is nothing but *the most general organization of the ruling classes, the basic function of which is the maintenance and extension of the exploitation of the suppressed classes.*" Contrary to the reformists, Marx had regarded the state not as an "eternal" phenomenon, but as a "historical category" characteristic of class society and the product of class struggle. A classless, Communist society would, by definition, be a stateless society. In the meantime, Bukharin continued, the structure and nature of the state reflected the changing economic base of class society. Each era had its specific form: laissez-faire capitalism found its expression in the liberal, noninterventionist state; finance capitalism (or state capitalism) had its expression in the "imperialist state." [102]

What set the modern state apart from its predecessors was its "colossal" economic powers. Repeating his theory of the emergence of the "state capitalist trust," Bukharin documented (wartime Germany being his main example) the way in which the state had intervened in every sphere of economic life, regulating and "militarizing" the whole economy. As a result, the pluralistic capitalism of the laissez-faire era had given way to a form of "collective capitalism," whose ruling "finance capitalist oligarchy" conducted its predatory affairs directly through the state: "*The state power thus sucks in almost all branches of production; it not only maintains the general conditions of the exploitative process, the state more and more becomes a direct exploiter, organizing and directing production as a collective capitalist.*" The new system differed radically from the old, particularly in having eradicated the anarchistic "free play of economic forces." As "statization" culminates in the "final form of the state capitalist trust . . . the process of organization continually eliminates the anarchy of the separate parts of the 'national economic' mechanism, placing all of economic life under the iron heel of *the militaristic state.*" [103]

While focusing on the economic aspects of "statization," and particularly on the unique "fusing" of political and economic functions in bourgeois society, Bukharin emphasized that the state, as though driven by an unquenchable lust, had spread its organizing tentacles into all areas of social life. The separation of state and society was being systematically destroyed: "It can even be said with some truth that there is not a single nook of social life that the bourgeoisie can leave entirely unorganized." All other social organizations were becoming mere "divisions of a gigantic state mechanism," until it alone remained, omnivorous and omnipotent. His portrayal was nightmarish:

Thus arises the final type of the contemporary imperialist robber state, an iron organization which envelops the living body of society in its tenacious, grasping paws. It is a New Leviathan, before which the fantasy of Thomas Hobbes seems child's play. And even more *"non est potestas super terram quae comparetur ei"* ("there is no power on earth that can compare with it").[104]

To summarize, this conception of national neo-capitalism—state capitalism—was at the heart of Bukharin's theory of imperialism. State capitalist Leviathans, in their separate imperialist searchings for greater profits, found themselves locked in a sanguinary struggle in the international arena. Imperialism in his understanding was "nothing but the expression of competition between state capitalist trusts," the "competition of gigantic, consolidated, and organized economic bodies possessed of a colossal fighting capacity in the world tournament of 'nations.' "[105] Hence the global scope and unprecedented ferocity of the first (imperialist) world war.

Taken as a whole, Bukharin's model of state capitalism and imperialism had considerable theoretical power and internal consistency. To Marxists living three decades after Marx and in a society notably unlike that which Marx had studied, it offered a compelling explanation of why capitalism had failed to collapse from its inherent contradictions, continuing instead to expand at a staggering rate at home and abroad. At the same time, it dutifully preserved the revolutionary breakdown supposition—the essential tenet of radical Marxism—by locating the causes of breakdown in the model of imperialism. World capitalism was now beset with fatal contradictions: it was doomed to revolutionary destruction, war being the catalyst and harbinger of ruin. But read literally, Bukharin's theory raised disturbing questions, some of which should have been evident at the time, others only as events unfolded.

His defenders would later argue that his writings on modern capitalism had to be understood as abstract analysis (similar to that presented by Marx in the first volume of *Capital*), as a "chemically pure" model designed not to correspond to every aspect of reality, but to reveal transitional tendencies in contemporary bourgeois society. It was a reasonable qualification, one that Bukharin now and then added.[106] For the most part, however, he gave every indication of meaning his theory, at least in broad outline, to be read literally. He restated it at length in his famous and controversial *The Economics of the Transition Period*, published in 1920, and again with some revisions in the late 1920's. Both times the essential elements of his original theory remained.[107]

The clearest evidence that Bukharin regarded his theory as an accurate portrayal of existing capitalist reality was the real horror aroused in him by the new militaristic state. His unusually emotional references to "the present-day monster, the modern Leviathan" were not the formulas of abstract analysis, but statements of passion.[108] Most striking was his repeated use of the image of the "iron heel of the *militaristic state*." He borrowed the expression from Jack London's novel *The Iron Heel*, a nightmarish account of the coming of a draconian, proto-fascist order, whose dictatorial "Oligarchy" mercilessly crushes all resistance and declares: "We will grind you revolutionists down under our heel, and we shall walk upon your faces. The world is ours . . . and ours it shall remain. . . ." The heel-boot image as a metaphor for despotic state power over citizen and society runs through anti-utopian literature from Jack London to George Orwell's epigrammatic "A boot stamping on a human face—forever." [109] Bukharin, it is clear from his impassioned language, also looked into the future, and what he saw, in the absence of socialist revolution, frightened him: "*a militaristic state capitalism*. Centralization becomes the centralization of the barracks; among the élites the vilest militarism inevitably intensifies, as does the brutal regimentation and bloody repression of the proletariat." [110]

In his description of an omnipotent "single all-embracing organization," Bukharin foresaw, however idiomatically, the advent of what came to be called the "totalitarian" state.[111] He also anticipated the agonizing question this development was to pose for Marxists. Was it theoretically conceivable that "statization" could become so pervasive—the economic base of society so fully subordinated to and controlled by the political superstructure—that spontaneous economic forces, crises, and thus the prospect of revolution would be eliminated? In short, was a third kind of modern society, neither capitalist nor socialist, imaginable? Unwilling to dodge unpleasant theoretical issues, Bukharin raised the question on four separate occasions between 1915 and 1928. Each time he answered affirmatively, though stressing that while conceivable in theory, such a society was impossible in reality. Two examples indicate the direction of his thinking. He first reflected on the possibility of a nonsocialist, marketless economy in 1915:

We would have an entirely new economic form. This would be capitalism no more, for the production of *commodities* would have disappeared; still less would it be *socialism,* for the power of one class over the other would have remained (and even grown stronger). Such an economic stucture would, most of all, resemble a slaveowning economy where the slave market is absent.

And again in 1928:

Here a *planned economy* exists, organized distribution not only in relation to the links and interrelationships between the various branches of production, but also in relation to consumption. The slave in this society receives his share of provisions, of the goods constituting the product of the general labor. He may receive very little, but all the same there will be no crises.[112]

Even in theory this was a dread potentiality. It suggested that history's destination was not necessarily socialism, that a post-capitalist society might bring another, crueler system of exploitation. If true, the certainty of a just order, and with it the Marxist doctrine of historical inevitability, vanished. Bukharin never acknowledged that such an outcome was a real possibility; but it lingered in his mind throughout his life. After 1917, when the danger had to be weighed in terms of the emerging Soviet order, the specter of the Leviathan state was to be a factor both in his Left Communism of early 1918 and in his gradualist policies of the twenties. And while the danger contributed to some of his most dishonest and tortuous rationalizations of Soviet developments, over the years it was a liberalizing element in his Bolshevism, part of what made Bukharin, despite his chronic public optimism, a man of private fears. It is further evidence that all Bolsheviks did not march to the same drummer.

His theory of state capitalism raised another and more immediate question. Although Bukharin exaggerated the extent and permanency of "statization" and trustification in 1915–16, he pinpointed a basic twentieth-century development. The following decades did witness the final disappearance of laissez-faire capitalism and the emergence of a new kind of economically active state, ranging in type and degree of intervention from administered capitalism and the welfare state to the highly mobilized economies of Soviet Russia and wartime Nazi Germany. Bukharin's theoretical instincts were modern and pertinent: in significant ways, his 1915–16 writings anticipated later literature (particularly that of social democratic origin) on state-regulated economies, much of which also revolved around the concept of state capitalism.[113] But in treating this development he was forced to revise seriously Marx's understanding of the coming of the anti-capitalist revolution. In dramatizing the organizing capabilities of "collective capitalism," he virtually eliminated the system's internal, crisis-producing contradictions. Bukharin's model gave no meaningful role to pre-monopoly market economies (not to mention pre-capitalist ones) and thus to the frenzied competition Marx had viewed as the source of capitalism's ruin.

> The individual capitalist disappears. He is transformed into a *Verbandskapitalist*, a member of an organization. He no longer *competes* with his "countrymen"; he cooperates with them, for the center of gravity of the competitive struggle is transferred to the world market, while inside the country competition dies out.[114]

As his party critics would later charge, this understanding strongly resembled the concept of "organized capitalism," which for Bolsheviks was the ideological underpinning of social democratic reformism.

To maintain the breakdown theory and the prospect of socialist revolution, Bukharin transferred capitalism's indigenous doomsday mechanism to the arena of world capitalism, or imperialism. Insisting that the internationalization of capital had created a genuine world capitalist system, he replicated Marx's picture of unorganized capitalism on an international scale. "World economy . . . is characterized by its highly anarchic structure," which "may be compared with the structure of 'national' capitalism typical until the beginning of this century. . . ." Capitalist crises were now international rather than national, war being their starkest manifestation.[115]

By interpreting war as the highest and final form of economic competition, however, Bukharin located the ultimate catalyst of revolution outside the national system. Previously, impregnable state capitalist régimes had used colonial "super-profits" to dampen domestic class struggle, "raising the workers' wages at the expense of the exploited colonial savages and conquered peoples." Because "the horror and shame" of imperialism had been confined to distant lands, a "bond of unity" had developed between the Western proletariat and the imperialist state, as evidenced by how deeply sentiments of the fatherland and patriotism had "penetrated into the souls of the workers." But world war, by turning imperialism's "true face to the working class of Europe," promised to "sever the last chain that binds the workers to . . . the imperialist state" and to mobilize them in a revolutionary "war against the rule of capital." "The additional pennies received by the European workers . . . what do they count compared to millions of butchered workers, to billions devoured by the war, to the monstrous pressure of brazen militarism, to the vandalism of plundered productive forces, to the high cost of living and starvation?" [116]

For a Bolshevik writing during the First World War, the proposition that proletarian revolution in advanced industrial societies was dependent on war presented no dilemma. Bukharin's main purpose was to refocus revolutionary expectations and to restore Marx's anti-statism to social democratic ideology. The movement was *"to emphasize strongly its hostility in principle to state power"*: the proletariat's immediate aim was to "destroy the state organization of the bourgeoisie," to *"explode it from within."* [117] But later, when the war had ended and the Bolshevik revolution remained alone in a capitalist world, Bukharin was left with the awkward assumption that further European revolutions were unlikely (if not impossible) without a general war. By the mid-twenties, this understanding was in painful conflict with his evolutionary domestic policies, which were predicated on a lengthy period of European peace: it implied a contradiction between the survival of the fragile Soviet régime and international revolution. He eventually lessened the dilemma by taking into account nationalist wars in colonial areas, a factor he did not stress in 1915–16. But the basic question—Was revolution in mature capitalist societies possible without a major war?—plagued him to the end; and in 1928–9, it became an issue in his controversy with Stalin over Comintern policy.

In sharp contrast to his earlier writings, Bukharin's ideas on imperialism and state capitalism broke new theoretical ground (at least in the Bolshevik context), had programmatic implications, and thus provoked serious controversies with Lenin. On the surface, there was little difference between his theory of imperialism and that set out a few months later in Lenin's *Imperialism*. Both presented the same general explanation of capitalist expansionism and ended with similar conclusions on the inevitability of war and revolution. Lenin read the manuscript of Bukharin's *Imperialism and World Economy* and used it in preparing his own study; he registered no serious objections and, in December 1915, wrote for its publication a highly laudatory introduction.[118] Nor did Bukharin, then or later, indicate any reservations about Lenin's work. Until his political defeat in 1929, when almost all of his theoretical writings came under attack, his book, like Lenin's, was honored in Soviet Russia as a classic Bolshevik statement on imperialism.[119] Nonetheless, there were significant dissimilarities in their treatment of modern capitalism, two of which were to be especially important.

First, Lenin's model of imperialism rested on a perceptibly different understanding of national capitalism. Though he, too, stressed the transformation of laissez-faire capitalism into monopoly capitalism, observing that "the main thing in this process is the displacement of . . . free competition," he was considerably less inclined to conclude that competition and production anarchy had been eliminated from the national economy. Rather, he argued that the monopolization of part of the economy intensified "the anarchy inherent in capitalist production *as a whole*." He saw a variegated picture—"something transient, a mixture of free competition and monopoly"—and concluded that "monopolies, which have grown out of free competition, do not eliminate the latter, but exist over it and alongside it, and thereby give rise to a number of very acute, intense antagonisms. . . ." For Lenin, the notion that trustification could abolish internal crises was "a fable spread by bourgeois economists." He therefore emphasized far more than did Bukharin the decay and decrepitude of neo-capitalism, an approach significantly unlike Bukharin's concept of organized state capitalism, which for the latter was synonymous with national capitalism.[120] Lenin's failure, as Bukharin eventually came to regard it, to understand the phenomenon of state capitalism was to be the subject of a long series of disagreements between the two men, beginning in 1917 and continuing into the twenties.

The second important difference involved the role of nationalism in the imperialist age. Bukharin's argument in *Imperialism and World Economy* was not incompatible with the subsequent rise of colonial wars of national liberation, as the fact that he was later able to take them into account showed. But in 1915–16, he was convinced that imperialism had rendered economic and political nationalism anachronistic (hence his habit of writing "national" in quotation marks). The era of imperialist wars was by definition a forcible remaking of the "political map," leading to the "collapse of independent small states." In this respect, despite their different theories of imperialism, his position was similar to the radical internationalism of Rosa Luxemburg.[121]

Bukharin's failure to see anti-imperialist nationalism as a revolutionary force was the most glaring defect in his original treatment of imperialism; he did not anticipate the historic development of the postwar period—the groundswell of national liberation movements. Lenin, on the other hand, partly because he was deeply interested in the colonial aspects of imperialism rather than the new structure of national capitalism, concentrated his attention on the possibility of nationalist colonial uprisings. In the extensive internationalization of capital, he found a factor preparing the way for imperialism's downfall—what he called "the law of uneven capitalist development," a pattern that explained both the intense competition for colonies and the growing resistance on the part of colonial peoples.[122] As he wrote far-sightedly a few months after completing *Imperialism*:

"colonial wars" are often national wars or national rebellions of these colonial peoples. One of the most basic features of imperialism is that it accelerates the development of capitalism in the most backward countries and thereby widens and intensifies the struggle against national oppression. . . . It follows from this that imperialism must very often give rise to national wars.[123]

Lenin's early enthusiasm for the potential revolutionary role of nationalism in colonial and noncolonial areas was reflected in his fervent advocacy of the slogan of national self-determination after 1914. This inevitably brought him into conflict with Bukharin and other young Bolsheviks who, like most radical Marxists, rejected appeals to nationalism as inappropriate and un-Marxist. The open dispute began in late 1915, ostensibly over control of the new journal *Kommunist*. The first (and only) issue contained an article by Karl Radek, an East European social democrat close to the Bolshevik émigrés. Radek's thinking on the national question was similar to that of Rosa Luxemburg, Piatakov, and by this time, Bukharin. Lenin objected to the article's viewpoint and refused to participate further in *Kommunist*, demanding that it be abolished. Theoretical disagreements immediately hardened into factional divisions. In November, Lenin's Central Committee in Switzerland deprived the Stockholm group—Bukharin, Piatakov, and Bosh— of the right to communicate unilaterally with Russia. In response, the Stockholm three dissolved themselves as a Bolshevik section.[124]

Later in November, the three sent to the Central Committee a set of documents outlining their position on self-determination and attacking Lenin's. The slogan, they stated bluntly, "is first of all *utopian* (it cannot be realized *within the limits* of capitalism) and *harmful* as a slogan which *disseminates illusions*." Imperialism had made international socialist revolution an immediate historic possibility; to approach social questions in a national, "'pro-state manner'" was to undermine the cause of revolution. The only correct tactic was to "revolutionize the consciousness of the proletariat" by "continually tossing the proletariat into the arena of *world* struggle, by placing constantly before it questions of *world* policy." Although Bukharin and his friends specifically excluded "*noncapitalist countries or countries with an embryonic capitalism* (for example, the colonies)" from their argument, they were in irreconcilable disagreement with Lenin on the whole principle of self-determination as a programmatic slogan.[125]

The controversy continued and grew increasingly acrimonious throughout most of 1916. The young Bolsheviks were outraged by Lenin's vehement response to their criticism. They reminded him that "all *extreme Lefts* who have a well-thought-out theory" were against the self-determination slogan: "Are they all 'traitors'?" Lenin, on the other hand, regarded their opposition on this single issue not only as theoretical nonsense, but as political disloyalty. Their ideas, he charged, "*have nothing in common either with Marxism or revolutionary social democracy*"; their request for open discussions reflected an "anti-party" attitude.[126] Although he apparently viewed Piatakov as the chief villain in the dispute over self-determination,[127] his attack on Bukharin was equally harsh and uncompromising. Correspondence between them served only to widen the gulf, and efforts at reconciliation by other Bolsheviks infuriated Lenin.[128] By some uncertain reasoning, he became convinced not only that Bukharin's heresies dated from the Bern conference, but that all the minor differences that had arisen since 1912, including those relating to Malinovskii, were of a piece: "Nikolai Ivanovich is a studious economist, and *in this* we have always supported him. But he is (1) credulous toward gossip and (2) devilishly *unstable* in politics. The war has pushed him toward semi-anarchistic ideas." [129]

Considering the many important issues on which they agreed, it is difficult to understand why Lenin allowed his relations with Bukharin to deteriorate so seriously. Nonpolitical factors were certainly at work. Lenin's well-known cantankerousness was particularly evident in 1916; he was in an "irreconcilable mood." Bolsheviks not directly involved in the dispute reproached him for his "unaccommodating disposition" and tactlessness in the affair; and Bukharin probably spoke for many when he expressed the hope that Lenin and Zinoviev did not treat Western comrades as rudely as they did Russians.[130] In addition, Lenin appears to have grown increasingly resentful and suspicious of his young follower's extensive associations with various non-Bolshevik groups. In Scandinavia, for example, Bukharin had become a popular and active figure in the anti-war socialist movement, which was composed mainly of young radical social democrats. The farther he drifted from the coterie around Lenin, the closer he became identified, at least in Lenin's mind, with the young European Left rather than the Bolshevik Party.[131] Generational friction between the forty-six-year-old leader and the twenty-eight-year-old Bukharin was never far from the surface. Lenin, in his best patriarchal manner, suggested that the "unpardonable" errors of "Bukharin and Co." were "due to their youth . . . perhaps in five years they will correct themselves." Bukharin, for his part, accused Lenin of being old-fashioned: "What is this? The sixties of the last century are 'instructive' for the twentieth century? . . . In regard to the slogan of self-determination, you stand on the viewpoint of the 'past century.' "[132]

At the same time, the leader's attitude confirms the impression that the "closer men were to Lenin, the more bitterly he quarreled with them."[133] For even during the worst period in their relationship, furtive evidence of their underlying mutual affection now and then appeared. Bukharin occasionally tried to appeal to this feeling. He begged Lenin not "to publish against me the kind of article that makes it impossible for me to answer cordially. . . . I did not want and do not want . . . a split."[134] Lenin was not totally unreceptive. In April 1916, Bukharin was arrested in Stockholm for his participation in an anti-war socialist congress. Learning of his trouble, Lenin dispatched an urgent appeal for help; and later in April, after Bukharin had been deported to Oslo (then Christiania), Lenin wrote to another Bolshevik in Norway asking him to convey best regards to Bukharin: "I hope from my heart that he will very soon take a rest and be well. How are his finances?" The message was terse, but, under the circumstances, warm, even fatherly. The benignity was short-lived. By July, Lenin was explaining to Zinoviev that "I am now so ill-disposed toward Bukharin, I cannot write."[135]

Whatever the exacerbating factors, the disagreement between Lenin and Bukharin on the national question was real and enduring; it flared up sporadically until 1919. This was not true of the even more divisive issue that now came to the fore. Earlier in 1916, Lenin had decided to publish a collection of programmatic articles under his own editorial control. He expected a contribution from Bukharin "on an economic theme." [136] Instead, Bukharin sent the essay "Toward a Theory of the Imperialist State" in which he depicted the "New Leviathan." The section that was to infuriate Lenin included Bukharin's exposition of the Marxist theory of the state, his call for the "revolutionary destruction" of the bourgeois state, and his provocative conclusion that the essential difference between Marxists and anarchists involved economic centralization, "not that Marxists are statists and anarchists anti-statists, as many maintain." [137] Rehabilitating the original anti-statism of Marxism had served two purposes for Bukharin. It followed from his horrified vision of the "New Leviathan" and satisfied his strong libertarian proclivities; second, it was the gravamen of his effort to re-radicalize Marxist ideology, which, in the hands both of Bernstein's reformists and Kautsky's orthodox school, had long since been purged of such militant tenets. A few left-wing Marxists—most notably Anton Pannekoek and the young Swedish social democrat Zeth Höglund—had earlier returned to the anti-statist theme.[138] But Bukharin was the first Bolshevik to do so, which alone was sufficient to guarantee Lenin's displeasure.

Lenin's first inclination was to publish the essay as "a discussion article." But, still incensed by their other differences, he soon changed his mind and decided that it was "undoubtedly not suitable." He postponed giving his reasons or informing Bukharin of this for two months. Finally, in September 1916, he wrote to him rejecting the article ("with sadness"). The section on state capitalism, Lenin explained, was "good and useful, but nine-tenths legal," and should be published elsewhere after a few "*very* small" corrections. The theoretical treatment of Marxism and the state, however, was "decidedly incorrect": Lenin objected to Bukharin's "sociological" (class) analysis of the state; quotations from Engels, he charged, had been taken out of context; above all, Bukharin's contention that Marxists and anarchists did not differ on the state, that "social democracy must strongly emphasize its hostility in principle to state power," was "either extremely inexact, or incorrect." Bukharin's ideas were "insufficiently thought out," even childish, Lenin implied. He advised him "*to allow them to ripen.*" [139]

Bukharin, until now unaware of Lenin's most recent displeasure, was hurt and angered by the rejection. After almost a year of polemics, he was in no mood to let his thinking on the state, which now stood at the center of his Marxism, "ripen." He defended his ideas in a series of letters to Lenin and the Central Committee. The battle by correspondence continued through September and into October; as before, each exchange further embittered and broadened the controversy.[140] Lenin (seconded by Zinoviev) accused Bukharin of "a very large error": that of "semi-anarchism," of ignoring the necessity for a post-revolutionary state, for the dictatorship of the proletariat, and of "mistakenly ascribing . . . to socialists" the goal of "exploding" the old state.[141] The new campaign against him persuaded Bukharin that Lenin's grievance was no longer a question of theory, but was more generalized. "It is clear," he wrote to Zinoviev, "that you simply do not want me as a collaborator. Don't worry: I won't be troublesome." Defiant, he began publishing his views on the state.[142] A final split with Lenin and the official Bolshevik leadership seemed imminent.

Meanwhile, in August 1916, Bukharin had moved from Oslo to Copenhagen, where he was again investigating a suspected double agent. He remained there until the inquiry was completed in late September, when he decided to go to the United States. What prompted his decision is not fully clear. While other considerations—his natural wanderlust and the possibility of party work in a citadel of modern capitalism—may have played a part, the deterioration in his relations with Lenin was probably a major factor. By this time, their squabbling had seriously affected Bolshevik activities in Scandinavia, where "despondency and grief prevailed." [143] In early October, Bukharin returned to Oslo to meet the steamer for America.

At that moment, Lenin began to worry that he had alienated Bukharin irrevocably. He anxiously instructed Aleksandr Shliapnikov, the chief Bolshevik organizer in Scandinavia: "Write *frankly*—in what mood is Bukharin leaving? Will he write to us or not? Will he fulfill requests . . . ?" [144] Lenin's sudden disquiet coincided with the arrival of a long letter from Bukharin. Intended as a farewell gesture, he again firmly rejected Lenin's accusations, reprimanding him for having fabricated and exaggerated their differences, and defended his views on the state as "correct and Marxist." Then, in a remarkable passage, he suggested how some socialists interpreted Lenin's campaign against him: they were saying "that in the last analysis I am being kicked out because 'your Lenin cannot tolerate any other person with brains.' " Bukharin characterized such speculations as nonsense; but, in a stroke, he had revealed an unspoken source of tension between himself and Lenin, as well as his own feelings about the obsequious coterie around the leader. He closed, however, with a moving plea:

I ask one thing of you: if you must polemicize, etc., preserve such a tone that it will not lead to a split. It would be very painful for me, painful beyond endurance, if joint work, even in the future, should become impossible. I have the greatest respect for you; I look upon you as my revolutionary teacher and love you.[145]

It was a strong appeal and Lenin responded favorably, albeit in his own peculiar fashion. He immediately wrote Bukharin a "soft" letter, which, while insisting that the charges were valid and the disagreements "fully" Bukharin's fault, praised him and affirmed: "We all value you highly." He concluded: "I wish with all my heart that the polemics had from the outset been only with P. Kievskii [Piatakov], and that disagreements with you were resolved." From Lenin, at least in personal terms, this was a major concession. Bukharin appreciated it as such and, before sailing, sent a last, conciliatory note reiterating his "absolute solidarity" with Piatakov, but deeply regretting that it had led to conflicts with Lenin. "Be well, think kindly of me. . . . I embrace you all," he closed.[146]

A final rupture had been avoided, but the startling denouement of their controversy over the state was yet to come. Lenin's criticism of Bukharin had been twofold: that he had distorted Marx's and Engels's views by quoting out of context; and that he had overlooked the need for a proletarian state. The latter charge was particularly curious since Bukharin had carefully stressed that his "anarchism" related to the ultimate communist society and not to the transition period between capitalism and communism. In the process of revolution, he had emphasized on several occasions, "The proletariat destroys the state organization of the bourgeoisie, utilizes its material framework and creates its own temporary state organization of power. . . ." [147] Bukharin was understandably baffled by Lenin's accusation. Among Scandinavian socialists, he pointed out, "I am considered to be at the head of the anti-anarchist company, and yet you criticize me as an anarchist." [148] Lenin's misrepresentation, it would seem, was a (conscious or unconscious) by-product of his initial hostility to Bukharin's innovating attempt to formulate a radical counterpoint to social democratic ideology by reinterpreting the Marxist theory of the state. Lenin had not thought about the matter before Bukharin raised it;

in December 1916, he promised "to return to this extremely important question in a special article." [149] The result was a volte-face in his thinking.

On February 17, 1917, Lenin suddenly notified another Bolshevik: "I am preparing . . . an article on the question of Marxism's attitude toward the state. I have reached conclusions much sharper against Kautsky than against Bukharin. . . . Bukharin is much better than Kautsky. . . ." Lenin still had reservations: "Bukharin's errors may *ruin* this 'just cause' in the struggle with Kautskyism." But two days later he again announced that despite "small errors" Bukharin was "*closer* to the truth than Kautsky," and that he was now prepared to publish Bukharin's essay.[150] His remaining doubts soon disappeared. When Bukharin returned to Moscow in May 1917, Lenin's wife, Nadezhda Krupskaya, relayed a message from the leader—"her first words were: 'V.I. asked me to tell you that he no longer has any disagreements with you on the question of the state.' " [151]

The fullest evidence of Lenin's complete turnabout came later in 1917, when he completed his famous treatise *State and Revolution*: its arguments and conclusions were Bukharin's. Lenin had decided that "the main, fundamental point in Marxism's teaching on the state" was that "the working class must *destroy, smash, explode* . . . the entire state machine." A new, revolutionary state was required temporarily, but one "constituted so that it rapidly begins to wither away. . . ." Therefore, "we in no way disagree with the anarchists on . . . the abolition of the state as the *goal*." Unabashed, he concluded: "Neither the opportunists nor the Kautskyists wish to see this similarity between Marxism and anarchism, because they have departed from Marxism on this point." [152]

Though it was to remain an inoperative promise after 1917, Lenin's *State and Revolution* made anti-statism a constituent part of orthodox Bolshevik ideology. Neither Bukharin, who said little about the dictatorship of the proletariat, nor Lenin, who commented on it extensively, foresaw the kind of state that was to rise out of the Bolshevik revolution. Bukharin imagined a revolutionary state responsible for little more than keeping "the overthrown classes in leash"; Lenin, a nonbureaucratic, "commune state" already in the process of "withering away." Both conceptions were simulacrums, remote from the post-1917 awareness that the Soviet state was an instrument of modernization, "the basic lever for the reconstruction of society." [153] Nonetheless, anti-statism was to play an important role in 1917: it helped to radicalize the party and to create a public insurrectionary opinion against the provisional government that had replaced the autocracy. Lenin's authority legitimized anti-statism, but the true initiative was Bukharin's.[154] In this way, as in his writings on modern capitalism and imperialism, he, as much as anyone, shaped the Bolshevik ideology that was emerging on the eve of the Russian revolution.

Bukharin's last months in emigration were spent in the United States. Arriving in New York in early November 1916, he divided his time, as he had elsewhere, between radical politics and local libraries.[155] His political activity centered at *Novyi Mir* (*The New World*), a Russian-language daily published by socialist émigrés in New York. In January 1917, he became its *de facto* editor, an apprenticeship for his ten-year editorship of *Pravda* after the October revolution. As would be the case with *Pravda*, he used the paper to popularize his favorite ideas. His articles on neo-capitalism, Marxism and the state, and the national question began to appear regularly and, predictably, to stir debate.[156] As for party work, his main purpose was to build support among the American Left for the Bolshevik-Zimmerwald attitude against the war, an undertaking that took him on occasional speaking tours across the country. Always a popular figure, who mingled easily outside Bolshevik ranks, Bukharin was credited with some success in converting American socialists to Bolshevik views, and particularly with having strengthened the anti-war position of *Novyi Mir*.[157]

Apart from his abiding respect for American technological and scientific achievements, Bukharin's short stay in the United States seems to have had little impact on his thinking. If anything, it reinforced his conviction that modern capitalism was a formidable system, whose vulnerability was most realistically measured in terms of the external pressures of war.[158] One New York association, however, did have lasting implications. In January 1917, Trotsky arrived and joined *Novyi Mir*'s editorial board. The sad history of the relationship between these two men—one to lead the Bolshevik Left, the other the Bolshevik Right in the twenties—was central to the collective tragedy that subsequently befell the old Bolsheviks. The two most gifted intellectuals of the original Soviet leaders, their personal affection would not survive their later political disagreements, which divided and finally destroyed them.

Bukharin had known Trotsky slightly in Vienna, but their close personal relationship began in New York.[159] At the same time, they were immediately at odds on the main political issue of the day. Trotsky, who did not join the Bolsheviks until July 1917, insisted that left-wing American socialists should remain in the American Socialist Party, striving to radicalize it from within. Bukharin (and Lenin, who followed the controversy from Europe) urged an organizational split and the formation of a new American party. The dispute, which imposed long-standing Russian disagreements on the fledgling American Communist movement, was sufficiently sharp to divide the New York émigrés into rival groups headed by Bukharin and Trotsky. Their political differences flared up publicly and privately in January and February, but probably were neither as intense nor as abrasive as subsequently depicted in party history.[160] It was characteristic of Bukharin to assume that political differences need not influence personal relations—one of his attractive features as a man and one of his considerable blind spots as a politician. Despite the dispute, he and Trotsky developed a warm friendship and collaborated politically at *Novyi Mir*.

The importance of such squabbles was suddenly and dramatically diminished by the news in February that bread riots in St. Petersburg had grown into a political revolution. The czar had abdicated, and a republic and provisional government had been established; the long years of exile were over. Unlike many Bolsheviks, whose radicalism focused on overthrowing the autocracy, Bukharin had been arguing the "inevitability of a *socialist* revolution in Russia" since 1915–16. From the outset, he therefore viewed the new Russian political order as only a first, transitional stage in a continuous revolutionary process; power, he predicted in March 1917, would soon pass from the weak Russian bourgeoisie to the rising proletariat, itself only "the first step of the world proletariat." [161]

A sea passage in wartime was difficult to arrange, and the delay must have been frustrating. Trotsky sailed in March, Bukharin in early April. His emigration ended as it had begun; he was arrested and detained for a week in Japan, and again upon entering eastern Russia ("for internationalist agitation among soldiers") by Mensheviks who controlled the area. In early May, he finally arrived in Moscow, where far greater controversies awaited him.[162]

CHAPTER II

The Triumph of
Radicalism in 1917

*When the old order begins to fall apart, many of the
vociferous men of words, who prayed so long for
the day, are in a funk.*

—ERIC HOFFER, *The True Believer*

BETWEEN THE FALL of the czar in February 1917 and the Bolshevik
takeover of the capital Petrograd in October, Russia experienced a
social revolution from below unequaled in modern history. Embittered by generations of official privilege, exploitation, and repression, radicalized by three years of war, and sparked by the
sudden collapse of czarism, the masses—workers, soldiers, and
peasants—seized the country's factories, garrisons, and great estates.
War-weary, land-hungry, and egalitarian-minded, they combined
to carry out a spontaneous, plebeian, anti-authoritarian upheaval
uncontrolled by any political party. By the summer of 1917, all
traditional forms of hierarchical authority and privilege, political
and economic, were crumbling under increasingly violent attack.
New, popular, decentralized institutions sprang up in their place:
local soviets electing representatives to higher soviets throughout
the country; workers' committees in the factories; rank-and-file
committees in the army; and peasant committees parceling out the
landlords' estates in the villages.

While popular sentiment grew more radical and turbulent
from month to month, the new provisional government in Petrograd constituted itself as a régime of moderation and legality. The
government began as a coalition of conservative and liberal politicians confronted on the left by the Petrograd Soviet, a socialist but
loyal opposition led by Socialist Revolutionaries and Mensheviks.

In the spring, under pressure of events in the country, it was reconstituted into a coalition of liberal democrats and moderate socialists from the Soviet and headed by Aleksandr Kerenskii, himself a Socialist Revolutionary. Despite its new complexion, however, the government continued to preach order and constraint, disapproving of the revolutionary turbulence, insisting that Russia remain in the war against Germany until victory or a negotiated peace was attained, and deferring great social issues, particularly the land question, until a national Constituent Assembly could be elected and convened later in the year.

Amidst revolution from below, a régime of moderation— liberal, socialist, or otherwise—stands no chance. Beset by the same social and military problems that had toppled the autocracy, living from crisis to crisis for eight months, the provisional government finally became their victim. By the fall of 1917, it commanded neither popular support nor troops sufficient to maintain order in the cities, stop the land seizures, conduct war, or even resist the feeble Bolshevik coup in Petrograd on October 25. The same unequal confrontation between official moderation and popular radicalism ruined the government's socialist supporters, transforming them into defenders of law and order and thus isolating them from their own disorderly constituents. By September, Socialist Revolutionary and Menshevik strength in the major soviets of Petrograd and Moscow had been replaced by Bolshevik majorities.

The spectacular history of Bolshevism in 1917—how a party with 24,000 members and little influence in February became a mass organization of 200,000 and the government of Russia in October—cannot concern us at length here. The idea that the party was the unrepresentative usurper of 1917, however, is misleading. The Bolsheviks were aided by their rivals' indecision and incomprehension, by Lenin's determination and ability to rally his party to his militant position, and by sheer good fortune. But it is also true that the party was the only significant political force consistently voicing and supporting the radical mass opinion of 1917. A minority party to the end (they received about 25 per cent of the votes for the Constituent Assembly in November), the Bolsheviks neither inspired nor led the revolution from below; but they alone perceived its direction and survived it.[1]

Bukharin's role in these events—his contribution to the party's success—requires special attention for two reasons. It accounted in large measure for his rise over older and higher-ranking claimants to the party's top leadership. At the same time, it also prepared the ground for his leadership of the Bolshevik Left's opposition to

Lenin's policies after only three months of party rule. Both developments derived from the fact that Lenin and the Bolshevik Left, of which Bukharin was the most prominent representative, found themselves in basic agreement on major questions confronting the party in 1917. This unanimity brought Bukharin, short of his twenty-ninth birthday, into Lenin's leadership council, the Bolshevik oligarchy that became the government of Soviet Russia. In February 1918, when Lenin abandoned his uncompromising radicalism of 1917, Bukharin and the Left returned to opposition.

The issues that had bitterly divided Bukharin and Lenin in emigration were resolved or rendered inconsequential in 1917 largely because the leader changed his mind. Even the resolution of their minor disagreements was significant. In campaigning for a mass Bolshevik following in 1917, for example, Lenin skillfully combined international defeatism with anti-war peace slogans similar to those Bukharin and the Baugy group had urged at the Bern conference. In addition, he reversed himself and through a series of conciliatory gestures enabled Trotsky and his followers to join the Bolshevik Party. Bukharin's 1915 call for unity among militant, anti-war Marxists prevailed, at least in this instance. Appropriately, it fell to him to welcome the Trotskyists at the Sixth Party Congress in July 1917. "In this hall," he reassured the assembly, "there is not a single person who does not feel the need to unite all the vital forces of social democracy." [2] But the essential factor in their new-found solidarity was Lenin's acceptance of the maximalist spirit implicit in Bukharin's call for the revolutionary destruction of the bourgeois state. In his famous April Theses, issued to startled party leaders upon his return to Russia in 1917, Lenin translated the anti-statist theme into a political program.

Until Lenin's return, party leaders in Russia, headed by Kamenev and Stalin, had regarded the post-czarist "bourgeois" republic as a long-term régime, and the Bolshevik role as that of a loyal opposition. They had formulated party policy accordingly. Lenin's April Theses set out an entirely different orientation. Insisting that the Russian revolution was already moving from its bourgeois phase "toward its *second* stage, which must put power in the hands of the proletariat and the poorest strata of the peasantry," he demanded "No support for the provisional government," neither for its war effort nor its domestic policies, whatever they might be. Lenin called instead for the destruction of the existing state—the "elimination of the police, the army, and the bureaucracy"—and the creation of "a revolutionary government" of soviets, a "commune state," which alone could wage a "revolutionary war" against all imperialist powers. Social democrats who regarded his proposals as unbridled anarchism or "the raving of a madman" were advised (just as Bukharin had earlier advised Lenin) to read *what* Marx and Engels said . . . about the *kind* of state the proletariat needs." Tersely and dramatically, the April Theses anticipated Lenin's *State and Revolution*, written in August and September, and set out his political program of 1917: Down with the Provisional Government! All power to the Soviets! [3]

Though elliptical over the question of timing, Lenin's argument meant insurrection and socialist revolution, an incitement that left most Bolshevik leaders "in a state of bafflement and perplexity." As Bukharin recalled seven years later: "Part of our own party, and by no means a small part of our own party, saw in this almost a betrayal of accepted Marxist ideology!" [4] Influenced by timidity, by a tacit acceptance of parliamentary democracy after so many years of opposing autocracy, and by a literal reading of Marxism which suggested that social conditions in peasant Russia were not ripe for proletarian or socialist revolution, many old Bolshevik leaders were either unenthusiastic or openly hostile to Lenin's insurrectionary call. Their resistance ranged from the public opposition of several of his senior lieutenants, among them Zinoviev, Kamenev, Aleksei Rykov, and Viktor Nogin, to widespread and persistent "vacillations . . . at the top of our party, a 'fear' . . . of the struggle for power." To make a socialist revolution, Lenin first had to radicalize his own recalcitrant party, an uphill struggle that occupied him from April until the final moment in October. [5]

He was able to do so in the end by bringing to bear his great persuasive powers, but also by promoting and relying on people previously outside the party's high command. Two groups were crucial in this respect: the Trotskyists, who assumed high positions immediately upon entering the party and played a major role in Petrograd; and the young left-wing Bolsheviks, of whom Bukharin was the most prominent, who were especially important in Moscow. Like most younger Bolsheviks, Bukharin was unsympathetic to the moderate, liberal admonitions of the new "bourgeois democratic" government, and looked forward to a second revolution from the outset. This united him so completely with Lenin that not even a brief literary skirmish over the theoretical section of the party program in the summer could seriously divide them.

Above all, Lenin's April Theses—confirmed by his personal

message sent through Krupskaya—had legitimized Bukharin's radical position on the state, "the fundamental and principal question of the entire practice of the revolutionary class." Armed by this perspective, both men stood "the entire time on the left flank" of the party in 1917.[6] As a result, Bukharin ceased to be a semi-outcast and became, at the Sixth Party Congress in July, a full member of its twenty-one-member Central Committee, the "general staff" of Bolshevism in 1917. With Lenin, Zinoviev, Kamenev, and Trotsky absent, he and Stalin delivered the main congressional speeches, an assignment signifying Bukharin's accession to the highest leadership.[7]

The arena of Bukharin's contribution to the party's radicalization, and the place where he emerged as a national party leader in 1917, was Moscow. Regularly ignored in Petrograd-oriented histories of the revolution, this city, the largest in Russia, gave the party some of its earliest and most important successes. In the beginning, however, Moscow Bolsheviks, like the party at large, were deeply split between advocates of moderation and radicalism. The Bolshevik Right was especially influential in the staid old capital, and its situation in the heart of peasant Russia reinforced their cautious outlook. "Here in the very center of bourgeois Moscow," mused one, "we really seem to be pygmies thinking of moving a mountain." [8] The Right's strength centered in the municipal party organization, the Moscow Committee, whose leaders included many proponents of moderation, among them Nogin and Rykov.[9]

On the other wing of the Moscow party, however, was a strong and vocal group of militant young Bolsheviks ensconced in the Moscow Regional Bureau. Formally responsible for all party organizations in the thirteen central provinces encircling Moscow, an area which encompassed 37 per cent of the country's population and (by October) 20 per cent of the party's total membership, the Bureau was the stronghold of the Bolshevik Left.[10] On returning to Moscow in early May, Bukharin resumed his seat on the Moscow City Committee. Equally important, he also became a member of the inner leadership of the Moscow Regional Bureau, where he was reunited with his pre-emigration friends; this Bureau became the base of his power and influence in 1917 and 1918.[11]

Bolshevik politics in Moscow in 1917 revolved around the struggle for supremacy between the cautiously inclined Moscow Committee and the radical, pro-insurrection Bureau.[12] Two circumstances further aggravated the rivalry. First, the Bureau had formal jurisdictional authority over the Moscow Committee, which it regarded as merely "one of the organizations of the Region," a situation resented and contested by the older, more prestigious city committee.[13] Second, relations between the two were regularly exacerbated by generational conflict. By early summer, the Bureau was in the hands of the Bolshevik generation of 1905. Also headquartered in the city, its major leaders were Bukharin, Vladimir Smirnov, Osinskii, Lomov, Iakovleva, Ivan Kizelshtein, and Ivan Stukov. Apart from Iakovleva, who was thirty-three, all were under thirty, a generation—ten to twenty years—younger than the leaders of the Moscow Committee (though it eventually included some younger leaders).[14]

While a majority of the Moscow Committee eventually supported insurrection, its response to the radical course set by Lenin and the Left was sluggish and halfhearted throughout. Most of its senior members believed, as one insisted, that "There do not exist the forces, the objective conditions for this." [15] Bureau leaders, constantly prodding their elders, remained worried as late as October that the "peaceloving" mood and "significant wavering" in the Moscow Committee would prove fatal "at the decisive moment." [16] Consequently, despite the radical support of some older Moscow Bolsheviks, the young Muscovites tended to regard the final victory in Moscow as their personal achievement, a *tour de force* of their generation. As Osinskii later put it, they had led the struggle for power "against significant resistance by a large part of the older generation of Moscow officials." [17]

This generational sense of identity and self-esteem, rooted in their shared experiences and friendships dating back to 1906-10, rendered the young Muscovites a distinct political group in the party in 1917 and after. As before, Bukharin was their ranking figure, with political and personal ties to the others. Osinskii, Smirnov, Lomov, Iakovleva, and her equally well-known brother Nikolai had been his close friends and associates before he emigrated. Lomov, for example, was an "ardent follower" of the more illustrious Bukharin, of whom he spoke "with love as well as reverence." [18] Less is known about Kizelshtein and Stukov, who arrived in Moscow only in 1917 but became loyal and enthusiastic supporters of the native Bureau leaders in the party disputes that followed.[19]

As indecision and caution eroded the authority of older Moscow party leaders, the power and influence of the young Muscovites grew. The pattern was established in early May, when Bukharin, Lomov, and Sokolnikov (another youthful friend from

1906–10) were added to the Bolshevik delegation in the Moscow Soviet to offset its rightist membership.[20] Influence over opinion in the Moscow party, however, involved control of its official publications. In early summer, the old 1909–10 trio of Bukharin, Osinskii, and Smirnov re-emerged to gain (or seize) command of the press organs. Headed by Bukharin, they formed a "working *troika*" inside the formal editorial board of *Sotsial Demokrat*, the party's daily newspaper. Their appointment seems to have been a virtual coup against four editors who had run the paper since its creation in March, and who were now deprived of a major voice.[21] A similar situation developed at *Spartak*, the party's theoretical journal. Bukharin became chief editor, Osinskii and Smirnov his deputies; older editors were again relegated to secondary positions as "contributors." [22]

These developments placed the Moscow party's publications in the hands of the young Left, and enabled the *troika* to shape Bolshevik opinion and policy during the crucial months of the Kerenskii government. Their growing political importance in the old capital was reflected in their representation on the all-party Central Committee elected in July. In addition to Bukharin, two other young Muscovites, Andrei Bubnov and Sokolnikov, were named full members, while Iakovleva and Lomov became candidate members. Their newly won parity with entrenched moderate leaders was formally acknowledged: a foursome of Bukharin, Lomov, Rykof, and Nogin was appointed to oversee party affairs in the Moscow area.[23]

At the same time, the rise of the young Left was mirrored in Bukharin's growing personal eminence among Moscow Bolsheviks. No one party leader dominated revolutionary politics in Moscow as Trotsky did in Petrograd; but in terms of prominence, Bukharin was second to none. A member of the Executive Committee of the Moscow Soviet, of the city Duma, and of the ill-fated State Convention, his became the predominant voice of radical Bolshevism in the old capital. A tireless and ubiquitous figure in the political campaign of 1917, he preached the mendacity of the provisional government and the necessity for socialist revolution in the soviets, factories, trade unions, schools, and streets of Moscow and the provinces.[24] His diminutive, boyish appearance belied his considerable oratorical powers, commented on by observers over the years:

He was quick and wiry . . . and stood very firm on his legs. . . . But you would never be prepared for the sparkling torrent of witty argument that flowed out of him. . . . He just strolled about, holding some paper in his hand, his blouse unflapped at the neck . . . and his whole being would become talk.

One admiring eyewitness listened as he taunted the liberals "with malicious and delicate irony," another as he railed at right-wing Bolsheviks before a gathering of workers: "Bukharin stood up, savage, logical, with a voice which plunged and struck, plunged and struck. . . . Him they listened to with shining eyes." [25]

As would be the case later, however, his reputation in 1917 spread mainly through his writings—a torrent of articles, editorials, proclamations, and manifestoes (including some of the party's most famous) published regularly in *Sotsial Demokrat* and *Spartak*.[26] Even his theoretical writing continued unabated. Marxists, he explained, do not "discontinue their theoretical work even at periods of the most violent class struggle." [27] (Lenin, it will be remembered, was similarly at work on *State and Revolution*.) In this spirit, throughout the turmoil of the summer and autumn, Bukharin published articles expounding to a Russian audience his ideas on imperialism and modern capitalism. He also undertook the only historical writing of his career, a vivid, popularized account of the current events entitled *Class Struggle and Revolution in Russia*. Patterned after Marx's famous essays on French politics and published in July 1917, the small book was widely read and later acclaimed by one Bolshevik admirer as "the best outline of the 1917 revolution." [28]

In subsequent years, 1917 would be looked back upon as the touchstone in a Bolshevik's political career, the time when his conduct forever enhanced or diminished his authority inside the party. In this respect, 1917 authenticated Bukharin's credentials as a party leader. By October, only a handful of Bolsheviks of any generation shared his stature in the party: veteran of 1905, underground committeeman, internationalist, theorist, editor, pamphleteer, and revolutionary tribune.

Bukharin's personal stature should not obscure the major, perhaps essential, role played by other young Muscovites in Bolshevism's victory in 1917, however. Individually, and collectively as leaders of the Moscow Regional Bureau, their radicalism, which sparked the party's remarkable popular success in Moscow Soviet and Duma elections, was instrumental in Lenin's effort to gain recalcitrant Bolshevik support for the Petrograd insurrection on October 25.[29] It was followed by the Moscow uprising, an episode dominated by Bureau leaders and their contemporaries.

More protracted and bloodier than the coup in Petrograd, the Moscow uprising continued against strong resistance until November 2.[30] Bukharin drafted, introduced, and defended the revolutionary decrees of the Moscow Soviet, in whose name the insurrection took place, and of the Military Revolutionary Committee, whose news bulletin he edited. Smirnov, who directed the military operations, Lomov, and two other young Muscovites, Nikolai Muralov and Usievich, were leading members of the Committee. (Osinskii was away from the city.[31]) Resistance suppressed and victory assured, the Moscow party chose two representatives to report formally to the new revolutionary government in Petrograd. The two chosen were Bukharin and Stukov, symbolizing the triumph of the Bureau and the generation of 1905.[32]

The role of Bukharin and his friends in the radicalization of Bolshevism was to have political ramifications after October as well. Their righteous militancy, disdain for cautionary voices, and occasional clannishness understandably offended older party leaders, who, in addition, resented having been pushed aside by their juniors.[33] Though subdued temporarily by victory, this lingering resentment was to make itself felt later when the young Left no longer represented the outlook of Lenin.[34] At the same time, their success in 1917 intensified the young Muscovites' confidence in their own political judgment and in the efficacy of uncompromising radicalism. Unlike Lenin (himself of the "older generation"), they were to be reluctant to abandon or dilute the maximalist spirit of 1917 when that seemed practical. Partly as a result, in early 1918 they emerged as the leaders of the first intra-party opposition in Soviet Russia—the Left Communists. As such, they would insist that the radicalism that had led to power was equally relevant to the party's uses of power, matters virtually ignored in 1917.

Central to the myth of a united, single-minded party is the notion that the Bolsheviks came to power with a preconceived, well-defined program to transform Russian society. The bitter disputes inside the party during the next twelve years stemmed in part from the fact that the opposite was true. In fact, they took office without a meaningful (much less consensual) program related to what they would eventually regard as their primary goal and the essential prerequisite of socialism—the industrialization and modernization of backward, peasant Russia. As Marxist socialists, the Bolsheviks wished to remake society, to "build socialism." These, however, were aspirations and promises, not operative plans or economic policies.

Insofar as the party spoke of the future in programmatic terms between February and October, the discussion was almost exclusively political. Lenin led the way. In domestic policy, he promised a "commune state," a republic of soviets, and a socialist government supported by and favoring the proletariat and poor peasants. (Even here, however, it was only later that this would be interpreted to mean a Bolshevik monopoly of power.) In foreign policy, he promised an end to Russia's participation in the European war, diplomatic hostility toward and revolutionary war against the belligerent imperialist powers, and support for anti-capitalist revolutions. Meanwhile, Lenin's remarks on economic policy were sketchy, infrequent, and incidental, amounting to three general proposals: nationalization of banks and syndicates, nationalization of the land, and workers' control of industry.[35] In addition to being elliptical and variously interpreted, even by Bolsheviks,[36] all three involved economic control and regulation, not the transformation and expansion of the country's economic foundations. Indeed, the Bolsheviks' "perfunctory attention" to economic questions amazed a Menshevik observer: "No economic program was even referred to. . . . [How] this backwardness, this petty-bourgeois, peasant structure, this extreme exhaustion and chaos could be reconciled with a socialist reorganization . . . not a word was said." The Bolshevik leadership, he believed, "simply almost forgot about it." Instead of an economic program in October, complained one Bolshevik who had recently joined the party, there was "almost a vacuum." [37]

Several reasons explain why Bolshevism—an avowedly doctrinal movement—came to power without a coherent program of economic and social revolution. Before 1917, the party had concentrated almost exclusively on the political struggle against czarism, not the seemingly remote problems of a socialist régime. The February revolt surprised its leaders, who then spent the remaining months before October debating the prospects of power rather than its uses. Second, there was little in traditional Marxism to guide their thinking about post-insurrectionary questions. Marx himself had viewed economic modernization as the historical function of capitalism, neither addressing nor even admitting the possibility of socialists in the role of modernizers. In addition, he generally declined to speculate about the post-capitalist period in specifics, a tradition his followers found congenial and respected. Third was Lenin's censorious attitude toward discussing future problems. He preferred Napoleon's advice, "On s'engage et puis . . . on voit," later acknowledging that the Bolsheviks had acted accordingly in

1917.[38] His disinclination hampered the few Bolsheviks who occasionally wanted to think ahead. In early 1916, for example, Bukharin praised the recent program of the Dutch social democrats, a moderate set of demands calling for the nationalization of banks and large industry, progressive taxation, welfare legislation, and an eight-hour working day. Lenin angrily denounced Bukharin's remarks, explaining: "Since at present . . . the socialist revolution in the designated sense has not begun, the program of the Dutch is absurd." [39]

None of these considerations, however, fully explains why independent-minded Bolsheviks like Bukharin—who was no more prepared for the domestic policy crises of the post-October period than Lenin—had failed to think seriously about an economic program. The problem ran deeper, touching on the major dilemma that soon confronted the victorious Bolshevik movement. Despite his persistent advocacy of socialist revolution, Bukharin understood that Russia was a profoundly backward society.[40] How could the two be reconciled? For him and for the Bolshevik leadership generally, the answer was (and remained for several years) the presumed organic relationship between revolution in Russia and revolution in advanced European countries. Instead of confronting the domestic implications of a socialist government in Russia, Bolsheviks fell back on the assumption, a revered verity for Marxists, that proletarian revolution, like its bourgeois predecessor, would be an international phenomenon. Russia's social and economic immaturity, they reasoned, would be offset and overcome by comradely aid and support from the West. This programmatic escapism, more than anything else, clouded Bolshevik thinking about economic modernization and other domestic problems that lay ahead.

Such escapism was particularly (though not uniquely) evident in Bukharin's thinking in 1917. In his first article published after the fall of the czar, he questioned how Russia's small proletariat, if victorious, could cope with the economic and organizational problems of a backward peasant society. And he answered: "There is no doubt whatsoever that the Russian revolution will spread to the old capitalist countries and that sooner or later it will lead to the victory of the European proletariat." Economic questions, in other words, were international in content, since international revolution would result in a single "fraternal economy." [41] Bukharin's reasoning remained unchanged during the course of 1917. Two days after the Bolshevik coup, he repeated the argument, making it even more explicit: "International revolution means not only the purely *political* reinforcement of the Russian revolution. It means the *economic reinforcement.*" While carefully speaking only of the "firm" and "final victory" of the revolution, his appraisal of the prospects of an isolated socialist Russia was unambiguous: "A lasting victory of the Russian proletariat is . . . inconceivable without the support of the West European proletariat." [42]

By tying Russia's economic future to successful European uprisings, the doctrine of international revolution distracted the Bolsheviks from domestic realities, obscured the need for industrial and agrarian programs, and riveted their attention obsessively on events in the West. The result was one of the party's main tenets in 1917: the belief in revolutionary war, by which a revolutionary Russia would, if necessary, escape its isolation and secure its lifeline to the advanced industrial countries of Europe. As Bukharin promised at the Sixth Party Congress in the summer:

[B]efore the victorious worker-peasant revolution will stand the decla-ration of a revolutionary war, i.e., armed help for those proletarians who are not yet victorious. This war can assume different characters. If we are successful in repairing the destroyed economic organism, we will go over to the offensive. But if we cannot muster the force to conduct an offensive revolutionary war, then we will conduct a defen-sive revolutionary war . . . a holy war in the name of the interests of the whole proletariat, and this will ring like a fraternal call to arms. By such a revolutionary war, we will kindle the fire of the world socialist revolution.[43]

Revolutionary war became an official, integral part of Bolshevik thinking in 1917 largely because it replaced the missing program of social change and economic development.[44]

No Bolshevik leader seemed more distracted by the prospects of European revolution than Bukharin. On the eve of October, to take only one example, his proffered theoretical model of the old order was still state capitalism, that is, the most advanced of capi-talist societies.[45] Its remoteness from Russian reality was underlined in 1917 by Bukharin's infrequent, strangely inappropriate references to Russia's increasingly revolutionary peasantry. In July, he argued that the war had so accelerated the concentration and centralization of capital in capitalist countries that small producers—the petty bourgeoisie—were rapidly ceasing to play a meaningful political or economic role.[46] This at a time when an anti-landlord revolution of unprecedented dimensions was transforming the Russian country-side, dividing the land, establishing the small peasant farmer as the predominant figure in the village, and deepening the petty bour-geois character of Russian agriculture.

Not surprisingly, then, Bukharin's conception of socialist revolution left little place for the insurgent Russian peasant and the agrarian revolution then under way. Viewing the peasantry as a "proprietary group," willing to fight only in "defense of its land," he, like most Bolsheviks, thought of the ongoing revolution as a two-stage process: "the first phase—with the participation of the peasantry which is striving to obtain land; the second phase—after the defection of the satiated peasantry—the phase of the proletarian revolution, when only proletarian elements and the proletariat of Western Europe will support the Russian proletariat." This implied that the two upheavals of 1917—rural and urban—would necessarily part company and, because of "the deep principled difference between the peasantry and proletariat," come into conflict.[47] Again, the Russian proletariat's supposedly indispensable ally was its European counterpart. Bukharin's subsequent revision of this awkward understanding—his discovery that the two revolutions had in fact been component parts of a single fortuitous upheaval—underlay much of his thinking in the 1920's. His conception in 1917, however, served only to compound the Bolshevik dilemma.

Whatever the reasons, the Bolsheviks' failure to think about an economic program before taking power became an important factor in the controversies that followed. It set the stage for the party's twelve-year search for viable economic policies commensurate with its revolutionary ambitions and socialist faith. It also assured that the search would be bitterly divisive, marked by an absence of consensus on basic principles. In particular, it set the stage for the central theme of Bukharin's political career after October—his persistent effort to develop a program and theory of "building socialism" in Russia. How little he—the party's leading theorist—was prepared for the task would soon be demonstrated by his participation in the Left Communist opposition, which revealed that, apart from revolutionary war, he had no long-range policies to offer a party that had suddenly become the government of Russia.

While elements of Bukharin's famous Left Communism were already present in 1917, the stereotype of him as a particularly doctrinaire proponent of extremist policies before 1921 requires some revision. Clearly, neither the Bolshevik Left nor Right began with doctrines easily applicable to domestic policy; improvisation was to be the rule. Nor, as we saw earlier, was Bukharin tempermentally incapable of moderation and compromise. The rumor that even in 1917 he was "more Left than Lenin" apparently derived from a misunderstanding of their brief literary debate over the updating of the party's 1903 program.[48] Bukharin wanted to replace the old theoretical introduction on pre-monopoly capitalism with a new description reflecting his ideas about state capitalism and imperialism. Lenin insisted that the old introduction was still relevant in its essentials. Though the dispute suddenly revealed the differences implicit in their understandings of modern capitalism, and to a lesser extent revived the controversy over self-determination, it did not involve actual party policy or tactics, on which they agreed.[49]

There was, moreover, recurring evidence even in 1917 that Bukharin's radicalism did not preclude realistic moderation and compromise. He was not, for example, among those several Bureau leaders who urged insurrection during the abortive street demonstrations in July. Nor were his views on the various tactical issues that divided moderates and radicals at the Sixth Party Congress consistently leftist: on one, he took a middle position, refusing to support "one tendency or the other"; on another, he argued, against objections from the Left, that the revolutionary tide in Russia was temporarily spent. He was even willing to amend his resolution on revolutionary war to accommodate doubts that Russia would be able to wage such a war.[50] And on one important occasion in September, he was plainly less radical than Lenin: he and the rest of the Central Committee voted to reject (and burn) Lenin's letters demanding immediate insurrection.[51] Finally, in a circumspect article published two days after the Bolshevik coup, he wrote in a tone less emboldened by victory than sobered by the "colossal" difficulties ahead. Clear-cut solutions, he warned, were not in the offing; the party would certainly make mistakes.[52]

This capacity for pragmatic moderation was to be diminished and obscured by the bitter controversies over foreign policy during the first months of Bolshevik rule. Later, as Bukharin became aware of the party's domestic problems and of the trauma inherent in prolonged social upheaval, such moderation would become the cornerstone of his thinking. For, in addition to having ignored the domestic implications of a Bolshevik government, he had not calculated what he would later call the "costs of revolution." In particular, he did not foresee the three-year Russian civil war, which was to compound the destruction and agony already inflicted on Russia by four years of European war and revolution. Least of all did he anticipate the human costs. The amorphous Marxist concept of class struggle figured in his pre-October writings as little more than the "expropriation of the expropriators," promising the transfer of property and redistribution of wealth, not the murderous consequences of marauding armies.

The bloody fighting in Moscow, where five hundred Bolsheviks alone died (compared to a total of only six people in Petrograd),[53] may already have alerted Bukharin to the impending "costs of revolution." Stukov later recalled their mood when he and Bukharin arrived in Petrograd to report on their victory: "When I started to speak about the number of victims something welled up in my throat and I stopped. I see Nikolai Ivanovich throwing himself on the chest of a bearded worker, and they start to sob. People start to cry." [54] The real revolution had begun.

CHAPTER III

The Politics of Civil War

*When hopes and dreams are loose in the streets, it is
well for the timid to lock doors, shutter windows and
lie low until the wrath has passed. For there is often
a monstrous incongruity between the hopes, however
noble and tender, and the action which follows them.
It is as if ivied maidens and garlanded youths were
to herald the four horsemen of the Apocalypse.*

—ERIC HOFFER, *The True Believer*

FROM 1918 to the end of the civil war in 1921, the Bolsheviks were
engaged in a desperate struggle against anti-revolutionary Russian
and foreign armies to survive as the government of Soviet Russia.
The impact of this fierce experience on the authoritarian party and
political system that emerged can hardly be overestimated. For
in addition to reimposing centralized bureaucratic authority, it
brought about a pervasive militarization of Soviet political life,
implanting what one Bolshevik called a "military-soviet culture," [1]
that lived on after the civil war itself had ended. Equally important,
by mid-1918 political survival had become intertwined with another, only slightly less consuming goal: the rapid, and in significant measure forcible, transformation of Soviet society along
socialist lines. And while this experiment also came to an end, it,
too, influenced political events for many years to come.

Having neither an army nor a program at the outset, the party
was unprepared for both challenges. For three years, it lived from
crisis to crisis, improvising strategy and makeshift solutions, the
meaning of the revolution becoming almost inseparable from the
"defense of the revolution," the actions and statements of party
leaders being inspired both by what had to be done and by half-
formed conceptions of what should be done. This was no less true
of Bukharin. A co-mingling of military expediency and ideological

conviction shaped his politics and thinking from his Left Communism in 1918, through his theoretical enshrinement of the party's warfare policies in 1920, to his role in the controversy that attended the collapse of those policies in 1920–1.

With radicalism still predominant in the party, Bukharin and the young Muscovites enjoyed a strong political position during the first months of Bolshevik rule. Almost immediately, they again provided Lenin with crucial support. Right Bolsheviks, together with several party leaders who had not opposed insurrection, now demanded a coalition government representing all socialist parties. Bolshevik opposition to Lenin's insistence on an all-Bolshevik régime ran high, including several Central Committee members and almost half of the Council of People's Commissars.[2]

Lenin finally prevailed, again partly by relying on the Moscow Left. Bukharin and Sokolnikov were named to head the Bolshevik delegation in the newly elected Constituent Assembly, displacing party moderates who opposed disbanding the Assembly.[3] Bukharin then spoke for the party at the Assembly's single meeting in early January 1918. Responding to the challenge of the majority, who were Socialist Revolutionaries, he voiced the mood of those Bolsheviks, headed by Lenin, who were determined to go it alone. Charging the other socialist parties with having participated in the discredited provisional government, he drew a clear line: "Comrades, before us . . . is that watershed which now divides this entire Assembly into . . . two irreconcilable camps, camps of principle . . . for socialism or against socialism." [4]

Their support for Lenin's maximalism brought Bukharin and his friends key posts, particularly in the emerging economic apparatus, which Bolsheviks regarded as the most important area. In November 1917, Bukharin was delegated to draft legislation on nationalization and on the creation of an agency to direct the country's economic life, which was approved in December. From his proposal emerged the Supreme Economic Council.[5] Osinskii, who with Smirnov had previously headed the new State Bank, became the council's first chairman, and was later joined on its executive bureau by Bukharin and Smirnov. Meanwhile, Lomov, who was also Commissar of Justice in the first Council of People's Commissars, supervised the nationalization of Moscow banks and industries and "the reorganization of the entire power apparatus in Moscow and the region." In January 1918 he, too, joined the presidium of the Supreme Economic Council, becoming its deputy chairman shortly later. When the council's official journal appeared, it was under the editorship of Osinskii, Smirnov, and Lomov.[6] The economic reins of Soviet Russia, it must have seemed to older Bolsheviks, had been placed in the hands of the young Muscovites.

Their collective prominence reflected Bukharin's growing authority in the party, as evidenced by his role as Bolshevik spokesman at the Constituent Assembly and in formulating the ruling party's first policy statements.[7] Particularly significant was Lenin's reliance on Bukharin in "socialist policies in the areas of finance and economics," a clear indication that this subject, later so divisive, did not yet separate them. Indeed, on November 27 (December 10), 1917, Lenin proposed that Bukharin and his friend Piatakov form a small commission responsible for "discussing fundamental questions of the government's economic policy." The nomination drew objections in the Central Committee, ostensibly on grounds that Bukharin was urgently needed at *Pravda*, the party's official newspaper. Lenin insisted that the all-important matter of economic policy required the full attention of "adept and able people" like Bukharin, but he was overruled. Bukharin therefore became editor of *Pravda*, a post he held, with one brief interruption, for the next twelve years.[8]

At the outset, then, Bukharin and the young Muscovites played an extraordinarily important role in the organization and direction of the new party-state.[9] In early 1918, however, their collective influence on official Bolshevik policy suddenly turned to collective opposition against Lenin and his new allies in the party. At issue was the leader's decision to terminate Russia's involvement in the European war by signing a separate and onerous peace with Germany.

To understand Bukharin's role in the Left Communist opposition, as it became known, it is necessary to understand that this movement actually went through two stages. From January through early March 1918, it was primarily an opposition directed against Lenin's peace proposals, advocating instead a revolutionary war against the advancing German army. Between the Left Communists and Lenin stood Trotsky and his supporters, whose simultaneous hostility to the treaty and skepticism about the prospects of military resistance produced their ambiguous formula, "Neither war nor peace." This phase of Left Communism ended in defeat with the signing of the treaty at Brest Litovsk in late February and its ratification after a bitter debate at the Seventh Party Congress in early March. The movement then entered a second stage, with the Left's fire switching to Lenin's revised economic policies. Bukharin's role was different in the two stages.[10]

He was the acknowledged leader of the movement against the peace treaty and for revolutionary war, speaking for the group in the culminating debate at the party congress in March.[11] Thus, for two months, at twenty-nine, Bukharin headed the largest and most powerful Bolshevik opposition in the history of Soviet Russia. At various times during the controversy, opponents of the treaty commanded a majority of the city and provincial soviets, several of the largest party organizations, a majority in the Central Committee (as long as Trotsky's group voted with the Left or abstained), and probably a majority of the party's rank-and-file membership. Even on the decisive vote, Lenin was unable to muster a majority in the Central Committee, and only Trotsky's abstention allowed him to outvote the Left. The final vote at the Seventh Congress—30 in favor of the treaty, 11 against, and 4 abstaining—did not reflect the opposition's real support within the party.[12]

Several factors made Bukharin the natural leader of the opposition. Relentless hostility toward the imperialist powers, expressed as the promise of a "holy war" against the European bourgeoisie, had been an emotional and popular part of the party's insurrectionary program. In abandoning it, Lenin moved away from the Bolshevik Left and toward those Bolsheviks who had opposed or resisted his course in 1917.[13] Radical Bolsheviks were thus left leaderless and in need of a ranking figure to defend their betrayed ideal. None was better suited than Bukharin, who, even before the dispute, had been closely identified with the idea of revolutionary war.[14] Of the seven Central Committee members who opposed the treaty unconditionally—himself, Bubnov, Felix Dzerzhinskii, Nikolai Krestinskii, Moshe Uritskii, Lomov, and Iakovleva—he alone had sufficient stature in the party to become a leader.

If Bukharin had any reservations about taking up the banner of revolutionary war—and there is circumstantial evidence that he was less than totally committed before mid-February [15]—the virtual unanimity of his generation of party leaders, especially his Moscow friends, probably dispelled them. As early as December 28 (January 10), the Moscow Regional Bureau had demanded "a cessation of peace negotiations with imperialist Germany as well as a breaking off of any diplomatic relations with all diplomatic robbers of all countries." Buoyed up by the success of their audacity in 1917, the young Muscovites were in no mood for conciliation or compromise. Their determination to challenge Lenin almost certainly prodded

Bukharin, who also believed that the lesson of the Bolshevik victory in Moscow, "when we went forward without organized forces," was applicable to the present situation.[16] This habit on the part of left-wing Bolsheviks of referring doubters to the "lessons of October" was to be a regular feature of intra-party disputes during the next decade.

The influence of long-standing personal, generational, and political associations on the Left Communist movement in general and Bukharin's leadership in particular was apparent throughout. While the movement included prominent representatives of party organizations throughout the country, Moscow, and especially the Bureau, became "the citadel of Left Communism." [17] The Bureau's youthful leaders of 1917 (Bukharin, Osinskii, Smirnov, Lomov, Iakovleva, Stukov, and Kizelshtein) were always in the forefront. The movement's roots in the more distant past were underscored by yet another appearance of the Bukharin-Osinskii-Smirnov *troika* (now supplemented by Karl Radek), which dated back to 1909, as the editorial board of the opposition's journal *Kommunist*, published by the Bureau.[18] As Left Communism grew into a nationwide movement, the Bureau began to function as its "Central Committee," its "organizing center." In this sense, despite its national strength, it was a native Moscow movement, with Bukharin, its indigenous leader, surrounded by political friends, many of whom he had known since his 1906–10 days as a Moscow committeeman. Understandably, the advocacy of revolutionary war came to be known as the "Moscow point of view." [19]

The generational motif also made itself felt again. Several older party figures—among them, Pokrovskii and Ivan Skvortsov-Stepanov, two of the most venerable—were Left Communists. But the opposition's leadership was strikingly youthful; the division that had characterized the left-right spectrum in Moscow in 1917 was now being duplicated in the party at large. While youthful righteousness fired the Left's opposition to Lenin and those Bolsheviks on whom he was relying for support, the leader adopted the stance of a sober-minded elder statesman, turning the youthfulness of the opposition leaders against them. "Youth," he said sardonically of the "young Muscovites," "is one of the most outstanding qualities of this group." The Muscovites were no less aware of the generational issue. Looking back at the controversy seven years later, Bukharin described himself and his allies as "we, 'the young,' 'the Left'. . . ." [20] In important respects, then, Left Communism was also the revolt of the generation of 1905 headed by its titular leader, Bukharin.

Indeed, the father-son element in the controversy probably

helps explain the opposition's eventual defeat. At the peak of their political strength against the peace treaty, the Left Communists represented an enthusiastic mass movement, probably a majority in the party. Although the threat of the German army increasingly undercut their position, theirs was really a failure of leadership, not of popular support. Left-wing Socialist Revolutionaries, who had joined the Bolsheviks to give the original government a semblance of coalition, for example, also opposed the treaty and offered their support in forming a new government to replace Lenin's. Left Communist leaders refused to do so, partly because of party loyalty but also because none among them regarded himself as an alternative leader of the Bolshevik revolution.[21] Bukharin complained bitterly that Lenin's policy was "fatal for the Revolution," and that a majority opposed him. But when asked by an acquaintance why he did not move decisively against Lenin, he reportedly exclaimed: "Am I of sufficient stature to become leader of a party and to declare war on Lenin and the Bolshevik Party? No, don't let us deceive ourselves!"[22]

Despite the coherence of the Left Communist movement, the political inclinations of its leaders were not identical. In particular, as the controversy developed, significant differences of outlook between Bukharin and more extreme Left Communists such as Osinskii and Stukov began to be apparent.[23] Obscured by the acrimony over the peace treaty, they were to be important in the second stage of the opposition. Nor did Lenin always share the views of his adherents. He was notably less pessimistic, for example, than those pro-treaty Bolsheviks who saw no prospect of revolution in the West and were already eulogizing Russia's revolutionary leadership. Indeed, beneath the mutual recriminations, Lenin and Bukharin shared "one and the same general premise: Without a world revolution we will not pull through."[24] What truly divided them lay elsewhere.

Historians usually record the advocacy of revolutionary war as Bukharin's folly, a "suicidal," "foolhardy" proposal born of emotion and ideological faith rather than sober judgment. Bukharin, however, insisted repeatedly that his conclusions, unlike Lenin's, were the product of "cold calculation."[25] In fact, both elements—an emotional commitment to cherished ideals and a logic grounded in Russian conditions—were combined in Bukharin's argument. The impassioned, quixotic features of his opposition to the peace treaty derived from his belief that European revolution was imminent and that without it the Bolshevik régime could not long survive. Most Bolsheviks shared this view, but Bukharin infused it with a desperate urgency: "The Russian revolution will either be saved by the international proletariat or it will perish under the blows of international capital." He saw no alternative: "Everything depends on whether or not the international revolution is victorious . . . the international revolution—and that alone—is our salvation." [26]

In the light of later controversies, it is significant that Bukharin explained this dire proposition not in terms of Russia's economic backwardness but of an external military threat. He drew an even more alarming picture of the external menace than did Lenin, arguing flatly that mutual antipathy to Bolshevism would inevitably unite the warring Western powers in a campaign to depose the Bolsheviks and "transform Russia into their colony." "Many facts," he maintained, "indicate that this agreement between the two hostile coalitions has already occurred." While Lenin emphasized the immediate threat of the advancing German army, Bukharin worried about a "union" of imperialist powers which would render meaningless any unilateral treaty. Only an international revolutionary front, he insisted, could withstand the inevitable united imperialist front against Soviet Russia. [27]

Despair for the Bolsheviks' survival—and it was widespread in the party in early 1918 [28]—and faith in an impending European revolution led Bukharin to regard the Russian proletariat as only "one of the detachments" of the international movement. Again, most Bolsheviks professed to share this view. Bukharin, however, implied that the broader movement should have priority over the Russian "detachment." Encouraged by strikes and civil disorders in Berlin, Vienna, and Budapest, he demanded that Soviet Russia abet revolution in Europe by an act of valiant defiance, "a holy war against militarism and imperialism." Negotiating with imperialist Germany, on the other hand, meant "preserving our socialist republic" by "gambling with the international movement." Not Russia's negligible military force, but the symbol of the Russian revolution was at issue. To stain its banner would be to undermine revolution abroad; to cease foreign revolutionary propaganda, as the German terms demanded, would be to silence the "bell resounding throughout the world, " to "cut off our tongue." [29]

Bukharin's conviction that Soviet Russia's power to influence European events derived from its ideals, not its army, produced his most quixotic gesture. In February, there appeared a slight chance that the allies would supply Russia to fight on against Germany. Acceptance was urged by Lenin and Trotsky when the issue came before the Central Committee. Bukharin opposed it as "inadmissible." He wanted a revolutionary war, but not with "the support of the imperialists." When the motion passed (6 votes to 5), he reportedly cried: "What are we doing? We are turning the party into a dung heap." [30] Lenin's willingness to deal individually with capitalist countries suggested temporary cohabitation with them. Bukharin, on the other hand, regarded "peaceful co-existence . . . between the Soviet Republic and international capital" as both impossible and inappropriate. A final reckoning could not and should not be avoided: "We always said . . . that sooner or later the Russian revolution would have to clash with international capital. That moment has now come." [31]

Two unspoken considerations probably also influenced Bukharin's willingness to wager everything on revolution in the West. The first was his understanding of modern capitalism, which implied the unlikelihood of revolution in mature capitalist societies without the external strains of war. Those strains were now present, and Bukharin may have worried that an abatement of hostilities would enable "state capitalist" régimes to stabilize themselves. Second, like many of his non-Marxist contemporaries, Bukharin had come to see in the continuing carnage of the European war a threat to civilization itself. Socialist revolution, which alone could end imperialism and militarism forever, was therefore the hope of "saving mankind's culture." [32] Internationalizing the revolution was for Bukharin not only Soviet Russia's salvation, but mankind's. If proposing revolutionary war to end imperialist war seemed contradictory, it was not unlike the sentiment expressed by the poet Kenneth Patchen: "Let us have madness openly, O men of my generation. Let us follow the footsteps of this slaughtered age. . ."

When Bukharin's case rested on appeals to world revolution, rhetoric prevailed. At the center of his argument, however, there was a hard kernel of logic derived from Russian conditions and the nature of the Russian revolution. It involved his understanding of the nature of revolutionary war as opposed to the notion of a "breathing spell," which by February had become the *raison d'être* of Lenin's peace proposal. Lenin insisted that the remnants of Russia's army were in no condition to fight the German war machine; the country first had to organize its will and repair its forces. The treaty, he hoped, would provide the necessary time: "I want to concede space . . . in order to win time." [33]

But Lenin and Bukharin were not talking about the same kind of warfare. The former thought in terms of conventional military operations, of well-organized armies confronting each other in traditional combat. Bukharin envisaged something very different, in effect guerrilla war:

Comrade Lenin has chosen to define revolutionary war only and exclusively as a war of large armies with defeats in accordance to all the rules of military science. We propose that war from our side—at least in the beginning—will inevitably take the character of a partisan war of flying detachments.[34]

Lenin sought a respite of weeks, even days. Bukharin maintained that in such a brief period Russia could neither repair her transportation system, establish supply lines, nor rebuild her army, and that therefore the military benefits of a "breathing spell" were "illusions." [35]

If the possibility of building a conventional army was closed to Soviet Russia, Bukharin argued, the development of a new kind of army was not. It would be a partisan force, emerging "in the very process of this struggle, during which more and more of the masses will gradually be drawn to our side, while in the imperialist camp, to the contrary, there will be ever increasing elements of further distintegration." Severe defeats at the outset were likely; but, he continued, not even the fall of major cities could destroy the revolution. Soviet power lay not merely in the Council of People's Commissars, but in countless local organizations of workers and peasants: "If our power is really of this type, then the imperialists will have to yank it by the roots from every factory, from every plant, from every rural hamlet and village. If our Soviet power is such a power, it will not perish with the surrender of Petrograd and Moscow. . . ." Bukharin did not contest Lenin's argument that the Russian peasant, the majority class, did not want to fight. He countered, however, that the peasant would fight when he saw that his newly acquired land was threatened: "These peasants will be drawn into the struggle when they hear, see, and know that their land, boots, and grain are being taken from them—this is the only real perspective." Others said that the pacific mood of the peasantry precluded revolutionary war. Bukharin answered: "But just this muzhik will save us. . . ." [36]

Bukharin's conception of irregular partisan forces encircling and defeating a conventional military invader reflected his faith in the popular base of the Bolshevik revolution. It also anticipated Soviet resistance to another German army two decades later, as well as the kind of guerrilla warfare that would become commonplace in other peasant societies. Even in 1918, as Bukharin's cause went down to defeat, it became clear that his judgment had merit. At that moment, Ukrainian peasants were resisting the German army in a similar fashion. Nor did the Brest peace treaty bring the kind of respite Lenin hoped for; in the end, a Soviet army had to be improvised in the course of combat.[37] Finally, the Bolsheviks' civil war victory eventually confirmed Bukharin's underlying assumption: The peasant would defend the revolutionary government as long as it guaranteed his tenure on the land.

The advocacy of partisan war—led by the proletariat but fought primarily by peasants—represented a new element in Bukharin's thinking. Previously, in traditional Marxist fashion, he had regarded the peasantry as a socially retrograde class whose support would expire as the revolution deepened into a proletarian or socialist phase. Now he seemed to be taking into account the central (and iconoclastic) fact of 1917—an agrarian revolution equal to if not greater than that in the cities. In looking to the peasantry to "save us" in 1918, Bukharin suggested that he was neither oblivious to nor disdainful of its class role, though it would be several years before he reinterpreted this role as part of a revised understanding of the Bolshevik revolution itself.

With the ratification of the Brest treaty in early March, the first phase of Left Communism came to an end. Throughout the next two months, the controversy focused on domestic issues as the embittered opposition turned against Lenin's proposal to moderate the Bolshevik government's initial economic policies. These policies had themselves been relatively moderate. In addition to limited nationalization, steps had been taken to eliminate inequities in housing and food distribution, an eight-hour working day was legislated, and private ownership of land terminated, though with the peasant's right to occupy and work his new holding affirmed. In the beginning, Bolshevik political radicalism did not further affect the economy, where the party was still cautious and in some respects reformist.[38]

At first, two of these initial policies—workers' control of industrial enterprises and selective nationalization—represented a happy coupling of expediency and ideology from the party's point of view. They at once gave legal sanction to the factory seizures of 1917, satisfied the party's commitment to the "expropriation of the expropriators," and struck at political and economic resistance to the Bolshevik government. By March 1918, however, they had seriously compounded the economic chaos and destruction wrought by four years of war and revolution, further crippling Russia's industrial production.

Lenin reacted to the worsening situation with characteristic decisiveness, announcing in early April 1918 his determination to change course. His plan called for an end to nationalization and expropriation, and a *modus vivendi* with large private capital. The new economic order would rely on limited state ownership, while preserving private (or joint) ownership and management in most enterprises. The Soviet state would regulate the private sector through financial and political suasion. The survival of his government, Lenin reasoned, required the technical collaboration of the large bourgeoisie, the termination of the revolution's destructive phase, and the reimposition of managerial authority. Centralized control was to be established over local soviets; labor discipline was to supplant workers' control. Lenin's commitment to economic recovery was absolute: wage incentives were to be restored. In short, as he frankly acknowledged, there was to be a "suspension of the offensive against capital." [39]

Searching for a conceptual definition of his proposals, Lenin described the projected mixed economy as "state capitalism," his model being Germany's wartime economy. State capitalism, he argued, would represent an enormous step forward for backward, petty bourgeois Russia, a giant step toward socialism:

I said that state capitalism would be our salvation; if we had it in Russia, then the transition to full socialism would be easy . . . because state capitalism is something centralized, calculated, controlled and socialized, and we lack this. We are threatened by the petty bourgeois element, which more than anything else has been prepared by Russia's history and her economy, and which prevents us from taking the very step on which the success of socialism depends.

To Lenin, state capitalism meant modern, efficient, and centralized industry; if Soviet Russia could attain it, it would be "three-fourths of socialism." [40]

The Left Communists responded to his proposals with an angry set of theses condemning them generally and specifically. Behind the new policies they saw the recreancy of "the right wing of the party" and "the psychology of peace." All of Lenin's proposals —his labor and wage policies, freezing of nationalization, agreements with "captains of industry," and his underlying idea of a rapprochement with private capital and the old administrative order

—were denounced as opening the way for "the complete supremacy of finance capital." Lenin's plan, they predicted, would lead to "bureaucratic centralization, the supremacy of various commissars, the loss by local soviets of their independence, and . . . the abandonment of . . . government from below—of the 'commune state.'" Scornful of compromise, the Left's theses demanded an entirely different course: relentless hostility to the bourgeoisie; an assault on capitalist economic relations; nationalization and "socialization" of industry; workers' control and preservation of the authority of local economic soviets; and support for poor peasants against rich, as well as the development of large-scale collective farming. In their criticisms and policy preferences, the Left Communists anticipated the platforms of other leftist oppositions to come. Their warning against traveling "the ruinous path of petty bourgeois policies" would be heard in the party many times again.[41]

Although short-lived, Lenin's "state capitalism" of April–May 1918 acquired retrospective significance because of its resemblance to what became known officially after 1921 as the New Economic Policy or simply NEP. Both were conceived as a mixed economy combining a limited public sector with a large private one. And even though the country and economy were very different in 1918 and 1921, Bolsheviks who later sought to legitimize NEP in the party mind could reasonably point out its similarities to Lenin's "state capitalism." [42] Since Bukharin was to be NEP's greatest defender, his position in this second phase of Left Communism is especially significant.

The ambiguity of Bukharin's political role and views throughout the economic controversy indicate that he lacked the fanatical certainty that had characterized his opposition to the Brest peace treaty. During the almost three-month-long economic debates, he published only one article directly related to the dispute, and this raised a theoretical, not a practical, objection to Lenin's policies.[43] Given the literary rather than organizational nature of the confrontation, his comparative silence was telling. Furthermore, during the controversy he completed a long pamphlet entitled *The Communist Program*, apparently designed to be the first popular exposition of Bolshevism in power. While it set out the radical aspirations of militant communism, its statements on immediate economic policy were strikingly moderate. The pamphlet's success—it was widely circulated as an official document and reprinted in most Western languages—suggests that its views reflected the mainstream of party thinking, as well as Lenin's.[44]

Thus Bukharin had ceased to be the leading spokesman and

chief animator of Left Communism. With the ratification of the peace treaty, the movement lost much of its nationwide following and became even more a Moscow operation. At the same time, Bukharin retired to the sidelines, issuing only sporadic objections to Lenin's proposals, while Osinskii took over the leadership of the Left Communists in the economic controversy. Always more radical than Bukharin on domestic affairs, he became Lenin's most implacable and extremist opponent.[45] It is clear that this juncture began the end of the Bukharin-Osinskii-Smirnov alliance; Osinskii and Smirnov were to be mainstays in party oppositions during most of the following decade.

Critical of conciliatory economic measures since December 1917, Osinskii now emerged as the chief advocate of radicalism. He wrote the Left Communists' programmatic theses, their most extensive and uncompromising indictment of Lenin's proposals. The document embodied his views, which he reiterated throughout April and May, and indeed long after the dispute had ended. He provided the impassioned tenor of the Left's accusation and demands, railing against any accommodation with the old order, against all centralized authority, labor discipline, and employment of bourgeois specialists, and demanding maximum nationalization and "socialization" of production. Osinskii, by his own account, "occupied the most 'left' position." [46]

Bukharin now found it necessary "to disassociate myself from those who embrace me." Acutely aware of the difficult problems created by the economic disorder, he refused to emulate the extremism of other Left Communists. On the issue of employing bourgeois specialists, for example, he saw no principle involved, announcing that he was "farther to the right than Lenin." Those oppositionists whose advocacy of workers' control bordered on syndicalism did not speak for Bukharin; he had sternly warned against the tendency in January. Nor did he sympathize with the semi-anarchistic resistance to a strong Soviet state, arguing instead: "In the interval between capitalism and communism . . . the working class will have to endure a furious struggle with its internal and external foes. And for such a struggle a strong, wide, well-constructed organization is required . . . the Proletarian State. . . ." [47] As for agriculture, Bukharin, like most Bolsheviks (including Lenin), endorsed the 1917 revolutionary redistribution of the land, but asserted that future progress required large-scale collective cultivation; he suggested no way of reconciling these two positions. Not surprisingly, midway in the economic dispute Lenin informed Bukharin that he was "nine-tenths in agreement with him." [48]

Nonetheless, Bukharin continued to side with the Left, speaking for them, however constrainedly, remaining an editor of *Kommunist*, and lending his name to their theses.[49] In part, this probably reflected his friendship with the young Muscovites, as well as the bitterness generated by the Brest controversy. But it also reflected his concern that the political outlook underlying the treaty decision would endanger "the economic program of October," that Bolsheviks who professed allegiance to proletarian revolution but who "instead of raising the banner 'Forward to Communism,' raise the banner 'Back to Capitalism,'" were getting the upper hand.[50] Although Bukharin's rhetoric, and presumably his mood, were still more radical than Lenin's, the recriminatory animus of the peace controversy was absent, and compromise on secondary issues had become possible.[51]

Bukharin did have practical objections to Lenin's economic proposals. The most important stemmed from his understanding of the nature of Russia's backwardness and how to cope with it:

The backwardness of Russia is not in the small number of large enterprises—on the contrary, we have quite a number. . . . Its backwardness consists in the fact that the *whole* of our industry occupies too little place in comparison with the vast areas of our rural districts. But . . . we must not belittle the importance of our industry. . . .

Therefore, he argued, if the party was to organize anything, the large-scale economic complexes, particularly the industrial and financial syndicates, had to be nationalized immediately. These "principal economic fortresses of capital" would serve as "the basic economic nerve"—"the basic bastions"—of the new Soviet economic system. The only modern and centrally organized components of the Russian economy, they had to be transformed into a state or socialist sector.[52]

Though critical of Lenin's plan to regulate large private capital, Bukharin did not advocate indiscriminate nationalization. He proposed to begin "with that which is not only easier to take, but easier also to organize . . . and which can be arranged in the smoothest way." Compared to Lenin's proposals, Bukharin's argument may have sounded radical, particularly in such slogans as "a socialist revolution, i.e., a revolution which expropriates capital," or "through the socialization of production toward socialism."[53] In fact, he apparently envisaged something similar to the future NEP, where state control would encompass only key sectors, or what was later called the "commanding heights." He specifically exempted small enterprises and subsidiary industries from nationalization, pointing out that the "economic fortresses" were sufficient, since "less important industries will also become dependent to a great extent on the greater ones even before any nationalization takes place." [54] The idea that an island of state industry could exercise influence throughout the economy was to be the basic concept of NEP. And in this sense Bukharin's proposals of 1918, more than Lenin's, anticipated the party's economic policies of the 1920's.

His attitudes toward workers' control, labor discipline, and managerial authority were less clear. These emotional issues were complicated by two factors. First, the tone of the original decree countermanding workers' control and giving "dictatorial powers" to the appropriate commissar was sufficiently extreme to provoke even the mildest critic of centralized authority.[55] Second was the ambiguity of the term "workers' control" itself: did it mean management by factory committees, local soviets, trade unions, the Supreme Economic Council, or merely a "workers' state"? There were almost as many Bolshevik opinions as possibilities, and Bukharin himself seemed to hold different ones on different occasions. Knowingly or not, for example, he had adumbrated the eventual statist solution as early as October 1917, when he defined workers' control as meaning that "state power is in the hands of another class," the proletariat. Similarly, he did not share the Left's unequivocal rejection of labor discipline, and in May 1918 even urged some form of "compulsory labor service." [56]

Here, too, however, Bukharin resisted Lenin's new course. He denied that responsibility for the economic chaos lay exclusively with factory committees and workers' control, pointing instead to the general breakdown in transportation and supply. Opposing the initial decree but offering no alternative solution, he could only plead for "the self-activity of the working class," and stop short before the dilemma: "There must be a conductor's baton, but it must be moved by the workers themselves." [57] Something other than pragmatism, it is clear, was behind his continuing opposition.

After the signing of the peace treaty, Bukharin's Left Communism was less a commitment to actual policies than to a vision of the new order as the antithesis of the old. In particular, the revolution promised the destruction of the monster Leviathan state and all that it represented in modern society. Whatever the outlook of other Bolsheviks, Bukharin took seriously the idea of a revolutionary "commune state"—a state "without police, without a standing army, without an officialdom," as Lenin (to Bukharin's enthusiastic applause) had sketched it in State and Revolution. The definitive feature of the "commune state" was to be its repudiation of bureaucratic political and economic authority. It would be a state without bureaucrats, "that is, privileged people alienated from the masses and standing *over* the masses." In short, it was to be a state without élites, the masses themselves becoming society's administrators so that "*all* will become 'bureaucrats' for a time in order that *nobody* will be able to become a 'bureaucrat.' . . ." [58]

In this vision, the soviets were to serve as the political structure of the "commune state," while workers' control, by creating a kind of grass roots industrial democracy, would function similarly in economic life.[59] With bureaucracy eliminated, the working class would have freedom and self-government at the most basic level— its place of labor. Thus, when Lenin moved to curtail the factory committees and reimpose bureaucratic authority from above, Bukharin evoked the dictum of the everyman administrator, the central image in *State and Revolution*. "It is good," he said, "that the cook will be taught to govern the state; but what will there be if a Commissar is placed over the cook? Then he will never learn to govern the state." [60] Here was the dilemma: an apparatus of everymen or of bureaucratic élites. It underlay two enduring fears of idealistic Bolsheviks: the potential emergence of a new ruling class, and the "bureaucratic degeneration" of the Soviet system.

The goal of a "commune state" reflected the utopian aspirations of Bolshevism. Arguably, it was doomed from the outset because it implied that a modern industrial society (to which the Bolsheviks, as Marxist socialists, were committed) lent itself to a simple, uncomplicated administrative order easily operated by nonspecialists. However, the process of economic modernization, in the Soviet Union as elsewhere, has accelerated quite the opposite development by promoting specialization and the formation of managerial élites. In 1918, this contradiction had not become apparent to many Bolsheviks, including Bukharin. The dream of a "commune state" still captivated its dreamers, of whom it could be said, as Goethe remarked of another crusader: "Napoleon went forth to seek Virtue, but, since she was not to be found, he got Power."

A combination of realism and idealism had placed Bukharin somewhere between Lenin and the extremist Left Communists in the controversy over economic-policy. In the end, however, it was not actual policy but a theoretical issue that provoked his sharpest outcry against Lenin. The argument centered on Lenin's description of the Soviet economy as "state capitalist," a semantic conflict which demonstrated once again that the two men had different understandings of modern capitalism. In applying the term to his policies, Lenin used "state capitalism" as a synonym for state regulation of private capital and modern economic management. He thus gave "state capitalism" a neutral connotation, devoid of class or historical content, and saw no contradiction in the proposition that a proletarian state might preside over a state capitalist economy.

Whatever the merits of Lenin's concept, it violated a theoretical understanding central to Bukharin's Marxism. For him, state capitalism *was* modern capitalism; it had defined his thinking about imperialism and, above all, the modern Leviathan state and its "penal capitalism" since 1915.[61] In Bukharin's mind, Lenin's application of the term to Soviet Russia was therefore outrageous. His single literary polemic after the treaty debates—pedagogically entitled "Some Fundamental Understandings of Contemporary Economics"—attacked the leader on this point. State capitalism, he explained, was not technique, but "a quite specific and purely historical category"; it was "one of the *varieties* of capitalism . . . a definite form of the power of capital." Lenin's usage made no sense:

State capitalism under the dictatorship of the proletariat—this is an absurdity, soft-boiled boots. For state capitalism presupposes the dictatorship of finance capital; it is the transfer of production to the dictatorially organized imperialist state. State capitalism without capitalists is exactly the same sort of nonsense. "Noncapitalist capitalism"—this is the height of confusion. . . .[62]

Bukharin's understanding of state capitalism had not changed since 1915, nor was it ever to do so. Underlying as it did his thinking about the contemporary world, about capitalism and socialism, it could not be compromised: "Because state capitalism is the fusing of the bourgeois state with capitalist trusts, it is obvious that one cannot speak of some kind of 'state capitalism' under the dictatorship of the proletariat, which in principle excludes such a possibility."[63] This seems to have been Bukharin's real quarrel with Lenin after the ratification of the peace treaty, and the main reason for his lingering presence among the Left Communists. A theoretical question exaggerated their actual policy differences and obscured Bukharin's thinking on the practical issues involved. For while he rejected Lenin's application of the term "state capitalism" to Soviet Russia, he clearly did not oppose in toto the moderate policies Lenin had assembled under that title.

The squabble over definitions also touched on a problem that would trouble Bolsheviks repeatedly. Bukharin and many others regarded socialism as "the antithesis of state capitalism." [64] How, then, was the new Soviet order to be described? Not even the most fanciful suggested that it was already socialism. Lenin's proposal, state capitalism, was widely unacceptable. Other possibilities included "a transition society" and simply "dictatorship of the proletariat." But the first was too imprecise, and the second a misnomer (not only because it ignored the increasing role of the vanguard party). More than a semantic question was involved. Behind the words lay a real uncertainty about the nature of the social order emerging out of the October revolution—an awkward, sometimes painful question that Bolsheviks would argue for years to come. In 1918, as later, however, the semantic issue served mostly to confuse things. In Bukharin's case, it made his views on domestic policy seem more radical than they actually were, leaving him open to the accusation that he ignored the "variety of social-economic structures which now exist in Russia." [65] Though unjust in general, the charge did illuminate an important truth: Bukharin's Marxism still had little to say about "building socialism" in backward peasant Russia.

Indeed, the striking feature of his opposition, and that of Left Communism generally, was its marginal relevance to the party's many internal problems. Bukharin's real cause was revolutionary war and opposition to the Brest peace treaty. At issue was whether a revolutionary socialist government could negotiate with a capitalist power. This principle, he later recalled, "shook our international conscience to the depths of our souls. . . ." [66] But when the controversy turned to economic policy, about which the party had thought much less, fewer clear-cut programmatic certainties were at stake. Most Bolsheviks were only beginning to think about workable economic policies.[67] Lenin's "state capitalism" sought to fill this vacuum, but his proposals amounted to little more than stopgap measures to halt the disintegration of the economy. They said little about the party's longer-range problems of industrialization and agricultural development, and still less about "building socialism."

Apart from elliptical comments on nationalization, Bukharin contributed almost nothing to the search for viable economic policies. He spoke vaguely of an end to market relations and the advent of planning, while virtually ignoring agriculture. Both components of his Left Communism—fervent advocacy of revolutionary war and halfhearted opposition to Lenin's economic proposals—reflected his own uncertainty and frustration over the party's domestic goals and problems. He suggested as much ten years later: "The external burdens, the greatest difficulties within—all this, it seemed to us, had to be cut with the sword of revolutionary war." [68]

In the early summer of 1918, the controversy over economic policy —and the Left Communist movement—suddenly ended. Lenin's moderate policies were discarded and a radically different course, known in retrospect as "war communism," was launched. The conciliatory "state capitalism" of early 1918 passed into history, a half-forgotten "peaceful breathing spell." [69]

The party's new economic radicalism did not originate, as is occasionally assumed, as a concession to the Left, but in response to pressing and perilous circumstances. In late June, fearful that large enterprises in occupied territories would be transferred to German ownership, the Soviet government resolved to nationalize "every important category of industry." Similarly, its new agrarian policies of May and June, based on promoting class strife and on forcible grain requisitioning, were spurred by a mounting threat of hunger in the cities. [70] Most important, June and July brought the onset of civil war and foreign military intervention. For the next two and a half years, encircled by White armies and the troops of Japan and the Western powers, blockaded and in control of only a truncated Russia, the Bolsheviks fought to survive by extending the party-state's control over all available resources.

The result was war communism, an extreme example of the economy of total war. In seeking to direct all resources toward military victory, the party-state abolished or subordinated autonomous intermediary institutions: thus trade unions were employed to accelerate production, the widespread network of consumer cooperatives to control distribution. Rationing, requisitioning, and primitive bartering replaced normal trade; the market, except for the black market, ceased to exist. Officially promoted, inflation spiraled, turning Soviet Russia into a "country of millionaire paupers": money ceased to have value or function. War communism, as described by a former Bolshevik, was above all the economics of military siege and political survival: "firstly, requisitioning in the countryside; secondly, strict rationing for the town population, who were classified into categories; thirdly, complete 'socialization' of production and labor; fourthly, an extremely complicated and chit-ridden system of distribution. . . ." [71]

The most characteristic feature of the 1918–21 period was the extensive "statization" of economic life, a term widely and accurately used to describe what was occurring. The state grasped every economic lever within reach, and a vast, cumbersome bureaucracy mushroomed into being. Cooperatives, trade unions, and the network of local economic soviets were transformed into bureaucratic appendages of the state apparatus. The Supreme Economic Council, now responsible for virtually all industrial production, created agency upon sub-agency. By 1920, the number of bureaucrats in relation to production workers was twice that of 1913.[72] The dream of a "commune state" expired in the fire of civil war, the only lingering similarity between the Soviet Republic and the Paris Commune being their beleaguered condition.

The experience of civil war and war communism profoundly altered both the party and the emerging political system. The party's democratic norms of 1917, as well as its almost libertarian and reformist profile of early 1918, gave way to a ruthless fanaticism, rigid authoritarianism, and pervasive "militarization" of life on every level. Victimized was not only internal party democracy, but also the decentralized forms of popular control created throughout the country in 1917—from local soviets to factory committees. Bolsheviks professed to see no choice because, as Bukharin declared, "The republic is an armed camp." [73] As part of this process, the party's attitude toward its political rivals changed, moving from reluctant tolerance at the outset, to expulsion of other socialist parties from the soviets in June 1918, and finally to an outburst of terror following the assassination of several Bolsheviks and an attempt on Lenin's life on August 30, 1918. Repression by the security police, the Cheka, added a new dimension to Soviet political life. Quoting St. Just several years later, Bukharin drew the apt analogy: "One must rule with iron when one cannot rule with law." [74]

These traumatic years also established a new reference point for future policy debates. All Bolsheviks, even those who later repudiated the measures of war communism, took pride in this era, when seemingly certain defeat was turned into victory. Bukharin captured the feeling of this moment when he wrote: "The proletariat stands in splendid isolation; everyone's hand is raised against it." Henceforth, 1918–21 would be "the heroic period," establishing a tradition of martial defiance in the face of the allegedly impossible, and of mobilized "mass upsurge and revolutionary enthusiasm." [75] A decade later, Stalin would call upon this tradition to storm other fortresses.

The coming of civil war and the disbanding of the Left Communists marked a turning point in Bukharin's party career. It ended his long political alliance with the young Moscow Left. Opposition movements in 1918–20 fluctuated according to the Bolsheviks' military situation. (Franklin's advice to American revolutionaries, "We must all hang together, or assuredly we shall all hang separately," was generally heeded.) Two significant oppositions did develop when military circumstances appeared less dire. In March 1919, a group called the Military Opposition attacked the reintroduction of traditional military discipline, privileges, and rank in the Red army. And beginning in 1919 the Democratic Centralists protested the reimposition of one-man managerial authority and the general bureaucratization and centralization in party and state affairs. Both factions were led by former Left Communists, notably Osinskii and Smirnov, and had their organizational base in Moscow.[76] Bukharin, however, was conspicuously absent from both oppositions, and at the Ninth Party Congress in 1920 he spoke against Osinskii in the name of the Central Committee.[77]

In February 1918, Bukharin and the Left Communists had resigned their party and state posts to go into open opposition against the Brest treaty.[78] Bukharin resumed his position on the Central Committee in May or June, and the editorship of *Pravda* immediately following an abortive uprising by Left Socialist Revolutionaries in early July. He later claimed to have been the first Left Communist "to admit my error," though a published statement to that effect did not appear until October.[79] By then revolution in Germany, and perhaps Vienna, seemed imminent, and the Brest treaty less onerous. With this in mind, Bukharin spoke with the admixture of hopeful expectation and prudence that was to characterize Soviet foreign policy for several years:

I must frankly and openly admit that we . . . were wrong, that Lenin was right, because the breathing spell gave us the opportunity to concentrate forces, to organize a powerful Red army. Now every good strategist must understand that we must not splinter our forces, but direct them against the strongest enemy. Germany and Austria are no longer dangerous. The danger comes from . . . the former allies—mainly England and America.

The German proletariat would be supported with "that which is dearest to us—our blood and our bread." But Soviet Russia was not to be risked; the main battleground was now the Russian civil war.[80]

From the summer of 1918 until late 1920, no important question divided Bukharin and Lenin. Two secondary disputes from the past were revived briefly, one over a theoretical description of modern capitalism, the other over Lenin's slogan of self-determination. The first was beyond resolution and simply dropped, the second finally settled by compromise, albeit a compromise weighted in Lenin's favor. Neither of these once-bitter issues, however, excited much passion because the two men again agreed on major decisions before the party.[81]

This ability to heal wounds after prolonged and bitter disputes reflected an important aspect of their relationship. No leading Bolshevik challenged Lenin's views more often than Bukharin; yet he had become Lenin's favorite. Affection, even love, and mutual respect bound them together.[82] The aftermath of Left Communism was no exception, though Lenin's full confidence in Bukharin's political wisdom was not immediately restored. On June 2, 1918, before Bukharin's departure for Germany to establish contact with radical Communists, Lenin warned the Soviet representative in Berlin: "Bukharin is loyal, but he went to sickening extremes in 'left-foolishness.' . . . *Prenez garde!*" [83] Nonetheless, his estimation of the youngest oligarch remained remarkably high, as evidenced by his remark to Trotsky early in the civil war: "If the White Guards kill you and me, will Bukharin and Sverdlov be able to manage?" Lenin may have worried, but he apparently thought of Bukharin as his replacement and of Iakov Sverdlov, then the party's chief organizer, as Trotsky's.[84]

Nor did Bukharin's brief opposition injure his standing in the party leadership. Unlike later times, a prodigal could return. At the Sixth Party Congress in 1917, he had been tenth in the voting for Central Committee members; at the Seventh Congress, at which he spoke for the Left Communists against the treaty, he had been fifth, evidence of his prestige even in opposition. One year later, at the Eighth Congress in March 1919, only six names appeared on every delegate's voting list: Lenin, Zinoviev, Trotsky, Bukharin, Kamenev, and Stalin, reflecting at least the party élite's feelings as to who rightfully comprised its high leadership. The Eighth Congress also created the first functioning Politburo, thereby institutionalizing the party oligarchy. It was composed of five full members—Lenin, Trotsky, Stalin, Kamenev, and Krestinskii—and three candidate members—Bukharin, Zinoviev, and Mikhail Kalinin.[85] These eight men were the real government of Soviet Russia.

Unlike Trotsky (for example), who as War Commissar was always center stage, it is difficult to get a precise picture of Bukharin's official activities during the civil war years, partly because he played several roles. His major responsibility was the editorship of *Pravda*, a position of great importance. In addition to being the ruling party's official voice at home and abroad, *Pravda* served as the definitive organ of internal party communication, a daily (except Monday) chronicle publishing official but also divergent points of view. Bukharin wrote most of the editorials and set the paper's general tone. And as *Pravda*'s offices gradually came to house a variety of party and nonparty publications, he assumed *de facto* responsibility for the Soviet press in general as well as overall Bolshevik propaganda.[86]

By late 1918, Bukharin was also deeply involved in international Communist affairs. His credentials as an internationalist made him a leading representative of the Russian party as foreign Marxists began their hopeful pilgrimages to the seat of successful revolution. In October 1918, on the eve of the abortive German uprising, he again journeyed to Berlin to confer with Karl Liebknecht and other German Communists. (The nature of his mission remains unclear.)[87] The German failure, however, did not thwart Lenin's 1915 aspiration for a new, Third International. On his instructions, Bukharin prepared a document outlining "the theory and tactics of Bolshevism"; it became a charter manifesto of the inaugural congress of the Communist International, or Comintern, in Moscow on March 4, 1919.[88] Henceforth, much of Bukharin's time was devoted to Comintern affairs. A member of its Executive Committee and deputy chairman of the "small bureau" which governed the organization, he and Zinoviev, its first chairman, shared responsibility for day-to-day operations.[89]

The fact that he combined these duties with a variety of other official and semi-official activities suggests that Bukharin played a special role within the Politburo. A remark attributed to Lenin implies what this was. When asked why Bukharin did not hold a formal state position, Lenin reportedly explained that the party needed at least one person "with brains without bureaucratic distortions." [90] Bukharin's reputation for honesty, fairness, and incorruptibility was a valuable asset in those days of unchecked authority and sometimes indiscriminate terror. He apparently assumed, or was delegated, the role of Politburo troubleshooter and righter-of-wrongs. He turned up constantly as the leadership's representative in troublesome situations: on a committee to combat anti-Semitism, at the Cheka to investigate questionable arrests of "bourgeois intellectuals," and at the trade unions when the party's labor relations became strained.[91] Not everyone thought that Bukharin performed this function well, one Bolshevik complaining that he had wrought more confusion than he resolved in the trade union affair. Whatever the case, he served enthusiastically, and "fluttered" ubiquitously about Moscow: "There is a saying about him. 'One can never tell where he will turn up next.' " [92]

None of these functions, however, compared with Bukharin's most influential role—that of Bolshevism's leading, and eventually official, theorist. Then, and for a few years to come, theorizing—and ideology in general—remained an important and meaningful endeavor. While the party's composition was changing rapidly, its leaders still regarded themselves as intellectuals. Political arguments were judged partly by their theoretical consistency and persuasiveness, and Bolsheviks took pride in their written work. Thus Lenin still gave "litterateur" as his profession, and Bukharin described himself and Lenin as "Communist ideologists." [93] The vaunted unity of theory and practice had not yet become jingoism. Bolsheviks respected theory and ideas as passionately as truth because they believed that the two were synonymous, and saw in this their capacity for leadership. Like Marx, they believed that "to be radical means to grasp the root of things." [94]

The body of theoretical work that earned Bukharin Lenin's praise as the party's "biggest theoretician" was largely completed by 1920. (*Historical Materialism* was published in 1921.) His two books written in emigration, *Imperialism and World Economy* and *The Economic Theory of the Leisure Class*, finally appeared in full in 1918 and 1919, bringing to a larger public the nature and extent of his achievements. Together with his other writings, they distinguished him as the party's leading student of neo-capitalism, a preeminence acknowledged by Lenin in 1919, when, bemoaning the impossibility of constructing "an integral picture of capitalism's collapse," he added: "I am completely certain that if anyone could do this, it is most of all Comrade Bukharin. . . ." [95] In 1920, in *The Economics of the Transition Period*, Bukharin extended his theoretical purview to contemporary Soviet Russia; and while the book was highly controversial, it established his claim as the foremost (and most audacious) theorist of the post-capitalist era as well.

Bukharin always distinguished between his "theoretical" and his "popular" writings, and it was one of the latter that brought him his greatest fame. Following the adoption of a new party program in March 1919, Bukharin and Evgenii Preobrazhenskii, another young theorist and former Left Communist, undertook "A Popular Explanation of the Program of the Communist Party of Russia." Completed in October, it was called *The ABC of Communism*, the best-known and most widely circulated of all pre-Stalinist expositions of Bolshevism. Preobrazhenskii's co-authorship half-forgotten, *The ABC* soon became inextricably associated with Bukharin, spreading his fame and giving rise to his reputation (in Communist circles) as "the golden child of the revolution." [96]

The ABC was notable less for its theoretical originality than for its encyclopedic coverage, readability, and extraordinary popularity. Observing that "older Marxist literature . . . is largely inapplicable to present needs," its authors tried to provide "an elementary textbook of communist knowledge" for party schools and "for independent study by every worker or peasant." Their text followed that of the program, expounding each point, omitting no contemporary question, foreign or domestic. Apart from its treatment of imperialism and state capitalism, it was not a specifically Bukharinist document.[97] Its views reflected those of the party as a whole and its novelty lay in its chronicling of almost every Bolshevik assumption in the year 1919.

For this reason, the book had and still retains considerable power. Its mood was that of war communism, a militant optimism invigorated by the belief that "what Marx prophesied is being fulfilled under our very eyes." [98] It was a statement of Bolshevik aspirations and utopian hopes in 1919, of party innocence, not Soviet reality. And although much of it was outdated by 1921, because *The ABC* spoke with the voice of "the heroic period," it became an instant and continuing success—"a party canon." By the early thirties, it had gone through no less than eighteen Russian editions and twenty foreign translations. For Russian and foreign Communists, *The ABC,* along with *Historical Materialism,* became "the two most standard books of Communist propaganda," carrying Bukharin's name to every corner of the earth, to wherever men and women were drawn to the revolutionary movement.[99] After *The ABC,* his fame approached that of Lenin and Trotsky.

At the same time, this eminence began to bring Bukharin an unfortunate sort of recognition. "Super-popular" writings like *The ABC* entitled him to praise as "one of the ablest pamphleteers . . . of our age." [100] But the longer the Bolsheviks ruled, and the more frequent dissent within the party, the more the leaders felt obliged to systematize and institutionalize their ideology. In the twenties, when party politics dictated the establishment of a well-defined fundamentalism, Bukharin's theoretical reputation and the biblical aura of writings like *The ABC* thrust him willy-nilly into the role of high priest of "orthodox Bolshevism." [101]

The pattern emerged even during the civil war. A charter member of the newly founded Socialist Academy, he acquired increasing responsibility and influence in shaping the ideological education of party members and the training of a party intelligentsia.

His works became required textbooks in party schools, and, beginning in 1919, he personally conducted seminars in economics and historical materialism at Sverdlov University. Though expressing Bukharin's natural proclivities, these pedagogical undertakings increasingly attained the status of official functions.[102] Still in his early thirties, he found himself surrounded by a growing number of disciples, many of whom would rise in the party and promote his enshrinement as keeper of the orthodoxy, a mantle Bukharin neither sought nor wore with ease.

An awareness that he was becoming responsible for the theoretical integrity of Bolshevism may have prompted Bukharin's decision, after two years of revolution, to undertake an analysis of the current transition from capitalism to socialism. No such effort had yet been made, partly because of the general party bewilderment over the improvised measures of war communism, and partly because Bolshevik attention remained fixed on Europe, where further revolutions were awaited "literally from day to day." [103] Bukharin's own fierce optimism about European prospects began to wane only in 1919, when he started to caution that international revolution should be viewed as a lengthy historical process made up of many parts, including anti-colonial rebellions in Asia, and that Communists should not seek "to force historical developments." [104] Though he would be hopeful again, particularly in the winter of 1920–1, Bukharin's euphoric certainty about the imminence of revolution in the West had passed. As a result, he and other Bolsheviks began to think more seriously about the economics of an isolated Soviet Russia.

In the economic debates of April–May 1918, Bukharin had been to the left of Lenin, but neither had foreseen or advocated policies like those of war communism. Indeed, some of these policies were contrary to what Bukharin had urged—for example, that only large, easily managed enterprises be nationalized. Nonetheless, within the year, he came to see in these extreme measures a validity beyond that imposed by military necessity. In the far-reaching "statization" of the economy, in the withering of intermediary institutions between state and society, he perceived a road along which Russia was speeding from capitalism to socialism. In March 1919, he put socialism "on the agenda of the day," and worried that the rapid tempo might shortly outdate sections of the party's new program.[105]

This expectant outlook brought an important change in Bukharin's thinking about the new Soviet state. Its "fundamental meaning," he now decided, "is precisely that it is the *lever of economic revolution.*" [106] While the acceptance of the state as the instrument to transform a backward society was essential for a Marxist modernizer, it called into question Marx's celebrated dictum that superstructural phenomena (including the state) were subordinate to the economic base of society. Bukharin's answer derived from his understanding of state capitalist societies, and constituted an important revision of Marxism:

> If the proletariat's state power is the lever of economic revolution, then it is clear that "economics" and politics must merge here into a single whole. Such a merging exists under the dictatorship of finance capital . . . in the form of state capitalism. But the dictatorship of the proletariat reverses all the relations of the old world—in other words, the *political* dictatorship of the working class must inevitably be its *economic* dictatorship. [107]

In 1919–20, this proposition rationalized war communism; later, it would lead Bukharin to a very different conception of "the road to socialism." In both instances, however, it meant postponing the state's "withering away" in favor of "strengthening the Soviet state," a tolerable perspective if it was a "workers' state." And in this, Bukharin's faith was unshakable. [108]

His enthusiasm for "statization" and war communism as the birth of an organized socialist economy was clearly based solely on the state's success in extending its control over industrial production, however meager, and the distribution of manufactured goods. [109] That this was a one-eyed view of a predominantly agrarian society was evident from Bukharin's own less fanciful remarks about peasant agriculture. Small peasants, he emphasized repeatedly, were not to be expropriated nor forcibly collectivized; "many intermediary forms and levels of agricultural production" were necessary. Acknowledging that "for a long time to come small-scale peasant farming will be the predominant form," he warned against the Bolshevik tendency "to spit on the muzhik," although spitting on the muzhik (forcible requisitioning) was in fact the linchpin of war communism. From the outset, then, Bukharin insisted that the country's millions of private peasant holdings should not be forcibly integrated into the new, organized economy, but "drawn in" through "a slow process, by peaceful means. . . ." How this would occur he left temporarily unanswered, urging only patience and pedagogy. [110]

If the economic reasoning behind Bukharin's acceptance of the policies of war communism as a viable road to socialism re-

THE POLITICS OF CIVIL WAR · 87

mains obscure, the historical circumstances influencing his thinking seem clear enough. Having come to office with no preconceived economic program, Bukharin, and Bolsheviks generally, embraced the first one that appeared to arise out of and correspond to actual events. An internal logic—what Marxists called lawfulness or "regularity"—seemed discernible in the kaleidoscopic developments of 1918–20 and the measures adopted to cope with them. Class war, civil war, foreign intervention, the economic and political monopoly of the "dictatorship of the proletariat"—each in its own way could be reconciled with the party's pre-1917 expectations. And if war communism was the product of improvisation, it meant only that reality was validating "gray theory." [111]

Bukharin was not alone in this. The notion (promoted by the Bolsheviks themselves after 1921) that only a few dreamers and fanatics accepted war communism as an enduring policy, as a direct route to socialism, is incorrect. It was the sentiment of the party majority; few resisted the general euphoria. Most notably, Lenin, despite his fabled pragmatism and subsequent deprecation of the follies of war communism, was no exception. "Now the organization of the proletariat's communist activities, and the entire policy of the Communists," he said in 1919, "has fully acquired a final, stable form; and I am convinced that we stand on the right road. . . ." [112] What set Bukharin apart from the others, what made him seem to be the most convinced, was his literary monument to the collective folly, *The Economics of the Transition Period*, a tract grounded in the worst error of the period, the belief that "Civil war lays bare the true physiognomy of society. . . ." [113]

The Economics appeared in May 1920, just as war communism was approaching its apogee. Bukharin intended it to be the theoretical half of a two-volume study of "the process of the transformation of capitalist society into communist society." The second volume, projected as "a concrete, descriptive work on contemporary Russian economics," never appeared. Originally, he planned to co-author the book with Piatakov; but "practical tasks" (Piatakov was at the front during most of the civil war) made this impossible and the latter contributed directly to only one chapter. Written rapidly and in extremely abstract language—as Bukharin noted apologetically, "almost in algebraic formulas"—key ideas and concepts were frequently not fully explained and occasionally inconsistent.[114] But as a first and audacious attempt to go beyond the existing body of Marxist thought the book was an immediate and lasting *succès d'estime*. And although its domestic policy implications were largely obsolete by March 1921, it continued to be a highly influential (and controversial) work. In 1928, Pokrovskii, the doyen of Soviet historians, cited it as one of the three great Bolshevik achievements in "social science" since the revolution.[115]

Western historians have tended to dismiss *The Economics* as a theoretical apology for war communism, which it was, though Bukharin's notion that it was a Marxist duty to analyze contemporary reality is surely a mitigating factor. Something more, however, accounted for the book's enduring esteem and for the fact that several of its arguments outlived war communism. Very generally, Bukharin dealt with three broad subjects or themes: the structure of modern capitalism on the eve of proletarian revolution; society in the midst of revolutionary breakdown, or the revolutionary "disequilibrated" society; and the process of establishing a new societal equilibrium out of the chaos as a phase in the transition to socialism. He mentioned Russia very rarely, but it was clear from his treatment of the second and third subjects that the Bolshevik experience was foremost in his mind. Just as Marx had posited his findings on English capitalism as general laws, so did Bukharin believe that he was formulating universal laws of proletarian revolution.

Bukharin's treatment of neo-capitalism in *The Economics* was largely a restatement of his views on state capitalism and imperialism. It occupied a large part of the book and generally followed his writings of 1915–17.[116] As earlier, he portrayed the state capitalist economy as an imposing assembly of productive, technological, and organizational achievements. This, however, raised a serious question about the desirability of revolution, which in Russia had reduced economic production to a virtual fraction of the 1913 level. In addition to the direct casualties of the civil war, thousands were dying from the most primitive of causes, hunger and cold. Consequently, the Bolsheviks were being assailed by European social democrats, particularly Karl Kautsky, as destroyers not builders. Marxists regarded themselves as harbingers of a socially just abundance, and this accusation hurt. A number of Bolshevik polemics had been produced in response,[117] but the charge required a more substantial and reasoned answer. *The Economics* sought to provide that answer by formulating "the costs of revolution" as a law of revolution.

Bukharin had observed earlier that the charge was reminiscent of the one leveled by the Girondins against the Jacobins, and which had driven Charlotte Corday to murder Marat. His point was that great revolutions were always accompanied by destructive civil wars, his favorite illustration being that when barricades are constructed out of railway cars or telegraph poles, the outcome is economic destruction.[118] But he was more intent on proving that a proletarian revolution inevitably resulted in an even greater temporary fall in production than did its bourgeois counterpart. Lenin's *State and Revolution* (and Bukharin's own writings before 1917) had established the doctrine that the bourgeois state apparatus had to be destroyed during the revolutionary process. Bukharin now argued that the merger of political and economic functions under capitalism, and the proletariat's desire to restructure "production relations," meant that the onslaught against the state had to become an onslaught against the economic apparatus of capitalism. "The hierarchical relations of capitalist society" are undone; "the *disorganization* of the 'entire apparatus' " results.[119]

Bukharin specified several "real costs of revolution," including the physical destruction or deterioration of material and human elements of production, the atomization of these elements and of sectors of the economy, and the need for unproductive consumption (civil war materials, etc.). These costs were interrelated and followed sequentially. Collectively, they resulted in "*the curtailment of the process of reproduction*" (and "negative expanded reproduction") and Bukharin's main conclusion: "The production 'anarchy' . . . , 'the revolutionary disintegration of industry,' is a historically inevitable stage which no amount of lamentation will prevent." [120]

This may appear to have been an obvious point, but it apparently came as a revelation to many Bolsheviks. It was directly opposed to the prevailing social democratic assumption that the transition to socialism would be relatively painless. Kautsky and Hilferding had fostered this belief, particularly the latter with his argument that if the proletariat seized the six largest banks it would automatically control the economy.[121] Even some "older" Bolsheviks accepted Bukharin's law only in connection with Russia, arguing that in England, for example, no serious fall in production would occur.[122] Bukharin disagreed, insisting on its universal applicability. After the introduction of NEP in 1921, he claimed that this was the basic point of *The Economics*: "The central thought of the whole book is that during the transition period the labor apparatus of society inevitably disintegrates, that reorganization presupposes disorganization, and that therefore the temporary collapse of productive forces is a law inherent to revolution." He had proved, he said in summary, "the necessity of breaking an egg to obtain an omelette." Profound or not, Bolsheviks generally came to accept the "law" and to regard it as a significant discovery by Bukharin.[123]

Bukharin's law solved another problem as well. Marxists were accustomed to believing that the "objective prerequisites" of socialism "ripen" within the seedpod of capitalist society, and that revolution occurs only after considerable ripening. Maturation was measured in terms of "the level of concentration and centralization of capital" of "the aggregate 'apparatus'" of capitalist economy; the new society, it seemed, arrived as a *deus ex machina.*" By arguing that this apparatus was invariably destroyed in the process of revolution, and that therefore "in toto it cannot serve as the basis of the new society," Bukharin subtly dismissed the nagging question of Russia's relative backwardness (unripeness). He emphasized the "human" rather than the "material" apparatus as the essential criterion of maturity, the decisive prerequisite being a certain level of "the socialization of labor" (the existence of a proletariat) and the revolutionary class's capacity to carry out "social-organizational" tasks.[124]

This argument led Bukharin to the heart of the dilemma of Bolshevik rule in an underdeveloped society, and to the previously unarticulated proposition that was to be at the center of party controversies in the twenties—"building socialism." He rejected the traditional Marxist assumption that socialism attains almost full maturity in the womb of the old order, and thus adapted Marxism to backward Russia. He contrasted the growth of socialism to the growth of capitalism:

They [the bourgeoisie] did not build capitalism, it built itself. The proletariat will build socialism as an organized system, as an organized collective subject. While the process of the creation of capitalism was spontaneous, the process of building communism is to a significant degree a conscious, i.e., organized process. . . . The epoch of Communist construction will therefore inevitably be an epoch of planned and organized work; the proletariat will solve its task as a social-economic task of building a new society. . . .[125]

Up to this point, Bukharin was describing a "disequilibrated" society, presenting a sophisticated and frequently ingenious account of the multiple rupturing of the social fabric. Now he had to treat the emergence of a new equilibrium. The concept of equilibrium runs through most of Bukharin's theoretical work, from *The Economics* to *Historical Materialism,* where he explained Marxist dialectics and social change in terms of the establishment and disturbance of equilibrium, to his famous 1928 attack on Stalin's five-year plan in "Notes of an Economist." It is important to note here only that he meant a "dynamic" or "moving" equilibrium, not a static system, and that the practice of viewing society (or at least economic systems) as being in a state of equilibrium had a genealogy, albeit a somewhat subterranean one, in Marxist thought.[126]

Bukharin's reliance on this precedent, and his understanding of equilibrium as a state of "evolution and growth," was spelled out in *The Economics*:

In theoretically mastering the capitalist system of production relations, Marx proceeded from *the fact* of its existence. Once this system exists it means . . . that social demands are being satisfied, at least to the degree that people are not only not dying off, but are living, acting, and propagating themselves. In a society with a social division of labor . . . this means that there must be a certain *equilibrium* of the whole system. The necessary quantities of coal, iron, machines, cotton, linen, bread, sugar, boots, etc., etc., are produced. Living human labor is expended in accordance with all of this in the necessary quantities in relation to production, utilizing the necessary means of production. There may be all sorts of deviations and fluctuations, the whole system may be enlarged, complicated, and developed; it is in constant motion and fluctuation, but, in general and in its entirety, it is in a state of equilibrium.

To find the law of this equilibrium is the basic problem of theoretical economics.[127]

Analyzing an existing equilibrium (or disequilibrium), however, was not the same as explaining how a new one could be forged out of the wreckage of the old.

Bukharin's answer was to endorse the coercive measures of war communism and give them theoretical expression. The new equilibrium was established by replacing the destroyed links between elements of production with new ones, by restructuring "*in a new combination the dismantled social layers. . . .*" This operation was performed by the proletarian state, which "statizes," militarizes, and mobilizes the productive forces of society. "The process of socialization in all of its forms" was "the function of the proletarian state." [128] Bukharin carefully pointed out that while there was a "formal" similarity between the proletarian system and state capitalism, since capitalist property was being transformed into "collective proletarian 'property,'" they were "diametrically opposite in essence." Because it was no longer "surplus profit" but "surplus product" that was being created, any sort of exploitation was "unthinkable" under the dictatorship of the proletariat. Labor conscription, for example, which under state capitalism was "the enslavement of the working masses," was now "nothing other than the . . . self-organization of the masses." [129]

Beneath this elaborate construction was the crux of Bukharin's argument: Force and coercion were the means by which equilibrium was to be forged out of disequilibrium. He did not avoid the harsh conclusion; an entire chapter on " 'Extra-Economic' Coercion in the Transition Period" defended the proposition:

> In the transition period, when one productive structure gives way to another, the midwife is revolutionary force. This revolutionary force must destroy the fetters on the development of society, i.e., on one side, the old forms of "concentrated force," which have become a counterrevolutionary factor—the old state and the old type of production relations. This revolutionary force, on the other side, must actively help in the formation of production relations, being a new form of "concentrated force," the state of the new class, which acts as the lever of economic revolution, altering the economic structure of society. Thus on one side force plays the role of a destructive factor; on the other, it is a force of cohesion, organization, and construction. The greater this "extra-economic" power is . . . the less will be "the costs" of the transition period (all other things being equal, of course), the *shorter* will be this transition period, the faster will a social equilibrium be established on a new foundation and the quicker will the . . . production curve begin to rise.

Here, too, revolutionary coercion was unlike previous " 'pure force' of the Dühring type," because it led toward "general economic development." [130]

It is easy to emphasize the ugly potentialities of Bukharin's reasoning that "proletarian coercion in all of its forms, beginning with shooting and ending with labor conscription, is . . . a method of creating communist mankind out of the human materials of the capitalist epoch. . . ." [131] All kinds of abuses could be and were rationalized with the argument, for example, that exploitation of the working class was impossible under a dictatorship of the proletariat. To argue that a workers' state could not by definition exploit a worker was to condone one set of evils because they were "progressive." Less obvious, perhaps, is the cogency and historical validity of his statement on the role of coercion in laying the foundations of a new social order. History provides few examples of a society in revolutionary upheaval being stilled or restored to order without the use of considerable force. Unfortunately, Bukharin's argument was obscured and weakened by a supplementary theoretical digression and also by an omission.

The digression dealt with his belief that political economy and its traditional categories were not applicable to post-capitalist society, an assumption which gave his treatment of the economics of the transition period an ultra-radical gloss. Marxism, in other words, employed "a dialectical-historical" methodology: categories and economic laws discussed by Marx related only to capitalist commodity production. Bukharin explained:

as soon as we take an organized social economy, all the basic "problems" of political economy disappear: problems of value, price, profit, and the like. Here "relations between people" are not expressed in "relations between things," and social economy is regulated not by the blind forces of the market and competition, but consciously by a . . . *plan.* Therefore here there can be a certain descriptive system on the one hand, a system of norms on the other. But there can be no place for a science studying "the blind laws of the market" since there will be no market. Thus the end of capitalist commodity society will be the end of political economy.[132]

This understanding of political economy was shared by many Marxists and, by the mid-twenties, by a majority of Bolshevik economists. It remained something of a "dogma," but also a topic of lively debate, until the thirties when it was officially repudiated in the search for "a political economy of socialism." [133] But, despite its currency, Bukharin's attempt to apply the proposition in 1920 caused considerable headshaking. In the chapter written with Piatakov, he observed that in analyzing the transition period, "the old understandings of theoretical economics instantly refuse to serve"; they even "begin to misfire." Examining each category (commodity, value, price, wages), and finding each theoretically obsolete, he proposed new concepts (instead of wages, "a social-labor ration"; instead of commodity, "product"; and so forth).[134]

As a result, *The Economics* sounded more radical than it was. For while Bukharin carefully stressed that the subject of political economy—commodity production—still existed in the transition period, and that therefore the old categories were still of practical value, his theoretical glimpse into the future seriously disturbed some readers. Two problems were involved: by discarding political economy, Bukharin seemed to be saying that man was no longer constrained by objective economic laws. Although not arguing this point, his failure to specify new objective regulators opened him to the charge of "voluntarism." Second and related was his disconcerting habit of discussing the future in the present tense.[135] In both respects, his presentation reflected the "leap-into-socialism" ideas associated with war communism.

But the most serious flaw so far as the programmatic implications of *The Economics* were concerned was Bukharin's failure to distinguish clearly between the period of disequilibrium and the period following the establishment of equilibrium. He spoke of the transition period as the transition to socialism, and also as the transition to a new social equilibrium, from which society would move on to socialism. Left unclear was whether the extreme measures used to forge a new equilibrium would continue to be the norm after equilibrium was established. Occasionally he implied that this would be the case.[136] But his breakdown of the transitional process distinguished between an initial period of mobilizing the fragments of the collapsed order, which he called "the economic revolution" or "primitive socialist accumulation" (a term borrowed from Vladimir Smirnov and later made famous in a different context by Preobrazhenskii), and a subsequent period of "technical revolution," which would witness an evolutionary, harmonious flowering of production.[137]

Put another way, Bukharin's understanding of equilibrium seemed to be in conflict with his analysis of the transition period. If a state of equilibrium, capitalist or otherwise, implied proportionality between elements and spheres of production, then the measures of war communism would have to become obsolete at some stage in the transition period. Bukharin's explanation, in which he tried to have it both ways, illustrates the confusion:

> *The postulate of equilibrium* is invalid. . . . There is neither proportionality between production and consumption, nor between different branches of production . . . nor between human elements of the system. Therefore it is radically wrong to transfer to the transition period categories, concepts, and laws adequate to a state of equilibrium. One may object that insofar as society has not perished, there is equilibrium. Such reasoning, however, would be correct if the period of time we are examining was conceived of as being of great length. A society cannot live *long* outside equilibrium, it dies. But this social system for a certain time can be in an "abnormal" state, i.e., outside a state of equilibrium.

This was open to two interpretations. Either the transition to socialism would be relatively brief; or Bukharin meant only the transition to a stabilized state from which socialism would evolve. It is reasonable to assume that in 1920 he believed the former. After 1921, however, he offered the second interpretation.[138]

The dilemma implicit in Bukharin's reasoning was again evident in his remarks on agriculture. The enormity of the agrarian problem was now clear to him. The need to re-establish equilibrium between town and country, he explained, was "decisive for the fate of mankind . . . the most important and *complex* question." His solution hardly suited this description of the problem. Here, too, he formulated the key role of coercion, especially in the forcible requisitioning of grain. It was most crucial, however, at an early stage of the revolution, when the transition period as a whole was characterized by "*a secret or more or less open struggle between the organizing tendencies of the proletariat and the commodity-anarchical tendencies of the peasantry.*" He did not specify the form of this struggle or its arena. Significantly, however, he did exclude collective forms of agricultural production as the primary means of bringing the peasantry into the "organizing process," arguing instead that "for the main mass of *small producers*, their drawing into the organized apparatus is possible mainly through *the sphere of exchange. . . .*" [139]

The remark was a tantalizing adumbration of Bukharin's later theory of "growing into socialism" through the market—but without its essential mechanism. For, while he excluded significant collectivization, he also excluded market and "monetary-credit" links between town and country. In 1920, he still accepted the state "organs of distribution and procurement" as the basic intermediary between the industrial city and the small-peasant countryside.[140] The problem should have been clear: Without a commodity market, what was to encourage the peasant to produce and deliver a surplus? Bukharin spoke of the average peasant's "two souls"— one inclined toward capitalism, one toward socialism—and presumably hoped that the good would volunteer surplus grain. The alternative to this dubious likelihood was a system of permanent requisitioning. One of the book's rare pessimistic notes suggested that Bukharin saw the quandary: "The Revolution [in Russia] triumphed easily because the proletariat, striving toward communism, was supported by the peasantry, who moved against the landlord. But this same peasantry turns out to be the greatest brake in the period of constructing communist production relations." [141] That, of course, was the Bolshevik dilemma, and the blind side of war communism.

Final judgment on a book like *The Economics*—so much a

product of its time—should take into account its contemporary reception. That its reputation outlived war communism was due to Bukharin's innovative treatment of themes which were compatible with the post-1921 view of war communism as a regrettable but necessary episode: the structure of neo-capitalism, the "costs of revolution," the concept of "building socialism," and the historical limitations of political economy. Although some Bolsheviks regarded parts of the book as "debatable from a Marxist point of view," none questioned its considerable influence.[142]

Indeed, in one quarter of the party it was greeted with undisguised hostility, because it did promise to be influential. A scathing attack by Mikhail Olminskii, one of the older Moscow committeemen edged aside by the young Left in 1917, appeared shortly after the introduction of NEP. Olminskii accused Bukharin of having abandoned Marxist political economy for "the Bukharinist method of penal servitude and shooting," and of "revising Marxism from the left." In the campaign to give the book the status of *The ABC*, he saw the further machinations of "that part of the party" who were delirious with "the enthusiasm of power," and for whom "nothing was impossible." Bukharin responded in a light vein, reprimanding Olminskii for his charges of "revisionism." [143]

With war communism then in the process of being dismantled and discredited, Olminskii scored some easy points. But he was mistaken or disingenuous in identifying the book's stance on war communism with Bukharin's generation, as was vividly illustrated by Lenin's private notes on *The Economics* and his "*recensio academica*," written on May 31, 1920, for the Communist Academy, which had published the book. Lenin's generally favorable evaluation was subsequently distorted by the circumstances surrounding the publication of his notes, which rested in an archive until Stalin's victory over Bukharin in 1929, when they were disinterred as part of the campaign to destroy Bukharin's theoretical credentials.[144] Stalinist commentators naturally dwelt on the negative comments, of which there were many, but which spoke more of the dissimilarities between Bukharin and Lenin as intellectuals than of the book itself.

The great majority of Lenin's objections centered on Bukharin's terminology. He particularly disliked what he called the use of "Bogdanovist gibberish" instead of "human language," and, closely related in Lenin's mind, Bukharin's penchant for the words "sociological" and "sociology." Over and over again he greeted them with "ugh!", "ha, ha," "eclecticism," and at one point: "it is good that the 'sociologist' Bukharin finally puts the word 'sociologist' in ironical quotation marks! Bravo!" [145] Lenin's reprimands reflected the very different intellectual orientation of the two men. Bukharin was deeply interested in contemporary sociological thought (as *Historical Materialism* would show) and regarded Bogdanov's more recent work on "organizational science" as interesting; Lenin instinctively distrusted modern schools of social theory and had an abiding dislike for anything associated with Bogdanov.[146] When Bukharin said something was "theoretically interesting," Lenin retorted scornfully. Lenin's other objections were more substantial. Some related to previous areas of disagreement such as the structure of modern capitalism; and some rightly focused on those parts of Bukharin's argument which were too abstract and in need of clarification or empirical evidence. They were pertinent comments from a friendly and sympathetic critic.

But all Lenin's reservations paled against his ecstatic praise for the most "war communist" sections of *The Economics*. Almost every passage on the role of the new state, on "statization" in general, and on militarization and mobilization met with "very good," often in three languages, as did Bukharin's formulation of disequilibrium and "building socialism." Most striking, Lenin's greatest enthusiasm was reserved for the chapter on the role of coercion. He filled these margins with superlatives and at the end wrote: "Now this chapter is superb!", a judgment more representative of his overall evaluation. He concluded his summary review with the hope that "small" shortcomings "will disappear from following editions, which are so necessary for our reading public and which will serve to the even greater honor of the Academy; we congratulate the Academy on the splendid work of its member." [147] Olminskii feared the book's influence; Lenin looked forward to future editions. There were to be no other Soviet editions, and Lenin's review remained unpublished.

Bukharin once said of Pokrovskii's historical work: "he who makes no mistakes, does nothing." [148] This was a fitting epigram for *The Economics*. Its critical shortcomings reflected the defect in war communism. Bukharin's analysis was mute on what were to be the long-term economic problems of Soviet Russia: those of investment and accumulation, of the relationship between industry and agriculture, and of expanding the entire economy, quantitatively and qualitatively. The "prose of economic development," as Olminskii put it, was absent. Hosannas to the advent of a "conscious regulator" did not constitute an economic program. *The Economics* was really about disequilibrium and the costs of revolution; and Bukharin's error, as he would soon realize, was to generalize on this experience for the entire transition period. His charge against social democrats applied to himself as well; for while he added a destructive stage in the transformation process, he, too, left the impression that socialism would come as a *deus ex machina*. It was indeed "as if ivied maidens and garlanded youths were to herald the four horsemen of the Apocalypse." [149]

Anyone impressed that the Bolsheviks, unlike traditional politicians, could act with political cunning and collective decisiveness whenever necessary should consider the demise of war communism. At least six months, if not more, intervened between the obvious bankruptcy of those policies and March 1921, when they were finally discarded.[150] Ultimately, war communism ended as it had begun—in response to crises and amidst an acrimonious party controversy, this time over the role of Soviet trade unions.

Anxiety about "economic construction" actually began in early 1920, when civil war victory seemed certain, only to be interrupted in the summer and autumn by a brief, unexpected war with Poland and a final campaign against the White armies. The dimensions of Soviet economic ruin, however, had been officially recognized as a catastrophe by January 1920.[151] By autumn, severe industrial and agricultural shortages were growing into a nationwide social crisis. The major cities, plagued by hunger, were half-deserted; rural unrest was turning into open hostility to the government, as peasant violence against requisitioners and other officials became more frequent and marauding peasant bands roamed the countryside. A new kind of civil war loomed before the party, which felt increasingly isolated from its one-time supporters, the toilers.[152]

Bolshevik leaders reacted with kaleidoscopic spurts of boldness and semi-paralysis. Unlikely people made unlikely suggestions. In February 1920, Trotsky proposed that arbitrary grain requisitioning—the linchpin of war communism—be replaced by a fixed tax in kind. (While not advocating the restoration of market exchange, his proposal predated the inaugural step of NEP by a year.) Rebuffed by Lenin and the Central Committee, he promptly "plunged back into the accepted folly," becoming the champion of the "militarization" of labor as a way out of the impasse.[153] Osinskii, now the great critic of undemocratic norms in party and state institutions, advocated intensifying coercive measures in the countryside, calling for compulsory, state-controlled sowing areas.

Lenin received worsening reports from provincial officials about the situation in the villages and the impact of bureaucratic mismanagement, only to respond by giving qualified approval to Osinskii's plan. Later, he appointed a Politburo commission to consider the "crisis in the peasantry," but otherwise did nothing. Abandoning requisitioning for a fixed tax with the peasant retaining his surplus seems not to have been discussed in the Politburo until early February 1921.[154] The leaders still regarded war communism "as the universal, general, and . . . 'normal' . . . economic policy of the victorious proletarian." [155] As if to reaffirm their faith by compounding its fallacy, in late November 1920 they nationalized all but the very smallest remaining private enterprises.

Like most rulers, the Bolsheviks preferred the status quo to the unknown. Skepticism may have been on the rise, but they remained committed to the existing system, which had produced military victory against great odds. They now hoped it would do the same for "peaceful construction." Despite everything, optimism prevailed, and no one was seemingly more its captive than Bukharin. *The Economics*, his ode to war communism, coincided with the deepening crisis, and projected him as a supreme optimist whose faith was undiminished. A closer look suggests this was not the full story.

Though Bukharin customarily showed sanguine confidence throughout his official career, we shall regularly encounter evidence of his private doubts and political anxieties. He was often a man of public optimism and private fears. Like the poet Heine, himself drawn to the apocalyptic radicalism of his own age and whom Bukharin admired, Bukharin was "prey to the secret fear of the artist and scholar." [156] After fervently lecturing an English acquaintance in 1919 on the certainty of world revolution, he suddenly confided: "Sometimes I am afraid that the struggle will be so bitter and so long drawn out that the whole of European culture may be trampled underfoot." [157] Without access to his private papers, it is never easy to judge Bukharin's private thoughts about Soviet developments. It is clear, however, that he had been troubled by aspects of war communism for a long time.

During these years, Bukharin produced some of the most gruesome statements legitimizing Bolshevik violence. Among them: "In revolution he will be victorious who cracks the other's skull"; and, dismissing people who did not distinguish between capitalist acts and those of a proletarian dictatorship—"humpbacks are only cured by death." [158] Personally, however, he had little taste for cracking skulls, on one occasion characteristically refusing to authorize the execution of an army deserter. More significant, he was frightened by the extent of Soviet police terror, and in 1919 urged that the Cheka's power of execution be curbed. As a result, Lenin appointed him to the collegium of the Cheka with "the right of veto." Worried about the recurring mistreatment of non-Bolshevik political figures and intellectuals, Bukharin often acted on their behalf and became known as a "liberal" among Bolsheviks, an "intercessor." [159] Ironically, he was speaking on this general subject at a Moscow meeting on September 25, 1919, when anarchists and dissident Left Socialist Revolutionaries exploded a bomb, killing twelve in attendance and wounding fifty-five, including Bukharin.[160]

Despite his rationalization of revolutionary coercion and violence, Bukharin had remarkably little to say about "class struggle," the rubric under which most Soviet acts of mass repression and terror would later be committed. Apart from his remarks on the Red army against the White, and proletarian states against capitalist ones, the concept of class struggle barely figured in his discussion of the transition to socialism. While allowing for an initial "de-formation of classes," he did not anticipate an enduringly hostile class enemy within nor permanent internal warfare.[161] His political opponents would later charge that this "error" stemmed from his conception of classes, which stressed their "general role in the production process" rather than their innate, mutual hostility.[162] Whatever the reason, Bukharin never shared the later Stalinist view of an "inevitable intensification of the class struggle" as socialism approached.

A similar ambivalence underlay his attitude toward the mushrooming Soviet state. Though the apostle of "statization," he understood the dangers of rampant bureaucratization in a backward, predominantly illiterate society. In that supremely optimistic document The ABC, he wrote: "This is a grave danger for the proletariat. The workers did not destroy the old official-ridden state with the intention of allowing it to grow up again from new roots." [163] Indeed, he was already troubled by what would become an abiding concern, that a new bureaucratic élite, a "caste," might grow out of a division between the laboring masses and a privileged "workers' aristocracy." Alert to the élite theories of Michels and Pareto, he quickly protested measures fostering stratification within the working class. One such proposal, he charged bitterly, would lead not to socialism but to Jack London's "Iron Heel." [164]

Optimism, however, drowned out any doubts during the civil war because the peril of the times permitted no despair, and be-

cause Bukharin had endowed the proletariat as a class with ideal-
ized powers of political consciousness and creativity. His own
warning in March 1918 that the proletariat was "disintegrating"
had quickly been forgotten.[165] Central to his conception of the
"transformation process" was the belief that while other social
groups decomposed, the proletariat preserved its internal "links,"
becoming even more united and thus "an inexhaustible reservoir
of organizational energy." A believer in masses rather than élites,
this assumption (or hope) allowed Bukharin to maintain that between "the vanguard" (the party) and the class there "is not a
grain." [166] Meanwhile, the Russian proletariat shrunk by half, as
industrial workers returned to the village and to a "petty bourgeois" way of life in order to exist. His disillusionment in this
respect became clear only in March 1921, when he admitted: "the
petty bourgeois element does not simply beat against the proletariat . . . , this petty bourgeois element runs through the proletariat." The working class had been "peasantized." [167]

By early 1920, Bukharin's faith in war communism began to
erode. He now emphasized "socialist construction" in a way that
he had not done earlier; he seemed weary and sick of civil war. To
theorize about the "costs of revolution" was one thing, to experience them another. The Polish war caught the Bolsheviks by surprise, and though Bukharin wished for the resources to carry the
campaign beyond Warsaw "right up to London and Paris," he
was glad when it ended, freeing the government to cope "with
our internal situation, with hunger and cold." For the first time he
wondered where future sources of economic development were
to be obtained, observing that the era of construction was "the
real period of social revolution" and "the greatest epoch." [168] His
discontent deepened. That officials produced optimistic reports
amidst a worsening situation was "a scandal"; he was pessimistic
about the prospects of a meaningful economic plan. Most of all,
the ever-growing bureaucratic apparatus appalled him. Control
was placed over control, he said, but served only to create a
"colossal ballast on the whole Soviet organism." He proposed a
new slogan: "It is better not to control a bad apparatus, but to
improve the bad so that it will become good," an interesting fore-
runner of Lenin's celebrated "Better Fewer, But Better." [169]

The basic crisis, however, involved agriculture, as Bukharin
began to emphasize in the second half of 1920. For the first time,
both aspects of the peasant problem figured prominently in most
of his major statements: how to establish stable economic relations
between the cities and the countryside; and how to reverse the

drastic fall in agricultural output. He still had no answer. While advising party officials to stop approaching the peasant with slogans about world revolution and appeal instead to his "reason," Bukharin continued to speak against "free trade," as did all the leaders.[170] But by January 1921, he saw the situation as clearly as anyone and was probably prepared to accept almost any solution: "Our situation is much more difficult than we think. We have peasant uprisings which must be suppressed with armed force and which will intensify in the future. . . . I maintain that the moment which the Republic is experiencing is the most dangerous that Soviet power has ever experienced." [171]

But at this critical moment the party leadership's attention was elsewhere. During the winter of 1920–1, as disaster threatened to engulf it, the Central Committee divided bitterly into opposing factions over the role of the trade unions after the civil war. The controversy was a model of obfuscation, only peripherally related to the real crisis in the country, and serving mainly to reveal the confusion, indecision, and dissension that permeated the party on the eve of NEP. Its full history need not concern us, only that it had roots in the widespread dissatisfaction with bureaucratic and authoritarian procedures. The argument contained a variety of elements, including concern over future economic policy, the desire of some trade union leaders to realize the promise of the 1919 party program that unions would gain authority in economic administration, and, behind the scenes, personal rivalries and resentments involving Zinoviev, Stalin, and Trotsky.[172]

The open dispute was triggered by Trotsky, whose plan to militarize the labor force and transform the trade unions into docile production units of the state enjoyed Lenin's support until the fall of 1920. The antipathy of Bolshevik trade unionists to militarization had been evident earlier, but erupted into open opposition in November, when Trotsky, never a diplomatic figure, called for a reorganization of the recalcitrant union leadership. Lenin now abandoned Trotsky and adopted a more moderate position, which recognized a role for the unions as links between the state and the masses ("schools of communism"), and which acknowledged that workers required union protection against the Soviet state. At this point, the Central Committee was so badly divided on the question that eight separate platforms were advanced. When the air cleared, the main antagonists were Lenin and his followers; Trotsky; and a group known as the Workers' Opposition, who spoke in a strong syndicalist voice against party and state domination of the unions and for independent union control over industry.[173] The compelling feature of the bitter controversy, however, was the deep split in Politburo ranks, most notably between Lenin and Trotsky.

Bukharin's ambiguous position in the affair reflected his troubled uncertainty on the eve of NEP. He reiterated some old ideas, but also groped for new ones. It also marked his debut as a political lone wolf in internal party struggles, having disassociated himself politically from his former Moscow allies. The Democratic Centralists, led by Osinskii and Smirnov, whose criticism of party bureaucracy was similar to that of the Workers' Opposition, were still entrenched in the Moscow organization. In November 1920, Bukharin made the break complete by calling publicly for "fresh forces" from outside Moscow to make the city organization "healthy" and establish a "businesslike" committee that would enforce the party line "in the present difficult conditions." [174] He spoke now as a representative of the party's high leadership. At the same time, he was neither insensitive to the Left's call for internal party democracy nor in full agreement with Lenin or Trotsky on the trade union issue. He therefore emerged as a compromiser, or, as he was characterized when he tried the role with equally disastrous results in 1923, a "peacemaker." [175]

Until the fall of 1920, Bukharin had advocated labor armies and "statization" of the trade unions, meaning by the latter that state and trade union organs would jointly manage the economy. He saw an important role for unions, but not one independent of the state. This had been the party's official attitude and, like Lenin, he had endorsed Trotsky's initial proposals. When the controversy broke out, he stopped speaking of militarization and took a stand between Trotsky and Lenin, combining elements of their program. He defined his conception of "statization" as a gradual process to distinguish it from Trotsky's "shaking up" by decree. In addition, he took seriously the party's pledge of September 1919 to encourage democratic procedures. Thus, when Lenin protested against the publicizing of the trade union dispute before a broader audience, Bukharin replied: "We have proclaimed a new sacred slogan—workers' democracy, which consists in the fact that all questions are discussed not in narrow collegiums, not in small meetings, not in some sort of corporation of one's own, but that all questions are carried to wide meetings." The open discussion, he insisted, was "a step forward." [176]

Bukharin first tried to mediate the dispute in the Central Committee by offering a compromise resolution. When this failed, he produced his own theses on the trade unions, which became known as the "buffer" platform. He explained: "when a train shows certain inclination toward a crash, then a buffer is not such a bad thing." The programs of Lenin (supported by Zinoviev) and Trotsky, he argued, were compatible and should be combined. Both production and democracy could be served; the trade unions were to be part of "the technical administrative apparatus," as well as "schools of communism." At the same time, his platform was a ringing endorsement of "workers' democracy," and called for a gradual "fusing" of trade union and state organs in a way that would not denigrate the unions:

If the general progressive line of development is the line of fusing the trade unions, then from the other side this same process is a process of "unionizing" the state. Its logical and historical end will not be the absorption of the unions by the proletarian state, but the disappearance of both categories, state and union, and the creation of a third—the communistically organized society.

To ensure equal standing for union officials, Bukharin proposed that trade union nominations for economic posts should be obligatory on the state, but that once in office these officials would be bound by state instructions.[177]

Compromise is usually regarded as a valuable part of politics, but Bukharin had offered the wrong program at the wrong time. A furious Lenin quickly singled him out as the leading villain: "Up to now Trotsky was the 'chief' in the struggle. Now Bukharin has far 'outstripped' . . . him . . . and has [achieved] a mistake one hundred times greater than all of Trotsky's mistakes taken together." He accused Bukharin of "syndicalism," of advocating workers' democracy at the expense of "revolutionary expediency," and of having "slipped into eclecticism." The last sin particularly impressed Lenin, who devoted part of an article to lecturing Bukharin on the meaning of dialectics. After a lengthy discourse including references to Hegel and Plekhanov, he concluded that by taking pieces from different platforms Bukharin had substituted "eclectics for dialectics." [178] Bukharin was probably surprised to learn that compromise was "undialectical," a pejorative usually confined to philosophical or at least theoretical discussions. Lenin, however, was serious. Three years later, in his "testament," he observed that Bukharin "has never studied and, I think, never fully understood dialectics," presumably an oblique reference to the trade union controversy.[179]

Rarely, if ever, had Lenin reacted with such bitterness toward

Bukharin. Before November 1920, they had collaborated closely on major political questions, including trade union affairs. Now Lenin evidently believed that Bukharin had failed as a loyal, unwavering supporter (a role currently being over-fulfilled by Zinoviev), and worse, that he was partial to Trotsky. Explaining Bukharin's "rupture with communism," he said:

We know all the softness of Comrade Bukharin; it is one of the characteristics for which he is so loved and cannot help being loved. We know that more than once in jest he was called "soft wax." It turns out that on this "soft wax" any "unprincipled" person, any "demagogue," can write whatever he pleases.[180]

Bukharin tried to prevent a split in the party leadership, an act Lenin viewed as disloyalty. Compromise no longer possible, Bukharin published a hurt rejoinder and shortly united with Trotsky in a common platform for the upcoming Tenth Party Congress, which was to decide the matter.[181] By January 1921, having abandoned militarization and moderated his other demands, Trotsky's revised position was similar to Bukharin's. Their joint platform endorsed "workers' democracy" and union management of industry, called for "statization" but defined it as a "long process," and agreed that trade unions should be "schools of communism" as well as production units. For his part, Bukharin dropped the idea of binding nominations and reaffirmed party control over trade union personnel. Some saw in this a capitulation to Trotsky, but Bukharin was satisfied that "we did not join Trotsky, Trotsky joined us." [182]

Here the matter stood in February 1921—surrealistically irrelevant to the real situation in the country. In terms of the actual crisis, the difference between Lenin on the one side and Bukharin and Trotsky on the other was minimal. Lenin's argument that unions had to protect their members from the state, a proposition Bukharin and Trotsky did not accept as formulated, was more in accord with the imminent end of war communism and the rebirth of private enterprises. Both sides, however, still thought in terms of the existing system; in this context, Bukharin and Trotsky at least tried to come to grips with the economic crisis through a restructuring of the administrative framework. But, by February 15, Bukharin was sufficiently exasperated by the irrelevancy of the discussions to editorialize in *Pravda* that the party should direct its attention to the real problem, "the crisis in agriculture" and the "fate of *our economy*." [183]

Gripped by "the great force of inertia," however, the leadership continued to procrastinate, as if inviting outside pressures to force its hand.[184] In late February, wildcat strikes swept Petrograd where, as in the new capital of Moscow, Socialist Revolutionary and Menshevik agitation began to find a receptive audience. As peasant uprisings in the countryside began to echo in the cities, the specter of a worker-peasant alliance against the party rose up to haunt the Bolsheviks. The dénouement came on March 2, when open rebellion against the government broke out at the Kronstadt naval base near Petrograd, once a Bolshevik stronghold. Speaking for "the toilers" of Russia and evoking the popular watchwords of 1917 against "the policeman's club of the Communist autocracy," the rebels charged the party with having betrayed the revolution.[185]

The Tenth Party Congress convened in the second week of March, as the Kronstadt uprising was being suppressed by government troops. On the eighth day, Lenin announced that grain requisitioning would be replaced by a fair tax in kind, leaving all surplus produce to the individual peasant.[186] Almost no debate attended this momentous change which, by abolishing requisitioning and necessitating some form of regularized trade between town and country, put an end to war communism. Though hotly debated for a month in the Politburo,[187] no one apparently understood that the decision would quickly lead to a radically different economic system—to the restoration of private capital, market and monetary exchange, the denationalization of many enterprises, and thus the diminishing of the socialist or state sector.

The system to be known as NEP entered surreptitiously, few at the party congress appreciating the enormity of what was happening. Lenin's trade union platform won easily, also with little debate. (A new resolution commensurate with the changed social circumstances would have to be drafted at the next party congress.) The delegates' attention was riveted on the traumatic events at Kronstadt. What should have been a triumphant congress of civil war victors was informed by one of its leaders, Bukharin: "now the Republic hangs by a hair." [188]

CHAPTER IV

Marxist Theory and Bolshevik Policy: Bukharin's *Historical Materialism*

It would be strange if Marxist theory eternally stood still.

—BUKHARIN

THE EVENTS OF EARLY 1921 mark a turning point in the history of Soviet Russia, the revolution, and in Bukharin's thinking about Bolshevism. In the wake of what he later called this "collapse of our illusions,"[1] he and other Bolsheviks began the painful process of rethinking their basic assumptions about the revolution. The new social conditions soon gave rise to new patterns of thinking, which for the next eight years commingled and competed with the ideological legacy of 1917–20. The superficial party unanimity evoked by civil war quickly dissolved into waves of profound disagreement and prolonged disunity. Until 1929, when dissent became dangerous and a harsher unity was imposed, instances of real party consensus were rare and fleeting. The underlying heterogeneity of the Bolshevik élite, partly subdued for three years, again emerged. Once, Bukharin lamented (the myth of an original Bolshevik unanimity was already entrenched) there had been "a single party, with a single psychology and a single ideology"; now the party was divided into "different parts, with different psychologies, with different deviations."[2]

Partly because of the party's great ideological and program-matic disunity, the Soviet twenties—the years between the intro-duction of NEP and the coming of Stalin's "revolution from above" in 1929—were to be a conspicuously rich and diverse decade of intellectual ferment. In philosophy, law, literature, economics, and other fields, wide-ranging theoretical controversies, both related and unrelated to the political debates under way in the party leadership, made this the most vital period in the history of Bolshevik thought and among the most interesting in the history of Marxist ideas.

Students of the era have naturally searched for patterns in the diversity, but often by positing dubious relationships between rival viewpoints in the various areas of intellectual controversy and political factions in the party. At its least persuasive, this approach has meant defining the equivalent to a left and right wing in each discussion, no matter how nonpolitical the topic. In the same vein, efforts have been made to establish a rigid correlation between an individual Bolshevik's interpretation of Marxism—his social or philosophical theory—and his politics. Always a difficult under-taking, this has been especially misleading in the case of Bukharin.

A widely held view maintains that the cautious evolutionary policies that Bukharin was to advocate in the twenties, which set him first against the Bolshevik Left and then against Stalin, may be explained largely by his mechanistic understanding of Marxist dialectics and his companion theory of equilibrium. His Marxism, it is argued, was sternly deterministic, emphasizing the hegemony of objective conditions over the interventionist capabilities of man. This view is contrasted with the voluntarism embedded in the Left's programs of the twenties and subsequently in Stalin's "great change" of 1929–33. Political and economic voluntarism is seen as being intimately related to the anti-mechanistic school in Soviet philosophy, centered around Abram Deborin, which unlike the mechanists (who disliked the Deborinist formulation of the propo-sition and its transcendent implications) argued that dialectics implied self-movement of matter and leaps from quantity to qual-ity. Where Bukharin is involved, this view represents a rare in-stance of agreement between Western scholars and Soviet writers. The latter also insisted, beginning with Bukharin's fall in 1929, when an official *post facto* campaign was launched to associate Stalin's defeated rivals with disfavored philosophical schools, that Bukharin's "right-wing" program was the logical outcome of his mechanism. In fact, the basic sources and inspiration of the Western interpretation were Stalinist critics of Bukharin.[3]

Of the several difficulties with this argument, the most troublesome is the most obvious: Bukharin's famous *Historical Materialism*, the systematic exposition of his social theory, appeared in the autumn of 1921, only months after the end of those extremist war communist policies he had supported enthusiastically.[4] Moreover, its writing coincided with his writing of *The Economics of the Transition Period*, a theoretical justification of voluntarism and social leaps. Overlooked is the fact that both *The Economics* and *Historical Materialism* contained Bukharin's celebrated mechanism and equilibrium theory, even though the former work exuded a cataclysmic ethos, the latter an evolutionary one.

As this suggests, the argument has rested less on the actual substance of Bukharin's social theory than on two false assumptions. The first is that there were "consciously formed connections" between the mechanist philosophers and the right wing in the party. This "legend" has since been disproved and the opposite shown to have been the case: there was "a widespread, conscious effort to keep the philosophical discussions separate from the Party factional quarrels," and specifically "to keep Bukharin out of the philosophical controversy."[5] The second is the assumption that Bolsheviks (or Marxists generally) who shared one theoretical position would likely agree on other issues, a misconception which ignores the diversity of Marxist thought, the intellectual heterogeneity of pre-Stalinist Bolshevism, and in this instance the maverick, contentious quality of Bukharin's *Historical Materialism*. The book contained something to please and displease almost everyone. Both Soviet and Western Marxists gave it a widely mixed reception; but Bukharin's least friendly Bolshevik critic was a fellow mechanist, who found much in the book that was "un-Marxist" and "undialectical." To confound the matter further, Bukharin and his critic accused each other of "determinism."[6]

Before the unanimity imposed by Stalinism in the thirties, agreement among Bolsheviks on one theoretical issue did not ensure affinity elsewhere, in theory or in politics. Many examples could be given, but suffice it to point out that while Trotsky, avatar of the party Left, rarely expressed himself on philosophical questions, when he did it was as a mechanist; and that Preobrazhenskii, later the foremost economist of the Left, employed the equilibrium model in analyzing capitalist and Soviet economics.[7] In short, one does best to heed the 1909 lament of a party leader that no two Bolshevik philosophers could agree.[8]

None of which is to say that Bukharin's social theory was wholly unrelated to his political and economic policies. Rather, it is to point out that in addition to misrepresenting the origins and nature of his subsequent gradualism, a simplistic formulation of the relationship between his social theory and his policies obscures what was truly interesting about his *Historical Materialism,* a book on which a generation of Bolshevik intellectuals were educated and which, in translation, was widely read outside the Soviet Union.

Although *Historical Materialism* originated as a textbook—there being "no systematic exposition of this 'basic of basics' of Marxist theory"—it was designed to break fresh theoretical ground. Aware that presenting new ideas in the form of semi-official pedagogy would again provoke the "conservatism" of his party critics, Bukharin opened with the assurance that, while he intended to "depart from the usual treatment of the subject," he remained faithful to "the tradition of the most orthodox, materialist, and revolutionary understanding of Marx." He wanted to systematize and make more precise a variety of Marxist tenets, but also to introduce "innovations." [9] Most of his reformulations and innovations were responses to contemporary social theorists critical of Marx. *Historical Materialism* was an extended intellectual counterpunch, and in this sense an important chapter in Bukharin's lifelong project to answer Marx's critics. As was his custom, in answering the challengers he borrowed from them.

It is curious that a rigid economic determinism should have been attributed to *Historical Materialism,* because Bukharin went to great lengths to exorcise this allegation and the notion of monistic causality from Marxism. An astute non-Marxist reviewer rightly observed that Bukharin strained toward monism but approached pluralism. [10] Indeterminism, historical teleology, and inexplicable accidents are rejected; but the book is studded with examples of the "if" in history, of instances where different historical developments are possible depending on a variety of factors, and of the multi-causal nature of change in general. "Social determinism" is not fatalism; it is "the doctrine that all social phenomena are conditioned, have causes from which they necessarily flow. . . ." Bukharin's Marxism, for example, does not deny human will or the superstructure; "it explains them." [11]

His pluralistic approach is most evident in the section on the superstructure, which Bukharin sees as "the widest possible" category—"as meaning any type of social phenomenon erected on the economic base." It is a complex, differentiated conception, including, in addition to the "social political order, with all its material parts," social psychology and ideology. The base defines and explains these phenomena; but, Bukharin points out (as had Engels earlier), they have a life and dynamics of their own as well, particularly during the long transition from one social structure to another, when there is "the process of a reversed influence of the superstructure. . . ." [12] It was hardly possible to argue otherwise, given the Soviet experience since 1917.

But Bukharin was equally aware that the superstructure plays a functional role in existing societies and in bringing about social change. He wanted to meet the challenge of psychologically oriented schools of economics and sociology, to show that Marxism takes less tangible factors into account. While he rejected Robinson Crusoe concepts then popular in the West, he acknowledged the major importance of psychology, ideologies, morality, and customs. They hold society together: they "coordinate men's actions and keep them within certain bounds, thus preventing society from disintegrating." And just as they are an adhesive force at one time, so the displacement of the prevailing psychology and ideology (the "mental revolution") marks the first stage in the collapse of the old social order. In short, Bukharin offered a variegated conception of causality: *a constant process of mutual cause and effect is in operation between the various categories of social phenomena. Cause and effect change places.*" [13]

Bukharin's treatment of the diverse components of the superstructure proved to be one of his most influential contributions. Apart from enhancing the role of the superstructure *vis-à-vis* the base, a proposition many Bolsheviks naturally welcomed, his formulations on science, philosophy, psychology, and the "accumulation" and "materialization" of culture were considered highly successful. Also satisfying and popular, for obvious reasons, was his treatment of class, party, and leaders, which gave positive theoretical expression to the important role of the latter two.[14] More than any other single work, *Historical Materialism* established Bukharin as the party's major theorist and probably the foremost Soviet systematizer of Marxism in the twenties.[15] But his most original contribution lay elsewhere.

Since the 1890's, the most formidable intellectual challenge to Marxism had come from the emerging schools of modern sociology. Sociology then, unlike its narrower and more empirical turn later, was directed toward broad social theorizing. Like Marxism, it was theory on a grand, often historical, scale, and it, too, viewed itself as science. Major figures of the new science—Durkheim, Pareto, Croce, Weber, Michels, to name a few—varied in their critical responses to Marxism; but each in his own way had to confront this imposing body of thought. Marx had posed central questions about society, and he had developed important analytical concepts. His conclusions could be dismissed, as could the remnants of German philosophy embedded in his thinking, but he could not be ignored. Said Pareto: "There is in Marx a sociological part, which is superior to the other parts and is very often in accord with reality." [16] Marx's contribution to sociology is now acknowledged, his reputation as a sociologist having become more commanding in some quarters than as either economist or prophet.[17] But his impact on the early theorists needs to be stressed. As H. Stuart Hughes has written: "The study of Marxism . . . offered them a kind of proving-ground. . . ." Marx's work was "the midwife of twentieth-century social thought." [18]

The new sociology had a profound impact on Bukharin, who, unlike many Bolshevik leaders, was in every respect a twentieth-century intellectual. It was evident in his émigré writings before 1917 and in much of his subsequent theoretical work. He recognized that contemporary scientific theories of society, many of which were formulated as critiques of Marxism, threatened to revise Marxism as social science and, presumably, to emasculate it as *Weltanschauung*. But he also appreciated their achievements. Contrary to later Soviet practice, Bukharin did not simply dismiss sociological thought; instead, he tried to meet it on its own ground. For him, historical materialism was sociology. In his book—the Russian edition of which was subtitled *A Popular Textbook of Marxist Sociology*—[19] he set out his understanding of the proposition:

Among the social sciences there are two important branches which consider not a single field of social life, but the entire social life in all its fullness. . . . One of these sciences is history; the other is sociology. . . . History investigates and describes how the current of social life flowed at a certain time and in a certain place. . . . Sociology takes up the answer to general questions, such as: What is the relation of the various groups of social phenomena (economic, legal, scientific, etc.) with each other; how is their evolution to be explained; what are the historical forms of society . . . etc.? Sociology is the most general (abstract) of the social sciences. . . . History furnishes the material for drawing sociological conclusions and making sociological generalizations. . . . Sociology in its turn formulates . . . a *method* for history.

Thus historical materialism "is not political economy, nor is it history; it is the general theory of society and the laws of its evolution, i.e., sociology." [20]

Bukharin believed (or said he believed) that all "social sciences have a *class* character" and that "proletarian sociology" therefore would be superior by definition. Bourgeois thinkers were limited by their class orientation. While they saw social interrelationships, they failed to emphasize society's contradictions. Still he regarded the entire school of "bourgeois sociology" as "very interesting." *Historical Materialism* was largely a tribute to its influence on him, and the book showed Bukharin locked in combat with its criticisms, striving to express orthodox Marxist tenets in sociological terms.[21]

He was not, of course, the first Marxist to promote the sociological component in Marxism. A pronounced movement in this direction and away from Marx's lingering metaphysics having been under way in Europe for more than two decades, several schools of Marxist sociology were already in existence by the time Bukharin's *Historical Materialism* appeared. The tradition was particularly strong in Vienna, as represented by the work of Max Adler and Karl Renner, where "Marx was discovered to have been primarily a sociologist—indeed the founder of modern scientific sociology." [22] In addition, nineteenth-century Russian radical thought, in its populist and Marxist manifestations, boasted a long and rich history of sociological theory. Even though the sociology associated with political movements dominated the scene, by 1917 academic sociology had established itself in the major universities of czarist Russia.[23]

Despite these credentials, contemporary sociology did not fare well among Lenin's Bolsheviks. Interestingly, Lenin's early study on *The Development of Capitalism in Russia* was not without sociological value, and he himself had argued in 1894 that Marxism "first made a 'scientific' sociology possible." [24] But the bitter 1908–9 philosophical battle with Bogdanov, who in his eyes had revised Marxism precisely by mixing it with bourgeois ideas, seems to have permanently prejudiced Lenin against all Western social theory. From that time onward, sociology (now always written in quotation marks) received only his derision. In rejecting Bukharin's

1916 article on the state, he had singled out for criticism the notion of a " 'sociological' (???) " theory,[25] and, as illustrated by his comments on Bukharin's *The Economics*, had grown still more hostile to sociological terminology by 1920. Although no reference to *Historical Materialism* appears in Lenin's published writings, we may be fairly certain that his objections began with the subtitle.

Not all Bolshevik intellectuals shared Lenin's disdain for sociology, though neither did they always agree with Bukharin's understanding of its role. Many preferred it to the argument that dialectical materialism was basically philosophy, a view held by the Deborinists and opposed by mechanists, who believed that positive science had virtually eliminated the need for philosophy. And, while non-Marxist sociology was excluded from Soviet universities in 1922, Bolshevik sociologists continued to publish serious theoretical and empirical work until the early thirties, when sociology suffered the fate of most social science under Stalin.[26] Even during the twenties, however, suspicion if not outright hostility to contemporary sociology appears to have been predominant among party intellectuals. Bukharin's designation of historical materialism as sociology was itself sufficient to outrage his early Bolshevik critics,[27] many of whom undoubtedly agreed with the verdict issued during the anti-Bukharin campaign in 1930:

Marx of course did not have a special "sociological method." . . . Marx's method was the method of dialectical materialism. . . . The representation of Marx as an advocate of a "sociological method" can only lead to a rapprochement of his teaching with the teaching of bourgeois "sociologists," which has nothing in common with Marxism.[28]

This was to be a constant refrain in Stalinist ideology, and only after the dictator's death were Soviet scholars again able to formulate a sociology. Against this background, Bukharin's attempt to develop a Marxist sociology takes on a unique boldness of conception and inquiry. He was referred to in the twenties by one Soviet writer as the "theoretician of proletarian sociology." And it is revealing that a reasonably friendly review of *Historical Materialism* came from Pitirim Sorokin, then living in Russia, who wrote that compared to other Bolshevik works it was "far more literate, interesting, and scientific." [29] An American sociologist has more recently confirmed Sorokin's appraisal: "It represents the one sophisticated effort by a major Marxist to come to terms with the emerging body of sociological theory and research." [30]

* * *

Of the various ways that contemporary sociology challenged Marxism as science, the most generally troublesome for Marxists involved the question of dialectics. Whether as method or as supposed presence in reality, the dialectical concept was deeply rooted in Marxist teaching about the nature and direction of social change. Its lingering Hegelianism made Marxism vulnerable. Moreover, the meaning of Marxist dialectics remained unclear. Marx, convinced that he had rendered dialectics consistently materialist, wrote little on the subject, confining himself to its application to history. It fell to Engels, late in Marx's life and after his death, to extend and systematize an understanding of the dialectic in history, nature, and human thought. In doing so, he laid the groundwork for an orthodox, universalistic doctrine of dialectical materialism. While several scholars have argued that Engels's finished system represented a sharp break with Marx's own philosophical materialism, it is generally agreed that in the end Engels's writings served to resurrect Hegel's idealist dialectics in a revised form, and to encumber Marxism with a vaguely metaphysical explanation of movement—a semi-mystical unfolding of the dialectic in history and in nature. The reborn Hegelianism strongly influenced Lenin's thinking about dialectics (as became clear when his *Philosophical Notebooks* were published in 1933) and became a central element in the dialectical materialism of the Deborinists.[31]

Bukharin turned his back on this tendency, stating his objections frankly: "Marx and Engels liberated the dialectic from its mystical husk in *action* . . . ", but it retains "the teleological flavor inevitably connected with the Hegelian formulation, which rests on the *self-movement* of 'Spirit.' " Bukharin's quest for a scientific ("radically materialist") sociology, his desire to counter the charge that Marxism embodied an ultimate idealism, led him instead to mechanism. Previously, he explained, Marxists had opposed mechanistic explanations in the social sciences; but this had derived from the old and discredited conception of the atom as "a detached isolated particle." The electron theory, with its new findings on the structure and movement of matter, disproved this and validated the language of mechanics as a means of expressing organic connections. Whether or not Bukharin fully understood modern physics is less important than his belief that the "most advanced tendencies of scientific thought in all fields accept this point of view." [32]

Mechanics, it seemed to him, demonstrated the scientific basis of Marxist materialism, and mechanistic materialism refuted those thinkers who persisted in "spiritualizing" and "psychologizing" social concepts. Bukharin defined each social category with an eye to preserving the imagery: society is viewed as "a huge working mechanism, with many subdivisions of the divided social labor"; production relations are "the labor *coordination of people* (*seen as 'living machines'*) *in space and in time*"; and so on. All that remained was to give a "theoretical-systematical exposition" of the dialectical method in mechanistic terms. "This," Bukharin believed, was "given by the theory of equilibrium." [33]

At the heart of *Historical Materialism* is his contention that dialectics and hence social change are explained by the equilibrium theory. His broad conception, not the multitude of subarguments he presents along the way, concerns us here.[34] According to Bukharin, the dialectic (or dynamic) point of view is that all things, material and social, are in motion and that motion derives from the conflict or contradiction internal to a given system. Equally true is that any system, again material or social, tends toward a state of equilibrium (analogous to adaptation in biology):

In other words, the world consists of forces, acting in many ways, opposing each other. These forces are balanced for a moment in exceptional cases only. We then have a state of "rest," i.e., their actual "conflict" is concealed. But if we change only one of these forces, immediately the "internal contradictions" will be revealed, equilibrium will be disturbed, and if a new equilibrium is again established, it will be on a new basis, i.e., with a new combination of forces, etc. It follows that the "conflict," the "contradiction," i.e., the antagonism of forces acting in various directions, determines the motion of the system.

By locating the source of motion in the conflict of forces and not in "self-development," Bukharin believed that he had purged Hegel's famous triad (thesis, antithesis, synthesis) of its idealist elements. His corresponding formula is original equilibrium, disturbance of equilibrium, and re-establishment of equilibrium on a new basis.[35]

Every system, he continued, is involved in two states of equilibrium: internal and external. The first refers to the relationship between different components within a system, the second to the entire system in its relationship with its environment. In neither case is there ever an "absolute, unchanging equilibrium"; it is always "in flux"—a dynamic or moving equilibrium. The key to Bukharin's theory is the relationship between internal and external equilibrium:

the internal structure of the system . . . must change together with the relation existing between the system and its environment. The latter relation is the decisive factor . . . *the internal (structure) equilibrium is a quantity which depends on the external equilibrium (is a "function" of this external equilibrium).*[36]

Applied to society, Bukharin's theory reads as follows: An existing society presumes a certain equilibrium between its three major social elements—things, persons, and ideas. This is internal equilibrium. But "society is unthinkable without its environment," that is, nature. Society adapts itself to nature, strives toward equilibrium with it, by extracting energy from it through the process of social production. In the process of adaptation, society develops "an artificial system of organs," which Bukharin calls technology and which constitutes "a precise material indicator of the relation between the society and nature." It is by identifying social technology with productive forces ("the combinations of the instruments of labor"), and by making the internal structure a function of the external equilibrium, that Bukharin is able, despite his pluralistic analysis of social development, to preserve monistic causality in economic determinism. Or as he acknowledges:

the productive forces determine social development *because* they express the interrelation between society . . . and its environment. . . . *And the interrelation between environment and system is the quantity which determines, in the last analysis, the movement of any system.*[37]

This theoretical model conveys Bukharin's historical materialism, systematizing social development. Social equilibrium is constantly being disturbed. It can move toward restoration in two ways: either by "a gradual adaptation of the various elements in the social whole (evolution)"; or by "violent upheaval (revolution)." As long as the envelope of social equilibrium, primarily the production relations as embodied in the classes directly participating in production, is sufficiently broad and durable, evolution occurs. In this way, for example, capitalism progressed through its several historical phases. But when the forces of production develop to where they come into conflict with "the fundamental web of these productive forces, i.e., property relations," revolution takes place. The "envelope is burst asunder." A new social equilibrium is established; "i.e., a new and durable envelope of production relations . . . capable of serving as an evolutionary form of the productive forces. . . ."[38]

* * *

If this abstract theory is pregnant with logical programmatic implications, as Bukharin's political opponents suddenly discovered in
1929, it is not immediately evident. A standard charge against
mechanism was that its understanding of motion precluded the
transformation of quantity into quality and "leaps" in general.
Here, allegedly, was the philosophical basis of political gradualism.
Bukharin, however, argued otherwise: "The transformation of
quantity into quality is one of the fundamental laws in the motion
of matter; it may be traced literally at every step both in nature and
society." He even drew the same political conclusion as his critics:
"the notion that nature permits of no such violent alterations is
merely a reflection of the fear of such shifts in society. . . ." [39]
Equally unconvincing is the claim that Bukharin's "naturalistic"
materialism—so designated because of his emphasis on society's
interaction with nature—could lead only to passive capitulation before objective conditions. This same "naturalism" was present in
The Economics, where he argued that internal and external equilibrium would be restored by willful force. [40]

When logic faltered, Stalinist critics tried to bolster their thesis
by proving deviation by association. They pointed to the fact that
Bogdanov, by now an official example of notorious political deviation, earlier had also rejected the Hegelian tradition of dialectics in
favor of a mechanical equilibrium model. They ignored, however,
the definitive dissimilarities between Bukharin's and Bogdanov's
theories, as well as Bukharin's long history of theoretical and political opposition to Bogdanov, before and after 1917. [41] The interesting
intellectual kinship between the two men is a separate issue, but the
commonplace view that Bukharin was his disciple should not go
unchallenged. Not only was there little of the elder thinker's influence apparent in Historical Materialism, but the book's long argument against "psychologized Marxism" as "a clear deviation from
the materialism in sociology emphasized con amore by Marx" was
aimed specifically at Bogdanov. [42]

It is more fruitful to recall that by the early 1900's, mechanical
equilibrium models (especially dynamic ones) had spread from
physics and biology to the social sciences, where they were widely
accepted and employed. It seemed to be the last word in science;
and then, as today, equilibrium theory was an important part of
Western sociological and economic thought. Sorokin noted one
relevant example in 1922: Bukharin's treatment of social equilibrium
was similar in several ways to Pareto's presentation in the second
volume of Trattato di Sociologia generale. [43] The "Bogdanovist

terminology," which so offended Bukharin's critics, was to a considerable extent the language of contemporary social theory, a fact which suggests the genuine underlying affinity between Bukharin and Bogdanov. Both regarded Marxism as an open-ended body of thought, vulnerable and receptive to new intellectual currents. Both believed it legitimate to refer their Marxist critics to the work of non-Marxists. Bogdanov's declaration of 1908, "The tradition of Marx-Engels must be dear to us not in its letter but in its spirit," was echoed by Bukharin in the preface to *Historical Materialism:* "It would be strange if Marxist theory eternally stood still." [44]

Nonetheless, *Historical Materialism* can throw some light on Bukharin's subsequent thinking about Soviet society. His sociology—his interest in the dynamics of social evolution and how existing societies function—presented a different dimension of his mind, which until 1921 had seemed to be tuned mainly to revolutionary disorder and cataclysmic change. To put it another way, the dissimilar tempers of *The Economics* and *Historical Materialism,* the latter an almost quietist tract by comparison, derived in part from the fact that they focused on different periods in society's life: the first portrayed a transitory state of revolutionary disequilibrium, the second the more usual state of equilibrated society. And it is here, in his discussion of equilibrated society, that Bukharin revealed an awareness that any stable, growing society must be a cohesively integrated aggregate, with at least a minimal harmony of its components.

Many radical Marxists, having dwelt on the apocalyptic vision in Marxism, tended to view pre-utopian society as little more than a battleground of irreconcilable forces and warring classes. Always searching for crises and omens of breakdown, they saw only a dysfunctional malformation. Usually, as one sociologist observed, they "shunned and even ridiculed" bourgeois notions of social interaction and cooperation.[45] While this image sustained revolutionary fervor, it did not advise social construction. As a Marxist, Bukharin naturally accented instances in which social conflicts were in the foreground, but he also understood that elements of harmony and "moments of cooperation" normally prevail. He saw society as a real totality, and marveled at "how truly tremendous is the Babylonian confusion of influences and mutual interactions in social life." The very fact that society was an aggregate of conflicting forces suggested to him the importance of adhesive elements, of "social bonds" and "rivets" that preserve the community. Nowhere was this clearer than in his picture of society's collective confrontation with nature: "It has taken man centuries of bitter struggle to place his iron bit in nature's mouth." [46]

This awareness of the prerequisites of a properly functioning society was to be reflected in Bukharin's thinking about domestic policy throughout the twenties. He believed that the Bolsheviks' initial task involved reconstructing the social fabric of a society torn and divided by revolution and civil war. Social integration meant "normalizing" Soviet authority and making it acceptable to as many segments of the population as possible. "Bridges" and "links," in the form of voluntary institutions, had to be built between the party-state and the masses, as well as among the atomized elements of the population itself. Beneath this emphasis on integration was Bukharin's basic assumption in the programmatic controversies that followed: that real growth, economic and otherwise, is predicated on civil peace, on cooperation and harmony; that a society at war against itself cannot be productive or prosperous. Hence his insistence, so characteristic of his policies in the twenties, that all classes and strata in Soviet society could, consciously or unconsciously, contribute to the building of socialism. And hence his relentless opposition to those Bolsheviks whose programs promised new discord and civil strife.

More difficult to assess is how the equilibrium theory itself conditioned Bukharin's way of looking at real social problems. The macro-sociological use of equilibrium in *Historical Materialism* must be distinguished from his advocacy of "dynamic economic equilibrium" during the planning controversy of the late twenties. This narrower (though related) argument spoke only of his belief in balanced or proportional economic development as opposed to the selective "leaps" and disproportions implicit in Stalin's first five-year plan.[47] That a growth model based on conditions of economic equilibrium could be derived from Volume II of *Capital* was not a unique point of view, and occasionally was even acknowledged obliquely by Bukharin's opponents.[48] What was more easily denounced as un-Marxist was Bukharin's extrapolation of this limited concept into a macro-sociological model, and his claim that "Marx already gives hint of such a formulation (the doctrine of equilibrium between the various branches of production, the theory of labor value based thereon, etc.)." [49]

This made his orthodoxy suspect from a number of perspectives. By giving a universal definition to society, and by applying the equilibrium model to all social formations, for example, he was open to the charge of having abandoned Marx's cherished historicism, which stressed the unique features and specific laws of different historical societies. Even though Bukharin insisted on the study of "*each form of society in its own peculiar terms*," he had acquired the sociological habit, which in his own words deals "not with the individual forms of society, but with society in general." [50] Furthermore, if the equilibrium model could be generalized, did this not imply the existence of a universal regulator or law operating in all societies? Bukharin only hinted at the answer in *Historical Materialism* when he spoke of "the expenditure of labor" as the law governing society's relations with nature; later, however, he would formalize "the law of labor expenditure" as "the necessary condition of social equilibrium *in each and every kind of social-historical formation*." [51]

But the fundamental criticism of Bukharin's sociological theory and its political implications was that equilibrium presupposes social harmony, while orthodox Marxism proves the prevalence of social conflict. Soviet writers are not alone in having contrasted a Marxist conflict model to an equilibrium model of society. A parallel can be found in recent criticisms of the present-day structural-functionalist school of sociology. Dissident Western sociologists have argued that (unlike Marxism) functionalism, with its homeostatic equilibrium concept, is unable to accommodate real social change from within and therefore puts a premium on harmonious stability. They have further suggested that equilibrium implies a normative (conservative) orientation, which looks askance on social conflict and regards disequilibrating elements as abnormal and pathological. One historian has even concluded that the "choice of an equilibrium model logically precludes a revolutionary ethic. . . ." [52] The association of political conservatism with equilibrium theory (even today a stable item in Soviet thought),[53] then, is not limited to Soviet Marxists.

Although he never seriously came to grips with it, Bukharin seems to have been aware of the paradox. He made a conscious effort to disclaim any notion of "perfect harmony," and a tinge of discomfort was discernible in his rejoinder to potential critics: "Examining a social system, and an irrational, blind one at that, from the point of view of equilibrium has nothing in common, of course, with *harmonia praestabilitata,* for it follows from the *fact* that this system exists and also from the *fact* that it develops." Development means that this is a "moving equilibrium, and not a static one." [54] Viewing equilibrium as a dynamic concept seemed to be fully compatible with the assumption that conflict and change are always present in society. Indeed, Bukharin believed that mechanics wedded to Marxism provided a powerful rebuttal to the biological organism model of society, which did represent disequilibrating elements as pathological.[55] Finally, he saw no contradiction between revolutionary Marxism and the view that social harmony will prevail during certain historical periods, because in pre-socialist societies the restoration of equilibrium would always be temporary and progressively less stable. Increasingly severe instances of disequilibrium will ensue until revolution occurred. In other words, here the prevalence of harmony, and the presence of homeostasis, is historically limited; only communism could provide the conditions for an enduring social equilibrium.

Still, it is questionable whether Bukharin's abstract theory really could account for deep-rooted social change originating from within. In the last analysis, as reflected in his treatment of technology, he made internal equilibrium dependent on the interrelations between society and nature. The impetus of pervasive change was external to the social system. In this and other respects, his "Marxist sociology" was frequently inconsistent and sometimes crude, though the validity of the mechanical equilibrium model continues to divide sociologists.

All this says little directly about Bukharin's politics. His abiding conviction that in the absence of harmony, "society will not grow but decline" [56] informed both *The Economics* and *Historical Materialism*, as did his faith that socialist revolution would bring an ultimately harmonious, productive, and durable equilibrium. Until 1921, he saw this promise emerging out of the policies of war communism. Shortly afterwards, he came to believe the opposite.

What *Historical Materialism* really illustrates is that Bukharin, like other "seeking Marxists" of the Soviet twenties, viewed Marxism not only as the ideology of the party-state, but as a system of living ideas competitive with and alert to the accomplishments of contemporary Western thought. With the eventual departure of these "seeking Marxists," politically in the late twenties and physically in Stalin's purges of the thirties, the tension between ideology and social science that had characterized Marxism from the outset was resolved in Russia in favor of the former, and the questing spirit went out of Soviet Marxism for many years to come.

CHAPTER V

Rethinking Bolshevism

*When I was a child, I spake as a child, I under-
stood as a child, I thought as a child: but when
I became a man, I put away childish things.*

—*1 Corinthians* (13:11)

*The transition to the new economic policies
represented the collapse of our illusions.*

—BUKHARIN

IN 1921 the Bolsheviks surveyed the bitter fruits of victory. Civil
war had brought, said one, an economic collapse "unparalleled in
the history of humanity." [1] The country lay in ruins, its national
income one-third of the 1913 level, industrial production a fifth
(output in some branches being virtually zero), its transportation
system shattered, and agricultural production so meager that a
majority of the population barely subsisted and millions of others
failed even that. Preventive measures came too late to avert the
final disaster. In the spring, famine descended upon once rich grain
areas, bringing more death, disease, and even incidents of cannibalism. Nor had the second horseman quit the land. War continued,
now against peasants who were rising in large numbers against the
government. The Kronstadt rebellion paled by comparison; and it
was only by the concessions of NEP and the military force of the
Red army that the rural insurrections were finally subdued in 1922.

It was in these unhappy circumstances that the party began to
discard the economic policies of war communism and to develop
willy-nilly over the next two and a half years a new course. The
new economic policies, known collectively as NEP, and the social
order to which they gave rise, "NEP Russia," as Lenin dubbed it,
lasted seven years, until the onset of Stalin's "great change" in
1928–9. Though the NEP years seem only a peaceful and, for most

of the population, increasingly beneficial interlude between upheavals, they comprised distinct periods with different official aims,
achievements, and developments. Above all, NEP was the great
discussion period in party history, when the course of the Bolshevik
revolution, the direction of Soviet society, and the fate of individual
Bolshevik leaders were decided.

NEP constituted a major turnabout in party policy, but like
war communism it did not develop in accord with a preconceived
plan. Indeed, its spontaneous unfolding, according to its own internal logic, later caused some Bolsheviks to fear that a Pandora's
box had been inadvertently opened. The inaugural establishment of
a fixed tax in kind replacing grain requisitioning in March 1921 was
conceived of as a limited step to encourage the peasant to produce
and deliver a surplus, on which depended the revival of industry
and the cities. Lenin's original intention was to confine normal
market relations to the "localities," which would exchange or barter
goods directly with the state. It failed immediately; by fall, "ordinary buying and selling" had swept across the country. As a result,
restrictions on free trade were soon removed and, properly speaking, NEP truly born.[2] The multitude of new policies that evolved
through 1923 logically followed, as nationwide free trade and market relations became the hallmark of NEP.

Gradually the tax in kind was reduced, then replaced entirely
by a monetary one. To encourage the peasant further, his tenure on
the land was guaranteed, though public ownership was maintained
in principle. Hiring labor and leasing land, with some restrictions,
was sanctioned. But the peasant's willingness to market his surplus
depended on the availablility and relative cost of manufactured
goods, and thus on the revival of industrial production, particularly
of consumer goods, and a stable currency. The principles of NEP
therefore came to permeate the whole economy. Small enterprises
were denationalized and returned to private ownership (or in some
cases leased). Remaining state enterprises underwent a process of
decentralization, trustification, and commercialization; cost ac-
counting was introduced to prepare them for entry into the market
on a competitive basis. The return to financial orthodoxy began in
November 1921 with the resurrection of the State Bank (it had
been abolished in 1920) and continued through the development
of traditional fiscal, credit, and savings institutions and practices.
Hard currency policies became the norm, especially after the stabilization of the ruble in 1923. NEP had become the antithesis of war
communism.

Thus, by late 1923, Soviet Russia had developed one of the first modern, mixed economic systems. The state sector, in the terminology of the time, controlled the "commanding heights"— most large enterprises, including all heavy industry, the transportation system, the central banking system, and insofar as the country was now trading with the outside world, a foreign trade monopoly. The predominance of the state sector in industrial production was assured: while private enterprises accounted for 88.5 per cent of the total number, they were extremely small, employing only 12.4 per cent of the industrial labor force while state industries employed 84.1 per cent.[3] Private capital, however, was ensconced in retail and wholesale trade in the form of the so-called nepman or private merchant, though as the twenties progressed, state and cooperative organs gained the upper hand in the former area. The great preserve of free enterprise, private capital, and anti-socialist tendencies was the countryside, where 100 million peasants reaped the fruits of the agrarian revolution on what grew to be 25 million small holdings.[4] The party's frequent reference to the state or socialist sector as an island in a sea of petty capitalism—an image reflecting the worry that the continuation of NEP might bring about a total submersion of the socialist sector—derived from this situation. As industrial and agricultural production climbed steadily toward prewar levels, the dimensions of NEP varied somewhat with changes in official policy, from the more permissive in 1924–6 to the more restrictive in late 1926 and 1927; but the general economic framework erected by 1923 remained until the end of the decade.

At the same time that the party-state began relinquishing its control over much of the country's economic life, it moved to solidify its political monopoly. Dangers inherent in the economic concessions were to be counterbalanced by political safeguards. The Cheka and the blandishments of NEP brought an end to the scattered activity of Mensheviks and Socialist Revolutionaries; some emigrated, others served the government as specialists, a few were imprisoned. The legitimacy of the one-party dictatorship, established and made more authoritarian by civil war, was no longer open to public question. But short of outright counter-revolutionary activity (anti-Bolshevism), a considerable degree of nonpolitical freedom remained. Economically, intellectually, and culturally, NEP Russia became a relatively pluralistic society. Indeed, apart from the suppression of uprisings and of the other socialist parties, the harshest measures instituted in 1921 were directed against dissident Bolsheviks, present and future.

The Tenth Party Congress in March 1921 marked the beginning of a far-reaching change in internal party politics. At the instigation of Lenin and other party leaders—themselves bitterly and publicly divided until the Kronstadt rebellion—the Congress endorsed two resolutions virtually banning dissent from below: one denounced the Workers' Opposition as a "petty bourgeois anarchist deviation" and "objectively" a counter-revolutionary element; the other, in the name of party unity, ordered the end of all factions at the risk of disciplinary action, including expulsion.[5] Though the ban on factions would be honored in the breach for years to come, the leadership's attempt to reassert its control gave the growing central party apparatus, whose head Stalin became in 1922, far-reaching punitive powers over individual members. The atmosphere of relaxation fostered in the country by NEP triggered an opposite course inside the party.

These two developments—the emergence of an uncertain economic policy and an increasingly authoritarian, bureaucratic pattern of oligarchical decisionmaking—set the stage for the great party controversies of the twenties. Both had provoked opposition by 1923. After Lenin's first stroke in May 1922, and his death in January 1924, they became the dominant issues in the succession struggle, a four-act drama of successive confrontations between shifting official majorities and dissenting oppositions led by Lenin's heirs: the triumvirate of Zinoviev, Kamenev, and Stalin against Trotsky in 1923–4; Stalin and Bukharin against Zinoviev and Kamenev in 1925, and then against the united opposition of Trotsky, Zinoviev, and Kamenev in 1926–7; and finally, Stalin's majority against Bukharin, Rykov, and Mikhail Tomskii in 1928–9. Each opposition found it necessary to combine its criticisms of party policy with an attack on the workings of the party apparatus; each fell victim to the apparatus. But the history of the prolonged struggle inside the party for Lenin's mantle, for political power, should not obscure the underlying issue. Whither the Bolshevik revolution and Soviet Russia?, Trotsky and the others asked. Where was NEP leading, to capitalism or socialism? [6] Indeed, could socialism be built in Soviet Russia; and if so, how? These were parts of a single question that structured the debates, which were regularly expressed as a search for "orthodox Bolshevism."

The Bolsheviks were distinguished by their belief in a revolution which "does not come to an end after this or that political conquest" but whose "only boundary is the socialist society." [7] After four years of upheaval and civil war, they could now reflect and act with premeditation on this commitment. Great but largely unplanned changes had shaped Soviet society since 1917. In the cities, the old ruling élites and the large bourgeoisie had been broken or driven from the country. The landlord had been swept from the countryside, the land divided, and the peasantry significantly equalized—the kulak (the most prosperous peasant, and the village exploiter in official eyes) greatly diminished, the poor enhanced, and the middle peasant (neither rich nor poor, neither exploited nor exploiter) established as the predominant figure. The party had presided over many of these changes, but it had not controlled them. Some could only be viewed as mixed blessings: how could the revolutionary division of the land be reconciled with the Marxist belief in large-scale agricultural production; and would this sea of small private holdings inevitably generate a new cycle of capitalist relations? All these developments profoundly altered property relations, but they did not basically affect the nature of the economy. Even at prewar levels, which were generally regained by 1926, the Soviet Union remained an underdeveloped, agrarian society. The party's commitment to socialism, therefore, had to be first a commitment to industrialization and modernization.

After decades of national revolutions arising out of and directed against the conditions of social backwardness, it has become commonplace to view the Bolshevik revolution as the opening chapter in this still continuing process in the underdeveloped world. In some respects, czarist Russia was not a representative pre-modern society, having a European cultural and diplomatic history, an imperialist past, and a significant level of industrialization. But neither was she entirely atypical—a semi-Asiatic country, predominantly agrarian and largely illiterate, where foreign capital had played a major role, ruled now by a party whose leaders were from the intelligentsia and looked upon the industrial West with a mixture of hatred and envy.[8] The situation has since become familiar: the revolutionary party yearned for modernity, it wanted to "catch up"; the country was afflicted with "accursed poverty." On hearing a plan for the country's electrification, Bukharin dreamed the dream of future modernizers everywhere:

Poor, starving and sheep-skinned Old Russia, Russia of primitive lighting and the repast of a crust of black bread, is going to be covered by a network of electric stations. . . . it will transform Russia into a unique economy, and the dismembered nation into an intelligent and organized section of humanity. The horizon is endless and beautiful.[9]

The transfiguration of Bolshevism from a movement of insurrection and revolutionary internationalism into a movement for social transformation was not instant. Bolsheviks understood the role played by Russia's backwardness in their political success, but they did not immediately grasp its future implications. Civil war and the hope of European revolution blurred their vision for a while. In addition, the prospect of performing the modernizing work of a bourgeois revolution went against their Marxist grain; like Bukharin, many initially saw the chance circumstance of a victorious socialist party in a backward peasant country only as "tragic." [10] But the failure of revolution in Germany in 1921 (and again in 1923) turned their attention inward even more, and after 1921, as "the prose of economic development" began to dominate party discussion, the modernization theme impressed itself on the Bolshevik mind. With the introduction of NEP, it became the overriding motif in Lenin's statements. To the party he said: We have made a political revolution, now we must make an economic and cultural revolution that will lead Russia from her "patriarchalism, Oblomovism, and semi-savagery" to modernity.[11]

Not all Bolsheviks were ever fully reconciled to the national task. Some sensed it in the end of revolutionary internationalism. Others simply did not believe that an isolated country could overcome such backwardness. But many were able to fuse their Communist faith with their role as modernizers, as indicated in a 1924 editorial (probably written by Bukharin):

It is as if history [were] saying to the communists: here is a country, backward, illiterate, impoverished, ruined, with a gigantic predominance of nonproletarian elements—here you will build socialism, here you will prove that even under such unprecedentedly difficult conditions you can lay firmly the foundation of a new world. If the future is yours—go toward your goal, in spite of everything.[12]

Once the task was acknowledged, however, the question became how to accomplish it. Not just industrialism but a socialist society was desired, a condition that complicated the debates of the twenties by making the nature of the program as important as its economic feasibility. It had to be "orthodox," that is, compatible with the ethos of the party's history. Bolsheviks, as Stalin reportedly declared, did not want "a modernizing Bolshevism without Leninism." [13]

But as the search for a domestic program began, the party quickly discovered that there was no orthodox Bolshevism related to building socialism, and that here its ideology was in total disarray. The absence of a consensual fundamentalism stemmed in part from the party's original heterogeneity, from a tremendous growth in membership, and (as Bukharin sadly observed) a specialization inside the ruling party which had created a multitude of occupational groups and tendencies, each viewing issues from different vantage points.[14] Lenin's stern resolution on party unity at the Tenth Congress was both an admission of this diversity and a quixotic attempt to suppress it. The main source of the doctrinal crisis, however, harked back to 1917, when the Bolsheviks had taken power without an authentic domestic program. Two had since been hastily improvised and failed: Lenin's state capitalism of early 1918 was half-born, then half-forgotten; war communism was thoroughly discredited (though for different reasons to different people). Even the official 1919 party program was outdated and irrelevant, as Bukharin bluntly informed the faithful in the editorial columns of *Pravda*.[15] Nor were pre-Bolshevik classics of much help, it now being thought the highest mark of realism to point out that Marx and Engels offered little advice on the transition period.[16]

Bolshevism after 1921 was a movement bifurcated by two conflicting ideological (and emotional) traditions, both embedded in "historical Bolshevism." The first, what may be termed the "revolutionary-heroic" tradition, derived its legitimacy and inspiration from the party's daring coup in October 1917 and its valiant defense of the revolution during the civil war. These successes seemed to verify the "fierce assault" as a fundamental Bolshevik *modus operandi*. Consistently revolutionary and uncompromisingly radical, the heroic strand exuded what one contemporary observer called "revolutionary romanticism."[17] The other tradition, more cautious and moderate, was only faintly articulated before 1921, though it found historical legitimacy and precedent in Lenin's limited economic policies of early 1918 and in the strategic concessions of the Brest peace treaty. It came of age, and became frankly evolutionary and reformist, with the introduction of NEP, whose prudent pragmatism was the antithesis of revolutionary heroism. In a limited way, the bifurcation of Bolshevism echoed a duality in Marxism itself, where voluntarism and determinism had been subtly interwoven.[18] In the Soviet twenties, the two traditions were to be reflected in the party's left and right wings.

The themes of the heroic tradition were sounded most often by left oppositionists. Trotsky, creator of the Red army and architect of the civil war victory, was its living symbol; his haughty demeanor and penchant for administrative solutions reflected the conquering spirit of the revolution. Though something of a reformist in domestic policy, more than anyone else he gave literary expression to the mystique of October. In his 1924 essay "Lessons of October" and elsewhere, he promoted 1917 as Bolshevism's moment of truth, insisting that the revolutionary audacity validated then was still relevant. In the official interpretation of NEP, he saw the first signs of Bolshevism's "degeneration." He sensed, and rightly, that Bolshevik doctrine was being deradicalized, and warned that a previous deradicalization of Marxism had produced the hated reformism of social democracy. While Trotsky's proposal for a single economic plan and the "dictatorship of industry" was mild compared to what one day followed, he prepetuated the heroic tradition by calling on the working class to sacrifice "blood and nerves" at home, and by linking the fate of Bolshevism in Russia inextricably to an international revolution. Though demagogically distorted by his opponents, his concept of "permanent revolution" was the metaphor that best captured his political personality. "We are . . . merely soldiers in a campaign. We are bivouacking for a day," he wrote in 1923. Heroic battles were ahead. When the civil war ended, Trotsky sensed an "anticlimax in his fortunes," and he was right.[19]

Other party leftists conveyed the legacy of October more clearly in economic policy. Economists like Preobrazhenskii and Piatakov were soon expressing their distrust of NEP, protesting the blanket denigration of war communism, warning of an inevitable clash with the petty bourgeoisie, and calling for new revolutionary offensives. Preobrazhenskii's theory of "primitive socialist accumulation," despite its insightful economic analysis and professed compatability with the political tenets of NEP, was a clarion call for a herculean effort to hurdle the dangerous "breathing spell between two battles." He was disdainful of reformist policies that weakened the proletariat's will "when it needs to continue to wage the heroic struggle of October—only now against the whole of world economy, on the economic front, under the slogan of industrializing the country." [20] To Piatakov, the concessions of NEP were almost a betrayal of October, when "the real spirit of Bolshevism" had been revealed. His Bolshevism recognized no restraining objective conditions, that being the difference between Bolsheviks and non-Bolsheviks: "What is impossible for them, for us is possible." [21] The heroic tradition tended to produce a military outlook—direct assaults and great campaigns; many left oppositionists had served at the front during the civil war. But the legacy of October knew no political boundaries, inspiring diverse men and varied programs. Advocates of teleological planning disarmed their more cautious colleagues in the late twenties with the argument that the primacy of teleology had been established in October, when the laws of capitalist development had been circumvented. And in 1929, Stalin's collectivization drive would be officially termed "a plan to realize the program of October in the countryside." [22]

Closely associated with the heroic tradition were two ideas that lingered on the periphery of party thinking throughout the twenties: the dream of a "third revolution" * and the specter of Thermidor. Revolutionary movements have usually embodied groups, who after apparent victory urged "one more final revolution" to settle tasks left undone. Babeuf was the voice of "second revolution" in France, and German fascism had its "second revolutionists" in Ernst Röhm and his *Sturmabteilungen*.[23] After October, anarchists in the Ukraine, the Kronstadt rebels, and the Workers' Truth (an underground Communist opposition) had raised the banner of "third revolution" against the Bolsheviks. But only during NEP, when the problem of acquiring new capital was acute, could talk of a third revolution—a sweeping expropriation of the rural bourgeoisie and the nepman, a final solution to political and economic problems—be heard in the party itself. Until Stalin adopted it in 1929, it remained outside the mainstream of party thought, the fantasy of people commonly regarded as the party's madhatters.[24] Leading Trotskyists shunned it, though their ambiguous attitude toward Stalin's revolution suggests that it was not wholly alien to their thinking. Most important, they haunted the party with prophecies of a Thermidorian degeneration, the hobgoblin of third revolutionists.

The analogy to the French revolution impressed almost everyone involved in the Russian experience. Bolsheviks advertised themselves as proletarian Jacobins; a Socialist Revolutionary wondered: "Who are we but Russian Girondists?"; and the historian of the French example, Albert Mathiez, lent his authority to the historical analogy in 1920.[25] The grip of French history on the Bolshevik mind is demonstrable: Trotsky resigned as War Commissar in 1925 to counter charges that he harbored Bonapartist ambitions.[26] It was natural, then, that various observers saw in NEP a disguised Thermidor. A British journalist regarded NEP approvingly, the *Smenovekhovtsy* (a group of pro-Soviet but non-Bolshevik spe-

---

* February 1917 being the first, and October the second. Occasionally it was referred to as a "second revolution," the count beginning with October.

cialists) hopefully, and the Mensheviks gloatingly.[27] To a Bolshevik, however, the prospect of Thermidor was a fearful apparition, the first step toward the end of revolution. A Zinovievist in 1925 seems to have been the first Bolshevik to raise the Thermidorian specter against the party's ruling majority, but again it was Trotsky who elevated it to a heuristic principle. After 1926, it stood at the center of his understanding of Soviet society and his opposition. He measured every omen of deradicalization, every policy, domestic and foreign, by a Thermidorian yardstick. "The odor of the 'second chapter' assails one's nostrils," he exclaimed in 1926.[28] The analogy would obsess and finally mislead Trotsky, blunting his perception of what was happening in the Soviet Union. But if permanent revolution captured the optimism of the heroic tradition, Thermidor symbolized its despair when reformism seemed to have seized the party.

In 1921, the revolutionary-heroic outlook dominated party thinking. The spirit of October and civil war, as well as the older image of Bolshevism as synonymous with maximalism, were still strong. Moreover, NEP, which was to give substance to the evolutionary-reformist position, had an ignominious birth. Forced on the party by internal uprisings and the failure of revolution abroad, consistently described by the leadership as a "retreat," it began in an aura of illegitimacy. Despite Lenin's insistence that no high-level disagreement attended their promulgation, the new policies generated widespread "despair," "demoralization," "indignation," and opposition in party and Komsomol ranks.[29] One prominent Bolshevik bitterly complained in 1921 that there were "no elements of socialism" left in the economy.[30] At the outset, it was possible at best to see in NEP an expedient maneuver, hardly sufficient to arouse enthusiasm or to inspire a long-term program. Two things, however, soon worked to make reformism and NEP more acceptable. First, the pacific mood of the party rank and file and the country, whose desire for civil peace after years of convulsions was manifest. Second, in the last years of his life, Lenin placed his immense authority behind the reformist tendency; then the party's leading theorist, Bukharin, developed it into a program and made it his own.

Lenin frankly presented the new economic policies to his followers as a retreat born of the failure of war communism. But he tried to legitimize them by stating that they had been adopted "seriously and for a long time," by describing them as a return to his correct aborted policies of early 1918, and, as if to convince the party that it was no longer in rout, by announcing shortly that the retreat was at an end (even though no change in policy accompanied the announcement). Meantime, he began debunking methods associated with war communism: the time of "furious assaults" was past; the notion that "all tasks . . . can be solved by Communist decree" was "Communist conceit." [31] And on the fourth anniversary of the revolution—twenty-five years after Eduard Bernstein, the father of deradicalized European Marxism, had made it anathema for radical Marxists—Lenin rehabilitated the concept of reformism. Condemning "exaggerated revolutionism" as the greatest danger in domestic policy, he wrote: "What is new at the present moment for our revolution is the need to resort to a 'reformist,' gradualist, cautiously roundabout method of activity in the fundamental questions of economic construction." He juxtaposed the new method and the old Bolshevik tradition: "Compared with the previous revolutionary one, this is a reformist approach (revolution is a transformation which breaks the old fundamentally and radically, and which does not remake it cautiously, slowly, gradually, trying to break as little as possible)." Lenin expounded reformism until he died. In 1922, he sent a brief greeting to *Pravda* in the form of a wish: "My wish is that in the next five years we will conquer peacefully not less than we conquered previously with arms." [32]

Neither Lenin nor Bukharin, who soon followed and went beyond his initiative, construed their evolutionism as a departure from the revolutionary precepts or ideals of October. Both, for example, would also find an enduring lesson in October: the need to preserve in a constructive form the historic *smychka* (alliance or union) between the working class and the peasantry, which in 1917 had been victorious in "the combination of a proletarian revolution and a peasant war." [33] Radical social transformation was still the goal. "Our revolution has not ended," Bukharin would promise. Evolutionism meant economic revolution not "by one stroke of the revolutionary sword," but by organic evolution along the "rails" of NEP. [34] Together Lenin and Bukharin had been largely responsible for radicalizing Russian Marxism before and during the world war; their writings on imperialism and the bourgeois state had given Bolshevism a militant ideological posture distinct from that of social democracy, and neither man ever openly repudiated the radical tradition. But while the main work of making reformism theoretically compatible with radicalism fell to Bukharin, only Lenin could have initiated what must have seemed to be a profound revision. For, in addition to the Thermidorians, Bolsheviks remembered Eduard Bernstein.

After Bukharin's defeat in 1929, Stalinist critics began referring to him as the Soviet Bernstein,[35] an interesting analogy but one which should have caused its supporters some discomfort. Shortly before his death, Engels, the surviving founder of Marxism and Bernstein's mentor, completed a prefatory essay which seemed to revise orthodox doctrine by suggesting that in certain countries the proletariat might come to power through legal processes, without revolution. Bernstein used this "last testament" defensively in his sweeping revision and deradicalization of Marxism.[36] Between January 2 and February 9, 1923, after suffering a second stroke in late December 1922, Lenin dictated five short, thematically connected articles: "Pages from a Diary," "On Cooperation," "Our Revolution," "How We Should Reorganize Rabkrin," and "Better Fewer, But Better." They were his last. Bukharin soon argued that they constituted a "political testament," a set of "directives," and that they marked an important change in Lenin's thinking about NEP Russia and building socialism: "Ilich . . . saw the inevitable end . . . he began to dictate his political testament and on the edge of the grave originated things which for decades will determine the policy of our party." [37] His own program, said Bukharin, was based on this "testament." The meaning of the five articles was debated throughout the decade, some Bolsheviks agreeing with Bukharin, others denying that Lenin had changed his mind on vital issues and quoting instead from an earlier Lenin. Still others insisted that his reformism was the work of a depressed, sick man and ought not to be taken seriously.[38] The bifurcation of Bolshevism was due in no small part to Lenin's ambiguous legacy.

Lenin set down his original understanding of NEP in May 1921 in an article called "The Tax in Kind." He defined the new course as a return to state capitalism, underlining its pedigree by quoting a lengthy extract from his May 1918 defense of state capitalism against the Left Communists. Once again, large capital, public and private, was to be aligned against less progressive petty bourgeois elements. This was the only feasible transition to socialism in a peasant country. He enumerated four forms of state capitalism present in the 1921 economy: foreign concessions (Lenin was optimistic that Western capitalists would invest generously in Soviet Russia); the cooperatives; private persons marketing state products; and the leasing of state property. He implied by omission that state-owned and operated enterprises were socialist, later describing them as being "of a consistently socialist type." [39]

Lenin's comparison of 1921 to 1918, when he had visualized a rapprochement between the new Soviet state and the private industrial establishment, was superficial and shaky. Unlike them, the state now controlled most industrial facilities, while large private capital was nonexistent. Moreover, in 1918 Lenin had not thought in terms of free trade, so his initial version of state capitalism had been silent on the question of market relations. [40] When he wrote "The Tax in Kind," trade was still restricted; but in 1922, when it had become a national phenomenon, he was forced to label ordinary trade as capitalism and include it in the overall system of state capitalism. Apart from rendering his theoretical conception inconsistent and all but incomprehensible, it drew a dire picture of Russia after four years of revolution. According to Lenin, as Bukharin later remarked, there seemed to be "a tiny island of socialism, and all the rest was state capitalism. . . ." [41]

This remained Lenin's general view of NEP Russia during the next year and a half. Bukharin (among others) immediately raised his previous objection that state capitalism was theoretically impossible under a proletarian dictatorship, again informing Lenin both publicly and privately, "you misuse the word 'capitalism.'" But because they concurred on the policies involved, and because each was unable to convince the other, both dismissed the terminological disagreement as abstract and unimportant. [42] Again fiercely pragmatic, Lenin was less concerned in 1921 and 1922 with theoretical definitions than with impressing on the party the importance and objectives of NEP: to appeal to the peasant's private initiative in order to set industry, large and small, into motion; to create through the medium of trade a durable economic and political *smychka* or union between the proletariat and the peasantry, between industry and agriculture; and to make state economic institutions efficient and capable of competing with their privately owned counterparts. To Bolsheviks who worried about where all this was leading, Lenin vaguely promised "to build solid gangways . . . to socialism through state capitalism" and "to build communism with non-Communist hands." [43] He did not explain how this would come about and it is doubtful that he knew how before late 1922, when his thinking began to change.

Three developments after May 1921 compelled Lenin to rethink his ideas on NEP and state capitalism. The ravages of war and famine were notably ameliorated and the economy, including the state sector, showed a steady advance, though heavy industry lagged seriously behind. The government's position was much improved. Second, Lenin had placed his hopes for new capital on foreign loans and concessions; it was his formula for recovery and industrialization. The plan proved to be an almost total failure. In September 1922, he admitted that sufficient foreign capital would not be forthcoming and concluded that the country would have to develop on its own resources through economizing measures and increased taxation. In addition to turning his attention inward, this development eliminated the major element of state capitalism in his original analysis. Third, as ordinary market relations unfolded, the cooperative societies, which had been numerous and very significant before October, and which had been transformed into state distribution organs during war communism, were gradually restored to autonomous status and began to capture an increasing amount of retail and wholesale trade. Bolsheviks were in the habit of scorning these producer and consumer societies as semi-capitalist, peasant, reformist institutions, dominated earlier by Socialist Revolutionaries and Mensheviks. In "The Tax in Kind," Lenin classified them as "a kind of state capitalism." [44]

Thus, by 1922, the cooperatives seemed to be the foremost element of state capitalism in Russia, wholly unlike the large industrial capital originally envisaged by Lenin. Since free trade was being assiduously and officially encouraged, marketing cooperatives were certain to develop further. Lenin probably began to change his mind just before his second stroke in late December 1922. On November 20, he delivered what was to be his final public speech. After a matter-of-fact appraisal of the country's situation, he concluded on a startlingly optimistic note: "Socialism is now no longer a question of the distant future . . . "; he was confident that "not tomorrow, but in a few years . . . NEP Russia will become socialist Russia." Within a month, he began preparing his last five articles, which (many would argue) translated this promise into a program.[45]

Taken as a whole, the articles rested on a single basic sociopolitical assumption—"in our Soviet Republic the social order is based on the collaboration of two classes: the workers and the peasants." A "split" between these classes, Lenin concluded, "would be fatal for the Soviet Republic." This unorthodox class alignment derived from the fact that the first socialist revolution occurred in a backward peasant country. But, Lenin insisted, the deviation from the expected historical pattern ("the German model") did not, as Mensheviks believed, preclude the construction of socialism in Russia. First, we will "create the prerequisites of civilization" and then "begin the movement toward socialism." Where is it written, he asked rhetorically, "that such modifications of the usual historical sequence are impermissible or impossible?" Quoting statistics putting the illiteracy rate at over 65 per cent, Lenin urged the party to begin with a "cultural revolution" to eliminate this "semi-Asiatic ignorance," and to expose the rural population to the pedagogical influence of the cities, but without "the pre-conceived goal of instilling communism in the countryside." This, too, would be "fatal for communism." [46] The peasant must be approached cautiously and patiently, on his own level of interest. And this admonition brought Lenin to the subject of cooperatives.

The article "On Cooperation" contained a statement of self-criticism: "we forgot to think about the cooperatives. . . ." Having now done so and decided that these societies represented the ideal combination of private interest and state regulation, Lenin concluded that they were the building blocks of Soviet socialism, the institutions which would allow "every small peasant . . . to participate in this construction":

Indeed, the power of the state over all large-scale means of production, state power in the hands of the proletariat, the alliance of this proletariat with the many millions of small and very small peasants, the guaranteed leadership of the proletariat in relation to the peasantry, etc.—is this not all that is necessary for constructing a fully socialist society out of the cooperatives . . . ? This is not yet the construction of socialism, but it is all that is necessary and sufficient. . . .

He envisaged at best "one or two decades" before the whole population would be participating in cooperatives, and before the peasant could be culturally transformed into "an intelligent and literate tradesman." But in Soviet conditions that would be socialism: "a system of civilized cooperators is the system of socialism." [47]

Lenin had executed a remarkable about-face in his own thinking as well as in the context of Marxist thought. He was speaking throughout of exchange or market societies, not (as Stalinists would later claim) production cooperatives. He was drawing on an old, pre-Marxist, "utopian" socialist tradition. Recognizing the departure, he added that the revolution had brought about a change in the nature of cooperatives. The cooperative socialism of Robert Owen and others had been a "fantasy, something romantic" because it failed to see the preliminary task of political revolution; in

Soviet Russia the fantasy "is becoming the most unvarnished reality." This, of course, was directly contrary to his position in "The Tax in Kind," where he had written: "Under existing Russian conditions, freedom and rights for cooperatives mean freedom and rights for capitalism. To close one's eyes to this obvious truth would be foolishness or a crime." Now he argued that (with "the 'small' exception" of concessions) "for us the simple growth of cooperatives is identical . . . with the growth of socialism." [48] He had turned the island of socialism into a sea, and little, if anything, remained of state capitalism.

It is not necessary to interpret these last articles as a "testament" to appreciate the profound change they represented. To be sure, intermingled with the positive themes was Lenin's growing disenchantment with the state and party bureaucracies; his last two articles were mainly an anxious warning against "repellent *chinovnik* * realities." But it was his optimistic evaluation of NEP as an advance toward socialism that stood out. He again expressed confidence that by diligent economizing, Russia's internal resources could provide the basis for industrialization. Equally important, by formulating, however sketchily, a type of indigenous cooperative socialism, and by raising this question separately from that of international revolution, Lenin implied that socialism in an isolated Soviet Russia was possible. His final directives to his party seemed neither internationalist nor radical, the heroic tradition being all but repudiated by his explicit acknowledgment of the new reformism:

we are forced to admit a radical change in our entire view of socialism. This radical change consists of the fact that earlier we placed, and had to place, the main emphasis on the political struggle, on revolution, on conquering power, etc. Now the main emphasis is being changed to such an extent that it is being shifted to peaceful organizational "cultural" work. [49]

Bukharin, too, was rethinking his Bolshevism during the early years of NEP. He published notably less in 1921 and 1922 (itself a sign of his silent deliberation); for the most part his tone was reflective and tentative. He brooded publicly on the great com-

* A literal translation of *chinovnik*, a term derived from the czarist system of bureaucratic hierarchy, would be simply "bureaucrat" or "functionary." For Bolsheviks, however, the word had an extremely pejorative connotation, meaning a state bureaucrat in the most obnoxious sense. To retain this important political meaning, I shall leave the term untranslated.

plexities facing a revolutionary party in power, comparing them
wistfully to the simple, clear-cut decisions of an earlier period.[50]
Evidence of his rethinking soon appeared, and by 1923 he had
articulated most of the major themes associated with his domestic
policies for the remainder of the decade. A year later, in a sort of
collective party *mea culpa*, he explained how the new wisdom had
dawned. Recalling Marx's statement that proletarian revolutions
would discover the correct policy through constant self-criticism,
he continued:

In the fire of this self-criticism the *illusions* of the childhood period are
consumed and disappear *without a trace*, real relations appear in all
their sober nakedness, and proletarian policy acquires in appearance
sometimes a less emotional, but therefore a more assured, character—
a solid one, adhering closely to reality and therefore much more truly
changing this reality.

From this point of view, the transition to the new economic policies represented the collapse of our *illusions*.[51]

Bukharin's own illusions about war communism had begun to
collapse in 1920, and by February 1921 he had accepted the need
for a drastic change. The end of grain requisitioning apparently
met with his full approval, his only objection during preliminary
Politburo discussions of the new course involving Lenin's insistence
on the term "state capitalism." In this respect, Bukharin was perhaps more easily able to incorporate the subsequent development
of free trade into his thinking than was Lenin. The essence of
capitalism, he argued, was "capitalist property," not market relations alone.[52] He seemed to be less enthusiastic about foreign
concessions (whether because he disliked the idea or thought it
unfeasible is not clear), and therefore quicker to emphasize the
importance of internal and foreign trade. But his full endorsement
of the new policies was evident; the official materials circulated in
the party to popularize them included his article, "The New
Course in Economic Policy." [53]

Though Bukharin did not mention it, the emerging economic
system resembled what he had advocated in early 1918. In the
beginning, however, he did not embrace NEP with a sense of its
enduring rationality or rightness. Like other leaders, he defended
it apologetically for several months, stressing the strategic expediency of the change and arguing that, while NEP involved risky
concessions, it was a response to a greater threat. Kronstadt and
the rural uprisings were omens of "a peasant Vendée"; economic

concessions were made to avoid political concessions—to restore a favorable social equilibrium and revive the economy. He encouraged his listeners to think of the move as "a peasant Brest." [54] But, while evasive as to the legitimacy and permanency of NEP, Bukharin flatly excluded a return to requisitioning and war communism. Commenting indirectly on his own justification of force in *The Economics*, he now stated that "extra-economic coercion" was limited to the destructive era of the revolution; once the old order was shattered, it lost "nine-tenths of its meaning." The constructive era was to be peaceful. [55]

Bukharin's enthusiasm for NEP began to emerge as his criticism of war communism broadened. In August 1921, he admitted that while the old policies had been militarily necessary, they were incompatible with economic development. [56] In December, he tied the economic irrationality of war communism to bureaucratic overcentralization. An "all-embracing apparatus" had been established to control the entire economy of a peasant country, but it had turned out to be economically "less rational than the anarchistic commodity structure." Bukharin now believed that there were severe limitations on what the proletariat could and should try to organize:

Taking too much on itself, it has to create a colossal administrative apparatus. To fulfill the economic functions of the small producers, small peasants, etc., it requires too many employees and administrators. The attempt to replace all these small figures with state *chinovniki*— call them what you want, in fact they are state *chinovniki*—gives birth to such a colossal apparatus that the expenditure for its maintenance proves to be incomparably more significant than the unproductive costs which derive from the anarchistic condition of small production; as a result, this entire form of management, the entire economic apparatus of the proletarian state, does not facilitate, but only impedes the development of the forces of production. In reality it flows into the direct opposite of what was intended, and therefore iron necessity compels that it be broken. . . . If the proletariat itself does not do this, then other forces will overthrow it.

This was to be Bukharin's position throughout the twenties, the origin of his conviction that in some areas the market performed more efficiently than the state and of his opposition to proponents of a "Genghis Khan plan." [57]

The argument was directly contrary to that in *The Economics*, where he had glorified the proletariat's organizing capabilities. Limitations on the efficiency of state control could be explained in part by referring to Russia's atomized peasant economy; but the problem ran deeper. It raised the question of the maturity of the Russian proletariat and therefore a larger one: Had Russia in fact been "ripe" for a socialist revolution? The possibility that they had acted prematurely in 1917, that their social revolution was doomed, haunted the Bolsheviks; it was on this premise that Marxist critics, from Bogdanov to the Mensheviks, challenged their right to speak and act in the name of Marxist socialism. In *The Economics*, Bukharin had dismissed Russia's relative backwardness by maintaining that since the old economic structure was destroyed in the process of revolution, the essential determinant of "ripeness" was the existence of a developed proletariat as a "social-organizing" class. The argument was no longer feasible. Everyone conceded that the proletariat had become "peasantized," a significant portion having rejoined the peasant in outlook and often in occupation. Bukharin therefore had to rethink the whole question of "ripeness." The product was a long article, "The Bourgeois Revolution and the Proletarian Revolution," written in late 1921 and published in the summer of 1922, which once again revised this crucial Marxist doctrine.[58]

Marxist expectations about socialist revolution were patterned on the historical example of capitalism's emergence from feudalism. As capitalism had ripened in the womb of feudal society, so socialism was expected to mature within the old capitalist order. Bukharin declared that the analogy was entirely wrong. The kernel of his argument was simple. In feudal society, the nascent bourgeoisie had an autonomous base in the new cities, where it could grow independently of and in opposition to the feudal landlord class, to create its own material, technical, and cultural foundations, and to develop its own administrative élites. The bourgeoisie was not an exploited or deprived class, and thus became in every way a qualified ruling and organizing class prior to its political revolution. The position of the proletariat in capitalist society, Bukharin continued, was altogether different. Lacking an independent economic base, its mass remained an economically and culturally oppressed and exploited class, despite the fact that it represented a potentially higher cultural principle. The bourgeoisie monopolized not only the means of production, but also of education (a point Bukharin thought had been overlooked). Throughout its pre-revolutionary history, the proletariat necessarily remained a backward class within a developed society. And therefore, unlike the bourgeoisie, it was unable *"to prepare itself for organizing all of society. It is successful in preparing itself for* 'the destruction of the old world' "; but "*it ripens as the organizer of society only in the period of its dictatorship.*" [59] Thus, class immaturity was not a peculiarity of the Russian proletariat, but a characteristic of proletarian revolutions in general.

By a single stroke, Bukharin had vanquished an assortment of ideological vexations confronting the Bolsheviks. Combined with his previous treatment of economic backwardness, the argument answered their Marxist opponents, provided a further explanation of the high "costs" of the Russian revolution (the inexperienced proletariat committing "a tremendous number of mistakes"), and presented economic and cultural modernization as a legitimate task of a Marxist party. It justified the employment of the old "technical intelligentsia" as a transitional measure pending the development of proletarian specialists. And above all, it rationalized on a higher level what Bolsheviks no longer bothered to disclaim—that the dictatorship of the proletariat was the "dictatorship of the party." The largely unqualified proletariat had to rule through its most advanced segment, the party, which was to the class what the head was to the body. The vanguard, however, was also heterogeneous and therefore required leaders, "through which the party expresses its will." Bukharin had traveled a long way from the myth of proletarian hegemony, and he did not shrink from the final fillip: because the working class was unable to cultivate its own intellectual élite in the womb of capitalism, initially its ranking leaders were necessarily drawn "*from a hostile class . . . from the bourgeois intelligentsia.*" [60] Soviet reality had been given theoretical expression.

Bukharin's argument could be dismissed as an ingenious piece of ideological chicanery were it not for two things. First, his treatment of "ripening" and the feudalism-capitalism analogy was more convincing than the orthodox doctrine, which was only an unstudied assumption. Second, he took his discovery seriously and did not ignore the peril to which it pointed. If, during the transition period, a slowly maturing but largely undeveloped proletariat remained politically, culturally, and administratively subordinate to a host of higher authorities, then the danger of a perversion of the socialist ideal was very great. Many Bolsheviks spoke during NEP of the danger of degeneration, usually thinking in terms of Russia's petty bourgeois economic base and the restoration of capitalism through the agency of the kulak and the nepman. It became a favorite augury of left oppositions and of Trotsky, who, somewhat incoherently, mingled it with his premonitions of Thermidor and "bureaucratic degeneration." Bukharin was among the first (if not the first) Bolshevik leaders to raise the question; [61] and while he occasionally referred to the "petty bourgeois danger," his real concern was more pertinent and less orthodox.

He feared that the "cultural backwardness" of the working masses might allow a new class to develop. If the advanced strata of the proletariat (its leading cadres) were to become "alienated from the masses" and "assimilated" with prevailing administrative élites, they could coalesce into a privileged and "monopolistic caste" and together "turn into *the embryo of a new ruling class.*" Bukharin was not consoled by the usual Marxist homily: "Appealing to working-class origins and proletarian virtue cannot in itself serve as an argument against the possibility of such a danger." He looked to two developments to undermine this "tendency to 'degenerate' "; the growth of the forces of production and the end of an educational monopoly. A "colossal overproduction of organizers" drawn from the working class would "nullify the *stability* of the ruling groups" and subvert "this possible new class alignment." [62]

Apart from its forthrightness, Bukharin's analysis was noteworthy for its implicit departure from the orthodox Marxist definition of class. The narrow association of class dominance with legal ownership of property would later hamper the critiques of anti-Stalinist Communists for decades. Even Trotsky, in his bitterly pessimistic *The Revolution Betrayed,* denied that the Stalinist bureaucracy constituted a social class. But thirty years before Milovan Djilas's *The New Class* revised the category and applied it to Soviet society, Bukharin was warning against "a new ruling class" based not on private property but on "monopolistic" authority and privilege. It was this problem—later expressed in Western theory in terms of "the managerial class" and "power without property"—that he had ignored in his 1915–16 study of modern capitalism, and which he now saw: an exploiting organizational class could emerge on the basis of nationalized property. How much this "enormous danger" alarmed him is illustrated by the fact that his discussion was prompted by the different élite theories of Bogdanov and Robert Michels.

Bogdanov long had argued that the ruling class in any given society is that group which organizes the economy, whether or not it actually owns the means of production. For him the essential source of exploitation lay in the relationship between organizer and organized.[63] Bukharin's contention that "the difference between technician and worker" cannot be eliminated within a capitalist society was directed against Bogdanov's conclusion that until the

proletariat ripened into a capable organizing class, socialist revolution was premature.[64] He did not, however, challenge the older
thinker's redefinition of class. Nor did he dispute the findings of
Michels's "very interesting book" (*Zur Soziologie des Parteiwesens
in der modernen Demokratie*), which showed that the "administration of boundless capital . . . assigns at least as much power to the
administrators as would possession of their own private property."
Instead, he tried to counter the conclusion that "socialists may be
victorious, but not *socialism*" by arguing that, in the future society,
"what constitutes an eternal category in Michels's presentation,
namely, the 'incompetence of the masses' will disappear. . . ." This
was his hope, but he was less than fully confident about the outcome. Class exploitation without private property was possible,
and he warned the party: "Our task generally is not to allow such
an 'evolutionary' return to exploitative relations." [65]

To characterize Bukharin's elliptical remarks on a new class
as a theory would be to exaggerate their substance. As though
fearful of pushing his logic further, he only hinted at this potentially "tragic outcome" of the revolution. But in various forms it
became perhaps his most serious private fear, offsetting to some
extent his public dogma that exploitation of the working class was
impossible in a "workers' state." Evolution of the revolutionary
régime into a new kind of exploitative bureaucratic state became
his personal bogie in the twenties, much as "petty bourgeois degeneration" became that of the Bolshevik Left.[66] In the Left's
economic programs he professed to see an institutionalization of
the official "arbitrariness" of war communism and the rise of
"privileged Communist groups"—a "new state of *chinovniki*"—
indifferent to the needs of the masses and enjoying "absolute
immunity" from recall. A rebirth of exploitation came to concern
him more than the fate of the urban masses alone: programs that
would "plunder" the countryside would lead, he predicted, not to
a classless socialist society but to "the eternal 'reign of the proletariat' " and to "its degeneration into a real exploiter class" in
relation to the peasantry. While others scanned the horizon for
ghosts of the French revolution, listening for "the footsteps of
history," Bukharin worried about a form of degeneration without
historical precedent.[67]

That he chose the first year of NEP to brood over this
gloomy possibility was not accidental. Kronstadt and the rural
uprisings had produced in him a profound sense of the party's
isolation, an awareness that the Bolsheviks now ruled as a tiny
minority, bolstered by armed force and lacking even the whole

support of the class they claimed to represent.[68] Once the leader and voice of revolutionary workers and peasants, the party was now "alienated from the masses." The people say, Bukharin told the Tenth Party Congress, "There is no bread and no coal—for this the Communist Party is to blame." In July 1921, he expressed uncertainty that the régime would survive, a situation starkly unlike 1917, when "all the soldiers and all the workers were on our side" and "it was joyous to live. . . ." [69] Although he continued to eulogize the party's dictatorship, sometimes quite unabashedly, élitism did not rest comfortably on him; henceforth, his thinking was predicated on the need to overcome the isolation that was the legacy of the civil war—to regain popular support and secure for the party's program the greatest number of allies.

From 1921 onward, Bukharin's attention focused on the "non-party masses," and his previous enthusiasm for revolutionary coercion shifted to an emphasis on persuasion and education.[70] He began to see in the "colossal" bureaucracy erected during war communism all that was symptomatic of the party's isolation, associating its growth with the "vacuum" that had opened between the Bolshevik government and the people. The equation resulted in one of his basic ideas. The antidote against bureaucracy consisted in filling this void with "*hundreds and thousands of small and large rapidly expanding voluntary societies, circles, and associations,*" which would provide a "link with the masses." They would promote "decentralized initiative" and collectively constitute a "transmission mechanism" through which the party could influence, but also be influenced by, public opinion. Their proliferation would express what Bukharin called "the growth . . . of the Soviet social structure (*sovetskaia obshchestvennost'*)," and would restore the disintegrated "social fabric." [71] This belief in voluntary organizations and "mass initiative at the lower levels," as opposed to "statization," was a characteristic part of Bukharin's rethinking.

The "masses," of course, meant the peasantry. Never having been an extremist among Bolsheviks on the "peasant question," Bukharin now accepted the fact that the party's stability depended on a lasting rapprochement with the rural population. The other problems that concerned him in 1921 to 1923—Russia's backwardness, bureaucratic overcentralization, and the Bolsheviks' isolation—were each a part of this larger one. The idea of a historic *smychka* between the proletariat and the peasantry (a euphemism for the party's relations with the peasant) quickly impressed him as "the fundamental question of our revolution," the "slogan of slogans," "*a conditio sine qua non* of the proletarian revolution."

After 1921, it was the basic factor in his policy thinking; and by April 1923, he could be identified in the Bolshevik leadership as the most convinced and consistent defender of the inviolability of the *smychka*.[72]

The insistence on the need to conciliate the peasant was not in itself unusual. Most Bolsheviks at least paid it lip service in the early twenties. What was distinctive about Bukharin's remarks on the *smychka* was his growing tendency to speak of the peasantry as a whole, as an undifferentiated class, and to skirt the orthodox Bolshevik distinction between peasant strata, between rural friends and enemies. In an address at Sverdlov University in early 1923, he admitted that the party knew little about contemporary village life and urged that new studies be undertaken and "clichés" avoided. He suggested that one such cliché involved the question of rural leveling and "the degree of stratification of the peasantry," to which, he added, there was "not a single answer." [73] How far his thinking had progressed at this stage is unclear. But his already pronounced habit of speaking of the proletariat and the peasantry as "two laboring classes" was the beginning of his hotly contested theory of Soviet Russia as "a two-class society" and his notion that "a worker-peasant bloc" had replaced the old ruling "land-lord-bourgeois bloc." [74] Both concepts were to be important in his domestic program.

Like Lenin, then, Bukharin had come to see in NEP the proper framework for Bolshevik economic policy and the conditions of social equilibrium in which the country might move toward socialism. He presented his views to the Fourth Comintern Congress in November 1922, where Lenin and Trotsky had emphasized the tactical considerations of NEP. Bukharin thought another perspective was needed. NEP, he said,

is not only a strategic retreat, but the solution to a large social, organizational problem, namely, the correlation between spheres of production which we must rationalize and those which we cannot rationalize. We will say frankly: we tried to take on ourselves the organization of everything—even the organization of the peasants and the millions of small producers . . . from the viewpoint of economic rationality this was madness.[75]

A few weeks later, he implicitly contrasted his new ideas with the still prevailing party sentiment; he called for a new party program, arguing that the 1919 program, as well as his own *ABC*, "which became a party canon," had been outdated by NEP. And shortly afterwards he declared: "we now see how we shall come to socialism . . . not as we thought earlier, but by a much more firm and solid path." [76]

In the process of rethinking, Bukharin also sounded three other principles of a new reformist Bolshevism. First and most general was that "civil peace *under the command of the proletariat*" should replace civil strife as party policy. From this followed his argument that class struggle in Russia would now be waged, not violently, but by peaceful market competition between socialist economies and private economies, and on the ideological and cultural fronts. Finally, in 1922 appeared the quintessential expression of Bukharin's gradualism, the theory of "growing into socialism." He launched it tentatively at the Comintern congress, dissociating it from "the revisionist understanding that . . . capitalism grows into socialism":

We shall not be able to fulfill our task by single decrees, by single compulsory measures . . . a prolonged organic process . . . a process of real growing into socialism will be required. But the difference between them and us is establishing when growing in begins. The revisionists, who do not want any kind of revolution, maintain that this process . . . occurs already in the bosom of capitalism. We maintain that it begins only together with the dictatorship of the proletariat. The proletariat must destroy the old bourgeois state, seize power, and with the help of this lever change economic relations. We have here a lengthy process of development, in the course of which socialist forms of production and exchange obtain an ever wider dissemination and, in that way, gradually displace all the remnants of capitalist society. . . .[77]

By 1923, he had specifically included peasant economies in this development "through the process of circulation," and was energetically expounding the "*evolutionary* path" as a reality of Soviet life. "For many decades we will slowly be growing into socialism: through the growth of our state industry, through cooperation, through the increasing influence of our banking system, through a thousand and one intermediate forms." [78]

The appearance of this theory as early as November 1922 calls into question the impression that the idea of "socialism in one country" resulted from the German fiasco of October 1923. While it is true that the German disappointment finally shattered Bolshevik hopes of an early European revolution, and that the idea of building socialism in isolation was first expressed formally by

Stalin in December 1924,[79] Bukharin's "growing-in" proposition indicates that the requisite reasoning had been expressed earlier. Though not yet facing the hard problems of industrialization (that began in 1924), his theory addressed the question of moving toward socialism in Russia, and was at no point dependent on internationalizing the revolution. (The same was true of Lenin's "On Cooperation," where he found "all that is necessary and sufficient.") Bukharin may have sensed the heretical implication of his argument; he hastened to assure his Comintern audience that "Russian socialism, in comparison with others, will look Asiatic," and that Russia's economic backwardness "will find expression in the backward forms of our socialism." [80]

He was not contrasting socialism in Russia with international revolution; nor, however, was he any longer making the former dependent on the latter. Like Lenin, he was groping for a vision of Bolshevism's future in peasant Russia. European revolution or no, the party had power, and one of two conclusions was possible: either it was building a socialist society or it was presiding over the evolution of capitalism. As Bukharin exclaimed in 1926, if the first was untrue, "then we went to the barricades in October for nothing." [81] In this sense, Stalin's future slogan of "socialism in one country" was far less innovating than is assumed. Indeed, in April 1924, eight months before Stalin's statement, Bukharin explained his theory of the "peaceful-economic-organic" class struggle as follows: *"A victory in this type* of class struggle (we abstract here from the problem of the external order) is the final victory of socialism." [82] Much of the controversy of the twenties revolved around the permissibility of just such an abstraction.

Bukharin's views on the outside world also changed in 1921–3, but less abruptly than on internal matters. Reluctant to conclude that the direct assault on European capitalism was over, in June 1921, with Zinoviev and Radek, he briefly opposed in preliminary meetings Lenin's proposal to introduce united front tactics at the Third Comintern Congress. Though offering no further opposition, in December he was still contesting assertions that European capitalism was overcoming its crisis. In 1922 and early 1923, he recognized that the "decelerated tempo" of European revolution meant it was "many years" away, but he continued to portray capitalism in a state of "economic chaos, social chaos, ideological chaos." [83] This outlook did not stem from a congenital leftism (it was Bukharin who informed—and scandalized—the Fourth Comintern Congress that the Soviet Union was sufficiently mature "to conclude a military alliance with one bourgeois country in order to crush with its help another bourgeois country" [84]). Rather, it probably related to what stabilization meant in terms of his understanding of state capitalism—a more powerful European capitalism vulnerable only to world war.

The new element in his thinking was the "world peasantry." Having abandoned his "foolish" position on the national question, and embraced the proposition that Soviet Russia was the defender "of all the oppressed and colonial peoples, the peasant class, the petty bourgeoisie, etc.," Bukharin discovered that the ratio between workers and peasants in Russia reflected a world phenomenon.[85] In April 1923, at the Twelfth Party Congress, he emerged as the Bolshevik leader most interested in the Eastern nationalist movements. Lenin had pointed in this direction earlier, and Bukharin followed enthusiastically. His congressional report on international revolution, including a detailed country-by-country analysis of a "whole Eastern world . . . in a period of the deepest revolutionary ferment," presented the awakening colonial peasantry as "a gigantic reservoir of revolutionary infantry," marching with the Western proletariat against world capitalism. The lessons of the Russian *smychka* were international, as his imagery sought to suggest: "If the state of things is examined on its universally historic scale, it may be said that the large industrial states are the *cities* of world economy, and the colonies and semi-colonies its *countryside*." The conclusion was obvious: "*a great united front between the revolutionary proletariat of the world 'city' and the peasantry of the world 'countryside.'* History has entered irrevocably upon this path." [86] Shortly thereafter, when he accepted the reality of European stabilization, this image became the pivot of his revised theory of international revolution.

Bukharin remarked in 1923 that he now thought differently than when in "swaddling clothes," implying that his rethinking was nearing completion and his illusions dispelled.[87] (Some would soon argue that he had exchanged one set of illusions for another.) The remark also reminds us that when war communism ended and NEP began, he was only thirty-two, not remarkably young in an era of revolutionaries, but sufficient for his opinions not yet to have hardened and become unshakable. On neither domestic nor foreign issues had Bukharin fully developed the new theories and programs which his party opponents would decry as neo-populism. But by 1923, when these issues became involved in the struggle for power, he had already developed a distinct orientation. He would choose allies accordingly.

*　　*　　*

The Politburo of the early twenties was a form of coalition government, and like most such arrangements serviceable in a time of crisis but unstable when danger passed. Lenin's uniquely authoritative presence gave its fractious membership a semblance of unity until his first stroke in May 1922, when a muted struggle for a ruling Politburo majority and, inevitably, the rank of *primus inter pares* began.

A triumvirate of Zinoviev, Kamenev, and Stalin was formed in late 1922 against the more illustrious Trotsky. Personal animosities and "biographical investigations," not policy, underlay the strife at the outset.[88] Zinoviev and Stalin despised and feared Trotsky, and inspired "whispering campaigns" to remind the party of his past Menshevism and potential Bonapartism. Trotsky, himself not above biographical politics, procrastinated, compromised, and guarded his political fortunes with unbelievable ineptitude. By 1923, he had been isolated from the effective sources of power. Later that year, he finally attacked, becoming the champion of internal party democracy and chief critic of the system of secretarial appointment and party bureaucracy now headed by Stalin. (The party's original doctrine of "democratic centralism," whereby centralized authority inside the party was to be combined with the election of lower and higher bodies, had become a rigid authoritarian system largely as a result of the civil war.) He was soundly defeated in December and January 1924, his authority further diminished. Though he later rose again in opposition, Trotsky's real political opportunity had passed.[89]

Bukharin was a noncontender in this opening round of the succession struggle. Until December 1923, when he conditionally threw his support to the triumvirs, he remained unaligned with either faction, an aspiring "peacemaker." His position in the Bolshevik oligarchy was anomalous. The senior members regarded him as their junior in age and tenure: "Our Benjamin," said Zinoviev; "the most distinguished forces (among the youngest forces)," said Lenin in characterizing Bukharin and Piatakov.[90] But, though formally only a candidate member of the Politburo between 1919 and 1924, along with Lenin, Trotsky, and the triumvirs, Bukharin was recognized by insiders and outsiders alike as one of the party's six "big" leaders. A foreign Communist visitor reported in 1922 that he was spoken of "as the eventual successor of Lenin."[91] The report was erroneous, but it testified to Bukharin's stature, as did the fact that after Lenin's stroke he functioned as a full Politburo member and then inherited Lenin's seat. His prestige rested less on powerful offices (though the editorship of *Pravda* was important) than on his reputation as the theoretical voice of Bolshevism, his great personal popularity in the party and Comintern, and his "tremendous authority" among the party youth.[92] Consequently, while he was not an immediate threat to any of the contending oligarchs, he was a valuable potential ally.

In an angry moment during the trade union debates, Lenin had described Bukharin as "soft wax," on which "any 'demagogue' can write whatever he pleases." Trotsky, the "demagogue" in question, repeated the remark many years later to explain Bukharin's subsequent alliance with Stalin. It has since become a familiar characterization, although it was inappropriate. In his political career to 1923, Bukharin had been singularly and fiercely independent, a maverick in emigration, leader of the young Left in 1917, head of the Left Communists in 1918, and a futile "buffer" between Lenin and Trotsky in 1920–21. No major leader had opposed Lenin so often. In the various factional disputes, only once had he aligned himself with another Politburo member (Trotsky in the second phase of the trade union controversy), his stand being determined each time by the issue, not the personalities. Bukharin's attempt to steer a course independent of the triumvirs and of Trotsky in 1922–3 was therefore characteristic. He was again a loner, but this time without ranking supporters. His personal friends and former political allies, among them Osinskii, Smirnov, Piatakov, and Preobrazhenskii, were in various ways becoming critics of the new policies and moving into opposition, for which Moscow would again provide organizational strength.[93]

If Bukharin was personally close to any senior Bolshevik at this time, it was the stricken Lenin. Evidence that by 1922 an unusually warm friendship existed between them is fragmentary but significant. Naturally, they continued to disagree on secondary matters, such as the meaning of state capitalism and proletarian culture, as well as on two points of greater importance. The first of these arose in April 1922, when Bukharin and Radek led a Comintern delegation to a Berlin conference of the three socialist internationals to explore the possibilities of united labor action in Europe. At the meeting, social democrats insisted on the condition that the Bolshevik government promise not to execute Socialist Revolutionary prisoners who were to be publicly tried in June for "terrorism" and "counter-revolution." Bukharin and Radek agreed. Lenin immediately protested the concession as a capitulation to "blackmail," though he conceded that the promise had to be honored. A sharply divided Politburo arrived at a compromise solution: the death penalty would be withheld as long as underground Socialist Revolutionaries refrained from "terrorist" activity.[94] A second and more abrasive agreement between Bukharin and Lenin developed in October 1922, when Bukharin, Stalin, and other Politburo members supported a proposal to relax the state's foreign trade monopoly. Lenin angrily intervened, castigated Bukharin, and blocked the proposal.[95]

Political dissension, however, was an integral part of their relationship. It had not spoiled their friendship earlier, and did not do so now. In his autobiography, Bukharin wrote of his relations with Lenin after 1918: "I had the good fortune . . . to stand close to him generally, as a comrade and a person." This personal note was unusual in the formal decorum of Bolsheviks, but it also appeared in Lenin's "testament," written on December 24, 1922:

Bukharin is not only the party's most valuable and biggest theoretician, he is also rightfully considered the favorite of the whole party; but his theoretical views can only with very great doubt be regarded as fully Marxist, for there is something scholastic in them (he has never studied and, I think, never fully understood dialectics).[96]

The leader's seemingly contradictory appraisal of Bukharin as the party's most valuable theorist, but one who did not understand dialectics, is open to various interpretations. It may have referred to what Lenin had regarded as Bukharin's unreliable political role in the trade union dispute of 1920–1. Or it may simply have reflected Lenin's passionate concern with Hegelian and Marxist philosophical dialectics (which he had "studied" intensely), a subject scorned by Bukharin for "sociology." Most important, however, was Lenin's unusual judgment of Bukharin as a person, the only such favorable appraisal in his "testament." It spoke less of Bukharin's general popularity in the party than of his position as Lenin's "favorite."

This lends further credibility to unofficial accounts of a letter Lenin is said to have written in early 1922 about their relationship. Bukharin was ill in 1921, and during the course of the year, Lenin dictated several concerned notes to different people on his behalf. One read: "Send the *best* doctor to *examine* the health of N. I. Bukharin . . . and inform me of the results." Doctors recommended medical treatment in Germany, but Bukharin was unable to obtain a visa. At this point, Lenin reportedly wrote to Krestinskii, the Soviet ambassador to Germany, asking him to approach Chancellor Wirth with a message that went something as follows: "I am an old man and I have no children. Bukharin is like a son to me. And I ask as a personal favor . . . that Bukharin be given a visa and the opportunity to receive treatment in Germany." [97] The visa was issued.

The letter cannot be verified, though circumstantial evidence of its existence can be found in official sources.[98] It is clear, however, that something approximating filial love bound the two men, and that this was particularly evident toward the end of Lenin's life. In the latter part of 1922, when the ailing leader had retired to his Gorki retreat, Bukharin was the only Politburo member who visited him frequently. He later recalled how "Lenin would summon me to come to see him . . . take me by the hand and lead me into the garden" to discuss political matters forbidden by the doctors. They spoke of "leaderology" and of Lenin's last articles, which Bukharin soon would interpret as a testament. Their views on NEP were now similar, and these confidences "on the edge of the grave" clearly fortified Bukharin's belief that he spoke for Lenin after 1924.[99] The meetings were not of great political importance, but rather a moving personal episode that probably prompted Bukharin to look with dismay upon the unseemly struggle among senior oligarchs to replace a leader who still lived.

His aloofness from the triumvirs, who were sanctimoniously wrapping themselves in the mantle of Leninism and "old Bolshevism," was revealed dramatically at the Twelfth Party Congress in April 1923. Since the autumn of 1922, a bitter struggle had been going on between Stalin and a dissident group of Georgian Bolshevik leaders who were protesting the mechanism through which the Georgian Republic would be federated into the new Soviet Union. Lenin supported Stalin's plan until late December 1922, when he discovered that the general secretary's representatives had brutally run roughshod over the dissenters. Lenin abruptly reversed his position. In a postscript to his "testament," dated January 4, 1923, he declared that Stalin was "too rude" to be entrusted with great power, and called for his removal as general secretary. He notified the Georgians, "I am with you . . . with all my soul," and prepared a set of notes denouncing this "Great Russian chauvinism." He dispatched the notes to Trotsky, asking him to take up the defense of the Georgian oppositionists. Trotsky suddenly had a weapon to strike back at the triumvirs by destroying the man on whom they relied for organizational power. He compromised instead. In return for empty gestures of repentance, he agreed to join Stalin, Zinoviev, and Kamenev in a conspiracy of silence at the Twelfth Congress.[100]

Only one Politburo member, Bukharin, refused to remain silent and rose at the congress to defend the doomed Georgians, who found themselves the victims of a well-orchestrated denunciation of "local chauvinism." His sympathy for their cause and intervention on their behalf had been known as early as October 1922; [101] now he, not Trotsky, spoke as Lenin wished. Criticizing Stalin and Zinoviev by name, and alluding to Lenin's suppressed notes, he exposed the official campaign against "local deviators" as a fraud. Why, he asked, did Lenin "sound the alarm" only against Russian chauvinism? Because that is "the main danger. . . . If Comrade Lenin were here he would give it to the Russian chauvinists in a way that they would remember for ten years." Bukharin appealed to the deaf assembly on two grounds: first, the Soviet nationalities were essentially peasant areas and centralist oppression threatened the *smychka;* second, this was a problem of international significance, which had to be solved justly if the Soviet Union were to appeal successfully to colonial peoples.[102] A few days after the congress had pilloried the Georgians, he exclaimed:

It is only people confirmedly myopic who will not see the whole vast gravity of the problem of nationalities. . . . In what manner can the Russian proletariat . . . gain the full confidence of the national and primarily the peasant sections?
. . . First and foremost, by ruthlessly combatting any survivals or resurrections of Great Russian chauvinism.

Throughout the twenties, non-Russian nationalities had few greater protectors than Bukharin, who saw in them a "bridge to the oppressed peoples of the East. . . ." [103]

His independent political posture was demonstrated again in 1923. In the fall, Trotsky belatedly raised the banner of internal party democracy against Stalin's manipulation of the party machinery. Here, too, Bukharin seemed to be out of sympathy with the triumvirs. He had made workers' democracy a "holy slogan" in 1920–1 and, probably because of his identification as a "liberal," had been chosen by the leadership to conciliate the opposition at the Tenth Party Congress. It was he who quipped irreverently in 1921: "the history of humanity is divided into three periods: the matriarchate, the patriarchate, and the Secretariat." [104] Not surprisingly, then, Bukharin appeared before a Moscow party meeting in 1923 to deliver a far-reaching criticism of the extensive bureaucratization of party life. He understood the "discontent" in lower party organs, attributing it to the system of secretarial appointment from above. The members of a party organization gather and are asked, he explained: " 'who is against?', and because they more or less

fear to speak against, the designated individual is appointed secretary . . . in the majority of instances elections in party organizations
are turned into elections in quotes . . . because to speak against
authority is bad. . . ." The same was true of "so-called discussion"
of policy: "The chairman asks: 'Who is against?'; no one is against.
The resolution is unanimously accepted. That is the customary type
of relations in our party organizations." [105]

On the surface, Bukharin seemed to be Trotsky's most likely
ally. Apart from the issues involved, they were the party's most
intellectual and cosmopolitan leaders, and were on good personal
terms when the struggle began.[106] Unlike other long-time Bolsheviks, Bukharin showed no jealousy of Trotsky's rapid rise; he had
urged Lenin to collaborate with him in 1915, welcomed him into
the party in 1917, and since defended him against detractors. Moreover, Bukharin seems to have disliked the senior triumvir Zinoviev,
whose ambition was exceeded only by his legendary vanity. Initially, however, Bukharin refused to side with either faction, seeking instead to reconcile them. He apparently believed that a unity
of all the successors was possible, and naïvely thought that personal
animosities and ambitions could be set aside.[107] Thus, in the summer
or early fall of 1923, when Zinoviev became envious of Stalin's
growing power, Bukharin "played the role of peacemaker" at a
bizarre meeting of vacationing Bolsheviks in a cave in the Caucasus.
There a plan was devised to "politicize" the Secretariat by reconstituting it with a membership of three top leaders—Trotsky, Stalin, and either Bukharin, Zinoviev, or Kamenev. Like Bukharin's
other "buffer" attempts, this one failed; but it again revealed his
studied neutrality in the worsening conflict.[108]

Why then did he join in the anti-Trotsky campaign when the
public confrontation came in December? The editorship of *Pravda*
clearly made further neutrality difficult; however equitably Bukharin tried to conduct the Central Committee's official organ,
there was mounting pressure from the triumvirs for selective edit-
ing in their favor.[109] But his decision to side with the triumvirate
requires a more complex explanation. First, Trotsky's own motives
and ambition were not above suspicion, his sudden commitment to
democratic procedures being suspect if only because previously he
had been among the most authoritarian of Bolshevik leaders. Moreover, Lenin had repeatedly asked him to become one of his deputy
premiers in 1922, and Trotsky had repeatedly refused. (Nor could
Trotsky's behavior in the Georgian affair have impressed Bukharin
with his commitment to principle or his sense of loyalty.) To
many, this was evidence of the haughty War Commissar's disdain

for collective leadership and proof that he coveted only the supreme position—"all or nothing." [110]

Trotsky was further compromised in Bukharin's eyes in October 1923, when forty-six prominent Bolsheviks, many of them former Left Communists and Democratic Centralists, submitted to the Central Committee a secret memorandum harshly critical of official policies. The signers included several of Trotsky's friends and supporters, and whether he desired it or not, the circumstances surrounding the document (it called for a new leadership) gave it a "Trotskyist" flavor.[111] It portended the emergence of a new left opposition and another major division in the party. By now, Bukharin had strongly repudiated his own earlier factionalism and become consistently hostile toward fresh moves in this direction, equating organized dissent within the party with a threat to the party's stability in the country. When opponents of the triumvirate pointedly compared current norms with the free discussions during the Brest controversy, Bukharin tried to discredit the earlier period by disclosing that Lenin's arrest had been discussed by Left Communists and Left Socialist Revolutionaries in 1918, and asserting that it had been "a period when the party stood a hair from a split, and the whole country a hair from ruin." [112] Factionalism, he was saying, is an evil in itself.

This new intolerance was related to the main reason behind Bukharin's decision to support the triumvirate: personal rivalries inside the leadership had been superseded in importance by far-reaching policy issues. Despite the country's overall improvement, an economic crisis had been deepening since 1923. Its most characteristic feature was the growing disparity between high industrial prices, arising in part from the monopolistic position of state industry, and low agricultural prices (the so-called scissors crisis). Peasant demand for manufactured products fell, industrial goods stockpiled, unemployment increased, and in the summer and fall a series of menacing strikes occurred in large cities. The response of the coalescing Left, notably Preobrazhenskii and Piatakov, was to accuse the leadership of lacking a long-term industrial policy and to demand an energetic and planned development of industry more or less independently of the current rural market. Though positions were not yet fully defined, Preobrazhenskii and Piatakov were already identified with the view that investment capital could be accumulated only through central planning and a policy of monopolistically inflated industrial prices. In this respect, their views were similar to Trotsky's, who since March had consistently urged the formulation of a single plan and an industrial "offensive." [113]

The Left's economic proposals propelled Bukharin into the anti-Trotsky campaign. For while endorsing Trotsky's emphasis on planning and industrialism at the Twelfth Congress, the triumvirs' policy of raising agricultural prices and lowering industrial prices reaffirmed economic concessions to the peasant as a definitive part of NEP. With Zinoviev and Kamenev in the "pro-peasant" phase of their erratic careers (it lapsed a year later), the majority's official position was that a prosperous peasant economy and expanding rural market were the prerequisites of industrial development. This corresponded fully to Bukharin's understanding of NEP and the *smychka*.[114] In his one important literary contribution to the anti-Trotsky campaign, he identified economic policy as the decisive question, dismissing the opposition's other charges as tactical subterfuges. The opposition really sought to institute their economic program, one based on a "paper" plan and "the dictatorship of industry." The "deviation" of Trotsky and his followers, Bukharin argued, stemmed from their failure to digest Lenin's "new" teaching on the worker-peasant bloc: "that we must . . . for a long time yet ride on a skinny peasant horse, and *only that way* save our industry and secure a solid base for the dictatorship of the proletariat. That is the root of the *present* disagreements." [115]

Having decided that "behind this struggle of people stands a struggle of political tendencies," Bukharin acted on what he saw as the overriding issue, while in effect closing his eyes to what he knew were the opposition's legitimate grievances about the bureaucratization of party life. Given his understanding of NEP and of the Left's economic proposals, he had perhaps no other choice. But five years later, when Stalin's apparatus was turned against him, he, like Zinoviev and Kamenev before him, would parrot Trotsky's accusations of 1923. Part of the tragedy of the old Bolsheviks lay here: for seven years they fought among themselves over principles, while an intriguer gradually acquired the power to destroy them all.

Bukharin's support of the triumvirate, however, was not unconditional. Significantly, his only major polemic against the opposition, a mammoth article beginning on December 28, 1923, and running through five issues of *Pravda*, appeared not under his name but as "the answer of the editorial board of the Central Organ to Comrade Trotsky." Though he was easily recognized as the author, it reflected his desire to intervene in the struggle impersonally.[116] Then, as again in the second anti-Trotsky campaign of October–December 1924, and later against the united opposition, Bukharin disclaimed "any personal appraisals, any personal sympathies or antipathies." The article itself, while not without outrageously dem-

agogic passages (he diligently recited the history of Trotsky's factional sins, each of which he also had committed), was in sharp
contrast to what he called "the foul-smelling" attacks of the Zinovievists.[117] More important, he repeatedly opposed the demand of
Zinoviev and Kamenev that Trotsky be expelled from the leadership and even arrested.[118] This restraint kept his relations with
Trotsky from being fully severed, and in early 1926 they again
established a short-lived, friendly "private contact." [119] But, as in
1923, it came to nothing, partly because Bukharin's politics were
now influenced by his new vision of Bolshevism's "historic role."

On January 21, 1924, Lenin died, and the official cult of his person
and words began in earnest. The quality of Soviet politics was
changed forever. "Leninism" became not only a course of instruction in educational institutions, but a largely undefined Scripture to
which every political proposal had to claim allegiance and make
reference. All Bolshevik leaders promoted the emerging cult in one
degree or another, though some objected to its more idolatrous and
sacerdotal manifestations. (Bukharin enthusiastically preached "orthodox Leninism," but protested the plan to mummify Lenin and
put his sarcophagus on permanent display, remarking of a similar
proposal to disinter Marx's remains for burial in Russia: "a strange
odor is coming from somewhere . . . in the party.")[120] As part of
the political ritual, each successor took occasion during the next
few months to memorialize Lenin and Leninism formally and at
length, and in so doing to establish his own fidelity and credentials.
Bukharin, as befitted his position as party theorist, presented his
memorial reflections on February 17 to the Communist Academy.
Entitled "Lenin as a Marxist," the speech contained his first explicit
attempt to associate his evolutionary theory with Lenin's last
articles.[121]

His ostensible purpose was to correct the "insufficient appreciation of Comrade Lenin as a theoretician." To do so, he divided the
history of Marxism into three eras: the radicalism of Marx and
Engels; the "Marxism of the epigones," that is, the reformism of the
Second International, in which "Marxist symbolics were preserved"
but from which "the revolutionary soul took flight"; and, finally,
the era of "Leninist Marxism," which represented an enrichment of
the original doctrine because it treated questions Marx could not
have foreseen, but which in its radical "methodology" was "a complete return" to Marx. Bukharin (partly to his own belittlement)
cited as Lenin's major theoretical contributions those on imperial-

ism, the national and colonial questions, the bourgeois and proletarian state, and the worker-peasant alliance. So far no one could
take exception, though his contention that the "best pages" of
Lenin's work were those on peasant matters may have raised a few
eyebrows.[122]

But it was in a final section on "fundamental theoretical problems which V.I. projected and which we must work out," that his
opponents later found the end of Leninism and the beginning of
Bukharinism. Sandwiched between unobjectionable remarks were
the two main theoretical innovations of Bukharin's rethinking:
Soviet Russia was *a two-class society*" (this being his first public
mention of the idea, which he attributed to one of his seminar students); and NEP Russia would "grow into socialism" through "an
organic period of development" and "the evolutionary struggle of
economic forms." Neither had been "formulated exactly" by Lenin,
but both, Bukharin insisted, were implicit in his writings, "especially
in his last articles." Here Bukharin returned to a thought he had
expressed in 1922: "different types" of socialist societies were to be
expected because "socialism is built *on that material which exists,*"
prelude to his argument several months later that Lenin had bequeathed "an original theory of 'agrarian-cooperative' socialism." [123]

On the eve of the great programmatic debates, then, Bukharin
already was committed to the proposition that the country's further
development toward socialism "proceeds along an evolutionary
path" and "cannot proceed otherwise." His acceptance of NEP and
opposition to revolutionary ("catastrophic") programs were now
unequivocal: "Here there can be no kind of third revolution." [124]
His reformist gradualism was still only a skeletal theory, but during
the next two years he would translate it into a comprehensive doctrine of Bolshevism and a program for the modernization of Soviet
Russia.

CHAPTER VI

Bukharinism and the Road to Socialism

Accumulate, accumulate! That is Moses and the prophets!
. . . save, save, i.e., reconvert the greatest possible portion
of surplus value or surplus product into capital! Accumula-
tion for accumulation's sake: by this formula classical
economy expressed the historical mission of the bourgeoisie,
and did not for a single instant deceive itself over the birth-
throes of wealth. But what avails lamentation in the face
of historical necessity?

—KARL MARX, *Capital*

THE ECONOMIC CRISIS of 1923 revealed that the party was again sharply divided on basic questions of economic policy and by implications on the future course of the Bolshevik revolution. At first, the conflicting responses and tendencies were overshadowed by the novelty of a public struggle for power among ranking Bolshevik leaders. But in the autumn of 1924, events reaffirmed and broadened this division between a cautious Central Committee majority and a left opposition: policy differences among the leaders and contradictory impulses within the revolution, international and national, urban and rural, came into the open. The great debates of the twenties, and most of all the industrialization debate, began in earnest.

The Left's ideological and programmatic features, real and alleged, took shape first. Trotsky's preachment about the "lessons of October" turned the wrath of the majority against his twenty-year-old theory of permanent revolution, now officially said to be the difference between "Trotskyism" and Leninism. Trotsky stood accused of "underestimating the peasantry" and of lacking faith in Russia's indigenous socialist potential, a pessimism countered in 1925 by the officially professed belief in the possibility (if necessary) of building "socialism in one country." [1] Meanwhile, Preobrazhenskii presented his new "law of primitive socialist accumulation," in essence a case for the need to expand state industrial capital rapidly at the expense of the peasant sector. Incongruously, perhaps, his argument was quickly identified as "the economic basis of Trotskyism." [2] (Few were struck by the contradiction between Preobrazhenskii's reasoning on socialist industrialization in an isolated Russia and Trotsky's emphasis on the crucial role of a European revolution.) Neither man seriously discouraged the association, and henceforth Preobrazhenskii's analysis was at the center of the Left's economic program.

The chasm between the Left's so-called super-industrialism and the majority leadership's position was dramatized in 1924-5, when the new economic policies were considerably extended. A disappointing crop and serious peasant unrest prompted the leadership (in the slogan of the day) to turn its "face to the countryside." Four economic concessions to the peasantry, above all to its middle and upper strata, were enacted in the spring of 1925: state fixing of grain-purchasing prices was relaxed and the agricultural tax reduced; the period of sanctioned land leasing was extended; wage labor, previously limited to the harvesting season, was legalized; and various administrative impediments to free trade were removed.[3] The measures were designed equally to pacify the peasantry and to stimulate further the economic revival brought by NEP. To their sponsors, they seemed a common sense extension of the permissive principles of NEP to the countryside. To the Left, they were evidence that "pro-peasantism," even a "kulak deviation," was in control.

This fundamental division over industrial and peasant policy, soon exacerbated by raucous disputes over foreign matters as well, structured the party debates of the twenties. Personal resentments, the struggle for power, and genuine disagreements about the nature and direction of the revolution were now thoroughly interwoven. Reconciliation between the left opposition and the official leadership was perhaps still possible as late as 1926-7, when both modified their positions, but it was never seriously attempted. As the controversy broadened, both sides escalated their polemics and disdained avenues of compromise, each portraying the conflict as a historic choice between alternative understandings of the revolution. Accordingly, each grew increasingly less tolerant and more certain of the other's apostasy.

This exclusive attitude was equally true of Bukharin, whose

part in the party's internal battles was radically altered by the events of 1924–5. From a supporting role in the anti-Trotsky campaigns, he moved to center stage when the triumvirate suddenly fell apart. Zinoviev and Kamenev, previously second to none in advocating conciliation of the peasantry, initially endorsed the new agrarian policies. But disturbed by second thoughts about their implications, and jealous of Stalin's growing power, they went into opposition in the fall of 1925. Like the Trotskyist Left, with whom they united the following year, they assailed Stalin's management of the party apparatus, the majority's economic policies, and the official interpretation of NEP, including the idea of socialism in one country.[4]

The end of the triumvirate thrust Bukharin into the co-leadership of the majority with Stalin, a natural development since Bukharin was the principal author of the controversial policies. By the summer of 1925, they had become integral to his own revised understanding of the revolution and building socialism in Soviet Russia. His economic program, and to some extent his broader programmatic theories, had become official party doctrine. Elevated to an exposed political position, identified as the architect of the majority's policies, and doubly conspicuous as official interpreter of the prevailing orthodoxy, he became the major target of opposition attacks. From 1925 onward, he was constantly embattled, a key participant in the factional conflicts, in which Bukharinism—the "Bukharin school," as it was called—was a central issue.[5]

These intensely political circumstances obviously affected both the presentation and substance of Bukharin's thinking about the great questions under discussion. Between 1924 and mid-1926, he developed a distinctive industrialization program and a theoretical explanation of how it would lead to Soviet socialism. Alone among the protagonists, he strove for a general theory of economic, political, and social development. His ideas, however, were rarely set out systematically or dispassionately, being scattered instead throughout dozens of hotly polemical speeches and articles.[6] As a result, as Bukharin tacitly acknowledged in 1926–7 when he introduced significant revisions, the initial version of his economic program, that of 1924 to 1926, was deficient in important respects. Some were the result of miscalculation; others, however, resulted from the belligerency of the debates. Determined to establish and defend what he now believed were a few rudimentary truths, Bukharin overstated his arguments and dismissed counterarguments. Caught up in the passions of revolutionary vision and righteousness, he, like the others, often responded to the challenges of his opponents rather than to the country's real economic conditions. And of these rival challenges, Preobrazhenskii's "law of socialist accumulation" was the most important.

Preobrazhenskii's "law" was an ambitious medley of far-sighted analysis, grand historical analogy, theoretical innovation, and economic policy. The first element made it a major contribution to the industrialization debates. Since 1921, official aspirations had centered on restoring the shattered economy, particularly industry, to its prewar (1913) levels, that is, on reactivating damaged and dormant productive facilities. Preobrazhenskii looked beyond this short-term goal to the time when the existing industrial plant would be operating at its full capacity. Arguing that the fate of socialism in the Soviet Union depended on rapid industrialization, he raised the problem of acquiring resources for intensive investment, especially in the capital goods sector. A large investment program was required not only to offset unproductive consumption and normal depreciation of fixed capital since 1913, but to provide for the expansion and technological reconstruction of the industrial base inherited from the old régime.[7]

Soviet Russia's underlying backwardness rather than her temporary destruction, further industrialization rather than simple recovery, were Preobrazhenskii's central concerns. For this reason, he formulated the long-term problems of industrialization more clearly than had previously been done, and forced a gradual reorientation in the discussions of economic policy. He interpreted official economic thinking as an illusory belief—fostered by the relative ease and low costs of the recovery period—that a surplus sufficient for extensive industrialization could be generated within the state industrial sector itself. He argued otherwise: before self-sustained, intra-industrial accumulation could ensue, there had to be an initial phase during which large sums of capital, derived mainly "from sources lying outside the complex of state economy," must be concentrated in state hands. Surveying the meager alternatives available to an isolated Soviet Russia, Preobrazhenskii concluded that the essential source of investment resources could only be the peasant economy. His solution for rapid industrialization was a massive preliminary transference of surplus value from the peasant to the state industrial sector.[8]

To dramatize his argument and give it theoretical coherence, Preobrazhenskii drew an analogy between this period of "primitive socialist accumulation" and the initial stage in capitalism's development which Marx had termed "primitive capitalist accumulation." He faithfully recalled Marx's account of how nascent capitalism had parasitically nurtured itself through "systematic plundering" (colonial robbery, expropriation, crushing taxation) of noncapitalist economic forms, acquiring surplus capital by "all methods of compulsion and plundering." Preobrazhenskii did not advocate the same methods for socialist accumulation; some were disqualified "on principle." [9] But he retained the terms "exploitation" and "expropriation" to characterize the extraction of surplus value from the peasantry, maintaining that one sector, socialist or private, must "devour" the other. Even less tactfully, his argument strongly implied that the relationship between state industry and the peasant economy was comparable to that between an imperialist metropolis and its colonies. The peasantry as an internal colony of the workers' state, his opponents charged, was Preobrazhenskii's vision. He later toned down the suggestive terms and images; but they were not forgiven or forgotten.

In fact, Preobrazhenskii's actual plan was less brutal than his analogy implied. Having rejected violence and confiscation as unacceptable methods, he proposed that new capital be accumulated through "nonequivalent exchange" in market relations between the two sectors, a means he considered more effective and less offensive than direct taxation. State industry should use its unique supermonopolistic position to pursue "a price consciously aimed at the exploitation of the private economy in all its forms." [10] The prices of industrial products would be artificially inflated while agricultural prices were relatively depressed, the state buying low and selling high. This proposal, in effect the Left's platform since 1923, was aimed directly at official policy. Preobrazhenskii scorned the leadership's efforts to close the discrepancy between industrial and agricultural prices. On the contrary, he endorsed the "scissors crisis" price structure of 1923 as a key device of social accumulation.

Independent of his recommendations and ill-fated analogy, Preobrazhenskii's analysis of the need for and sources of new fixed capital was an important insight into the problems of industrialization. The question had been all but ignored before his contribution in late 1924. His diagnosis seemed even more perceptive after 1925, when the leadership slowly perceived that the chronic malady of the Soviet economy was not the under-consumption evidenced in 1923, but a recurrent "goods famine"—state industry's inability to meet consumer demand effectively. Viewed in this light, the analogy was not essential to his underlying argument. Although

Preobrazhenskii probably thought it expressed his hard-headed approach to the problem, it really served his theoretical ambition to formulate "primitive socialist accumulation" as the "fundamental law" or regulator of the socialist sector, as opposed to the law of value governing the private sector.[11] This was a separate and theoretical issue related, as we shall see, to the discussion of political economy initiated by Bukharin in 1920. But Preobrazhenskii chose to let his model stand as a piece, and as such it was a formidable achievement, providing the Left with powerful ideas and an economic spokesman of the first rank. Understandably, Bukharin struggled with Preobrazhenskii's "law" for the rest of his career as a policymaker, even in 1928–9 when he thought Stalin had adopted it.

Though Bukharin's belief in a different method and pattern of economic development had been evident before the autumn of 1924, the publication of Preobrazhenskii's arguments forced him to spell it out. The task of defending the majority's extempore policies and providing them with a sense of purpose and coherency fell to Bukharin, the only accomplished economist in the leadership. In the process of answering Preobrazhenskii and the Left generally, his own program emerged.[12] Because he presented it largely as a critique, Bukharin tended to express it in terms of his objections to Preobrazhenskii's proposals. Viewed broadly, he raised three objections, all interrelated: an economic, a political, and what may be understood as a moral or ethical objection. While economic arguments naturally dominated the discussions, the latter two strongly influenced Bukharin's economic reasoning and will be discussed first.

His political objection was stated in a dictum: "A proletarian dictatorship which is in a state of war with the peasantry . . . can in no way be strong." [13] Preobrazhenskii's program, he insisted, would alienate the peasantry, undermine the *smychka*, and endanger the régime's survival. By 1924, everyone accepted that peasants would not voluntarily produce or deliver surplus grain without adequate incentives. The introduction of NEP was tangible recognition of this fact of Soviet life. Yet Preobrazhenskii's "nonequivalent exchange" seemed to eliminate market incentives, leaving unanswered what would happen when the peasant, confronted with a manifestly unfavorable price structure, refused to market a surplus. Bukharin believed that it would necessitate a return to requisitioning and again set the party on a collision course with the rural population. That, he maintained, was where the Left's " 'ferocious' logic"—"the psychology of desperate gestures, superhuman pressures, and willful impulses"—led.[14] Preobrazhenskii's historical analogy only further convinced him that the Left's programs promised civil strife and disaster.

Any policy that risked a conflict with the peasantry, no matter how compelling its economic reasoning, was unacceptable to Bukharin. He was certain that the party would be the loser in such a confrontation. The indispensability of the peasantry's support—the inviolability of the *smychka*—he now saw as the cardinal lesson of Russia's revolutionary history: "The revolution of 1905 was a failure because there was not a *smychka* between the urban movement and the agrarian-peasant movement." That was "the supreme lesson for us all," underlining "the whole importance of the union of workers and peasants." The events of 1917 validated this historic truth, success having resulted from a happy combination of "a *peasant war* against the landlord and a *proletarian revolution*." This "quite peculiar and original situation was the basis for the entire development of our revolution." Initially a destructive *smychka*, NEP had translated it into a constructive alliance, without which the party's dictatorship was doomed: "If this especially favorable combination of class forces is lost, then the whole basis for developing the socialist revolution in our country collapses." [15]

Bukharin's peasant war–proletarian revolution interpretation of 1917, developed from an aside by Lenin, served three collateral purposes. It presented the "great agrarian revolution" of that year as a constituent and salutary part of "our revolution," not as an alien movement as had been Bolshevik custom earlier. It thus, secondly, countered the interpretation of 1917 associated with Trotsky's theory of permanent revolution. And, finally, it enabled Bukharin to argue that the relationship between the proletariat and the peasantry was analogous to the earlier collaborative alliance between the industrial bourgeoisie and the landlords, not, as Preobrazhenskii suggested, to the relationship between an exploiting and an exploited class.[16] But the central instruction of the interpretation was caution and conciliation—the watchwords of Bukharinism. It taught that anti-peasant policies were suicidal and underlay Bukharin's repeated warning that his party had to "walk on the razor's edge." [17]

It is perhaps curious that Bukharin, who in 1915–16 had portrayed the modern capitalist state as an omnipotent Leviathan, should now have seen the Soviet state as resting precariously on the continued tolerance of the peasantry. Impressed by the fierce independence of private peasant farmers during the rural uprisings of 1920–1, he did not clearly perceive that their very dispersal and individual autonomy was their collective weakness. Between 1929 and 1933, the Soviet state would wage and win a determined civil war against the rural masses, proving that their alienation was not fatal to the régime. And yet Bukharin's was only a partial error. He understood, or at least sensed, what a forced confrontation with the peasantry would entail, a prospect that horrified him and became another of his enduring fears. As even an unsympathetic writer has said: "he had a strong premonition of the furies that would descend upon the land" [18] if "willful impulses" were to prevail.

Bukharin's analysis of the party's political situation was, however, only a part of his opposition to anti-peasant policies, and he never relied on it alone. Between 1924 and 1929 he also sounded, not consistently or always clearly it is true, a moral objection to any systematic political or economic mistreatment of the peasantry. This element in his thinking is to be approached cautiously, if only because Bukharin conceivably would have denied its importance, and because there was a strong tradition in original Marxism and in Bolshevism against injecting moral values into social judgments.

The tradition derived from Marx himself. Despite the unmistakable moralism that infused much of his writing, Marx insisted formally on a rigidly nonethical approach to the study of society and to history generally. His stern refusal to reason other than in terms of the laws of a given epoch was expressed in his famous statement: "Right can never be higher than the economic structure of society and its cultural development conditioned thereby." This, he believed, distinguished his scientific socialism from the fantasies of utopian socialists. Early Marxists, familiar with Marx's scathing ridicule of the 1875 Gotha Program—whose demands for "equal right" and "fair distribution" he dismissed as "verbal rubbish" and "ideological nonsense about right and other trash so common among the democrats and French Socialists"—were strongly influenced by this bias against ethical judgments.[19] Bernstein's later revisionist effort to wed a Marxist socialism purged of "scientific" certainties with Kantian ethics showed the close connection between the anti-ethical and scientific assumptions in original Marxism, and made further moves in this direction doubly suspect.

In this respect, Bukharin's pre-October position was entirely orthodox. He reminded his readers in 1914: "There is nothing more ridiculous . . . than the attempt to make Marx's theory an 'ethical' theory. Marx's theory knows no other natural law than that of cause and effect, and can admit no other such law." "Ethical rhetoric," he added, was something "which we need not take seriously." [20] After 1917, the anti-ethical tradition became involved with Bolshevik decisionmaking, frequently being expressed in a disdain for moral inhibitions in the face of "objective conditions." Reasoning of this sort was commonplace during the civil war, when the party's excesses were consolingly rationalized as historical necessity or as means justified by socialist ends (a mode of rationalization encouraged in no small way by Bukharin's *The Economics*). This outlook did not end with the civil war. Speaking for the defense at the trial of Socialist Revolutionaries in 1922, Bukharin refused to base his acquittal plea on "moral" grounds, resting his case instead on the only admissible standard, "political expediency." And in 1924, responding to anti-Bolshevik statements by Ivan Pavlov, he proclaimed his allegiance "not [to] the categorical imperative of Kant and not [to] a Christian moral commandment, but [to] revolutionary expediency." Some people, he complained a year later, "very often replace sober reasonings with moral ones, which have nothing to do with politics." [21]

The same complaint was to be leveled at Bukharin himself during the twenties. For, contrary to the old tradition, and his own statements notwithstanding, an ethical standard began to figure prominently in his position on domestic policy. From the moment in December 1924 when he first denounced Preobrazhenskii's law as "a monstrous analogy" and "a frightful dream," to his charge in 1929 that Stalin's program amounted to "military-feudal exploitation of the peasantry," "ethical rhetoric" was part of his opposition to anti-peasant policies. It was to this that Preobrazhenskii referred when he reproached Bukharin for an "outburst of moral indignation." [22] Marx once said of the working class: "they have no ideals to realize. . . ." For Bukharin, an ideal had become central to Bolshevism's historical task.

This new element in his thinking related to his awareness, evident already in 1923, that the Soviet proletariat's minority status was not a national peculiarity. With the enthusiasm of a man who has belatedly uncovered an overlooked truth, and armed with supporting statistics, Bukharin seized every opportunity in 1924 and 1925 to impress on his audiences that globally "the proletariat . . . constitutes an insignificant minority," while peasants, mostly in agrarian countries of the East, "are the huge majority on our planet." His revised understanding of international revolution was based on an extrapolation of the Russian experience; hence his repeated image of "a world city and a world countryside," of a world "*smychka* between the Western European and American industrial proletariat and . . . the colonial peasantry," and of a global version of "proletarian revolution and peasant war." [23] Given the leadership of the proletariat, he prophesied in 1925, the peasant "will become —is becoming—the great liberating force of our time." But, as in the Soviet Union, "the decisive problem" would remain: a victorious world proletariat still would be a minority, and "after its victory will have *to get along* with the peasantry *no matter what,* for it is the majority of the population with great economic and social weight."[24]

On one level, Bukharin's remarks represented an effort to adjust Marxist theory, which traditionally viewed the peasantry as a reactionary relic of feudalism, to the revolutionary agrarian movements initiated by the First World War. They were also directed against the resurgence of anti-peasant sentiment within the party. He was challenging the conviction, his own in 1917 and now officially attributed to Trotsky, that the peasantry served the revolution "only as cannon fodder in the struggle with the capitalist and the large landowners." Instead, the proletariat required peasant support throughout the whole transition period: "it is compelled, in building socialism, to carry the peasantry with it."[25] While Bukharin's position was not "pro-peasant" in the populist sense of a glorification of the muzhik and village life, but rather a pragmatic appraisal of class forces, he did want the urban Bolsheviks to regard their ally sympathetically and appreciate that social backwardness "is not the peasant's 'guilt,' but his misfortune." Approach the peasant, he urged, not with "disgust and contempt" but "seriously with love." Anti-peasantism was incompatible with "proletarian duty," especially in an age when the proletariat and the bourgeoisie were competing "for the soul of the peasant."[26]

This view of Soviet Russia as a microcosm of world classes spurred Bukharin's imagination in another, more important direction. His reflections on the "world countryside" coincided with the Bolsheviks' growing perception of themselves as modernizers. By 1924–5, "capitalist stabilization" had dashed their hopes for an early European revolution, and the onset of the economic controversies reflected the party's realization that, for the time being anyway, Soviet Russia would have to industrialize on its own. Bukharin related these two questions and found a larger implication: economic backwardness was an international phenomenon, and great parts of the world, like Soviet Russia, were mainly pre-industrial. The Bolshevik experiment thus acquired for him an additional significance. Not only was it the first proletarian revolution, but for the first time in history a country had embarked on a "noncapitalist path" to industrialism. The question of whether Russia's peasant masses and their pre-capitalist economies could "bypass the capitalist path" was therefore relevant to all backward countries. In this, and in the "unheard-of and unprecedented" fact that the experiment was being undertaken "without those who have commanded for tens and hundreds of years," Bukharin saw "the most enormous significance not only for us, but for the toilers of the whole world." [27]

His ethical objection to anti-peasant policies took shape in this context. The Bolshevik revolution had shattered the old Marxist assumption that industrialization was the exclusive task of capitalism. In its place, Bukharin advanced the idea of a historic comparison between the process of "socialist industrialization" (or "socialist accumulation") and the past history of "capitalist industrialization." The former was to prove radically different in nature. His conception of an atrocious capitalist example was borrowed from Marx. It originated in the period of "primitive capitalist accumulation" and the merciless expropriation of noncapitalist producers, when "conquest, enslavement, robbery, murder, briefly force, play the great part." This, capitalism's equivalent of "original sin," was "the historical process of divorcing the producer from the means of production," the "transformation of feudal exploitation into capitalist exploitation," out of which, in Marx's words, "capital comes dripping from head to foot, from every pore, with blood and dirt." The subsequent history of capitalist accumulation, according to Bukharin, followed a similar pattern: its "driving motive" was "ever higher profits—exploitation, destruction, and ruin, that is the real mechanism of relations between the capitalist and the noncapitalist milieu"; imperialism based on "colonial exploitation is only *the world scope of this phenomenon*." [28]

The essential feature of capitalist industrialization was for Bukharin its "parasitic" impact on agriculture and the peasant. Cities had enriched themselves by "devouring" and impoverishing the villages:

Capitalist industrialization—this is the parasitism of the city in relation to the countryside, the parasitism of a metropolis in relation to colonies, the hypertrophic, bloated development of industry, serving the ruling classes, along with the extreme comparative backwardness of agricultural economics, especially *peasant* agricultural economics.

Hence the "accursed legacy" of this "bloodsucking process"— "poverty, ignorance, cultural backwardness, inequality," what Marx called "the idiocy of rural life." [29] And it was in this regard that there was to be a fundamental difference "in the type of *our* industrialization." As Bukharin insisted repeatedly between 1924 and 1929:

we must constantly keep in mind that our socialist industrialization must differ from capitalist industrialization in that it is carried out *by the proletariat*, for the goals of *socialism*, that its effect upon the peasant economy is different and distinct in nature, that its "attitude" toward agriculture generally is different and distinct. Capitalism caused the *debasement* of agriculture. Socialist industrialization is not a parasitic process in relation to the countryside . . . but the means of its greatest *transformation and uplifting*.[30]

It was this vision that he tried to convey in constant references to Bolshevism's "historic task." Soviet industrialization, unlike its capitalist predecessor, was obliged to develop the rural sector economically and culturally, to "*open a new epoch* in relations between the city and the village, one which puts an end to the systematic retardation of the village . . . which turns industry's 'face to the countryside' . . . leading it from history's backways to the proscenium of economic history." The venture was historic because it was unprecedented, a theme on which Bukharin rhapsodized before a Komsomol gathering in January 1925:

It stands for the first time in human history . . . because in not a single period, in not a single cycle of human history—not in the epoch of Oriental despotisms, nor in the period of the so-called classical world, nor in the Middle Ages, nor under the capitalist régime—never was there such an example where the ruling class posed as its fundamental task the overcoming and destruction of the difference between the predatory city and the village on which it preys—between the city, which reaps all the benefits of culture, and the village, which is sacrificed to ignorance.[31]

Bukharin was groping toward an ethic of socialist industrialization, an imperative standard delineating the permissible and the impermissible. Believing that the Soviet experience would be viewed in the mirror of capitalist history, and wanting the reflection to be more humane and beneficial as well as more productive, he saw an epic judgment in the making. Could Soviet Russia industrialize without emulating the atrocities of the capitalist model? If not, he seemed to suggest, the outcome would not be socialism. The means would shape the end. "We do not want to drive the middle peasant into communism with an iron broom, pushing him with the kicks of war communism," he explained in January 1926. This had been and was now "untrue, incorrect, unsuitable from the point of view of socialism." Bolsheviks were "pioneers, but we do not carry out experiments, we are not vivisectionists, who . . . operate on a living organism with a knife; we are conscious of our historic responsibility. . . ." [32]

This special understanding of Bolshevism's role in history accounts significantly for the intensity of Bukharin's opposition to anti-peasant policies (and, as we shall see, for his initial economic complacency). He emotionally denounced "third-revolutionists" as advocates of a "pogrom"—"cranks who would propose to declare 'a St. Bartholomew's night' for the peasant bourgeoisie." [33] It also illuminates his outraged reaction to Preobrazhenskii's ideas, in whose invocation of bygone plundering and expropriation he saw not an interlude of "primitive socialist accumulation" but a permanent system of exploitation "on an expanding basis." Preobrazhenskii's formulation, Bukharin contended, would apply in only one circumstance:

if the discussion was not about moving toward a classless Communist society but toward strengthening forever the proletariat dictatorship, toward conserving the supremacy of proletariat, and toward *its degeneration* into a real exploiting class. *Then* the conception of exploitation would correctly apply without reservation to such an order. Equally, it would also be correct to designate the petty bourgeois peasant economy . . . as a "proletarian" colony.

But, he asked rhetorically, "May one . . . call the proletariat *an exploiting class* . . .? No! And a thousand times no! And by no means because this 'sounds bad.' . . . But because such a 'name' does not correspond . . . to objective reality and to our historic task." It was "to lose sight of the *originality* of the process" of socialist industrialization; "it means not to understand its *historic essence*." [34]

Apart from its ethical underpinnings, Bukharin's juxtaposition of capitalist and socialist accumulation concealed a significant inconsistency. Despite his bleak portrayal of the capitalist model, he was aware that in at least one country, the United States, industrialization had been accompanied by a prospering agriculture.[35] What really seems to have provoked his generalization about previous exploitation of the countryside was the unhappy history of the Russian peasantry. The image of a rapacious autocracy preying on the muzhik had been a powerful theme in pre-Marxist Russian radical thought, and Bukharin adopted it. Before the February revolution, he recalled, "a half-destitute peasantry," subject to *"medieval forms of exploitation,"* had suffered "under the iron heel of the landlord" and an autocracy which "constituted nothing but an enormous parasite on the body of the nation." Czarism rather than capitalism itself seems to have been the real source of Bukharin's "parasitic" model. As he warned in an angry and revealing polemic, super-industrialist programs would "put the USSR in the historical line . . . of *old Russia*," with its "backward, semi-serfdom agriculture, pauper-peasant . . . and merciless exploitation of the muzhik. . . ."[36]

While, for obvious reasons, he never isolated it from his other arguments or called it by its proper name,[37] this ethical consideration influenced Bukharin's economic thinking throughout the disputes of the twenties. His conviction that socialist industrialization must benefit the peasant masses was reflected in his central economic proposition that "mass consumption"—the "needs of the masses"—was "the real lever of development, that it generates the most rapid tempos of economic growth." Or, as he expressed it programmatically: "Our economy exists for the consumer, not the consumer for the economy. This is a point which must never be forgotten. The 'New Economy' differs from the old in taking as its standard the needs of the masses. . . ."[38] This proposition subtly combined an ethical and an economic argument. As a Bolshevik, however, Bukharin had to convince the party that it was economically sound, not ethically preferable.

Economics naturally formed the main substance of the debates. Here we must begin by understanding that Bukharin agreed with Preobrazhenskii and the Left in two important respects. First, like all leading Bolsheviks, he accepted industrialization as the party's foremost goal. This was for a variety of reasons, including national pride and security, the Marxist association of industrialism with socialism, and the attendant worry that a proletarian régime would be forever insecure in a predominantly agrarian society. And, like the Left, he wanted in particular an industrialization process that would yield a large capital goods sector: "metal industry . . . this is the basic spine, the backbone of our industry."[39]

Second, Bukharin and Preobrazhenskii agreed that Soviet industrialization would have to rely mainly on internal resources.[40] Moreover, Bukharin concurred that industrialization required a transfer of resources from the agrarian to the state industrial sector, or what Preobrazhenskii called "pumping over" from the peasant economy. The real disagreement, Bukharin insisted, was over methods and limits:

It would be wrong to argue that industry should grow only on what is produced within the limits of this industry. But the whole question involves *how much* we can take from the peasantry . . . *to what extent* we can carry this pumping over, *by what methods*, where are the *limits* of this pumping over, *how* . . . to receive the most favorable result. . . . Here is the difference between us and the opposition. . . . Comrades of the opposition stand for pumping over excessively, for such intense pressure on the peasantry which . . . is economically irrational and politically impermissible. Our position in no way renounces this pumping over; but we calculate much more soberly. . . .[41]

The crux of Bukharin's economic objections to Preobrazhenskii's proposals, and the basis of his own program, was his belief that industrial growth depended on an expanding consumer market. He first broached the argument in a roundabout way in the spring of 1924, in a series of theoretical articles ostensibly unrelated to the emerging party debates. Among his targets was the economist Mikhail Tugan-Baranovskii, whose earlier theory of economic crises was relevant to the party discussions. In arguing his "disproportionality" explanation of crises, Tugan-Baranovskii had denied a necessary dependency between production and mass consumption, maintaining that, given the planning of correct proportions among different branches of production, capital accumulation could grow regardless of the level of social consumption. Industry, he said in effect, could provide the effective demand for its own output. Bukharin flatly rejected Tugan-Baranovskii's "lunatic utopia," in which production was isolated from consumption. The "chain" of production, he insisted, must always "*end* with the production of means of consumption . . . which enter into the process of personal consumption. . . ." [42]

At first glance, his inflexible approach to Tugan-Baranovskii's arguments seems curious. Bukharin himself, after all, had frequently emphasized the regulatory powers of state capitalist systems, later even theorizing that under "pure" state capitalism (without a free market), production could continue crisis-free while consumption lagged behind.[43] The presence of a hopeful "ought" is perhaps discernible in his insistence that production must in the end be oriented toward satisfying social wants. Whatever the case, it became evident a few months later that Bukharin was speaking less to old controversies than to new ones when he set out his major economic axiom: "if there is given such a system of economic relationships where industry has *already* worked for the peasant market, where it cannot exist without a connection with this market, then the situation in industry, the tempo of accumulation, etc., cannot be independent from the growth of the productive forces of agriculture." He was referring, of course, to Russia, going on to suggest that Preobrazhenskii's "law" constituted a program based on "applied Tuganism," a charge he repeated throughout the twenties.[44]

Bukharin believed that the Left's call for "a dictatorship of industry" ignored the crucial problem of peasant demand. (This problem, he added, had been instrumental in the downfall of czarism.)[45] Hence his main economic argument, tirelessly reiterated between 1924 and 1926: "Accumulation in socialist industry cannot occur for long *without accumulation in the peasant economy.*" Thus "the capacity of the internal market . . . is the central question of our economics." If the problem was properly resolved, the outlook was hopeful: "the greater the buying powers of the peasantry, the faster our industry develops." Or as Bukharin succinctly promised: "kopeck accumulation in the peasant economy is the basis for ruble accumulation in socialist industry."[46]

The Left's "super-industrialism" suggested to Bukharin the opposition's failure to see that the urban and rural sectors were "a single organism." If agriculture and industry were prevented from interacting, "you will have silent factories . . . you will have a declining peasant economy; you will have general regression." Accordingly, he insisted that the true indicator of growth was not industrial investment alone, but "the sum of the national incomes, on the basis of which everything grows, beginning with production and ending with the army and the schools."[47] NEP had solved the crucial problem of linking the two sectors by creating "an economic *smychka* between socialist state industry and the millions of peasant economies." That economic *smychka* was trade, through which "a bridge is erected between the city and the countryside."[48]

The reciprocity of the two sectors was expressed for Bukharin in mutual demand and supply. Rural demand was twofold: the peasant desired first of all consumer goods and simple agricultural implements; but as accumulation in the peasant economy progressed, he would also require complex producer goods such as tractors. Peasant demand therefore served to stimulate all branches of industry, light and heavy. At the same time, the technological advancement of peasant agriculture depended on the availability of industrial products, especially fertilizers and machinery.[49] Viewing the process from the city, Bukharin continued, state industry received in return its prime essentials: grain and industrial crops, the former to feed urban workers and to export abroad in exchange for needed equipment, the latter to supply further industrial production.[50] Thus did the interdependence of the two sectors work to solve what he thought were the major problems of Soviet economic growth—grain collection and the weak capacity of the internal market.

It was this rationale that Bukharin offered for the controversial agrarian reforms of 1925, which extended NEP in the countryside by eliminating most of the remaining legal barriers to peasant farming.[51] The linchpin of his program was the encouragement of private peasant accumulation, thereby broadening the rural demand for industrial products and increasing the marketable surplus of peasant agriculture. He hoped that the peasant sector could be transformed from "a natural consumer economy into a commodity-producing economy." This meant encouraging the prosperity of all rural strata, but particularly the middle and better-off peasant, a prospect that the Left, whose sympathies went out only to the poor peasant, considered politically dangerous and ideologically repugnant. Bukharin's defense of the reforms also reflected his ethical understanding of Bolshevism's "historic task." The party's goal, he maintained, was not "equality in poverty," not "reducing the more prosperous upper stratum, but . . . pulling the lower strata up to this high level." Taking aim at the Left, he added: "poor peasant socialism is wretched socialism. . . . Only idiots can say there must always be the poor." [52]

His essential argument, however, was pragmatic. A meaningful increase in rural demand and marketed produce would necessarily rest, at least in the beginning, on those stronger peasants capable of monetary accumulation and expanded production. But these were the peasant households, whose economic development was specifically fettered by legal restrictions and capricious administrative practices left over from war communism. As Bukharin explained:

the prosperous upper stratum of the peasantry and the middle peasant who also aspires to become prosperous *are at present afraid to accumulate*. There is a situation where the peasant is afraid to install an iron roof for fear of being declared a kulak; if he buys a machine, then he does it in such a way that the Communists will not notice. Higher technique becomes conspiratorial.

The reforms were to remedy this situation. They would apply to all segments of the rural population, as Bukharin made explicit in a proclamation that provoked the political scandal of 1925: "we must say to the whole peasantry, to all its strata: enrich yourselves, accumulate, develop your economy." [53] Politics compelled him to retract the "enrich yourselves" slogan, but not its meaning. It was, he said: "a mistaken formulation of an entirely correct position." And that position was: "we do not hinder kulak accumulation and we do not strive to organize the poor peasant for a second *expropriation* of the kulak." [54]

The larger aim of the reforms was "unleashing commodity turnover," a goal which Bukharin termed "the general line of our economic policy." He believed that a flourishing of trade would result in the fastest and surest economic growth. Broadening the absorption capacity of the market, raising the total volume of commodities, and accelerating their circulation between industry and agriculture, and within industry and agriculture, "is the main method of accelerating the tempo of our economic life." It "would provide space for the fullest development of productive forces." [55] For this reason, manufactured goods originating outside the state sector were to be welcomed. The reforms applied not only to peasant farming but also to the vast network of small handicraft industries, which manufactured a great variety of goods and whose development would contribute to the total national income. Similarly, Bukharin urged that industrial products be imported if necessary to meet internal demand, because an imported tractor, to use his example, would increase the capacity of the home market and eventually generate additional demand for Soviet industrial products.[56]

Bukharin rightly observed that his program differed from that of the Left, who put the first emphasis on production, in that it meant moving "from circulation (money, prices, trade) to production." This was the substance of his hotly contested theory (to be discussed in more detail below) of "growing into socialism through exchange." As he explained in 1925: "Accelerating turnover, expanding the *market*, and on this basis expanding production—from this comes the possibility of further lowering prices, further expanding the market, etc. That is the path of our production." [57] A program of this sort required that the party follow three basic policies: promulgating and enforcing the agrarian reforms; restoring normal conditions and minimizing state interference at places of trade, from central markets to local bazaars; and constantly forcing down industrial prices.

Controversy over the large questions of the revolution in 1924–6 frequently centered on the immediate, practical matter of official price policy. The ratio between industrial and agricultural goods related not only to the prospect of rural unrest, but also to the question of which class woud bear the burden of industrialization and to the level of "pumping over" from the peasant sector. Thus while Preobrazhenskii and the Left demanded relatively high industrial prices, Bukharin offered two arguments for the opposite policy.

First, he assumed (apparently unlike Preobrazhenskii) that peasant demand for industrial goods was highly elastic. Lower prices would result in a larger volume of sales and greater total profits. In addition, they would allow for faster capital turnover and a variety of cost reductions derived from maximizing output and rationalizing production. Conversely, Bukharin warned that an artificially high price policy would have disastrous effects, diminishing the capacity of the peasant market, creating a repetition of the 1923 "selling crisis," and—having deprived industry of its market and raw materials—leading to "industrial stagnation." Preobrazhenskii's proposal meant "killing the goose that lays the golden egg." [58] Although Bukharin once declared that "it would be nonsensical on our part *to renounce the utilization* of our monopolistic position," during the mid-twenties he plumped solely for "cheaper prices in each successive cycle of production," promising that the most rapid tempo of industrial growth emanated not from "cartel super-profits" but from "the minimum profit per unit of merchandise." [59]

To this argument against high industrial prices he added another: "Any monopoly conceals within itself . . . *the danger of decay*, of resting on its laurels." The capitalist firm had been "spurred by competition" to produce more cheaply and more rationally. Soviet industry lacked this inner dynamic:

if we, who in essence . . . have a state super-monopoly, do not push, press, and whip our cadres, spurring them to cheapen production, to produce better, then . . . we have before us all the prerequisites of monopolistic decay. The role played by competition in capitalist society . . . must with us be played by the constant pressure arising from the needs of the masses.[60]

Bukharin's remarks on this danger, sometimes referred to as "monopolistic parasitism" and "bureaucratic degeneration," were prompted by more than the economic costs of "bureaucratic mismanagement." They reflected, as we have seen, his abiding fear of a new class—"our managers are proletarian fighters but they are

transition to socialism, relations between the private and public sectors would be maintained and governed through the operation of the semi-free market, whose functioning varied with the exercise of the state's regulatory powers.

In addition to linking the two sectors, distributing commodities, and helping to allocate resources, the market permitted the Soviet state to benefit from the private pursuits of its "mass of semi-friends and semi-enemies and open enemies in economic life." [69] According to Bukharin, the NEP market economy had established "the correct combination of the private interests of the small producer and the general interests of socialist construction." By stimulating the personal incentives of peasants, artisans, workers, "and even the bourgeoisie . . . we put them objectively to the service of socialist state industry and the economy as a whole." His attitude toward the kulak peasant ("we help him but he helps us") typified his attitude toward private capital generally. Its development served willy-nilly—"independent of its will"—the interests of socialism.[70] And in the end, the state sector stood to benefit most; through its greater market competitiveness, efficiency, and resources it would gradually displace private capital from trade and production. How Bukharin envisaged "overcoming the market through the market" will be discussed below; what is important here is that his acceptance of the mixed economy and the market determined his position on three key issues under debate: planning, growth proportions between branches of industry, and the rate of economic growth itself.

The idea of planning, with its promise of "economic rationality," agitated every Bolshevik's imagination. All were agreed on its virtues and desirability, few on its meaning or implementation.[71] A single industrial plan was the Left's great cause, so compelling that it united the several different tendencies within the opposition. Partly for this reason, and partly in reaction to the centralizing excesses which had passed for planning during war communism, Bukharin's remarks on the subject were frequently negative between 1924 and 1926. He ridiculed the notion of an instant general plan imposed from above—materializing "like a *deus ex machina*"—as a remnant of those war communist illusions which should have expired "when the proletarian army took Perekop." More to the point was his criticism of an industrial plan calculated independently of market forces, of the demand and supply of the peasant sector, as "unthinkable": "*the correlation . . . inside state industry is determined by the correlation with the peasant market.* That 'plan' which misses this correlation is not a plan, because this *correlation* is the basis of the entire plan." [72]

His positive remarks, on the other hand, drew upon the new wisdom of NEP. A "real" or "exact" plan could be formulated only gradually, as state economies ousted private ones through market competition and as large socialist production grew. The road to a planned economy was "a long process." Meantime, however, Bukharin saw a "planned beginning" in the state's regulation of the economy through manipulation of its "commanding heights," and in the planning of wholesale and retail prices. And while his hostility to "economic futurism" tended to give his thinking on the subject a negative cast, he did adumbrate the philosophy behind his more ambitious planning proposals after 1926. In April 1925, he explained the direction of genuine planning: "Toward establishing the proportions between various branches of production within industry on the one hand, and the correct relations between industry and agriculture on the other." The two were inseparable: "Proportionality of the separate parts of production without the establishment of a certain proportionality between industry and agriculture is a complete abstraction, merely noise." Planning, he believed, began by maintaining proportionality, not, as he thought the Left was advocating, "by systematically breaking socially necessary proportions." [73]

The Left viewed planning as a way to promote immediate and extensive investment in heavy industry. Bukharin's program envisaged a different pattern of industrial growth. Looking to mass consumption as the spur, and to the capacity of the internal market to determine proportions within industry, made necessary "the adaptation of industry to the peasant market." [74] It meant beginning with the development of industries producing for personal consumption (textiles, for example), and allowing heavy industry to grow as a result of the chain process. Bukharin argued that this pattern, which he also contrasted to the follies of war communism, had been proved viable by the industrial recovery attained since 1921: "We began by raising the lightest branches of industry, with those that obtained a commodity *smychka* with the peasant economy; through it light industry began to pick up, then middle, and the end of this process reached the basic production link, the production of basic capital, i.e., metal." He projected this balanced growth pattern into the future, foreseeing a steady development of light industry and the continued dependency of heavy industry on a "full *smychka* with the peasant economy." [75]

Finally, there was the question of tempo. Its importance in the debates fluctuated with the party's perception of Soviet Russia's security among nations, and it was usually discussed in terms of speculative philosophy. Everyone, of course, wanted the fastest attainable rate of industrial growth. The Left exhibited a particular sense of urgency, while being as imprecise in its pronouncements as the majority leadership. Bukharin's public statements added to the confusion. Throughout 1924 and 1925, he insisted that his program, not the Left's, would "achieve a very rapid tempo of development," contrasting Soviet development to the economic situation in European capitalist countries. Thus, in early 1924, he declared: "in five or six years the USSR will be the most powerful European state." [76] The "stabilization" of European capitalism by mid-1925, however, prompted a second and more sober thought: "we are growing and *they* are growing, this is something new . . ."; "we therefore must grow faster, significantly faster, than a number of our neighbors." This would be guaranteed by "unleashing commodity turnover." [77]

During the same period, however, Bukharin repeatedly employed imagery that seemed to imply a much slower growth rate. Seeking to emphasize the need to progress industrially in conjunction with the peasant sector, he expressed it variously: as "moving ahead slowly . . . dragging behind us the cumbersome peasant cart," or "dragging behind . . . the enormous heavy barge of the entire peasantry." [78] How could this image of "tiny steps," as he put it elsewhere, be reconciled with his simultaneous promise of a "very rapid tempo"? Partly because the imagery referred to the prolonged process ("decades") of preparing the peasantry, economically and psychologically, for socialism, while "rapid tempo" referred only to economic growth. But the distinction was neither clear nor satisfactory. The Left's polemics predictably focused on the implication of "tiny steps," especially after Bukharin told a party congress in December 1925 (two weeks after reiterating that "we will grow very rapidly"): "we can build socialism even on this wretched technical base . . . we shall creep at a snail's pace. . . ." [79] If this meant that industrialization would proceed at a "snail's pace," it satisfied no one, including Bukharin.

He was on firmer ground when he chose, as he often did, to combine the issues of tempo and "pumping over," and to take a more long-range perspective. Preobrazhenskii's plan of "pumping over inordinately," contended Bukharin, might bring an initial upsurge in capital expenditures, but a "sharp" fall would certainly follow. Instead, "our policies must be calculated not on the basis of one year, but a number of years," in order to "guarantee every year a greater broadening of the whole economy." He summarized this more tenable argument in July 1926:

The most rapid tempo of industrial development is in no way ensured by taking the maximum amount from agriculture. It is not at all that simple. If we take less today, we thereby promote a larger accumulation in agriculture and thus ensure for ourselves tomorrow a larger demand for our industry's products. By ensuring a larger income for agriculture, we shall be able to take more from this larger income next year than we took last year, and to ensure for ourselves in future years even greater growth, even greater revenue for our state industry. If in the first year . . . we move at a somewhat less rapid tempo, in return the curve of our growth will *then* rise more rapidly.[80]

The discussion of tempo underlined a significant fact about the economic debates generally. They were intimately connected with and influenced by noneconomic considerations, among them domestic and foreign politics, and, equally important, Bolshevik ideology. This was especially true in the case of the theoretically minded Bukharin. For, while he raised political, ethical, and economic arguments against the Left, his own program was only part of a broader theory of social change in the Soviet Union.

The public Bolshevik ideology that had served so well from 1917 to 1920 was in shambles by 1924. The rude dismantlement of war communism, the emergence of NEP with its "extraordinary confusion of . . . socioeconomic relations," the "psychological depression" caused by the failure of European revolution, Lenin's death, and the spectacle of his successors claiming allegiance to different Leninisms—all shattered or seriously undermined earlier beliefs and certainties.[81] The "collapse of our illusions" had been the collapse of dearly held assumptions, of old theories. Disenchantment and pessimism came in the aftermath. There were many signs, some petty, some portentous: workers resented the finery of the nepman's wife; rural Communists were disoriented by the permissive agrarian policies; and, most serious, among the party faithful, especially the youth, NEP brought "a sort of demoralization, a crisis of ideas." [82]

In a sense, the sequence of disillusionments put an end to the Bolsheviks' innocent faith in the omnipotence of theory. Even Bukharin now liked to quote: "Theory, my friend, is gray, but green is the eternal tree of life." [83] Nonetheless, party leaders felt strongly the need to rebuild and reassert Bolshevism as a coherent ideology. The literate public, Bukharin warned in 1924, was expressing growing "demand . . . and inquiries in the sphere of ideology"; if the party did not provide answers, others would.[84] Answers were particularly important in the context of the party debates, where rival factions sought to appeal to the party's broader membership and to its labor constituency at large. Both the official leadership and the opposition were committed to ideological communication, each claiming that its program alone was inspired by and consistent with "orthodox Bolshevism" (Leninism), or what Bukharin disingenuously called "historical Bolshevism." Content to wrap its proposals in the existing ideological banner of the revolutionary-heroic tradition, the Left appealed largely to previous values and understandings. It saw no need for extensive theoretical innovation, preferring instead to scorn the majority's "spiteful disbelief in bold economic initiative" as opportunism in practice and revisionism in theory.[85]

On the other hand, the "crisis of ideas" presented Bukharin with a special responsibility. As official theorist and chief defender of the new economic policies, he was doubly responsible for the reconstruction of Bolshevik ideology, at least where large contested questions were involved. After 1923, he contributed little to intellectual discussions unrelated to the party dispute, devoting his attention instead to explaining the new policies and his program theoretically, and in the process trying to to prove them compatible with "historical Bolshevism." Here again he faced a special problem. While the Left could effectively evoke established (if tarnished) ideas, Bukharin was busy debunking many of those ideas as past illusions. He dismissed, for example, three years of Bolshevik fervor with the judgment that in economic practice war communism had been "a caricature of socialism." [86] His constant contempt for ideas gained from "old books" meant that he had to build anew. For if it was true that the party's essential understandings had radically changed, new theories were required. And though Bukharin, too, could refer effectively to Lenin's writings, especially the reformism of his last articles, he was quick to admit that to intone *magister dixit* was not enough.[87]

Nor were statesman-like apothegms a solution. Consistent with his new pragmatism, Bukharin now inveighed regularly against "hysterical" policies, praising a course that was "neither right nor left, but . . . correct." The trouble with this kind of middle-of-the-road maxim, and declarations such as "I say 20,000 times that we absolutely must not depart from the principles of NEP," [88] was that they smacked of conservatism and thus fed the suspicion that the majority's policies were a betrayal of revolutionary ideals. The hopeful prognosis of some non-Bolsheviks, "the angel of revolution is flying quietly from the country," had to be refuted, because it was also the opposition's opinion.[89] Bukharin himself had reflected in 1922: "History is full of examples of the transformation of parties of revolution into parties of order. Sometimes the only mementoes of a revolutionary party are the watchwords which it has inscribed on public buildings."[90] The opposition called this "Thermidorian reaction."

In short, not only new theories but optimistic ones were needed. Bukharin understood that NEP had generated pessimism partly because it was not outwardly heroic.[91] The surface tawdriness of the mixed economy made him vulnerable to the charge that his ideas were "an idealization of NEP," that he was not the theorist of revolutionary socialism but, as one opposition wit dubbed him, "the Pushkin of NEP."[92] Having originated as a retreat, the new policies seemed to many to remain only that. It was necessary to convince party members that in fact they represented the forward march of socialism, not "backward movement." All those "concealed skeptics" who "consider it a mark of bad form to speak of our forward advance," had to be refuted.[93] In 1923, on the twenty-fifth anniversary of the party, Bukharin had written: "We set out upon a voyage the like of which not even Columbus ever dreamt."[94] Now he had to show that the voyage continued, that his acknowledged reformism, his "new economics," were leading to socialism.

Before the details of socialist development could be broached, it was still necessary to establish whether it was permissible even to aspire to socialism in an isolated agrarian country. As we have seen, earlier Marxist-Bolshevik theory, with its central expectation of an international proletarian revolution arising out of the contradictions of mature industrialism, clearly suggested otherwise. The party's Left, not always consistently or comfortably, defended the old position, even though its spokesmen carefully allowed that the *process* of building socialism in Soviet Russia was possible. They passionately rejected, however, the assertion that the process could be completed in a single, economically backward country. Their position, they insisted, was orthodox, realistic, and unflaggingly internationalist.[95] But the logic of events since 1917—the Bolsheviks' national success in October and in the civil war, the widespread succumbing to "leap into socialism" ideas during war communism, and the encouraging reappraisal of NEP initiated by Lenin in 1922–3

—pointed to a different conclusion.[96] This was drawn by the Stalin-Bukharin majority, in the doctrine of "socialism in one country."

Stalin, in the campaign against the "permanent revolutionists," was the first to advance the doctrine explicitly; but it was Bukharin who turned it into a theory and thus defined the official understanding of "socialism in one country" in the twenties.[97] As we have seen, he had been approaching such a conception since November 1922, it being the implicit assumption of "growing into socialism." But only in April 1925, three months after Stalin's statement, did Bukharin begin to address the question publicly and explicitly.[98] He occasionally denied that the doctrine represented a revision of earlier views, though his disclaimers were halfhearted, and properly so: from 1917 to 1921, he, like everyone else, had been on record as believing that socialism in Russia alone was impossible.[99] Although the logic of "socialism in one country" could be traced to the October coup, and legitimate paternity to Lenin's 1922–3 articles, formal expression of the doctrine did constitute a radical departure in official Bolshevik thought, as Bukharin tacitly acknowledged: "it turned out that the question was not so simple as it seemed earlier, when we thought less about it." [100]

Having thought about it, he now presented a two-part formula in answer to the question, Can socialism be built in Soviet Russia in the absence of European revolution? The first part of the formula dealt with the country's internal circumstances, her resources and classes. Here Bukharin's conclusion was unequivocally affirmative. Rejecting the supposition that "we must perish because of our *technical backwardness*," he issued his famous assurance: "we *can* build socialism even on this wretched technical base . . . we shall creep at a snail's pace, but . . . all the same we are building socialism and we shall build it." [101] This, he argued, was Lenin's position in his "testament," where he had found "all that is necessary and sufficient" for socialism. If true, it meant that "there can be no . . . point at which this construction can become impossible." One potential obstacle did exist and was accounted for in the second part of Bukharin's formula: the Soviet Union would be secure from foreign capitalist intervention and war only when the revolution became international. Thus, in terms of a guarantee from external threat, *"the FINAL practical victory of socialism in our country is not possible without the help of other countries and the world revolution."* [102]

This formula was Bukharin's way of reaffirming his internationalism while responding optimistically to the immediate question, Where are we going? By distinguishing between internal potential and external menace, he was focusing in effect on the prospects of economic modernization, a reasonable approach. For beneath the rhetoric about "building socialism" stood the essential, nondenominational issues of industrialization and modernization. It required no special vision of socialism to argue, as Bukharin did, that "we can stand firmly on our own feet," that "daily, monthly, and yearly we will be overcoming this technical-economic backwardness." [103] In other words, "socialism in one country" was in large measure a debate about the possibility of industrializing without foreign assistance, whether from a victorious European proletariat or, in present-day terms, from a wealthy patron nation.

Although Bukharin defended his formula throughout the controversy, its unavoidable whiff of nationalism clearly made him uneasy. He apparently believed that he had reconciled "socialism in one country" with his own abiding commitment ("not platonic . . . but real") to international revolution; [104] but he also knew that the Left's charge of "national narrow-mindedness" pointed to a real and growing danger. Though personally free of nationalistic fervor, he did not speak for the average party member, many of whom saw in the doctrine primarily a promise of Russia's national destiny. Recognizing this, Bukharin tried to discourage the nationalist tendency in three ways. First, by stressing that socialism was "several decades" away "at a minimum." Second, by repeating that even then Soviet socialism would be "backward socialism." And, finally, by lashing out at the view that the Soviet undertaking "is what might be called a 'national' task," and warning against the danger inherent in his own ideas about building socialism:

if we exaggerate our possibilities, there then could arise a tendency . . . "to spit" on the international revolution; such a tendency could give rise to its own special ideology, a peculiar "national Bolshevism" or something else in this spirit. From here it is a few small steps to a number of even more harmful ideas.[105]

Discomforting or not, the doctrine cleared the way for a theoretical explanation of how NEP Russia would evolve into socialist Russia. Bukharin always insisted that the debate over "socialism in one country" was really about the "nature of our revolution," that is, the nature and mutual relations of those classes involved in the revolutionary drama. This Marxist perspective meant that Bukharin's theory had to begin with an analysis of Soviet Russia's classes. Three were said officially to be present in NEP society, landlords and large capitalists having been eliminated as forces during the civil war: the proletariat, the peasantry, and the "new bour-geoisie." [106] The urban population caused no theoretical problem or serious disagreement, all Bolsheviks assenting that the industrial proletariat was the progressive class, the carrier of socialism. Nor was there difficulty in defining the urban reactionary, the nepman, who traded and speculated for "anti-social gain" within officially proscribed limits: he, along with his rural counterpart the kulak, was part of the "new bourgeoisie." Unanimity ended, however, at the city limits.

Disagreement centered on the differentiation within the peas-antry, on applying the old tripartite classification of poor peasants, middle peasants, and kulaks to a countryside drastically trans-formed and leveled by the revolutionary events of 1917 to 1920. Not only were the categories vague (kulak, for example, had be-come more of a pejorative than a precise sociological category) but the statistical evidence was unreliable, conflicting, and regularly subjected to political manipulation. An official 1925 calculation estimated poor peasant households at 45 per cent of the total, middle peasants at 51 per cent, and kulaks at 4 per cent. Each figure was challenged and widely revised during the twenties, but especially the last. Opinion as to the percentage of kulaks ranged from zero (some arguing that the hated pre-1917 type of village exploiter had ceased to exist) to 14. Since 20 to 25 million house-holds were involved, even small variations in informed estimates, which put the kulak at about 3 to 5 per cent of the village population, had important implications for political and economic policy.[107]

The Left habitually accepted and polemicized on the basis of the higher kulak figure. This was true of the few extremists who anticipated an anti-kulak expropriation, as well as of the mainstream oppositionists who believed that NEP had unleashed a new process of rural differentiation similar to that under capitalism. They fore-saw increasing polarization between rich and poor peasants, the emergence of the exploiting kulak as the dominant force in the village, and a spreading of capitalist relations which would en-danger not only revolutionary gains in the countryside but also in the cities. This was the heart of the Left's repeated contention that NEP, particularly its extension in 1924–5, threatened to bring about a restoration of capitalism.[108]

Not all of the opposition's claims were rejected outright by Bukharin. He agreed that since 1923–4 differentiation had again been under way in the village. But he maintained that the national-ization of the land structurally limited the process of differentiation and that the constraints associated with the state's "commanding heights" guaranteed that the process would not acquire serious dimensions.[109] Also like the Left, though with some qualification, he accepted in theory the crucial dogma that poor and landless peasants, regarded as an agricultural proletariat, were the party's natural rural "support" and the kulak "our enemy." [110] But his treatment of the kulak and, equally important, of the middle peasant, a category which tended to disappear in the Left's analysis of polarization, suggested a very different understanding of village stratification and its implications.

The term "kulak" typified a larger problem faced by Bukharin in trying to adapt existing Bolshevik theory to a reformist program. The lexicon of the ideology—"dictatorship of the proletariat" and "class war" being examples—was provocatively bellicose. Bolshevism's watchwords had been born in the anticipation and conduct of civil strife, and were not easily adaptable to policies based on peace. Most of the radical terminology came from original Marxism, or more properly, French revolutionary history; part, as in the case of the term "kulak," came from Russian tradition. During the party's brief promotion of rural class war in 1918, Lenin had declared a "merciless war" against kulaks, depicting them as "bloodsuckers, vampires, robbers of the people." In his 1922–3 "testament," however, he did not even mention the kulak, recognizing presumably that civil war had reduced the rural population to a largely undifferentiated mass of poverty-stricken peasants.[111] Still, the heinous connotation of kulak lived on, conjured up by the Left to hint darkly that Bukharin proposed a recreant economic collaboration with "bloodsuckers" and "robbers of the people." [112]

Bukharin understood the problem. From 1924 onward, he methodically prefaced his policy statements with somber warnings about a potential "kulak danger" in the party, claiming (justly, it would appear) to have been the first to define this danger and to caution against translating the new policies into a "wager on the kulak," and asserting that he saw the kulak "perfectly well." [113] Behind these strictures, however, he was seeking to reorient the party's thinking on the subject. He seems to have toyed briefly with the idea of arguing that the Soviet kulak was unlike the "old type." Instead, he chose the safer argument that the kulak and well-to-do peasant constituted only "about 3, not more than 3 to 4 per cent" of the total, while at the same time distinguishing between the rapacious "well-to-do innkeeper, village usurer, kulak" and the "strong proprietor who employs some agricultural workers. . . ." The distinction reflected his unwillingness to label every enterprising peasant a kulak.[114]

Most important, however, was his argument that the kulak alone did not represent a serious economic or political threat. While rural capitalists might temporarily flourish, they could do so only alongside the expanding state sector, whose "commanding heights" contained and directed their economic development. For this reason, insisted Bukharin, the advantageous policy of encouraging kulak production was not in itself dangerous. And "in the end, the kulak's grandson will probably thank us for having treated his grandfather this way." [115] The political threat, if misunderstood, was more serious, since it involved whether or not the kulak could exercise influence and leadership over the peasant masses, particularly the middle peasantry. The danger, Bukharin explained, was in direct proportion to rural satisfaction or dissatisfaction with Soviet power. When official malpractices generated widespread dissatisfaction, "the middle peasant sees in the kulak, expressing it patriarchically, a father-benefactor. . . ." Occasional kulak successes in local soviet and cooperative elections were attributable to this kind of middle-peasant disgruntlement, which, if allowed to become a mass phenomenon, would give the kulak hegemony over an "overwhelming majority of the population." [116]

Bukharin was arguing, as he would throughout the twenties, that the party's primary concern should be not the so-called kulak danger but the uncertain sympathies of the middle peasantry. The old militant Bolshevik adage *Kto kogo?* (Who will do in whom?), he said, no longer applied; now it was *Kto s kem?* (Who will be allied with whom?) [117] The party's strategic need to reconcile those peasants who were neither rich nor poor had been emphasized since 1918. But the coming of NEP infused the issue with a new urgency, as evidenced by Lenin's declaration that the middle peasant had become "the central figure of our agriculture." This sociological perspective was the alpha and omega of Bukharin's thinking. His agrarian program, he once remarked, was in part a "wager on the middle peasant." The opposition retorted, not inappropriately, that Bukharinism was "middle-peasant Bolshevism." [118]

In describing the middle peasant as the "most important stratum" and "basic mass," Bukharin wanted to convey three related ideas to the party. The first was sociological: the destruction of landlords and kulaks and the redistribution of land during "our great agrarian revolution" had resulted in the "*middle-peasantization of the countryside*"—the middle peasant had become the majority figure on the land. The second was economic: middle-peasant economics were the backbone of Soviet agriculture. And, finally, a political idea: the allegiance of the middle peasant was the pivotal factor in the contest for hegemony in the countryside. These, Bukharin thought, were empirical observations pointing to an irrefutable conclusion: "the basic line of our policy consists in winning this stratum to the side of Soviet power." [119] In his mind, peasant policy meant policy toward the middle peasantry. And on this equation, he built his theory of socialism and the peasant.

Bukharin saw the middle peasant standing at a historic "crossroads." One led to capitalism (kulak economics), the other to socialism. Opposition spokesmen had implied that middle-peasant undertakings were capitalist, a suggestion Bukharin contested vigorously. In Marxist analysis, he explained, the middle peasant was a "simple commodity producer": "he engages in trade but he does not exploit wage labor." Therefore, he was not a capitalist, but, in class terms, petty bourgeois. Under capitalism, petty bourgeois economies tended to grow into capitalist ones, the simple commodity producer becoming a small capitalist, or, failing that, a proletarian. In Soviet society, however, his future evolution was open, because there existed the possibility of a "noncapitalist path." [120] This unprecedented option was conceivable because, as Bukharin put it, the peasant had "two souls": a "laboring soul," identifying with socialist aspirations, and a "nonlaboring soul," residing in the small owner who "has a certain respect for the large owner." Which soul would prevail depended on the "social-economic context." [121]

It is clear that for Bukharin the middle peasant had become not just the "most important stratum" but a symbol of the peasantry as a class. The ambi-tendency within the middle peasant's "soul" was characteristic of the peasantry generally, "even the laboring peasant." [122] This unorthodox association found reflection in Bukharin's habit of dropping "middle" and speaking of "the peasantry," as, for instance, when he elaborated on the worldwide "struggle for the peasantry's soul." Similarly, neither his analogy with the "landlord-capitalist bloc" nor his contention that the Soviet worker-peasant *smychka* originated in a "combination of proletarian revolution and peasant war" left room for traditional Bolshevik differentiation between peasant strata.

But the clearest evidence of his tendency to think in terms of an undifferentiated village population was his conception of NEP Russia as "basically a two-class society." Despite pro forma references to three classes, the theory of a "two-class society"—a social order based on the "collaboration of two laboring classes"—revealed his underlying understanding of the transition period and its main problems: "the problem of the city and the countryside, industry and agriculture, large and small production, the rational plan and the anarchistic market, and . . . relations between the working class and the peasantry." [123] What each of these dualisms omitted, his opponents quickly pointed out, was any perception of capitalist economies and the "new bourgeoisie," particularly the kulak. Equating the middle peasant with at least the "peasant masses," however, was theoretically indispensable to Bukharin. It explained, for example, his objection to Bolsheviks who urged "neutralization" rather than a "firm alliance" with the middle peasant. This, too, was contrary to Bolshevism's "historic task" of "guaranteeing to every small peasant the possibility of participating in the construction of socialism." [124]

The reverse side of class theory was economic. In Marxist thought, social classes evolved and acted as representatives of different forms of economic activity, each prevalent in different historical societies. Collective labor, epitomized by the industrial factory, was embryonically socialist, while private ownership and individual labor were thought to be incompatible with socialism. Of Bukharin's two "basic classes," the proletariat therefore should have posed no theoretical or organizational problem, since it represented the economic future of socialism. But in 1925, determined to counteract what they regarded as the majority's idealization of NEP, the Zinovievists suddenly inferred that Soviet state industry was not socialist but state capitalist.[125]

Why they chose this self-defeating tactic is something of a mystery. As Bukharin pointed out, the earlier controversy over state capitalism had been "another question *entirely*." It had concerned the presence of large private capital in the Soviet economy and not the nature of nationalized industry, which Lenin described as being of "a consistently socialist type." The opposition apparently failed to perceive the ramifications of its own criticism, because, as Bukharin asked, if state industrial enterprises were state capitalist, "where is our hope?" It would mean that the Bolshevik régime was an "*exploiting* system and not at all a proletarian dictatorship." Were this true, he added with dramatic flourish, "I would quit the party, begin building a new party, and begin propagating a third revolution against the present Soviet power. . . ." [126] From the Bolshevik point of view, his argument was unassailable, because it rested on an assumption crucial to leadership and opposition alike: "speaking in Hegelian language, socialism does not 'exist' here but it 'is becoming,' is *im Werden*, and it already has a strong foundation, our socialist state industry." [127] Bukharin won this exchange easily.

Peasant agriculture was a more troublesome matter. The Bolsheviks had come to power believing in the doctrinal sanctity and economic superiority of large-scale, collective agricultural production. The 1917 revolution, however, had the opposite effect, breaking up large estates and creating millions of new, minuscule peasant holdings. War communism witnessed a brief and unsuccessful campaign for various types of collective farms; but with the coming of NEP, the immediate feasibility of such endeavors on a broad scale was dismissed as another illusion, though the verbal commitment to a future collectivized agriculture continued, most pronouncedly among Left Bolsheviks. After 1921, official disinterest combined with peasant hostility to reduce the amount of land under collective cultivation to around 2 per cent in 1925. That same year, however, in connection with the debates over "building socialism," and with the desire to offset the growth of rural capitalism by establishing a socialist "commanding height" in the countryside, collective farming again came under discussion and found a small group of enthusiastic supporters in the party.[128]

Proponents of the collective farm suffered a resounding (though temporary) defeat, no one contributing to this defeat and the generally "anti-collective farm mood" in the party [129] more than Bukharin. Not all of his remarks were flatly negative. He insisted, for example, that Bolsheviks still believed that large enterprises were "more rational than small ones" in agriculture as well as in industry. And, conceding that "the collective farm is a powerful thing," he held out the prospect that some poor and landless peasants, because of their destitution, would "gravitate" spontaneously toward collective farming. But, he added, even where these lowest strata were concerned, the peasant's traditional proprietary soul—"old habits inherited from grandfathers and fathers"—worked against the acceptability of collective farming. It was therefore "scarcely possible to think that the collective farm movement will capture the *whole* wide mass of poor peasants." [130]

That the movement would have any success whatsoever in the foreseeable future, among Soviet Russia's "basic peasant mass" —the middle peasantry—was unthinkable. This was for Bukharin "an arithmetic truth." Collectivized agriculture was at best a distant prospect, whose eventuality depended on the ability of voluntary, mechanized, self-sustaining collective farms to prove their economic superiority in competition with private farming on the open market. It would be a mistake, he warned, to create collective farms artificially; they would become "parasitic Communist institutions," living off state funds and serving only to reinforce the peasant's conviction "that private economy is a very good thing." [131] Having set out the obvious case against collective farming, Bukharin proceeded to abandon an entrenched Bolshevik assumption: "Collective economics is not the main highway, not the high road, not the chief path by which the peasantry will come to socialism." To emphasize its importance, he restated this pronouncement almost verbatim at four auspicious official gatherings in March and April of 1925, one of them the inaugural conference of collective farmers. [132]

Since state farms were even less attractive to the peasant, Bukharin's declaration meant that socialism in the village would "not begin . . . from the angle of production." [133] Given the Marxist understanding of the decisive role of the mode of production in shaping social relations, this was a novel assertion. How, then, would the peasant come to socialism? Bukharin answered: through "ordinary cooperatives—marketing, buying, credit." Here he was greatly dependent for theoretical legitimacy on Lenin's "original theory of 'agrarian-cooperative' socialism," the "Leninist plan which was bequeathed to us as directives, as a route, as a high road. . . ." [134] For although an official rehabilitation of the cooperatives had been under way since 1921, they remained in the eyes of many Bolsheviks essentially capitalist institutions. To Bukharin, however, they were the key to the peasantry's "noncapitalist evolution," and the "high road to socialism" in the countryside. His program, as he pointed out regularly from 1924 onward, was also "a wager on the cooperatives." [135]

The common wisdom of NEP taught that the proprietary interest of the peasant had to be accommodated. This, according to Bukharin, was the great virtue of cooperatives. They appealed to the peasant "as a small owner" and gave him "immediate benefits":

If it is a credit cooperative, he should receive cheaper credit; if it is a marketing cooperative, he should sell his product more advantageously and emerge from this the gainer. If he wants to buy something, he should do it through his cooperative and . . . receive a better and cheaper commodity.

In pursuing his private interests, the peasant would discover that "it is more advantageous to be organized in cooperatives . . . than to remain outside cooperatives," and would thus become amenable to other collective ventures, including collective farming.[136]

But agricultural cooperatives also performed a higher function in Bukharin's scheme of things. With their "innumerable threads leading to the individual peasant undertakings," they served as "the organized bridge . . . by which state industry is united with the peasant economy." In other words:

> *the intermediate link between the proletarian city and the laboring village is the cooperative*, which stands precisely at the junction where the city and the village meet, embodying first of all the economic *smychka* between the working class and the peasantry. . . .

By their close association with state economic organs, cooperatives provided a means of "linking up," through the market, centralized state industry and millions of scattered peasant economies, and of setting the latter on a socialist course. Calling upon yet another metaphor, Bukharin explained: "Our proletarian steamer, i.e., our state industry, will drag behind it first the cooperative; and the cooperative, which will be a barge heavier than this steamer, will drag behind it by millions of threads the enormous heavy barge of the whole peasantry." [137]

Few Bolshevik sensibilities were seriously offended by the suggestion that market and credit cooperatives, unlike collective farms, could appeal successfully to the peasant. They had done so on a very broad scale before the revolution. More novel, and to many shocking, was Bukharin's contention that the whole "ladder" of these formerly bourgeois (at best, petty bourgeois) institutions would "grow into socialism," that their growth was "the continuous and systematic growth of the cells of the future socialist society." [138] While continuing to profess optimism that "ordinary cooperatives" would one day lead the peasant to collective cultivation, his main point was: "we will come to socialism here through *the process of circulation*, and not directly through the process of production; we will come there through the cooperatives." This, as a Stalinist critic later said, was "the alpha and omega of Bukharin's cooperative plan." [139] It was controversial not only because it seemingly ignored the exalted role of production in Marxist thought, but because of the cooperatives' long association with Russian populist socialism and Western Marxist revisionists.

Bukharin tried to turn the suspect past of the cooperatives to his advantage, arguing as follows: Populists and Marxists who had projected a noncapitalist path for agriculture in the theory of "so-called 'agrarian-cooperative socialism' " were purveyors of "a miserable reformist Utopia" because they had imagined a socialist evolution of cooperatives within the capitalist system. In fact, cooperatives existing alongside and dependent on capitalist banks, industry, and the bourgeois state inescapably "fall under the influence of capitalist economics"; they "gradually become fused to capitalist economic organizations," and finally themselves "are transformed into capitalist enterprises." In short, "they grow into capitalism." Through the same process, however, Soviet cooperatives, functioning within the dictatorship of the proletariat, relying on and connected with socialist industry and banks, inevitably "become part and parcel of the proletarian economic body." "Independent of their will," they must "grow into socialism": "The cooperatives will grow into the system of *our* institutions, just as in capitalist society they grew into the system of *capitalist* relations." Thus agrarian-cooperative socialism "becomes a *reality* under the dictatorship of the proletariat." [140]

Bukharin's theory of NEP as the road to socialism rested heavily on this analogical reasoning. Positing the cooperative as the vehicle of transition, it enabled him to argue that, again paralleling the process in capitalist society, "the small owner inevitably will grow into our state-socialist system. . . ." [141] This theory of "growing in" clearly derived from his decade-old conception of modern state capitalism, in which a dominant state sector absorbs and subordinates smaller and formerly autonomous economic units through a centralized amalgam of bank and finance capital. Indeed, his earlier implicit revision of the Marxist proposition that the productive base of society governs its superstructure was now made explicit in his discussion of the Soviet case. The proletarian state, he reasoned, was "not merely a political superstructure," but, because it included the "economic commanding heights," a "*constituent part of the productive relations* of Soviet society, i.e., a part of the 'base.' " Hence, "the *originality* of the relationship between base and superstructure" in Soviet society: "the 'secondary' (the superstructure) regulates the 'primary' (the base). . . ." [142] This logic underlay Bukharin's argument that the state socialist sector would through natural evolution bring "the seething, unorganized economy under socialist influence." Given the "socialist commanding heights," Soviet petty bourgeois and cooperative economics would evolve along socialist lines. More specifically, it rationalized his insistence that no separate "commanding height" (the collective farm, for example) was required in agriculture: "*the commanding height in the countryside . . . is the city.*" [143]

The essential mechanism in this "growing in" process was the Soviet banking and credit system. The "threads" of financial and credit dependency assured the economic hegemony of the state sector, "knitting" nonsocialist organizations to the socialist sector and creating a " 'community of interests' " between cooperatives and *the credit organs of the proletarian state.*" [144] Faith in the economic omnipotence of the state's bank credit "commanding height" brought Bukharin to his most controversial conclusion: "even the kulak cooperative [credit cooperatives] will grow into our system." Anticipating the objections this idea would provoke, he first broached it tentatively in the spring of 1925. A few weeks later, however, summing up his cooperative theory, he wrote with greater certainty:

the basic network of our cooperative peasant organization will consist of cooperative cells not of a kulak but of a "laboring" type, cells growing into the system of our general state organs and thus becoming *links in a single chain of socialist economy.* On the other hand, the kulak cooperative nests will in exactly the same way, through the banks, etc., grow into this same system; but they will be to a certain extent an alien body. . . . What will become of this type of kulak cooperative in the future? . . . If it wants to prosper, it must inevitably be linked . . . with state economic organs; it . . . will deposit its spare cash in our banks in order to receive a fixed interest. Even if their own banking organizations should arise . . . they unavoidably would have to be linked with the powerful credit institutions of the proletarian state, which have at their disposal the country's basic credit resources. In any event, the kulak and the kulak cooperative will have nowhere to go, for the general pattern of development in our country *has been determined beforehand as the system of the proletarian dictatorship.* . . . [145]

Four years later, this passage would be cited as supreme evidence of Bukharin's heresy.

One important Marxist concept, that of class struggle, remained to be integrated into his theory of the evolutionary road to Soviet socialism. From a vaguely ethereal notion about the exploitative nature of nonsocialist economics, it had been transformed by the events of 1917 to 1920 into a euphemism for civil war. The most Sorelian image in Bolshevik ideology, it pictured society as a battlefield of warring and irreconcilable classes, a divided, strife-ridden arena in which only a single victor could emerge. In the context of the Soviet twenties, class struggle was a potentially explosive *idée fixe*, the antithesis of civil peace. References to its continuing presence and inevitable intensification came naturally and frequently from the Bolshevik Left, particularly its anti-kulak wing. On the other side, Bukharin tried to defuse the dogma by making two revisions in its understanding.

First, he maintained that the advent of Soviet society made possible a new relationship between antagonistic classes: "the dictatorship of the proletariat serves as an envelope for a certain 'collaboration of classes,' which expresses the unity of the social whole. . . ." [146] This proposition combined two of Bukharin's basic ideas. Soviet society (and its economy) was a single entity or a "unity of opposites," a truth he thought the Left did not perceive: "Preobrazhenskii sees the *contradictions* but does not see the *unity* of the national economy, he sees the *struggle* but he does not see the *collaboration*. . . ." Social "unity" implied a significant degree of class harmony or collaboration, which for Bukharin meant that the proletariat and the peasantry were joined in a maximum economic collaboration in which the new bourgeoisie could participate "within limits" to perform a "socially useful function." [147] Thus, economic class collaboration prevailed over, or at least tempered, the disruptive aspects of class struggle.

Collaboration did not mean, Bukharin explained in his second revision, that class struggle had ended in Soviet Russia. Rather, it meant that its previous violent forms—"the mechanical 'knocking out of teeth' "—no longer applied, and that class struggle now expressed itself as "an economic competition" between socialist (state and cooperative) enterprises and capitalist ones. In this "unprecedented and extremely original" process, socialist victory appeared in many guises: in the displacement of private trade through market competition; in providing the peasant with cheaper credit than did the village usurer; and, generally, in winning over the "soul" of the peasantry. In all respects, the new class struggle differed from the old in being "peaceful" and "bloodless"; it was conducted "without the clanging of metal weapons." To war against the private merchant, Bukharin cited as an example, was "not to trample on him and to close his shop, but . . . to produce and to sell cheaper and better . . . than he." Cheaper and better goods, cheaper and larger credit were "the weapons we should bring to . . . our struggle with the exploiting elements in the countryside." [148]

Both revisions were expressed in angry objections to the idea that socialist development presupposed a deepening of class conflict, particularly in the countryside. Conceding that class struggle might intensify sporadically in the near future, Bukharin insisted that progress meant "the class struggle would begin to subside," begin "dying out." Incidents of violent confrontation would not proliferate, but "become ever more rare and finally will disappear without a trace." [149] Above all, he denounced the argument that the party should "kindle the class struggle" rather than seek its "softening." As he declared at a party conference in 1925: "Can it be said that our general line, the Bolshevik line . . . consists in a conscious forcing of the class struggle? I do not think so. . . ." Or, as he said elsewhere: "I am not at all in favor of sharpening the class war in the countryside." [150] In his mind, movement toward socialism presupposed an easing of class conflict.

Rendering the class struggle as a depersonalized competition between economic forms capped Bukharin's evolutionary theory and resolved what seemed to be its internal contradiction. Marxist socialism anticipated a planned marketless economy, but Bukharin's program called for "economic growth *on the basis of market relations.*" [151] To reconcile the two propositions, he again referred analogically to capitalist societies where, through market competition, "*large production finally ousts small, medium capital retreats before larger capital* . . . the number of competitors decreases," and there is "a vanquishing of the market by the market itself, free competition changing into monopoly. . . ." The process would be replicated within the NEP framework. As larger and more efficient socialist units displaced private capitalists from their strongholds in retail and wholesale trade, "we will outgrow the market" and approach a planned economy: "Through the struggle on the market . . . through competition, state and cooperative enterprises will oust their competitor, i.e., private capital. In the end, the development of market relations destroys itself . . . and sooner or later the market itself will die off. . . ." The irony was dialectical: "It turns out that we will come to socialism precisely through market relations. . . ." [152]

Whatever else, Bukharin's theory was optimistic. Within the discouraging economic pluralism of NEP society, it found an "organic evolutionary road" to socialism. The "rails" were laid, no cataclysmic upheaval, no final solution, no "third revolution" was required; even the kulak's fate was cheerfully predetermined. The essential assumption on which this optimism rested was that "ordinary" peasant cooperatives were socialist "cells." Identifying market cooperatives with the socialist sector allowed Bukharin to cite the yearly proportionate increase in state and cooperative trade over private trade as proof of socialism's advance, evidence "that despite the absolute growth of private capital . . . the socialist elements of our economy are growing relatively stronger all the time." [153] The same reasoning promised the spontaneous emergence of economic planning as the socialist sector "keeps increasing its strength and gradually absorbs the backward economic units. . . ." Together these assumptions meant that the mere "growth of productive forces . . . in our conditions is movement toward socialism. . . ." [154]

His theory, in the Bolshevik context, also was new because while embracing revolutionary ideals, it repudiated the prevailing revolutionary-heroic tradition and opted frankly for gradualism and reformism. By these methods rather than previous ones, said Bukharin, "step by step we will overcome all the evil which still exists here." A fundamental alteration in Bolshevik thinking and practice was required. As he put it in 1925: "We now see clearly our road to socialism, which runs not where, or rather, *not quite where* we searched for it earlier." [155] Not only a "new economics" and new theory were needed, but a new politics as well.

In asking the party to travel an evolutionary road in economic policy, Bukharin was also calling for a far-reaching change in Bolshevik political thinking and practice. Economic policies based on social harmony, class collaboration, voluntary performances, and reformist measures were by definition incompatible with the pre-1921 politics of "mechanical repression" and "bloodletting." He summarized the desired changes in domestic politics by declaring that Bolsheviks were no longer "the party of civil war, but the party of civil peace." [156] Insofar as Bukharin articulated a political program in 1924 to 1926, civil peace was its basic plank and constant watchword. He was not, however, advocating fundamental structural changes in the Soviet political system that had emerged by 1921. Above all, he did not question the Bolsheviks' one-party régime. Even a second pro-Soviet party was impermissible. The existence of two parties, he said in a famous quip, suggested that "one must be the ruling party and the other must be in jail." [157] Nor was an alteration in the professed class nature of the régime thinkable. Soviet power was "supported by the muzhik, but it is a proletarian power." The *smychka*—"collaboration in society"—did not mean "collaboration in power." In short, Bukharin's political premise was the virtue and legitimacy of the Bolshevik dictatorship: "first, a necessary alliance between the workers and the peasants . . . second, the leading role in this alliance must belong to the working class; third, the leading role within the working class . . . must belong to the Communist Party." [158]

Like other Bolsheviks and most modernizers who followed, Bukharin was not a democrat in a recognizable Western sense. Indeed, despite his wish to extend the franchise gradually, and (if unconfirmed reports can be believed) his preference for some kind of bill of rights protecting Soviet citizens against state abuse, he accepted the existing prophylactic provisions of the 1922 Soviet constitution, which, in addition to excluding "bourgeois" segments from political life, favored the minority urban proletariat to the disadvantage of the peasantry.[159] As would be true of other twentieth-century modernizers, democracy was for him first an economic concept; democratization meant "drawing the masses into socialist construction." He never publicly challenged the Bolshevik dogma that the "dictatorship of the proletariat is at the same time the broadest democracy." [160]

Nonetheless, under the slogan of civil peace, Bukharin was proposing far-reaching changes in Soviet political life. Most important, the state was no longer to be chiefly "an instrument of repression." Instead, it was to promote the peaceful conditions necessary for "collaboration" and "social unity," finding breathing room and toleration for the many unwilling but pacific fellow travelers of the revolution, its "semi-friends and semi-enemies." Only incorrigible protagonists of the old order (and Bukharin seemed to see few) would encounter the mailed fist of the state. For the rest of the population, the state was devoted to "peaceful organizational work." As for terror, "its time has passed." [161]

This formulation of the state's new "function" rested partly on Bukharin's evaluation of the political situation in the Soviet Union after 1924. His prognosis differed notably from that of the Bolshevik Left and, in retrospect, dramatically from that officially proffered during the Stalin era, when class struggle and conspiracy were said to be intensifying murderously. Convinced that the party had broken out of its dangerous isolation of 1921–2 and recaptured popular confidence, Bukharin claimed modestly in 1925 that "generally the majority of the population is not against us," and more positively: "the peasantry was never so friendly . . . as it is today." His essential political argument, however, was that the revolution's internal enemies had disappeared or been disarmed: "All is 'peaceful'; there are no uprisings, no counter-revolutionary acts, no conspiracies in the country." [162] Moreover, he argued, occasional acts of violence against Soviet officials were due, not to intrinsic anti-

Bolshevik sentiment, but to defects in Soviet officialdom itself. Episodes of peasant violence, for example, were provoked by "lower agents of power"—"little Shchedrin heroes"—who abused power in a fashion reminiscent of czarist satraps.[163]

Throughout the twenties, Bukharin never wavered in his conviction that the main organized forces of counter-revolution in Soviet Russia were dead. He was saying in effect that objective conditions for lasting civil peace were at hand, and that the party-state should adjust its practices accordingly. He called this adjustment "*forced 'normalization'* of the Soviet régime,"[164] by which he meant that "revolutionary legality" was no longer to be a euphemism for "administrative arbitrariness" and official "lawlessness." These persistent "remnants of war communism" were to yield to "firm legal norms": local party and Komsomol organs were to stop issuing decrees—lawmaking was the prerogative of the Soviets alone; Communists were to lose their *de facto* "immunity" from prosecution and were to act lawfully, not "outside the law." Revolutionary legality meant "introducing revolutionary order where earlier there was chaos." The noun, not the adjective, was to be operative: "*Revolutionary legality* should replace all remnants of administrative arbitrariness, even if the latter should be revolutionary."[165] Bukharin was thinking primarily of the countryside: "The peasant must have before him Soviet *order*, Soviet *right*, Soviet *law*, and not Soviet arbitrariness, moderated by a 'bureau of complaints' whose whereabouts is unknown."[166]

In addition to developing from a "military proletarian dictatorship" characterized by command, coercion, and official caprice to a "normalized" one-party system based on law and order, Bukharin demanded a "decisive, full, and unconditional transition to the methods of persuasion." The party was to abandon force as its *modus operandi* and henceforth "stand for persuasion and only for persuasion" in dealing with the masses.[167] No theme better reflected Bukharin's political thinking and his reformism. In addition to industrialization, social revolution involved educating and remaking people, undertakings that required a new kind of political leadership which, for Bukharin, was pedagogical. Addressing party and particularly Komsomol activists, who outnumbered their elder comrades in the countryside and therefore often represented the party in the village, he explained that "the task of political leadership is in the broadest sense of the word . . . a social pedagogical task."[168] If the new economics was evolutionary, the new politics was pedagogical—paternalistic, benevolent, and gentle.

In a real sense, this expressed Bukharin's understanding of the

Soviet constitutional order as a whole. He viewed the nationwide pyramid of soviets as a grassroots teaching "laboratory"; upper levels were to be dominated by party members, assuring "secure proletarian leadership from above"; lower levels (village soviets mainly), however, were to be populated increasingly by "nonparty masses," because local soviets constituted "the laboratory in which we convert the peasants, overcome their individualist psychology, win them over, teach them to work in harmony with us, educate and lead them along the . . . socialist road." [169]

But to be effective, local soviets, which (Bukharin lamented) had "died off" during the party's military régime of 1918 to 1921, had to be resuscitated, again becoming popularly elected, functioning bodies—"small laboring 'parliaments' " where the awakening peasant could find political satisfaction and guidance.[170] Bukharin was therefore an enthusiastic advocate of the party's 1924–6 campaign to "revitalize the soviets" through new and freer elections. That fewer party members were elected did not trouble him. He interpreted the results as confirming the virtues of "ideological persuasion" over "administrative pressure," reasoning that one genuinely elected Bolshevik enjoyed real support, while ten who had been "fictionally elected . . . had no authority among the population." [171]

Bukharin's faith in political and ideological persuasion was closely related to his emphasis on competition in the economic arena. Both bespoke his certainty that within the pluralism of NEP society, Bolshevik goals—economic, political, and ideological— were advanced best through peaceful, nonadministrative methods of "bloodless struggle." Indeed, he had come to see the principle of competition between socialist and nonsocialist tendencies as a valuable "molecular process," guaranteeing that Bolshevik gains would not be the artifices and false victories of monopolism. The depth and inclusiveness of his commitment to the competitive principle may be judged from Bukharin's stand in a 1924–5 controversy over party policy in literature, an issue seemingly far removed from coping with private capital and winning local elections.

The party had avoided legislating in literary matters for seven years. But, with the flowering of a diverse and popular "nonrevolutionary" belles-lettres after 1921, Bolshevik partisans of proletarian literature began calling for a *dictatorship of the party* in the field of literature," with their writers' organization, known as VAPP, as its "instrument." They sought official favor for themselves and war against literary fellow travelers. After months of discussion, their demands were rejected by the leadership in a Central Committee resolution dated July 1, 1925. Written by Bukharin and embodying his opinions, the resolution repudiated systematic party intervention in literature, endorsed the principle of literary diversity, and guaranteed the protection and encouragement of nonparty writers.[172] What made Bukharin's position interesting was his long and continuing association with the idea of a separate "proletarian culture," of which he was the only Politburo sponsor. Though the catholicity of his own cultural tastes and attitudes was well known, he occupied a radical position on "proletarian culture," eagerly welcoming a "proletarian" novel or theatrical production as "a first swallow." [173]

Despite his theoretical sympathies for proletarian culture, however, Bukharin vigorously opposed the suggestion that a new literature could be achieved by "methods of mechanical coercion" and official favoritism. "If we . . . stand for a literature which should be regulated by the state . . . then . . . by this we shall destroy proletarian literature." Proletarian writers had to "win literary authority for themselves" by relying on "the principle of free, anarchistic competition" with other movements. While the party offered guidance, its role was not to curtail competition but to encourage "maximum competition"; to foster "multi-varied groups, and the more there will be, the better." Declared Bukharin: "Let there be 1,000 organizations, 2,000 organizations; let there be alongside MAPP and VAPP as many circles and organizations as you like." [174]

Though the literary dispute did not relate or correspond to political divisions inside the party, Bukharin saw identical principles at stake. The claimants of VAPP, he said, stood for "the monopolistic principle" and thus occupied "in literary policy the place occupied by Preobrazhenskii in economic policy." And just as the "super-monopoly" principle in economics invited industrial and agricultural ruin, so was monopolism "the best way to destroy proletarian literature." While advocating a well-defined party orientation "in all areas of ideological and scientific life, even in mathematics," Bukharin nowhere favored "taking to the cannon" or "stifling" rival tendencies. Nowhere was the party "to squeeze everybody into one fist"; everywhere it was "to make possible competition." As with recalcitrant peasants, Bolsheviks were to woo nonproletarian writers, not "bludgeon them senseless" or "clutch them in a vise." [175] Here, as in other areas of domestic policy, he preached progress through diversity, persuasion, and peaceful competition, and against the false gains of political repression.

This emphasis on civil peace, legality, official constraint and toleration, and persuasion (all the strictures Bukharin gathered under the heading of "normalization") represented a dramatic turnabout from his 1920 eulogy of "proletarian coercion in all of its forms." Clearly, his new political thinking was strongly influenced by his economic program. Growth based on market relations, on transforming the peasant into an efficient market producer and consumer, was incompatible with governmental caprice, which, he argued repeatedly, "stood in full contradiction to the needs of economic development and developing the peasant economy." The peasant, who was being asked to farm rationally, could no longer be subjected to old practices, "when today we took one tax, tomorrow another, when today we issued one decree, tomorrow another"; the "development of commodity exchange is possible only with the eradication of the remnants of war communism in administrative-political work." Bolsheviks had to understand, insisted Bukharin, that "arbitrary . . . interference in the course of economic life can have an extraordinarily sad effect on this economic life." [176]

But something more lay behind his new political thinking. Again, it was his concern about the potential tyranny latent in the Bolsheviks' one-party system. His manifold warnings against official "arbitrariness" (proizvol) provides the key. Proizvol, as the image of czarist officialdom willfully running roughshod over peasant Russia, had been a persistent theme of nineteenth-century Russian radical thought. It served Bukharin both as reminder and foreboding.[177] He equated proizvol with "remnants of war communism"; with party officials acting as if they had "some kind of absolute immunity"; with the psychology of "I can do what I please"; with the arrogant "Communist conceit" of Bolsheviks "who say we are the salt of the earth"; and with the attitude that party rule meant "being rude to everyone who is not a member of the All-Union Communist Party or the Communist Union of Youth." [178] Within the limits of his commitment to the party's dictatorship, Bukharin perceived the dangers inherent in political monopoly, fearing a new despotism of institutionalized proizvol.

The fear was related, as we have seen, to his ethical understanding of Bolshevism, but also to his distinction between evil "bureaucratism" and bureaucracy as an organizational necessity. Proizvol or official caprice was for him the psychology and modus *operandi* of bureaucracy as Lenin had condemned it in *State and Revolution*, an officialdom "alienated from the masses." In the twenties, it was the threat of what he had called "a new state of *chinovniki*" ruling by "false mandates." It was the specter of a "new class." When the Left spoke of Bolshevism's possible degeneration, they pointed to "petty bourgeois influences" or to the regimentation of party life. Bukharin also worried about the latter; but for him it was the *proizvol* of Bolshevik officialdom that truly portended the movement's degeneration:

For our whole party and for the whole country, the remnants of arbitrariness on the part of any Communist groups present one of the major possibilities of real degeneration. When for a group of Communists no law is written, when a Communist can . . . "arrange things," when no one can arrest or prosecute him if he commits any crime, when he is still able to escape revolutionary legality through various channels— this is one of the largest bases of the possibility of our degeneration.[179]

Bukharin knew that warning against abuse of power was not enough. Insofar as he had a safeguard, it was still promoting independent "voluntary organizations" to fill the "vacuum" between the party-state and the people. From cooperative and literary societies to chess clubs and temperance leagues, these "subsidiary organizations" collectively were to provide "direct links with the masses," foster "mass initiative at lower levels," open "channels" through which popular opinion could influence the government and, when necessary, through which the whole population could be mobilized around the government.[180] Bukharin apparently hoped that thousands of such "associations of people," beyond safeguarding against a new bureaucratic tyranny, would repair the "degeneration of social fabric" witnessed in 1917–21, bind the fragmented nation into a unified society, and broaden and solidify the popular basis of the Bolshevik dictatorship.[181]

Believing in "voluntary organizations" as the "small pieces" of Soviet democracy, he was especially concerned, for economic reasons as well, that cooperatives be truly voluntary and elective societies, not mere replicas of state institutions.[182] His personal favorite, however, was the nascent organization of worker and village correspondents, amateur journalists who contributed reportage about their places of labor to local and central newspapers, and who numbered over 189,000 in 1925. Operating under the auspices of *Pravda*, the movement was the recipient of Bukharin's special interest and influence. For five years, he waged an uphill battle against moves to transform the worker correspondents into a "stratum of *chinovniki*." Conceding that they should be more than only "a gramophone, a reflector of what is happening below," he nonetheless insisted that to "bureaucratize" them would undermine their "basic job" as "antennae" transmitting popular moods and dissatisfactions to the government, and their essential freedom to criticize officialdom.[183] Stalinist opponents would later charge that this typified Bukharin's "opportunistic" philosophy of bowing to the "backwardness and dissatisfaction" of the masses. To this, and to the bureaucratization of Soviet society then underway, Bukharin would again respond with the slogan: *"all possible associations of workers, avoiding by all means their bureaucratization."* [184]

In many respects, Bukharin's political thinking mirrored the social reality of NEP society. Believing in the one-party system, he hoped for Bolshevik "hegemony" in economic, cultural, and ideological life; but he was also tolerant of, and even applauded, the pluralism that characterized these areas during the NEP years. Sensitive to auguries of a "New Leviathan," alarmed in retrospect by the excesses of war communism, he opposed making the dictatorship's "basic organizations" omnipresent and omnipotent, and transforming all other social institutions into "organizational fists." [185] No longer a proponent of "statization," he was a most un-"totalitarian" Bolshevik. His faith in a leadership that was consensual and pedagogical rather than imperious, in "comradely persuasion" rather than force, and in social harmony spoke of a society that was both weary of civil strife and predominantly illiterate. His more sympathetic opponents sometimes suggested that Bukharin was wrong because he offered gentle solutions to the harsh problems of industrialization and modernization. This charge would be raised again in 1928-9, when he found himself leader of the right opposition. It was not without insight, echoing, after all, the prophecy of Matthew: "And he shall set the sheep on his right hand, but the goats on the left."

By the middle of 1926, Bukharin had set out his revised doctrine of Bolshevism. It was, as befitted an official Marxist theorist, comprehensive. He had projected an economic and a political program and related both theoretically to the "broad, general, strategic purpose" of building socialism in NEP Russia.[186] Assuming the party wished to pursue peaceful, evolutionary development, Bukharin's theoretical achievements were considerable. Most generally and importantly, he had reconciled in theory the two revolutions of 1917. By presenting the anti-landlord agrarian revolution as part of "our revolution," and the dual upheaval of 1917 as the fortuitous origin of a victorious "worker-peasant *smychka*," he had laid to ideological rest the specter of a third revolution, either as peasant or "proletarian nemesis." [187] If nothing else, his argument that anti-peasantism was politically, economically, and ethically alien to Bolshevism's "historic task"—"a song from an entirely different opera" [188]—gave Bolsheviks a way to reconcile their unexpected role as modernizers with their socialist ideals.

The campaign to enshrine his new theory as party orthodoxy, however, was certain to encounter resistance, even among non-oppositionists. The revolutionary-heroic tradition was still alive, its sympathizers more widespread than the numerically small Left. Many rural officials had been educated in the spirit of war communism, and some remained hostile to the new agrarian policies and skeptical of Bukharin's claim that NEP was not "a departure from glorious revolutionary traditions." [189] In addition, much of his theorizing—from his treatment of market cooperatives to his concept of organic evolutionism—recalled the heresies of social democratic reformism, while his rendering of the *smychka*, of workers and peasants as comradely "toilers," impressed some as an unholy lapse into Russian populism (*narodism*). Though always critical of populist thought and never echoing its idealization of village life, Bukharin was trying to adapt urban Marxism to Russia's peasant reality, and thus inevitably sounded pre-Marxist themes. That he had perceived the peasantry's role as a revolutionary destructive force in the twentieth century did not eliminate the ideological suspicion shrouding his ideas nor the charge that he espoused a "Communist *narodism*." [190]

In the end, however, Bukharin's doctrine had to stand or fall not on its ideological acceptability but its economic practicability. His program called for industrialization through the broadening and intensification of commodity exchange between state industry and peasant agriculture. A steady increase in peasant demand for industry's goods was to assure grain surpluses and spur continuous industrial growth. Here, at both ends of the "economic *smychka*," his assumptions were open to serious question.

Led by Preobrazhenskii, the Left quickly pinpointed the essential weak spot in his industrial program, accusing him of a delusive "restoration ideology." [191] While a program of encouraging consumer demand to stimulate industrial output may have sufficed during the period of industrial recovery, which had started in 1921 and was drawing to a close in 1926, the Left argued that it was totally unsuitable for the ensuing period, when the existing industrial plant would be operating at full capacity, and when expansion and technological retooling of fixed capital ("reconstruction") would become the central problem. As the relatively cheap costs of recovery were exhausted, the hard problem of new investment could no longer be avoided. In focusing on demand, his critics charged, Bukharin was chasing a deadly chimera. The consumption and depreciation of fixed capital in 1914–21, coupled with the fact that the revolution had freed peasants from their heavy financial obligations and enabled them to put greater demands on Soviet industry, meant that industry's structural inability to meet consumer demand was the real malady, not a weak internal market. Until industry was reconstructed, no equilibrium between supply and demand was possible. Instead, there would be a chronic industrial "goods famine." [192]

The Left's critique was clearly valid in important respects. Bukharin had projected a long-term program on the basis of short-term industrial successes. Dazzled by the "stormy economic growth" of 1923–6, when industrial output increased one year by 60 per cent and the next by 40, he anticipated "enormous perspectives for unleashing industry." That his strategy involved reactivating existing facilities rather than creating new ones was evident: "The whole art of economic policy consists in forcing into motion ('mobilizing') the factors of production which are lying hidden as 'unemployed capital.' " [193] Although 75 per cent of industry's "unemployed capital" was "in motion" by 1925, it was not until March 1926 that Bukharin began to worry publicly about "additional capital." He was virtually silent on the mild goods famine of 1925, until February 1926, when he dismissed it as a "spasm of our economic development." [194] His disinclination to envisage a radical and immediate expansion of industry was also obvious in secondary ways. Bolsheviks understood, for example, that the source of their mounting urban unemployment was rural overpopulation. Preobrazhenskii's solution was new industry to absorb the migration to the city; Bukharin's was to generate new agricultural employment in the countryside. [195]

His thinking about agriculture was also vulnerable. Bukharin's assumption that whetting peasant consumer appetites and commercializing the peasant economy would generate grain sufficient to feed the cities and support industrialization obscured the inherent backwardness and low productivity of Russian agriculture, the primitive, fragmented nature of which had been worsened by the revolutionary breaking up of large surplus-producing estates and kulak farms in 1917–18. Two solutions were possible. One was to allow private consolidation of land and the formation of a rural capitalist sector capable of high productivity. To Bukharin, as to most Bolsheviks, this "kulak solution" was ideologically un-acceptable.[196] While wanting to spike the kulak bogey, his tolera-tion of kulak farming did not include condoning land consolida-tion or the emergence of a rural bourgeoisie. In telling peasants to "enrich yourselves," he was hoping for a uniformly prosperous, middle-peasant countryside, probably a delusive proposal. An alternative solution was the creation of larger, productive collective or state farms. But consistent with his negative attitude in 1924–6, the period of Bukharin's greatest influence witnessed an official neglect and decline of all forms of collective cultivation.[197]

Even if Soviet agriculture regained its pre-revolutionary pro-ductivity, there still remained the problem of marketed produce. The leveling of the countryside had reinforced the self-sufficiency of the peasant economy, and the abolition of the peasant's arrears had given him greater freedom in deciding how much and what to produce and market.[198] Bukharin hoped that favorable prices and an abundance of cheap industrial goods would entice a steady in-crease in marketed surplus, a prospect constantly jeopardized by the threat of goods famine. If shortcomings in his industrial pro-gram imperiled his agricultural program, the reverse was also true. The first omens appeared in 1925, when, despite a good harvest, grain collections fell considerably below official expectations, seriously impairing the government's export-import schedule.[199]

All of which is to say that Bukharin's economic thinking in 1924–6 underemphasized the need for state intervention in both industrial and agricultural production.[200] Instead of planned capital investment, he urged lower industrial costs and prices; instead of pointing toward the eventual creation of a supplementary, collec-tive grain sector, he depended wholly on the "collaboration" of the small peasant. In each instance, he minimized the interventionist capabilities of the state's "commanding heights," relying instead on the spontaneous functioning of the market. Throughout 1924–6, he posed what were essentially market goals, such as displacing private traders and speeding up commodity exchange. These goals were often achieved, but the country's productive capacity was left untouched.

This orientation underlay other difficulties associated with Bukharin's policies. His thinking on the rate and pattern of indus-trial growth also reflected the recovery period, when output surged forward dramatically and light industry was left to spur heavy. But, while speaking of a "snail's pace" movement toward socialism, and once arguing that "a slow tempo" need not be "a fatal danger," [201] Bukharin, like the Left, strongly desired "a very rapid tempo," and one that would not permit heavy industry to "lag behind." Finally, to many Bolsheviks his policies seemed to deprive the party of its industrializing initiative and to place it in the suspect hands of the peasant or the foreign market. For this reason, a rankling feeling of political impotence combined with economic objections to generate opposition to his program.

Why did Bukharin linger with important misconceptions and remain stubbornly indifferent to the Left's analysis? Certainly, he was misled by the government's dramatic successes during the period of economic recovery. In addition, certain that the opposition's policies meant political disaster, and himself engaged in a bitter struggle inside the party, he closed his mind to valid criticism and, like his opponents, grew more convinced that his policies—and only his policies—were wise. More than anything, however, his ethical understanding of Bolshevism's "historic task" seems to have been responsible. It wed him to the proposition that mass consumption would be the driving force of Soviet industrialization. This perspective occasionally served Bukharin well, alerting him, for example, to the dangers inherent in political and economic monopoly. But it also misled him. Outraged by Preobrazhenskii's "lunatic Utopia," that would feed industry by exploiting the peasantry, he indulged in moral sloganizing when hard-headed reasoning was needed. To the Left's call for higher industrial prices, he retorted: "our industry must give the village economy cheaper products than did the capitalists." [202] However gratifying morally, this did not answer Preobrazhenskii. At its worst, the ethical understanding led Bukharin to imagine the impossible: industrialization without scarcity or terrible burdens—a painless road to modernity.

Whatever the reason, his original economic program was already in trouble by 1926, the year industrial recovery drew to a close. Within months, he would begin to rethink and revise his policies,[203] though his revised thinking would remain faithful to the general theoretical, political, and ethical arguments he had set out in 1924–26. Then, as before, politics as well as economic conditions would influence his proposals, if only because Bukharin and his ideas were now at the center of a political storm.

CHAPTER VII

The Duumvirate:
Bukharin as Co-Leader

*I now see, comrades, that Comrade Stalin has
become a total prisoner of this political line, the
creator and genuine representative of which is
Comrade Bukharin.*

— LEV KAMENEV, 1925

We stand, and we shall stand, for Bukharin.

— IOSIF STALIN, 1925

IN THE FIRST HALF OF 1925, at the age of thirty-three, Bukharin
gradually joined with Stalin in a new leadership of the Central
Committee majority, and entered upon the period of his greatest
influence on Soviet policy. Their coalition originated in the dissolu-
tion of the anti-Trotsky triumvirate, which began to disintegrate
in late 1924 and collapsed in 1925, when Zinoviev and Kamenev,
first covertly, then openly, challenged Stalin's management of the
party apparatus and Bukharin's ideological and policy formulations.[1]

The logic of the new duumvirate was arithmetical. Seven
full members sat on the Politburo in 1925: Trotsky, Zinoviev,
Kamenev, Stalin, Rykov, Tomskii, and Bukharin, who had risen to
full membership upon Lenin's death. The first three were now
opposed to official policies, though they did not unite until the
spring of 1926. Rykov and Tomskii were in general agreement
with those policies, of which Bukharin was the main spokesman.
By joining with Bukharin, Stalin reconstructed a Politburo majority
of four (with Trotsky temporarily in sullen abstention) against his
former allies, Zinoviev and Kamenev. In turn, Bukharin secured

an official majority for those policies in which he fervently believed. Again disclaiming any personal antagonisms, he commented indirectly on the origins and nature of the duumvirate: "people must struggle for a majority if they want to guarantee the execution of their policies, which they consider to be correct." [2]

As this suggests, coalition—or, in the terminology of the twenties, "bloc"—best describes the Politburo majority led by Stalin and Bukharin. It was a conditional alliance of convenience between different "groupings," not a single group of wholly likeminded oligarchs.[3] Like the former triumvirate and later the united left opposition of Trotsky, Zinoviev, and Kamenev, the Stalin-Bukharin majority was held together as much by fear of common foes as by shared views. On this basis, despite signs of internal strains, the coalition survived its inaugural contest in 1925, as well as the bitter factional controversies of 1926–7, which eventually encompassed almost every issue of domestic and foreign policy. Then, after the organizational destruction of the Left at the Fifteenth Party Congress in December 1927, it fell apart.

What Stalin brought to the coalition was organizational power. Since becoming head of the party Secretariat, or general secretary, in 1922, he had assiduously and skillfully cultivated the far-reaching powers of the central party machinery. He did not yet control the entire party, which in the mid-twenties frequently resembled a federation of "principalities" dominated by baronial leaders.[4] But through his powers of secretarial appointment and removal, Stalin had already laid the foundations of what defeated oppositionists, one after the other, would decry as "the dictatorship of the Secretariat." [5] The central party bureaucracy gave him the most formidable power base of any contending oligarch; through it he built and manipulated loyalist voting strength in lower party organizations, in the Central Committee, at party congresses, and eventually on the Politburo itself.

Stalin's machine power was demonstrated at the Fourteenth Party Congress in December 1925. Zinoviev and Kamenev, their strength based in what the former believed was his "impregnable" Leningrad "fortress," rose at the congress to oppose the duumvirate's policies and leadership. They were crushed, 559 congressional votes to 65. Within the week, representatives of the victorious leadership swept into Leningrad, deposing Zinoviev's supporters and establishing the "loyalty" of the Leningrad party.[6] Stalin had put down the first major challenge to Bukharin's policies. In the process, he had extended the Secretariat's influence over another "principality." This set the pattern for the next three years.

Bukharin's role in the coalition was more complex but equally important, at least at the outset. First and foremost, he developed and articulated the general economic policies and ideology of the leadership between 1925 and 1927. His leading part in the decision to expand NEP was no secret; he referred to it and to his ideological initiatives openly. He not only inspired the industrial and agrarian philosophy of the majority, but personally wrote the "principal parts" of the controversial 1925 resolutions on agricultural policy.[7] His theoretical propositions on the disputed issues of the day—peasant strata and rural social development, the nature of state industry and its proper relationship with agriculture, market cooperatives, NEP as a transitional system, and other questions related to "building socialism"—constituted the professed ideology of the duumvirate, and hence of the party. Official Bolshevism in 1925–7 was largely Bukharinist; the party was following Bukharin's road to socialism.[8] Nor was his influence limited to the Soviet party and internal affairs. He systematically wrote his theories into the resolutions of the Comintern, as for example at the meeting of its Executive Committee in April 1925, where he presented sixty-three new "Theses on the Peasant Question." [9] From 1926 onward, he, almost alone, shaped official Bolshevik understanding of the outside world, of international capitalism and revolution.

There was, generally speaking, a rough division of labor between Bukharin and Stalin, between policy formulation and theory on one side and organizational muscle on the other.[10] Stalin, of course, was neither ignorant of nor indifferent to policy or theory. Always the cautious politician, he disassociated himself from his ally's occasional indiscretions, most notably the "enrich yourselves" slogan. Sensitive to the political vulnerability of some of Bukharin's theories, he was careful not to identify with him on interpretations where Lenin's legacy was particularly uncertain.[11] But while Stalin sometimes eulogized industrialism (especially heavy industry) and the virtues of Soviet economic autarky more than did Bukharin, he did not seem to harbor a separate industrial or agrarian program. From the initial elaboration of Bukharin's program in 1924–6, through its revision in 1926–7, Stalin was a Bukharinist in economic policy.[12] With those policies under fierce attack at the Fourteenth Congress in 1925, he declared: "we stand, and we shall stand, for Bukharin." Of this the opposition had no doubt. Said Kamenev at the same congress: "I now see, comrades, that Comrade Stalin has become a total prisoner of this political line, the creator and genuine representative of which is Comrade Bukharin." [13]

Bukharin also contributed more practical political assets to the duumvirate. The most important was his control of the party's central publications. To his editorship of the daily *Pravda* was added in April 1924 the Central Committee's new biweekly journal, *Bolshevik*, whose announced purpose was "the defense and strengthening of historical Bolshevism against any attempts at distorting and perverting its foundations." [14] Control of the Central Committee's two principal organs of opinion gave Bukharin an important weapon in the factional struggle, as evidenced by Zinoviev's futile campaign to establish rival publications in Leningrad in 1925, and by Stalin's all-out effort to take them from Bukharin in 1928. [15] Through *Pravda* and *Bolshevik*, Bukharin reigned over a far-flung press and propaganda empire. Both published under their auspices a variety of other widely circulated periodicals, newspapers, and pamphlets, while Bukharin sat also on the editorial boards of numerous other journals, encyclopedias, and publishing houses. Most important politically, the local party press took its editorial lead and often its articles directly from *Pravda*. [16] In the 1920's, the central organs were more than the authoritative channels of party communication. Their responsibility for interpreting party resolutions inevitably gave them a significant role in the ultimate formation and implementation of policy. Kamenev exaggerated only slightly when he complained that Bukharin and his followers (who staffed the publications) exercised a "factual monopoly over the political-literary representation of the party" and over "all political educational work." [17]

Bukharin's other institutional post represented a different kind of political asset. He and Zinoviev had co-managed the workings, policy, and doctrine of the Comintern since 1923. Although Zinoviev lingered on formally as chairman until October 1926, his defeat in December 1925 soon made Bukharin the actual authority in the international organization. Upon Zinoviev's formal dismissal, Bukharin became general secretary of the Executive Committee and thus the *de jure* head as well (the chairmanship having been abolished). [18] The post added nothing to the duumvirate's organizational power within the Soviet party; but because both the majority and the opposition still valued the sympathies of foreign Communist parties, leadership of the Comintern had its advantages. It enhanced Bukharin's personal prestige as well as the prestige and authority of the duumvirate. It also expanded his sphere of influence, enabling him to place his Soviet followers in the Political Secretariat of the Executive Committee of the Comintern and advance his foreign sympathizers.[19] Throughout the party debates, particularly when discussion turned to foreign policy in 1926–7, the Comintern provided Bukharin with another official platform.

These domains, the central organs and the Comintern, were Bukharin's "principalities." They corresponded to his general role in the majority's struggle against the opposition: while Stalin conducted the organizational war, Bukharin waged the ideological war, his ideas and counter-arguments composing the substance of the leadership's attack and defense. As an ideological warrior, he was indispensable during the early stages of the duumvirate. Neither Stalin nor his personal followers were a match for the luminaries of the opposition, which had in Trotsky, Kamenev, Preobrazhenskii, Piatakov, Smirnov, Smilga, and Radek dexterous theorists, talented economists, and eloquent publicists. All were men of ideas and wit, gifted and comfortable in public debate and ideological combat.

Whenever the debates settled on a reasonably elevated intellectual plane, only Bukharin among high majority leaders was their equal (though Rykov was good at practical economics). His acknowledged theoretical acumen and erudition, his "oratory art," and his sometimes abused skills as a "merciless polemicist" [20] gave the majority an eminent spokesman capable of coping with the oppositionists. It was Bukharin who answered Preobrazhenskii; he who at the Fourteenth Party Congress wrecked Zinoviev's belated attempt to gain stature as a Bolshevik theorist and virtually destroyed whatever ideological authority that fading figure may have had; and it was he who journeyed to proletarian Leningrad in February 1926 to defend the leadership's peasant policies.[21] In one sense, the programmatic debates of the twenties were a prolonged political campaign: significant battles, though perhaps not the decisive ones, were won and lost on the hustings. Bukharin did not always win these confrontations; but when the majority could claim a respectable intellectual victory, the achievement was largely his.

Ideological warfare, like any other, however, requires legions as well as field marshals. And it was in these legions, in the young party intellectuals of what became known as the "Bukharin school," that Bukharin had his most unique and controversial political instrument. The school was catapulted onto the center of the political stage in 1925, amidst a cascade of denunciation. Labeled variously as the rising incarnation of "petty bourgeois decay," a "kulak deviation," and "a *Narodnik* spirit," the school, together with Bukharin, became the opposition's chief villain at the Fourteenth Congress.[22] Complaining that its representatives controlled the "entire press" and sought "to terrorize anybody who points out their distortions and perversions of . . . Leninism," Zinoviev and Kamenev charged: "around Bukharin there is now forming a whole 'school,' which endeavors to conceal reality and to retreat from the class point of view." Indeed, concluded Kamenev, the "school is founded on deviations from Lenin." Krupskaya, temporarily a supporter of the two former triumvirs, saw a long-term danger: "the Red Professorate grouped around Comrade Bukharin is a succession which is being prepared, a training of the theorists who will determine our line."[23] Henceforth, similar accusations against "the theoretical school under Bukharin's patronage" were rarely absent from the Left's account of official perfidy. They would be repeated and embellished by Stalin in 1928–9.[24]

The subject of this anxiety was a small band of young party ideologists, most of them graduates of the Institute of Red Professors, who regarded Bukharin as their intellectual and political mentor and themselves as his disciples. Though they became politically controversial only in 1925, the existence of Bukharin's "neophytes" had been noted as early as 1922.[25] The presence of young Bolsheviks around a Politburo member was not in itself unusual. Most major leaders—Trotsky, Zinoviev, and Stalin, for example—employed a few young party members to staff their personal secretariats and serve as aides. (Comparable arrangements exist in all political systems.) These secretaries, as they were usually called, were frequently recruited from the leader's special area of responsibility. Thus, Bukharin's own personal secretariat was headed by Efim Tseitlin, a founder and one-time national leader of the Komsomol.[26] But what distinguished the men of the Bukharin school from an ordinary entourage of aides (in addition to their number) was their education in higher party institutions, their sought-after intellectual and literary abilities, their common ideological identity, and the political role they came to play. This role derived from the fact that while they sometimes served as personal aides to Bukharin, they performed mainly and increasingly in official positions.[27]

There seem to have been three reasons why so many able young Bolsheviks clustered around Bukharin. First was his unrivaled fame as a Marxist thinker; he was to them a "theoretical

Hercules," an idol.[28] Second, and closely related, was Bukharin's "tremendous authority" among party youth, especially those chosen for advanced preparation as future Bolshevik intellectuals. For several years, he had been the Politburo member most closely associated with Komsomol affairs, quipping in 1923: "I ask you not to think that this has become my speciality or profession." [29] In addition, "hundreds of thousands of people" were being educated on the basis of his writings, such as *Historical Materialism*. He was therefore particularly admired and influential, as both a Marxist thinker and political leader, in the party's educational institutions.[30]

Nowhere was this more true than in the Institute of Red Professors, one of the great Marxist intellectual centers of the Soviet twenties. Offering three-year graduate programs in economics, history, and philosophy, the Institute was established in 1921 with the purpose of producing "Red Professors" to replace eventually the nonparty academicians who still dominated Soviet universities. In a milieu combining aspects of a university, a political salon, and a monastery, the party's best older minds met in seminars and lectures with a small select group of students. In fact, a considerable number of Institute graduates ended up not primarily in academic pursuits, but in party political-literary work.[31] Many of these moved into Bukharin's circle; most of the leading figures of the Bukharin school were members of the Institute's first graduating class of 1921–4.

Finally, the Bukharin school is not fully comprehensible apart from the personality of its inspirer. Those who encountered him over the years testify that the gentle, open, good-humored Bukharin, who in his traditional Russian blouse, leather jacket, and high boots conveyed the aura of Bohemia-come-to-power, was the most likable of the Bolshevik oligarchs. (Trotsky remarked that "Bukharin remained at bottom an old student.") There was about him none of Trotsky's intimidating hauteur, Zinoviev's labored pomposity, or the intrigue and mistrust surrounding Stalin. He was "lovingly soft in his relations with comrades," and "beloved." Exuding an "impervious geniality," he brought infectious gaiety to informal gatherings and, in his best moments, an ameliorating charm to politics.[32] Bukharin, observed Lenin, was among those "people with such happy natures . . . who even in the fiercest battles are least able to envenom their attacks." Bolshevik opponents, as if to confirm ritually Lenin's deathbed judgment that Bukharin was "the favorite of the whole party," prefaced their attacks on him with declarations of personal affection for "Bukharchik." [33] Even Stalin, a malicious enemy in 1929, found it necessary to echo Brutus: "We love Bukharin, but we love the truth, the Party, and the Comintern even more." [34]

Testimony to Bukharin's likeableness is such that it might be said, to paraphrase Ford Madox Ford, that here was The Good Bolshevik. An older party figure, neither disciple nor hagiographer, characterized him as "one of the most beloved figures of the Russian revolution," explaining that he was also a man of many and varied enthusiasms: "He is lively and animated, like quicksilver; he thirsts for all of life's manifestations, beginning with a new and profound abstract thought and ending with a game in town." [35] He had "all the attributes to capture and enthrall the imagination of the youth," said a foreign Communist admirer, and young Bolsheviks were naturally drawn to him. A part of his grace was a warm and generous receptiveness to young and subordinate comrades, who found him easy to talk to and readily accessible. Where Bukharin presided over promising "neophytes," at *Pravda* for example, "an atmosphere of harmonious, comradely collaboration, of faith in and respect for one another" prevailed.[36] Only slightly their senior in years, he met and encouraged "my young comrades" as equals, without the pretense of rank. In return, they were tied to him by personal as well as political bonds, regarding him as their "dear teacher" and "with love." [37] When his fall became certain in 1928–9, only one, Aleksei Stetskii, defected to Stalin.

At the peak of its celebrity, the Bukharin school numbered perhaps fifteen easily recognizable members. Among the best known were Aleksandr Slepkov, Valentin Astrov, Stetskii, Dmitrii Maretskii, Petr Petrovskii, Aleksandr Aikhenvald, D. P. Rozit, E. Goldenberg, Tseitlin, and Aleksandr Zaitsev. Except for Stetskii and Petrovskii, who became known during the civil war, little is recorded of these men's biographies, their careers having been cut short by Bukharin's defeat and their lives by Stalin's purges, which only Astrov seems to have survived.[38] They were in their middle and late twenties; most had joined the party in 1917 or after, and had served in minor capacities before entering the Institute of Red Professors in 1921. Like all but a few Institute students, they were of middle-class origins. Their political backgrounds varied. Petrovskii was the son of the old Bolshevik and Ukrainian party leader Grigorii Petrovskii. Slepkov, whispered the opposition, had been a Monarchist-Cadet as late as 1918.[39] Aikhenvald was the son of the famous literary critic and Constitutional Democrat Iurii Aikhenvald, whom he visited in Berlin in the hope of reconciling "my incorrigible father" to the Bolshevik régime. Only Goldenberg seems to have had an oppositionist past, having sympathized briefly with Trotsky in 1923.[40] Several had established scholarly reputations before becoming political figures in the mid-twenties, Slepkov and Astrov as historians, Maretskii as an economic historian, and Aikhenvald and Goldenberg as economists.[41]

But it was as tireless and ubiquitous publicists for Bukharinism that they gained notoriety. In hundreds of monographs, pamphlets, articles, and speeches—in the press, schools, party meetings, and other public forums—they propagandized and defended (and sometimes expanded) Bukharin's ideas and policies.[42] They reviewed his books, composed his biography, and cried his praise.[43] Everywhere, sneered one critic, they "sang . . . with the voice of N. I. Bukharin." In their diverse operations, grumbled another, they functioned as Bukharin's personal "agitprop." [44] Above all, they fought the Stalin-Bukharin leadership's ideological war against the opposition, not, of course, in the name of Bukharinism, but in that of "orthodox Bolshevism." Bukharin naturally denied the "screeching about a 'new school,' " as did his Stalinist allies, who profited from its activities. Said one of Stalin's men in its defense:

Bukharin does not have any kind of special school; the school of Bukharin is the Leninist school. Bukharin's service is that he has educated in theory and in the spirit of Leninism a large number of young comrades, who conduct propaganda, agitation, and literary work in our party.[45]

The opposition passionately dissented from the first assertion, and bitterly lamented the truth of the last.

As already noted, what made the young Bukharinists more than merely one oligarch's intellectual coterie was their rise to important party and state positions. Foremost was their "monopoly" of the party's central publications. Astrov and Slepkov became editors of *Bolshevik* in September 1924, and with Bukharin ruled that authoritative Central Committee journal until mid-1928. All published with remarkable frequency in both *Bolshevik* and *Pravda*, for with Bukharin they also controlled the latter, first informally and later formally; by early 1928, Astrov, Slepkov, Maretskii, Tseitlin and Zaitsev had become editors of *Pravda* as well.[46] These were the school's strongholds. In addition, their articles and editorials appeared regularly in almost all major party and Komsomol publications, especially those edited in the capital. When *Komsomol*

Pravda, in effect a new central organ, was created in May 1925, Stetskii was its first editor-in-chief. Though the opposition forced his removal a few weeks later, following a series of politically indiscreet articles by himself and Slepkov, one Bukharinist, Maretskii's brother, remained on the editorial board.[47] Their political role extended even to Leningrad. After the ouster of Zinovievists from *Leningrad Pravda* in January 1926, Astrov, Petrovskii, and Goldenberg represented Bukharin at various times as its editors.[48]

Nor were their operations confined to the press. In addition to the Comintern and the worker-peasant correspondents movement,[49] two of Bukharin's special preserves, they were notably influential in the growing network of Communist universities and educational institutions. One young Bukharinist was a university rector; others supervised curricula, taught courses, and wrote widely used textbooks; still others dominated the party cells of such important institutions as Moscow's Industrial Academy, the Institute of Red Professors, the Communist Academy, and the Academy of Communist Education.[50] They were also active in state economic institutions responsible for planning and industrial development. Aikhenvald and Goldenberg, for example, occupied high posts in Gosplan, the State Planning Commission, the latter rising to deputy chairman of its Russian Republic division.[51] Only in Stalin's central party apparatus was their role less substantial. Two, Stetskii and Rozit, sat on the disciplinary body, the Central Control Commission. In addition, Stetskii headed the agitprop bureau of the Leningrad party, and became a full member of the Central Committee in 1927. Slepkov was a "responsible instructor" of the Central Committee, a benign title for powerful ideological Nestors who toured the country watching over the fidelity of lower party organizations and the local press.[52]

In a variety of ways, the Bukharin school had become an important force in Soviet politics by 1925. Political liabilities as well as benefits, however, accrued to its inspirer. The righteous aggressiveness of his disciples, for example, frequently irritated older party intellectuals; and in some quarters Red Professor reportedly was "a curse word."[53] Of greater political consequence, they sometimes pushed Bukharin's ideas beyond the point of political discretion (though he himself had set this precedent), thus becoming easy targets for oppositionists who offered their excesses as proof of the majority's heresy. An example was the controversy generated by Stetskii and Slepkov when they elaborated on Bukharin's 1925 "enrich yourselves" slogan in the official press. There was another problem. The opposition was quick to identify any offending young publicist with the Bukharin school, as happened in the famous Bogushevskii affair of 1925. Bogushevskii, until then an obscure journalist, published an article in *Bolshevik* arguing that the kulak was a "bogy." [54] For the next two years, the Left cited his *faux pas* as evidence of the duumvirate's "kulak deviation." In fact, Bogushevskii apparently had no association with Bukharin, his article appearing uncensored due to a series of editorial mishaps.[55]

Nevertheless, the school gave Bukharin an unusual political base that for a time served him well. No other oligarch had his own personal "agitprop," least of all one of such size and quality. This phalanx of talented men enabled him to place dedicated followers in those agencies where policy, ideology, and future cadres were being shaped, and to popularize and defend his own policies with great effectiveness. He and his disciples, who met every opposition-ist polemic with a dozen Bukharinist retorts, were mainly responsi-ble for the ideological victory of the majority. It was the school that abetted Bukharin's rise to hierophant of orthodox Bolshevism, sustaining him there and institutionalizing Bukharinism as official party ideology.

Bukharin brought all these real political assets to his coalition with Stalin in 1925. In addition, he contributed something less tangible but of equal importance—the weight of his personal authority, a contribution understandable only in the context of the "succession struggle" that followed Lenin's death. In one sense, this is a mis-nomer. For, while the internal party battles of 1923–9 constituted prolonged attempts to reconstruct the power and authority pre-viously exercised by Lenin, the idea that there could be a successor —a "Lenin of today"—was impermissible. Lenin's authority within the leadership and in the party generally had been unique. Among other things, it had derived from the fact that he was the party's creator and moving spirit, from his political judgment which had been proved correct so often and against so much opposition, and from the force of his personality, which united and persuaded his fractious colleagues. In no way did it derive from an official post. As Sokolnikov pointed out: "Lenin was neither chairman of the Politburo nor general secretary; but, nonetheless, Comrade Lenin . . . had the decisive political word in the party." It was, as has recently been argued, a kind of charismatic authority, inseparable from Lenin as a person and independent of constitutional or insti-tutional procedures.[56]

Some of his heirs intuitively understood this and commented

on it in different ways. "Lenin was a dictator in the best sense of the word," said Bukharin in 1924. Five years later, describing Lenin as the singular "leader, organizer, captain, and stern iron authority," and contrasting his pre-eminence with Stalin's brute machine power, Bukharin tried to explain further:

But he was for us all *Ilich*, a close, beloved person, a wonderful comrade and friend, the bond with whom was indissoluble. He was not only "Comrade Lenin," but something immeasurably more. Such was our bond. . . . This was not at all simple "command," "administrative fiat," etc.[57]

This mixture of sentiment and real insight about Lenin's unique role led to a natural loathing, inside and outside the leadership, for thinking in terms of a "succession." A delegate at the Fourteenth Congress in 1925 objected that "individual representatives . . . are beginning to try on his mantle. This mantle does not fit anyone. . . ." Added another: "I think we should abandon the idea of succession and successors." Whatever the secret aspirations, and however impractical, it was assumed publicly that the post-Lenin leadership should be genuinely oligarchical or, as Bukharin insisted in 1925, collective:

because we do not have Lenin, there is not a single authority. We can now have only a *collective* authority. We have no person who could say: I am sinless and can interpret Leninist teachings absolutely to a full 100 per cent. Everyone tries, but he who expresses a claim to a full 100 per cent attributes too big a role to his own person.[58]

A group of inheritors, then, was to replace the dead chieftain. In the beginning, collective leadership was an exclusive conception, not necessarily including all leading Bolsheviks or even all members of the Politburo. Instead, it referred to that "basic nucleus of Leninists," [59] five of the six men discussed by Lenin in his "testament": Trotsky, Stalin, Zinoviev, Kamenev, and Bukharin. Though rarely said publicly, it was nonetheless widely appreciated that these were the men who individually represented a part of Lenin's legacy, who together embodied the party's legitimate authority, and who therefore, all or some, should rule collectively. Rykov and Kalinin, to take two prominent examples, were high-ranking figures but not essential in this respect. Neither conveyed in his person the *gestalt* of Bolshevik or party authority. That a few Politburo members were *primi inter pares* was not advertised but understood. They were, as observers sometimes put it, the "Bolshevik Olympia." [60] Stalin, who possessed a crude but reliable sense of such distinctions, alluded to it with a similar metaphor in 1928. Speaking to Bukharin about the nine-man Politburo, which no longer included Trotsky, Zinoviev, or Kamenev, he declared: "You and I are the Himalayas; the others are nobodies." [61]

In 1925, however, there were five "Himalayas," or what may be called "authoritative" Leninist heirs.[62] Each qualified by having some combination of four legitimizing credentials: (1) membership in Lenin's inner circle before and after 1917; (2) a revolutionary-heroic biography, 1917 being the crucial touchstone; (3) stature as a revolutionary internationalist; (4) recognition as an "outstanding Marxist," which meant as a theorist. No oligarch's credentials were in perfect order. Zinoviev and Kamenev (who were regarded as a hyphenated entity) were strongest in the first but weakest in the second, having opposed insurrection in 1917; Trotsky, on the other hand, had no peer in the second and third, was second only to Bukharin in the fourth, but was critically vulnerable in the first, having joined the party late. None of Bukharin's credentials was deficient: he overshadowed everyone in theory, had great stature in connection with 1917 and as an internationalist, but could not boast Zinoviev's tenure as Lenin's cohort prior to 1917, nor his fidelity afterward. Stalin's were the least impressive: he had no standing whatsoever in the third and fourth, and ranked behind Trotsky and Bukharin in the second.

Though increasingly chimerical (since the least imposing now held the most power), these considerations were taken very seriously, as seen in the fact that the politics of the twenties so often revolved around political biography, party history, and efforts by various oligarchs to embellish their credentials. Zinoviev and Kamenev wished desperately to live down their shame of 1917; their opponents would not allow it. Zinoviev labored to emerge as a theorist in 1925, only to be rebuffed by Bukharin. Trotsky tried to compensate for his Menshevik past; his adversaries used it against him and, in addition, challenged the orthodoxy of his pre-1917 ideas. Stalin slowly achieved a kind of recognition in the Comintern by ousting his rivals; but he was entirely unknown as a man of theory. He was painfully aware of this, as Bukharin discovered in 1928: "He is consumed with a craving to become an acknowledged theoretician. He thinks that this is the only thing he lacks." [63]

Viewed in this context, Bukharin's important role in the duumvirate is clear. The original triumvirs had united in the fulfilled hope that their collective stature would offset Trotsky's enormous authority in the party. They succeeded in making him seem to be a false and arrogant pretender. Now, however, Zinoviev and Kamenev had abandoned Stalin and were shortly to join with Trotsky. The illusion of their collective authority moved Kamenev to assure Trotsky: "It is enough for you and Zinoviev to appear on the same platform, and the party will find its true Central Committee." Trotsky remembers "laughing at such bureaucratic optimism," [64] but Kamenev's expectation was doubtless Stalin's nightmare. The least illustrious, he was now opposed and denounced by three of the five heirs: the grave threat of appearing the usurper hung over his head, a prospect made more serious by Lenin's still unpublished but widely known "testament."

Bukharin's accession to the co-leadership helped Stalin avert this danger. He bestowed at least a semblance of legitimate Leninist authority and thus made possible the perpetuation of the majority's "collective authority." Despite his relative juniority and the suspicion that his forte was ideas rather than practical politics, both of which probably qualified his stature as a political leader, his validating role in the duumvirate is not to be minimized. Unlike Stalin's, his was an authoritative voice on foreign and domestic issues, from the feasibility of soviets in revolutionary China to capital investment and literary policy at home.[65] At the same time, he in effect vouchsafed for the general secretary, lending his popularity to a man opposed as much out of personal dislike as for policy differences, and, to give a more specific example, "creating an atmosphere of confidence in the Comintern for him." [66]

The question of past association with Lenin was especially sensitive in 1925. Krupskaya, at whom Stalin had directed "an unusually rude outburst" and "vile invectives" three years earlier, openly supported Zinoviev and Kamenev. Her presence at their side symbolized their long intimacy with her dead husband and reminded knowledgeable Bolsheviks of the damning postscript to Lenin's "testament," which had condemned Stalin as "too rude" and recommended his removal from the Secretariat.[67] Here, too, Bukharin furnished a countervailing symbol, Lenin's youngest sister Mariia Ulianova. There was between them a warm personal relationship, as well as a professional one. Ulianova was an old and close friend of Bukharin and, since 1917, executive secretary of *Pravda*. His fall in 1929 ended her political career, and she died in semidisgrace in 1937, a few months after his arrest. But in 1925, Ulianova lent her name to Bukharin and thus to Stalin. Photographs showing her and Bukharin working side by side at *Pravda* were prominently circulated.[68] And at the Fourteenth Congress, after Krupskaya had publicly challenged Bukharin's interpretation of Lenin's last articles, Ulianova rose to deliver a terse rejoinder:

Comrades, I take the floor not because I am Lenin's sister and therefore lay claim to a better understanding and interpretation of Leninism than all other members of our party. I think that such a monopoly by Lenin's relatives . . . does not exist and cannot exist.[69]

In the last analysis, however, Bukharin's authority rested on his standing as Bolshevism's greatest living Marxist, or, as he was officially heralded in 1926, the man "now acknowledged as the most outstanding theorist of the Communist International." [70] He was accorded that most dubious status, "classic" in his own time. His writings were anthologized in official volumes dedicated to Marxist economics, philosophy, sociology, and literary and art criticism. When a Soviet writer wished to give evidence of the "international fame" of Bolshevik intellectual achievement, he would say: "It is sufficient to point only to the outstanding sociological and economic works of N. I. Bukharin. . . ." [71] A charter member of the Communist Academy and its presidium, he was the party's leading nominee and only political leader elected to the Soviet Academy of Sciences in 1928–9, a final, honorific testimony to his pre-eminence.[72]

On such acclaim (however sycophantic), coupled with his other credentials as an heir, was Bukharin's political authority built; and from 1925 to 1928, Stalin was its co-beneficiary. That this kind of authority carried considerable political weight in the twenties was still evident as late as 1928, when the general secretary began his surreptitious campaign against Bukharin by attacking his reputation as party theorist. Unlike later, when Stalin made nonsense of all such credentials by officially attributing each and every one to himself alone (a phenomenon later called "the cult of the personality"), party theory mattered greatly. The rival claimants to Bolshevik orthodoxy regarded it as the surest guide to proper policy and the truest indicator of revolutionary correctness generally. Politics and theory, they agreed, were of a piece. Or, as the Stalinist Lazar Kaganovich exclaimed in 1929: "Treachery in politics always begins with the revision of theory." [73]

This was the profile of the Stalin-Bukharin duumvirate. As Leninist heirs, Stalin and Bukharin were the majority's ranking party leaders, but not its only important representatives. Two other Politburo members had now acquired special importance as staunch supporters of the majority's Bukharinist policies and determined foes of the

Left. One was Aleksei Ivanovich Rykov, who as Lenin's successor as chairman of the Council of People's Commissars (or premier) and, replacing Kamenev in 1926, chairman of the Council of Labor and Defense, combined the two most important and powerful government offices. The other was Mikhail Pavlovich Tomskii (born Efremov) who, except for a brief interlude in Lenin's disfavor in 1921-2, had been the leader of the Soviet trade unions since 1918.[74] Both of these major (and neglected) figures of the revolution were old Bolsheviks, full members of the Politburo since 1922, and now committed to NEP as the proper framework for industrialization. Together with Bukharin, they would form the leadership of the right opposition against Stalin in 1928-9.

Rykov was the most illustrious representative of the moderate strain in Russian Bolshevism. On becoming premier in 1924, at the age of forty-three, he carried an unbroken identification with the party's right wing, beginning with his opposition to Lenin's April Theses in 1917 and his advocacy of a coalition socialist government in October. A gifted administrator—he headed the Supreme Economic Council during war communism and again briefly in 1923, and was a deputy premier from 1921 to 1924—he was identified primarily with the state and economic organizations. He executed party policy loyally and skillfully throughout the civil war, but (he once confided) had never abandoned the political spirit of Lenin's 1905 slogan of a "democratic dictatorship of the proletariat and the peasantry."[75] He was a not uncommon type among early Bolsheviks, a Marxist whose real political cause had been anti-czarism, and whose socialism related to the "toilers" rather than just the proletariat. Himself of peasant origin, Rykov enjoyed a reputation for "his loving and attentive attitude toward the needs of the peasantry."[76]

The coming and expansion of NEP elicited his full approval and found in him a natural and unwavering advocate. A perennial foe of grandiose economic projects and teleological planning schemes, he shared Bukharin's abhorrence of Preobrazhenskii's "law" as "a scandalous theory" which, if implemented, would "mortally compromise socialism." In addition to his programmatic hostility to the Left he seems to have harbored a special dislike for Trotsky and the people around him.[77] No major Bolshevik, including Bukharin, personified so unambiguously the political and economic philosophy of NEP and the *smychka*. Though much less given to theoretical generalizations, by 1925 his industrial and agrarian policy preferences were virtually indistinguishable from

Bukharin's; and with the formation of new political alignments in 1924–5, he emerged as one of Bukharin's strongest defenders.[78]

Tomskii, a radical trade unionist since 1905 and the only Politburo member with an authentic proletarian background, represented a different component of Bolshevism; his commitment to NEP is less easily explained. In viewing the urban labor force as its essential constituency, the party instinctively thought of the trade unions as the "backbone" of its social base. Consequently, while no longer expecting the managerial power they had anticipated during the early days of the revolution, Bolshevik trade union leaders remained an influential group. Sharing a common background and identity, they were the most homogeneous element in the party élite, a self-perceived "party within the party." [79] Tomskii—chairman of the All-Union Trade Union Council—was their official leader and highest ranking political spokesman. Around him gathered almost the entire upper echelon of the Soviet trade union movement, which was to be ousted in toto by Stalin in 1928–9: G. N. Melnichanskii, A. I. Dogadov, Iakov Iaglom, V. M. Mikhailov, Boris Kozelev, Fedor Ugarov, and Vasilii Shmidt, the Commissar of Labor, a post controlled and filled by the trade unionists. These men, remarked Tomskii later, were "comrades who had become accustomed in the course of years to see in me their leader." Indeed, they made him the subject of a minor cult, eulogizing him both as a trade unionist and an old Bolshevik, and promoting him as the "personification of party leadership of the trade union movement"—their emissary on the Politburo.[80]

Tomskii's views reflected the rise, fall, and reconciliation of their aspirations. Earlier, he had been a strong opponent of "statizing" the unions and an equally persistent defender of a trade union role in industrial management.[81] The first cause was won with the collapse of war communism; the second had been irrevocably lost by 1920. With the full development of NEP, Tomskii reconciled himself to the unions' new dual role as the party-state's "transmission belt" to the working class and, simultaneously, the protector of workers' interests in the mixed economy. While faithful to party policy, he zealously embraced the second and more traditional function. Writing in 1925, he made clear that, within the limits of this structural ambiguity, the trade unionists took seriously their revived commitment to the welfare of their membership:

Before the trade unions always stands . . . one fundamental task. This task, which defines the very role and meaning of trade unions, is that of comprehensively serving and continuously working for the up-lifting and betterment of the material and spiritual level of their members. This is the task which, throughout the history of the trade union movement, has stood and will stand before the unions.[82]

This understanding determined Tomskii's support for the Bukharin-Rykov economic policies. He apparently foresaw what the Left's (and later Stalin's) program of forced industrialization and investment priority in capital goods production would mean for the unions and their constituents. Whatever his reservations about official policy, he preferred the promise of gradually rising consumption and real wages, and the preservation of the unions' remaining autonomy. From 1923 onward, he voted with Bukharin and Rykov; and, partly motivated by the memory of Trotsky's 1920 attempt to militarize labor and "shake up" the union leadership, he and his people formed a solid bastion of opposition to the Left.[83]

A second consideration also influenced Tomskii's allegiances. On the question of international working class or socialist unity, the trade unionists were the most ecumenical-minded group in the party. Most had favored a coalition socialist régime in 1917; similarly, they now wanted reconciliation, de facto or de jure, with their European social democratic counterparts grouped around the Amsterdam International.[84] The high point of their strivings was 1925, which brought increasing contacts with Amsterdam and the advent of the first important organizational manifestation of re-union, the Anglo-Russian Trade Union Unity Committee.

The committee commanded the full enthusiasm of Bolshevik trade unionists, particularly Tomskii. A frequent visitor to European trade union gatherings, he emerged as an international figure during the committee's short lifetime, and was its major defender in the Soviet party.[85] These activities, only the most notable of various gropings toward cooperation with European social democracy, were (we shall see) compatible with Bukharin's new views on international politics. They were, however, profoundly repugnant to Trotsky (and to a lesser degree to Zinoviev), who saw in them further evidence of the majority's reformism. Thus domestic and foreign orientations combined to place Tomskii squarely in the majority's camp. He made a special point in 1925 of objecting to those who wished "to discredit Bukharin" as the party's economic spokesman, and, shortly later, to "wholly and fully agree" with Bukharin's ideas on foreign policy.[86]

Exactly when Bukharin, Rykov, and Tomskii began to view

themselves as a separate group within the ruling Politburo majority is not certain.[87] It is clear, however, that circumstances soon distinguished them as a threesome. First, all three were issue-oriented leaders united by a durable adherence to specific policies (as would be demonstrated in 1928). Second, in the nine-man Politburo elected in January 1926, which saw Kamenev demoted to candidate status and Molotov, Voroshilov, and the lightly regarded Kalinin elevated to full membership, they were the only important majority leaders who did not owe their high positions in some way to Stalin. (Molotov and Voroshilov had long been identified with the general secretary.) Significantly, Bukharin, Rykov, and Tomskii each took occasion at the Fourteenth Party Congress or shortly after to condemn publicly the principle of a dominant Politburo member ("a single authority"), a disapprobation relevant only to Stalin, who was already being touted by his supporters as *primus inter pares.*[88] Third, for personal, policy, and institutional reasons, Rykov and Tomskii had cause to prefer Bukharin to Stalin if a choice between the duumvirs became necessary.

On the surface, it might seem that as administrators and practical politicians, Stalin, Rykov, and Tomskii were natural allies. The contrary seems to have been true. The gracious and popular Rykov in no way resembled Stalin as a personality; he apparently distrusted the general secretary and was in turn disdained by him.[89] More important, they headed rival organizations, the state and the party, and were therefore locked in an inherently fractious situation. Tomskii and Stalin were also unlikely associates, their mutual dislike, probably dating from 1921, becoming evident in 1928.[90] In addition, Tomskii wished to enhance the independence of trade unions, while Stalin sought to increase their submissiveness to the party and extend the Secretariat's appointment power to Tomskii's organizational "principality." Finally, Tomskii's growing involvement in foreign affairs brought him into conflict with the Stalinist head of the Red International of Trade Unions (Profintern), Solomon Lozovskii, who resented the Soviet trade unions' unilateral activities abroad.[91] Not surprisingly, neither Rykov nor Tomskii exhibited any public enthusiasm for Stalin, and it was periodically reported that they were at odds with him.[92] Bukharin, on the other hand, was on record as strongly favoring a restoration and preservation of the official division between state and party functions; and, beginning in 1926, he was effusive in his praise of trade union activities at home and abroad.[93]

Circumstances rather than design made Bukharin, Rykov, and Tomskii a discernible if not fully defined political trio at least by

1926. They may conveniently be termed the Politburo Right, meaning that they—"150 per cent Nepists," in Piatakov's mocking words—were committed to policies thought to be antithetical to the Left's, and that Stalin, while defending those policies, occupied a center position, keeping his own counsel and protecting both of his political flanks.[94] The three complemented one another as political leaders. Rykov's detailed, matter-of-fact approach to economic problems was a valuable correlative to Bukharin's penchant for philosophical economics, while Tomskii's support helped dispel the "pro-peasant" aura of their policies. At the same time, they were men of differing inclinations. Tomskii undoubtedly would have preferred policies more immediately beneficial to unions and labor, and less obviously concerned with the peasant. And neither he nor Rykov shared Bukharin's revolutionary ebullience in foreign policy (the premier necessarily speaking in a tone different from that of the Comintern head). As was true of all "groupings" within the leadership, theirs was a political identification shaped not by full accord but by that which separated them from others. As Tomskii later explained: "I am thirty kilometers to the right of Bukharin on international matters, but I am one hundred kilometers to the left of Stalin. . . ."[95]

Three other features further distinguished the Politburo Right. In contrast to the predominantly Jewish Left and the increasingly Transcaucasian complexion of Stalin's group, all of its major and second-rank leaders were Russians. Although this fact did not go unnoticed, its actual political significance is not clear. Conceivably, it influenced their receptiveness to peasant Russia. But the seemingly probable was not always the case: during the ascendency of the Politburo Right, for example, non-Russian nationalities enjoyed their greatest freedom under Soviet rule.[96] The second feature was particularly striking in contrast to Stalin: Bukharin, Rykov, and Tomskii had reputations as popular Bolshevik leaders. Tomskii, who apparently conducted trade union affairs with bureaucratic dispatch, may have profited by being the only leader of a nonparty, mass organization on the Politburo. But, as with Bukharin, Rykov's "popular backing" was genuine. All three (memoirists recall) were men who walked unguarded in crowds.[97] Their personal popularity, their reconciliatory and peasant-oriented policies, and the fact that Rykov, Tomskii, and the rightist Kalinin (titular head of the Soviets and thus president of the Soviet Union) represented the main nonparty organizations combined to give the Right a semblance of popular support, or of aspiring to it. One observer remarked: "They tried to appear as people's leaders."[98]

However tenuous this impression, it points to the Politburo Right's third political distinction: the great support their leadership obtained in Commissariats (particularly Agriculture, Finance, Labor, and Trade) and other state organs (the Supreme Economic Council, the State Bank, and Gosplan) responsible for preparing and administering economic policy. These institutions, by nature sympathetic to the return to orthodox economic practices, and with their importance revived by NEP, were staffed largely by former anti-Bolshevik intellectuals, so-called nonparty specialists.[99] In particular, both former Mensheviks working in the Supreme Economic Council and Gosplan and Socialist Revolutionaries in the Commissariat of Agriculture strongly preferred Bukharin and Rykov as party leaders to either Stalin or the Left. Their preference rested on two related assumptions: that the Right's economic policies were the most desirable; and that a victorious Stalin or Trotsky, each in his own way, would mean an end of civil peace and a resumption of the political strife and intolerance of war communism. While viewing Bukharin sympathetically, their rallying figure was Rykov. Both as premier and as an individual, he was renowned as the patron and protector of nonparty specialists.[100] Their considerable service and influence in the Soviet government would terminate with his fall from power.

The Supreme Economic Council was of special importance in this connection as the center of right-wing industrial strategy in 1924-6. As nominal manager of the state sector, the Council's main responsibility was for heavy industry, its growth and planning. With Rykov's appointment to the premiership in February 1924, Felix Dzerzhinskii, chief of the secret police, became its chairman. Confuting the fears of the specialists, he turned out to be their reliable friend and, most important, a passionate advocate of Bukharinist economic policies. An ardent believer in the *smychka*, his faith in the efficacy of basing heavy industry growth on the peasant market and accumulation within the state sector through lowering costs and prices and increasing turnover was even more single-minded than Bukharin's. He shared the essential article of Bukharinism: "It is not possible to industrialize ourselves if we speak with fear about the prosperity of the village." [101]

A strong chairman of the Council, candidate Politburo member, and still head of the police, Dzerzhinskii gave the Right an organizational toughness many of its other representatives lacked. In some ways the majority's angriest and most effective voice in the debates with industrializers of the Left, he died on July 20, 1926, hours after a bitter exchange with the opposition. Whether Dzerzhinskii would have stood with Bukharin, Rykov, and Tomskii against Stalin in 1928 can only be guessed. But his death soon deprived them of a key stronghold. His successor was Valerian Kuibyshev, a supporter of Stalin and zealous believer in large investment projects and rapid industrialization. Within weeks, the philosophy and personnel of the Supreme Economic Council began to undergo a far-reaching transformation.[102]

The Right, it will have been noticed, enjoyed considerable support outside the party machine. With one exception, no major party organization can be specifically identified with its policies or leaders. The exception, however, was an important one—Moscow, the party's largest single organization. The political history of the Moscow Committee during this period is somewhat unclear. Although its leadership had been loyal to the triumvirs in 1923–4, Trotsky's opposition had attracted numerous sympathizers at lower levels, primarily among students and remnants of the 1917 Moscow Left. Probably because of this embarrassing unruliness in the capital, the first secretary of the Moscow Committee was replaced in September 1924 by a Leningrad party secretary, Nikolai Uglanov.[103]

Uglanov, who quickly rose to candidate membership on the Politburo and a full seat on the Secretariat and Orgburo, assured that during the next three years Moscow was the majority's (and the duumvirate's) vociferous partisan. In 1928, he, his co-secretary Vasilii Kotov, and most of the Moscow Committee leadership— E. F. Kulikov, Mikhail Riutin, Nikolai Mandelshtam, Nikolai Penkov, G. S. Moroz, V. A. Iakovlev, and V. M. Mikhailov—stood adamantly and fell collectively with the anti-Stalin opposition led by Bukharin, Rykov, and Tomskii.[104] Historians have assumed that Uglanov was originally Stalin's agent in Moscow, and that his subsequent opposition represented a change of heart. In actual fact, considerable evidence suggests that by 1925, the Moscow party leadership identified with the policies of the Politburo Right, and with Bukharin in particular.

First signs that Bukharin's economic program was finding an unusually receptive audience in the capital appeared at the time of the duumvirate's formation. By mid-1925, the struggle with the Zinovievists had acquired a Moscow-versus-Leningrad slant, with the opposition implying that the ascent of "pro-peasantism" in "provincial" Moscow was no accident and that its own authentic proletarian line was consistent with the singular revolutionary traditions of "Leningrad—this salt of the proletarian earth." Part of the inter-city rivalry was a replay of the pre-1917 chauvinisms of the two Russian capitals; part was inspired by Zinoviev, who had opposed the transfer of the capital to Moscow in 1918, and who now found himself cut off from the central party and state machinery.[105]

It also had, however, a sociological basis. Moscow and the surrounding province housed over a fifth of all Soviet industry; but light industry accounted for 84 per cent (in 1926) of the area's total output, including almost half of the nation's textile production. Accordingly, Moscow's industry had revived dramatically since 1921, and its wages were the highest in the country. This situation contrasted markedly with Leningrad, where metal was the pivotal industry and where the four-year emphasis on consumer goods production had been felt adversely. While the Muscovites paid lip service to "transforming calico Moscow into metal Moscow," it is clear that NEP and Bukharin's industrial program favored their city.[106] Significantly, Uglanov opposed the Dnieprostoi project, the harbinger of an eventual massive shift of investment funds to heavy industry. And a favorite complaint about the Moscow Committee leaders was their "idealization of 'calico Moscow.'"[107]

In a roundabout but significant fashion, the Moscow Committee's industrial bias coincided with that of Tomskii and his trade unionists, and pointed to a secondary connection between the Politburo Right and Moscow. Uglanov, as a secretary, was identified with the party apparatus after 1921; previously, however, he had been equally if not more prominent in trade union affairs.[108] His past association with Tomskii remains vague, but their friendship was said to have been a factor in 1928, and he reportedly declared that Tomskii deserved to lead the trade unions for as long as he lived.[109] Further, though several of Tomskii's co-leaders (like Tomskii himself and Uglanov) had made their earlier careers in Leningrad, many union leaders were Muscovites. One was Mikhailov, chairman of the important Moscow Provincial Trade Union Council, who was also a full member of Uglanov's Moscow Committee Bureau. Another was Melnichanskii, chairman of the Textile Workers' Union, whose members made up 55 per cent of the working-class rank and file of the Moscow party.[110] Whether this web of personal and organizational contacts was politically decisive or only circumstantial is unclear: that a community of identity—what enemies called the "calico" point of view—had developed in Moscow by 1925 is not.

But in a politics of jealously contested authority and rival "principalities," it was the association with a Leninist heir that mattered. That Bukharin and his native city, where he had begun his career and later risen to power, continued to hold each other in special esteem was manifested in a variety of revealing ways: in Bukharin's reflecting on this or that "feat of which Moscow can be proud"; in the proliferation of Moscow public places renamed in his honor, including a thoroughfare, a tram depot, a park, a library, a workers' education faculty, a custom house, and several factories; and in his personal popularity as an "honorary member" of the Moscow Soviet.[111] More than casual sentiment was involved: between December 1924 and November 1927, Bukharin delivered at least fourteen speeches to official Moscow gatherings, twelve of them to important convenings of the Moscow party and Komsomol, all of which were partisan and controversial policy statements.

This was an unusually large number of major addresses by a national leader who held no post in the Moscow party and in a city where the local leadership had its choice of resident Politburo members. (During the same period, Stalin spoke at only four Moscow meetings, once apparently without an official invitation.)[112] An example of the exceptional political relationship between the Moscow Committee leaders and Bukharin occurred at the Moscow Provincial Party Congress in December 1925, a few days before the national party congress. Bukharin delivered a highly individualistic restatement of his theories of NEP and its certain socialist evolution, as well as an attack on the Leningraders who had been challenging his ideological authority for months.[113] The Moscow conference then adopted a lengthy resolution and an open letter to the Leningrad organization. Together the documents amounted to an unprecedented, sweeping, point by point defense and endorsement of Bukharin and Bukharinism. One passage even incorporated his theoretical trademark: "'Lenin . . . clearly emphasized the possibility of the *direct* socialist development of the cooperatives." This was the linchpin of Bukharin's agrarian theory, a contentious formulation that had not yet appeared in a Central Committee resolution. Its unequivocal endorsement by the Moscow party leadership signaled the beginning of a distinctly Bukharinist orientation in that organization's public ideology.[114]

Moscow had not again become Bukharin's bailiwick or "principality." The city's leaders, it would seem, regarded themselves as a semi-autonomous force in the party and not (the example of Zinoviev's reign in Leningrad was before them) as vassals of an individual leader. Uglanov had become a powerful and important figure in his own right, and several of his co-leaders sat on the Central Committee. Like many party secretaries at that time, they were not creatures of Stalin, but independent-minded men capable, within limits, of steering their own course.[115] But given Moscow's semi-autonomy (comparable, perhaps, to that of the trade unionists), their partiality for Bukharin and the Right seems clear. Theirs, too, was an identification determined largely by issues rather than political patronage, which so far was what distinguished the Stalin group. They, too, refrained from eulogizing the general secretary, at a time when his role in the party was growing ever larger, referring to him only as "one of its workers, one of its leaders."[116] When the break between the Politburo Right and Stalin finally came, Uglanov would be among the first, if not the first, to throw down the gauntlet.

Bukharin was therefore elevated to a lofty position of leadership and influence between 1925 and 1928 because of a convergence of allies around his policies, an expedient coalition with Stalin, and a vacuum created by the defection (and then exclusion) of the three other Leninist heirs. During these three years, he distinguished himself as a ruler in some respects, and considerably less so in others. Though he eventually lent his authority to mean and self-defeating acts, he was neither an unattractive politician nor a malicious abuser of power. Where the broad population was involved, his conception of Bolshevism's modernizing role and its attendant "grandiose responsibility" led him to advocate a benevolent form of party rule. He implored party members to inculcate themselves "in this spirit of responsibility," to understand that "a true Communist . . . never forgets for a moment the hard conditions under which the working people, who are our flesh and blood, are living. . . ." Compassion for the people, he knew, was not always the natural state of the party mind: "We must cultivate in ourselves, high and low, a feeling for the masses . . . a feeling of constant and uninterrupted caring about these masses. . . . We must again and again cultivate a feeling of responsibility."[117]

At another level of social life, Bukharin's tenure as a ruler coincided with a remarkable flurry of Soviet intellectual and artistic creativity, inside and outside the party. He was not its sole protector, but his high leadership guaranteed official toleration for it during the twenties. He was a knowledgeable patron of artistic and scientific accomplishment, the rare party leader who enjoyed good relations with men as diverse as Osip Mandelstam, Mikhail Pokrovskii, Maxim Gorky, and Ivan Pavlov. Party intellectuals had in him one of their own, a political oligarch who was not suspicious of diversity and innovation. Like many old Bolsheviks, he believed in genuine learning, ridiculing as an "ugly . . . 'Talmudic' deviation" the person who "crams Volume One of *Capital* . . . but if asked the whereabouts of Sweden can easily confuse it with North Africa." [118] To Bukharin's credit he warned, vainly as it turned out, against allowing the bitter and sterile epithets of the political struggles to flow over into and eviscerate the party's intellectual life.[119]

Nor did the non-Bolshevik intelligentsia, specialist or poet, have reason to fear him. In addition to protecting several of them, notably the poet Osip Mandelstam, he was tolerant of their pursuits, and if not ideologically, at least personally appreciative of their achievements.[120] He disliked intensely (to take another example from literature) Sergei Esenin's poetic idealization of "the most negative features of the Russian village." Yet he understood that the poet was popular—that "under a Komsomol member's *The Communist Companion* quite frequently lies a small volume of Esenin's poems"—partly because "we serve up an astonishingly monotonous ideological food . . . which immediately sickens the unaccustomed person." Party writers, he pointed out, "have not touched those chords in the youth which Esenin touched. . . ." A persistent opponent of cultural regimentation, Bukharin sought a humanistic Communist art, "to which nothing human is alien": "We do not need walking icons, not even of the proletarianized type, who feel obligated to kiss machines or to erect a ghastly 'urbanism.' . . ." [121]

Where he ultimately failed, as did his rivals, was in his unwillingness or inability to extend equal understanding and tolerance to his party opponents, in his underlying assumption that the economic and cultural pluralism of Soviet society should be accompanied by some kind of operative unanimity within the party. From the onset of the duumvirate, Bukharin had misgivings about the vindictiveness of the internal party battles and the direction they were taking. At a meeting after the Fourteenth Congress in December 1925, at which he endorsed Stalin's organizational reprisals against the Leningraders, Kamenev indignantly remarked that Bukharin had opposed similiar measures against Trotsky in 1923-4. Said Trotsky from his seat: "he has begun to relish it." Bukharin answered in a letter a few days later: "You think that I have 'begun to relish it,' but this 'relishing' makes me tremble from head to foot." [122] That he sanctioned the reprisals anyway, despite reservations, is perhaps explainable. For six months, Zinovievists had made him their special target of harsh abuse; they had, he complained without exaggeration, ignored "elementary fairness" and "baited me unprecedentedly." He was "utterly tired out," depressed, and

angry. He knew that a victorious Zinoviev, who earlier had demanded even sterner measures against Trotsky, would have been
no more charitable.[123]

But the true test of Bukharin's remaining temperance—since
Zinoviev brought out the worst in everybody—was in his relations
with Trotsky. He had entered the 1923-4 campaigns against Trotsky reluctantly, without personal animus, and without emulating
the "foul-smelling" attacks of the Zinovievists; he had privately
urged making it possible for Trotsky to remain in the leadership,
repeatedly opposing efforts by Zinoviev and Kamenev to expel him
from the Politburo or worse.[124] Little had passed between them
since then, as Trotsky watched the controversies of 1925 from the
sidelines. Now, in two speeches in early 1926, presumably hoping
to dissuade Trotsky from joining Zinoviev and Kamenev, Bukharin
reminded him of his previous restraint and that "I was always
against . . . saying that Trotsky is a Menshevik. Of course Trotsky
is not a Menshevik . . . the party is much indebted to him. . . ."[125]
At the same time, a private correspondence developed between the
two men. Initiated by Bukharin in January 1926, and including
several frank letters and notes, it lasted only three months, until
Trotsky united with his two former detractors and the factional
disputes were set on their final course.

The correspondence was revealing and pathetic, showing two
old comrades still capable of mutual warmth and friendliness, but
unable to strike the slenderest genuine political accord. The ill-
fated history of the old Bolshevik leaders was epitomized in these
letters. Bukharin urged Trotsky to reconsider the "big social questions" of the revolution debated during 1925. Trotsky, however,
was intent on discussing only the bureaucratization of the party.
"Think for a moment," he insisted: "Moscow and Leningrad, the
two major proletarian centers, pass simultaneously and unanimously
(think of it—unanimously!) . . . two resolutions directed against
each other." It was, he thought, proof that his warnings about the
"system of apparatus terror" had been fully justified. Bukharin, on
the other hand, wanted Trotsky to judge which resolution was
right on the political and economic issues involved.[126]

Neither could empathize with the other's vital concern. The
correspondence ended with Trotsky asking Bukharin to investigate
anti-Semitic slurs that were creeping into the official campaign
against the Left. Bukharin's response (he was an outspoken critic
of Soviet anti-Semitism) is not recorded.[127] Faint echoes of their
renewed affection continued a few months longer, as each refrained
from vilifying the other. Soon, however, the factional bitterness

engulfed them both; by 1927, they were reduced to exchanging shouts of "lie . . . slander . . . Thermidor." In the eyes of Trotsky, who now saw all political issues in terms of the perfidy of party bureaucracy, Bukharin became the supreme recreant: "the little Bukharin swells up until he becomes a gigantic caricature of Bolshevism." As for Bukharin, he finally allowed himself to ask, and then answer negatively, whether Trotsky had ever "become a real Bolshevik." [128]

In his reasoning about the opposition generally after 1925, Bukharin succumbed to the potential logic of a single-party philosophy. He advised the Left in 1926: "hold to your principles, defend your opinions, *speak at party meetings.* . . . Argue, but do not dare form a faction. Argue, but after decisions are made, submit!" Because "if we legalize such a faction inside our party, then we legalize another party and . . . then we in reality . . . slip from the line of the proletarian dictatorship. . . ." It was an impossible exhortation, because his rivals also wished "to struggle for . . . their policies" and band together; "nobody," Bukharin had observed, "enjoys being in a minority." [129]

Thus arose the perilous equation that persistent dissent augured a faction, a second party, and ultimately counter-revolution. It produced much of the political obscenity and dishonesty that wracked the old Bolsheviks after 1925. It led Bukharin, in a paroxysm of violent allusions to expulsion, to reverse himself at the party conference in November 1926, and to demand repentance from the opposition: "come before the party with head bowed and say: Forgive us for we have sinned against the spirit and against the letter and against the very essence of Leninism." Forgotten was his concession to their principles. "Say it, say it honestly: Trotsky was wrong. . . . Why do you not have the common courage to come and say that it is a mistake?" Even Stalin was impressed: "Well done, Bukharin, well done. He does not speak, he slashes." Though not characteristic, it was, perhaps, Bukharin's worst moment. [130]

The underside of his degenerating relations with his opponents was, of course, his partnership with Stalin. Despite premonitory rumblings of their future disagreements (including Stalin's increasing emphasis on the primacy of economic autarky and military security, and his manifest disinterest in his ally's quest for new combinations of revolutionary mass support in Europe and Asia), as well as Bukharin's lingering reluctance as late as 1927 to believe Stalin's worst charges against the opposition, the duumvirate endured. [131] It must rank among the least likely alliances in political history, joining together leaders who were almost wholly dissimilar in temperament, values, gifts, and ambition.

Archives, hopefully, will one day tell its full history, certainly a complex and tortuous one. (There is fragmentary and inconclusive evidence of a plan in 1925 or 1926, presumably involving Bukharin, Rykov, and Tomskii, to remove Stalin as general secretary and replace him with Dzerzhinskii.)[132] But after a shaky start in mid-1925, when Stalin disavowed Bukharin's "enrich yourselves" slogan and the related exuberances of two young Bukharinists,[133] the duumvirs presented a united public face, each defending the other. As was true throughout, the opposition held them together. By December 1925, Stalin had dismissed Bukharin's indiscretion as "not worthy of attention" and had embraced his key formulation that overestimating the kulak danger was a more serious deviation than underestimating it. This convinced the Zinovievists that he had "become a total prisoner" of Bukharin's "political line," and henceforth they treated the duumvirs as co-evils. Stalin did nothing to discourage the association: "You demand Bukharin's blood? We will not give you Bukharin's blood. . . ."[134] In fact, it was never clear whose blood the opposition did want.

Even discounting the possibility that there was discussion about ousting Stalin, it may be safely assumed that Bukharin did not stand beside him unconditionally or without misgivings. For one thing, he continued to criticize publicly the pervasive authoritarianism of party life and the conduct of responsible party officials. His repeated denunciations of the "arbitrariness" and "lawlessness" of "privileged Communist groups" unavoidably reflected on Stalin's management of the apparatus. As did his charge in March 1926 that party authority was becoming patterned "along the lines of military command" and "military discipline," and his condemnation of this "tendency of transforming our party into such a hierarchical system."[135] Moreover, Bukharin had, as early as the civil war, pinpointed a crucial, ramifying aspect of Stalin's personality: "Stalin can't live unless he has what someone else has. He will never forgive it"; he has "an implacable jealousy of anyone who knows more or does things better than he." While the general secretary's other rivals consistently mistook him for "just a small-town politician" and "the outstanding mediocrity in the party," Bukharin apparently perceived the inner demon that fed Stalin's private ambition.[136] It should have alerted him to his own danger as Bolshevism's "most outstanding theorist." Whether it did or whether he knew before 1928 that his ally was "an unprincipled intriguer who subordinates everything to the preservation of his own power," remains uncertain.[137]

But there would seem to be little question why Bukharin persisted in the alliance. Still disclaiming any "personal antipathies," he remained immovable in the conviction that at stake in each and every round of the party controversies, "sometimes in a secret form, sometimes in an open form," was the pivotal issue of *"the relationship between the working class and the peasantry."* He believed—and to this he subordinated all else—that between himself and the Left there was *"a radical programmatic disagreement,"* and that the fate of the revolution hung in the balance.[138]

The opposition believed no less. In its polemics, it had linked the offending official policies inextricably with Bukharin's name. His alliance with Stalin was thus required to assure majority sanction for those policies and negate "the impression that I am a white horse among members of the Central Committee, the Politburo, etc." [139] From 1926 onward, resentments and disagreements, central and marginal, proliferated, as the debates were conducted increasingly in a "pogrom atmosphere" (manipulated, some said, by Stalin to prevent a rapprochement between the Right and Left).[140] The ground and will for reconciliation dwindled. Thus by the time Bukharin had modified his economic program in 1926-7, seemingly narrowing his distance from the Left, the latter had already shifted its main opposition and indignation to foreign policy, where chances for consensus were slimmer and passions ran even higher.

CHAPTER VIII

The Crises of Moderation

And though I have the gift of prophecy, and understand all mysteries, and all knowledge; and though I have all faith, so that I could remove mountains, and have not charity, I am nothing.

—1 Corinthians

FROM 1924 TO 1926, Bukharin had discussed economic policy in very broad, frequently abstract terms. Theory was his arterial pursuit, a manner of exposition he found congenial. The main reason for his abstract style, however, was his determination to establish general economic, political, and (as has been argued) ethical principles about the nature of Soviet industrialization and of Bolshevism in power. His treatment of economics tended to be philosophic, because he refused to separate it from his broader philosophy of the worker-peasant *smychka*. He never entirely abandoned this approach to policy questions, usually preferring to leave the recitation of details and statistics to Rykov. But beginning in 1926, Bukharin's discussion of economic issues became notably more pragmatic, specific, and problem-oriented.

The change in style reflected one of substance, coinciding with a reconsideration and significant modification of his policies. It began in the spring of 1926, with Bukharin's awareness that some of his economic assumptions had been flawed or were becoming obsolete, and continued through 1927, when he spelled out his new proposals more fully. It culminated in December 1927 at the Fifteenth Party Congress, whose resolutions embodied his and his allies' revised program and their understanding of the new period in Soviet economic development.

Bukharin stressed, and correctly, that these modifications did not represent a fundamental departure from the principles he had elaborated in 1924–6. Indeed, he redoubled his emphasis on all those "historic truths" of the *smychka* and on his various objections to the Left's economic policies. His revised thinking remained squarely in the context of NEP, presupposing as before the indefinite continuation of a large private sector, individual peasant farming, private accumulation, and the prevalence of market relations. Nonetheless, the revisions constituted an important alteration in his original program. They represented a shift away from full reliance on the automatic functioning of the market toward greater state intervention in the economy in the form of planned investment, increased regulation of private capital, and the restructuring of the productive foundations of agriculture.

The state of industry prompted his first public reconsiderations. By April–May 1926, Bukharin and the official leadership had recognized the two related problems confronting the state sector. The existing plant was operating at almost its full capacity. The immediate problem was therefore no longer mobilizing "unemployed capital," but acquiring "additional capital"; it had ceased to be only a question of speeding "blood . . . through our economic organism," but was also and essentially one of enlarging the "organism" itself.[1] Second, he gradually acknowledged Preobrazhenskii's prognosis that a dearth of industrial products rather than insufficient consumer demand was the chronic economic malady. At first, Bukharin presented the goods famine as a temporary "spasm" that could be readily overcome through an emergency effusion of domestic goods and manufactured imports. Shortly, however, he sensibly began to treat it as a long-term problem, though (unlike Preobrazhenskii) not one that was irremediably or disastrously disequilibrating. Arguing that it could be alleviated from year to year, he added that it was actually a blemish of health because it reflected, in contrast to capitalist societies where supply exceeded demand, a broadening internal market for industrial goods. Since demand and consumption were to be the driving forces of industrialization, excessive demand was a positive if troublesome symptom.[2]

While both of these acknowledgments were accompanied by cheerful estimates of past gains and future prospects, Bukharin understood that together they threatened the course of industrialization generally and his program of market exchange between state industry and peasant agriculture specifically. By the fall of 1926, and consistently thereafter, he spoke frankly of a new period of "reconstruction" as opposed to the concluding era of "restoration," and of the inevitable hardships and complexities that would go with it. The transition meant that new industrial construction could no longer be deferred, that "the expansion of the basis of production . . . the construction of . . . new enterprises, to a considerable extent on a new technical basis" was required. It was, he warned in a tone significantly less complacent than before, "a task of the greatest difficulties." The easy years of reactivating idle factories were past; the party was forewarned that future increases in industrial output would not be as cheap, painless, or as rapid.[3]

In short, Bukharin now accepted the need for an industrial investment program that differed in two important respects from that of the early twenties. Far greater expenditures were necessary; and, second, allocation could no longer be determined mainly by the market, with heavy industry lagging behind. Recognition that further growth depended on expanding and retooling the existing plant, concern over the sluggish response of metallurgy, and, be-ginning in early 1927, a growing fear of war brought Bukharin and the leadership much closer to the Left's position that sizable ex-penditures in heavy industry were urgent. Bukharin, however, was careful to insist that this more ambitious investment program be judicious and balanced:

We think that that formula which calls for maximum investment in heavy industry is not quite correct, or rather, quite incorrect. If we must put the main emphasis on the development of heavy industry, then we must still combine this development with a corresponding develop-ment of light industry, which has a more rapid turnover, which real-izes profits more rapidly, and which repays those sums expended on it sooner. We must, I repeat, strive for the most favorable combination.

These two guidelines—a proportional fostering of light industry and strict avoidance of freezing too many funds in costly, time-consuming projects—were to govern investment in existing facili-ties as well as new construction.[4] Bukharin hoped that a steady growth of the state's consumer goods sector, combined with the output of private industry and handicrafts, would alleviate the goods famine during reconstruction; the Left's "naked formula," he pointed out, would only intensify it.[5]

Though he had reordered its priorities, Bukharin's program still called for evolutionary, balanced industrial development.[6] The ambiguity, as before, involved the question of tempo, an issue com-plicated further in November 1926, when the leadership resolved "to catch up and surpass" the "levels of industrial development of the leading capitalist countries in a relatively minimal historical period." Said Bukharin: "it is possible to do this." [7] The opposition saw it as a repudiation of his 1925 "snail's pace" utterance, even though Bukharin had always demanded a growth rate higher than that prevailing in Europe. Indeed, his readjustment in 1926–7 arose partly because he had decided: "we are proceeding far too slowly." [8] The new slogan was later to create serious "strains" throughout the economy and a psychological atmosphere unconducive to prudent, balanced investment, largely because it coincided with the fear of an imperialist war against the Soviet Union in 1927, a specter rarely absent from majority or opposition speeches after January. Bukharin's own anxiety about the "war danger" peaked in the summer and autumn, when he warned that the régime's breathing spell might be abruptly terminated.[9] Since he allowed that this would necessitate emergency reallocations and thus affect anticipated growth rates for light and heavy industry, it was never clear exactly what he (or anyone else) regarded as an acceptable overall tempo.

Generally, however, he now urged the long view and policies that would bring "a rising curve" from year to year.[10] He did not envisage a sudden, radical expansion of the industrial sector, as was evident in his approach to the problem of urban unemployment. By 1927, unemployment had grown to alarming proportions and become one of the most compelling arguments favoring the "super-industrializers." Cautioning against their "one-sided" solution, Bukharin again maintained that moderate industrial growth had to be coupled with measures designed to slow rural migration to the cities, among them the gradual industrialization of agriculture and the promotion of labor-intensive farming. To those who called for an industrial expansion sufficient to absorb surplus urban labor, he answered that the "expansions in question would have to be so great that no sane person could possibly demand them." [11] Henceforth, until silenced in 1929, his objections to the industrial proposals of his opponents focused not on the necessity of significant new construction, but on what he regarded as the immoderate targets of "madmen," be they Trotskyists or Stalinists.[12]

Having accepted the indispensability of substantial outlays, Bukharin was forced to return to "the major problem: how is a poverty-ridden country to scrape together the abundant capital for industrialization . . .?" [13] Here he made no serious revisions in his original program, contending that none of the three internal sources of investment funds had yet yielded its full potential. The primary source remained surplus profits within state industry and from other nationalized undertakings, as did the "central idea, our *central economic directive* . . . speeding up commodity turnover" by lowering retail prices. Insofar as Bukharin offered fresh thoughts on this subject, they revolved around the "régime of economy" campaign launched by the government in 1926 to minimize costs and maximize output in the state sector. The campaign became his great hope for adequate accumulation during reconstruction. He emphasized its themes repeatedly: "rationalization of the economy" through a reduction of production, managerial, and administrative overhead, increased labor productivity, and improved technique.[14] A parallel effort was to be undertaken to "rationalize circulation," to eliminate unproductive costs in state and cooperative marketing agencies and to close the "scissors" between retail and wholesale prices.[15]

The other two sources were more restricted by political considerations, but Bukharin remained convinced that they also would produce additional revenue. As of 1926, private capital was subjected to heavier and better-calculated taxation. At the same time, energetic attempts were to be made to attract private savings in state and cooperative banks by promoting confidence in those institutions and in the ruble.[16] Finally, his realization of the enormous industrializing funds needed spurred in Bukharin a somewhat greater interest in the possibility of foreign assistance, a prospect immediately diminished by deteriorating relations between the Soviet Union and the capitalist powers.[17] In the end, he rested his case on the country's internal resources. Speaking on the eve of the Fifteenth Congress in 1927, he anticipated a period of stringent belt-tightening, but reaffirmed his faith that if the available resources were carefully husbanded and properly utilized, successful industrialization was possible without foreign credits and without exacting a cruel tribute from the population: "we propose and we believe that given . . . rationalization, economizing, the reduction of costs, and the mustering of swelling savings in the city and the village, we shall overcome these difficulties." [18]

Each revision in Bukharin's industrial program pointed to the need for economic planning. This alone could ensure the desired pattern and rate of growth, as well as the fullest utilization of existing resources. It was also ideologically attractive, Bukharin having never ceased to equate socialism with a planned economy. His earlier negative attitude, largely a reaction to the excesses of war communism and to the Left's call for a separate industrial plan, now gave way to a cautious optimism about the rewards of more comprehensive planning. In 1927, he and the leadership embraced the idea of a five-year plan for the whole economy. General "directives," but not the actual control figures, were presented and ratified at the Fifteenth Party Congress in December. This failure to legislate actual figures in congressional resolutions would be significant in 1928–9, when Bukharinists and Stalinists disputed what goals had actually been adopted by the congress. Already aware that some Bolsheviks "think that the growth of planned economy means that it is possible . . . to do as you please," [19] Bukharin tried during the period before the congress to sketch out the meaning of "real" planning.

His understanding included three related fundamental propositions. First, that target figures be calculated on the basis of scientific statistics, and that they be "realistic" rather than a "mere combination of figures accepted . . . as ideal." Second, on both formulating and implementing projected targets, that "the approximate nature of our five-year plan be kept in mind." Planning targets were to be regarded as flexible guidelines, not mandatory decrees imposed from above come what may. They were to allow for such uncertainties as the size of annual harvests and grain collections, and all "those corrections which may be introduced by life." Third, the developmental philosophy of the plan was to be strict maintenance of the country's "basic economic proportions," namely, the necessary proportions between light and heavy industry, between industry and agriculture, and between calculated output and anticipated consumer and producer demand. To guarantee that development would be "more or less crisis-free" and would not generate a spiraling series of disproportions and bottlenecks, figures for each branch of the economy were to presuppose and aim for the creation of reserves, both monetary and natural.[20]

Bukharin, to his eventual regret, developed his planning ideas fully only after the Fifteenth Congress, when in the course of his 1928–9 battle with different "madmen" he tried to educate the party in his conception of a plan predicated on balanced growth and "moving economic equilibrium." But at the beginning of his renewed interest in planning in 1926, on the occasion of another dispute with Preobrazhenskii, he stated in theoretical form his central assumption. Both he and Preobrazhenskii, it will be recalled, held the view that the categories of political economy were historically limited; the law of value, they agreed, was peculiar to capitalist-commodity systems. What law, if any, would succeed it in a post-capitalist economy remained unanswered until Preobrazhenskii advanced his "law of socialist accumulation." This principle, he contended, already regulated the Soviet public sector and was currently locked in mortal competition with the law of value prevailing in the private sector.[21] Since Preobrazhenskii's law impressed many as an invitation to economic voluntarism rather than an "objective regulator," he was vulnerable to the same charges leveled earlier against Bukharin's *The Economics of the Transition Period.*

Preobrazhenskii, however, had at least formulated a new regulator, while Bukharin, the doyen of Bolshevik theoretical economics, had left the question unanswered in 1920. In July 1926, Bukharin tried to remedy the omission and refute his former collaborator. Drawing somewhat remotely on Marx, he argued that the same regulator actually governs all economic systems: he called it the "law of proportional labor expenditures," defining it as "the general and universal law of economic equilibrium." He squared this assertion with his historical understanding of political economy by explaining that the law takes different forms in different societies. In a capitalist-commodity economy, "it clothes itself in the fetishistic costume of the law of value." Only in a socialist economy, with the growth of the planning principle, does it emerge as its "defetished," rationalized self. Therefore, Bukharin concluded, Preobrazhenskii's error had been to imagine two antagonistic regulators at work, while in truth the Soviet economy was witnessing *"the process of the transformation of the law of value into the law of labor expenditures, the process of the defetishization of the fundamental social regulator."* [22]

More than theory was at stake here. Bukharin was emphasizing the continued existence of objective economic conditions, and insisting that the "economic futurism" of those who construed planning as an opportunity "to do as you please" was dangerous folly. He elaborated the "law of labor expenditures" as a theoretical retort to Preobrazhenskii; but he reasserted what he understood to be its elementary truths time and again, especially in 1928 when Stalin's planners were proposing to feed industrial accumulation by starving agriculture:

the law of value may grow into . . . anything you please except into a law of accumulation. The law of accumulation itself presupposes the existence of another law on whose basis it "functions." What it is— the law of labor expenditures or something else—is a matter of indifference to us here. But one thing is clear: if any branch of production systematically does not receive back the costs of production plus a certain additional increment corresponding to a part of the surplus labor and adequate to serve as a source of expanded reproduction, then it either stagnates or *regresses.*[23]

This dictum—"if any branch of production does not receive nourishment . . . it decays," as he put it elsewhere [24]—defined the limits and the nature of Bukharin's revised program of planned industrial development.

Whether revisions were required in Bukharin's agrarian program was less clear, and on this subject he was considerably slower to decide and propose changes. Part of the reason was that his policies seemed to be paying off. Harvests, marketings, and state collections met or exceeded expectations in 1925, 1926, and the first three-quarters of 1927. Moreover, as Bukharin had predicted, state and cooperative organs were "squeezing" private traders from the grain market. From 1926 until November 1927, when first signs that collections had dropped sharply began trickling in, Bukharin's remarks on the grain question were self-congratulatory. Occasional difficulties in collection campaigns, he said, had been due to faulty pricing policies and related mistakes by responsible agencies, not (as the opposition suspected in 1926) to a kulak "grain strike." His excitement that state and cooperative enterprise (the "socialized sector") had won a virtual "grain monopoly" apparently delayed his response to the underlying problem: [25] the annual growth of agricultural output was lagging seriously behind industry, an ominous disparity on the eve of projected industrial expansions.

In October 1927, Bukharin announced a major change in the official agrarian policies operative since 1925. Explaining that during the past two years the state's "commanding heights" had been strengthened, the *smychka* with the peasant masses secured, and the kulak socially "isolated," he declared that it was possible to begin a "forced offensive against the kulak," to begin to limit his "exploiting tendencies." [26] This reasoning did not persuade Trotsky: "Today, 'Get rich!' and tomorrow, 'Away with the kulak!' That is easy for Bukharin. He picks up his pen, and is ready. He has nothing to lose." [27]

Bukharin, however, meant something else. He was exceptionally careful to stress that he did not mean a "hysterical" maneuver —"not a bullet . . . shot from a revolver"—but prudent actions compatible with the principles of NEP. Apart from a single political sanction (loss of voting rights in land societies), the "offensive" involved measures only to limit the kulak as a prosperous farmer, including heavier taxation, a crackdown on surreptitious buying and selling of land, and stricter limitations on rural wage labor and the period of land leasing. None of the measures were to affect poor or middle-peasant farming, which, on the contrary, were to be encouraged even more assiduously.[28]

The announcement constituted a partial abrogation of the 1925 agrarian reforms, and effectively closed the door (if in fact it had ever been opened) to a "kulak solution" of Soviet Russia's agriculture problems. The era of "we do not hinder kulak accumulation" was at an end. Bukharin's policies were still based on individual farming and private accumulation, on the "commercialization of agriculture," and on "combining large socialist industry with the millions of peasant holdings . . . through the market"; [29] but "enrich yourselves" no longer applied unconditionally to the upper peasant stratum. Considering his new industrial ambitions, it seemed an odd time for Bukharin to dissuade expanded production on the part of the most productive farmer. He hoped to compensate for the lost output and gain further surpluses through two additional policies, both of which aimed at enlarging the productive capacity of Soviet agriculture.

The first called for energetic state aid to overcome the individual peasant's "extraordinarily barbaric, primitive working of the land." Improved cultivation implements, fertilizers, irrigation, the development of varied and labor-intensive crops, elementary agronomic enlightenment—all were steps that had been neglected and were now advocated by Bukharin to "rationalize" and uplift private farming at relatively little cost: "even within the limits of this budget it should be possible to achieve much greater productivity." [30] The second was a longer-term, more far-reaching, and costlier venture, and represented an important change in Bukharin's thinking. It called for the gradual creation of a collectivized agricultural sector, mainly large-scale, mechanized production cooperatives. Neither he nor other leaders elaborated publicly on the decision to move toward moderate collectivization until after the Fifteenth Congress. But Bukharin's conception of the undertaking was clear. He did not regard it as a decision against individual cultivation or market cooperatives, but an attempt, through greater investments and inducements to voluntary association, to build a supplementary grain-producing sector as a means of increasing agricultural output during the impending stage of industrialization. Private farming, he insisted, would remain the backbone of Soviet agriculture for "several decades." [31]

These were the principal changes Bukharin introduced into his economic program on the eve of the Fifteenth Party Congress. His revised policies were ambitious, but tempered by realism and caution.[32] Gone was the complacency that the Left had derided as a "restoration ideology." A characteristic component of his new sobriety was his increased emphasis on "cultural revolution" as an integral part of economic modernization—on the lengthy, painstaking task of surmounting age-old traditions of backwardness, "Oblomovism," in production and administration, on educating new workers, managers, and technicians, and on scientific and technological advancement generally.[33]

Beyond this, however belatedly, Bukharin had recognized the deep-rooted deficiencies of Soviet industry and agriculture as well as the growing ramifications of these deficiencies. He had, he thought, adjusted his policies accordingly. His revised developmental strategy relied considerably more on state intervention in the whole economy—on stricter regulation of private capital, long-range planning, and reconstructing the productive base of NEP society. Inconsistencies and uncertainties remained, as, for example, in the contradiction between heavier direct taxation and increased private savings, between constricting the kulak and increasing total agricultural output, and between reducing industrial costs and the rising worker's living standard Bukharin seemed to anticipate. Neither was it certain that "rationalization" could soon generate the sizable surpluses needed for investment, nor that meanwhile the goods famine could be alleviated sufficiently to induce a continuous growth in agricultural marketings.

But while his revised solutions were belated and may not have been wholly adequate to his analysis, Bukharin no longer obscured the problems ahead. In confronting them, he proposed to utilize the mixed economy and its variety of forms to the utmost: to maximize the cheaper expansion opportunities of existing production facilities and construct new facilities; to extend the "socialist sector," but to continue to employ "semi-friends and semi-enemies and open enemies" in the private sector; to plan and regulate, but also to take advantage of market economies and rationalities. Though prepared to move in new directions, he rejected either-or solutions, preferring, it has been observed, to walk on as many legs as possible.[34] Because of its evolutionary methods, moderate goals, and long-term solutions, Bukharin's program depended on a substantial period of time free from serious domestic or foreign crises. Both were in the making. The former, the severity of which became clear in November–December 1927, was partly a result of the leadership's tardy response to underlying economic problems. The latter, of which the war scare was part, was largely beyond its control.

"We are children of the world revolutionary movement," Bukharin reassured a Communist audience in 1926.[35] The Soviet Union's prolonged isolation may have persuaded some that the birth of the first worker's state had been premature or that orphanhood seemed likely, but no Bolshevik would have publicly contested the statement. It was an article of profound faith, which strongly influenced the party's thinking and behavior for six years. While the international nature of the revolution continued as a revered verity, 1923 brought a lull in the party's obsessive attentiveness to omens of revolution abroad. Prospects in Europe dimmed and the Bolshevik leaders turned their attention almost exclusively to urgent domestic issues. Comintern policy played no meaningful role in the shaping of party factions or in the controversies of 1924–6, and came to the fore belatedly and obscurantly only in 1927, when the opposition seized upon the Stalin-Bukharin leadership's failures in England and China.

Compared to his earlier attention to the subject, Bukharin was therefore little concerned with customary questions of international revolution between 1924 and the latter part of 1926. His main efforts in this connection were toward refining and popularizing an understanding of the revolutionary process that belied the supposition that the absence of European revolution, the Communist setbacks in Eastern and Central Europe, and the onset of "stabilization" in the major capitalist countries signified the "dead end" of world revolution. This "naïve" misconception, he explained, stemmed from the "usual bookish, scholastic" notion that conflagration would take place "everywhere simultaneously," from a failure to see the process as "a gigantic process involving decades." Though international proletarian revolution was expected to unfold in a shorter historical period, it was also to be remembered that its bourgeois counterpart had occurred in different places at different times, even in different centuries.[36]

Above all, the revolutionary process was to be understood as a global drama, and not a specifically European one. Here Bukharin simply expanded on the imagery he had first used in 1923, of the European and American "industrial metropolises" as representing a "world city" and the "agrarian colonies" a "world countryside." The ultimate destruction of world capitalism (imperialism) would come about through an eventual global *smychka* between proletarian insurrections in the "metropolises" and "the colonial movement, in which the peasantry plays a large role," in the East. They were equally important "component parts" of a single, ongoing world revolution. For the moment, colonial-nationalist uprisings promised to deprive imperialist nations of markets and materials, and were thus powerful factors in capitalism's universal crisis initiated by the war of 1914–18. Stabilization in Europe indicated only that capitalist development continued to "ebb and flow," not that the revolutionary process had ended. Rather, it was currently centered in Soviet Russia, where the imperialist front· had been breeched and a rival civilization was being built, and increasingly on capitalism's Eastern "colonial periphery," where "a giant flame is flaring up, and it is reflected in the windows of the London and Paris banks." [37]

As far as it went, this was a pleasing definition of ongoing international revolution, offsetting to some extent Communist despair caused by civil tranquility in the West. Apart from Bukharin's highly personal idiom (inspired by his understanding of the Russian revolution), and his unusually strong emphasis on the "world peasantry" as a "great liberating force," it was essentially an extrapolation and embellishment of the Eastern orientation sketched out by Lenin in 1920–3. Bukharin apparently encountered no significant opposition when he wrote it into the official resolutions of the Comintern in 1925. At best, however, it could suffice only as a general conceptual framework. It did not seriously address a variety of problems which had become controversial matters by 1926, particularly the disconcerting economic upsurge under way in leading capitalistic countries. The Sixth Comintern Congress was tentatively scheduled for early 1927 (it eventually convened in the summer of 1928), at which a Comintern program was finally to be adopted. A definitive Bolshevik statement on the nature and long-range implications of stabilization could no longer be postponed. It fell to the official theoretician, Bukharin, who had already produced two draft programs in 1922 and 1924 (both outdated), and who was now responsible for a third.[38] From late 1926 through the summer of 1928, amidst his reappraisal of Soviet domestic policy, much of his time was given over to questions of "capitalist stabilization and proletarian revolution." [39]

Of all Bukharin's theories of the 1920's, his treatment of contemporary capitalism required the least innovation. To explain its stabilization, he revived his controversial eleven-year-old concept of state capitalism, or to call it by its forbidden name, organized capitalism. He seemed hesitant at first to recall the term "state capitalism," probably because of its gloomy implications for European revolution, its association with the ideas of Hilferding and other social democrats, and its role in his own past disagreements with Lenin. But though he did not explicitly speak of "state capitalism" until December 1927 (and then only of "tendencies in the direction of state capitalism"), it is clear that from 1926 onward it underlay his thinking about the nature of postwar national capitalism.[40]

A "second round of state capitalism," Bukharin reluctantly concluded, was under way. This meant that stabilization was not, as some Communists believed, an "accidental" occurrence, but the result of "deep, internal structural changes" within capitalist society. Armed with statistics, he related the renewed monopolization of capitalist economies, the unprecedented concentration and centralization of capital through more sophisticated and larger forms of combined ownership and management, and the re-emergence of the bourgeois state as a powerful regulating, organizing, and planning force in the economy. Once again, Bukharin admitted, national capitalism was overcoming its "anarchical nature" and rapidly reconstituting itself on yet another and higher foundation, further "replacing the problem of irrational elements with the problem of rational organization." His full argument need not be restated: it was almost identical to the one he had presented in 1915–16.[41]

Bukharin resuscitated his theory of state capitalism, but with an important amendment. Originally, he had stressed the European war as the primary impetus in the "statization" of economic life. The "second round," however, was developing as a " 'peaceful' economic system" and thus on a "new basis" that differed in two essential ways from the old. First, unlike the extensive, direct state control imposed from above during the war, the current "process of the fusing of the largest centralized enterprises, concerns, trusts, and the like with organs of state power" was proceeding largely "from below." The state was becoming "directly dependent on large and powerful concerns or combinations of these concerns," a development Bukharin called " 'trustification' of state power itself." The prevalence of fusion from above and from below varied from country to country (Germany, Japan, Mussolini's Italy, and France being his main examples), but the direction was the same: "all this reflects a peculiar form of state capitalism, where the state power controls and develops capitalism." [42]

The emerging system was also distinguished from its predecessor by its higher technological base. Bukharin marveled at the "truly remarkable" innovations in capitalist production and economic organization. Capitalism, he exclaimed, "is again revealing the staggering wonder of technological progress, transforming scientific knowledge . . . into a powerful lever of technological revolution." Its ability to "permeate all the pores of its being with

the spirit of 'scientific management of the enterprise' " was bringing about an unprecedented "rationalization" of economic life.
That Bukharin regarded this peacetime state capitalism as a more
advanced, formidable phenomenon was expressed in a striking
analogy: "the present state capitalism . . . is to the state capitalism
of 1914–18 as the present system of growing socialist economy in
the USSR, planned at decisive points, is to the economy of so-
called war communism." In this sense, it was "growing as a 'normal'
capitalist system." [43]

The point of his analysis, as in 1915–16 was its implications for
the coming of revolution. As organized capitalism eradicated free
competition and other internal economic contradictions, the likelihood of a "direct revolutionary situation" arising from essentially
internal crises grew more remote. Bukharin emphasized capitalism's
continuing internal problems, and carefully disassociated himself
from Hilferding's recent contention that the organizing process
could be effective on an international scale as well; but he left no
doubt that he thought "the 'prewar' Hilferding" was now doubly
valid.[44] Modern capitalism, Bukharin concluded for the second time
in a decade, had become unlike the capitalism of Marx's time. Its
fatal, crisis-producing contradictions were at work outside the
country rather than within:

Its anarchical nature creeps over to . . . *international* economic relations. The problems of the market, of prices, competition, and crises
increasingly become problems of *world* economy, being replaced inside the "country" by the problem of *organization*. The most painful
and bleeding of capitalism's wounds, its starkest contradictions, are
unleashed precisely here, on the world "field of battle." Even the problem of problems, the so-called "social question," the problem of class
relationships and class struggle, is a problem . . . connected with the
position of this or that capitalist country *on the world market*.[45]

Right or wrong in his conclusions, it was this kind of intellectual integrity that put Bukharin in awkward political corners.
Hilferding and other social democratic theorists of peaceful or
"ultra-imperialism," he said, erred in failing to understand that
organized capitalism brings " 'not peace, but the sword' ": that "the
dying out of competition *inside* capitalist countries" results in "the
greatest *intensification* of competition *between* capitalist countries," thus making war and revolution inevitable.[46] Bukharin was
again arguing that catastrophic external forces would be decisive
in bringing down state capitalist systems. He was implying, but he

denied and did not wish to be saddled with, the argument that future proletarian revolutions were likely only in the event of war, a proposition which had been academic in 1915–16, but which now posed a real dilemma for the Soviet régime, whose need for peace in Europe was equal to (or surpassed) its professed desire for companion revolutions.

Bukharin's enemies would seize upon this implication in 1928. Pressed, he would point out that dating from the Paris Commune, revolutions had come in the aftermath of war, quickly adding, however, that he did not exclude the possibility of the former without the latter. "I would formulate it like this: direct revolutionary situations, say in Europe, are possible and perhaps even likely *without war*. . . . But *in the event* of war, they are absolutely inevitable." [47] Given his understanding of state capitalism, it was a lame and unconvincing answer. The political motives of his adversaries aside, Bukharin did not believe that "direct revolutionary situations" were developing in the "metropolises." [48]

It is easy to comprehend why he attached such great importance to the ersatz (peasant) wars on capitalism's "colonial periphery." Short of world war, they were striking "a great blow" at the "metropolis," hopefully offsetting its renewed organizing vigor at home.[49] At the same time, Bukharin's search in the East for forces capable of triggering the collapse of Western capitalism gave him some insight into the nationalist movements set into motion by the First World War. He saw that an era of "anti-imperialist revolutions" had been inaugurated, and that in these awakening "colonial and semi-colonial countries" (China being the major example in the twenties) the alignment of revolutionary classes differed significantly from traditional Marxist expectations based on European or even Russian history. Because nationalist revolution combined a struggle against a partially feudal agrarian order with one against foreign domination, the enormous peasantry, the small proletariat, and the native bourgeoisie were swept into "a single nationalist revolutionary current." Bukharin expected the bourgeoisie to drop out eventually, but he never doubted that the "colonial peasantry," intent on agrarian revolution, had permanently entered history as a "great liberating force," and that this "majority of mankind" would in the end "decide . . . the whole struggle." [50]

He continued, of course, to express faith in the eventual revolutionary hegemony of the native proletariat. But as social unrest in the East spread and stabilization in the West increased, Bukharin, like Lenin before him, came to view nationalist revolution as a thing in itself, to look, with scant concern for class content, to "Eastern-Asiatic peoples" and their "people's revolution" for Soviet Russia's allies.[51] Thus, as the Kuomintang marched from victory to victory in China in 1926–7, he dreamed of "one huge revolutionary front stretching from Archangel to Shanghai and comprising a population of 800 millions." And, as Lenin had done, he began to picture a world divided into oppressed and oppressor nations, and Soviet Russia, with its "unique position across the gigantic European-Asiatic continent," as the rallying center of the former.[52]

Finally, as the likelihood grew in 1925–7 that a victorious "people's revolution" in China would precede a socialist one in Europe, Bukharin took up Lenin's briefly articulated idea of a "noncapitalist development" of colonial countries. The possibility of other peasant societies "bypassing the capitalist road" was for Bukharin closely related to his thinking about the future of the Soviet peasantry and its pre-capitalist economy. Where colonial countries were concerned, it remained an ill-defined concept, but one that bespoke a new vision of a world in revolutionary flux. In the "suppressed and humiliated colonial masses" of the "world countryside," Bukharin had found the "guarantee of our final victory" over the imperialist, state capitalist "world city."[53] His imagery and vision would be revived forty years later by Chinese Communists.[54]

Better than most Bolsheviks, Bukharin perceived, in a special perspective it is true, two developments that were to shape much of the twentieth century. Despite a great depression (which he did not foresee), Western capitalism reconstituted itself on a new basis and endured; anti-capitalist régimes emerged in Europe only in the wake of war, and then not solely through indigenous revolutionary upheavals. Popular mass revolutions, on the other hand, have continued to move relentlessly through the "world countryside," old orders being swept away and new movements catapulted into power by the "destructive force" of the peasantry, much as Bukharin anticipated. What his analysis lacked was the prospect of Western capitalism, surviving the loss of its colonies, of organized capitalism's capacity to obtain from other sources and by other means the "super-profits" which, Bolsheviks believed, warded off insurrection at home. Even this dire possibility was apparently impressing itself on Bukharin by 1928.[55] Many future developments would have disappointed him; few would have confounded him.

Insight into long-range tendencies was, however, of marginal political value to a Bolshevik politician in the second half of the Soviet twenties. At issue was Comintern policy and the immediate tactics of foreign Communist parties. On this question, East and West, Bukharin was guided by a single thought: Communists should avoid quixotic political postures that would alienate them from the mainstream of social protest and invite a return to their isolation of the early twenties.[56] Much as Bolsheviks now sought broad support in Soviet society for their domestic programs, so should foreign Communist parties strive to rally the greatest number of allies for their goals. In China, this meant participation in and preservation of the "anti-imperialist bloc" as represented by the Kuomintang, a broadly based movement led by the nationalist bourgeoisie. Looking ahead, it necessitated a patient and enlightened "struggle for influence over the colonial and semi-colonial peasantry." [57]

In the West, it meant a sustained effort to win the allegiance of the working class, particularly through participation in its "most important and largest mass organizations," the trade unions. The British strikes of 1925–6 (among other things) persuaded Bukharin that "these citadels of social democracy" were the backbone of any meaningful proletarian movement, the Communists' lifeline and direct route to building a mass party. Working in trade unions, concerning themselves with "small deeds," gave Communist parties their best opportunity to expose social democratic reformism and radicalize and convert its rank-and-file membership. (In addition, he seemed to regard strong, consolidated unions as the only possible bulwark against labor's powerful new enemy, "trustified capital.") In 1925–26, Bukharin's enthusiasm for the unions' revolutionary potential became the cornerstone of his Comintern policies in the West.[58] Beyond his belief that they were the key to a mass following, it reflected his desire to see Communist parties establish genuine roots (as leaders) in the European labor movement, and to see "the tragedy of the working class, its internal schism" overcome. He became and remained an advocate of policies based on working-class unity. As he pleaded vainly in 1928, when those policies were on the verge of being discarded, "the banner of unity is no mere maneuver. . . . *This banner of unity from below, of unity against the capitalists, must not be lowered for one instant by the Communists*." [59]

The operative aspect of this general outlook was Bukharin's commitment to the Comintern's united front policies, in force in one form or another since 1921. Officially, there were said to be two kinds of united front politics: those "from above," which

meant Communist Party collaboration with European social democratic leaders, as in the case of the Anglo-Russian Trade Union
Committee or electoral alliances in England and France; and those
"from below," which meant working with lower, primarily rank-
and-file social democrats while scorning their leaders. In 1925–6,
Bukharin and Comintern policy were oriented, at least in specific
cases such as England, toward the first. In mid-1927, however,
Bukharin, as head of the Comintern, sponsored and presided over
a moderate "left turn" (analogous in some respects to that under
way in his domestic policies), toward united front policies "from
below." Prompted by various factors—including Communist setbacks, alarm over growing right-wing sentiment in some Communist parties (notably the French and British), pressure from the
Bolshevik Left, and probably his own hostility to European social
democratic leaders—it primarily involved ending Communist electoral support for socialist parties in England and France.[60]

United front policies expressed Bukharin's enduring belief
that mass movements alone were truly revolutionary, and that the
necessary constituency of communism was "the broadest masses of
the working class and the toilers of every race and every continent." His optimism that Bolshevism was shaking the world in
1925–7, when international Communist influence briefly seemed to
be on the rise from England to China, was considerable: "Our
army is the majority of mankind, and that army is on the move." [61]

By their nature, however, collaborative policies depended not
only on the perseverance of foreign Communist parties, but also
on the strategy of their non-Communist allies. It was inevitable
therefore that they would produce spectacular and embarrassing
failures as well as apparent successes. For example, the sudden
collapse of the British general strike in 1926, the sharp rightward
turn of British trade unionists and their subsequent withdrawal
from the Anglo-Russian Committee in September 1927 were
serious though not calamitous setbacks.

The kaleidoscopic turn of events in China (a society about
which Bolshevik leaders, including Bukharin, knew little), on the
other hand, was disastrous. Bukharin had strongly supported Communist cooperation within the Kuomintang since 1923. It was, he
thought, the organizational embodiment of the "anti-imperialist
bloc" that was fueling the ongoing Chinese revolution. Its victories
in 1925–7 further convinced him of this—he imagined "Canton,
the capital of a revolutionary China, becoming a kind of 'Red
Moscow' for the awakening masses of the Asiatic colonies"—and

he sternly opposed (until it was too late) suggestions that the Chinese Communists should part company with the forces of Chiang Kai-shek for an independent course.[62] Certain that the Kuomintang was the "peculiar," indispensable vehicle of further social revolution and future Communist influence in China, he set aside his worry that the bourgeoisie might "desert" the revolution.[63] Chiang Kai-shek's massacre of his Communist allies in Shanghai in April 1927 caught Bukharin and the Soviet leadership unprepared; on the eve of the coup, they had instructed the Chinese party to bury its arms. Still unwilling "to hand over the flag of the Kuomintang," he and Stalin ordered support for the separatist left-Kuomintang régime in Wuhan (Hankow). In July it, too, turned against the Communists. Finally, in the fall, after futile attempts to rally dissident Kuomintang elements around radical Communist action, Bukharin belatedly concluded: "the Kuomintang and all its groupings has ceased to exist as a revolutionary force." [64]

The Chinese debacle was among Bukharin's worst political experiences as a leader. Charged (together with Stalin) by the opposition with having aborted the real Chinese revolution, he found himself improvising tactics that were immediately outdated by events, blaming the Chinese Communists for having "sabotaged" Comintern instructions, and generally engaging in the ugly subterfuges inherent in the defense of policies that, whatever their original wisdom, had come to ruin.

Not all of his post-mortem arguments, however, were mere sophistry. His China policies had been based on conviction, and he was probably sincere in saying that, apart from "partial errors" (presumably the fatal unpreparedness leading up to the destruction of Chinese cadres), he still believed "in all conscience" that the Comintern's general line was the "only correct line." Its perfidy notwithstanding, "the Chinese bourgeoisie had been assisting in the unleashing of popular forces, it helped bring the people into the independent arena, and in this lies the justification of our tactics. . . ." Nothing, Bukharin insisted, could negate that historic accomplishment, which ensured a future revolutionary upsurge in China. And while agreeing that tactics in China could not be "mechanically" transferred to other colonial revolutions, he denied that the idea of an "anti-imperialist bloc" and collaboration with a nationalist bourgeoisie had been discredited: "If the Devil himself came out against the imperialist god, we should thank him." [65]

Although the fiasco in China was of greater magnitude, it was the united front setbacks in the West (in England and to a lesser degree that resulting from Pilsudski's coup in Poland in 1926) that impressed some Bolsheviks as being particularly instructive. Here, too, Bukharin refused to renounce united front policies flatly, even those "from above." The collapsed alliance with "opportunist" British trade unionists, he maintained, had contributed to the radicalization of the workers and increased the influence of the small British Communist Party.[66] And even while initiating the 1927 leftward turn away from united fronts "from above" to ones "from below," he did not completely exclude the former, leaving open the possibility of new alliances with socialist parties and European trade unions.[67] It was predictable therefore that in 1928, when Stalinists began to close the door on any form of united front or collaboration with social democrats, even (or especially) against fascism, Bukharin would oppose them. His insistence on working-class unity assured that, despite his personal hostility toward social democratic leaders, he would resist the folly of equating social democracy with "social fascism" and designating it the primary enemy.

Though self-serving in his relations with the left opposition, Bukharin's contention that defeats should not be interpreted as heralding the bankruptcy of the united-front principle was tenable. By definition, those policies presumed that maximum Communist goals lay at the far end of a long and tortuous road. But this did not mitigate the profound impact of the failures abroad on Soviet internal affairs. Among other things, they prompted opposition leaders, themselves seriously divided over tactics in England and China but understandably outraged by the slaughter of Chinese Communists and their followers, to include Comintern affairs in their condemnation of the Stalin-Bukharin leadership.

Virtually silent publicly on foreign policy before the China catastrophe, the Left, spearheaded by Trotsky, now charged the duumvirs with having betrayed the international as well as the Russian revolution.[68] Henceforth, the widening split between the leadership and the left opposition was probably irreversible. At the same time, Comintern failures combined with Soviet diplomatic setbacks and new international tensions—notable events included the breaking of diplomatic relations by the Conservative British government in May 1927, and the assassination of the Soviet ambassador to Poland in June—to create the war scare and an acute sense of Soviet isolation. From the summer of 1927 onward, the party was enveloped in an atmosphere of deepening crisis. This threw the leadership's moderate domestic and foreign policies into question, intensified the factional struggle and prepared the way for the Left's expulsion, and began to open up rifts in the Stalin-Bukharin majority itself.

For Bukharin and the Politburo Right, 1927 began as a year of optimistic reappraisal. It ended in a series of interrelated crises, which undermined their economic policies and reverberated adversely upon their political fortunes. In several respects, the war scare was the nexus of their troubles. Its immediate effect on economic policy was to accentuate more dramatically than ever before the perceived need for a significant expansion of capital goods industries, particularly those on which national security depended, and to transform the party slogan of "catch up and surpass" (the capitalist countries) into an urgent, perilous imperative. In short, the adequacy of both the projected pattern and tempo of industrialization was brought into question, provoking (it soon became clear) deep dissatisfaction in new quarters. Short-term military preparedness had played little part in Bukharin's economic thinking before 1927; for all his talk of an "epoch of wars and revolutions," he had reckoned in terms of a prolonged "breathing spell." [69] Though he and his allies now framed their economic recommendations in the context of a possible war, the crisis atmosphere, which was to outlive the transitory international tensions of 1927, could only work against Bukharinist policies.

The second economic consequence of the war scare did not make itself felt fully until the end of the year, when it aggravated a crisis whose origins lay elsewhere. Alarmist speeches by party leaders, including Bukharin, had triggered widespread hoarding during the summer and early autumn of 1927. Food queues sprang up in the cities and the goods famine was seriously exacerbated. The leadership believed at the time that the worsening goods famine was temporary and that the satisfactory grain collections then in progress, which continued into October, would remedy the food shortages. But in November–December, the inadequacies of the leadership's past agrarian policies suddenly struck with a vengeance. Deprived of cheap goods and faced with an unfavorable price structure, the peasant sharply reduced his marketed produce: state grain procurements fell drastically, totaling only half those of the previous November–December. [70]

The ominous news—shortly to be declared a "grain crisis"—was scarcely mentioned at the Fifteenth Party Congress in December, though secret discussions on how to meet the situation were already under way in the Politburo. Caught "asleep" [71] and without reserves, unable to flood the village with enough goods to draw peasant stocks onto the market or even guarantee increased marketings in the near future, and unwilling to disrupt its industrial investment plans by raising grain prices sufficiently, the leadership would resort to "extraordinary measures" in January 1928. Many things were to follow from this momentous decision "on the grain front," including an open break between the Politburo Right and Stalin and the onset of the collective farm revolution of 1929–33.

The impact of the war scare on internal party politics was no less far-reaching. Governments customarily react to a real or imagined crisis by seeking either to rally opposition around a single unifying standard or to suppress it. The Stalin-Bukharin leadership chose the second course, questioning the opposition's loyalty and trying to stifle its criticisms of failures abroad. Beginning in the summer of 1927, the Left was subjected to increasingly repressive reprisals, threats of expulsion, and, for the first time, systematic police harassment. Trotskyists and Zinovievists were partially responsible for the crackdown, giving no hint of a willingness to rally around the duumvirate. Though differences on economic policy had narrowed considerably, the Left's indictment was by now total, condemning with unprecedented bitterness all of the majority's domestic and foreign policies, past and present, as Thermidorian perfidy. Openly challenging the duumvirs' capacity to lead in wartime, the Left demanded no less than a change of leaders (a demand dramatically underlined by Trotsky's approving reference to Clemenceau's wartime conduct).

Because they were forbidden party channels of protest, oppositionists turned (not without some revolutionary nostalgia) [72] to public demonstrations, clandestine pamphleteering, and other illegal methods. This produced a sequence of tragi-comic incidents, a mixture of secret police provocation and futile Left heroics, and a final majority ultimatum to recant and disband or face worse. Defiant, Trotsky and Zinoviev were expelled from the party on November 15, eight days after the tenth anniversary of the Bolshevik revolution. The rout of the Left was completed at the Fifteenth Party Congress in December, which ratified the decision and expelled the remaining opposition leaders. Broken, the Zinovievists finally capitulated. A few weeks later, Trotsky and his unrepentant followers were banished from the capital. [73]

In retrospect, it is clear that only Stalin profited from these events of April–December 1927. If, as reported, the Politburo

Right had resisted his previous attempts to expel the opposition, the war scare was a blessing. It helped to engender the "pogrom atmosphere" and enabled him to wheel out the "dry guillotine." [74] By so vehemently attacking Comintern policy in China and England, the Left had forfeited the remaining sympathies of the two Politburo leaders least disposed to favor expulsion, Bukharin and Tomskii. In the autumn, no longer inclined toward restraint, Bukharin joined in the strident indignation over the opposition's "illegal" escapades. Aware that oppositionists frequently had been provoked into "saying things they do not believe . . . and going farther than they would have liked," and hoping "with all our souls" that they would give in to the leadership's ultimatum, he nonetheless concluded: "there is no place in our party for people with such views." [75]

The Politburo Right would soon regret its acquiescence in the final destruction of the Left. With the Right's assistance, Stalin had eliminated the common foe tying him to his erstwhile allies. They probably did so confident of their own political strength. On the surface, it was formidable. (Trotsky predicted that they would shortly "hunt down Stalin.")[76] The major symbols of revolutionary authority were in their hands: the premiership, the party's theoretical mantle and ideological organs, the Comintern, and the trade unions. A Soviet Bagehot would have understood, however, that these were "dignified," apparent sources of power, and that real, "efficient" power lay increasingly with Stalin's party machine.

This separation of real and apparent authority—which had characterized Soviet politics from the beginning, but which had grown during the twenties as the Secretariat's power fed on the factional struggles—had been on display at the Fifteenth Party Conference in October 1926. Bukharin, Rykov, and Tomskii, in that order, reported first; only then, at the tenth session, did Stalin deliver the report on the party, traditionally the keynote address. The unusual agenda seemed to signify the Right's supremacy. But that same month, two more of Stalin's associates, Ian Rudzutak and Kuibyshev, became full members of the nine-man Politburo. Though the Right still regarded Kalinin and Voroshilov as convinced supporters of their policies, it was at this point that Stalin obtained a potential Politburo majority independent of Bukharin, Rykov, and Tomskii.

A shift in the balance of power was not the only development setting the stage for a confrontation between Stalin and the Politburo Right. The domestic and foreign troubles of 1927 had cast grave doubt on the continuing viability of Bukharinist policies, even in their revised and more realistic form. The difficulties probably shook Stalin's confidence in the economic sagacity of his "150 per cent Nepist" allies, reinforcing his inclination to heed other counsel and set his own course. By 1927, future Stalinist industrializers, headed by Kuibyshev, already occupied strategic economic posts, most notably at the Supreme Economic Council, and were moving toward industrialization policies of their own. Moreover, by initiating policy revisions toward planning, larger capital investment, and collectivization, Bukharin and Rykov had opened the door to varying interpretations of the projected changes. In state planning agencies, for example, very different understandings of the five-year plan had already crystallized. Even before the Left's expulsion, a Stalinist planner, S. G. Strumilin, had uttered the philosophical slogan of Stalin's industrial revolution: "We are bound by no laws. There are no fortresses the Bolsheviks cannot storm." [77]

Exactly when economic policy began to divide the Stalin-Bukharin majority is not known. While sharp and systematic disagreements between the Politburo Right and those who would compose Stalin's new majority seem not to have occurred before late January or February 1928, it does seem clear that contrary positions on collectivization, investment policy, and the tempo of industrial growth were taking shape on the eve of the Fifteenth Congress, even before news of the grain crisis. The congressional resolution on collectivization, and perhaps others, apparently represented unpublicized compromises within the leadership.[78] Whatever the nature and extent of early differences, they were not sufficiently divisive to subvert the united Politburo front which expelled the Left and presided over the Fifteenth Congress. The economic resolutions, compromise or no, reflected the revised views of Bukharin and Rykov, setting out the new goals in language that cautioned against excesses and accented prudence, balanced development, and the inviolability of NEP. (They were, however, general enough to suggest different things to different people.)[79]

Further hints of something less than full unanimity in the Politburo appeared in the congressional speeches of the leaders. Stalin and Molotov sounded a noticeably harsher note on the kulak question than did Kalinin or Rykov, who gave the main economic report.[80] In addition, Stalin defined the necessity of collectivization in a considerably less flexible way than had Bukharin or Rykov before the congress, arguing that only collective cultivation could

THE CRISES OF MODERATION · 267

solve the problems of Soviet agriculture. "There is no other solution," he concluded. He also proffered an evaluation of European
capitalism strikingly different from Bukharin's, predicting an
imminent end of stabilization and "a new revolutionary upsurge in
both the colonies and the metropolises." [81] But these and other
intriguing nuances did not yet reflect separate and distinct schools
of thought. (Stalinists were just beginning to grope toward positions of their own.) Indeed, they stood out only because all of the
leaders, including Stalin, addressed the congress in the cautious,
moderate, and pro-NEP tone of Bukharinism. Nor were the variations in emphasis consistent. Bukharin, after all, had been the first
to formulate and announce the "forced offensive against the
kulak." And both he and Rykov were also now committed to a
serious if limited collectivization effort.[82]

More ominous signs of disharmony at the congress involved
not policy but personalities. For the first time, spokesmen associated
with Stalin openly, though cautiously, criticized Bukharin. In the
discussion following his report on Comintern affairs, two junior
officials closely identified with the general secretary, Lazar Shatskin and Beso Lominadze, as well as the Profintern head, Lozovskii,
sharply objected to Bukharin's description of Western capitalism
as state capitalist, and, more to the point, accused him of ignoring
an incipient "right danger in the Comintern." [83] Their criticism,
from which Stalin pointedly disassociated himself, was portentous.
Not only did it involve a questioning of Bukharin's management of
the Comintern; it struck obliquely at him as the party's theorist.
The state capitalism theory was the weakest link in his Leninist
armor, and later a favorite target of Stalin's anti-Bukharin campaign. Finally, the sorties by these second-rank surrogates marked
the beginning of Stalin's adroit use of the Profintern and Komsomol organizations to undermine the Right's authority and
power.[84]

So it was that in December 1927, at the moment of apparent
triumph, having just legislated their revised program and expelled
their ideological adversaries, the Politburo Right found their
policies beset with crises and their political position threatened.
Bukharin bore a large part of the responsibility for what became
their desperate situation. That he waited so long to heed the valid
economic criticisms of the Left, and then failed to set out fully
his modified policies in time for the important Fifteenth Congress,
were matters of poor judgment. That he aided in the "civil execu-

tion" of the Left represented a different kind of failure.[85] It was not only an unwise political decision, but a failure of the restraint and minimal decency he had exhibited earlier. He participated in this final dance of vengeance undoubtedly still not "relishing it" and "trembling from head to foot." He had not expected "that the logic of struggle would bring this to the fore so rapidly and in such an accentuated form," and was deeply relieved when Zinoviev and Kamenev capitulated. Bukharin was not without some empathy for "this tragedy of the opposition leaders." [86] Nonetheless, he lent his authority to and abetted their destruction.

Bukharin did not come to these destructive actions suddenly. An uninterrupted theme of Bolshevik politics after 1921 had been the waning of official toleration of party dissidents; the leaders, including Lenin, had expelled lesser oppositionists before.[87] Nor was it Bukharin's first personal sanctioning of the "dry guillotine." In 1924, he had presided over the excommunication of, among others, his wartime friend Zeth Höglund from the Comintern. Now he condoned the expulsion, jailing, and then banishment of two of his oldest friends, Vladimir Smirnov and Preobrazhenskii, a close comrade and fellow exile, Mikhail Fishelev, several former Left Communists whom he had led in 1918, and dozens of other Bolsheviks with whom, as he said, he had once "gone into battle." As an intellectual, a man sensitive to arbitrary abuses of power and far from the meanest of Bolsheviks, Bukharin should have known better. Power had not dulled all of his critical faculties. He saw and condemned in the Soviet Union Communist privilege, anti-Semitism, Russian chauvinism, and bureaucratic abuses. But he outlawed his former friends as "enemies" with whom "we have nothing in common." [88]

He did so, once again, apparently because he still believed that the Left's ideas and programs were alien and fatal to everything he had come to identify with Bolshevism. Trotsky had warned him in 1926: "the system of apparatus terror cannot come to a stop only at the so-called ideological deviations, real or imagined, but must inevitably spread throughout the entire life and activities of the organization." [89] Bukharin did not respond to this; neither the "militarization" of the party, which he openly deplored, nor Stalin's growing power and ambition impressed him as much as did his *radical programmatic disagreement* with the Left. He was not the only important Bolshevik caught up in this one-eyed folly. When Bukharin finally discovered in 1928 that "the disagreements between us and Stalin are many times more serious than all of the disagreements we had with you," Trotsky, convinced that Bukharin was the avatar of Thermidor, would declare: "With Stalin against Bukharin?—Yes. With Bukharin against Stalin?—Never!" [90]

Hounded, defamed, banished, and mesmerized by his special harkening to "the footsteps of history," Trotsky's blindness was perhaps understandable. Bukharin had less excuse, and ample warning. In November 1927, he received from a former comrade a letter denouncing him as a "jailer of the best Communists," a man who allowed heroes of October to be judged by secret policemen like Iakov Agranov. The writer closed with an all too prophetic taunt:

Take care, Comrade Bukharin. You have often argued within our party. You will again probably have to do so. Your present comrades will then give you Comrade Agranov as your judge. Examples are infectious. [91]

CHAPTER IX

The Fall of Bukharin and the Coming of Stalin's Revolution

You must conquer and rule,
Or lose and serve,
Suffer or triumph,
Be anvil or be hammer.
— GOETHE

IN 1928–9, in the eleventh year of Bolshevik rule and for the second time in just over a decade, Russia was again on the eve of revolution. Though no one anticipated it, by the winter of 1929–30 the country and its 150 million inhabitants would be in the frenzy of Stalin's "revolution from above," a process as momentous in its consequences as history's great upheavals "from below," including that of 1917.[1] Like other great social revolutions, Stalin's would shatter and then sweep away the old order, bringing about a new, radically different kind of society. Here, however, there was to be a novel development: the order destroyed was NEP society, itself the recent product of a great revolution. And, therefore, as we approach the events that preceded "revolution from above," it is appropriate to take a final look at the "old order," at NEP Russia on the eve of its destruction.

Compared to the Stalinist order that followed, the distinctive feature of NEP—of the Soviet twenties—was the existence of significant social pluralism within the authoritarian framework of the one-party dictatorship. For, while the party's monopoly of political power was zealously defended, pluralism and diversity in other areas was officially tolerated and even encouraged. The chief example lay, of course, in the country's economic life, where 25 million peasant holdings accounted for virtually all agricultural produce; where millions of small artisans produced about 28 per cent of all manufactured goods and between half and three-quarters of the basic consumer items; and where countless small merchants and traders still played an essential part in the flow of commodities (many of their wares being advertised in the official Communist press).[2] Despite the growing weight of the state sector, private undertakings continued to define the tenor of Soviet economic life at the end of the twenties. Most citizens, particularly the immense peasant majority which still constituted over 80 per cent of the population, lived and worked remote from party or state control.

Nor did the party monopolize all other areas of social life. Indeed, even within the political system, throughout lower and administrative levels nonparty people and views were encouraged to participate on a very broad scale. The central state bureaucracies, for example, which recommended, administered, and thereby helped shape official policy, were staffed largely by non-Bolsheviks, many of them previously opponents of the revolution. In 1929, less than 12 per cent of all state employees were Communists; and though the formal heads of Commissariats and important agencies were usually party members, Communists comprised a small percentage of their ranking personnel.[3]

In part the widespread employment of "bourgeois specialists," as the nonparty intelligentsia was known, was a result of the dearth of qualified party cadres, and a source of official anxiety. The party was eager to train and promote its own people, especially in areas such as education where it was represented by only 3 per cent of the country's teachers.[4] But, as may be seen in the number and prominence of nonparty people as well as in their willingness to participate, it also reflected the conciliatory spirit of NEP, the counterpart of the régime's collaborative economic policies. Thus, non-Bolsheviks also played a major role in sensitive areas which the party could have monopolized had it wished. Of all official press personnel, for example, at least one-third were non-Bolsheviks in 1925.[5] And at the local elective level, as a result of the decision in 1924–5 to allow relatively free elections, only 13 per cent of all members of local soviets belonged to the party or to the Komsomol, and only 24 per cent of their chairmen.[6]

But perhaps the truest reflection of the pluralism of NEP society was to be found in its cultural and intellectual life, always a barometer of genuine diversity and state toleration. For here the twenties were a decade of memorable variety and achievement. In the party's own intellectual life, in its academic institutions, societies, and scholarly publications, in the intense debates in social theory from education and science to law, philosophy, and historiography, it was a period not of imposed, arid orthodoxy but of contrary theories and rival schools, a kind of "golden era of Marxist thought in the USSR." [7]

Outside the party, despite the large cultural emigration as a result of the revolution, the Soviet twenties brought a remarkable explosion of artistic ferment and creativity in almost every field. In an atmosphere invigorated by revolution and uninhibited by any official artistic doctrine, and with state, cooperative, and private sponsorship, a great diversity of artists expressed their varying esthetics, theories, and visions in a dazzling array of forms. It was an era when party-oriented artists and "fellow travelers" competed, when national and minority cultures prospered, thick journals and salons revived, cultural circles, associations, and manifestoes proliferated. Soviet artists, moving to and from Western capitals, saw themselves as part of an international cultural upsurge. Above all, it was a time of experimentation, when the modernism of the cultural avant-garde flourished spectacularly if briefly under the lenient reign of the political avant-garde. [8]

NEP culture is most often remembered for its prose fiction and poetry. Among the many writers who produced much of their major work in the twenties were Pasternak, Babel, Olesha, Kataev, Fedin, Esenin, Akhmatova, Vsevolod Ivanov, Sholokhov, Zamiatin, Leonov, Pilniak, Bulgakov, Mandelstam, Zoshchenko, and Mayakovsky. The list is much longer, a virtual roster of the great names of Soviet literature, many of whom would perish, physically or artistically, after NEP.

Literature, however, was only part of the picture. For it was also during the NEP years, again to recall but a few examples, that Eisenstein, Vertov, Pudovkin, and Dovzhenko pioneered the modern cinema, that the experimental productions of Meyerhold and Tairov revolutionized the theater, and that Tatlin, Rodchenko, Malevich, Lissitzky, Ginzburg, the Vesnin and Sternberg brothers, Melnikov, Leonidov, and many others helped create modern painting, architecture, and design in Russia. Looking back, it is clear not only that the Soviet twenties were a "golden era" in Russian culture, but that NEP culture, like Weimar culture, was a major chapter in the cultural history of the twentieth century, one that created brilliantly, died tragically, but left an enduring influence.[9]

That the social pluralism and state liberality of NEP were relative and frequently ambiguous is also true. Some artists were publicly traduced and semi-blacklisted; nonparty specialists were often harassed; peasant proprietors were occasionally abused by local officials; and sudden police raids on ostentatiously prosperous nepmen were not unknown.[10] But in contrast to what followed, and in its own right, NEP was a comparatively pluralistic and liberal order. Its spirit—what Stalinists would shortly condemn as "rotten liberalism"—was conciliatory and ecumenical.[11] The party-state did not deny its many "semi-friends and semi-enemies" the designation "soviet," a concept which in the twenties, unlike later, was defined mainly by territory rather than mindless fidelity to party strictures.[12] And it was this toleration of social diversity, as well as the official emphasis on social harmony and the rule of law, as opposed to official lawlessness, that thirty years later would commend NEP to Communist reformers as a model of a liberal Communist order, an alternative to Stalinism.

But as the twenties drew to a close, and the party found itself confronted by serious difficulties, NEP was judged not by its future appeal but by its current realities. In important respects, its achievements were impressive. NEP had brought civil peace, political stability, and economic recovery; and it had done so while preserving the Bolsheviks' political monopoly and, judging by the decline of "counter-revolutionary acts" in the twenties, while extending the party's authority and influence among the population.

Beyond this, the twenties witnessed the further development of the progressive social legislation initiated by the revolution (and largely undone after NEP)—in welfare, education, women's rights, divorce, and abortion.[13] The civil peace of NEP also enabled the government to make progress against the social ills which traditionally afflicted its main constituency, the poor. Thus, by the late twenties, literacy had increased notably and enrollment in primary and secondary schools was double the prewar level; and the death rate had decreased by 26 per cent, infant mortality by about 30 per cent, and instances of venereal disease by almost half.[14] Many of these, as in education, were small first steps in what remained a profoundly backward society; others, as with many welfare provisions, were still more promise than reality. Nonetheless, considering the scarcity of resources, the Bolshevik government had made significant advances in the few years since the end of the civil war.

Indeed, there is little question that Russia's industrial workers and peasants, who had made the social revolution of 1917, now lived better than they had under the old régime. In short-term gains, the peasant had emerged as the chief beneficiary of the upheaval. Though the average peasant continued to live a hard existence, farming subsistently with primitive tools and few animals, the revolution had removed the landlord, given him land, abolished his burdensome arrears, and established him as an independent producer. All this had come with few political liabilities. By the early twenties, when the smoke of revolution cleared, the peasant had reverted to his traditional way of life and governance. Few party officials intruded into the village, which, as late as 1928–9, was effectively governed not by the local soviet but by the traditional commune, now discreetly called the "village society." [15] As a result, and due to its welfare efforts on the peasant's behalf, the Soviet government had probably gained acceptance if not affection among the majority of the rural population, and the party's prestige and influence were on the rise, especially among the younger village generation. According to one foreign observer in 1927: "the old village, however slowly, is passing away before our eyes." [16]

The gains of the industrial working class, in whose name the party ruled, were more ambiguous. While the Bolsheviks' initial promise of political and economic power to the workers had not been realized, their general situation was considerably better than before the revolution, when industrial conditions had been almost Dickensian. By the late twenties, when the cities and proletariat regained their prewar size, the average workday had decreased from ten hours to seven and a half; real wages, though low by West European standards, had risen about 11 per cent over the 1913 level; and the factory worker, like the peasant, was eating better than before the revolution. In addition, comprehensive (though frequently inadequate) social insurance, trade union benefits, and free medical care and education had improved the worker's position. On the other hand, urban unemployment had reached 1½ million in 1927, double the 1924 figure; factory conditions remained very poor and the accident rate high; food and clothing were exceptionally costly; and housing conditions had deteriorated seriously since the revolution.[17]

It is, of course, impossible to calculate precisely the gains and losses of Soviet workers and peasants after a decade of revolution.

Account must be taken of the millions who died in the civil war and famine, as well as the demoralizing impact of the Bolsheviks' unfulfilled promises on the survivors. On the other side, credit must be registered for the social mobility acquired by workers and, to a lesser extent, peasants, as well as their "revolution of status" in the new order. The psychological importance of the exalted citizenship conferred upon industrial workers and poorer peasants by the Bolshevik ideology cannot be measured but should not be discounted. Whether it took the form of glorification in official propaganda, the performing of some minor functions as a "representative of the worker's state," or simply of access to the former sanctuaries of the privileged classes (museums, theaters, grand buildings, and the like), this elevated status probably compensated in part for the still low level of material rewards.[18] Whatever the precise balance, Soviet workers and peasants lived better in the last years of NEP, on the eve of Stalin's revolution, than they had before 1917, and than they would for years to come.[19]

None of these achievements, economic, cultural, or otherwise, however, diminished the serious problems still facing NEP Russia. Two were of special importance. First was the primitive, laggardly state of peasant agriculture, which had only barely surpassed its prewar productivity and whose marketed surplus was still ominously below the 1913 level. The second also involved the over-populated, underproductive countryside: rural migration was flooding the cities with unskilled, discontented laborers, swelling the ranks of the unemployed and further worsening urban living conditions.[20] Both problems, accentuated by the party's meager administrative and ideological influence in the countryside, frustrated the Bolsheviks' industrial ambitions and threatened to disrupt market relations between town and village, the basis of NEP. In December 1927, the Fifteenth Party Congress had resolved to attack these problems head-on through more ambitious planning and industrial investment coupled with partial voluntary collectivization and state assistance to private peasant farmers.[21] In its Bukharinist spirit and resolutions, the party congress had reaffirmed its commitment to "NEP methods." But, as the events of 1928 were to show, sentiment was growing in some party quarters that these policies, only just adopted, were too little and too late.

Viewed through the party's aspirations, then, NEP presented a mixed picture. Soviet Russia in the twenties was a country of dramatic contrasts: of the traditional and the modern, the wooden plow and the machine, widespread disrepair and great construction projects, cultural brilliance and persistent illiteracy, unemployment and ostentatious affluence, free primary education and roaming bands of perhaps a million homeless children, socialist hopes and rampant alcoholism.[22] The positive features bolstered confidence in NEP and the leadership's Bukharinist policies. The negative ones bred doubt and disillusion, as did the still strong current of revolutionary militancy, especially at lower party levels. For despite the defeat and discrediting of the Left, the party's "revolutionary-heroic" tradition lived on, feeding not only on the nostalgia for 1917 and the civil war, but also the seedier aspects of NEP society.[23] With economic and urban recovery had come a revival of widespread prostitution, gambling, drug traffic, corruption, and profiteering. These features offended Bolshevik sensibilities, gave NEP "a sinister grimace," and aroused the party's "violent zealots of proletarian purity" against the régime's "semi-friends and semi-enemies"—nepman, prosperous peasant, non-party specialist, and artist alike.[24]

Nonetheless, it is important to understand that despite its ignoble origins, blemishes, and problems, by the mid-twenties NEP had achieved a general (if sometimes grudging) consensus among Bolshevik leaders as the proper transition to socialism. Bukharin and his allies were its greatest defenders—"150 per cent nepists" as Piatakov called them; but, as this suggests, all the rival party leaders and factions of the twenties accepted NEP and were "nepists." The common view that the Left was strongly anti-NEP is incorrect. Thus, Preobrazhenskii, the sternest critic of the leadership's economic policies, formulated his own program ("primitive socialist accumulation") in terms of the continuation of NEP's economic pluralism, of private farming and market relations. And Trotsky, for many the embodiment of Bolshevik zealotry and intolerance, was at the same time a leading defender of NEP's cultural diversity.[25] Indeed, the ultimate evidence that NEP had become an all-party policy and model of Communist rule was the fact that not even its eventual destroyer, Stalin, openly advocated its abolition.[26]

The years 1928–9 were a turning point in the conduct and nature of Soviet leadership politics. They marked the transition from the predominantly overt intra-party politics of the twenties and earlier to the covert politics of the thirties and after. Until the expulsion of the Left in 1927, political conflict within the party was substantially a matter of public record. Though (like politicians everywhere) Bolshevik leaders piously deplored acts of manifest disunity, rival factions quarreled and sought support in public—in the press, at mass party meetings and congresses, and even in the streets. In this respect, the leadership's overt politics was part of the more general, if limited, openness of Soviet political life during the NEP years, which ranged from the diversity of opinion expressed in official and nonofficial institutions and publications to the irreverent caricaturing of Bolshevik leaders in popular magazines.[27] After 1929, however, this atmosphere was to disappear, as political conflict within the party leadership grew increasingly covert and, apart from furtive signs, receded from public view.

The confrontation between the Politburo factions of Bukharin and Stalin in 1928–9 was the transitional episode in this development. For, while both sides continued the practice of seeking broader party support, they did so more secretly than had been the case before. Open conflict was confined to select and largely unpublicized meetings of the high leadership. And public debate, while long and intense, was conducted not in candid political language but in the discreet idiom of oblique polemics known in the party from pre-revolutionary times, when it was used to elude the czarist censorship, as "Aesopian language." [28] Indeed, throughout the bitter struggle, both factions publicly denied its existence, and it was not until mid-1929, after the outcome was settled, that the antagonists were officially identified.

This does not mean that the fateful struggle over power and policy inside the Stalin-Bukharin leadership was unknown in wider party circles. Accounts of dissension within the Politburo and Central Committee quickly if imperfectly filtered down to lower officials; and "every literate party member" understood the Aesopian debate.[29] But the most momentous struggle in the party since 1917–18 was the least public and most covert. Its conduct was virtually clandestine; important programmatic documents, including several of the right opposition (as Bukharin and his allies became known), were never published.[30] And, as a result, the political events leading to Stalin's "revolution from above" were then and remain even today obscure in significant respects.

Not the least is the moment when the Stalin-Bukharin coalition that had led the party for three years fell apart. It did not happen suddenly. The concealed divisions accompanying the leadership's leftward turn in economic and Comintern policy in late 1927 had been evident in the varying emphases, uneasy compromises, and political maneuverings at the Fifteenth Party Congress in December. They intensified and then erupted in the early months of 1928. If the final defeat of the Left removed the political rationale of the alliance between the Politburo Right and Stalin, the precipitous drop in grain collections in late 1927 destroyed whatever consensus remained on domestic policy.

The decision in early January 1928 to resort to "extraordinary" or "emergency" measures was the pivotal event. Taken unanimously, its consequences almost immediately, and irreparably, divided the Politburo. Bukharin, Rykov, and Tomskii supported the decision as a regrettable, short-term necessity. They appear to have envisaged an orderly, limited campaign—punitive fiscal and mainly judicial measures aimed exclusively at "kulak speculators." The harshest aspects of these would be limited to selective confiscation of hoarded grain as specified in Article 107 of the criminal code.[31] Conduct of the operation was left to Stalin, as general secretary, and what followed was very different. Within weeks, major grain areas were struck by a wave of administrative "excesses," including armed requisitioning squads, arbitrary and illegal grain seizures and arrests, peremptory dismissal of local authorities, closing of markets, and even isolated attempts to drive peasants into communes. To the rural populace, the onslaught smacked of war communism, a memory accentuated by the arrival of thirty thousand urban plenipotentiaries in less than three months. Panic and rumors of NEP's abolition swept the countryside.[32]

Some of the consequences of initiating ill-defined "extraordinary measures" were predictable, and for these the whole Politburo shared responsibility. But Stalin's role in the excessive severity and scope of the campaign was central. As early as January 6, its nature was shaped by the belligerent, "exceptional" directives sent from his office to local party officials.[33] His closest associates— among them Mikoyan, Lazar Kaganovich, Andrei Zhdanov, Nikolai Shvernik, and Andrei Andreev—took charge of regional operations.[34] Most remarkable, since he rarely traveled about the country, Stalin personally departed on January 15 on a three-week mission through Siberia and the Urals, where grain collections were low despite a good harvest. His trip resembled a military expedition. Summoning local authorities at each stop, and rudely dismissing explanations of local conditions and legal procedures, Stalin assaulted them as incompetent and cowardly, and sometimes accused them of being kulak agents. He left the shaken and purged party organizations with an ultimatum to collect large quantities of grain or suffer worse reprisals.[35]

On February 6, Stalin returned to Moscow and an angry confrontation in the Politburo. Bukharin, Rykov, and Tomskii apparently reaffirmed their support for the original decision but attacked the "excesses" of Stalin's implementation, particularly the victimizing of middle peasants, the degree of coercion, and the disruption of local markets. The root causes of the grain crisis were probably also argued. Both sides agreed that the kulak was withholding stock from the market to force up grain prices, though Stalin presented a more dramatic picture of the size and perfidy of this "hoarding." More important, in Siberia he had suddenly rejected the viability of peasant agriculture, concluding: "we can no longer make progress on the basis of small individual peasant economy." Though Bukharin and Rykov now accepted the need for a limited collectivization program, this dire formulation was unacceptable. For them the immediate source of the crisis was not the structure of peasant agriculture, but the state's errors in price policy and calculating the market situation.[36]

Whatever the range of discussion at this point, the result was a retreat by Stalin and a compromise strongly favoring the Right. Directives from the leadership, while continuing the harsh anti-kulak rhetoric of the original decision, now included stern denunciations of "excesses" and emphatic denials that the "extraordinary measures" were in any way part of the general line adopted at the Fifteenth Congress or a repudiation of NEP. Mikoyan, Stalin's chief operative in the grain campaign, was obliged to repudiate publicly its offending features as *harmful, unlawful, and inadmissible.*[37] Compromise was also apparent elsewhere on the "grain front," as it was becoming known. At the same time in February, the rightist Commissar of Agriculture of the Russian Republic, Aleksandr Smirnov, was removed; but his replacement was another moderate, and Smirnov himself was appointed to the party Secretariat, presumably to help restrain Stalin.[38]

In addition to dividing the Politburo, the grain campaign had other unpredictable and far-reaching consequences. For the first time since NEP's inauguration, the state had challenged the peasant's right to dispose of his surplus as he pleased. This was to have two effects. It undermined the farmer's confidence that the government would treat him fairly and thus made more difficult the resumption of normal market relations and the free flow of grain on which Bukharinists counted. And because the measures were temporarily successful—their renewal in the spring brought mid-year collections to the 1926–7 level—they encouraged thinking about nonmarket, even coercive solutions to the grain problem. Equally portentous, despite official disavowals, the "extraordinary measures" never really ceased. As the crisis continued and deepened, they eventually grew "month by month" into an ad hoc system of procurement which inflamed the countryside and led to the all-out showdown between state and peasantry in late 1929.[39] Finally, the discrepancy between the original decision in January and the turmoil that followed illustrated Stalin's great advantage over his opponents: the Politburo made policy; but Stalin, through the Secretariat, implemented and thereby could transform it.[40]

While of singular importance, the grain controversy was only part of a more general dissension that unfolded in early 1928. News of the collection difficulties revealed two very different moods in the leadership as early as January. Kuibyshev, whose super-industrializing views Stalin was to share, exhorted the party to disregard the market setbacks and "to swim against the current . . . as never before." Uglanov, whose Moscow party was to provide the Right's main organizational support, urged conciliation in the village and prudence in industry. Large construction projects initiated in 1927, he told the Moscow Committee, should be curtailed, and investment in consumer industries, so vital to market relations with the peasant, increased.[41] Caution was also the watchword of Bukharin and his "school," who took the occasion of the fourth anniversary of Lenin's death to fill the central press with reminders of the importance of the small farmer and the primacy of "cultural revolution." [42]

Then, tentatively and stealthily, Stalin began to probe the political strongholds of the Right. In February, he tried to intervene in the affairs of the Moscow Committee. He was rebuffed, and Uglanov tightened his control. Shortly after, a Stalinist minority temporarily failed to dislodge the Bukharinist party bureau at the Institute of Red Professors. Bukharin himself again clashed with Stalin's protégés, including Lominadze, in the Comintern's Executive Committee in February, while the following month Tomskii and his associates found their conciliatory policy toward European trade unions challenged by the Stalinist Lozovskii.[43] In the Politburo, however, the leadership continued to function in manageable if strained accord. Rykov's proposal in early March to limit allocations to heavy industry and collective farms was contested but a compromise reached. And though rumors of conflict were now spreading, the leaders gave no overt sign of discord.[44] Indeed, the only public controversy to touch Bukharin during the first half of 1928 was sparked by the publication of an old photograph showing him with a cigarette. The junior Communist league, the Pioneers, demanded to know if he had violated his month-old "pioneer pledge" to quit smoking.[45]

Into this simmering dissension and shadowy political scene now came another explosive issue. On March 10, it was announced that the security police had uncovered a counter-revolutionary plot involving technical specialists and foreign powers at the Shakhty mines in the Donbass industrial complex. Fifty-five people were accused of sabotage and treason; many confessed. Stalin's purpose in promoting what appears to have been a frame-up into a national political scandal is clear. Through it he sought to discredit Bukharin's collaborative policies and emphasis on civil peace, Rykov's management of the state apparatus, to which most non-Bolshevik specialists were attached, and Tomskii's leadership of the trade unions, which were nominally responsible for overseeing their work. In its social impact, the Shakhty affair was to be almost as significant as the grain crisis. It provided the initial occasion for Stalin's murderous thesis that as the Soviet order approached socialism, its internal enemies would increasingly resort to open and conspiratorial resistance, necessitating ever greater vigilance and state repression.[46] By 1929, alongside the escalating coercion in the countryside, the nonparty intelligentsia was to be caught up in a mounting witchhunt of mass dismissals and arrests.

At the outset, Shakhty did not provoke a straight factional response. Some of Stalin's supporters were alarmed by the promise of rampant "specialist-baiting," for which the general secretary already had a reputation.[47] But the Right was threatened most. Upon hearing the news in March, they called an urgent Politburo meeting to defend the essential role of nonparty experts in the country's modernization effort. Everyone agreed on the need to accelerate the training of Communist specialists, a cause now espoused furiously by Stalin; but Bukharin, Rykov, and Tomskii maintained that it was neither a class matter nor reason to abuse nonparty personnel.[48] They did not question the facts of the Shakhty affair. But, unlike Stalin, they publicly insisted that it was an isolated case, that bourgeois specialists were overwhelmingly loyal and indispensable and that responsibility for Shakhty as well as other kinds of official corruption lay also with local party secretaries under Stalin.[49]

Though Stalin's interpretation of Shakhty's significance was still a minority view in the leadership,[50] its value to his political ambitions was quickly evident. In the weeks that followed, hinting darkly of political malfeasance in high places and class enemies everywhere else, he devised a powerful weapon out of the party's old slogan of "self-criticism." Under its banner, he launched a

major crusade against official "bureaucratism" and "conservative
tendencies," particularly in the state and trade union apparatuses.[51]
It became an irresistible wedge in the hands of Stalin's agents; a
minority in the various strongholds of the Right, they now had a
legitimate way to attack and mobilize support against the entrenched rightist leaderships. "Self-criticism" being a traditional
Bolshevik shibboleth, the Bukharinists were obliged to endorse the
campaign and found themselves reduced to cautioning against its
"abuses." [52]

So matters stood on April 6, when the Central Committee
gathered in plenary session for the first time since the Stalin-
Bukharin coalition had begun to crack. Though individual leaders
seem to have addressed the closed meeting in varying tones, the
Politburo strained to present a unanimous front and compromise
resolutions. The mood of the delegates, many of them provincial
officials, was still favorable to the Right, as were the plenum's
resolutions. The emergency grain measures were defended as a
success and said to be at an end; but their "excesses" were roundly
condemned and all future policy, including the "offensive against
the kulak," defined in terms of NEP and largely in a Bukharinist
spirit.[53] On one matter, Stalin experienced a clear defeat. Presumably in connection with the Shakhty affair and without warning, he proposed to transfer the training of new specialists from
the Commissariat of Education, headed by the liberal Lunacharskii and under Rykov's jurisdiction, to Kuibyshev's Supreme
Economic Council. The proposal was defeated, reportedly by a
two-thirds majority.[54] When the Central Committee adjourned,
then, the grain crisis seemed past and the Right's views and
political strength confirmed. It was an illusion.

How little the leadership's feigned unanimity reflected its
internal discord was dramatized immediately after the plenum.
Speaking on the same day in Moscow and Leningrad respectively,
the Politburo's two pre-eminent leaders, Stalin and Bukharin, gave
radically different accounts of party policy and the situation in
the country. Reviving his earlier bellicosity on the "grain front,"
announcing that Shakhty was not "something accidental," and
unveiling his "self-criticism" crusade, Stalin's theme was starkly
uncompromising: "We have internal enemies. We have external
enemies. This, comrades, must not be forgotten for a single
moment." His target was unnamed but identifiable leaders who
"think NEP means not intensifying the struggle," who wanted "a
policy in the countryside that will please . . . rich and poor alike."
Such a policy had "nothing in common with Leninism"; and such

a leader was "not a Marxist, but a fool." [55] Meantime, speaking in a very different tone on the same issues, Bukharin was expressing his first public apprehension over the "tendency" of "certain people" to regard the "extraordinary measures" as "almost normal" and "to negate the importance of the growth of individual economies and in general to exaggerate the use of administrative methods." [56]

At this point the grain crisis broke out anew. A severe winter, depletion of village reserves, and peasant withdrawal from the market suddenly brought another sharp drop in collections. In late April, the emergency measures were revived with greater intensity and scope than before. The role of Bukharin, Rykov, and Tomskii in this decision is not known; but if they supported it they must have done so with great misgivings. Kulak surpluses had been exhausted by the first campaign; now the measures would fall squarely on the middle—or majority—peasant, who held what stocks remained. During the next two months, the expanded collection measures and accompanying "excesses" provoked widespread discontent and sporadic rioting in the countryside. Reports of rural disturbances and food shortages stirred industrial unrest in the cities.[57] The strain was too much for the fragile accord in the Politburo. In May and June, the split between Bukharinists and Stalinists became complete.

Until the spring of 1928, Bukharin, Rykov, and Tomskii seem to have regarded differences in the leadership as negotiable, and tried to resolve them in the Politburo. Now, however, they (and especially Bukharin) were alarmed by the Stalin group's increasingly radical, uncompromising posture. Differences of opinion were becoming large and systematic. At the center of the dispute were contrary analyses of the régime's current problems exemplified by the grain shortages and the Shakhty affair. The Bukharinists insisted that they were the result of secondary factors: the state's unpreparedness, poor planning, inflexible price policies, and negligent local officials.[58] On the other hand, Stalin and the people around him were portraying the difficulties as having derived from structural or organic causes, and thus from the nature and deficiencies of NEP itself. In addition to kulak hoarding, Stalinists maintained, the grain crisis reflected the cul de sac of peasant agriculture; both it and the Shakhty episode were not transitory by-products of "faulty planning and chance mistakes," but evidence of an unavoidable intensification of the class war, a battle which had to be fought to the end.[59]

Bukharin's analysis recommended moderate remedies, including assistance to private farmers, flexible price policies, and improved responsiveness by official institutions. Stalin's pointed to radical solutions. He had as yet no comprehensive alternative to prevailing Bukharinist policies, but he was moving in another direction: toward asserting and legitimizing the "will of the state," including coercive "extraordinary measures," on all fronts. In relation to this, he began to disparage private farming while heralding collective and state farms as "the way out."[60] Though the dispute still focused on agriculture, its implications for industrial policy and the five-year plan then in preparation were equally great. Kuibyshev's reconstituted staff at the Supreme Economic Council was already challenging the cautious planners of Gosplan, whose views on proportional development and equilibrium market conditions were similar to Bukharin's. By May, echoes of the planning controversy could be heard in the Politburo.[61] At stake, therefore, was the party's entire economic program and, once again, the future course of the Bolshevik revolution.

Taken together, Stalin's policy initiatives threatened the prevailing Bukharinist understanding of NEP as a system of civil peace and reciprocal market relations between town and country. They conflicted rudely with the Right's belief that problems could and should be solved "in the conditions and on the basis of NEP."[62] More immediately, Bukharin complained, they distorted the party's general line ratified only four months earlier at the Fifteenth Congress. Embodying the Right's revised program, the congressional resolutions had promised a leftward turn toward an "offensive against the kulak," the creation of a partial, voluntary collectivized sector, and planned industrial development with greater emphasis on capital goods production. But each goal had been stated in a moderate, Bukharinist fashion, pointedly excluding extreme policies. Now, however, Stalin was seeking to legitimize his new militancy by reinterpreting those resolutions, portraying, for example, the "extraordinary measures" as a "normal" consequence of the congress's anti-kulak resolution.[63]

Convinced that Stalin's overtures had "disoriented the party ideologically" and were becoming "a new political line different from the line of the Fifteenth Congress," Bukharin was roused to battle in May and June. He warned the Politburo that the grain campaigns were turning the entire peasantry, not just the kulak, against the régime, a development that jeopardized both the party's industrialization program and its political survival. Imagining "all salvation in collective farms" was dangerous nonsense; he urged termination of the emergency measures, meaningful aid to peasant farmers, and a normalization of market conditions.[64]

Bukharin and his followers also opened an Aesopian public attack on Stalin's ideas. Speaking at the Eighth Komsomol Congress on May 6, Bukharin criticized promiscuous sloganeering about "class war" and "some kind of sudden leap" in agriculture; and in an emotional article three weeks later, he lashed out at the sponsors of a "monstrous" industrialism, "parasitic" in its impact on the village.[65] Young Bukharinists such as Maretskii and Astrov were less discreet, attacking by name junior Stalinist officials who, eager to "provoke the party" to a showdown with the muzhik, had written off private farming for a collectivization based on the "absolute ruination of the peasantry," and who saw "extraordinary measures" as "a system of policies," a way "to socialism through Article 107." [66]

Relations between Bukharin and Stalin deteriorated accordingly. Their joint public appearances, while maintaining the formal charade of unity, were becoming thinly veiled confrontations.[67] The duel was accentuated on May 28, when Stalin ventured boldly into Bukharin's ideological bailiwick, the Institute of Red Professors, to speak "On the Grain Front." Castigating the arguments of unnamed opponents as "liberal chatter" and a "break with Leninism," he issued his most extreme public statement to date on peasant agriculture. His audience, precisely aware of his target, was astonished. About the same time, Bukharin began describing Stalin privately as the representative of neo-Trotskyism.[68]

Meanwhile, Bukharin tried to assert his influence in the Politburo. In notes to its members in late May and again in June, and endorsed by Rykov, Tomskii, and Uglanov, he criticized Stalin's course and detailed his own recommendations. As a result of its dissensions, he argued, the Politburo no longer had "a line or a general opinion"; it was improvising policy from day to day. A full discussion should therefore be undertaken at the upcoming Central Committee plenum scheduled to open on July 4. While accepting "nine-tenths" of Bukharin's policy recommendations, Stalin resisted, insisting that the leadership again present unanimous resolutions, as was finally the case. His tactics inside the Politburo, Bukharin complained, were evasive and deceitful, combining empty concessions and false comaraderie but designed "to make us appear to be the splitters." [69]

By late June, despite its public facade, there was neither pretense nor grounds for unity within the leadership. On the 15th,

Moshe Frumkin, the rightist Deputy Commissar of Finance, sent
the Politburo an anxious letter evaluating the situation in the
countryside in terms even more pessimistic than Bukharin's. He
reported that his views were supported "by many Communists."
The Politburo voted to circulate his letter among Central Committee members with a collective reply. Stalin immediately violated
the decision, sending a personal reply through the Secretariat.
Outraged, Bukharin accused him of treating the Politburo as "a
consultative organ under the general secretary." Stalin tried to
placate Bukharin: "You and I are the Himalayas; the others are
nobodies," a remark Bukharin quoted at a "savage" Politburo
session to Stalin's shouts of denial. No longer on speaking terms,
the personal breach between the former duumvirs was total.
Bukharin now refused to distribute written recommendations to
the Politburo, reading them instead: "You can't trust him with a
single piece of paper." He spoke of Stalin with the "absolute
hatred" born of revelation—"He is an unprincipled intriguer who
subordinates everything to the preservation of his power. He
changes theories depending on whom he wants to get rid of at the
moment." [70]

Controversy over policy had become, once again, a struggle for
power in the Bolshevik leadership. On the eve of the Central
Committee's July plenum, both Politburo factions had mobilized
their outside supporters—their "periphery," as Stalin put it [71]—
and were engaged in furious battle. Ten years earlier, Bukharin
had led the Moscow-based Left Communists. Now, for a different
cause with different allies, the center of Bukharinist activity was
again the Moscow party. Utilizing their position in the capital,
Uglanov and his lieutenants on the Moscow Committee Bureau,
whose support for Bukharin, Rykov, and Tomskii was eager and
complete, provided the organizational base for the drive against
Stalin's policies and conduct. They caucused with government and
party allies, lobbied the uncommitted, and combatted Stalin's
apparatchiki with their own apparatus methods.[72] Elsewhere, in
the state ministries, trade unions, central party organs, and educational institutes, Bukharin, Rykov, and Tomskii moved to tighten
their control, rally supporters, and blunt the "self-criticism"
crusade, which (lamented one of their allies) had become for
Stalin "what the Jewish pogrom was for czarism." [73] The covert
struggle was accompanied by a war of words, as newspapers loyal

to the rival factions stepped up their Aesopian polemics and both sides circulated clandestine documents.

The purpose of all this activity was to win over a majority of the seventy-one full members of the Central Committee. As its July plenum approached, the campaign grew more intense. Uglanov and the Muscovites seem to have conducted most of the Right's lobbying, meeting regularly with delegates from the provinces.[74] But Bukharin also dispatched personal emissaries. Thus, in June, Slepkov journeyed to Leningrad, a key party organization, where his fellow Bukharinists Stetskii and Petrovskii, head of the city's agitprop department and editor of *Leningrad Pravda* respectively, had already begun to organize.[75]

The Bukharinists' appeal to Central Committee members focused on the urgent need to end the "extraordinary measures" unequivocally, and on Stalin's abrasive role in their implementation. Arguing that the measures were yielding diminishing economic results while generating an increasingly dangerous political situation in the countryside, they insisted that Stalin's misconduct of the collection campaigns, as well as his other initiatives, violated the decisions of the Fifteenth Congress and subsequent plenums, and were largely responsible for the dire situation. Their case against his political freewheeling and "Asiatic policies" was strongly worded and, it appears, directed at removing him as general secretary. (Tomskii evidently aspired to the post, though Uglanov, who pressed hard for Stalin's ouster, was also a logical candidate.)[76] Although uncommitted delegates were "terribly afraid of a split" and grew frightened when "talk turned to the possibility of replacing Stalin," the Bukharinists were initially encouraged by their response on policy issues, a receptiveness doubtless influenced by fresh reports of peasant rioting.[77]

Indeed, the Right's political strength must have seemed formidable in the spring and early summer of 1928, and belies the notion that Stalin was already the omnipotent general secretary of later years. In addition to the prestige and authority of their combined official positions, Bukharin, Rykov, and Tomskii exercised substantial voting power in the party's executive councils. On the nine-man Politburo, relying on the support of the rightist Kalinin and the neutrality or wavering of Voroshilov, Kuibyshev, and Rudzutak, they anticipated a working majority against Stalin and Molotov.[78] Sizable Muscovite and trade union representation also gave them a majority on the Orgburo and a strong minority— two to Stalin's three—on the Secretariat itself.[79] In the event of a showdown in the Central Committee, the picture was less clear: Bukharin probably expected to begin by dividing about 30 of the 71 votes evenly with Stalin, regarding the others as uncommitted.[80]

Outside the party's leadership institutions, the Right's strength appeared even more impressive. Tomskii's trade union "principality," which claimed to speak for 11 million workers, provided another organizational base and operated as an influential opinion group. The central state ministries under Rykov's Council of People's Commissars (particularly Agriculture, Labor, Finance, Education, and Gosplan), and on which the party depended for preparing and administering social policy, were still predominantly Bukharinist in outlook.[81] Rightist influence even extended to the security police, now called the OGPU. Stalin had already begun to develop personal connections in the police that were to serve him later. (Bukharin complained that his phone was tapped and that he was being followed in 1928.) But while its chief, Viacheslav Menzhinskii, supported the general secretary, his two deputies, Genrikh Iagoda and Mikhail Trilisser, leaned toward the Right.[82] Finally, and of considerable importance at this stage, Bukharinists still controlled the party's opinion-making institutions. In addition to the educational academies and the Central Committee's two official organs, *Pravda* and *Bolshevik,* Bukharin and his allies controlled almost all the major newspapers published in the capital, as well as the second city's main daily, *Leningrad Pravda.* Only one important Moscow paper was in Stalin's hands, *Komsomol Pravda,* the organ of the Young Communist League.[83]

As events were to reveal, the Right's political position was far more vulnerable than its array of posts and allies suggested. Among other things, the advantages of Stalin's six-year manipulation of the party's Secretariat soon became evident in crucial ways: in the presence of strong Stalinist minorities in each of the Right's "principalities"; in the fact that virtually all initially uncommitted leaders went over to him; and in his overwhelming following among second-ranking leaders, especially party secretaries who currently sat as candidate members of high bodies, including the Politburo and Central Committee.[84] If Bukharin and his friends formally prevailed in the high offices of the party-state, and monopolized its symbols of power, Stalin controlled a potent shadow government, "a party within the party." [85] When the balance at the top, particularly in the Politburo, shifted to Stalin, his forces everywhere began to oust and replace entrenched leaders loyal or sympathetic to the Right, a process abetted by a decade of bureaucratic centralization and deference to orders from above.

But to participants and observers alike, the balance of power still appeared to be with the Right when the Central Committee assembled on July 4, a fact that helps explain Stalin's unwillingness to risk an open confrontation and his repeated concessions on major issues.[86] It also explains Bukharin's shocked reaction to events at the plenum, whose public decisions bore little relation to what actually occurred during the week-long proceedings. On the surface, the Bukharinists emerged victorious. The principal resolution, while a compromise, spoke (for the last time) in the voice of the Right. It assured peasant farmers of their security and essential role under NEP, promised a final cessation of the emergency campaigns, and resolved, against Stalin's opposition, to raise grain prices. It was so conciliatory that exiled Left oppositionists lamented the Right's triumph. Trotsky predicted that Bukharin and Rykov would shortly "hunt down Stalin as a Trotskyist, just as Stalin had hunted down Zinoviev." [87]

In fact, as Bukharin understood, the plenum represented a major setback for the Right. The rift was now partially exposed before the Central Committee.[88] While the Politburo leaders continued their labored diplomacy, mostly criticizing each other only indirectly, their supporters exchanged sharp and explicit attacks. Molotov, Mikoyan, and Kaganovich spoke for Stalin; Stetskii, Sokolnikov, and Osinskii for the Right (Osinskii, after years on the party Left, thereby rejoined Bukharin in a political friendship dating back to their Moscow youth). As the heated debate over peasant policy unfolded, the Right's hope for a majority faded. Bukharin had counted on the support of the important Ukrainian and Leningrad delegations; both failed to intervene, the Leningraders openly disassociating themselves from Stetskii, a member of their own delegation.[89] Many delegates, genuinely worried about the rising tide of peasant unrest, spoke ambivalently; but they were unwilling to censure Stalin or endorse unlimited concessions to the peasantry at the expense of the industrialization drive. Their mood was not Stalinist, but it had shifted from the Right; at best, Bukharin reasoned, they "still don't understand the depth of the disagreements." Worse, it was also clear that the Right had lost its Politburo majority. Kalinin and Voroshilov, as their conduct revealed and Bukharin confided, "betrayed us at the last moment. . . . Stalin has some special hold on them." [90]

Sensing the delegates' mood, the Stalin group became more daring. While Molotov openly criticized *Pravda*'s editorials on the procurement campaigns, and thus by implication Bukharin himself, Kaganovich defended the "extraordinary measures" so extravagantly as to justify them "at all times and in any circumstances." [91] As the plenum drew to a close, Stalin and Bukharin rose to deliver the main addresses. The disheartened Bukharin tried to rouse the Central Committee. No sustained industrialization, he insisted, was possible without a prospering agriculture, which was now declining as a result of the requisitioning. Moreover, faced with a "wave of mass discontent" and "a united village front against us," the régime was on the verge of a complete break with the peasantry: "two bells have sounded, the third is next." [92] Stalinists retorted with hoots of "panic-monger." The general secretary was similarly unmoved. Dismissing the Right's admonitions as a "cheerless philosophy" and "capitulationism," he spoke instead of class war and collectivization, and suddenly introduced the theoretical rationale for a new, unspecified peasant policy: since Soviet Russia had no colonies, the peasantry would have to pay "something in the nature of a 'tribute'" to fund industrialization. Bukharin was stunned. His former ally had appropriated not only Preobrazhenskii's reasoning, but his draconian rhetoric as well.[93]

Formally the plenum had decided nothing. Bukharin and his allies had not been directly defeated; the resolutions were largely theirs, and most delegates were perplexed rather than rigidly partisan. But Bukharin sensed the Right's perilous situation. A minority in the Politburo and unable to rally the Central Committee, they faced a ruthless, skilled adversary determined "to cut our throats" and whose policies were "leading to civil war. He will have to drown the uprisings in blood." [94] Frightened by this turn of events, Bukharin took a desperate step, one that was to have adverse repercussions when it became known. Violating "party discipline," he made personal contact with the disgraced Zinoviev-Kamenev opposition. On July 11, the day before the plenum closed, he paid a secret visit to Kamenev.

What passed between them comes to us through Kamenev's elliptical notes acquired and published clandestinely by Trotskyists six months later.[95] Bukharin, believing rumors inspired by Stalin of the general secretary's own impending reconciliation with the Left, had come to convert Zinoviev and Kamenev, or persuade them to remain aloof. He, Rykov, and Tomskii agreed: "it would be better to have Zinoviev and Kamenev in the Politburo now than Stalin. . . . The disagreements between us and Stalin are many times more serious than were our disagreements with you." As the "extremely shaken" Bukharin related the history of the rift, Kamenev had "the impression of a man who knows he is doomed." Bukharin was obsessed by Stalin's villainy—"a Genghis Khan" whose "line is ruinous for the whole revolution." Trapped in a Hamlet-like posture, Bukharin wanted, but was unable, to carry the struggle into the open because a fearful Central Committee would turn against any perpetrator of an open split. "We would say, here is the man who brought the country to famine and ruin. He would say, they are defending kulaks and nepmen." Bukharin could only hope that his discreet efforts or outside events would convince the Central Committee of Stalin's "fatal role." On this note, he left, swearing Kamenev to secrecy and warning that they were under surveillance. They were to meet twice again that year in equally melancholy and pointless sessions.[96]

The July plenum was a pivotal episode in the struggle. Though it gave Stalin neither a decisive political victory nor a programmatic mandate, it emboldened him and reduced the Right to minority status in the leadership. With Stalin still groping toward alternative policies and uncertain of his political strength, and the Right's acquiescence in concealing the split, the pretense of Politburo unity continued. But the advantage was now Stalin's. He used it first in a different arena. On July 17, the Sixth World Congress of the Communist International opened in Moscow. It sat for six weeks, during which Bukharinists and Stalinists were locked in fierce battle for control of the international organization and the direction of Communist policy abroad.

At stake, as became clear when the issues crystallized in the summer of 1928, were the Comintern policies of the past seven years and particularly Bukharin's conduct of its united front strategy since 1925–6. The history of the dispute paralleled that over domestic policy. Revision of the Comintern line had also begun under Bukharin's sponsorship in 1927 in the aftermath of setbacks in China and the West. Here, too, he had conceived of the leftward turn not as a radical break but as a moderate revision toward more independent Communist activity and less high-level collaboration with European social democrats. Voices demanding greater militancy were raised in late 1927; but it was not until 1928, with Stalin's backing and then active intervention, that Bukharin's Comintern authority and policies were directly challenged. Preliminary skirmishes occurred covertly in February and March, at a meeting of the Comintern's Executive Committee and at the Fourth Profintern Congress.[97] By July, probably at the Central

Committee plenum, Stalin had openly criticized Bukharin's draft of the Comintern program (his third and most ambitious since 1922), which was to be adopted at the upcoming congress. "Stalin had spoiled the program for me in many places," he told Kamenev.[98]

The struggle over international policy revolved around conflicting estimates of the health of Western capitalism and the likelihood of imminent revolutionary situations. It thus became a controversy over the nature of the "third period," the onset of which had been officially proclaimed and variously defined in 1927. In brief, Stalinists now asserted that advanced capitalist societies, from Germany to the United States, were on the eve of profound internal crises and revolutionary upheavals. This led them to three tactical demands. First, foreign Communist parties should prepare to reap the whirlwind by charting a radically independent course, refusing any collaboration with social democrats, and, more specifically, by creating rival trade unions everywhere. They should in the process destroy reformist influence on the working class by attacking social democratic parties, which according to the Stalinists were passing from token reformism to "social fascism," as the main enemy of the labor movement. Third, all Communist parties should gird for revolutionary battle by purging their ranks of dissenters, particularly "right deviationists" who in the new circumstances were now the main danger within.[99]

This amounted to a sweeping repudiation of Bukharin's Comintern policies. As we have seen, his understanding of advanced capitalist systems, updated and restated in 1926–7 and again at the Sixth Comintern Congress, derived from his prewar theory of "state capitalism." For him, capitalism's "third period" witnessed not internal breakdowns but further stabilization on a higher technological and organizational level. Revolutionary upheavals were inevitable; but they would come in the West from "external contradictions," on the wings of imperialist war, not from isolated internal crises. Therefore, for Bukharin and his followers, the assertion that Western capitalism was on the brink of revolutionary breakdown was "radically wrong, tactically harmful, and crudely mistaken theoretically"; it meant "to lose contact with real relations." [100] The continuing development of state capitalist systems called for working-class unity, not quixotic sectarian adventures that promised "isolation" for Communist parties and "tragedy" for the working class.[101]

The chimera of social democracy as "social fascism," a notion developed by Zinoviev in the early twenties but made into policy by Stalin, was to have especially tragic consequences. In 1928, fascism was for Communists only a vague and little-studied reactionary phenomenon identified chiefly with Mussolini's Italy; the menace of Hitlerism was still very remote. Unlike most of his Comintern initiatives, the idea that socialists were somehow akin to and a greater evil than fascists seems to have appealed to Stalin much earlier. In 1924, he had uttered what was to become the ritualistic catch phrase of the Comintern disaster of 1929–33: "Social-Democracy is objectively the moderate wing of fascism. . . . They are not antipodes, they are twins." [102]

Though the unpublicized 1928 debate over social fascism remains obscure, Bukharin's opposition to the concept as a guide to policy seems clear.[103] He had contributed greatly to the Bolshevik animosity toward social democratic leaders since 1914, and his present thinking did not exclude traducing them as renegades and bulwarks of the capitalist order. It did exclude, however, writing off social democratic parties and trade unions, which represented the overwhelming majority of European workers, as "social fascist" and the labor movement's primary enemy. Political compromise at the Sixth Comintern Congress apparently obliged him to concede that "social democracy has *social fascist tendencies*." But he quickly added: "it would be foolish to lump social democracy together with fascism." Moreover, he anticipated and opposed the implication that Communists might ally with fascists against socialists: "Our tactics do not exclude the possibility of appealing to social democratic workers and even to some lower social democratic organizations; but we cannot appeal to fascist organizations." [104]

Each of these policy disputes was fiercely contested in closed meetings during the Sixth Comintern Congress, in reality the occasion of two congresses. As its political secretary and titular head, Bukharin reigned over the official, public congress. He opened and closed its proceedings, delivered the three main reports, and received its accolades and enthusiastic ovations. On the surface, it was the high point of his career in the international movement. Behind the scenes, however, echoed faintly in the disparate public speeches, a "corridor congress" was under way against his authority and policies. It began when Stalin's majority in the Russian delegation recalled and amended Bukharin's keynote theses, and spread quickly to the major foreign delegations who divided (for reasons of principle, careerism, and the habit of emulating the Russian party) into Bukharinist and Stalinist factions. Rumors swept the congress as Stalin's agents whispered of Bukharin's "right deviation" and "political syphilis," and that he was condemned to Alma Ata, Trotsky's place of exile. After two weeks, the "corridor congress" had grown so clamorous that the Soviet Politburo felt compelled to issue a collective denial of a split in its ranks. No one seems to have believed the disclaimer, and the "anti-Bukharin caucus" went on unabated.[105]

The outcome of the official congress has been frequently misinterpreted. It did not legislate a new, ultra-left course; that came a year later under Stalin's exclusive auspices. In the summer of 1928, the leadership of the major foreign parties still included strong or majority groups allied with Bukharin or otherwise unsympathetic to Stalin's radical proposals. Among them were the German Communists around Heinrich Brandler, August Thalheimer, and Arthur Ewert; the official American leadership, headed by Jay Lovestone; and the Italian leadership of Palmiro Togliatti (Ercoli).[106] The congress's unanimous resolutions on disputed issues (as well as the program) therefore resulted from hard-fought compromises and, despite striking inconsistencies, were predominantly Bukharinist.[107] Bukharinists would later protest justifiably that the extremist course of 1929–33 was a distortion of the Sixth Comintern Congress.[108]

Nonetheless, the congress was another important victory for Stalin. It gained three things for him. First, the ambiguities in its resolutions seriously compromised Bukharin's international policies and provided a semblance of legitimacy for Stalin's extremist line already in the making. Second, the "corridor congress" brought many foreign Communists to his side, mobilized strong Stalinist factions in the major parties, and virtually ended Bukharin's control of Comintern affairs. After the congress closed on September 1, only three significant figures in its permanent Moscow apparatus remained loyal to him: the Swiss Jules Humbert-Droz, the German Klara Zetkin, and the Italian Angelo Tasca (Serra).[109] Third and most damaging, however, was Bukharin's main concession at the congress. Reversing himself, he endorsed Stalin's axiom that "the *right deviation* now represents the central danger" in the Comintern. He tried to minimize the concession, construing right deviationism as an impersonal tendency, to be fought with ideological rather than organizational methods, and quoting from an unpublished letter written by Lenin to him and Zinoviev in the early twenties: "If you drive out all the not especially obedient but clever people, and are left with only the obedient fools, you will *most certainly* ruin the party." His qualifications helped not at all.

It remained only for Stalin to transfer the damning category of "right deviation" to the Russian party, and victimize Bukharin himself.[110]

The end of the Comintern congress left Bukharinists and Stalinists bitterly divided over international policy and refocused the dispute on domestic affairs. One important policy issue still remained outside the controversy, the rate and pattern of industrialization. This came to the fore on September 19, when Kuibyshev, speaking for Stalin's faction, proclaimed a new industrializing manifesto. Bukharin's revised program, adopted at the Fifteenth Party Congress, was ambitious but restrained. In stressing balanced industrial and agricultural development, and consumer and capital production, it explicitly rejected "that formula which calls for maximum investment in heavy industry." [111] Kuibyshev wholeheartedly embraced the formula, until now the clarion of the Left. Crises and perils at home and abroad, he said, demanded a radical acceleration and concentration of investment in heavy industry at any price, including economic imbalances and "discontent and active resistance" among the population.[112] Stalin, revealing his own thinking, cast the new industrializing philosophy in historical perspective a few weeks later. The imperative of "maximum capital investment in industry," he explained, was dictated by Russia's traditional backwardness. He referred his party audience to Peter the Great, another revolutionizer from above, who in an effort to break out of this backwardness "feverishly built mills and factories to supply the army and strengthen the country's defenses." [113]

Bukharin responded in a famous article entitled "Notes of an Economist." [114] Kuibyshev's Supreme Economic Council, with Stalin's encouragement and to the Right's dismay, was already escalating its proposed five-year plan targets. "Notes of an Economist" was a definitive policy rejoinder. Bukharin reiterated the Right's belief in proportional, "more or less crisis-free development" and a plan that specified and observed "the conditions of *dynamic economic equilibrium*" between industry and agriculture, and within the industrial sector itself. Defending the current level of investment but opposing any increase, he went on to a detailed indictment of Stalin's and Kuibyshev's "adventurism."

Two features particularly infuriated him. To increase capital expenditure without a requisite improvement in agriculture, indeed amidst an agricultural crisis, was to disregard industry's essential base and invite overall "ruin." Furthermore, in addition to the shortages of grain and technical crops, industry was already lagging behind its own expanded demand, creating acute shortages of materials and widespread bottlenecks. A further overstraining of capital expenditure could only disrupt construction already under way, reverberate adversely throughout the entire industrial sector, and "in the last analysis reduce the tempo of development." Instead, "upper limits" on industrial expansion had to be set, and that level of expenditure utilized efficiently for "real" construction, if only because "it is not possible to build 'present-day' factories with 'future bricks'." Addressing the bravado of Stalinist industrializers, Bukharin added: "You can beat your breast, swear allegiance and take an oath to industrialization, and damn all enemies and apostates, but this will not improve matters one bit."

"Notes of an Economist" caused a major stir in the party when it appeared in *Pravda* on September 30, 1928. Though its target remained anonymous " 'super-industrialists' of the Trotskyist type," the long, strongly worded polemic was a transparent assault on Stalin's group and as close as Bukharin had come to making public the struggle. His supporters circulated and recommended the article as "showing the path that must be taken," while Stalinists, secretly trying to proscribe it, launched a press campaign defending their industrial line. On October 8, Stalin's Politburo majority, over the objections of Bukharin, Rykov, and Tomskii, reprimanded its "unauthorized" publication.[115] The policy dispute was now total and seemingly beyond compromise. Its outcome awaited a political showdown.

With a Politburo majority to sanction his offensive, Stalin moved relentlessly against the Right's political bases in the late summer and autumn of 1928. Rykov's authority in high state councils was rudely challenged and a number of pro-Right officials in Moscow and the republican governments dismissed. Tomskii was savaged privately by Stalin as "a malicious and not always honorable person"—surely a classic piece of pharisaism—and his trade union leadership criticized in the Stalinist press for assorted sins, among them obstructing productivity.[116] Much the same was afoot in the Moscow party organization in August and September, where Uglanov and his district secretaries were under the fire of a "self-criticism" campaign against "right opportunism." [117] Meanwhile, the Bukharinist party bureau of the Institute of Red Professors was finally toppled by Stalinists. And in the Comintern, the dwindling band of Bukharin loyalists was locked in a losing battle for control of the Executive Committee apparatus, while

Bukharin found himself powerless to stop the drive against Comintern "rightists," notably in the important German party.[118]

Equally significant was Stalin's seizure of the party's leading press organs. Petrovskii, after criticizing the general secretary's "tribute" speech, was summarily transferred from the editorship of *Leningrad Pravda* to a tiny provincial newspaper.[119] About the same time, probably in August or September, the young Bukharinist editors of *Pravda* and *Bolshevik*, Slepkov, Astrov, Maretskii, Zaitsev, and Tseitlin, were ousted and replaced by Stalinists. Bukharin remained editor-in-chief of *Pravda,* and with Astrov still sat on the seven-man board of *Bolshevik;* but he no longer decided their editorial policy or contents.[120] This was an important development. Until the autumn, these authoritative publications of the Central Committee had interpreted disputed policy in a Bukharinist spirit, thus moderating the party leadership's official voice and its communication with lower officials.[121] Now, though occasional dissonant articles and speeches by Bukharinists continued to appear, the party's official voice became Stalinist. The turnabout coincided in mid-September with the beginning of a strident press attack on a still unidentified "right danger" in the party. No such thin anonymity adorned the covert anti-Right campaign; by October, Stalinists were surreptitiously "working over" Bukharin as a "panic-monger" and "enemy of industrialization and collective farms." [122]

Damaging as these developments were, they did not directly alter the uncertain balance of power in the Central Committee, where the struggle had ultimately to be completed. Here the key was the Moscow party organization, which continued to oppose Stalin with impunity, a fact no doubt carefully observed by party secretaries elsewhere. Since the July plenum, the Muscovites had persistently defended Bukharinist policies, including their own special interest in light industry. Indeed, Uglanov, a tough and determined adversary, was fighting back. Mounting their own press campaign, he and his associates had encouraged anti-Stalinists not to fear the word "deviation," denounced talk of a right danger as "slanderous rumors" by "intriguers," and suggested obliquely that Stalin was a negligent general secretary.[123] Their daring worried even Bukharin, who cautioned Uglanov against giving Stalin a pretext to intervene in Moscow.[124]

Considering the past efficiency of Uglanov's machine, Stalin's overthrow of the Moscow party leadership was remarkably swift. In the first weeks of October, Uglanov found himself besieged by rampant insubordination in lower ranks, unable to make personnel changes in his own organization, and forced to dismiss two of his most outspoken district secretaries, Riutin and Penkov. His hopeless situation was displayed at a full Moscow Committee meeting on October 18–19. Incited and sanctioned by directives from Stalin's central apparatus, insurgents censured Uglanov's conduct of the Moscow party and his toleration of "deviations from the correct Leninist line." On October 19, in the tone of a conqueror, Stalin personally addressed the gathering. His "message" was the urgency of conducting a relentless fight against the "Right, opportunist danger in our Party" as well as Communists who exhibited "a conciliatory attitude towards the Right deviation." Allowing that the apostasy was still only "a tendency, an inclination," and naming no offenders, he nonetheless magnified the peril: "the triumph of the Right deviation in our Party would unleash the forces of capitalism, undermine the revolutionary positions of the proletariat and increase the chances of the restoration of capitalism in our country." [125]

Outgunned and humiliated, Uglanov and several aides issued semi-recantations, but to no avail. Further high-level dismissals ended their control of the Moscow organization on October 19. Uglanov and his deputy Kotov lingered on in their posts until November 27, when they were replaced formally by Molotov and Karl Bauman. A sweeping purge of Bukharin's Moscow supporters and sympathizers, high and low, followed.[126] The overthrow of the old Moscow leadership was complete, its thoroughness symbolized by the disgrace of even Martyn Liadov, rector of Sverdlov University and a venerable Moscow committeeman who had been a member since the party's inception and a founding father of Moscow Bolshevism.[127]

Stalin's rout of the Muscovites was a devastating blow to Bukharin, Rykov, and Tomskii, and probably the decisive episode in the power struggle. In addition to depriving them of their most important organizational base, it proved an exemplary incident for neutral or wavering Central Committee members elsewhere. Coming a month before the November plenum, it demonstrated that even the country's largest party organization, led by a candidate Politburo member and seven full members of the Central Committee, and allied with the prestigious Politburo three, could not withstand Stalin's central apparatus. All party organizations were instructed to study the Moscow documents.[128] None, whatever their reservations about Stalin's policies, were prepared to run the same risk.

All this Bukharin had watched impassively from afar. His

customary summer vacation delayed by the Comintern congress, he had left Moscow for Kislovodsk, a spa in the Caucasus, in early October. Behaving rather like Trotsky in 1924, he had remained there while his allies and friends were routed, offering neither overt resistance nor (so far as the record shows) even any symbolic gesture to hearten them. His Olympian detachment broke finally in the first week of November, when he learned that Rykov was retreating in the Politburo debate on the 1928–9 industrial plan. Bukharin departed immediately for Moscow, only to have his plane trip interrupted twice en route by Stalin's agents professing concern over his health. He finally arrived on around November 7, his combative spirit restored.[129]

A week of stormy Politburo sessions, preparatory to the Central Committee plenum on November 16, ensued. They brought another round of angry clashes between Bukharin and Stalin. Bukharin called for a radical turnabout in policy, including a reduction of Stalin's proposed capital expenditure and alleviation of excessive, punitive taxation on better-off peasants. He followed with a political "ultimatum" demanding a resolute cessation of the campaign and organizational reprisals against himself and his supporters. When Stalin reneged on a formal discussion of the demands, Bukharin cursed him as a "petty Oriental despot" and stalked from the room. Moments later he, Rykov, and Tomskii submitted their resignations, written beforehand. Stalin is said to have received them "paling and with trembling hands." Unprepared to risk the Bukharinists' open opposition to his still inchoate policies, he agreed to a compromise.[130]

Once again, ineluctably, Stalin's concessions and Bukharin's gains proved empty. In return for the trio's nominal support of Politburo resolutions at the plenum, and Rykov's formal presentation of the industrial theses, Stalin apparently consented to reduce capital expenditure slightly and halt the anti-Bukharinist persecution. His first concession was so minimal as to constitute a major setback for the Right; the second he simply ignored.[131] The agreement evidently also involved Uglanov's appointment as Commissar of Labor. This, too, was a dubious gain, since he replaced another ally, Tomskii's associate Shmidt; in any case, Uglanov's tenure was powerless and brief.[132]

Compromise enabled the Politburo factions to perpetuate their mock unanimity at the Central Committee plenum; but the guise was halfhearted and the proceedings a clear defeat for the Right. Rykov's cautionary report on industry was received with vocal disapproval by the general secretary's partisans.[133] Stalin then delivered his strongest words yet on the theme of "maximum capital expenditure" (or perish), and on the menace of the "right deviation." More significant, the plenary resolutions, while reflecting Bukharin's influence (or Stalin's indecision) on agriculture, were for the first time largely Stalinist in content. They ratified his industrial perspective, proclaimed the "right deviation and conciliationism" to be the main danger, and ordered the first general purge of the party—at this time a bloodless weeding out of undesirables —since 1921. Formally directed at "alien elements," there was no mistaking the implicit target of the latter resolution.[134] Powerless to alter the proceedings but unwilling to sanction them by his presence, Bukharin boycotted the plenum.[135]

If further evidence was needed, the futility of compromise with Stalin was demonstrated amply the following month when he completed his conquest of Bukharin's and Tomskii's "principalities." In a rare Comintern appearance, he personally signaled the seizure of the international organization at a meeting of its Executive Committee presidium on December 19. At issue was the persistent opposition of anti-Stalinists in the German party leadership. Denouncing the "craven opportunism" of Bukharin's supporters on the Executive Committee, Humbert-Droz and Tasca, Stalin read the German Rights and "conciliators" out of the party: "the presence of such people in the Comintern cannot be tolerated any longer." [136] Over Bukharin's protests in the Politburo, a wave of expulsions soon followed, including those of Brandler and Thalheimer. Parallel reprisals were in the making in other parties, leading in 1929 to a mass expulsion of foreign Communist leaders allied with or sympathetic to Bukharin.[137] Stalin's takeover of the Comintern's central apparatus was symbolized by Molotov, who assumed control and whose international credentials were as neglible as his own.

Tomskii's downfall, preceded by subversion similar to that in the Moscow party, came at the Eighth Trade Union Congress on December 10–24. By early November, Stalin's campaign to discredit his leadership had led union officials to complain of "an atmosphere making it completely impossible to work." [138] When the congress opened, Tomskii and his fellow leaders found themselves a minority in the party caucus which controlled the agenda, and were defeated on two crucial issues. One involved endorsement of the Central Committee's November resolutions, and thus official trade union acquiescence in industrial policies bitterly opposed by its leadership.[139] The fight was decided in the caucus, but it spilled over into a debate by innuendo at the public congress. While Stalinists led by Kuibyshev extolled all-out heavy industrialization, Tomskii and his associates objected to the prospect of an industrial drive that would victimize the working class and transform unions into "houses of detention." It was the Tomskii leadership's swan song, a defense of the traditional NEP role of unions: "Trade unions exist to serve the working masses," a conception now rejected as "narrow shop stewardism" and apolitical. The incoming order was heralded by a new Stalinist slogan: "Trade Unions— Face Toward Production!" [140]

Tomskii's other defeat ended his decade-long control of the trade union organization. On Politburo instructions, the caucus voted to co-opt five Stalin appointees onto the Central Trade Union Council. Tomskii tried to block one nomination, that of the unpopular Kaganovich, charging that it created a "dual center" and imposed a "political commissar" on the unions. Defeated, Tomskii again submitted his resignation on December 23. It was rejected, but he remained trade union head in name only, refusing to return to his post.[141] He and virtually the entire union leadership (most of them, like Tomskii, pioneers of the Bolshevik trade union movement) were removed officially in June 1929. This overthrow was so wholesale and arbitrary that it elicited an explanation by Kaganovich: "It could be said that this was a violation of proletarian democracy; but, comrades, it has long been known that for us Bolsheviks democracy is no fetish." [142]

By November–December, Bukharin, Rykov, and Tomskii were no longer leading members of a divided leadership making decisions by compromise, but a minority opposition in Stalin's Politburo, powerless and with dwindling influence over policy. Apart from Rykov, their roles had become less than minimal. Formally still editor of *Pravda* and political secretary of the Comintern, Bukharin, like Tomskii, quit his posts in protest in December and never returned.[143]

They had been reduced to this state by fighting and losing where Stalin excelled, in covert organizational politics. Except for "Notes of an Economist," published after much soul-searching in July, Bukharin had avoided public opposition: "calculation dictates prudence," he explained to Kamenev.[144] Now, with complete silence the only alternative, he changed his mind. On three occasions in late 1928 and January 1929, he spoke out publicly against Stalin's "general line." All three protests appeared in *Pravda*, directed to the policy sense and conscience of the Central Committee. And while Bukharin refrained from attacking Stalin explicitly, his angry words bore the unmistakable stamp of fervent opposition.

The first came on November 28 in a speech to worker-peasant correspondents, the grass roots association Bukharin had promoted to countervail official misdeeds.[145] He began, in terms more explicit and less technical than "Notes of an Economist," with a denunciation of the industrial "policies of madmen," who dreamed only of gluttonous, giant projects that for years would *"give* nothing but *take* enormous quantities of the means of production . . . and the means of consumption." Indifferent to agriculture, not caring that consumer goods were needed to obtain peasant grain, that peasants "are taking up arms in some areas," they could only shout: " 'Give us metal, and don't worry about grain.' " Their stupidity invited disaster: "if some kind of madmen propose to build immediately twice as much as we are now doing, this truly would be the policies of madmen because then our industrial goods famine would intensify several times over . . . and mean a grain famine."

But this "stupidity" in policy, Bukharin went on, reflected an even greater evil: "party officials are turning into *chinovniki.*" Like provincial officials under the old régime, they postured as "bureaucratic idols," "doing whatever they please," usurping authority and suffocating initiative when "more local, group, and personal initiative" was needed, and protecting themselves in "companies of 'friends' " answerable to no one. Worst of all, party bureaucrats forgot that "the fate of many millions of living people depends significantly on our policies." For them, "there is no difference in principle between a person and a log; for the bureaucrat it is important only that he himself be clean in the eyes of authority." And because "a piece of paper is one hundred per cent justification," party bureaucrats were ready to accept any concoction of "Communist conceit," any "fraudulent, bureaucratic 'creation,' " including "policies of madmen." Echoing Trotsky but more directly his own long-standing fear that party functionaries would become an abusive, privileged élite, Bukharin's speech was a scathing condemnation of the degeneration of party officialdom under Stalin.

"Communist conceit" was the theme of his next public attack, an article in *Pravda* on January 20, 1929.[146] On one level it analyzed the technological revolution in the West. On another it implicitly accused the Stalinist leadership of economic irresponsibility and incompetence, of conceiving an industrial drive based not on the most recent achievements of science and technology and "objective statistics adapted to reality," but on "bureaucratic memoranda," "subjective aspirations," and "Communist yahooism." The negative consequences, predicted Bukharin, would be monumental because in a planned, centralized economy with "an unprecedented concentration of the means of production, transportation, finance, etc. in state hands . . . any miscalculation and error makes itself felt in a corresponding social dimension." A *"historic truth"* was being ignored: *"we shall conquer with scientific economic leadership or we shall not conquer at all."*

Bukharin's most dramatic protest, however, came the following day in a long speech commemorating the fifth anniversary of Lenin's death. Its sensational title, "Lenin's Political Testament," alerted readers to its importance when it appeared in leading newspapers on January 24.[147] For, while Bukharin was talking about Lenin's deathbed articles on party policy, his title recalled the dead leader's other "testament," unpublished but not unknown, with its damning postscript calling for Stalin's removal as general secretary. In the context of 1929, Bukharin's actual subject was no less provocative. He wanted to show that Stalin was violating Lenin's programmatic "testament" as well. The device was a straightforward exposition of the famous five articles that had inspired Bukharin's programs, and official policy, since 1923–4. Their legacy, he began, was "a large, long-range plan for all of our Communist work . . . the general paths and high road of our development. . . . To set out Ilich's entire plan as a whole—that is my task today."

Point by point, "adding absolutely nothing of my own," Bukharin reiterated Lenin's "last directives": The revolution's future depends on a firm collaborative alliance with the peasantry; party policy must center now on *"peaceful, organizational, 'cultural' work,"* on conciliating peasant interests, not on a "third revolution"; capital accumulation and industrialization must proceed on the "healthy base" of expanding market relations, with prospering peasant farmers joining into market-oriented cooperatives (which were not collective farms), and on a rational utilization of resources combined with a relentless cutback in unproductive and bureaucratic expenditure. The watchwords of Lenin's "testament" were caution, conciliation, civil peace, education, and efficiency. Its central directive was preventing a "split" with the peasantry, for this would mean *"the destruction of the Soviet Republic."*

Composed largely of Lenin's words and signed by Bukharin,

"Lenin's Political Testament" was a ringing, anti-Stalinist manifesto, a defense of the NEP philosophy and policies being jettisoned by the general secretary. A year earlier it would have been an official homily. In January 1929, it was an opposition platform, attacked by the Stalinist majority as "a revision and distortion of the most important principles of Leninism," an attempt to portray Lenin as "a common peasant philosopher." [148] It was also the last explicit statement of Bukharin's thinking and policies to be published in the Soviet Union. Sensing what was to come, he appealed to Bolshevism's tradition of critical thought, imploring party officials "to take not a single word on trust . . . to utter not a single word against their conscience." He added, plaintively, "conscience, contrary to what some think, has not been abolished in politics." [149]

Bukharin's outcry reflected the worsening situation in both the leadership and country. Disagreements between the two Politburo factions now included even the fate of the foe who had once united them. In mid-January, with Bukharin, Rykov, and Tomskii protesting bitterly, Stalin's majority voted to expel Trotsky from the Soviet Union. The deportation was carried out on February 11, when the great tribune was escorted to a steamer bound for Constantinople, banished forever.[150] Meanwhile, as Stalin's industrial ambitions soared, the agricultural crisis worsened. By early 1929, grain collections had again begun to fall sharply; incidents of peasant violence were on the rise. The Stalinist leadership had no new solution. There was a heightened campaign inciting rural officials to war against kulaks and "kulak agents." Over the objections of Bukharin and Rykov, "extraordinary measures," though officially banned, were repeated in euphemistic guise in key grain areas. They helped little since there were few peasant stocks left to confiscate. Market relations and the whole grain delivery system were rapidly approaching a total breakdown.[151]

It was in these circumstances that Stalin moved toward a showdown in the leadership. The appearance on January 30 of an underground Trotskyist pamphlet containing Kamenev's account of his July talk with Bukharin was the pretext. Dissembling righteous indignation, Stalin convened a joint meeting of the Politburo and several leaders of the Central Control Commission, the party's disciplinary body headed by his supporter Ordzhonikidze, to censure Bukharin's "factional activity." The trial, as Bukharin characterized it, opened on January 30 with Stalin and a chorus of intimates in the role of prosecutor. Charging "Bukharin's group"—but primarily Bukharin—with opposition to the party line, a "right-opportunist, capitulatory platform," and connivance "to form an anti-party bloc with the Trotskyists," Stalin's tone grew increasingly menacing as he recited his opponent's "crimes." [152]

Unintimidated, Bukharin had come prepared. Justifying his meeting with Kamenev as necessitated by "abnormal conditions" in the party, he retaliated with a thirty-page counter-indictment of Stalin's political conduct and policies. His defiant statement apparently surprised Stalin; at this point the Politburo adjourned while a small commission composed of Bukharin and a Stalinist majority considered the charges. On February 7, it produced a "compromise" which, in exchange for dropping the censure motion against Bukharin, required him to admit the "political error" of his meeting with Kamenev, to retract his counter-accusations of January 30, and to return to his posts. Declining to denounce himself, Bukharin rejected the compromise. He then drafted another detailed attack on Stalin which was signed by Tomskii and Rykov, who read it to the final Politburo session of February 9.[153] This "platform of the three" seems to have been virtually identical to Bukharin's statement of January 30. Considered as a single document, it was his most important declaration of opposition, the strongest condemnation of Stalin and nascent Stalinism ever to originate in the Politburo. Never published and known solely from fragmentary accounts, it can only be partially reconstructed.

Its political theme was that behind a spate of participatory slogans, Stalin and his coterie were "implanting bureaucratism" and establishing a personal régime inside the party. The official line called for self-criticism, democracy, and elections. "But where in reality do we see an elected provincial secretary? In reality, elements of bureaucratization in our party have grown." Indeed, "the party doesn't participate in deciding questions. Everything is done from above." The same situation prevailed in party councils, where Stalin was usurping power: "We are against that practice where questions of party leadership are decided by one person. We are against that practice where collective control has been replaced by the control of one person, however authoritative." [154]

Bukharin then specified Stalin's abuses of power. Among them were gross violations of party decorum, as in the surreptitious campaign against Bukharinists who were being "politically slaughtered" and subjected to "organizational encirclement" by Stalin's henchmen, "political commissars" like Kaganovich, "a wholly administrative type." These "abnormal conditions" made it impossible to discuss urgent problems. To point out that there was a grain shortage was to be "worked over" and accused of "every filth" by "a swarm of well-nourished, satiated functionaries." Meanwhile,

Stalin was arbitrarily disregarding official party resolutions. Despite unanimous and repeated decisions to assist private farmers, for example, policy proceeded quite differently and these directives "remained merely literary artifacts." A similar process was under way in the Comintern, where policy was being revised "with scorn for the facts," and where Stalin's tactics of "splits, splinters, and groups" were leading to the "decomposition" of the international movement.[155]

Turning to domestic policy, Bukharin charged Stalin with an irresponsible failure of real leadership in conditions of national crisis.

Serious, urgent questions are not discussed. The entire country is deeply troubled by the grain and supply problems. But conferences of the proletarian, ruling party are silent. The entire country feels that all is not well with the peasantry. But conferences of the proletarian party, *our party*, are silent. The entire country sees and feels changes in the international situation. But conferences of the proletarian party are silent. Instead there is a hail of resolutions about deviations (all in the very same words). Instead there are millions of rumors and gossip about the rightists Rykov, Tomskii, Bukharin, etc. This is petty politics, and not politics that in a time of difficulties tells the working class the truth about the situation, that trusts the masses, and hears and feels *the needs of the masses.* . . .[156]

Those economic measures actually advocated by the Stalin group, continued Bukharin, were only a disastrous "going over to Trotskyist positions." Industrialization based on the "impoverishment" of the country, the degradation of agriculture, and the squandering of reserves was impossible—"all our plans threaten to collapse." But Bukharin's harshest words dealt with peasant policy. Stalinists had written off private farming and talked only of collectivization; but "in the next few years . . . collective and state farms cannot be the basic source of grain. For a long time, the basic source will still be individual peasant economies."[157] Then, in a never-to-be-forgotten "slander," Bukharin perceived a dark impulse behind the "overtaxation" and requisitioning in the countryside. Since the plenum of July 1928, he charged, Stalin had advocated industrialization based on "the military-feudal exploitation of the peasantry."

What in fact has determined subsequent policy? . . . Comrade Stalin's speech about tribute. At the Fourteenth Party Congress, Comrade Stalin was completely against Preobrazhenskii's idea of colonies and the exploitation of the peasantry. But at the July plenum, he proclaimed the tribute slogan, that is, the military-feudal exploitation of the peasantry.[158]

The dramatic confrontation of January 30 to February 9, highlighted by Bukharin's intransigence and counterattack on Stalin, completed the breach in the leadership. By rejecting the "compromise" of February 7, Bukharin refused to continue the pretense of Politburo unity, and for the first time was denounced formally by the Stalinist majority. Brushing aside his call for a return to conciliatory policies to pacify the peasantry and ease the supply crisis, the expanded Politburo meeting, in a secret resolution on February 9, strongly censured his "factional activity" and "intolerable slandering of the Central Committee, its internal and foreign policies, and its established leadership." (Tomskii and Rykov were also reprimanded, but in milder terms.) Employing the standard equation, the document construed his opposition to the Stalin group as opposition to "the party and its Central Committee." [159]

But despite this major victory, Stalin appears to have encountered resistance among his own supporters and gained less than he had hoped from the showdown. There is evidence that he wanted to expel his opponents, and primarily Bukharin, from the Politburo.[160] The censure resolution, the language and specifics of which were notably less harsh than his own, not only refrained from such drastic reprisals but demanded that Bukharin and Tomskii return to their posts. Adding to its ambiguity, the resolution was not published. As the proceedings ended, Stalin suggested his dissatisfaction: "we . . . are treating the Bukharinites too liberally and tolerantly. . . . Has not the time come to stop this liberalism?" [161]

At least two worries seem to have constrained several, perhaps a majority, of Stalin's supporters among the twenty-two or so high leaders in attendance. While they endorsed his leadership and industrial goals, they must have been troubled by his uncertain rural policies, as well as by the grave situation in the countryside. Some undoubtedly shared Bukharin's anxieties. Moreover, those who were the general secretary's supporters but not his personal devotees—unlike Kaganovich or Molotov, for example—were still unwilling to grant him the singular pre-eminence that the ouster of Bukharin (the only other "Himalaya" still in the Politburo) would bestow. Tradition and prudence inclined them toward collective authority at the top, however vestigial, rather than a supreme leader. Or as Kalinin confided: "Yesterday, Stalin liquidated Trotsky and Zinoviev. Today, he wants to liquidate Bukharin and Rykov. Tomorrow, it will be my turn." [162]

Nevertheless, Bukharin and his Politburo allies had suffered a severe defeat. They were in an incongruous and precarious position. Since the struggle and their censure remained unpublicized, their official esteem was unaffected. Bukharin continued to be elected to honorary presidiums of party and state gatherings, accorded the requisite "noisy ovation," and celebrated as a new member of the Academy of Sciences, the only important political figure to be chosen.[163] In closed meetings and party corridors, however, they were the victims, in Bukharin's expression, of "civil execution," as Stalinists spread word of their recreancy with intensified vigor. Simultaneously, the press campaign against the anonymous "right danger" redoubled and grew more strident. Officially (if secretly) censured, privately vilified, stripped of organizational leverage, and (presumably) deprived of uncensored access to the press, the trio had become "prisoners of the Politburo." [164] The strain began to tell. Despite their show of solidarity on February 9, Rykov was again wavering; while Bukharin and Tomskii became more adamant, he withdrew his resignation, though he continued to resist Stalin's policies at Politburo meetings. Further evidence of the pressure, as well as the Stalinist groundswell, came in early March when Stetskii, a renowned Bukharinist, defected to Stalin.[165]

Events now awaited the first uninhibited confrontation before the full Central Committee, the next plenum of which was scheduled for April 16–23, the eve of the Sixteenth Party Conference. In the interim, as their public protests grew more Aesopian and thus fainter, the Bukharinist trio tried to function as a loyal opposition—exercising "passive resistance"—inside the Politburo.[166] During March and the first half of April, their objections centered on Stalin's five-year plan for industry, which was to be adopted at the upcoming plenum and party conference. Its goals, expressed in minimal variants immediately discarded for escalated optimal ones, had soared enormously. They now envisaged a tripling or quadrupling of investment in the state sector, 78 per cent earmarked for heavy industry, and an increase in capital goods production of at least 230 per cent in five years.[167]

Aghast, Bukharin and Rykov tried to constrain Stalin's industrial aspirations. Rykov proposed a supplementary two-year plan to "liquidate the discrepancies between agricultural development and the needs of the country." Embodying the Bukharinist principle of industry's dependency on agriculture, it called for "the most rapid rectification of the agricultural sector" through a series of tax, price, and agronomical remedies. Rykov's plan was brusquely rejected as a ploy to discredit the five-year plan, as were similar criticisms and counterproposals then submitted by Bukharin. Even token compromise being no longer possible, Bukharin, Rykov, and Tomskii abstained in the formal Politburo vote on the industrial figures on April 15.[168]

Meanwhile, Bukharin was privately pursuing a tactic that the right opposition had thus far resorted to only hesitantly and haphazardly. In preparation for the Central Committee meeting, he was gathering evidence to document Stalin's personal unfitness for the general secretaryship, a post now being equated with that of party leader. His intention, it seems, was to revive and reaffirm the judgment Lenin had expressed in his "testament" in 1923:

Stalin is too rude. . . . Therefore I propose that the comrades think of a way to remove Stalin from that position and appoint to it another person who in all respects differs from and is superior to Comrade Stalin —namely, that he be more tolerant, more loyal, more polite, and more considerate toward comrades, less capricious, etc.[169]

After six years of complicity in suppressing Lenin's "testament," Bukharin was compiling testimony from victims of Stalin's "rudeness." Among them was Humbert-Droz, who had clashed with Stalin in the Comintern and to whom Bukharin wrote on February 10, 1929: "Please write to me whether it is true that at a meeting of the presidium, during the discussion of the German question, Comrade Stalin shouted at you the words 'Go to Hell.' " Humbert-Droz confirmed the incident.[170]

To remind the party of Lenin's last wishes in the circumstances of 1929 required courage; but it was too late for such a "trivial matter," as Stalin labeled it, to stem the political tide.[171] When the plenum opened on April 16, Bukharinists were engulfed by an assembly presided over by Stalinists eager to pillory and crush the opposition. Dramatizing their isolation, the Central Committee met jointly with the full Central Control Commission, swelling the attendance to over three hundred. Bukharin and his supporters numbered about thirteen.[172]

For the first time, the party's highest body was informed fully and explicitly of the year-long struggle, and exhorted to denounce the man who was still its most illustrious member. After Stalinists had presented for approval the Politburo's resolution censuring Bukharin, and Bukharinists had spoken in their own defense, Stalin gave his version of Bukharin's "right deviation" and "treacherous conduct." It went considerably beyond the resolution of February 9. Bukharin, he said, advocated a line completely hostile to the Central Committee's on every major issue from Comintern affairs to domestic policy; its implementation would mean "to betray the working class, to betray the*revolution." Asserting that Bukharin's "mistakes" were not accidental, Stalin struck at the basis of his authority in the party. In a section on "Bukharin as a Theoretician," he resurrected Bukharin's pre-1917 controversy with Lenin on the state to reveal that his reputation as party theorist was "the hypertrophied pretentiousness of a half-educated theoretician." Moments later Stalin took a more ominous tack: he hinted that during the peace treaty dispute of 1918, Bukharin had conspired with Left Socialist Revolutionaries "to imprison Lenin and carry out an anti-Soviet *coup d'état.*" In April 1929, this malicious innuendo was designed to make credible Stalin's claim that Bukharin—whom Lenin (the assembly would recall) had described as "the favorite of the whole party"—now headed "the most repulsive and the pettiest of all the factional groups that have ever existed in our Party." [173] Nine years later it became the criminal charge that Bukharin had conspired to assassinate Lenin.

It was remarkable that the Bukharinists found the will to resist insistent demands for their recantation in this pogrom atmosphere. Moreover, they fought back defiantly, particularly Bukharin, Tomskii, and Uglanov. (Rykov evidently restated his opposition in a more moderate tone.) [174] Only Stalin's address was ever published. But judging by fragments later quoted, Bukharin's speech to the plenum was among his greatest. He began, it seems, with Stalin's personal misconduct and "rudeness," and by denying angrily that he and his allies were opposed to "the general line." [175] Rather, it was Stalin who had violated the authorized line with policies incompatible with its NEP tenets. Much of Bukharin's argument was similar to his Politburo declarations of January 30 and February 9. But here, before the Central Committee, he focused on the crux of the struggle over policy—the fate of NEP.

There was, he exclaimed, "something rotten" in Stalin's line; and it had led the country into a vicious circle. While grain deliveries fell, rural violence increased, and open revolt broke out in Soviet borderlands, Stalin preached intensified class war, more "extraordinary measures," the necessity of "tribute," and "new," direct forms of the *smychka* between the state and the peasantry.

This reflected "a clear exaggeration of the possibility of influencing the basic peasant masses without market relations," and promised a "monstrously one-sided" relationship with the peasant. "And what is all this from the standpoint of our struggle with Trotskyism? It is a complete ideological capitulation to Trotskyism." Bukharinists supported rapid industrialization; but Stalin's plan, like a plane without an engine, was doomed because it rested on agricultural decay and the destruction of NEP: "The extraordinary measures and NEP are contradictory things. The extraordinary measures mean the end of NEP." Tomskii put it with equal bluntness: "What is this new form of *smychka?* . . . There is nothing new here; it is the extraordinary measures and the ration book." [176]

But the plenum's outcome was never in doubt. Characterizing Bukharin's views as incompatible with the party's general line, the Central Committee upheld his censure and endorsed Stalin's five-year plan. Bukharin and Tomskii were relieved of their official posts at *Pravda,* the Comintern, and the trade unions, and warned that persistent "factionalism" would bring further reprisals. [177] To this extent, the April plenum brought to an end the struggle for power—for the leadership of the party—between Stalin and the Bukharinists. Both sides regarded the Central Committee as the court of last resort, and it had confirmed Stalin's victory overwhelmingly.

And yet the outcome was also strikingly inconclusive. Despite the Central Committee's stern denunciation of the Bukharinists, Stalin had again gained less than their complete political destruction. Bukharin, Rykov, and Tomskii remained on the Politburo, full if impotent members of the leadership; Rykov continued as premier. [178] Furthermore, neither the removal of Bukharin and Tomskii from their posts nor the anti-Bukharin resolution, whose charges were again less extreme than Stalin's own, were made public. If this suggested that the Central Committee was still reluctant to disgrace and expel Bukharin and his friends from the leadership, its economic decisions, ratified at the Sixteenth Party Conference which opened on the day the plenum closed, reflected a similar restraint in policy. The adoption of Stalin's industrialization plan, made retroactive to October 1928, was a major break with the party's Bukharinist policies. But it was tempered by the April plan's agricultural goals, which were very similar to Bukharin's. Collectivization was still viewed as a modest, supplementary undertaking: collective and state farms were to encompass 17.5 per cent of all sown areas in five years compared to about

3–5 per cent in 1928–9; private farming, therefore, was to remain the mainstay of agriculture.[179] The entire plan, whatever its implications, was formulated in the context of a continuing NEP.

In short, contrary to the extreme events and fraudulent claims that shortly followed, Stalin's victory over Bukharin in April 1929 mandated neither personal dictatorship nor "revolution from above." The Central Committee, that is, had neither repudiated NEP nor politically destroyed its greatest defender. It had arrived at an uneasy accommodation. Voluntary grain deliveries, the foundation of NEP, were in virtual collapse; and Stalin's pronouncements disparaging private farming and legitimizing "extraordinary measures," together with the upward revision of industrial targets, did not encourage moderate NEP solutions.[180] If nothing else, Stalin's limited mandate was incommensurate with his political ambitions. Immediately after the plenum, his personal entourage began threatening Bukharinists with expulsion from the party and promoting privately the Stalin cult that was to blossom officially eight months later: "Our party . . . has at last found a true, strong-minded, courageous leader. This leader is Comrade Stalin! . . . Lenin's one and only successor. . . ." [181]

All this augured ill for Bukharin. His ambiguous status was apparent at the April party conference, the last before the onset of the "great change." Showing no sign of bending to Stalin's will, Bukharin seems not to have attended. Nonetheless, he, Tomskii, and Rykov, who delivered a compliant but unenthusiastic report on the five-year plan, were respectfully elected to its honorary presidium. In a closed session midway through the conference, delegates were informed by Molotov of the Central Committee's sanctions against the Bukharinists; but there was no public mention of their defeat or of dissension in the leadership.[182] Nor was there more than a hint of the furious defamation that would shortly descend upon Bukharin. While speaker after speaker urged "a merciless rebuff to right opportunism," an air of uncertainty about the agricultural crisis and Bukharin's fate hung over the proceedings. David Riazanov, the venerable Marxian scholar and irrepressible critic of sordid politics, seemed to allude to Bukharin's plight. "Marxists aren't needed in the Politburo," he remarked.[183] It was, some later thought, an epitaph for the impending age.

Bukharin's defeat, unlike that of the Left opposition, was to have momentous social consequences. Viewed historically, it was political prelude to "revolution from above" and to the advent of what became known as Stalinism. Why Stalin won, and the meaning of his political victory, are therefore major historical questions. Their answer rests partly on the nature of the policy argument between Bukharinists and Stalinists. Through the middle of 1929, the dispute frequently seemed to revolve chiefly around alternate means toward shared goals; both sides were eager to transform Soviet Russia into a "metal country," to achieve economic and military security in a hostile capitalist world, while moving toward a socialist society. In the longer view, it is clear that they offered the party and the country a fateful choice not only between radically different programs, but different destinies as well.

Before 1928, Stalin was largely a Bukharinist in economic philosophy; in 1928–9, as he groped toward policies that were in effect counter-Bukharinist, he began to become a Stalinist. Despite his pessimistic diagnosis of the current economic crisis, however, he did so without openly repudiating NEP, the foundation of Bukharinism. Indeed, well into 1929 his specific prescriptions were remarkably few and elliptical. Rhetoric aside, they were two: maximum investment in heavy industry and the creation of collective and state farms. Apart from his "tribute" concept and the gradualism he still attributed to collectivization, Stalin said little or nothing about the actual sources of capital investment, the nature of economic planning, or the process of socializing agriculture, omissions prompting Bukharin to insist that he had no long-term economic policy at all.[184] What made Stalin's nascent program so radical was less his concrete proposals than the political and ideological themes of his advocacy. Martial in spirit, their central imagery was that of civil war.

Bolshevism had always contained a faintly martial strain. Lenin's *What Is to Be Done?*, the movement's charter document, abounded with military analogies. But unlike Communist parties that have since come to power through prolonged guerrilla warfare, the Bolsheviks remained strikingly civilian in ethos until 1918. A major change came during the civil war years, whose imperatives imposed a far-reaching militarization of party norms. NEP then brought the reverse, a process of demilitarization or demobilization. Though eclipsed in the twenties by the reformist, evolutionary principles of NEP, the military habit did not disappear completely. "Administrative arbitrariness" and "remnants of war communism," criticized regularly by Bukharin and other leaders, testified to its tenacity. More intangibly, it lived on also— with the memory of 1917—in Bolshevism's "revolutionary-heroic" tradition. Trotskyists gave it occasional literary expression; but it was Stalin who in the crisis atmosphere of 1928–9 revived the war-fare tradition, gave it new meaning, and began to remake the party-state in its spirit.

From the onset of the grain crisis and his expeditionary dash across Siberia and the Urals, the imagery, analogy, and inspirational validity of the civil war were rarely absent from Stalin's public remarks. They composed his great programmatic theme of 1928–9. His response to the fall in grain collections was a call for mobilization: "throw the best forces of the party, from top to bottom, onto the procurement front." In the aftermath, with Stalin and his entourage setting the tone, the party's official outlook and methods underwent a steady militarization. Policy areas became "fronts"— the "grain front," "planning front," "philosophy front," "literary front," and by the thirties included such exotic battlements as the "vernalization front." Goals and problems became fortresses to be stormed by assaults. And, said Stalin in April 1928, "there are no fortresses that the working class, the Bolsheviks, cannot capture." [185] If war is politics by extraordinary means, what had originated as temporary, "extraordinary measures" acquired in the emerging Stalinist vision a legitimate, permanent status. Though Stalin himself rarely evoked 1917, the civil war precedent inevitably fused with that of October, joint evidence that "Bolsheviks can do anything," and became part of the ideology of "revolution from above" in late 1929.[186] It would lead, for example, to the portrayal of wholesale collectivization as "the storming of the old countryside" and "a rural October." [187]

The revival of civil war thinking was in some measure a natural response to the party's difficulties of 1928–9. But Stalin, its chief inspirer, infused it with special meaning. The civil war years, which he had spent enviously in Trotsky's shadow as a political commissar at the front, seem to have been a crucial experience in his life; and warlike approaches to social problems were congenial to what has been described as his "warfare personality." [188] Whatever the psychological reasons, it was Stalin who furnished the theoretical underpinning and novel feature of the "mobilization" of 1928–9—the argument that as socialism draws nearer, the resistance of its internal enemies, and thus the class struggle, will intensify. Bukharin's view was the opposite: progress toward socialism required and presupposed a diminishing of class conflict and civil strife. On this disagreement rested profoundly different understandings of the nature and development of Soviet society.[189]

Military rather than traditionally Marxist in inspiration, Stalin's intensification theory was perhaps his only original contribution to

Bolshevik thought; it became a *sine qua non* of his twenty-five-year rule. In 1928, applied to kulaks, "Shakhtyites," and anonymous "counter-revolutionaries," it rationalized his vision of powerful enemies within and his "extraordinary," civil-war politics. By the thirties, he had translated it into a conspiratorial theory of "enemies of the people," and the ideology of mass terror.[190] Its murderous implications were clear to Bukharin when he first heard the theory in July 1928: "This is idiotic illiteracy. . . . The result is a police state."[191]

The warfare themes of nascent Stalinism were central to the struggle between Bukharin and Stalin. They constituted a radical counterpoint to Bukharin's fundamental arguments—class collaboration, civil peace, and evolutionary development; systematic "extraordinary measures" were antithetical to the conciliatory, peaceful policies he called "NEP methods." Stalin's themes gave his otherwise elusive proposals a willful, extremist quality. The complexities of economic planning were dismissed as "vulgar realism" and reduced to the storming of "fortresses"; and, warned Bukharin as early as July 1928, even a circumspect collectivization program threatened to degenerate into a frenzied attempt "to drive the muzhik into the commune by force."[192] Their polemics reflected this civil war–civil peace confrontation. Bukharin accused Stalin of "war communist" and "military-feudal" policies "leading to civil war."[193] Stalinists boasted of having "put into the archives" Bukharinist notions of peaceful development and "other liberal rubbish," charged that Bukharin had turned Lenin into "an apostle of civil peace," and denounced his calls for caution and "normalization" as wartime sins of "defeatism," "pessimism," and "demobilizing moods."[194]

Although Bukharin complained bitterly that his former ally's sudden conversion to "super-industrialization" and exploitative peasant policies was "a complete ideological capitulation to Trotskyism," he understood that in Stalin's hands these ideas, convulsed by his warfare politics and stripped of the Left's analytic sophistication, represented a danger of a different and far greater order.[195] He responded by restating and defending anew the policies and thinking about Soviet development that he had set out against the Left since the early twenties. Again structured around political, economic, and moral objections to "wilful impulses," and enhanced by his revisions of 1927, his views and critique of Stalin's new course in 1928–9 acquired special importance in the light of what followed.

Underlying Bukharin's political thinking, as before, was his

conviction that intemperate agrarian policies would violate the
legacy of 1917, the *smychka* between town and countryside, and
trigger a fatal civil war with the peasantry. This no longer meant
for him economic concessions to the nascent village bourgeoisie.
He continued to support an offensive against the kulak, but of the
sort he had defined in 1927: nonviolent, "NEP methods" to curtail
kulak accumulation and influence, and which would in no way
touch the nonkulak masses.[196] Stalin's anti-kulak campaign, insisted
Bukharin, was something entirely different: a war—however euphe-
mistically labeled—against the peasantry at large. Moreover, his
intensification theory was a disingenuous rationalization of measures that had inflamed the countryside and created "a united village
front against us." The rising tide of peasant riots in mid-1928 reaffirmed Bukharin's certainty that Stalin's policies were leading to
civil war. For the first time, he seems to have suspected that given
the ruthlessly repressive methods of a "Genghis Khan," the party
might actually survive the showdown. This was the implication of
his remark that Stalin "will have to drown the uprisings in blood,"
a sudden presentiment that neither consoled him nor diminished his
objection.

A related argument figured in his case against Stalin's rural
policies. Even though the war scare of 1927 had subsided, the
prospect of a foreign attack on the Soviet Union was among the
perils invoked by Stalinists as necessitating all-out heavy industrialization at any cost. Bukharin, while committed to the development
of defense-oriented industries, replied that an equally decisive prerequisite of Soviet security was "the confidence of the peasantry."
An actively hostile or even passively disaffected rural population
would jeopardize the government in the event of war.[197] It was a
sensible concern, one revived in the thirties when the war scare was
more real, and validated in the catastrophe of 1941 when peasants
on the western frontier initially welcomed German invaders as
liberators.

Bukharin's economic objections to Stalin's emerging policies
were no less adamant. They ranged on several levels, from the
durability of NEP to the nature of planning. In construing the
grain shortage of 1928 as symptomatic of an organic crisis of peasant agriculture, Stalin had implicitly challenged prevailing Bukharinist assumptions about NEP's long-term viability. His analysis
of the crisis varied. On the one hand, he argued that the kulak,
grown prosperous and powerful and seeking to impose his will on
the government, was hoarding vast quantities of grain and had

thereby declared war on NEP and the Soviet state. On the other, he pointed to the persistently low productivity and marketed surplus of peasant agriculture.[198] While contradictory in their estimates of the volume of grain production, both arguments suggested that private farming was no longer compatible with the party's industrial aspirations.

Bukharin strongly disagreed, maintaining that the grain shortage was due not to "an iron law" or organic causes, but to "temporary disproportions" and transitory conditions. He rejected out of hand Stalin's conjuration of " 'terribly enormous' grain reserves. . . . Nobody believes these fairy tales any longer." The real problem was not concealed grain riches, but laggardly grain production. It had two primary causes, both serious but neither irreparable. One was the government's "madhouse" price policies, which had willy-nilly created a situation making grain farming unprofitable by comparison to other crops as well as nonagricultural pursuits. (Off-farm occupations accounted for almost half of village income.) A responsive price policy, advantageous to grain, would stimulate increased production and, coupled with progressive taxation and a steady abatement of the industrial goods shortage, marketed surplus. The second cause of the grain lag, Bukharin agreed, was the primitive state of peasant agriculture. But he continued to believe that relatively modest financial and agronomical assistance to small farmers would yield a significant increase in output.[199]

Private farming was still the foundation of Bukharin's agricultural program; but unlike 1924-6, it was no longer its exclusive feature. He now believed in the need and possibility of a voluntary collective sector that, properly advertised and supported, would evolve gradually, supplying one-fifth or so of surplus grain in five to ten years, and eventually, after "an entire historical period," supplanting peasant farming. Through mid-1929, Stalin officially advocated similar goals. But as early as May–June 1928, Bukharin saw in his warlike tone and Manichean disregard for private farming and market cooperatives indications of a disastrous "sudden leap." Peasant farms were to be the mainstay of grain in the immediate future; yet as a result of Stalin's "extraordinary measures," Bukharin pointed out, peasant agriculture was "regressing" because "the basic peasant masses have lost any stimulus to produce." Moreover, Marxists traditionally understood viable collectivization to require trained personnel, "a certain accumulation in agriculture," and mechanization, prerequisites absent from the Soviet countryside: "a thousand wooden plows cannot replicate a single tractor."

Did Stalin, he demanded angrily, propose to collectivize "on the basis of poverty and decay?" This, added Rykov, "would be to discredit the work of socialization and ruin the whole affair." [200]

Stalin's course in the countryside was for Bukharin economic folly precisely because it was "shutting off alternatives" by destroying NEP's diverse potential. His own agricultural program sought to maximize different opportunities and find "the correct combination of collective and individual agriculture." [201] He urged a variegated approach: "an uplifting of individual peasant economies, especially those producing grain, a limiting of kulak economies, the construction of state and collective farms, in conjunction with a correct price policy and development of the cooperatives of the peasant masses. . . ." [202] In this way, NEP—specifically, peasant agriculture and market relations—would continue to serve the cause of Soviet industrialization. Official party policy as late as 1929, it was abruptly jettisoned at the year's end, Bukharin's reasoning unrefuted and untried.

Bukharin's agrarian program determined his opposition to Stalin's boundless heavy industrialization funded by tribute-like extractions from agriculture. He seems now to have recognized that "applied Tuganism" (a parasitic industry producing almost exclusively for itself) could in the hands of a latter-day Genghis Khan be successful in its own cruel and transitory fashion.[203] But sustained "healthy" industrialization, he insisted again in 1928-9, was possible only if based on the expanding consumer market and resources of a prospering agriculture. This axiom no longer reflected complacency about the development of heavy industry or its costs. As a result of his rethinking in 1926-7, Bukharin (and Rykov) was now committed to sizable capital expenditures, reconciled to the inevitability of "temporary, partial disproportions," and aware that "we shall have to make sacrifices for some time to come." [204] Capital outlays, however, were to be limited by proportional investment in agriculture and in consumer industries serving the peasant market, and by actual reserves. Sacrifices and disproportions, he hoped, could be minimized by encouraging small private industries to contribute (especially to the alleviation of the consumer goods famine), by avoiding over-investment in costly long-term projects, and by bringing to Soviet industrialization the increased productivity and general rationality of "scientific management" and the technological revolution in the West.[205]

Unavoidably, the economic dispute became also a clash between different conceptions of planning and specifically of the first five-year plan. In the spirit of its warfare politics, the Stalin group had adopted an extreme version of what was called teleological planning, an approach that extolled the primacy of willful exertion over objective constraints, and became under Stalinist auspices a cascade of chiliastic commands and escalating targets. Bukharin's views on planning, set out in 1928–9 were naturally very different. They may be summarized briefly.

First, economic planning means the rational use of resources to achieve desired goals; the plan must therefore be based on scientific calculation and objective statistics, not "doing whatever you please" or an "acrobatic *salto mortale*." Second, planning seeks to eliminate from economic development the anarchy and crises (disequilibrium) inherent in capitalism; the plan must therefore foster and operate within "conditions of *dynamic economic equilibrium*," defining and adhering to "correct proportions" throughout the whole economy, taking into account and providing for reserves, and "leveling down to bottlenecks." Third, planning, especially in a backward agrarian society, must be tentative, allowing for "the very significant elements of *incalculable spontaneity*," among them the vagaries of harvests and the market; it cannot be one hundred per cent planning or (remarked another Bukharinist) "a five-year bible." [206] Finally, the planning process must in every respect avoid "over-centralization" or "over-bureaucratization." The negative ramifications of a wrong decision in such circumstances "may be no less than the costs of capitalist anarchy"; and, by eradicating flexibility and initiative from below, it leads to "economic arteriosclerosis," to "a thousand small and large stupidities," and what Bukharin termed "organized mismanagement." Instead,

centralization has its limits and it is necessary to give subordinate agencies a certain independence. They should be independent and responsible within prescribed limits. Directives from the center should be confined to formulating the task in general terms; the specific working out is the business of lower agencies, which act in accordance with actual conditions of life.[207]

Contrary to Stalinist legend, then, the struggle was not between champions and foes of planned industrialization, but between different approaches to the problem. The dispute frequently centered on questions of degree: the level of "pumping over" from agriculture, of capital expenditure, of the projected growth rate. For Bukharin, however, these constituted the difference between "more or less crisis-free development" and "adventurism." He defended the ambitious investment level set early in 1928—calling for almost 20 per cent annual increase in industrial output—and abandoned by Stalin as inadequate. The correct course, he argued, was "to *maintain* (but not push higher!) this rate"; to strive for real growth and not (as Rykov put it) "make a fetish of tempo." This, he promised, rather than the "policies of madmen," would produce "the highest *sustained* tempo." [208] In its revised form, Bukharin's economic thinking still advised restraint and balance against the excesses of over-investment, over-straining, over-planning, and over-centralization. If his economic and planning strictures seem unremarkable, it is because they have been widely accepted, even in Communist countries. More remarkable is that they were to be so completely ignored, and indeed, in the aftermath of his downfall, officially scorned as "alien" to Bolshevism.

More than political apprehension and economic philosophy, however, underlay Bukharin's bitter hostility to Stalin's new course. A major factor was still his moral objection to "monstrously one-sided" peasant policies as incompatible with socialism and Bolshevism's "historic task." In his polemics against Preobrazhenskii in the mid-twenties, Bukharin had expressed this view mainly as a comparative ethic of Soviet industrialization. He defended it against Stalin as well: "our industrialization must differ from that of capitalism. . . . Socialist industrialization is not a parasitic process in relation to the countryside." This in turn influenced his economic argument against the principle of " 'production for the sake of production' " and for the principle of "the development of mass consumption as the basic economic principle" of Soviet industrialization.[209]

But, at the same time as his dismay over Stalin's "policy of tribute" grew, Bukharin began to express his moral protest in the somewhat different context of Russian history. The shame of czarist Russia, he wrote angrily in September 1928, was its "merciless exploitation of the muzhik"; Stalin "wants to put the USSR in this historical line of . . . *old Russia*." [210] Nothing conveyed this historical indictment so clearly as his remarkable description of Stalin's peasant policies as "military-feudal exploitation." The adjectival term (or its variations) had special implications for a Russian revolutionary. It recurred in the writings of pre-revolutionary radicals (and liberals) as a malediction characterizing the uncommonly despotic nature of the czarist state, the legacy of the Mongol conquest, and its plunderous treatment of the enserfed peasantry.[211] For Bukharin and his followers, Stalin's "extortions from the population" and "policies of the Tartar khans" augured a rebirth of this tradition.[212] And in charging the general secretary with the "military-feudal exploitation of the peasantry," Bukharin was indicting him in the name not only of the Bolshevik revolution but of the anti-czarist intelligentsia that preceded it. Accordingly, his "gross slander" has never been officially forgotten nor forgiven.[213]

Indeed, his foreboding of reborn czarist practices went even further. For Bukharin, as for Russia's pre-Marxist radicals, the political quintessence of czarism had been its "*chinovnik* state" ruling despotically over a hapless people through official lawlessness or "arbitrariness." Revolution promised a break with this tradition— the advent of a non-*chinovnik* state of and for the people, what Lenin had called a "commune state" and what was for Bukharin the hopeful antithesis of contemporary history's drift toward a "New Leviathan." Throughout the early and mid-twenties, having rejected his own brief enthusiasm for "statization," Bukharin had worried aloud about the possibility of "a new state of *chinovniki*" and a new "official lawlessness" in Soviet conditions. He had seen this danger in the Left's "monopolistic philosophy" and "willful impulses"; but he had looked above all to the party to guard against the natural *chinovnik* habits and abuses of state officialdom, and to be the paladin of the people.[214]

The events of 1928–9 transformed his persistent concern into unconcealed alarm, and shattered his romance of the party. In Stalin's protracted "extraordinary measures," he saw the epitome of "administrative arbitrariness" and a renascent system of official lawlessness exemplified by a Soviet official, revolver displayed on the table, extorting grain from assembled peasants. That was why, as Stalin remarked contemptuously, "Bukharin recoils from extraordinary measures as the Devil from holy water." [215] Worse, Bukharin knew that party officials, responding to orders from above, were the direct agents of the new "arbitrariness." His outcry against party cadres who had become "*chinovniki* of the Soviet state" and "forgotten about living people" revealed his disillusion. Party cadres, he was saying, had been corrupted by power and themselves become its abusers, like "provincial officials under the old régime," obediently "servile and groveling" before superiors, capricious and "swaggering" toward the people.[216] "The party and the state have become one—this is the misfortune: . . . party organs are indistinguishable from state organs." [217] Silent as to whether this was the cause or outcome of Stalin's new course, but despairing over its emulation of "old Russia" and where it was leading, Bukharin evoked Lenin's "commune-state" ("from which, sadly, we are still very, very far") to underline what he regarded as the historical thrust and betrayed promise of Stalin's policies: "in a word, the people for the *chinovnik*, and not the *chinovnik* for the people." [218]

Seeing Stalin's line as ruinous for the party and the country, as well as incompatible with Bolshevism, Bukharin's outrage exceeded even his earlier animosity to the Left. The historical legacy of failed opposition at major turning points in history is, of course, that of a what-might-have-been, ponderable but not really calculable; and so it is with the alternative course of development represented by Bukharin's economic policies. Part of his critique of nascent Stalinism, however, was soon verified. As early as mid-1928, a year and half before "revolution from above," Bukharin perceived in Stalin's warfare policies, whatever their economic feasibility, the prospects of "third revolution," civil war in the countryside, bloody repression, and "a police state," consequences unanticipated by others, including supporters of the general secretary. This prescience alone was to gain him stature even in defeat during his remaining years in Stalin's Russia; it was also to earn him Stalin's special animus.

How, then, is Stalin's lopsided political victory over Bukharin to be explained? Of the several circumstances favoring the general secretary, the most important was the struggle's narrow arena and covert nature. This situation, abetted by Bukharin, Rykov, and Tomskii, confined the conflict to the party hierarchy where Stalin's strength was greatest, and nullified the Bukharin group's strength, which lay outside the high party leadership and indeed outside the party itself.

For, unlike the Bolshevik Left, which remained to the end a movement of dissident party leaders in search of a social base, the Right was an opposition with potential mass support in the country. That its rural policies were preferred by the peasant majority was clear to almost everyone, Bukharinists, Stalinists, and noncombatants alike.[219] In addition, the purges that ravaged administrative agencies, from central commissariats to local soviets and cooperatives, echoed in the prolonged press campaign against "rightism in practice," indicated that Bukharin's moderate views were widely shared by nonparty officials, especially those involved with the countryside and outlying republics.[220] Nor was the appeal of Bukharinism exclusively rural. Even after Tomskii's disgrace, rightist sentiment among rank-and-file trade unionists (and presumably the urban working class itself), expressed chiefly in stubborn resistance to Stalin's industrial policies, was a persistent fact. Its extent may be judged from the wholesale reconstitution of factory committees in 1929–30: in the major industrial centers of Moscow, Leningrad, the Ukraine, and the Urals, 78 to 85 per cent of their membership was replaced.[221]

Latent Bukharinist support was also considerable inside the party itself, again as evidenced by the clamorous attack on "right opportunism" at all levels. Beyond its acknowledged following among Communist administrators and intellectuals in the capital, where (according to Frumkin) "hundreds and thousands of comrades" regarded Stalin's line as "ruinous," significant pro-Right sentiment seems to have existed in party organizations throughout the country.[222] It was, predictably, most evident among rural cadres, who had accommodated themselves politically, and perhaps economically, to the lenient practices of NEP. While the all-party purge of 1929–30 brought about 170,00 expulsions, or 11 per cent of the party's total membership, 15 per cent of all rural Communists were expelled and an equal number reprimanded.[223] Not all the purge's victims were Bukharin's supporters or even sympathizers; but nor did its results represent the full extent of Communist opposition to Stalin's course. An undetermined but sizable number of party officials were expelled during the "extraordinary measures" of 1928, before the formal purge began. More important, its figures did not reflect the "secret rightist moods" which, as Stalinists complained repeatedly, were widespread in party and Komsomol ranks. Intimidated by the vehement anti-Right campaign, many Communists ceremoniously endorsed the new line, while sympathizing silently with the Bukharinist opposition.[224]

No preferential voting having occurred outside the Central Committee, it is, of course, impossible to gauge accurately the opposition's support. Nonetheless, the judgment of a foreign observer, even if exaggerated, confirms that it was very substantial: "the country and the Party were overwhelmingly Right and accepted Stalin's unexpected course in a sullen and frightened spirit." A Trotskyist, and thus no friend of the Bukharinist opposition, was of the same opinion: "at certain junctures it included the great majority of officials and enjoyed the sympathy of the nation." [225]

Bukharin's tragedy, and the crux of his political dilemma, lay in his unwillingness to appeal to this popular sentiment. Where the general population was concerned, his reluctance is simply explained. It derived from the Bolshevik dogma that politics outside the party was illegitimate, potentially if not actually counter-revolutionary. This was an outlook intensified by the fear, shared by majority and opposition groups alike, that factional appeals to the population might trigger a "third force" and the party's destruction.[226] From it came the axiom that intra-party disputes ought not even to be discussed before nonparty audiences. It was, as one Trotskyist said in explaining the Left's plight, a matter of "party patriotism: it both provoked us to rebel and turned us against ourselves." [227] So, too, with the Right, who were additionally constrained by a crisis in the country. Certain that Stalin's course was dangerously unpopular as well as economically disastrous, Bukharin, Rykov, and Tomskii remained nonetheless silent before the nation. Public opinion intruded into the struggle only obliquely, in a running debate over the significance of letters pouring into the center to protest the new rural policies. For Bukharinists they were "the voice of the masses," for Stalin unrepresentative manifestations of "panic." [228]

But Bukharin was restrained by another consideration as well. In Marxist eyes, the social groups thought to be most receptive to his policies, notably peasants and technical specialists, were "petty bourgeois" and thus unseemly constituencies for a Bolshevik. Their occasional expressions of Bukharinist sentiment in 1928–9, eagerly seized upon by Stalinists, were therefore damaging, as for example the *obiter dictum* of a self-proclaimed spokesman for the non-Communist intelligentsia: "When Bukharin speaks from the soul, nonparty fellow travelers on the right may keep silent." [229] Indeed, it was their prospective social base in the country that led Stalin to stigmatize Bukharinists as "rightist," an epithet repugnant to all leftists, including Bukharin. His strenuous efforts to dispel the charge inhibited him politically and produced an assortment of preposterous maneuvers, among them his decision personally to draft the resolution condemning "right deviationism" for the crucial Central Committee plenum of November 1928. "I had to notify the party that I was no rightist," he told an astonished Kamenev.[230] Here again Bukharin was trapped by Bolshevik assumptions, many of them mythical and partly of his own making.

His reluctance to carry the fight against Stalin to the party-at-large derived from similar inhibitions. For party politics outside the leadership arena had also become suspect and atrophied. Its membership swollen from 472,000 in 1924 to 1,305,854 in 1928, the party was no longer the politicized vanguard of revolution but a mass organization of rigidly stratified participation, privilege, and authority. At the bottom was a newly recruited rank and file, acquiescent and in large part politically illiterate, not knowing "Bebel from Babel, Gogol from Hegel," nor one "deviation" from another. In the middle was a bloated administrative officialdom, party *ap-*

paratchiki regarded by all oppositionists, left and now right, as a "quagmire" of obedient bureaucrats. Above sat the high leadership, arrogating to itself all prerogatives of party opinion-making and decisionmaking.[231] As Trotsky had warned and Bukharin sporadically feared, the party's political life had been choked off, supplanted by a system of hierarchical command fostered and legitimized by the leadership's animadversions against "factionalism," that is, politics outside its own ranks.

By 1929, Bukharin had come to share most of Trotsky's criticisms of the party's internal régime. Unlike Trotsky, however, having sanctioned its development, he was its prisoner. His dissent and accompanying pleas for the toleration of critical opinion in 1928–9 were regularly rebuffed with quotations from his own, earlier sermons against the Left's "factionalism," and his attacks on Stalin's "secretarial régime" with derisive jeers: "Where did you copy that from? . . . From Trotsky!"[232] Still, despite his complicity in imposing the proscriptive norms, Bukharin was tempted to appeal to the whole party. He agonized over his dilemma: "Sometimes at night I think, have we the right to remain silent? Is this not a lack of courage? . . . Is our 'fuss' anything but masturbation?"[233] Finally, believing that the party hierarchy he sought to win over would "slaughter" any leader who carried the struggle beyond its councils, he conformed to "party unity and party discipline," to the narrow, intolerant politics he had helped create. He shunned overt "factionalism," and so was reduced to ineffectual "backstairs intrigues" (like his Kamenev visit) easily exploited by his enemies.[234] His position was politically incongruous: driven by outraged contempt for Stalin and his policies, he remained throughout a restrained, reluctant oppositionist.

Apart from public appeals too Aesopian to be effective, Bukharin, Rykov, and Tomskii therefore colluded with Stalin in confining their fateful conflict to a small private arena, there to be "strangled behind the back of the party."[235] And it is in this context that Stalin's decisive victory must be explained. The customary explanation is uncomplicated: his bureaucratic power, accumulated during six years as general secretary and fed by successive victories over party dissidents, was omnipotent and unchallengeable; effortlessly and inexorably, it crushed the Bukharinists. The full truth is more complex. For while this interpretation emphasizes an important part of the story, it exaggerates Stalin's organizational power in 1928, underestimates the Right's, and discounts the substantive issues that hung in the balance and influenced the outcome.

Stalin's control of the central party bureaucracy was, of

course, a major factor. Through its appointment powers, he had promoted loyalists throughout the party, especially provincial secretaries who sat also on the Central Committee. Like a fourteenth-century Muscovy prince, he had gathered party "principalities" and barons into his orbit. They were the backbone of his support in 1928–9.[236] Equally important was the central bureaucracy's secretarial apparatus, which served the general secretary as a nationwide shadow government. On one level, its direct communication with all party organizations allowed him to interpret policy, manipulate party opinion, foster "pogroms," and generally offset the Bukharinist press. On another, its network of subordinate organs—whose secretarial cadres (133,00 to 194,00 strong)[237] were sufficiently ubiquitous to obstruct Bukharin's return from Kislovodsk in November 1928—functioned as virtual Stalinist caucuses in every institution headed by the opposition and its sympathizers. Minorities when the struggle began, these caucuses subverted and replaced rightist leaderships in places as diverse as the Moscow organization, the trade unions, the Institute of Red Professors, and even foreign Communist parties.[238] Their collective ascendency in 1928–9 imposed the hegemony of the party bureaucracy over "principalities," among them Rykov's governmental apparatus, previously outside its control.

The carrot and stick of Stalin's machine, from the lure of promotion to the threat of reprisal, also influenced undecided Central Committee votes. On the eve of the July 1928 plenum, for example, Stalin withdrew Kaganovich, probably the ablest and most despised of his lieutenants, as general secretary of the Ukrainian party. The latter's three-year tyranny in Kharkov had outraged Ukrainian delegates, who were now grateful for his removal.[239] A similar largess involved new capital construction scheduled under the five-year plan. Provincial party leaders, including the Ukrainians and Leningraders on whom Bukharin was counting, wanted a large share for their own regions. If this inclined them toward Stalin's policy of "maximum investment," it likewise alerted them to his control over its location. Their intense competition for allocations and its effect on the political struggle was noted by Riazanov at the party conference in April 1929: "every speech ends . . . 'Give us a factory in the Urals, and to hell with the Rights! Give us a power station, and to hell with the Rights!' "[240] The general secretary's stick was no less effective, from his rout of the Muscovites and authority to investigate party organizations to his habit of using the Secretariat's personnel records for "defamatory revelations." [241]

All this comprised the "heavy bludgeon of the Center's authority."[242] That it gave Stalin an enormous advantage over Bukharin, who once described himself as "the worst organizer in Russia," is unquestionable.[243] But machine politics alone did not account for Stalin's triumph. In terms of the Central Committee, it served mainly to guarantee him the allegiance or acquiescence of low- and middle-ranking delegates who had risen through his patronage, and about whom a disillusioned Stalinist remarked: "We have defeated Bukharin not with argument but with party cards."[244] Their Central Committee membership notwithstanding, however, these junior officials played a secondary role in 1928–9. In effect, they ratified an outcome already decided by a smaller, informal group of senior Central Committee members—an oligarchy of twenty to thirty influentials made up of high party leaders and heads of the most important Central Committee delegations (notably those representing Moscow, Leningrad, Siberia, the North Caucasus, the Urals, and the Ukraine).[245]

And within this select oligarchy, Stalin's bureaucratic power was considerably less imposing. Its actual limits were evidenced by the Right's own high-level strength (reaching even to the Secretariat and Orgburo), and by the number of uncommitted leaders whose wavering kept the outcome in question for months. It was also limited by the oligarchs themselves. Typified by men like Ordzhonikidze, Kuibyshev, the Ukrainians Stanislav Kosior and Grigorii Petrovskii, and the Leningrad party chief Sergei Kirov, they were the party's "practical politicians," who had risen to high "military-political" authority in civil war and presided over the country's key provinces and resources ever since.[246] As administrators and politicians, they were often associated with the general secretary. Most of them, however, were not his mindless political creatures, but important, independent-minded leaders in their own right.[247] Tough, pragmatic, and concerned primarily with domestic affairs, their collective outlook was dominated increasingly by the problems of transforming Soviet Russia into a modern industrial society, an aspiration intensified by the war scare of 1927 and imperiled by the grain crisis of 1928. In significant measure, the struggle between Bukharin and Stalin was a contest for their support, one in which issues and "argument" played an important part.

By April 1929, these influentials had chosen Stalin and formed his essential majority in the high leadership. They did so, it seems clear, less because of his bureaucratic power than because they preferred his leadership and policies. To some extent, their choice doubtless expressed their identification with the general secretary as a forceful "practical politician," compared to whom, perhaps,

the gentle, theoretical-minded Bukharin seemed "merely a boy." [248]
But it also expressed their doubts about the further efficacy of
Bukharinist policies and negative reaction to the Right's programmatic dilemma in 1928–9. Despite Bukharin's commitment to the
revised industrial and agricultural goals of the Fifteenth Party Congress, the worsening grain crisis placed him and his allies in an awk-
wardly equivocal position. Insisting that no economic programs
consistent with the congress's "NEP methods" were possible until
the rural situation was "normalized," they called repeatedly for
temporary concessions to the peasantry and for industrial restraint.
However sensible, these demands created an aura of retreat and
pessimism around the Right and reinforced Stalin's contention,
tirelessly reiterated, that Bukharin, Rykov, and Tomskii were
timid men incapable of resolute leadership, wedded to antiquated
thinking and a "theory of continuous concessions," and, above all,
prepared to jeopardize the pace of industrialization.[249] Neither the
ambitious long-term programs of the Bukharinists, nor their plea
for "a distinction between optimism and stupidity," [250] dispelled
this impression. It, as much as anything, proved their undoing.

For the salient political fact of 1928–9 was a growing climate
of high party opinion impatient with the Right's cautionary sermons and receptive to Stalin's assiduous cultivation of Bolshevism's
heroic tradition. This was conspicuous among younger, rising party
officials and Komsomol leaders who, despite Bukharin's long association with their organization, stood almost unanimously with Stalin
and contributed significantly to his victory.[251] Most important, this
impatience was the prevailing sentiment among party influentials.
Their mood and disenchantment with the Bukharin group was
summarized by Kuibyshev: "History will not allow us to proceed
quietly . . . by timid steps." He was echoed by Kirov: "In a word,
don't be in a hurry. . . . In a word, the Rights are for socialism,
but without particular fuss, without struggle, without difficulties."
And Ordzhonikidze, conceding Bukharin's good intentions, stated
their worry: "it is not a question of wishing but of policies. And
Comrade Bukharin's policies will drag us backward, not forward." [252] Determined to "catch up and surpass" the industrial
West quickly, frustrated by the current crisis, the party oligarchs
chose Stalin's "optimism" over the Right's "hopeless pessimism." [253]

In so doing, they were not voting for what Bukharin had
called "policies of adventurers." Rather, they were endorsing the
bold but still NEP-oriented policies Stalin advocated against the
Right, and which the Central Committee ratified in April 1929.
These policies enshrined the primacy of rapid industrial growth

and planning over market equilibrium; but they did not anticipate what actually followed—forcible wholesale collectivization, "de-kulakization," and the end of NEP.[254]

In short, Stalin built an anti-Bukharin majority and emerged as *primus inter pares* inside the leadership not as the reckless archi-tect of "revolution from above," but as a self-proclaimed sober-minded statesman pledged to a "sober and calm" course between the timidity of the Right and the extremism of the Left—as the true defender of the line of the Fifteenth Congress.[255] For all his warfare rhetoric, he won in his familiar role of the twenties as the man of the golden middle, who had impressed fellow administrators with his pragmatic efficiency, "calm tone and quiet voice." [256] Seven months later, he was to set out upon a wholly different course with unimagined goals and risks: a "great change," which for many Bolsheviks, including some who had supported him against Bukharin, was to come, like the day of the Lord, as a thief in the night.

The turbulent months between April 1929 when Bukharin was defeated and December were among the most important in Russian history. They brought three large, related events: an abrupt radi-calization of Stalin's policies, accompanied by his emerging prac-tice of making major decisions autocratically; a further worsening of the state's relations with the peasantry; and the onset of a furious official campaign against the Right opposition and Bukharin per-sonally, which grew into a repudiation of political moderation generally. Together these developments led to policies unlike any-thing ever advocated by any Bolshevik group, including the Left, to the final destruction of NEP, and to the coming of Stalin's "revolution from above."

Emboldened by his overwhelming victory in the Central Com-mittee, Stalin began to transform party policy during the summer and autumn of 1929. His first major departure came in the Comin-tern. At the tenth plenum of its Executive Committee in July, presided over by Molotov, the year-old decisions of the Sixth Con-gress were discarded in favor of the radical new course sponsored by Stalinists since 1928. The "third period" was redefined to mean the end of capitalist stabilization, an upsurge of proletarian mili-tancy, and the certainty of revolutionary situations in the West. Socialist parties, indeed reformists generally, were designated the chief enemy—their "fascization" said to be complete. Amidst the widening purge of Comintern moderates, foreign Communist parties were instructed to sever ties with social democratic movements, expose their "social fascism," and establish rival trade unions—in effect, to split the European labor movement.[257] Thus began the Comintern's ill-fated journey into extremism. It was to end disastrously five years later, having contributed to the destruction of the once-powerful German labor movement, both its socialist and Communist parties, and thus abetting Hitler's rise to power.

Stalin's further leftward turn at home was no less extreme. During the months following its adoption in April–May, both the industrial and agricultural goals of the five-year plan were revised drastically upward, and the nature of the overall plan transformed. Encouraged by a sharp increase in industrial production over the summer, but in the face of growing economic strains, the Stalin group suddenly turned optimal figures into minimal ones, increasing the annual growth target from 22.5 to 32.5 per cent and doubling the number of new factories to be built. By autumn, it was insisting that the entire five-year plan be fulfilled, and then overfulfilled, in four years. The result was to strip the original plan of its conditional features, its provisions for balance, and its coherence generally.[258] What remained was no longer a plan but a kaleidoscope of escalating figures, an ersatz rationalization of the breakneck heavy industrialization of the next three years.

Meanwhile, the situation in the countryside continued to deteriorate. Confirming the Right's predictions, summer and autumn brought a new wave of peasant unrest; in Moscow province alone, 2,198 rural disturbances, many of them violent, were recorded between January and September.[259] Equally serious and predictable, peasant sowings continued to decline. Grain as well as industrial crop shortages grew more acute and consumer rationing, reintroduced early in 1929 for the first time since the civil war, more stringent.

His industrial goals threatened by the deepening supply crisis, Stalin responded with still more coercive and ambitious measures. By the autumn of 1929, the "extraordinary measures" had become (as Bukharin feared) a regularized system of state requisitioning. Simultaneously, Stalin's thinking about large-scale collective farms grew more daring. Central planners and rural officials were instructed to regard collectivization not as supplementary to private farming and market cooperatives (as envisaged in the original plan), but as an immediate solution to the régime's agricultural problems. As state agents—their methods increasingly coercive—swarmed the countryside procuring grain, promoting collectives, and inciting against the kulak, the percentage of collectivized households rose significantly from 3.9 in June to 7.6 in early October. The infant collectives were small, often unstable and of poor quality, and still represented only a fraction of the country's 25 million holdings; but this increase seems to have decided Stalin on an all-out drive. The central press began to speak hopefully of mass collectivization in select areas, though there was still no hint of the great assault that was to come in December.[260]

At first, these developments did not affect the defeated opposition. Tomskii and his followers were formally removed from the trade unions in June, and Bukharin and his foreign allies from the Comintern's Executive Committee in July.[261] In June, Bukharin had been appointed director of the Scientific-Technological Department of the Supreme Economic Council, which administered a network of industrial research institutes. Though later an effective platform for his views, the position was obviously incongruous for a Politburo member, a place of political exile.[262] None of these steps, however, exceeded the Central Committee's decision in April to relieve Bukharin and Tomskii of their important offices (bowing, in effect, to their resignations) but to maintain them as Politburo members formally in good standing. Accordingly, despite the heightened anti-Right campaign in early summer, Bukharin, Rykov, and Tomskii were still not openly attacked.

For their part, the trio seems to have avoided public acts that would undermine their already precarious position as a dissenting minority in the leadership. For Rykov, who lingered on as premier until December 1930, this meant signing decrees he opposed. For the less adaptable Tomskii, it meant virtual silence. Bukharin, on the other hand, continued to speak out for a time, though with dwindling opportunities and necessarily greater restraint. Addressing a congress of atheists in June, he subtly protested the growing climate of official intolerance and Stalinist demands for uncritical party obedience. Marxism, he reflected, was critical thought, not dogma and dead formulas; he recommended Marx's favorite slogan: "Subject everything to doubt." [263] His own critical attitude toward Stalin's Comintern and economic policies was expressed obliquely in a two-part essay in May and June, the last even cautiously dissonant article he was able to publish in 1929.[264] Ostensibly a critique of Western theories of large-scale organization, it reiterated his argument that capitalist stabilization continued in the West and, on domestic issues, his warnings about the dangers of over-centralization and rampant bureaucratization.

But despite their self-restraint and effort to "legalize" their dissenting status on the Politburo,[265] it was clear by August that

Stalin was determined to destroy the trio, and especially Bukharin, as political leaders. His extremist course and the unrest in the countryside were creating a potentially explosive situation. And while they had persuaded many banished Trotskyists to capitulate and return—"half-hanged, half-forgiven," in Trotsky's disdainful words [266]—to serve his industrialization drive, they were also generating alarm and dissension among Stalin's own supporters.[267] In these circumstances, the defeated but not disgraced Bukharin remained a formidable rival, whose warnings and programs were acquiring new validity and whose political stature still stood between Stalin and supreme leadership.

The decision to disgrace Bukharin and all he represented, apparently taken solely on Stalin's initiative, was an integral part of "revolution from above." The public attack began on August 21 and 24, when *Pravda*, now the general secretary's mouthpiece, published sweeping denunciations of Bukharin as "the chief leader and inspirer of the right deviationists." [268] It was immediately taken up by virtually every official newspaper and journal, growing during the last four months of 1929 into a systematic campaign of political defamation unsurpassed in party history. (It was also unprecedented in that Bukharin, unlike earlier oppositionists, was unable to reply or publicize his views.) In an almost daily spew of articles, exhumed archive documents, pamphlets, and books (many composed by Stalinist "theory brigades" as early as 1928),[269] Bukharin's entire political and intellectual biography was condemned variously as un-Marxist, anti-Leninist, anti-Bolshevik, anti-party, petty bourgeois, and pro-kulak. No significant episode or writing escaped traducement, from his disputes with Lenin in emigration and Left Communism of 1918 to his opposition to Stalin, from his wartime essays on modern capitalism and the state, *The Economics of the Transition Period* and *Historical Materialism*, to "Notes of an Economist" and "Lenin's Political Testament." [270]

The campaign's purpose was to discredit irrevocably Bukharin's authority as a Bolshevik leader, and particularly his reputation as "the favorite of the whole party" and its greatest theorist. Its ramifications, however, were far greater. Unlike Trotsky, Bukharin had exercised enormous intellectual influence in many areas of party life; his writings had been official doctrine for over a decade, educating "hundreds of thousands of people." [271] The campaign "to eradicate Bukharinist influence" therefore became an assault on major components of Bolshevik ideology, on the party's intellectual institutions, on the education of a generation. Vilified and repudiated were not merely the central principles of Bukharinism—class cooperation, civil peace, and balanced, evolutionary growth—but also philosophical, cultural, and social outlooks only remotely associated with him. In the process, the warfare themes and policies of Stalinism were enshrined in their place as official ideology.

By November, the pillorying of Bukharin, "the right deviation," and "conciliationism" had become an ideological terror directed at policy moderation in general. Coupled with the purge (which was now victimizing all of Bukharin's known sympathizers, even Lenin's widow Krupskaya and his sister Mariia Ulianova),[272] its immediate political consequence was to impose zealotry on a still predominantly recalcitrant party. Among other things, it repressed the widespread hostility to Stalin's agricultural policies and drove terrified party officials to the frenzied excesses that produced the rural catastrophe of the winter of 1929–30.[273]

More generally, the campaign constituted an official repudiation of NEP's moderately tolerant, conciliatory practices, now assailed as "rotten liberalism" or, occasionally, "Bukharinist liberalism."[274] It echoed a major transformation underway in Soviet cultural and intellectual life since mid-1929. Paralleling the persecution of private farmers, small merchants, artisan producers, and the nonparty intelligentsia, cultural diversity was falling prey to the "class struggle on all fronts." In the Manichean spirit of its warfare politics, the Stalin group began by elevating one of the several groups or schools as its instrument to silence the others: dialectical philosophers over mechanists (incriminated by their casual affinity with Bukharin's philosophical theories); "proletarian" writers and artists over fellow travelers; teleological planners over geneticists; "red" specialists over "bourgeois" specialists.[275] The goal and eventual outcome, however, was simply the suppression of heterogeneity and the imposition of a monopolistic orthodoxy still in the making. Here, as in economic life, the principles and foundations of NEP society were under attack.

None of these radical developments during the second half of 1929 resulted from a formal party decision. Far exceeding the April resolutions of the Central Committee, which was scheduled to reconvene on November 10–17, they were initiated by Stalin and his chief lieutenants, notably Molotov and Kaganovich, who now dominated the party's executive bodies in Moscow.[276] On November 7, in a *Pravda* article that for cowed party officials carried the force of a decree, Stalin went still further. He proclaimed "a great change" in agriculture and the central myth of his "revolution from above." Contrary to party legislation (as well as to the actual situation), he asserted that the peasant masses, including middle peasants, were voluntarily quitting their private plots and "joining collective farms . . . by whole villages, groups of villages, districts, and even regions." [277] It was a call for immediate wholesale collectivization.

The Central Committee convened three days later. Exactly what occurred during this crucial November plenum remains obscure. Despite serious misgivings even among Stalin's supporters,[278] the assembly was no longer able or willing effectively to deny the general secretary, who demanded ratification of his related *faits accomplis*: the political destruction of Bukharin and the turn toward mass collectivization. On November 12, following a barrage of Stalinist threats that they recant or face possible expulsion from the party, Bukharin, Rykov, and Tomskii read a circumspect but unrepentant statement to the plenum. While acknowledging certain "successes," it criticized Stalin's methods in the countryside and their impact on urban living standards. It was immediately denounced by Stalin and Molotov; and on November 17, Bukharin was expelled from the Politburo.[279]

Even though public defamation had made Bukharin's continuation in the leadership untenable, the Central Committee appears to have acquiesced in his ouster without enthusiasm.[280] (Rykov and Tomskii, attacked less harshly in the press, temporarily retained their seats.) The assembly then endorsed Stalin's call for mass collectivization, but anxiously and with some reservations. Unlike his spokesman, Molotov, who urged the incredible goal of complete collectivization in key areas by the summer of 1930, the plenum was vague on the tempo, stating ambiguously that events "now confront separate regions with the task of mass collectivization." Still hoping for some semblance of order and moderation, it also recommended that a special commission be established to work out specific guidelines.[281]

One political triumph eluded Stalin at the plenum, but only briefly. Demoralized and broken, Bukharin's remaining Moscow supporters on the Central Committee had recanted during the proceedings.[282] Bukharin, Rykov, and Tomskii, however, continued to refuse with "extraordinary obstinacy." [283] But a week later, on November 25, they finally relented and signed a brief statement of political error. Published the next day, the conceding passage read:

We consider it our duty to state that in this dispute the party and its Central Committee have turned out to be correct. Our views . . . have turned out to be mistaken. Recognizing our mistakes, we will . . . conduct a decisive struggle against all deviations from the party's general line and above all against the right deviation. . . .[284]

Though considerably less than the abject self-renunciation demanded by Stalin, it was political surrender and the end of the Bukharinist opposition.

Why Bukharin, reportedly less willing than Rykov or Tomskii, signed is uncertain.[285] That it was neither a genuine conversion nor a failure of courage was to be demonstrated by his defiant conduct in the months to come. One factor in his decision seems to have been the plight of his young adherents of the "Bukharin school," particularly Slepkov, Maretskii, Tseitlin, Petrovskii, Zaitsev, and Aikhenvald. Withstanding banishment and enormous pressure, they had emulated Bukharin's defiance, refusing to renounce him or their anti-Stalinist views. They were now threatened with worse reprisals, including arrest. Bukharin's concession apparently spared them temporarily, or at least freed them to issue similar statements.[286] Another consideration was probably "party patriotism." For better or worse, the country was on the verge of a momentous, hazardous upheaval not without heroic overtones. In these circumstances, Bukharin's duty, as he saw it, was to his party, which meant "party discipline," the pretense of unity and the gesture of repentance.

Whatever its motivation, the capitulation of Bukharin—the greatest representative of an alternative "general line"—completed the general secretary's rise to unrivaled leadership. It was celebrated officially with the birth of the Stalin cult. On December 21, his fiftieth birthday, the press was filled with fulsome eulogies of Stalin, "the most outstanding continuer of Lenin's work and his most orthodox disciple, the inspirer of all of the party's chief measures in its struggle for the building of socialism . . . the universally recognized leader of the party and the Comintern." Among his accomplishments was said to be the exposing of Bukharin's "kulak, anti-proletarian" ideas.[287] In the years ahead, the cult would become a full-throated glorification, ascribing to Stalin alone every quality and achievement once attributed to the party and its collective leaders. By the same token, at the age of forty-one, Bukharin's career as a leader of the Bolshevik revolution and a "Leninist heir" had come to an end. An important political afterlife remained; but it was to be only an afterlife, nonetheless.

Wendell Phillips once observed: "Revolutions are not made; they come." Revolutions from above, however, are made, as in the Soviet Union in December 1929. Ignoring frantic reports of rampant official lawlessness and mounting chaos in the countryside, Stalin now bombarded rural cadres with uncompromising directives to accelerate the pace of collectivization. Their essential message was: "Anyone who does not join the collective farm is an enemy of the Soviet régime." The commission on collectivization sat between December 8 and December 22, its eight subcommittees proposing a series of procedures and timetables to regulate the transition. All were flatly rejected by Stalin in favor of collectivization "without any limitations." On December 27, again without party sanction, he announced the final, murderous ingredient: "the liquidation of the kulaks as a class." Augmented by the hastily devised concept of *podkulachnik*, or "kulak agent," "dekulakization" authorized the forcible collectivization of the country's 125 million peasants, and all-out war against any who resisted.[288] It was the death knell of NEP society, and the end of an era.

CHAPTER X

The Last Bolshevik

There is a shadow of something colossal and menacing that even now is beginning to fall across the land.

— JACK LONDON, *The Iron Heel*

In accord with eternal, iron
Great laws
Must we all
Complete the cycles
Of our life.

— GOETHE, QUOTED BY BUKHARIN IN 1932

To UNDERSTAND the last eight years of Bukharin's life, it is necessary to understand the nature and full impact of Stalin's "revolution from above." In all its dimensions, it lasted a decade, from the onset of forcible collectivization in 1929 to the ebbing of Stalin's blood purge in 1939. By any criterion of social change, it was a truly momentous process that radically transformed not only the economic and social foundations of Soviet society but the nature of the political system as well. It was during this process of the 1930's that the present-day Soviet Union, with its great military-industrial power, took shape, and that Stalinism, a new political phenomenon, was established.

From 1929 to 1936, the period of the first and second five-year plans, Stalin's "great change" was primarily an economic revolution, a farrago of brutal coercion, memorable heroism, catastrophic folly, and spectacular achievement. Few of the targets of the first plan were attained on schedule; but its actual accomplishments, consolidated and expanded at an annual rate of 13–14 per cent during the more pragmatic and modest second plan, nonetheless created the foundations of an urban, industrial society.

By 1937, heavy industrial production was three to six (depending on the indices used) times greater than in 1928: steel production had quadrupled, coal and cement production more than tripled, oil production more than doubled; electrical output had grown seven-fold, that of machine tools twentyfold. While old plants were expanded and retooled, new cities, industries, power stations, iron and steel complexes, and technologies came into being, many in formerly undeveloped areas. The industrial labor force and urban population doubled. The total number of students grew from 12 million to over 31 million; by 1939, illiteracy among citizens under fifty had been eliminated.[1]

The costs of this leap into economic modernity were no less spectacular. For a zealous minority—mostly party members but also ordinary men and women—it was a time of genuine enthusiasm, feverish exertion, and willing sacrifice.[2] For the majority, including several millions whose fate was deportation, forced labor camps, and death, it was one of repression and misery. The concentration of resources in heavy industry, the suppression of private manufacturing and trade, the virtual collapse of agriculture during the years of collectivization, and the epidemic of waste generated by mismanagement, chronic breakdowns, overstrained and abused equipment, and unskilled labor had a devastating and lasting impact on Soviet life. In the cities, which suffered less, housing space declined sharply and per capita consumption of meat, lard, and poultry in 1932 was only a third of what it had been in 1928. Factory workers lost the right to change jobs without official permission and incurred severe penalties for absenteeism, while real wages dropped by perhaps as much as 50 per cent in the early thirties.[3] Rationing and queues became the norm; consumer goods and services all but disappeared.

Far heavier blows fell on the countryside during the four-year civil war known as collectivization. Great revolutions almost always victimize a social class; in this case, it was 25 million peasant families. Most did not want to relinquish their meager plots, tools, and animals, and become collective farmers. They were forced to do so by the party-state which, in addition to fiscal and administrative compulsion, resorted to prolonged confiscations, mass arrests, deportations, and military assaults by rural cadres, urban brigades, police, and even army detachments. The peasants fought back, often in sporadic pitched battles, occasionally in mass uprisings, but mainly in traditional rural fashion by destroying their crops and livestock.[4]

The nature of the struggle was determined in January–

February 1930. Driven by Stalin's menacing directives and purge of "rightists," local authorities unleashed a reign of terror against recalcitrant kulaks, middle and poor peasants alike. Half of all the households—more than 10 million families—were collectivized by March. The holocaust, however, compelled Stalin to call a temporary halt in a remarkable article blaming local officials for the "excesses" and for having grown "dizzy with success." A mass exodus from the collective farms followed, plummeting the percentage of enrolled households from 57.6 in March to 23.6 in June.[5] But the retreat had come too late to stave off disaster. Figures published in 1934 revealed that more than half of the country's 33 million horses, 70 million cattle, 26 million pigs, and two-thirds of its 146 million sheep and goats had perished, most during what one official history now disparages as the "cavalry march" of January–February 1930.[6] A greater catastrophe could hardly befall an agrarian society. Twenty-five years later, livestock herds were still smaller than in 1928.

Later in 1930, with more deliberation but hardly less coercion, the state resumed its offensive. Repression "on an extraordinary scale" still swept the countryside in 1933.[7] By 1931, 50 per cent of the households had again been collectivized, and by 1934, 70 per cent; the remainder followed shortly. What finally broke the peasant resistance, ending the unequal war, was the deliberately created famine of 1932–3, one of the worst in Russian history. Having procured the meager harvest of 1932, the state withheld grain from the countryside. Firsthand accounts tell of deserted villages, burned-out houses, cattle cars still carrying deportees northward, roaming hordes of begging, starving peasants, incidents of cannibalism, and the uncollected bodies of men, women, and children; in short, a ravaged, totally defeated countryside.[8] At least 10 million peasants, possibly many more, died as a direct result of collectivization, about half during the imposed famine of 1932–3.[9]

When it was all over, 25 million private enterprises had been replaced by 250,000 collective farms, controlled by the state and compelled to deliver a high percentage of their considerably reduced crop at very low prices. Forcible collectivization was the linchpin of Stalin's economic revolution, and his singular innovation. No Bolshevik had ever advocated anything remotely like what happened in 1929–33. All had viewed collectivization as a form of highly productive, mechanized agriculture developing at a later stage of industrialization; none had conceived of it as a procurement device and primitive instrument of crash industrialization.[10] (If a spiritual precedent is to be found, it is in the czarist tradition, as Stalin himself occasionally suggested by his admiration for Peter the Great.) Almost any other agricultural program would have been more productive and far less destructive. But Stalin's boasted one accomplishment: it brought the once autonomous peasantry, the majority of the population, under state control, and made possible what was indeed a kind of "military-feudal exploitation." Statistics for 1933 tell the story: while the grain harvest was 5 million tons less than in 1928, state procurements had doubled.[11]

The worst extremes of industrialization and collectivization were over by 1934; two years of relative relaxation and economic improvement followed. Meanwhile, the early thirties had also brought significant political changes, whose direction recalls Kliuchevskii's aphorism about czarist history: "The state swelled up; the people grew lean." [12] Against the background of social violence and militarization, centralized bureaucracies proliferated to administer the expanding state economy, police a growing labor camp population, control the activities and movements of citizens (the internal passport having been reintroduced), and regulate intellectual and cultural life. A transmogrification of the party-state's ideology and social policies had also begun. When completed in the late thirties, the revolutionary experimentalism, progressive legislation, and egalitarianism in education, law, family life, incomes, and general social behavior of 1917–29 had been officially repudiated. They were replaced by traditional, authoritarian norms, which augured the paradoxical outcome of Stalin's revolution: the creation of a rigidly conservative, highly stratified society. Other features of mature Stalinism were similarly on the rise, including the Stalin cult and the falsification of party history, an official resurgence of Russian nationalism and rehabilitation of czarist history, and the abandonment of other important Marxist outlooks.[13]

But in spite of these developments, no political change comparable to the economic revolution of 1929–33 had yet occurred. The Bolshevik Party—its chief organs and traditions—was still the center of the system; its major figures (many demoted but still in responsible positions) and its substantially pre-Stalinist élites and cadres remained on the scene. In this respect, Stalin's blood purge of 1936–9 constituted the second, political stage of his revolution from above. The three-year terror of mass arrests and executions—directed by Stalin and his personal coterie operating through the secret police, or NKVD—savaged Soviet society. At least 7–8 million people were arrested, of whom about 3 million were shot or died from mistreatment. Prisons and remote concentration camps swelled to 9 million inmates by late 1939 (compared to 30,000 in 1928 and 5 million in 1933–5). Every second family suffered a casualty. Every ruling élite—political, economic, military, intellectual, and cultural—was decimated.[14]

The party was hit hardest. Of its 2.8 million full and candidate members in 1934, at least a million, anti-Stalinist and Stalinist alike, were arrested and two-thirds of them executed. Its old leadership, from bottom to top, was destroyed: entire local, regional, and republican committees disappeared; 1,108 of the 1,966 delegates to the Seventeenth Party Congress in 1934 were arrested and most of them shot; 110 of the 139 full and candidate members of the 1934 Central Committee were executed or driven to suicide. After Trotsky's murder in Mexico in 1940, from Lenin's high council only Stalin remained alive.[15] The official explanation of the terror was that its victims were "enemies of the people," participants in a vast anti-Soviet conspiracy of sabotage, treason, and assassination. Elaborated most fully at three show trials of old Bolsheviks in 1936, 1937, and 1938—of which the last, that of Bukharin, was the most important—all of the criminal charges were false.[16]

Stalin's blood purge constituted a revolution "as complete as, though more disguised than, any previous changes in Russia."[17] The Bolshevik Party was destroyed and a new party with a different membership and ethos created. Only 3 per cent of the delegates to its last pre-purge congress in 1934 reappeared at the next congress in 1939. Seventy per cent of the party's full membership in 1939 had joined since 1929, that is, during the Stalin years; only 3 per cent had been members since before 1917.[18] By the late thirties, the Soviet political system had ceased to be a party dictatorship or government in any meaningful sense. Behind a facade of institutional continuity and official fictions, Stalin had become an autocrat, reducing the party to one of his several instruments of personal dictatorship. Its deliberative bodies, the party congress and Central Committee, and eventually even the Politburo, rarely met after 1939. Indeed, until the dictator's death in 1953, the party's power remained less than that of the police, and its official esteem less than that of the state.[19]

If the far-reaching impact of Stalin's "revolution from above" is clear, its internal political history is considerably less so. Partly in response to the social upheaval and perils of 1929–33, politics inside the high leadership were now almost completely hidden.

Dissension and conflict were scrupulously concealed from the public behind a facade of enthusiastic unanimity. This, along with the violent death of most of its chief figures and a continuing censorship of history in the Soviet Union, has left us with a fragmentary knowledge of the political history of the thirties. Many important episodes and issues are still obscure. Enough evidence has appeared, however, to dismiss the once prevailing assumption that Stalin ruled essentially unchallenged after Bukharin's defeat in 1929. It shows that by 1933 a muted but fateful struggle over policy had developed between what may be termed moderates and Stalinists in the Politburo itself, and that its outcome was settled only by Stalin's purge of 1936–9.[20]

The programmatic thinking of this moderate or (to use Stalin's pejorative) "liberal" group coalesced in 1933,[21] but its origins go back to the rural disaster of early 1930. Indeed, cracks in Stalin's own Politburo and Central Committee majority appeared within weeks of Bukharin's ouster from the leadership. The source was Stalin's radical departure from the economic platform on which he had won a majority and defeated Bukharin, initiatives that had suddenly produced the gravest threat to the régime since the civil war. It was an alarmed Politburo group that persuaded or compelled Stalin to call a temporary halt to collectivization on March 2. Some Politburo members then objected to his face-saving device of placing full responsibility for the debacle on local officials.[22] As they knew, it was Stalin and his intimates in Moscow, not local cadres, who had been "dizzy with success" and had initiated the frenzied assault on the peasantry.

Though limited, these early strains in Stalin's own Politburo reflected a far greater unrest among high Stalinist officials throughout the country, as evidenced a few months later by the Syrtsov-Lominadze affair. Sergei Syrtsov was premier of the Russian Republic and a deputy Politburo member; Lominadze, a Central Committee member, was now head of the important Transcaucasian party organization. Once Stalin's ardent supporters against Bukharin, they had been profoundly shocked by the consequences of his new course. Discussing the "catastrophic situation" privately in Moscow in mid-1930, they began separately circulating memoranda and lobbying in official channels for a change of policy, including an end to forcible collectivization and the curtailment of industrial investment. Their proposals and criticism of Stalin's line were strikingly similar to Bukharin's in 1928–9. While Syrtsov criticized the consequences of "extraordinary centralization" and "rampant bureaucratism," dismissing vaunted industrial projects as "eyewash" and "a Potemkin village," Lominadze echoed Bukharin by denouncing the régime's "baronial-feudal attitude toward the needs and interests of workers and peasants." [23] Stalin's easy suppression of the two—both were condemned as "double-dealers" who had "capitulated to right opportunism," and stripped of their posts in December—should not obscure the significance of their ill-fated protest. It signified a widespread disillusionment and crisis of confidence among many of Stalin's original supporters, high and low.[24]

Purged of his major rivals, the Politburo, however, stood with Stalin, thereby preventing any change of course or leadership. Throughout the social trauma of the next three years, its members supported the resumption of imposed collectivization and Stalin's continuous reprisals (still bloodless) against dissident and "passive" party members. In addition to their complicity in his rise to supremacy and in his policies, they did so, it seems, for at least three reasons. They were committed to the industrialization drive. They believed that it was too late, politically and economically, to turn back from all-out collectivization. And at a time when virtual civil war threatened the régime's survival, they feared the consequences of open conflict at the top, much less a change of leadership.[25]

Publicly, all Politburo members therefore praised Stalin, defended the "general line," and contributed to the sustained pillorying of defeated oppositionists, above all Bukharin, that had become an *idée fixe* of his politics. Privately, however, several tried to moderate his policies and constrain his increasingly arbitrary actions. Ordzhonikidze, for example, opposed the terrorizing of the old technical intelligentsia that produced two show trials of non-Bolshevik "wreckers" in 1930–1, protecting those he could. As Commissar of Heavy Industry, he—and other leaders—began to urge, and eventually achieved in 1933, greater "realism" and moderation in the second five-year plan.[26] Most important, he and two other Politburo members, Kirov and Kuibyshev, had begun to protect various prominent Bolsheviks from Stalin's wrath.[27] And it was in this connection, in the fall of 1932, that the emergence of a coherent resistance to Stalin within his own Politburo became clear.

Earlier in 1932, the deposed Moscow secretary Mikhail Riutin, joined by several younger Bukharinists including Slepkov, Maretskii, and Petrovskii, had drafted and circulated clandestinely a 200-page anti-Stalin platform. A bitter assault in a Bukharinist vein on Stalinist policies, the document called Stalin "the evil genius of the Russian Revolution, who, actuated by vindictiveness and lust for power, had brought the revolution to the edge of the abyss." [28] Stalin, without basis, insisted this was a call for his assassination. Challenging the deep-rooted Bolshevik tradition against resorting to the death penalty in intra-party disputes, he demanded Riutin's (and possibly his collaborators') execution. The case came first before the Central Control Commission, the disciplinary body which had already offended Stalin by reinstating on appeal many party members expelled since 1930.[29] Declining to act, it passed the case to the ten-member Politburo, where Stalin again demanded Riutin's execution. He was defeated by a Politburo majority of Kirov, Ordzhonikidze, Kuibyshev, and probably Kosior and Kalinin. Riutin and his associates were simply expelled from the party and banished from Moscow.[30]

The "Riutin affair," as it became known, was a turning point in the politics of the thirties. On one level, Stalin's defeat merely reaffirmed the sacrosanct prohibition against shooting party members. On another, however, it demonstrated that Politburo moderates were now determined to resist his grasp for greater, more arbitrary power within and over the party. Headed by the Leningrad party chief Kirov, an independent-minded and popular figure, and Ordzhonikidze, and with the support or sympathy of many Central Committee members, by 1933 they were also advocating general policies unlike those preferred by Stalin and his Politburo devotees, Kaganovich, Molotov, and Voroshilov. At the same time, as later became clear, the Riutin affair dates Stalin's determination to rid himself of all such restraints represented by the existing Bolshevik Party, its élite, and its political traditions.[31]

Despite its covert existence, the nature of this moderate Politburo group is reasonably clear. Its members, typified by Kirov, had been Stalin's adherents in the succession struggle and energetic executors of his "general line." Their collective oligarchical support had enabled him to defeat Bukharin in 1929 and survive the crisis of the early thirties. Nor were they now anti-Stalinists in the conventional sense. They sought neither to remove him nor to diminish his pre-eminence and official adulation as leader (though some of their sympathizers did, voting against his re-election to the Central Committee in January 1934).[32] Rather, their purpose was twofold. First, it was to preserve the Leninist practice of collective or oligarchical decisionmaking by the Politburo and to a lesser extent by the Central Committee: to preclude the kind of autocratic rule by *fait accompli* that Stalin had exercised during the early months of collectivization. Second, arguing that the industrial leap and mass collectivization were largely complete and the worst over, they proposed, and sought Stalin's support for, a general change in policy. They urged a new course based on an end to official terror and civil strife, on relaxation and reconciliation with the population and with former oppositionists inside the party. Their policy of reconciliation was related to foreign affairs as well, and particularly to the need to rally the population in light of the new danger posed by Hitler's accession to power in Germany in January 1933.[33]

If Stalin's "revolution from above" revived one Russian governmental tradition, the Politburo moderates revived another—that of reform from above. Their growing influence was seen in the changes that followed. Mid-1933 brought an end to the "saturnalia of arrests" and deportations in the countryside, and the beginning of concessions to the collectivized peasantry, including the legalization of small private plots within the collective structure and an alleviation of the exploitative system of delivery prices and quotas. In 1934, in connection with the revised second five-year plan, living standards and consumer goods were given higher priority, and food rationing ended. Abuse of the nonparty intelligentsia and former party oppositionists declined, and many of the latter, most symbolically Bukharin, were appointed to prominent (though still secondary) positions. The tone and substance of official statements grew less warlike and more conciliatory. A curbing of police excesses and constitutional reforms were promised. By 1934, the dramatically changed atmosphere suggested that a "Soviet spring" had arrived.[34]

The moderates' political success and popularity was evident at the Seventeenth Party Congress in January–February 1934. While formally a celebration of Stalin's policies and wise leadership (a theme voiced by all speakers, including his critics), the proceedings reflected the new balance of forces and new party mood. Unlike Stalin, the moderates spoke in an unmistakably conciliatory spirit; and Kirov, their chief spokesman, was accorded "an extraordinarily enthusiastic reception" second only to (some said equal to) Stalin's.[35] Defeated opponents, notably Bukharin, addressed the assembly and were received politely, even approvingly.[36] Furthermore, at the customary post-congress meeting of the Central Committee, Kirov, in addition to his Leningrad post and seats on the Politburo and Orgburo, was elected a full member of Stalin's erstwhile stronghold, the Secretariat. His elevation was clearly designed to check Stalin's autocratic use of that powerful institution and its network of agents.[37]

Stalin's response to the emerging reform faction within his

own leadership later prompted Bukharin to call him "a genius of [political] dosage." [38] Though leaving little doubt about his own ideas, expressed in his repeated insistence that the class struggle— that is, the battle against enemies in the country and now even in the party itself—continued to grow sharper, he did not "directly oppose" the moderate policies but tried "merely to limit the practical consequences." [39] Meanwhile, through his personal cabinet or secretariat, various cadres departments, and the police, he was building "a positive machinery of despotism . . . outside of and independent of the official political organs." To operate it and supplement his old guard loyalists, he was promoting a new generation of personal followers, men like Nikolai Yezhov, Aleksandr Poskrebyshev, Andrei Vyshinsky, Andrei Zhdanov, M. F. Shkiriatov, Lavrenti Beria, Grigorii Malenkov, Nikolai Bulganin, and Nikita Khrushchev.[40] Some were to remain shadowy operatives; others eventually became his political heirs.

Thus, while Politburo moderates sought a reform consensus in the party and strove for *"influence over Stalin,* for his soul, so to speak," [41] Stalin himself prepared in other ways. At the high point of their policy success, on December 1, 1934, Kirov was shot dead by an assassin in the corridor of his Leningrad office. That Stalin plotted the murder through his police agents is no longer seriously in doubt.[42] In a single stroke, his major rival had been removed and the pretext created for a new and greater terror. Amidst official mourning (led by Stalin) for Kirov, thousands were being arrested and charged with direct or indirect complicity in the crime, among them a group of former party oppositionists that included Zinoviev and Kamenev. This first wave of terror soon passed; but in the years to come tens of thousands would be shot as conspiratorial accomplices in Kirov's assassination, leading one victim of the high purge of 1937 to say: "The year 1937 really began on the 1st of December 1934." [43]

During the next two years, Politburo and Central Committee moderates continued to press their policies and resist falteringly the approaching terror. Their temporary successes in 1935–6 belied a progressively unequal struggle between irresolute, miscalculating reformers relying on persuasion, and "a genius of dosage" bent on —and controlling the instruments of—terror. One by one, prominent moderates and sympathizers disappeared from the scene: Abel Enukidze as a victim of Stalin's intrigue in January 1935, Kuibyshev by a mysterious death the same month, the influential writer Maxim Gorky probably murdered in June 1936, and Ordzhonikidze as a suicide or murder victim in February 1937.[44] As the struggle entered its final stage, it became the ultimate confrontation between the old Bolshevik Party and Stalinism.[45] The moderates' last, desperate stand against the terror was an attempt to save Bukharin, whom both sides had come to regard as the pre-eminent symbol and representative of old Bolshevism, in the winter of 1936–7. With their failure and Bukharin's arrest in February 1937, Stalin's assault on the party began in earnest.

It was in this context, as protagonist, symbolic figure, and victim, that Bukharin lived out the last eight years of his life. As with the general political history of the period, important aspects of his thinking and conduct between 1930 and 1938 remain obscure, to be illuminated only when Soviet archives are finally opened. Until that time, we cannot delineate the Bukharin of the thirties with the detail and certainty that we can bring to the Bukharin of the twenties. But sufficient evidence is now available to dispel the impression that after 1929 he was merely a servant of Stalin and Stalinism. Rather, his career in the thirties was closely related to, indeed part of, the covert three-act struggle within the Stalinist leadership. During the social upheaval of 1930–3, Bukharin continued to be a target of official opprobrium, relegated to a minor post and without a significant voice in affairs of state. In 1934–6, the interlude of relaxation and reconciliation, he resumed a position of official eminence and authority (though not of power), becoming an important spokesman and symbol of those policies. And with their failure, he became the chief defendant at the famous Moscow trial of March 1938.

The fundamental circumstance defining each of Bukharin's varying roles in 1930–8 was that even in defeat he remained a figure of "immense authority" and importance in the party.[46] It is sometimes thought that for Bolsheviks Trotsky was the arch-representative anti-Stalinist of the thirties. In fact, despite his eloquent attacks on the Stalinist leadership from foreign exile and his considerable following abroad, Trotsky and his ideas were no longer of political importance in the party. For several reasons, Bukharin and what he represented were. One was simply that unlike Trotsky (or Stalin's other rival of the twenties, Zinoviev), Bukharin had always enjoyed great personal popularity in the party, an affection perhaps diminished but not destroyed by his defeat.[47] Another was his continuing intellectual influence. After months of the anti-Bukharin campaign, Stalinists still complained: "Bukharinist theory lives. Its sprouts, its manifestations, are revealed now here, now there on the theoretical front. . . ." [48]

Most important was the fact that the consequences of Stalin's policies had amply confirmed Bukharin's warnings of civil war, agricultural disaster, and chronic industrial disproportions, and renewed the widespread appeal of Bukharinist policies. This was the meaning of Stalin's prolonged insistence that "the right opposition is the most dangerous—greater fire to the Right!",[49] as well as the extraordinary spectacle of the Sixteenth Party Congress in June–July 1930, the primary business of which involved an orchestrated outcry against resurgent Bukharinist sentiment and "right opportunism" in the party. Equally significant, virtually every oppositionist trend in the party during the early thirties—including anonymous leaflets and sporadic protests, the Syrtsov-Lominadze affair in 1930, the Riutin group in 1932, and the small opposition of government administrators led by Aleksandr Smirnov in 1932–3—was Bukharinist in economic outlook.[50] At the Sixteenth Congress, a Stalinist speaker quoted anxiously an example of dissident party opinion in the provinces: "Stalin's policy is leading to ruin and misery . . . the proposals of Bukharin, Rykov, and Uglanov are the only correct, Leninist ones; only they . . . are capable of leading the country out of the dead end. . . ." [51] Even a majority of the Central Control Commission, once a Stalinist stronghold, reportedly had been converted to "a Bukharinist position," convinced by events that "Bukharin is right, Stalin is ruining the country." [52]

These developments did not restore Bukharin to power; but they gave him, even after 1933 when the crisis had passed and confidence in Stalin grown,[53] a unique stature as the party's quintessential representative of non-Stalinist Bolshevism. This circumstance helps to explain the ferocity of the Stalinist attack on him during the early thirties, the important role he was to play in the moderates' "policy of reconciliation," and eventually the criminal charges brought against him. It also helps to explain his own ambiguous conduct, and particularly his determination to remain in the party as a force for change.

By conventional political standards, the collectivization disaster of early 1930 should have toppled the Stalinist leadership and returned the Bukharinists to office.[54] Instead, because the party oligarchs, however reluctantly, stood with Stalin, the vilification and persecution of Bukharin and his followers intensified in direct proportion to the worsening crisis. Nonetheless, Bukharin contrived on two occasions to tell the party his opinion of Stalin's rural policies. In an article in *Pravda* on February 19, 1930, in the veiled language that was his only recourse, he tacitly ridiculed the official myth of collectivization as a carefully premeditated continuation of NEP based on an upsurge of mass peasant support. Rather, he wrote, it was a forcible termination of NEP, "entered into . . . through the gates of the extraordinary measures and rapidly developing grain crisis." Its "significant costs," he added, derived from the state's use of "the most severe means of extra-economic coercion." [55]

On March 7, 1930, five days after Stalin's sudden indictment of local officials, Bukharin in effect responded by pinpointing the real political and moral responsibility for the rural holocaust. In a historical polemic ostensibly directed against a recent papal encyclical on Bolshevism, he developed a subtle but unmistakable analogy between the "corpselike" obedience, "ideological prostitution, and unprincipled toadyism" imposed by Loyola's Jesuit Order, and Stalinism. The analogy established, he then condemned Stalin's collectivization by quoting from a critical, "humanist" history of the papacy:

If they (the popes, N.B.) kill the soul, what right have they to call themselves the vicars of Christ? Where is the similarity of their institutions? He once said to Peter: "Feed my flock." But what do the popes do? Do they not drive the Christians, *impoverished by papal plundering*, to starvation—do they not unceasingly fleece their flock and cut into their flesh while shearing them? [56]

Stalin's "plundering" of the peasantry, in other words, had nothing in common with Lenin's legacy or Bolshevism.

This damning judgment ended Bukharin's access to the central press. It would be three years before he was again permitted to write on political themes in either *Pravda* or *Izvestiia*. He resorted first therefore to a different form of protest, officially decried as "Bukharin's conspiracy of silence." As a result of the collectivization crisis, the statement of political error signed by himself, Rykov, and Tomskii in November 1929 had soon been deemed unsatisfactory. Stalin now demanded that Bukharin renounce fully each of his oppositionist policies and accusations, as well as his followers at home and abroad. [57] Bukharin refused, and at one point in early 1930 may have countered with a threat of suicide. [58] The uneven duel between a mobilized press stridently clamoring for his recantation and the defiantly mute Bukharin continued through most of 1930. It provided the major drama at the Sixteenth Congress. While speaker after speaker insisted that the "great silent one" join Rykov and Tomskii in their penitence before the assembly, Bukharin boycotted the congress, even though it incongruously re-elected him to the Central Committee. His nine-month silence, raged one Stalinist, was "supremely significant" for others who shared his views.[59]

On November 19, 1930, after prolonged "negotiations," Bukharin finally signed another ambiguous statement.[60] He again vaguely acknowledged "my mistakes," disowned "any attempts at secret struggle against the party leadership," and called for "solidarity around the Central Committee." His chief concession was to repudiate all "deviations from the party line"; but he did not, as was demanded, explicitly renounce his own policies or his charges of 1928–9, and indeed pointedly refused to retract his views on European capitalism and thus his scorn for Stalin's Comintern line. Nor did he bow to the custom of praising the general secretary, or even mention him, making it clear that his overture was to "the Central Committee of the party," not Stalin. A compromise document grudgingly accepted as "the minimum," it did little to improve relations between Bukharin and the Stalin group. When Molotov suggested at a Central Committee meeting the following month that the statement was still inadequate, Bukharin remarked contemptuously: "you have power; if you wish, you can interpret it as you please." [61]

But in the political context of 1930, another even nominally contrite gesture by Bukharin was an important event, demoralizing to his supporters and useful to Stalin.[62] Why Bukharin obliged, even in this minimal fashion, again must be deduced from fragmentary evidence. While the fate of his young protégés was still a concern, other considerations seem now to have been paramount. By November, the Syrtsov-Lominadze episode had demonstrated conclusively that the party oligarchs would not desert Stalin and therefore that meaningful opposition inside the party was hopeless, at least for the time being.[63] Without public access to the party or the country, Bukharin was thus faced with a choice between some form of acquiescence to Stalin and a futile resistance ("secret struggle")—a course which meant risking expulsion from the party and any future role he might otherwise play.[64]

Beyond this, but closely related, was the larger dilemma that confronted Bukharin repeatedly in the years that remained. His outraged hostility to Stalin's brutal policies was clear: he "pitied" the besieged peasantry from "humanitarian motives," and he saw wasteful, costly industrial projects "as monstrous gluttons which consumed everything, deprived the broad masses of articles of consumption. . . ." [65] But, at the same time, he retained faith in the revolution and the party, and thus was wed, psychologically and politically, to the system. Moreover, however brutally and wastefully, Stalin was pursuing goals—industrialization, collectivization of agriculture, technological progress, new forms of labor organization—that were common to all Bolsheviks, including Bukharin.

If his opposition to Stalinism during his last years was therefore to acquire some tragic dimension, it was often also to seem hopelessly inadequate and pathetic. As Bukharin later explained, this amalgam of objectionable Stalinist methods and shared Bolshevik goals produced in him "a peculiar duality of mind," a "dual psychology" aggravated further by a situation in the countryside that endangered not merely Stalin's policies but the Bolshevik government itself during the years of collectivization. If Stalin's leadership had confirmed Bukharin's worst fears, its consequences had also placed him and his followers "literally in twenty-four hours, on the other shore" as advocates of an aroused peasantry. Its resistance threatened the Soviet system and its anger, Bukharin now feared, could no longer be reconciled even to his own moderate policies.[66]

Given his special status, his loyalty to the party and the revolution, and the political situation, Bukharin apparently saw little choice. A short time later, with obvious personal implication, he quoted Engels on the dilemma that Goethe had faced: "to exist in an environment which he necessarily held in contempt, and yet to be chained to it as the only one in which he could function. . . ." [67] By signing a compromise statement in 1930, Bukharin adopted an "intermediate position" between avowed resistance and the effusive glorification of Stalin's leadership and abject recantation that were becoming political norms.[68] He maintained this posture for the next two years, prefacing his occasional public utterances with perfunctory affirmations of the "victories of socialism," shunning and advising against organized opposition, and warning those whom he had earlier defended, such as nonparty specialists, that he could no longer protect them and that they, too, must now choose between "two camps." [69]

This political stance did not end the official invective against Bukharin and his policies; anti-Bukharinism was now an integral component of Stalinist ideology. But it did enable him to function energetically throughout the upheaval of 1930–3 in his minor post of director of research first under the Supreme Economic Council and then, when the Council was abolished in 1932, under the new Commissariat of Heavy Industry. This, in turn, enabled him to play a leading role in the Academy of Sciences, to head the Soviet delegation to the International Congress of the History of Science and Technology in London in mid-1931 (where his appearance impressed the audience but scandalized the Conservative press, which tried to use it against the Labour government), to publish essays on cultural and scientific themes, and to found and co-edit a related journal. These functions made him an unofficial but eminent spokesman for the Soviet scientific community, its representative to a not always appreciative officialdom and to foreign visitors.[70] Despite his continuing presence on the party's Central Committee, such activities were of course inconsequential compared to his past career. As with other exiles from power, the imposed leisure returned him to private pursuits that he had sacrificed for politics: to painting and to his long study, begun in emigration, of Marx's influence on modern thought.[71]

It was also during this period that Bukharin acquired a new family, an otherwise prosaic fact that later became politically important. He had separated from his first wife, Nadezhda Lukina, in the early or middle twenties, and then lived for several years with Esfir Gurvich, herself a party member and well-known economist, who bore him a daughter, Svetlana. This relationship had ended by the early thirties; in 1932 or 1933, at forty-five, Bukharin married Anna Mikhailovna Larina, "a young girl of rare beauty," the daughter of an old Bolshevik. A son, Iurii, was born to them in 1934. Bukharin is said to have loved his young wife and child very much. Concern for their well-being was to influence his conduct in 1937-8.[72]

Politically, then, Bukharin's role in 1930-3 was his least important since the revolution. Because of his stature, however, even his minor activities were of some significance. In his essays on culture, philosophy, and science, on Goethe, Heine, Darwin, and the poets Mayakovsky and Bruisov, for example, he kept alive an authentic Marxist perspective in a society increasingly bereft and disdainful of serious Marxism.[73] His long article on "Marx's Teaching and Its Historical Influence," written in 1933 for the fiftieth anniversary of the founder's death, was perhaps the last statement of classical Marxism to be published in Stalin's Russia. Among other things, it reaffirmed Marx's thesis that "the basic function of state power is to guarantee the process of exploitation," a reminder uncongenial to the official statism of the thirties and promptly censured as such.[74]

The subject that most engaged Bukharin, however, was science and its development in the Soviet Union. As director of industrial research, he presided over the great expansion of scientific institutes and facilities during the early thirties, and wrote extensively on the problems involved. These writings are noteworthy in two respects. The early Soviet thirties witnessed the first attempt in any country to implement the planning of scientific research and development, an endeavor whose importance is now recognized. Bukharin played a leading part in this pioneering undertaking, and his writings and speeches on methodological and theoretical aspects of the planning of science, according to one Western historian of science, were of genuine significance and "even now would be pertinent reading for science administrators, including those in democratic countries." [75]

In addition, his flow of pronouncements on scientific and technological matters gave Bukharin a politically circumspect way to continue to protest Stalin's first five-year plan, and to defend his own, now disgraced, views. He did this in two ways. One was to argue repeatedly in 1929–33 that a technological revolution must be the basis of genuine industrialization, and that therefore *the scientific-research network must grow faster than even the leading branches of socialist heavy industry*." [76] This proposition at once challenged Stalin's principle of the priority of heavy industry, rejected his prevailing "gigantomania," and argued for neglected "qualitative indicators" of industrial development. Bukharin's other critical device involved his definition of the "sensible" planning of science, which was simply a specific application of his conception of economic planning generally. A scientific-research plan, for example, was to avoid "bureaucratic distortion" by combining centralized guidelines with decentralized autonomy; it was to be based on "*flexibility and elasticity*," allowing for the incalculable and providing "reserve" time for fulfillment. Little imagination was required to see that these prescriptions and Bukharin's accompanying criticism of "the Gothamite, bureaucratic, bungling *method* of planning" represented his continuing objections to Stalin's first five-year plan and his recommendations for the second.[77]

Indeed, Bukharin's relationship with the emerging moderate faction in the leadership probably originated in this connection. Ordzhonikidze, the influential Politburo moderate who regularly befriended defeated oppositionists, had taken over the Supreme Economic Council from Kuibyshev in 1930, and become head of the important Commissariat of Heavy Industry on its creation in 1932. He was therefore Bukharin's administrative superior in 1930–3. And it was about the time that Ordzhonikidze began his successful campaign for a more balanced, realistic second five-year plan that Bukharin acquired increasing prominence in the Commissariat, occasionally even representing it officially in Ordzhonikidze's absence.[78] By 1932, he had become a member of its governing presidium and of the commission appointed to formulate the new plan, a remarkable turnabout for a man whose planning and industrial philosophy had been labeled "alien" by Stalin.[79]

A few months later, Bukharin took a step that shortly changed his position in the party as well. Speaking before the Central Committee in January 1933, he abandoned his "intermediate" stance and repented more fully his "guilt" and "absolutely incorrect" stands of 1928–9. He alluded to two of the reasons behind his decision that "intermediate positions" were no longer tenable, and that all segments of the party must rally around the existing leadership: they were the "extreme dangers" represented by peasant resistance and the famine, now in its most murderous phase, and by developments in Germany which were to bring Hitler to power two weeks later.[80]

Another, unspoken, consideration also lay behind his act. Three months earlier, in the Riutin affair, Politburo moderates had shown their readiness and ability to resist Stalin. (Among those implicated with Riutin and saved by their intervention were three of Bukharin's personal protégés.[81]) Now, at the Central Committee meeting in January, the moderates were beginning to assert themselves on larger questions of policy.[82] It was evident to Bukharin that the party and the country were entering a new period of uncertainty but also of possible changes in Soviet domestic and foreign policy. To participate in and influence these events, he, too, had to adhere to the facade of unanimity and uncritical acceptance of Stalin's past leadership behind which the muted struggle over the country's future course was to be waged. For Bukharin, this required first the fuller recantation he issued in January 1933. Within a few months, for the first time in three years, articles by him on major political issues began to reappear in the central press. Their theme, cautiously stated, was that the warfare period of "revolution from above" was ending, and "a new period" beginning.[83]

The essential features—though not the full story—of Bukharin's relationship with the moderate group in Stalin's Politburo are clear. While the fact that neither Kirov nor Ordzhonikidze had been virulent anti-Bukharinists in 1928–9 probably mattered,[84] the basic factor was the affinity between their political thinking in 1934–6 and Bukharin's of the twenties. Though conditions in the country were now different, the moderates' "policy of reconciliation" and civil peace echoed Bukharin's conception of NEP as the "normalization" of the Soviet order after the excesses of war communism. Similarly reminiscent were their advocacy of better living conditions and a "prosperous collective farmer," and their crucial argument that the threat of war (now from Nazi Germany) made it imperative to assure the population's willingness to defend the Soviet system. These underlying affinities with discredited Bukharinist ideas were not, of course, explicitly acknowledged.[85] But they were reflected in various political developments. One, for example, involved the young Bukharinist and former editor of *Leningrad Pravda*, Petr Petrovskii. An uncompromising anti-Stalinist, he had been implicated in the Riutin affair and his party membership suspended in 1932. Two years later, he reappeared in Kirov's Leningrad organization as head of its ideological department and, again, an editor of *Leningrad Pravda*.[86]

But it was Bukharin's own political comeback that, in the eyes of the party, symbolized the moderates' success. The scene of his return was the Seventeenth Party Congress in January 1934, the first he had addressed since 1927. His speech, which combined the obligatory endorsement of Stalin's leadership with (as we shall see) a critical appraisal of his foreign policy, received prolonged applause from the assembled party élite.[87] When the Central Committee convened after the congress, Bukharin's significance in the secret tug-of-war between Politburo moderates and Stalinists became still more apparent. Though demoted from full to candidate membership on the Central Committee, he was appointed chief editor of the government newspaper *Izvestiia*. The daily being second only to *Pravda* as an authoritative voice of official policy, Bukharin's appointment was particularly significant.[88] Dramatic evidence of the moderates' progress, it established him as both a symbol of and an illustrious spokesman for their reconciliatory program.

Two subsequent events further illustrated Bukharin's special role in the reformist policies. The first was the inaugural Congress of Soviet Writers, which met amidst great fanfare in August 1934 to celebrate the formation of a new organization embracing all Soviet writers. In retrospect, the congress is seen as the beginning of a far harsher regimentation of literature, based on the imposed doctrine of "socialist realism." At the time, however, after four years of party-sponsored "class struggle on the literary front," writers and artists welcomed it as initiating an official relaxation, an occasion for "great hopes and beautiful expectations." [89] A major reason for this optimism was Bukharin's appearance as one of the three official speakers. Renowned as an opponent of party dictates in literature and, even in the thirties, as an "intercessor" on behalf of disfavored writers,[90] his presence on the rostrum seemed to confirm expectations of a reconciliation between the régime and the cultural intelligentsia.

His remarkable three-hour address to the congress accentuated this impression, overshadowing the other featured speeches by Gorky and Stalin's future cultural enforcer, Andrei Zhdanov. Bukharin's topic was Soviet poetry; but his real subject was the danger that the party's "compulsory directives" in literature since 1929 would lead to "the bureaucratization of creative processes and serve badly the whole development of art." The "paraphrasing of newspaper articles" and "rhymed slogan" (favored by the Stalinist leadership), he said, "is, of course, not art at all." A socialist civilization required a "powerful, rich, and variegated art," whose animating spirit was a "humanism" enveloping "the entire world of emotions—love, happiness, fear, anguish, anger, and so on to infinity—the entire world of desire and passion. . . ." Such an art, he still insisted, could grow only from "diversity and quality" and from "a wide freedom of competition in creative questing." To emphasize his argument, he dismissed officially acclaimed "agitational poets" as obsolete, and praised at length disfavored lyrical poets, particularly the defiantly apolitical Boris Pasternak.[91]

The startling candor and liberalism of Bukharin's remarks infuriated "agitational" writers but elated the great majority of his audience, who cheered his speech enthusiastically. "Many writers," it is said, "literally fell into each other's arms and, breathless with delight, spoke of the prospects of a real emancipation of art." [92]

In the end, however, the relaxation and cultural "spring" symbolized by Bukharin's address to the writers' congress turned out to be short-lived. Three years later, the Politburo moderates destroyed, Bukharin in jail, and many writer-delegates themselves victims of the terror, the Stalinist press would single out Bukharin's speech as a malevolent attempt to "disorient and demoralize nonparty writers." [93]

The other major event associating Bukharin with reform from above was the establishment in February 1935 of a commission to prepare a new Soviet constitution. Chaired formally by Stalin, the thirty-member panel included Bukharin, who later confided that he alone, with a little assistance from Radek, had written the document "from first word to last." [94] Given the participation of the legal profession and the lengthy public discussion preceding its ratification in December 1936, this is probably misleading, though it is likely that Bukharin prepared or edited the final draft. Whatever the case, his central role in the preparation of the charter (officially dubbed the "Stalin Constitution" and still in force today), and particularly its new provisions for universal suffrage, secret balloting, the possibility of multi-candidate elections, and explicit civil rights of citizens, seems to have been widely known at the time.[95] And though few people, including Bukharin, took seriously the official claim that the constitution guaranteed real "democratization," it provided for many inside and outside the party further evidence that an era of civil peace and legality had begun, that "people will have more room. They can no longer be pushed aside." [96]

But dramatic (and ultimately futile) as the writers' congress and new constitution were, it was Bukharin's editorship of *Izvestiia* that gained him real prominence and public influence in 1934–6. For the first time since the twenties, his signed articles and unsigned editorials on pressing political issues appeared regularly in a newspaper read faithfully by the ruling élites and educated Soviet society generally. Within a few months, he had created at *Izvestiia*'s editorial offices the same comradely, intellectual spirit that had characterized his tenure at *Pravda*. He recruited talented writers, among them his boyhood friend Ehrenburg and the repentant Trotskyist Radek, and acquired for the daily a reputation as the liveliest, most critical-minded of all Soviet newspapers.[97]

For this, as for the revival of his political fortunes generally, Bukharin naturally had to pay a price, of which his recantation, reiterated at the Seventeenth Party Congress, was only a part. Stalinist politics, a survivor has said, "not only exterminated honest people, but corrupted the living." [98] Even during the relatively liberal interlude of 1934–6, participation in politics required adherence to the rituals of the Stalin cult, the falsification of party history, the defaming of reputations and oppositionist ideas, and the misrepresentation of events of the magnitude of collectivization.

These were ceremonies that Bukharin, a famous but powerless politician and now editor of the government newspaper, could not avoid. Instead, he tried to limit his compliance ("corruption"), and to abide by some standard of "political morals." [99] Thus, like the Politburo moderates who bowed to Stalin's "weakness for such adulation" while pursuing their dissident policies, Bukharin agreed "to burn incense before Stalin and extol his person," but frequently in a manner so ambiguous as to invite skepticism.[100] When Stalin staged an elaborate Congress of Collective Farmers in February 1935 to eulogize "the victory of socialism in the countryside," the renowned foe of imposed collectivization consented to address the convention, but in a very different tone. And when Pokrovskii and his once orthodox historiography were repudiated posthumously, Bukharin contributed a polemic, but one whose main criticism deplored merely the abstractness of Pokrovskii's treatment of Russian history.[101] In other respects, Bukharin simply refused to comply, contributing nothing to the neo-nationalistic rehabilitation of czarism or to the rewriting of party history.[102] Above all, he refused to denounce Bolsheviks imperiled by Stalin's vindictiveness. While other former oppositionists, including Rykov, exhorted the court to show "no mercy" to Zinoviev and Kamenev in 1936, Bukharin remained silent.[103]

The price he did pay must have seemed acceptable in return for a central and hopefully influential role, through his writings and presence in public life, in the momentous struggle between the factions of reconciliation and terror. The stakes, Bukharin believed, were very high—the future course of the Bolshevik revolution, the country, and world affairs; and his articles and editorials in 1934–6 were a major part of the moderates' effort to develop a consensus in the party for civil peace and reform in the country.[104] This did not mean, it must be remembered, that Bukharin could write explicitly about these issues and conflicts at the top. Like other participants in the covert struggle, he was obliged to communicate in the discreet Aesopian language that had been an occasional feature of party politics in the twenties and had now become the primary mode of public debate and political dialogue.[105]

There was nothing strange nor peculiarly Soviet about this esoteric communication. The language of disguised polemics, allegorical symbols, metaphoric allusions, code words, significant emphases and omissions, as well as the practice of reading between the lines, have been part of political discourse throughout history, especially in authoritarian societies where official censorship is imposed and heterodoxy persecuted. Students of political philosophy and even of biblical texts are accustomed to reading "aesopianly," mindful of what could not be said openly in a given historical context.[106] Politicized Soviet citizens who had grown up in censorious czarist Russia were particularly adept at the "language of Aesop," and none more so than Bolsheviks whose own revolutionary ideas had once circulated in this surreptitious fashion. In *What Is to Be Done?*, Bolshevism's charter document and still obligatory reading in party schools, Lenin had written:

In an autocratic country with a completely enslaved press, in a time of desperate political reaction when even the slightest outgrowth of political discontent and protest is persecuted, the theory of revolutionary Marxism suddenly makes its way into the *censored* literature, expounded in Aesopian language but understood by all the "interested." [107]

Like dissenters in czarist Russia, Bukharin wrote obliquely for the "interested"—first and foremost, for party members—about what should be done in Stalin's Russia in 1934–6. The ideas and policies he advocated were based on his general evaluation of the situation in the country, which he urged upon his readers. It carried special weight because of his stature as an opponent of Stalin's policies. The previous programs and conduct of party oppositionists, he argued, were no longer viable or relevant. They had been outdated by the events of 1929–33. Whatever the "costs" and wisdom, the far-reaching changes wrought by Stalin's four-year "revolution from above"—the abolition of NEP, collectivization, heavy industrialization, and the defeat of "other strategies"—were irreversible facts. The Soviet Union had become a different country, and there now could be no talk of returning to the pre-1929 situation. Anti-Stalinists should therefore stop lamenting the past and begin "studying actual tendencies of development." The end of the first five-year plan opened a "new crossroads" in Soviet history. And it was time for all Bolsheviks to accept the existing leadership so that they could confront the two related problems of the present: the rise of fascism and the need to reform the new Soviet order created by Stalin's imposed revolution.[108]

Fascism—as both the menace of Nazi Germany and a new political phenomenon—was central to Bukharin's thinking in the thirties. Hitler's rise to power had left Stalin's Comintern policies a shambles. While it is arguable whether collaboration between German Communists and socialists in 1929–33 would have prevented the Nazi victory, or whether Stalin's anti-socialist line was the only impediment to such collaboration, many Soviet and foreign Communists believed it to be true.[109] Moreover, Stalin abandoned his discredited policies reluctantly and slowly, only in 1934 and formally at the Seventh Comintern Congress in mid-1935, which called for a united front between Communist and socialist parties against fascism. The belated turnabout was part of a broader re-orientation of Soviet diplomacy toward European collective secur-ity against Germany, symbolized by Soviet membership in the League of Nations in September 1934. Behind the scenes, however, a deep split had developed in the Soviet leadership over policy to-ward the new Germany, one which continued even through the Soviet decision to intervene on the side of anti-fascism in the Span-ish civil war in the fall of 1936.[110]

The division, as Molotov confirmed in a rare public disclosure in 1936, was between advocates of "thoroughgoing irreconcilabil-ity" toward fascism and Nazi Germany specifically, and the Stalin group, which wanted "an improvement in Soviet-German rela-tions." [111] Like most European statesmen, Soviet leaders held di-verse and often dim understandings of fascism. All saw it as a product of the crisis of capitalist society and the bourgeoisie's desperate need for an open, as opposed to a disguised parliamentary, "dictatorship of capital." This assumption, however, left room for important disagreements. For Stalin, it meant that the advent of Nazism—simply another capitalist régime—need not terminate the special relationship, begun in 1922, between the two outcasts of postwar Europe, the Soviet Union and Germany. He stressed this point to the party (and to Hitler) at the Seventeenth Congress in January 1934: "fascism is not the issue here, if only because fascism in Italy, for example, has not prevented the USSR from establish-ing the best of relations with that country." [112] Whether, as early as 1934, Stalin foresaw the kind of collaborative alliance that he obtained in the Nazi-Soviet Pact of August 1939 is unclear. What is clear is that even during the Soviet Union's pro-Western orienta-tion of the mid-thirties, he preferred, and initiated secret diplomacy toward, a Soviet form of appeasement and "the best of relations" with Hitler.[113]

Bukharin championed the opposite outlook. Convinced from the outset that Hitlerism had "cast a dark and bloody shadow over the world," [114] he became an ardent defender of uncompromising anti-fascism and collective resistance to Nazi Germany. At the same party congress which witnessed his return to political promi-nence, he tacitly rejected Stalin's assertion that the nature of fascism did not matter. Exemplified by Hitler's *Mein Kampf*, fascist ideology, he insisted, had to be taken seriously. Its espousal of "open robbery, a frankly *bestial philosophy*, the bloodstained dag-ger and an open era of throat-cutting" were already being practiced inside Germany. Hitler's avowed anti-Bolshevism, his demand for German living space in Russia and "open call for the destruction of our state," made his foreign intentions "completely clear." German designs on the Soviet Union's western territories and Japanese ambitions in Siberia, Bukharin remarked with prophetic gallows humor, "apparently mean that we shall have to find a place for our Union's entire population of 160 million somewhere in one of the furnaces of the Magnitogorsk Works." He ended by challenging Stalin's acceptance of the Nazi régime: "This is the *bestial face of the class enemy!* This, comrades, is who confronts us, and whom we shall have to face in all those historic battles that history has placed on our shoulders." [115]

Throughout the next three years, in private talks, public speeches, and in *Izvestiia*, Bukharin hammered away at the inevitability of war with Germany and the need for a "policy of security" with Western governments. To appeasers in the Soviet leadership, he emphasized the fundamental irreconcilability between the nature of communism and the "bestialism and racism" of fascism, as well as the implacability of Hitler's Germany, which had made "war the basis of foreign policy" and the conquest of Soviet Russia its goal. He reminded Bolsheviks that "compared to the Middle Ages and to fascism," bourgeois democracies were " 'good.' " [116] To appeasers in the West, he emphasized the "historical lessons" of 1914, and the mutual Nazi peril to England, France, Austria, Czechoslovakia, the Baltic countries, Finland, and even the United States. Should the Soviet Union fall to Germany, he warned in 1935, it would give Hitler "a powerful resource base . . . beginning the *second round* of the operation by 'the German Sword,' this time in the West." [117]

Bukharin's foresight requires no commentary. It seems sufficient to place him with that handful of important political figures who understood the extraordinary menace of Nazi Germany from the beginning, and who were heeded too late. But anti-fascism was for him more than a strategy of foreign policy. It figured prominently in his thinking about developments inside the Soviet Union as well. The most immediate connection in his mind, of course, involved preparing for war by eliminating the "enormous . . . discontent among the population," particularly among the peasantry.[118] Resistance to German fascism and "reforms" inside Soviet Russia—especially in the direction of "a prosperous life" and "democratization"—were, he believed, of a piece, and he linked them regularly in 1934-6.[119]

The advent of Nazi Germany, however, also influenced Bukharin's thinking about internal Soviet trends in more complex ways. The similarities between the party-state dictatorships of Hitler's Germany and Stalin's Russia, already the subject of discussion abroad, did not escape his attention. Formally, of course, he had to dismiss them as superficial resemblances between antithetical societies; but in his articles (and privately) he communicated to "the interested" a more problematic and alarmed analysis. Unlike all too many Marxists, Bukharin recognized that the Nazi order was something new. It represented, he believed, the actualization of the "New Leviathan," the nightmarish potentiality in modern society that he had adumbrated in 1915, the "state of Jack London's *The Iron Heel*." [120] And as his portrayal of Nazi Germany, its "totalitarian" order, "statism and Caesarism," in 1934–6 seemed to suggest, and as he confided privately, he feared that Stalinist policies and practices since 1929 were leading to a similar development in the Soviet Union.

Unlike some thinkers—including the émigré philosopher Nikolai Berdiaev, whose book on the "process of dehumanization" in the "two Leviathans" he criticized but singled out as being of remarkable interest [121]—Bukharin did not identify the evil with the nature of modern, large-scale organizations. Rather, he saw it in "the idea of violence, of coercion as a permanent method of exercising power over society, over individuals, over man's personality," in "terroristic dictatorships" based on "permanent coercion" and "a real gulf between . . . a small group of ruling exploiters and the exploited masses." Such a régime, "with all its organizational efforts, *blind* discipline, cult of Jesuitical obedience, and suppression of intellectual functions, creates a dehumanized populace." [122] He applied this characterization to Germany, but in a way that implied its relevance to the emerging Soviet cults of Stalin, the Russian state, and iron discipline:

Fascism . . . has established an omnipotent "total state," which dehumanizes everything except the leaders and "supreme leaders." The dehumanization of the masses here is in direct proportion to the glorification of the "Leader." . . . The great majority of people are thereby transformed into simple functionaries bound by a discipline imposed in all areas of life. . . . Three ethical norms dominate everything: devotion to the "nation" or to the "state," "loyalty to the Leader," and the "spirit of the barracks." [123]

The possible degeneration of the Bolshevik revolution into a new exploiting order had troubled Bukharin before. But the current potential, represented by Stalinism, for a Soviet system of "permanent coercion" must have seemed desperately real, and horrified him. When he began his outcry in 1934, he evidently believed that the reality in Nazi Germany could still be averted at home. This hope, which underlay his fervent support for the moderates' reforms, inspired his own concept of "proletarian" or "socialist humanism." Humanistic slogans, associated largely with a school of nonparty writers, had been denounced (along with "rotten liberalism") by the Stalinist leadership in 1929–30 as "one manifestation of the vacillation and panic of . . . groups who, unable to keep up with the rush of events, cannot find their place in the ranks of the fighters for socialism." [124] By 1934, however, Bukharin had made "socialist humanism," along with anti-fascism, one of his two major themes. [125]

Echoing his moral objections to anti-peasant policies in the twenties, it represented a frankly ethical outlook. The "principle of socialist humanism," Bukharin explained, meant "a concern for all-round development, for a many-sided ('prosperous' material and spiritual) life." It meant a society where "the machine is only a means to promote the flowering of a rich, variegated, bright, and joyful life," where people's "needs, their growth, the broadening and enrichment of their life, is the goal of a socialist economy," where the "criterion is the *freedom of maximum development of the maximum number of people*." [126] In formulating "socialist humanism" as "diametrically opposed to fascist bestiality," Bukharin also wanted to persuade reluctant Western critics to unite with the Soviet Union "against anti-humanist fascism." [127] But his first concern was apparently Soviet society itself, and his real audience the Bolshevik Party.

In one sense, his doctrine of humanism was unremarkable, little more than a restatement of original socialist aspirations. In Soviet circumstances of the mid-thirties, however, it amounted to a radical critique and manifesto, a plea for a humanistic socialism that would be taken up by Communist reformers two decades later. Against the background of Stalin's "revolution from above," amidst official celebrations of what Bukharin viewed as "features of a *military order*," hierarchical bureaucratic power, and "cruel, un-cultured provincialism," he was reminding the party that the social-ist mission was a new civilization, preserving and transcending the best achievements and values of the modern age. [128] Fascism as well as Stalinism, he seemed to be saying, threatened these values by their reliance on violence and contempt for human achievement, epitomized for him by the Nazi poet who exclaimed: "When I hear the word culture, I reach for my Browning." [129] He was re-minding the party, its vision and outlook transformed by seventeen years of civil war, bitter internal conflict, imposed industrialization and collectivization, that "a creative, happy, human society is for us an end in itself. . . ." [130]

As he confided privately, Bukharin worried most about the brutalizing impact of collectivization—"a mass annihilation of completely defenseless men, together with their wives and children"—on the party. Some Communists had remained aloof, some had revolted, and some, including Stalin's own wife Nadezhda Alliluyeva, had committed suicide in protest. Many, however, had become acclimated and obedient to violence as a normal system of rule, transformed, he feared, into "cogs in some terrible machine . . . the 'iron heel.' " Advocating socialist humanism was evidently Bukharin's way of warning and appealing to the party against this pathology. He remained hopeful that party members were acting badly "not because they are bad, but because the situation is bad. They must be persuaded that the country is not against them, but only that a change of policy is necessary." [131] Thus his articles of 1934–6 urged them to embrace the tentative reforms—the end of terror in the countryside and of rationing; the beginning of larger expenditures on agriculture, consumer goods, and welfare; the cultural spring promised by the writers' congress; and the legality and democratization brought by the new constitution—as *the first flowering of socialist humanism,*" the moment "to realize ideology in living practice." He was pleading, it seems, that socialist humanism, not Stalinism, *become the ideological axis of our time.*" [132]

It is difficult to judge Bukharin's real optimism about the possibility of decisive reform and resisting Stalinism, or to know exactly when it turned into despair. His revival of the iron heel metaphor, which had always meant an omnipotent despotism rooted in social conditions, implied an underlying pessimism all along. Moreover, even during the success and popularity of the reforms and anti-fascism, there was regular evidence of Stalin's intentions and arbitrary power. Kirov's assassination in December 1934 stunned Bukharin, and he may already have suspected the real hand behind it.[133] Whatever the case, he knew about Stalin's political use of the killing in the weeks that followed, and probably about his secret directives (some obliquely implicating Bukharin himself) against concealed "enemies" in the party. Subsequent events in 1935—the first trials of Zinoviev and Kamenev, the abolition of the Society of Old Bolsheviks, and the removal from libraries of books by several former oppositionists—augured clearly the threat to the moderates' policies and to the old Bolshevik Party.[134]

In addition, despite his revived political fortunes, Bukharin's personal standing with Stalin remained "the very lowest." [135] His only contact with the leader's entourage during the early thirties seems to have been his close friendship with Stalin's young wife.[136] Her Bukharinist views on collectivization and her suicide in November 1932 could only have worsened matters. Nor apparently did Bukharin seriously share the optimism of Politburo moderates that "burning incense before Stalin" would win his trust. As in 1928, he saw an insatiable psychological as well as political compulsion at work. Stalin, he explained, "is wretched because he cannot convince everyone, not even himself, that he is greater than everyone else . . . his wretchedness compels him to take revenge on people, all people, but particularly those who are in some way superior or better than him. . . ." Bukharin understood that his own stature in the party made him a prime target of this "wretchedness," and that his personal danger grew with the popularity of what he represented politically.[137] Stalin's public conduct was occasionally friendly, as at a banquet in 1935 where he toasted "Nikolai Ivanovich Bukharin. We all know and love him, and whoever remembers the past—get out of my sight!" [138] Meantime, however, his police agents were already preparing a dossier on Bukharin's "past." And on February 10, 1936, for the first time in several years, the Stalinist organ *Pravda* ominously attacked his present views.[139]

Two weeks later, already "certain that he will devour us . . . he is only waiting for a more opportune moment," [140] Bukharin traveled to Paris on his last visit abroad. Accompanied by his wife, he was part of a three-man Soviet delegation seeking to purchase the unique archives of the destroyed German Social Democratic Party. The archives, which included Marx's manuscripts, were in the safekeeping of Boris Nicolaevsky, an émigré Menshevik historan residing in Paris who had helped smuggle them out of Nazi Germany. Including stopovers in Prague and Berlin, and an excursion to Copenhagen, Bukharin remained abroad two months. It soon became clear that he had come on what he suspected would be his last journey "with his obituary in mind." [141] He spoke to friends and old political foes alike with startling candor and scant regard for the party's tradition of political secrecy. During a surprise visit to Fedor Dan, leader of the émigré Russian Menshevik Party, he discussed Stalin—"this small, malicious man, no, not a man, a devil"—with unconcealed "fear and loathing." Strolling with André Malraux in the Place de l'Odéon, "he confided to me absently, 'And now he is going to kill me.' . . ." [142]

It was to Nicolaevsky, however, that he chose, "obituary in mind," to confide important historical facts and his own views for posterity. He trusted Nicolaevsky, despite his Menshevism, presumably because of his reputation as an archivist and Marxist historian, but also because he was Rykov's brother-in-law. At first, Bukharin spoke cautiously of mutual friends, distant events, and philosophy. But as their private conversations stretched through March and April and grew more intimate, he related, sometimes hesitantly and elliptically, major aspects of the struggle inside the Soviet leadership since the Riutin affair, and of his own role and thinking on domestic and foreign policy. On the basis of these talks (and possibly a subsequent communication from Bukharin), six months later Nicolaevsky published anonymously the famous *Letter of an Old Bolshevik*, a remarkable document and the source of much of our knowledge about Soviet politics in the thirties.[143] To Nicolaevsky and others, including an old Comintern friend who wanted him to remain abroad and establish an anti-Stalinist newpsaper, Bukharin left the impression of despair for himself and for the Soviet Union under Stalin. Why then, they asked, was he returning? His answer suggested his determination to play out his political and symbolic role in the party: "How could I not return? To become an émigré? No, I couldn't live as you, as an émigré. No, come what may. . . ."[144]

Bukharin returned to Moscow in late April 1936, as Stalin's preparations for a great terror were nearing completion. It was to begin with the trial and execution of Zinoviev and Kamenev, already under arrest, on charges of having formed a "Trotskyite-Zinovievite Terrorist Centre" that murdered Kirov and plotted the assassination of the Stalinist leadership. In his first article in *Izvestiia* upon returning, Bukharin alerted "the interested" to the desperate situation. Ostensibly a contribution to the nationwide discussion of the new constitution, he began by quoting Machiavelli, a familiar Aesopian device, and then introduced a new theme: All fascist régimes operate behind a facade of "*political fiction* and ideologically fraudulent decoration." [145] On June 18, Gorky, an influential opponent of the impending terror, died under mysterious circumstances. In his eulogy, Bukharin mourned the death of "the great proletarian *humanist*" and "singer of reason." [146] In the weeks that followed, the accused in the "investigation" of Zinoviev and Kamenev began to crack and confess to false charges.

On July 6, Bukharin published what he evidently knew would be his last article. The title, "Routes of History: Thoughts Aloud," again alerted readers to its exceptional importance as a kind of final testament.[147] Its recurrent theme was the "real" direction of events at home and abroad. He began with a post-mortem. "Everyone is talking about the Stalin constitution"; but the development of real importance was the "consolidation" of the Stalinist régime behind the scenes and the impending destruction of all resistance to it. Lest anyone mistake his analysis of fascism's "beastly bullying, oppression, violence, and war," as applying only to Germany, Bukharin again pointed out: "An intricate network of decorative deceit (in words and deeds) is an extremely essential characteristic of fascist régimes of all kinds and complexions."

A political testament, however, must also address the future. And here, alongside his despair over the present, Bukharin seemed to offer an ultimately hopeful "perspective." He had returned from Europe doubly convinced of the stability and menace of Nazi Germany, and the need to orient Soviet diplomacy toward England.[148] Now, he implied, Stalin was preparing to abandon anti-fascism in foreign policy as well. But these "adventuristic illusions" could not avert the inevitable clash with Germany, nor the Soviet Union's eventual destiny as a bulwark *against fascist war and fascist counter-revolution.* In the "great historical drama" that lay ahead, every Soviet citizen must remain loyal and confident in the eventual victory of socialism in the Soviet Union which, he evidently still believed, Stalinism also could not prevent.

Régimes of the Stalinist type, Bukharin seemed to be predicting, were doomed by a "paradox of history." They were based on an "ideology of *hatred* toward the masses . . . for them the masses are '*Untermenschen*,' 'subhumans,' 'inferiors.' . . . The *masses, however, have already entered the historical arena*, and there is no way that they can be driven completely underground." Such régimes must therefore "create the illusion of mass participation in power. . . . But it would be extremely shortsighted not to see the historical limits of this organized deception. . . . Sooner or later this deception must be exposed." The Soviet revolution had laid the "basis of *socialism*" and brought "enormous changes in the entire internal structure and life of the country." Despite the Stalinist régime, ordinary people were maturing politically; economically, and culturally, already ceasing to be "mere '*instrumenta vocalia*' ('tools with a voice,' as slaves in Rome were called)" and becoming "a conscious mass of conscious personalities." This guaranteed the future of socialism, because "living history is made by living people, by millions of these living people. . . ." On the eve of his own destruction, Bukharin retained his faith in the people and in history. Or as he told Nicolaevsky: "One is saved by a faith that development is always going forward . . . like a stream running to the shore. . . . The stream goes through the most difficult places. But it still goes forward. . . . And the people grow, becoming stronger in it, and they build a new society." [149]

The trial of Zinoviev, Kamenev, and fourteen co-defendants began on August 19, and promptly established that Stalin had in mind victims other than those in the dock. Carefully tutored by his "interrogators," several defendants immediately gave testimony implicating Bukharin, Rykov, Tomskii, and a number of former Trotskyists in their alleged "counter-revolutionary crimes." On August 21, Vyshinsky, the Stalinist prosecutor guiding the accused through their pre-arranged confessions, announced the beginning of an investigation of Bukharin and the others implicated. [150] On seeing the published announcement the following day, Tomskii committed suicide. Father of the Soviet trade union movement and still a candidate member of the Central Committee, he wanted to escape the abuse and degradation heaped on Zinoviev and Kamenev. He chose, wrote a friend abroad, "a dignified end." [151] All sixteen defendants in the Zinoviev trial were pronounced guilty on August 24, and executed a few days later. Meanwhile, the press filled with "workers'" demands that Bukharin's ties with "these liquidated double-dealers, murderers, spies, and rabid enemies of the working class" be exposed. [152]

Politburo opponents of the terror, notably Ordzhonikidze and probably the Ukrainians Kosior, Chubar, and Pavel Postyshev, now began their last resistance. They apparently had agreed reluctantly to the trial of Zinoviev and Kamenev, already sentenced to prison terms twice previously, on Stalin's promise that the defendants would not be executed. Betrayed, they moved to save Bukharin and Rykov, far more popular and important political figures. [153] At a series of high-level meetings, possibly of the Central Committee but probably of Politburo members, in late August and early September, they obtained several important decisions. One evidently authorized Soviet intervention in the Spanish civil war. Another ended the proceedings against Bukharin and Rykov. On September 10, Pravda announced that Vyshinsky's office, having "failed to establish legal facts," had terminated the investigation. [154]

Though still at liberty and even able to travel inside the country, Bukharin could hardly have been consoled by the reprieve. He certainly knew that he stood foremost among those, as the poet Evtushenko has written, "with death sentences shining inside them like white crosses on the doors of the Huguenots." [155] Although his name remained on the editorial masthead through January 16,

1937, he had lost control of *Izvestiia*, probably in August, and not regained it.[156] Nor had Stalin's intrigue terminated with the criminal investigation. At the end of September, he managed to replace the police chief Iagoda, whose connection with the Bukharinists in 1928-9 now disposed him against their persecution, with Yezhov, the zealot of terror who was to conduct Stalin's main assault on the party in 1937-8. Yezhov's appointment accelerated preparations for a second public trial of old Bolsheviks, this one featuring Radek and Bukharin's friends Piatakov and Sokolnikov, and involving additional charges of espionage and wrecking.[157]

Bukharin was now trapped in "an atmosphere of relentless terror" manipulated by the "genius of dosage." [158] On November 7, as he and his wife viewed the anniversary celebrations from the stands rather than from the platform for dignitaries atop Lenin's mausoleum, they were approached by a guard. Bukharin's wife remembers thinking "he would tell Nikolai Ivanovich to leave or that he was coming to arrest him, but the guard saluted and said: 'Comrade Bukharin, Comrade Stalin asked me to inform you that you are not in the right place and he begs you to go up on the tomb.' " [159] A month later, Bukharin's name was dropped from the final constitutional commission, and the press again began implying his involvement with "enemies of the people." [160]

The trial of Piatakov, Sokolnikov, Radek, and fourteen others opened on January 23, 1937. Once again the accused immediately gave prepared testimony incriminating Bukharin and Rykov, now in sabotage and treason as well as murder. After seven days of false charges and bizarre confessions, the court found all seventeen defendants guilty, sparing (temporarily) only Radek, Sokolnikov, and two others the death penalty.[161] During the next two weeks, several lesser Bukharinists were "worked over" in police cellars and their "confessions" delivered to Bukharin as "a sort of psychic torture." Probably already a virtual prisoner in his Kremlin apartment, Bukharin began a hunger strike, a forlorn protest to inspire Central Committee opponents of the terror who were gathering for their "last stand." [162]

The most fateful meeting of the Central Committee since 1917 convened on February 23, 1937. To stop the terror, its opponents knew they had to prevent Bukharin's expulsion from the party and arrest, still a prerogative of the Central Committee. If Bukharin could be condemned as an "enemy of the people," no one was safe. For the same reason, Stalin had prepared carefully for the showdown. Five days before, Ordzhonikidze, the most powerful opponent of the terror, had been murdered or forced to commit suicide.

The plenum therefore opened with depleted moderates competing against emboldened Stalinists for an already intimidated Central Committee majority. Several matters were scheduled for discussion; but "there was, in reality, only one item on the agenda—the expulsion of Bukharin and Rykov." [163] Still candidate members of the assembly, both were in attendance.

Distributing police depositions against Bukharin and Rykov, Stalin and his men took the floor to demand their arrest as "hired murderers, saboteurs, and wreckers in the service of fascism." Stalin's nine-year-old thesis that class enemies intensify their resistance as socialism grows nearer, had been triumphantly vindicated, he and his associates claimed, by the exposure of these conspirators "hiding behind a party card and disguised as Bolsheviks." Their demands that Bukharin confess produced a remarkable exchange between Bukharin and Molotov. Bukharin: "I am not Zinoviev or Kamenev, and I will not tell lies about myself." Molotov: "If you don't confess, that will prove you're a fascist hireling. Their press is saying that our trials are provocations. We'll arrest you and you'll confess!" [164] Knowing that arrest was imminent, when Bukharin returned home after the session he composed a last letter "To a Future Generation of Party Leaders," which he asked his wife to memorize.

"I feel my helplessness," it began, "before a hellish machine, which . . . has acquired gigantic power, fabricates organized slander, acts boldly and confidently. . . ." Stalin's police, he continued, were

a degenerate organization of bureaucrats, without ideas, rotten, well paid, who use the Cheka's bygone authority to cater to Stalin's morbid suspiciousness. . . . Any member of the Central Committee, any member of the party, can be rubbed out, turned into a traitor, terrorist, diversionist, spy, by these "wonder-working organs."

Declaring himself innocent of any crime, Bukharin wrote that accusing him of being an enemy of the revolution and a capitalist agent was like discovering that the last czar "devoted his whole life to struggle against capitalism and monarchy, to the struggle for . . . a proletarian revolution." He appealed to future party leaders,

whose historical mission will include the obligation to take apart the monstrous cloud of crimes that is growing ever huger in these frightful times, taking fire like a flame and suffocating the Party. . . . In these days, perhaps the last of my life, I am confident that sooner or later the filter of history will inevitably sweep the filth from my head. . . . I ask a new young and honest generation of Party leaders to read my letter at a Party Plenum, to exonerate me. . . . Know, comrades, that on that banner, which you will be carrying in the victorious march to communism, is also my drop of blood.[165]

When the Central Committee meeting resumed, Bukharin read an angry, emotional statement on behalf of himself and Rykov. According to an account that circulated in Moscow, much of it confirmed by other sources, Bukharin agreed that there was "a monstrous conspiracy" afoot—one headed by Stalin and Yezhov, who sought to establish a personal dictatorship based on police power "over the Party and the country. . . . That is why we are to be eliminated." Turning toward Stalin, he charged:

By political terrorism, and by acts of torture on a scale hitherto unheard of, you have forced old Party members to make "depositions." . . . You have a crowd of paid informers at your disposal. . . . You must have the blood of Bukharin and Rykov in order to carry out the *coup d'état* which you have been planning for a long time. . . .

Insisting that the issue was not his fate but the country's, Bukharin implored the Central Committee

to return to the traditions of Lenin and to call to order the police plotters who conceal themselves behind the authority of the Party. It is the NKVD, and not the Party, which today governs the country. It is the NKVD, and not the followers of Bukharin, which is preparing a *coup d'état*.[166]

When he demanded an investigation of police practices, Stalin interjected: "Well, we'll send you there, and you can take a look for yourself."[167]

The choice clear, Postyshev, a candidate Politburo member, rose to speak for opponents of the purge: "I personally do not believe that . . . an honest Party member who had trodden the long road of unrelenting fight against enemies, for the Party and for socialism, would now be in the camp of enemies. I do not believe it. . . ." At this point, Stalin reportedly interrupted in a way so menacing that Postyshev's determination was shattered. He and like-minded speakers began to retreat and retract their doubts, though some evidently did not. Seeing he had the advantage, Stalin now resorted to a familiar tactic. Feigning neutrality, he left the continuing attack on Bukharin and Rykov to his proconsuls of terror, and appointed a commission dominated by these same loyalists to decide their fate.[168]

The commission reported its verdict to the meeting on February 27: "Arrest, try, shoot." It was endorsed by a majority of the Central Committee, 70 per cent of which would perish in the months ahead. Bukharin and Rykov were arrested where they sat and removed to the main political prison, Lubianka.[169] They reappeared thirteen months later as the chief defendants in the last and most important of the Moscow purge trials.

History sometimes remembers its important actors in inappropriate ways. For many years after his death, Bukharin was defined in the Western political imagination not by his role in the Bolshevik Party or by what he represented in Soviet history, but almost exclusively by his show trial of 1938. The grim fascination of an illustrious founding father pilloried and executed as a "rabid enemy" of the Soviet Republic is understandable. It was made doubly compelling, however, by a widespread misconception—that Bukharin willingly confessed to hideous, preposterous crimes in order to repudiate what he himself represented, to repent sincerely his opposition to Stalinism, and thereby to perform a "last service" to the party and its myth of infallibility. Derived from a misinterpretation of his conduct at his trial, this notion gained popularity with Arthur Koestler's famous 1940 novel, *Darkness at Noon,* whose fictional purge victim, Rubashov, an old Bolshevik modeled largely on Bukharin, is persuaded by his police interrogator (and by himself) of the necessity and rightness of such a "last service." Owing largely to Koestler's powerful art, this image of Bukharin-Rubashov as repentant Bolshevik and morally bankrupt intellectual prevailed for two generations.[170] In fact, however, as some understood at the time and others eventually came to see, Bukharin did not really confess to the criminal charges at all.[171]

His courtroom behavior must be understood in terms of the political meaning of the trial itself, and of the unhappy choices that faced him during his year-long imprisonment. In some respects, the eleven-day judicial travesty was simply a grander version of the previous two. It began on March 2, 1938, in the columned auditorium of the Trade Union House, once an ornate ballroom of the Nobles' Club, before a three-judge tribunal of the Military Collegium of the Supreme Court. The two notorious adjudicators of Stalin's terror, V. V. Ulrikh and Vyshinsky, were again in charge as presiding judge and prosecutor. In addition to Bukharin and

THE LAST BOLSHEVIK · 373

Rykov, nineteen defendants sat in the dock, including the deposed police chief Iagoda, the famous Bolsheviks and onetime Trotskyists Nikolai Krestinskii and Khristian Rakovskii, five People's Commissars and high economic administrators with no record of opposition, and three republican party and state leaders. The remainder were nonpolitical men, alleged instruments of the main plotters: an agronomist, a trade official formerly posted in Berlin, the private secretaries of Iagoda and the deceased Gorky and Kuibyshev, and three elderly Kremlin doctors. The confession of each, painfully extracted, was tailored to the bizarre indictment. Everything had again been rehearsed, including the three hundred or so spectators who, apart from a few foreign diplomats and reporters, were mostly police employees posing as indignant citizens.[172]

In scope and political design, however, the trial differed significantly from its predecessors. According to the indictment, prepared under the personal supervision of Stalin, who then observed the proceedings from a curtained window above the courtroom,[173] the accused were part of a vast criminal conspiracy comprising virtually all oppositionist and faintly dissident Bolsheviks past and present. Its ringleaders were Bolshevik rightists headed by Bukharin and Bolshevik leftists guided from abroad by the exiled Trotsky. This concept of an all-Bolshevik amalgam inspired the official name of the trial: "The Case of the Anti-Soviet 'Bloc of Rights and Trotskyites.'" The indictment attributed to the "Bloc" responsibility not only for the assorted acts of terrorism, wrecking, and espionage laid to previous defendants, but a wide range of still more fiendish crimes. They included plotting successfully to murder, among others, Kuibyshev and Gorky and unsuccessfuly Stalin and his "most remarkable comrades-in-arms"; to undermine Soviet security and open the country's frontiers to Germany and Japan; to relinquish Soviet territories to various foreign powers; and to sabotage the economy and restore capitalism.

Individual counts in the indictment served various purposes. Some attributed actual crimes of which Stalin himself was suspected —the assassination of Kirov, for example—to his rivals. Others were clearly fabricated to explain away spectacular failures of Stalin's leadership since 1929, for example, the charge that Bukharin and others organized "kulak uprisings" and poisoned livestock during collectivization, and conspired to deprive the urban population of consumer goods, partly by instructing their agents to mix glass into foodstuffs.[174] Collectively, however, their overall purpose, and that of the trial, was to discredit and condemn forever all anti-Stalinist ideas and the entire old Bolshevik leadership except Stalin (and somewhat grudgingly Lenin) as a "foul-smelling heap of human garbage"—to be, in effect, a macabre coronation of Stalin and Stalinism. The general secretary's dictum on the occasion of Bukharin's arrest in 1937 became, through his spokesman-prosecutor Vyshinsky, the political gravamen of the trial:

The historic significance of this trial consists before all in the fact that at this trial it has been shown . . . that the Rights, Trotskyites, Mensheviks, Socialist Revolutionaries, bourgeois nationalists, and so on . . . are nothing other than a gang of murderers, spies, diversionists, and wreckers, without any principles or ideals. . . .

The Trotskyites and Bukharinites, that is to say, the "bloc of Rights and Trotskyites" . . . is not a political party, a political tendency, but a band of felonious criminals, and not simply felonious criminals, but of criminals who have sold themselves to enemy intelligence services, criminals whom even ordinary felons treat as the basest, the lowest, the most contemptible, the most depraved of the depraved.[175]

Stalin's plan called for Bukharin to play the leading role in this incrimination of the old Bolshevik movement. The major symbol of pre-Stalinist Bolshevism and the most important party leader to stand trial (Trotsky being tried and sentenced in absentia), he was for party members and all knowledgeable citizens the central figure in the trial.[176] His criminality, the subject of a great part of the 800-page trial proceedings, was to symbolize Bolshevism's. To Bukharin, an eyewitness recalls,

belonged the role of archfiend. . . . He had been behind every villainy, had had a hand in every plot. Each prisoner, as he blackened himself, was careful at the same time to blacken Bukharin. . . . Lurking memories of a glorious past were obliterated.

Abetted by compliant defendants, Vyshinsky labored on every occasion to transform the entire political biography of the party's onetime "favorite" into "the acme of monstrous hypocrisy, perfidy, jesuitry and inhuman villainy." Indeed, Vyshinsky concluded, "the hypocrisy and perfidy of this man exceed the most perfidious and monstrous crimes known to the history of mankind." [177] Finally, to Bukharin alone was attributed the supreme crime of attempted patricide: plotting to kill Lenin during the Brest peace controversy in 1918.

During Bukharin's year in prison, Stalin and his police interrogators demanded his full cooperation—his confession and courtroom participation—in this grim charade. Throughout the great purge, indeed until Stalin died, similar demands were made of thousands of equally innocent prisoners. Why so many confessed is no longer a mystery. By 1937, Soviet political prisons had become the scene of the cruelest methods of physical torture, continual debilitating interrogation (the "conveyor" system) for weeks on end, and countless summary executions. Brutal atrocities were inflicted on men and women, young and old alike. It was, concludes one Soviet historian, "probably the most terrible page in Russian history." [178] Many prisoners somehow held out, finally tortured to death or shot without confessing. Those who "confessed" did so for the most human of reasons: they were physically or otherwise compelled. A few Bolsheviks may have confessed because of Rubashov-like motives; but for the great tormented majority, a survivor tells us, *Darkness at Noon* "would have been the subject of gay mockery." [179]

In these surroundings, Bukharin, reportedly not tortured, held out "with remarkable vigor" for three months against the continual threats and interrogation directed by Yezhov on Stalin's instructions. On around June 2, 1937, he finally relented, "only after the investigators threatened to kill his wife and newborn son." [180] This was no idle threat. "Wives of Enemies of the People," with their children, were routinely arrested and used as hostages (particularly in cases of major Bolsheviks scheduled to appear in show trials), sentenced to long prison terms, or shot. Within weeks of his arrest, Bukharin's wife and son had been exiled with relatives of other "politicals" to Astrakhan.[181] To save them—they spent the next twenty years in prison camps—he had to "confess" and stand trial.

At the same time, Bukharin had, or soon developed, an additional reason for agreeing to stand trial. Saving his own life was not a factor. He knew that whatever his behavior, however little or much he complied, he would be shot with or without the trial; Stalin's scenario required it.[182] The question thus arose, as he explained obliquely in the courtroom: " 'If you must die, what are you dying for?'—an absolutely black vacuity suddenly arises before you with startling vividness." [183] The trial, he realized, would be his last public appearance and opportunity to give meaning to his death, for himself and others. He would accept the symbolic role of representative Bolshevik: "I bear responsibility for the bloc," that is, for Bolshevism.[184] But through whatever subterfuges were available to him in the courtroom, and a final exercise in Aesopian communication, he would infuse the role with a meaning and "historic significance" different from what Stalin intended.

Bukharin's plan, as another writer has pointed out, was to turn his trial into a counter-trial (a well-known practice of Russian revolutionaries) of the Stalinist régime, and his own indictment into an indictment of Stalin as the executioner of Bolshevism.[185] Briefly stated, his tactic would be to make sweeping confessions that he was "politically responsible" for everything, thereby at once saving his family and underlining his symbolic role, while at the same time flatly denying or subtly disproving his complicity in any actual crime. The real political meaning of the criminal charges would then be clear to "the interested." Stalin's court would automatically return a verdict of guilty. But Bukharin was going on trial to testify before another, higher court, that of history and the "future generation" to which he had addressed his last letter. Or as he said in the courtroom: "World history is a world court of judgment," and the one that mattered.[186]

From Stalin's viewpoint, the predictable risks of allowing Bukharin a final public forum must have been outweighed by the fact that there could be no trial as conceived without his participation.[187] Preparing him for trial therefore became a long and grim process of negotiation. After seeing Stalin's personal revisions in the text of his initial confession, which had been agreed upon in a session with Yezhov and Stalin's emissary Voroshilov in June, Bukharin repudiated it. His interrogators had to begin anew, working "day and night." The final script was still being revised on the eve of the trial. In the process, Stalin's agents tried to guard against any initiatives Bukharin might be planning. To discourage hope of secretly communicating the falsity of the charges, for example, they showed him Lion Feuchtwanger's recent book recounting the writer's observation of the 1937 trial and his assurances that the charges and confessions were authentic. Throughout the interrogation, and at the trial itself, however, Stalin's strongest argument remained the fate of Bukharin's family.[188] Nonetheless, Bukharin flatly refused to agree to certain charges, particularly espionage and attempting to assassinate Lenin, which were incompatible with his intention to stand trial as the symbolic Bolshevik. Meanwhile, by way of his own preparation in prison, he "worked, studied, and retained my clarity of mind." [189]

When the trial began under the glare of klieg lights on the morning of March 2, it became clear that Vyshinsky wanted to keep Bukharin off the witness stand for as long as possible, and with good reason. For three days, he led other defendants through their testimony condemning themselves and Bukharin. Everything went according to plan, an observer recalls, "so long as Bukharin himself took no part in the proceedings." But when he finally gained the floor, during his persistent cross-examining of prosecution witnesses and other defendants, during his own examination by Vyshinsky on March 5 and 7, and in his final statement to the court on March 12, "things did not go so smoothly." [190] In a dazzling exhibition of doubletalk, evasion, code words, veiled allusions, exercises in logic, and stubborn denials, Bukharin regularly seized the initiative from an increasingly flustered Vyshinsky and left the case of the real prosecutor, Stalin, a shambles.

His strategy became apparent the moment his examination began: "I plead guilty to . . . the sum total of crimes committed by this counter-revolutionary organization, irrespective of whether or not I knew of, whether or not I took a direct part in, any particular act." For anyone failing to see that the second half of this statement made nonsense of the first, Bukharin later devalued his entire "confession" with a single aside: "The confession of the accused is a medieval principle of jurisprudence." [191] As the trial progressed, he was careful—for his family's sake—to emphasize repeatedly his extravagant confession of responsibility for all "the crimes of the bloc," while specifically, in one manner or another, disclaiming each and every one. The most outlandish he simply denied outright, as may be seen from the following exchanges:

Vyshinsky: Did you talk to him [co-defendant Ikramov] about wrecking activities? . . .

Bukharin: No, I did not . . .

Vyshinsky: Did you talk to Ikramov about wrecking activities and acts of diversion in subsequent years?

Bukharin: No, I did not.

• • • •

Vyshinsky: I repeat, tell the Court . . . of connections between your conspiratorial group and Whiteguard circles abroad and the German fascists.

Bukharin: I do not know of this. In any case, I don't remember.

• • • •

Vyshinsky: Accused Bukharin, do you plead guilty to espionage?

Bukharin: I do not.

Vyshinsky: After what Rykov says, after what Sharangovich says?

Bukharin: I do not plead guilty.

• • • •

Vyshinsky: I am asking you again, on the basis of testimony which was here given against you: do you choose to admit before the Soviet

Court by what intelligence service you were enlisted—the British, German, or Japanese?

Bukharin: None.

· · · ·

Vyshinsky: And what about the assassination of Comrades Stalin, Sverdlov, and Lenin?

Bukharin: Under no circumstances.

· · · ·

Vyshinsky: There was a plan to assassinate Vladimir Ilyich Lenin?

Bukharin: I deny it.

· · · ·

Bukharin: I categorically deny any complicity in the assassination of Kirov, Menzhinsky, Kuibyshev, Gorky, and Maxim Peshkov.[192]

Some charges and evidence Bukharin had to refute more subtly. Cross-examining a defendant whose testimony incriminated him in wrecking, he elicited dates that contradicted the indictment itself. As for Ivanov and Sharangovich, co-defendants who swore that he had led them in sabotage and espionage, they were, he observed, "two agents-provocateurs." At one point, a "strange corpselike" witness, the old Socialist Revolutionary Vladimir Karelin, was brought from police dungeons to testify about the plot to kill Lenin. Asked by Vyshinsky if he knew the witness, Bukharin cleverly implied the tortures that had broken the man: "Well, he has changed so much that I would not say that he is the same Karelin." At another point, Bukharin struck at the whole conspiracy edifice on which the trial rested by insisting that he had never met or heard of five of his fellow conspirators: "in order to be a gang, the members of the gang of brigands must know each other. . . ." And, turning to what Vyshinky "calls logic," he philosophized: "This is what in elementary logic is called tautology, that is, the acceptance of what is yet to be proved as already proven." [193]

Protecting Bolshevism's historical legacy by refuting the criminal indictment was Bukharin's main objective. But he wanted also to use his courtroom testimony to make a last political statement on the two major issues confronting the country—war with Germany and the advent by terror of Stalinism. The prosecution welcomed his comments on the first, so it posed no problem. From "the fragments of real life" reaching him in prison, Bukharin knew that the European crisis was deepening and war nearer. On trial, as before, he therefore implored discontent Soviet citizens to forsake "a defeatist orientation" and defend the Soviet Union, even a Stalinist one, as "a great and mighty factor" against German fascism. Between Stalinist Russia and Nazi Germany there could be only one choice.[194]

Speaking for Bolshevism and to future generations, however, Bukharin believed it equally important that he challenge the official myth, enshrined at the trial, that Stalin's régime and Stalinism were the rightful heirs and culmination of the revolution. To do this, he simply adopted the prosecution's bizarre terminology for his own purposes. "In my terminology," he made clear on several occasions, "anti-Soviet bloc," "counter-revolutionary organization," or "forces of counter-revolution" really meant the old Bolshevik movement or party; "illegal," "insurrectionary," and "conspiratorial" activities meant legitimate opposition to Stalin or merely unofficial meetings.[195] In this way, he had no trouble demonstrating throughout that the real "historic significance" of Stalin's purge, of which the trial was only the visible tip, was the destruction of the Bolshevik Party—"the internal demolition of the forces of counter-revolution." [196]

To indicate the real ideals and programs of Bolshevism was more difficult, because Ulrikh and Vyshinsky persistently cut off his discursions into "the ideological and political stand of the criminal bloc." [197] Bukharin managed nonetheless: "in the economic sphere, state capitalism, the prosperous muzhik individual, the curtailment of the collective farms, foreign concessions, surrender of the monopoly of foreign trade, and as a result—the restoration of capitalism in the country." Vyshinsky quickly aborted Bukharin's attempt "to decipher one formula, namely, what is meant by the restoration of capitalism," but its meaning was evident anyway.[198] Bukharin personally, and Bolsheviks generally, had believed in some kind of NEP-like transition to socialism. Revolution imposed from above, "the military-feudal exploitation of the peasantry" and all that ensued from it, was Stalinism, not Bolshevism or Leninism.

Given all this, it is difficult to explain how any reader of the daily press accounts or verbatim trial report published in large foreign editions could have missed the drama of Bukharin's struggle. Stalin and Vyshinsky, of course, understood that Bukharin had "a system, a tactic" and was trying "to attach a special meaning" to the trial.[199] Alarmed and infuriated by his "preposterous circus acrobatics," Vyshinsky and Ulrikh tried every bullying device to save the script, threatening at one point to silence Bukharin completely if he did not stop "following definite tactics . . . hiding behind a flood of words, pettifogging, making digressions into the sphere of politics, of philosophy, theory and so forth. . . ." [200]

Firsthand accounts confirm vividly that Bukharin "was fighting for his reputation before the world and his place in history." At forty-nine, his features aged and small beard grayed, he seemed "strangely like Lenin" in appearance and manner.[201] Openly contemptuous of Vyshinsky and "thoroughly enjoying his fighting role," Bukharin "was on his toes every minute, reading from his notes, which he has carefully taken throughout the trial," turning on his accusers "with flashes of logic and scorn, which held the court spellbound." After Vyshinsky's summation portraying him as "that damnable cross of a fox and a swine," Bukharin rose to make his final statement before the court. Again admitting the case against him, he then "proceeded, uninterrupted this time, to tear it to bits, while Vyshinsky, powerless to intervene, sat uneasily in his place, looking embarrassed and yawning ostentatiously." [202] When Bukharin finished, an American correspondent wrote:

Mr. Bukharin alone, who all too obviously in his last words fully expected to die, was manly, proud and almost defiant. He is the first of the fifty-four men who have faced the court in the last three public treason trials who has not abased himself in the last hours of the trial. . . .

In all of Mr. Bukharin's speech there was no trace of bombast, truculence or cheap oratory. It was a brilliant composition, delivered in a matter-of-fact manner, and he was tremendously convincing. He was making his last appearance and last utterance on the world stage, where at times before he has played great parts, and he seemed simply and intensely an earnest man completely unafraid but merely trying to get his story straight before the world.[203]

Three decades later, a Western specialist would write that Bukharin's trial, "degrading though it was in many respects, may fairly be called his finest hour." [204] Bukharin hoped that this would be history's verdict; he knew it would not be the court's. Vyshinsky's demand that he and the others be "shot like dirty dogs" was echoed in *Pravda*'s daily editorials on the trial: "By exterminating without any mercy these spies, provocateurs, wreckers, and diversionists, the Soviet land will move even more rapidly along the Stalinist route, socialist culture will flourish even more richly, the life of the Soviet people will become even more joyous." [205] Accordingly, at 4:30 A.M. on March 13, after a decorous six-hour "deliberation," Ulrikh reconvened the court to read the sentences: Bukharin, Rykov, and seventeen others "to be shot." On March 15, 1938, the Soviet government announced that the executions had been carried out. By a grim stroke of irony, news of Bukharin's death was overshadowed by Hitler's march into Austria three days earlier.[206]

No authoritative description of Bukharin's execution is available. According to one account that circulated in Moscow, "Bukharin and Rykov died with curses against Stalin on their lips. And they died standing up—not groveling on the cellar floor and weeping for mercy like Zinoviev and Kamenev." True or not, the report comforted those, inside and outside the Soviet Union, who mourned the end of Bukharin and Russian Bolshevism.[207]

EPILOGUE

Bukharin and Bukharinism in History

Stalinism cannot be regarded as the Marxism-Leninism or the Communism of three decades. It is the perversions that Stalin introduced into the theory and practice of the Communist movement. It is a phenomenon profoundly alien to Marxism-Leninism, it is pseudocommunism and pseudosocialism. . . .

The process of purifying the Communist movement, of washing out all the layers of Stalinist filth, is not yet finished. It must be carried through to the end.

—ROY A. MEDVEDEV

BUKHARIN'S POSTHUMOUS REPUTATION in official Soviet society may be briefly summarized. Five months after his execution there appeared a new official history of the party and the revolution. Known to its millions of readers during the next two decades by its subtitle, the *Short Course*, it depicted Soviet development since 1917 as the triumphant struggle of virtue, personified by Stalin, over "the Bukharin-Trotsky gang of spies, wreckers, and traitors." [1] Few who could bear personal witness to the falsity of this Manichean fable survived. By the time of Hitler's invasion in 1941, most old Bolsheviks, oppositionist and non-oppositionist alike, and their political associates and friends, had been shot or were soon to perish in Stalin's concentration camps. (Only one of Bukharin's personal followers, Valentin Astrov, is known to have survived.) [2] Many older Soviet citizens, of course, knew the truth. [3] But until Stalin's death in 1953, the Soviet Union was a society silenced by terror, where none but an official voice could be heard. The names of Bukharin and all but a few of the original Bolshevik leaders remained anathema, uttered publicly only in conjunction with such standard imprecations as "a common band of enemies of the people." [4]

After Stalin died, and with him the terror, the reformation of Soviet society known as destalinization began, and was accompanied by a slow—and still inconclusive—official reevaluation of Bukharin and other martyred Bolsheviks. In the course of his rise to power, Khrushchev's campaign to restore the party to the preeminent position it had occupied before 1936 led him to a far-reaching exposure and denunciation of Stalin's "crimes" against the party. His famous secret speech to the Twentieth Party Congress in February 1956, while carefully defending the political defeat of the Bukharinist opposition in 1928–9, condemned Stalin's terror of the thirties and thus implicitly exonerated its victims. [5] The late nineteen fifties and early sixties witnessed a sustained reexamination of party history and the political rehabilitation of thousands of Stalin's victims. Most of those honored posthumously, however, were either Stalin's onetime supporters who had subsequently perished in his indiscriminate terror, or lesser party oppositionists. Neither Bukharin nor Stalin's other important rivals of the twenties were among them.

By 1961, Khrushchev's increasingly radical anti-Stalinism had brought the question of Bukharin, the representative anti-Stalinist in party history, to the fore. Late that year, four surviving old Bolsheviks petitioned the Politburo for his full rehabilitation. "A man whom Lenin called *the rightful favorite of the Party*," they wrote, "cannot remain in the list of traitors and outcasts from the Party." [6] Though their petition went unanswered, a year later Bukharin's widow, who with her son had been freed in the fifties after almost twenty years in prison camps, obtained a personal audience with Khrushchev. She asked that the criminal charges against Bukharin be officially repudiated, that she and her son be allowed to resume their lives in Moscow, and that her husband's memory be restored to party honor. Khrushchev granted the first two requests, and promised to consider the third. [7] In December 1962, an official spokesman succinctly dismissed the criminal charges: "Neither Bukharin nor Rykov, of course, was a spy or terrorist." [8]

Political rehabilitation, however, did not follow. The "Bukharin question," which unavoidably involves the legitimacy of Stalin's imposed collectivization and thus the structure of present-day Soviet society, apparently had already become a source of controversy between Khrushchev and his opponents in the Soviet leadership. With his ouster in 1964 and the advent of a conservative leadership determined to limit reform and reimpose at least a partial silence concerning the Stalinist past, the question of Bukharin's rehabilitation was closed. Criminal charges against him are no longer mentioned, and his name occasionally appears without pejorative comment;[9] but some thirty-five years after his execution, Bukharin, still excluded from mention in Soviet encyclopedias, remains the object of intense official opprobrium—an "anti-Leninist," a "pseudo-Bolshevik," it is said, whose political ideas and "right opportunism" jeopardized the revolution and threatened to restore capitalism in the Soviet Union.[10]

Bukharin's treatment in official Soviet literature, however, does not accurately reflect the status of his ideas in the contemporary Communist world. During the twenty years since Stalin's death, the central issue in Eastern Europe has been the reformation of the Stalinist order created in the Soviet Union in the nineteen thirties and imposed on countries coming under Soviet hegemony after the Second World War. In each of those societies where anti-Stalinist reformism has become an effective force, in or out of power, Bukharinist-style ideas and policies have revived. In Yugoslavia, Hungary, Poland, and Czechoslovakia, Communist reformers have become advocates of market socialism, balanced economic planning and growth, evolutionary development, civil peace, a mixed agricultural sector, and tolerance of social and cultural pluralism within the framework of the one-party state. For many, "socialist humanism" has become a slogan and a vision.[11] Bukharin's official reputation has been significantly upgraded in some of these countries.[12] It would be a mistake, however, to think that it is specifically his memory or writings that have inspired contemporary reformist ideas. Rather, and no less a tribute to his enduring relevance, such ideas have arisen—along with renewed interest in NEP and the Soviet twenties—as a natural result of the search for a non-Stalinist Communist order.[13]

This has also been true in the Soviet Union itself. During the high tide of Khrushchev's reformism and relaxation of censorship in 1959–64, the far-reaching critique of Stalinist history and practice produced an outburst of what may be termed pseudonymous Bukharinism—a rebirth of Bukharinist ideas and approaches that could not be, and were not, identified with his name. Many examples could be given. The Khrushchev leadership itself repudiated Stalin's class struggle thesis and adopted a variation of Bukharin's view that Soviet society should evolve peacefully, should "grow into" communism.[14] Reformist planners and economists began to echo Bukharin's famous admonitions concerning scientific planning, proportional development, the utility of the market, and social consumption.[15] Proponents of cultural liberalism held up as a model the party's policies during the NEP years and its 1925 resolution on literature, written by Bukharin.[16] Meanwhile, Soviet revisionist historians, freed from Stalinist myths and now gaining access to archives, developed a critique of peasant agriculture under NEP and of Stalin's collectivization policies remarkably similar to Bukharin's; historians of Stalin's industrialization and, to a lesser extent, his Comintern policies did the same.[17] Though the point should not be unduly stressed, it seems fair to conclude that three decades later, anti-Stalinist Communism is again—however pseudonymously—significantly Bukharinist in spirit.[18]

Since the fall of Khrushchev, critical discussion of Stalinism under official auspices has largely ended. Nonetheless, the definitive shattering of the twenty-year myth that Stalinism was synonymous with the Bolshevik revolution makes it unlikely that the official moratorium on revisionist thinking can continue for long. Eventually, perhaps when the present generation of Soviet leaders— whose outlook was shaped by the experience of the Stalin years— has passed from the scene, historical censorship will be lifted and Soviet writers, with more evidence and insight than is now available to us, will openly explore the great issues and alternatives that faced the party during the crucial twenties and thirties. Like Western students of the Soviet experience, they will disagree on fundamental questions, debating whether there was in fact a viable Bolshevik alternative to Stalin's "revolution from above"; whether Bukharin's agricultural policies were adequate to the needs of a growing population and the necessities of industrial expansion; whether the long-run impact of his conception of socialism and his programs was compatible with the party's political monopoly; and, a central point to the Soviet political mind, whether a country led by Bukharinists would have been more prepared or less for the Second World War. Also like their Western counterparts, many Soviet analysts will probably conclude that some form of Bukharinism would have been both viable and preferable—that while Stalin's course produced spectacular achievements at spectacular costs, Bukharin's, producing neither, would have been more successful (and acceptable) in a less mountainous but also less painful way.[19]

That Bukharinist views may someday dominate Soviet historical opinion is suggested not only by the direction of revisionist writing during the Khrushchev years, but also by the growing body of uncensored literature, typed and circulated by hand,

known as *samizdat*. It is in these unofficial "publications" that critical discussion of Stalinism, as part of the reformers' search for an
authentic non-Stalinist tradition in the Soviet past, has continued
since the mid-sixties. Here, too, dissident Marxist-Leninists, some
of them the grown children of martyred Bukharinists and other
Bolsheviks,[20] have revived the Bukharinist tradition. Some now
flatly insist that Bukharin's agricultural policies were "the only correct ones, in contrast to the incorrect policies of Stalin." [21] Others
simply echo his criticism of Stalin's "unreal and adventurist" policies, condemning "Stalin's barracks Communism" and concluding,
as did Bukharin, that "without Stalin we undoubtedly could have
attained much greater success." [22]

While historical in nature, these are, as we have seen, also
questions of great contemporary importance. Politically, the future
of Bukharin's reputation and of what he represented in the Bolshevik revolution depends largely on the fate of Communist reformism, especially in the Soviet Union. If reform is overruled,
Bukharinism will probably be remembered as an isolated impulse in
the history of the revolution, a failed alternative to Stalinism in the
modernization and shaping of Soviet Russia. If, on the other hand,
reformers succeed in creating a more liberal communism, a "socialism with a human face," Bukharin's outlook and the NEP-style
order he defended may turn out to have been, after all, the true
prefiguration of the Communist future—the alternative to Stalinism
after Stalin.

NOTES AND
SELECTED
BIBLIOGRAPHY

NOTES

To keep the notes manageable, I have adopted the practice of giving most titles in full only when first cited, and in a shortened but clear form thereafter. I have handled Bukharin's many periodical publications in a somewhat different fashion. They are cited in full on first mention or where it seemed most appropriate, but thereafter only by reference to the newspaper, journal, or collection in which they appear. All shortened titles, including Bukharin's, are also cited in full in the bibliography. (More extensive notes to the material presented in Chapters I–VII are available in my doctoral thesis: "Bukharin and Russian Bolshevism, 1888–1927," Columbia University, 1969.)

In addition, I have used the following abbreviations and symbols in the notes:

BSE	*Bol'shaia sovetskaia entsiklopediia* (1st ed.; 66 vols; Moscow, 1926–47)
Inprecor	*International Press Correspondence*
MSE	*Malaia sovetskaia entsiklopediia* (edition cited)
PSS	V. I. Lenin, *Polnoe sobranie sochinenii* (5th ed.; 55 vols; Moscow, 1958–)
PZM	*Pod znamenem marksizma*
Soch.	V. I. Lenin, *Sochineniia* (3rd ed.; 30 vols; Moscow, 1928–37)
T——	The Trotsky Archives (unpublished materials, Houghton Library, Harvard University)
VKA	*Vestnik kommunisticheskoi akademii*

PREFACE

1. In addition to my own doctoral dissertation, studies of Bukharin include two monographs and two unpublished doctoral theses: Peter Knirsch, *Die ökonomischen Anschauungen Nikolaj I. Bucharins* (Berlin, 1959); A. G. Löwy, *Die Weltgeschichte ist das Weltgericht. Bucharin: Vision des Kommunismus* (Vienna, 1969); John E. Flaherty, "The Political Career of Nicolas Bukharin to 1929" (unpublished Ph.D. dissertation, New York University, 1954); and Sidney Heitman, "Bukharin's Conception of the Transition to Communism in Soviet Russia: An Analysis of His Basic Views, 1923–1928" (unpublished Ph.D. dissertation, Columbia University, 1963). Heitman has published a valuable bibliography, *Nikolai I. Bukharin: A Bibliography* (Stanford, Calif., 1969). Bukharin is also treated at some length in more general studies of the period, including Alexander Erlich, *The*

Soviet Industrialization Debate, 1924–1928 (Cambridge, Mass., 1960); Robert V. Daniels, *Conscience of the Revolution: Communist Opposition in Soviet Russia* (Cambridge, 1960); N. Valentinov, *Doktrina pravogo kommunizma* (Munich, 1960); M. Lewin, *Russian Peasants and Soviet Power: A Study of Collectivization* (Evanston, Illinois, 1968); and in E. H. Carr's multi-volume *History of Soviet Russia,* whose volumes are cited in the bibliography.

2. Warren Lerner in *The Russian Review* (April 1969), p. 202.

3. Isaac Deutscher, *The Prophet Unarmed: Trotsky, 1921–1929* (London and New York, 1959), p. ix. Rudolf Schlesinger has remarked earlier, and rightly, that the work of E. H. Carr represented a break with the "traditions of the Trotsky-Stalin feud." See *Soviet Studies,* April 1960, p. 393.

CHAPTER I

1. For another critique of the legend, see Daniels, *Conscience,* pp. 4–8. Daniels presents instead a dualistic view of Bolshevism, which (as will be clear) I do not share.

2. Bukharin in *Desiatyi s"ezd RKP(b). Mart 1921 goda: stenograficheskii otchet* (Moscow, 1963), p. 230.

3. M. Gaisinskii, *Bor'ba s uklonami ot general'noi linii partii: istoricheskii ocherk vnutripartiinoi bor'by posleoktiabr'skogo perioda* (2nd ed.; Moscow and Leningrad, 1931), p. 4.

4. See, for example, George F. Kennan, *Russia and the West Under Lenin and Stalin* (Boston, 1960), Chapter xvii.

5. The prevailing view was stated by Victor Serge, a onetime Bolshevik who should have known better: "the brains of the revolution . . . spoke the same Marxist language." *Memoirs of a Revolutionary: 1901–1941* (London, 1963), p. 135. Similarly, see Deutscher, *The Prophet Unarmed,* p. 12.

6. Indeed, there was controversy over whether Marx's economic categories applied to post-capitalist Soviet Russia. See the debate in *VKA,* Book II (1925), pp. 292–346.

7. S. V. Utechin, "Bolsheviks and Their Allies After 1917: The Ideological Pattern," *Soviet Studies* (October 1958), p. 113.

8. Bukharin, *K voprosu o trotskizme* (Moscow and Leningrad, 1925), p. 11.

9. J. M. Thompson, *Leaders of the French Revolution* (New York, 1967), p. ix. Or, as John Adams said of the American example: "The principles of the American Revolution may be said to have been as various as the thirteen States that went through it, and in some sense as diversified as the individuals who acted in it." Quoted in Jack P. Greene, *The Ambiguity of the American Revolution* (New York, 1968), p. 2.

10. Unless otherwise noted, this account of Bukharin's life before 1905 is based on his "Avtobiografiia," in *Deiateli soiuza sovetskikh sotsialisticheskikh respublik i oktiabr'skoi revoliutsii* (3 vols; Moscow, 1925–8), I, pp. 52–6. Brief Soviet biographical sketches of Bukharin include D. Maretskii, "Nikolai Ivanovich Bukharin," *BSE,* VIII, pp. 271–84, and those by N. Meshcheriakov in *MSE,* Vol. I (Moscow, 1929), pp. 912–15; S. Vol'fson in *Literaturnaia entsiklopediia,* Vol. I (Moscow, 1929), pp. 631–4; and V. Zalezhskii in *MSE,* Vol. II (2nd ed.; Moscow, 1934), pp. 173–6. Valuable information about Bukharin's family not available elsewhere is

contained in the czarist police dossier reprinted in *Bol'sheviki: dokumenty po istorii bol'shevizma s 1903 po 1916 god byvsh. moskovsk. okhrannogo otdeleniia* (Moscow, 1918), pp. 186–7.

11. *Bol'sheviki*, pp. 186–7.

12. Louis Fischer, *The Life of Lenin* (New York, 1964), p. 6.

13. Without encouraging them, Bukharin's father seems to have tolerated his son's revolutionary activities and occasionally even allowed the use of the family home for party meetings. See Michael Futrell, *Northern Underground* (New York, 1963), p. 137.

14. "Avtobiografiia," pp. 52–3; and Bukharin quoted in Boris I. Nicolaevsky, *Power and the Soviet Elite* (New York, 1965), p. 15.

15. Ypsilon, *Pattern for World Revolution* (Chicago, 1947), p. 62; Svetlana Alliluyeva, *Twenty Letters to a Friend* (New York, 1967), p. 31; and Nicolaevsky, *Power and the Soviet Elite*, pp. 14–15.

16. Markoosha Fischer, *My Lives in Russia* (New York, 1944), p. 198. See also Nadezhda K. Krupskaya, *Memories of Lenin* (2 vols; New York, n.d.), II, p. 112. Examples of his political caricatures are reproduced in Jules Humbert-Droz, "*L'oeil de Moscou*" *à Paris* (Paris, 1964), pp. 144–5; the same author's *De Lénine à Staline: dix ans du service de l'internationale communiste, 1921–1931* (Neuchatel, 1971), frontispiece and before pp. 129, 284; and Gunhild Höglund, *Moskva tur och retur: En dramatisk period i Zeth Höglunds liv* (Stockholm, 1960), pp. 39, 197, 199.

17. "Avtobiografiia," pp. 52–4; Maretskii, "Bukharin," p. 275.

18. "Avtobiografiia," p. 54. For the gymnasium, see also Bukharin's "Vospitanie smeny," in *Kakim dolzhen byt' kommunist—staraia i novaia moral': sbornik*, edited by A. Borisov (2nd ed.; Moscow, 1925), p. 23; and Ilya Ehrenburg, *People and Life: 1891–1921* (New York, 1962), pp. 30–4.

19. "Avtobiografiia," p. 54; and Bukharin, "Professor s pikoi," *Pravda*, October 25, 1928, p. 3.

20. Maretskii, "Bukharin," p. 271; and B. A. Dunaev, "V iunosheskie gody," in *Piatyi god: sbornik vtoroi*, edited by M. Miliutina (Moscow and Leningrad, 1926), pp. 19–32.

21. "Avtobiografiia," p. 54.

22. J. L. H. Keep, *The Rise of Social Democracy in Russia* (London, 1963), Chapters v–vii.

23. Bukharin, *Mikhail Ivanovich Kalinin: k 60-letiiu so dnia rozhdeniia* (Moscow, 1936), p. 10.

24. Eva Broido, *Memoirs of a Revolutionary* (London, 1967), p. 122; Ehrenburg, *People and Life*, p. 36; N. Popov, *Outline History of the Communist Party of the Soviet Union* (2 vols; New York, 1934), I, p. 212. Bukharin and Ehrenburg were close boyhood friends, "Avtobiografiia," p. 54. He appears only as "Nikolai" in the latter's censored memoirs.

25. Maretskii, "Bukharin," p. 275.

26. *People and Life*, p. 37.

27. *Shestoi s"ezd RSDRP (bol'shevikov). Avgust 1917 goda: protokoly* (Moscow, 1958), p. 295.

28. *People and Life*, p. 37.

29. Maretskii, "Bukharin," p. 271; "Avtobiografiia," p. 54.

30. *People and Life*, p. 46. Similarly, see B. A. Dunaev, "V iunosheskie gody," in *Piatyi god: sbornik vtoroi*, pp. 20–1.

31. For these activities, see Maretskii, "Bukharin," p. 271; Ehrenburg, *People and Life*, p. 39; Dunaev (cited above, note 30), pp. 47–55; L. Shatskin, "VLKSM," *BSE*, XI, p. 636; and Sokolnikov's autobiography in *Deiateli*, III, p. 74.

32. Maretskii, "Bukharin," p. 271; Bukharin, "Avtobiografiia," p. 54; Ehrenburg, *People and Life*, p. 43.

33. Maretskii, "Bukharin," p. 272; "Avtobiografiia," p. 54.

34. Osinskii's autobiography in *Deiateli*, II, p. 92; Ivan Kheraskov, "Reminiscences of the Moscow Students' Movement," *The Russian Review* (October 1952), pp. 223–32.

35. Bukharin, "Avtobiografiia," p. 54; Osinskii's autobiography in *Deiateli*, II, p. 93; Maretskii, "Bukharin," p. 276.

36. "Avtobiografiia," p. 54; Maretskii, "Bukharin," p. 272; Lenin, *Soch.*, XXIII, p. 601.

37. "Avtobiografiia," p. 55; Maretskii, "Bukharin," p. 272.

38. Leonard Schapiro, *The Communist Party of the Soviet Union* (New York, 1960), p. 101; and Bertram D. Wolfe, *Three Who Made a Revolution* (Boston, 1959), p. 478. Also see *Gody reaktsii (1908–1910)*, Vol. I, edited by V. I. Orlov (Moscow, 1925).

39. Maretskii, "Bukharin," p. 272; *Politbiuro TSK VKP(b): biografii* (Moscow, 1928), not paged.

40. Wolfe, *Three Who Made a Revolution*, p. 540; David Shub, *Lenin* (Garden City, N.Y., 1949), pp. 114–15.

41. These events remain somewhat obscure. This account is based on "Avtobiografiia," p. 55; Maretskii, "Bukharin," p. 272; and *Bol'sheviki*, p. 187.

42. For some recollections of Bukharin before 1917, see above, note 30; Rosa Meyer-Leviné, quoted in editor's Introduction to Rosa Luxemburg and Nikolai Bukharin, *Imperialism and the Accumulation of Capital*, edited by Kenneth J. Tarbuck (London, 1972), p. 8; Löwy, *Die Weltgeschichte*, pp. 27, 147, 149, 279; Höglund, *Moskva tur och retur*, p. 49; Fischer, *My Lives in Russia*, pp. 198–9; and D. Shub, "Iz davnykh let," *Novyi zhurnal*, No. 101 (1971), pp. 203–4. For another woman's opinion, see Claire Sheridan, *Russian Portraits* (London, 1921), p. 88. For a police description, see *Bol'sheviki*, pp. 186–7.

43. "Avtobiografiia," p. 55.

44. For the first article, which appeared in a student journal, see Maretskii, "Bukharin," pp. 275–6; for the second, see Bukharin, *Ataka: sbornik teoreticheskikh statei* (2nd ed.; Moscow, 1924), pp. 25–50. He always considered political economy to be "the field of science with which I am most familiar." See his "O formal'nom metode v iskusstve," *Krasnaia nov'*, No. 3, 1925, p. 253.

45. Maretskii, "Bukharin," p. 276.

46. "Avtobiografiia," p. 54.

47. For Lenin's work, see *Soch.*, XIII. For Bogdanov and the philosophical dispute, see S. V. Utechin, "Philosophy and Society: Alexander Bogdanov," in *Revisionism: Essays on the History of Marxist Ideas*, edited by Leopold Labedz (New York, 1962), pp. 117–25; and Wolfe, *Three Who Made a Revolution*, Chapter xxix.

48. "A. A. Bogdanov," *Pravda*, April 8, 1928, p. 3. Their intellectual relationship will be discussed further in Chapter IV.

49. Osinskii and Smirnov are discussed below, and other young Muscovites in Chapter II. Little information about their early careers is available. Some appears in the heavily edited memoirs of Polina Vinogradskaia, their friend and contem-

porary: *Sobytiia i pamiatnye vstrechi* (Moscow, 1968); and in her "Oktiabr' v Moskve," *Novyi mir*, No. 4, 1966, pp. 143–86. In the latter (p. 163), she dates their group affiliation from 1905.

50. Lukina was born in 1887, joined the party in 1906, and worked in the Moscow organization until she emigrated, probably in 1911. She and Bukharin apparently separated in the twenties. Arrested in 1937, she died in 1940, presumably in a Soviet concentration camp. See *Protokoly: desiatyi s"ezd (RKP(b)* (Moscow, 1933), pp. 912–13; *Vos'maia konferentsiia RKP(b): protokoly* (Moscow, 1961), p. 296; *Soch.*, XXIX, p. 129; and Krupskaya, *Memories*, II, p. 118. For her brother Nikolai, see N. M. Lukin, *Izbrannye trudy*, I (Moscow, 1960), pp. 5–12.

51. See Osinskii's autobiography in *Deiateli*, II, pp. 90–8; *Put' k oktiabriu: sbornik statei vospominanii i dokumentov* (5 vols; Moscow, 1923–6), III, p. 205; *Soch.*, XXII, p. 651; and Bukharin, "K voprosu o zakonomernostiakh perekhodnogo perioda," *Pravda*, July 7, 1926, p. 2. For the "trio," see *Put' k oktiabriu*, I, p. 241.

52. Ehrenburg, *People and Life*, p. 50; Bukharin in *Pravda*, December 12, 1922, p. 3. An older party member referred to Bukharin's generation as "urchins playing at revolution." Quoted in Ralph Carter Elwood, "Trotsky's Questionnaire," *Slavic Review* (June 1970), p. 299.

53. *Gody reaktsii* (1908–1910), Vol. I, edited by V. I. Orlov (Moscow, 1925), p. 270.

54. Maretskii, "Bukharin," p. 273.

55. "Avtobiografiia," p. 55.

56. Four of his emigration articles were reprinted in *Ataka*, pp. 1–88. The two books were first published in full after the revolution: *Politicheskaia ekonomika rant'e: teoriia tsennosti i pribyli avstriiskoi shkoly* (Moscow, 1919), translated as *The Economic Theory of the Leisure Class* (New York, 1927); and *Mirovoe khoziaistvo i imperializm* (Petrograd, 1918), translated as *Imperialism and World Economy* (New York, 1929). An abridged version of the second book appeared in the Bolshevik collection *Kommunist* (Geneva, 1915), pp. 4–44.

57. See his remarks in "Krizis burzhuaznoi kul'tury," *Pravda*, November 7, 1922, p. 7; and in "Lenin i zadachi nauki v sotsialisticheskom stroitel'stve," *Pravda*, January 20, 1929, p. 3.

58. Maretskii, "Bukharin," p. 272; Bukharin, "Orlitsa," *Pravda*, July 5, 1927, p. 1; and Krupskaya, *Memories*, II, p. 112.

59. Krupskaya, *Memories*, II, p. 112; Fischer, *Lenin*, p. 82; Shub, *Lenin*, pp. 119–20; Wolfe, *Three Who Made a Revolution*, Chapter xxxi; and Flaherty, "Nicolas Bukharin . . . ," p. 8.

60. *PSS*, XLIX, p. 194.

61. See his "Pamiati Il'icha," *Pravda*, January 21, 1925, p. 1; and Bukharin quoted in Nicolaevsky, *Power and the Soviet Elite*, p. 12.

62. *Soch.*, XXI, p. 546, and XXIII, p. 601; Maretskii, "Bukharin," p. 272; *Leninskii sbornik* (33 vols; Moscow, 1924–40), XIII, p. 212; *PSS*, XLIX, p. 253. Bukharin's first article appeared in *Prosveshchenie*, No. 8–9, 1912. For Lenin's visit, see Krupskaya, *Memories*, II, p. 118.

63. *Economic Theory of the Leisure Class*, pp. 7, 17.

64. *Ibid.*, p. 7; "Avtobiografiia," p. 55. For marginalism's challenge to orthodox Marxism, see Peter Gay, *The Dilemma of Democratic Socialism: Eduard Bernstein's Challenge to Marx* (New York, 1962), pp. 174–84.

65. See his articles on Petr Struve, Tugan-Baranovskii, Böhm-Bawerk, and Franz Oppenheimer, reprinted in *Ataka*.

66. *Economic Theory of the Leisure Class*, pp. 8, 23–32. Also Rudolf Hilferding, *Böhm-Bawerk's Criticism of Marx*, edited by Paul M. Sweezy (New York, 1949).

67. See Hermann Duncker's review in *Inprecor*, X (1930), No. 33, p. 607. Also Rudolf Schlesinger, "A Note on Bukharin's Ideas," *Soviet Studies* (April 1960), pp. 419–20.

68. *Bol'shevik*, No. 10, 1924, pp. 87–9. Also see Maretskii, "Bukharin," p. 279; and Meshcheriakov, "Bukharin," p. 914.

69. See, for example, his *Historical Materialism: A System of Sociology* (New York, 1925); and "Uchenie Marksa i ego istoricheskoe znachenie," in *Pamiati Karla Marksa: sbornik statei k piatidesiatiletiiu, 1883–1933* (Moscow, 1933), pp. 9–99. The latter item was apparently part of a larger manuscript he was working on in the thirties. According to one source, he was still working on the project during the last year of his life in prison. Abdurakhman Avtorkhanov, *Stalin and the Soviet Communist Party* (New York, 1959), p. 24.

70. *Economic Theory of the Leisure Class*, pp. 8–9, 160; *Ataka*, pp. 51, 77. For contemporary social theory and Marxism, see H. Stuart Hughes, *Consciousness and Society: The Reconstruction of European Social Thought, 1890–1930* (New York, 1961), Chapter iii; and Bukharin, "Uchenie Marksa . . . ," pp. 16–17.

71. His *Historical Materialism*, which is discussed in Chapter IV, was largely an attempt to come to grips with the modern sociologists. For his admiring references to Weber, see *Historical Materialism*, p. 178 and *passim*; "Uchenie Marksa . . . ," p. 54; "Nekotorye problemy sovremennogo kapitalizma i teoretikov burzhuazii," in *"Organizovannyi kapitalizm": diskussiia v Komakademii* (2nd ed.; Moscow, 1930), p. 174; and Nicolas J. Boukharine, *Les problèmes fondamentaux de la culture contemporaine* (Paris, 1936), p. 22.

72. See George Lichtheim, *Marxism: An Historical and Critical Study* (New York, 1962), Chapter vii.

73. Bukharin's later attitude was that they were the best of a bad lot. See, for example, his "The Austrian Social Democrats' New Programme," *The Communist International*, October 15, 1926, pp. 2–6. They apparently regarded him similarly. See Ruth Fisher, *Stalin and German Communism* (Cambridge, Mass., 1948), p. 279. The differing attitudes of Lenin and Bukharin toward Hilferding are discussed below. Among other Bolsheviks, Trotsky, for example, had a low opinion of the Austrians. See his *My Life* (New York, 1960), pp. 206–12.

74. *PSS*, XLVIII, pp. 242, 263, 403 n.272. Pressed, Lenin finally allowed an investigative commission to look into the charges against Malinovskii. Bukharin testified. Again, however, Lenin "donned the armor of his steel will" and refused to believe the accusations. See Bukharin's account in *Pravda*, January 21, 1925, p. 1; Krupskaya, *Memories*, II, pp. 131–2; and Wolfe, *Three Who Made a Revolution*, pp. 500–1.

75. *PSS*, XXV, p. 458. Several writers—Leon Trotsky, *Stalin* (New York, 1941), pp. 157–8, and Wolfe, *Three Who Made a Revolution*, pp. 581–2—have suggested that Bukharin played a large role in preparing Stalin's article. I have found no evidence to substantiate this view. Nor is there any evidence to support the customary view that Bukharin and Lenin were already divided on the national question.

76. Meshcheriakov, "Bukharin," p. 913; Maretskii, "Bukharin," p. 272; and Bukharin, *Economic Theory of the Leisure Class*, p. 7.

77. *Pravda*, July 7, 1927, p. 3. Similarly, see *Pravda*, January 21, 1925, p. 1.

78. Olga Hess Gankin and H. H. Fisher, *The Bolsheviks and the World War*:

The Origin of the Third International (Stanford, Calif., 1940), pp. 136–7; Bukharin, *Economic Theory of the Leisure Class*, p. 7; *Soch.*, XXIX, p. 129.

79. See the memoirs of Evgeniia Bosh in Gankin and Fisher, *Bolsheviks*, pp. 180–1; *Leninskii sbornik*, XI, p. 135; and I. I. Mints, *Istoriia velikogo oktiabria*, I (Moscow, 1967), p. 241.

80. *Leninskii sbornik*, XI, p. 135; Krupskaya, *Memories*, II, p. 156; and Bukharin's letter quoted in D. Baevskii, "Bor'ba Lenina protiv bukharinskikh 'shatanii mysli'," *PR*, No. 1 (96), 1930, p. 23.

81. Krupskaya, *Memories*, II, p. 156; and Bukharin quoted in Baevskii, "Bor'ba Lenina . . . ," p. 23.

82. Thus, on Lenin's instructions, the Central Committee Bureau explained to Bukharin that such initiatives had to be decided "collectively," and "not by just several comrades." Quoted in Mints, *Istoriia velikogo oktiabria*, p. 241. For Rozmirovich and the Malinovskii affair, see Wolfe, *Three Who Made a Revolution*, pp. 548–50.

83. Since Bukharin's speeches to the conference remain unpublished, his arguments are known largely from later, distorted Soviet accounts. See *Bol'shevik*, No. 15, 1929, pp. 86–8; and D. Baevskii, "Bol'sheviki v bor'be za III internatsional," *Istorik marksist*, XI (1929), p. 38. His theses and the Baugy group's resolution are reprinted in Gankin and Fisher, *Bolsheviks*, pp. 187–91.

84. The original inspiration of subsequent Soviet accounts, which Western scholars have generally followed, was Lenin's own distortion of Bukharin's Bern position a year later. See his letters in Gankin and Fisher, *Bolsheviks*, pp. 241–2, 245. Prior to 1929, Soviet historians put no special emphasis on their differences at Bern. See, for example, D. Baevskii, "Partiia v gody imperialisticheskoi voiny," in *Ocherki po istorii oktiabr'skoi revoliutsii*, edited by M. N. Pokrovskii (2 vols; Moscow, 1927), I, pp. 366, 444. With Bukharin's fall in 1929, however, his position at Bern was portrayed as ultra-leftist, anti-Leninist factionalism. See, for example, Baevskii's new interpretation in his "Bor'ba Lenina . . . ," pp. 18–46, and in his "Bol'sheviki v bor'be . . . ," pp. 12–48.

85. Gankin and Fisher, *Bolsheviks*, pp. 174, 179, 181–8.

86. *Ibid.*, p. 181; Mints, *Istoriia velikogo oktiabria*, p. 241.

87. "Avtobiografiia," p. 55.

88. Krupskaya, *Memories*, II, p. 179. The date is unclear. Only Lenin's letters are available. See *PSS*, XLIX, pp. 86–8, 108.

89. Krupskaya, *Memories*, II, p. 166; Gankin and Fisher, *Bolsheviks*, p. 215.

90. Maretskii, "Bukharin," p. 273; *Kalendar' kommunista na 1929 god* (Moscow and Leningrad, 1929), p. 690; Futrell, *Northern Underground*, p. 91; *PSS*, XLIX, p. 108.

91. An abridged version of Bukharin's study appeared in September 1915. See above, note 56. Lenin received the book-length manuscript in late 1915. He wrote a laudatory introduction, dated December 1915, which along with the manuscript was sent to Russia for publication. Both were then lost in a police raid. Bukharin's book was finally published in 1918, but Lenin's introduction was recovered only later. It first appeared in *Pravda*, January 21, 1927, p. 1, and is included in the English translation, *Imperialism and World Economy*, pp. 9–14. Lenin began researching his own *Imperialism* in late 1915, completing the writing in June 1916. See Krupskaya, *Memories*, II, p. 175; and Fischer, *Lenin*, p. 95. The published edition contained a reference to Bukharin's manuscript, see *Soch.*, XIX, pp. 104, 463 n. 76. For other evidence that Lenin used Bukharin's manuscript in preparing his own study, see *Leninskii sbornik*, XXXVII, pp. 162, 188, 198.

92. Rudol'f Gilferding, *Finansovyi kapital: noveishaia faza v razvitii kapitalizma* (3rd ed.; Petersburg, 1918). First published in Russian in 1912, it had gone through four editions by 1923. Despite his subsequent position as an anti-Bolshevik "reformist" after 1917, Hilferding's influence on Soviet students of imperialism was very great.

93. *Ibid.*, p. 332.

94. E. M. Winslow, *The Pattern of Imperialism: A Study in the Theories of Power* (New York, 1948), p. 159. Hilferding's discussion of imperialism was confined to the concluding section of *Finansovyi kapital*, pp. 438–553.

95. He fully acknowledged his debt. See *Imperialism and World Economy*, pp. 36, 64, 71, 107, 123, 135, 136, 142.

96. *Ibid.*, pp. 84–5, 104, 114, 140, and Chapter ix.

97. *Ibid.*, pp. 95, 103, 121, 133, 139, 142, and *passim*. Hilferding, on the other hand, while arguing that militaristic policies were an inevitable consequence of imperialism, seemed to leave open the possibility that radical political action could prevent war. *Finansovyi kapital*, Chapter xxv.

98. In his *Imperialism*, Lenin prefaced his discussion of imperialism and colonialism with an analysis of monopoly capitalism. He did so, however, briefly and without any notable additions to Hilferding. He was interested mainly in international developments. One reflection of Bukharin's and Lenin's differing interests was Lenin's heavy reliance on J. A. Hobson's *Imperialism* (1902), a volume concerned exclusively with imperialist developments. Bukharin made no mention of Hobson; his essential source was Hilferding.

99. *Imperialism and World Economy*, pp. 73–4, 108, 118–20, and Chapter xiii. Though the term was already in use, primarily in connection with Germany's wartime economy, Bolshevik writers frequently gave Bukharin credit for having elaborated the Marxist understanding of state capitalism. See, for example, Osinskii's review in *Kommunist* (Moscow), No. 2, 1918, p. 24; and L. Kritsman, *Geroicheskii period velikoi russkoi revoliutsii* (2nd ed.; Moscow and Leningrad, 1926), p. 19. Bukharin claimed authorship of the term "state capitalist trust." See his *Ekonomika perekhodnogo perioda* (Moscow, 1920), p. 10.

100. *Imperialism and World Economy*, p. 129; also pp. 124–9, 148–9, 151, 155.

101. Though extracts and summaries of its argument appeared in 1916 and 1917, the full article—minus a conclusion which was lost—was not published until 1925. "K teorii imperialisticheskogo gosudarstva," in *Revoliutsiia prava: sbornik pervyi* (Moscow, 1925), pp. 5–32.

102. *Ibid.*, pp. 6–14.

103. *Ibid.*, pp. 15–18, 21–2, 25, 27.

104. *Ibid.*, pp. 18, 28, 30.

105. *Imperialism and World Economy*, pp. 120, 135.

106. See, for example, Maretskii, "Bukharin," pp. 276–7; Bukharin, "The Imperialist Pirate State," translated in Gankin and Fisher, *Bolsheviks*, pp. 238–9; and his "Gosudarstvennyi kapitalizm i marksizm," *Novyi mir* (New York), December 2, 1916, pp. 4, 6.

107. *Ekonomika perekhodnogo perioda*, Chapters i–iii; and his two articles of May–June 1929 reprinted in "*Organizovannyi kapitalizm*," pp. 168–99.

108. "The Imperialist Pirate State," p. 238; also *Imperialism and World Economy*, p. 129.

109. Published in 1908, London's novel was well known among socialists. Bukharin was to refer to it many times in the years that followed. He first used the

term "iron heel" in *Imperialism and World Economy*, p. 62, and frequently thereafter. For London and Orwell, see Max Lerner's introduction, *The Iron Heel* (New York, 1957), p. ix.

110. "K teorii imperialisticheskogo gosudarstva," p. 31.

111. Other social institutions, he wrote, "*have a tendency to fuse with one another and to become transformed into one organization of the rulers. . . . So there comes into being a single, all-embracing organization, the modern imperialist pirate state, an omnipotent organization of bourgeois dominance, with innumerable functions*," with gigantic powers, with spiritual . . . as well as material methods. . . ." "The Imperialist Pirate State," p. 238.

112. *Imperialism and World Economy*, p. 157 n. 2; "O nekotorykh voprosakh iz pervoi chasti proekta programmy K.I.," *Kommunisticheskii internatsional*, No. 31–2, 1928, p. 35. For his other two posings of the question, see "K teorii imperialisticheskogo gosudarstva," p. 26; and his *Imperializm i nakoplenie kapitala* (4th ed.; Moscow and Leningrad, 1929), p. 82.

113. It was frequently discussed in connection with Nazi Germany and Stalin's Russia. See, for example, Frederick Pollack, "State Capitalism: Its Possibilities and Limitations," *Studies in Philosophy and Social Sciences*, IX, No. 2, 1941, pp. 200–25; and Franz Neumann, *Behemoth* (New York, 1966), pp. 221–34. Hilferding, the inspirer of later Marxist definitions of state capitalism, rejected the concept in regard to Germany and Soviet Russia. See his "State Capitalism or Totalitarian State Economy?," in *Verdict of Three Decades*, edited by Julian Steinberg (New York, 1950), pp. 445–53.

114. "K teorii imperialisticheskogo gosudarstva," pp. 17, 25; also *Imperialism and World Economy*, pp. 53, 119–20, 124, 164.

115. *Imperialism and World Economy*, pp. 53–4; also pp. 87, 106–7, 119, 120, 123–4.

116. *Ibid.*, pp. 164–7; "The Imperialist Pirate State," p. 239.

117. "K teorii imperialisticheskogo gosudarstva," pp. 30–2.

118. See above, note 91.

119. Which is to say that both were required reading in party educational institutions. See also I. I. Skvortsov-Stepanov's introductory remarks in Hilferding, *Finansovyi kapital* (3rd ed.; Moscow, 1923), p. v.

120. Lenin, it should be noted, was not always consistent in his remarks on monopoly capitalism. See V. I. Lenin, *Selected Works* (3 vols; Moscow, 1960), I, pp. 723–4, 728, 731, 740, 781, 790, 812. But the extent of their disagreement on this point was to be made clear in 1920, when Bukharin published his *The Economics of the Transition Period*. There he wrote: "Finance capital destroys the anarchy of production inside large capitalist countries." Lenin corrected him: "does not 'destroy.'" *Leninskii sbornik*, XI, p. 350. Beginning in 1929, this difference in their understandings of monopoly capitalism became the substance of the Stalinist attack on Bukharin's theory of modern capitalism. See, for example, M. Ioel'son, "Monopolisticheskii kapitalizm ili 'organizovannyi kapitalizm'?," *Bol'-shevik*, No. 18, 1929, pp. 26–43.

121. *Imperialism and World Economy*, pp. 120, 144–5; see also his "Gde spasanie malen'kikh natsii?," *Novyi mir* (New York), December 20, 1916, p. 4. He thought, for example, that the continued independent existence of Belgium was doubtful.

122. *Selected Works*, I, pp. 705, 788, 812. Bukharin allowed for uneven development, but was more inclined to emphasize "the leveling of economic differences," *Imperialism and World Economy*, p. 107.

123. *Soch.*, XIX, p. 324.

124. Gankin and Fisher, *Bolsheviks*, pp. 215–16.

125. The documents are reprinted in *ibid.*, pp. 219–33.

126. *Ibid.*, p. 221, *Soch.*, XXX, p. 251; and *PSS*, XLIX, p. 214.

127. See Krupskaya, *Memories*, II, p. 188; and Lenin's suggestion that it was possible to work with Bukharin despite the controversy, *PSS*, XLIX, p. 253.

128. Aleksandr Shliapnikov and, on at least one occasion, Zinoviev tried to mediate the dispute. See Gankin and Fisher, *Bolsheviks*, p. 249; and *PSS*, XLIX, p. 231.

129. *PSS*, XLIX, p. 194; also see pp. 205, 246–8. Bukharin's letters to Lenin on self-determination have not been published. Their contents may be judged from Lenin's correspondence and from the draft of an article in *Soch.*, XXX, pp. 250–6.

130. Krupskaya, *Memories*, II, p. 197; Gankin and Fisher, *Bolsheviks*, p. 239; and Bukharin's letter to Zinoviev published in *Bol'shevik*, No. 22, 1932, p. 86.

131. For Bukharin in Scandinavia, see Futrell, *Northern Underground*. A good example was Lenin's criticism of Bukharin's favorable reference to the Dutch Left's program, *Soch.*, XXX, pp. 251–6.

132. *PSS*, XLIX, p. 194; see also Lenin's paternalistic appeal for tolerance of wayward young Marxists—advice he himself rarely heeded—in *Soch.*, XIX, pp. 294–7. For Bukharin's remarks, see his unpublished letter quoted in Baevskii, "Bol'sheviki v bor'be . . . ," p. 37.

133. Bertram D. Wolfe, "Leninism," in *Marxism and the Modern World*, edited by Milorad N. Drachkovitch (Stanford, Calif., 1965), p. 51.

134. From an unpublished letter quoted in *Soch.*, XXIX, p. 261; similarly, see his letter written later in 1916 and published in *Bol'shevik*, No. 22, 1932, pp. 87–8.

135. *PSS*, XLIX, pp. 213, 220, 260; once again his references to Bukharin were embittered (pp. 254, 255, 283).

136. *Ibid.*, p. 222.

137. "K teorii imperialisticheskogo gosudarstva," p. 13.

138. For a discussion of the ways in which Marxism has been alternatively de-radicalized and re-radicalized, see Robert C. Tucker, *The Marxian Revolutionary Idea* (New York, 1969), Chapter vi. Bukharin praised both Höglund and Pannekoek in this connection. See "K teorii imperialisticheskogo gosudarstva," p. 30; and his letter to Lenin in October 1916, *Bol'shevik*, No. 22, 1932, p. 87. He was a friend of Höglund and a contributor to his journal *Stormklockan*. See Futrell, *Northern Underground*, pp. 91–2; and Maretskii, "Bukharin," p. 273.

139. *PSS*, XLIX, pp. 271, 287, 293–4.

140. Several letters relating to this dispute have not been published, including some of Lenin's, as is clear from *ibid.*, pp. 297, 478, 541 n. 378; and *Bol'shevik*, No. 22, 1932, p. 88 n. 1 and 4. Contents of the missing letters, however, may be judged from those published in this issue of *Bol'shevik* (pp. 86–93) and from Lenin's letter of October 14 in *PSS*, XLIX, pp. 306–10.

141. *PSS*, XLIX, pp. 293–4; and Lenin's attack on Nota-Bene (Bukharin) in *Soch.*, XIX, pp. 295–6.

142. *Bol'shevik*, No. 22, 1932, pp. 86–7. Nine years later, in a footnote to his original article, he explained his decision to defy Lenin and publish his views. "K teorii imperialisticheskogo gosudarstva," p. 5.

143. See Shliapnikov's memoirs in Gankin and Fisher, *Bolsheviks*, p. 250.

144. *PSS*, XLIX, p. 302.

145. *Bol'shevik*, No. 22, 1932, pp. 87–8.

146. *PSS*, XLIX, pp. 305, 306–10; *Bol'shevik*, No. 22, 1932, p. 93.

147. "K teorii imperialisticheskogo gosudarstva," p. 32; also pp. 13, 30. Similarly, see *Imperialism and World Economy*, p. 166; and *Novyi mir* (New York), December 2, 1916, pp. 4, 6.

148. *Bol'shevik*, No. 22, 1932, p. 88. Bukharin's alleged anarchism and Lenin's misrepresentation are discussed in Sidney Heitman, "The Myth of Bukharin's Anarchism," *The Rocky Mountain Social Science Journal* (April 1963), pp. 39–53.

149. *Soch.*, XIX, p. 296.

150. In letters to Aleksandra Kollontai and Inessa Armand, *PSS*, XLIX, pp. 388, 390–1.

151. Bukharin appended this information to the published edition of his article in 1925, "K teorii imperialisticheskogo gosudarstva," p. 5 n. 1. His account of Krupskaya's message was never challenged. Even in 1929, Stalin thought that "Quite possibly Nadezhda Konstantinovna did tell Bukharin what he writes here." But, explained Stalin, it meant only that Lenin believed that *Bukharin* had changed his views. J. Stalin, *Works* (13 vols; Moscow, 1952–5), XII, p. 82. Bukharin may have learned of Lenin's change of mind before Krupskaya told him, either from Lenin's fragmentary writings after the February revolution or from Kollontai, who was also in New York. Indeed, Lenin may have communicated it to him in a letter of February 17, 1917, which has not been published. See *PSS*, XLIX, p. 479.

152. *Soch.*, XXI, pp. 385, 388, 406, 411, 444, and *passim*. Entitled *State and Revolution: The Teaching of Marxism on the State and the Tasks of the Proletariat in the Revolution*, it was the product of Lenin's decision in December 1916 to write an article on the subject.

153. Compare Bukharin's remarks in *Imperialism and World Economy*, p. 166; and in *Ataka*, p. 268.

154. That Bukharin had been the first to revive Marx's anti-statism, and that that initiative prompted Lenin's subsequent formulation, was generally acknowledged in the Soviet Union until 1929. See, for example, *Leninskii sbornik*, II, p. 284 n. 7. Maretskii made the claim in his 1926 biographical sketch of Bukharin—"Bukharin," pp. 276–7—and it went unchallenged until after Bukharin's fall from power, when Lenin or occasionally Pannekoek received the credit. See Baevskii, "Bol'sheviki v bor'be . . . ," p. 42. Even after 1929, however, Lenin's well-documented debt to Bukharin was sometimes acknowledged, though grudgingly and obliquely. See *Soch.*, XIX, p. 479 n. 155. In the mid-twenties, while recalling the dispute and noting Lenin's initial "incorrect" position, Bukharin gave him credit for having worked out "the concrete form of the dictatorship of the proletariat." "K teorii imperialisticheskogo gosudarstva," p. 5 n. 1; *Ataka*, pp. 267–70. On this question, see also Robert V. Daniels, "The 'Withering Away of the State' in Theory and Practice," in *Soviet Society: A Book of Readings*, edited by Alex Inkeles and Kent Geiger (Boston, 1961), pp. 113–26.

155. "Avtobiografiia," p. 55; Trotsky, *My Life*, p. 273.

156. Maretskii, "Bukharin," p. 273; Theodore Draper, *The Roots of American Communism* (New York, 1957), pp. 76–7; D. Shub, "Iz davnykh let," *Novyi zhurnal*, No. 102 (1971), p. 202. See, for example, the exchange between him and S. Novomirskii in *Novyi mir*, November 23, December 2 and 12, 1916. For a list of his *Novyi mir* articles, see Sidney Heitman and Peter Knirsch, *N. I. Bucharin* (Berlin, 1959), pp. 19–23.

157. *Novyi mir*, February 28, 1917, p. 5; *PSS*, XLIX, p. 387; *Politbiuro*, not paged.

158. This was to be his position on the likelihood of an American revolution in the twenties.

159. Trotsky, *My Life*, p. 273. Generally speaking, Trotsky's retrospective account of their relationship, which will be discussed in Chapters V and VIII, is unreliable.

160. See Draper, *Roots of American Communism*, pp. 80–5; and the recollections of Ludwig Lore in *One Year of Revolution* (New York, 1918), pp. 7–8, and of Sen Katayama in *The Revolutionary Age*, July 26, 1919, p. 6.

161. "Perspektivy revoliutsii," *Novyi mir*, March 27, 1917, p. 4; see also his "The Russian Revolution and Its Significance," *The Class Struggle* (May–June, 1917), pp. 14–21. For his earlier thinking, see "Avtobiografiia," p. 55; and Maretskii, "Bukharin," pp. 276–7.

162. See Draper, *Roots of American Communism*, p. 85; "Avtobiografiia," p. 55; and *Spravochnaia knizhka zhurnalista* (Moscow, 1924), p. 289. His arrival in Moscow is occasionally given as late April.

CHAPTER II

1. Despite a growing number of Soviet and Western monographs, there is still no adequate social history of the 1917 revolution. A dated but still valuable account is William Henry Chamberlin, *The Russian Revolution: 1917–1921* (2 vols; New York, 1960). See also *Revolutionary Russia*, edited by Richard Pipes (Cambridge, Mass., 1968); and for the party, Robert V. Daniels, *Red October: The Bolshevik Revolution of 1917* (New York, 1967).

2. *Shestoi s"ezd*, p. 72.

3. For the Theses, which summarized an unpublished speech Lenin gave upon his return, see *Soch.*, XX, pp. 87–90. For social democratic reaction, see N. N. Sukhanov, *The Russian Revolution 1917: Eyewitness Account* (2 vols; New York, 1962), I, pp. 286–7.

4. Sukhanov, *Russian Revolution*, I, Chapter xii; and Bukharin, *Ataka*, p. 269.

5. Lenin quoted in Daniels, *Red October*, p. 65, which provides a detailed account of the leader's struggle to radicalize and unite his party in 1917. For different outlooks in the party, see also Alexander Rabinowitch, *Prelude to Revolution: The Petrograd Bolsheviks and the July 1917 Uprising* (Bloomington, Ind., 1968).

6. See Bukharin's review of *State and Revolution* in *Kommunist* (Moscow), No. 1, 1918, p. 19; and his "Avtobiografiia," p. 55.

7. "Avtobiografiia," p. 55; *Shestoi s"ezd*, pp. 99–105. Bukharin's speech on "The War and the International Situation" was given first and appears to have been the main report.

8. Rykov quoted in Leon Trotsky, *The History of the Russian Revolution* (3 vols; New York, 1937), III, p. 151.

9. Lenin, *Soch.*, XX, p. 650 n. 136.

10. G. A. Trukan, *Oktiabr' v tsentral'noi Rossii* (Moscow, 1967), Chapter i and *passim; Voprosy istorii KPSS*, No. 10, 1967, p. 15.

11. Neither Bukharin in his autobiography nor Maretskii in his official biography later mentioned Bukharin's membership on the Bureau, presumably because of the organization's subsequent role in the Left Communist opposition. For evidence that he was a member, indeed in the Bureau's "inner circle" of leaders, see G. Lomov, "V dni buri i natiska," *Proletarskaia revoliutsiia*, No. 10, 1927, pp.

166–7; Stukov's memoirs in *Oktiabr'skoe vosstanie v Moskve*, edited by N. Ovsiannikov (Moscow, 1922), p. 40; and Leonard Schapiro, *The Origin of the Communist Autocracy* (Cambridge, Mass., 1956), p. 108.

12. Daniels, *Conscience*, p. 41. There is no satisfactory political history of the Moscow party in 1917. In addition to the articles, memoirs, and monographs cited in this chapter, see *Ocherki istorii moskovskoi organizatsii KPSS: 1883–1965* (Moscow, 1966), Chapter vi; and *Oktiabr' v Moskve* (Moscow, 1967).

13. *Proletarskaia revoliutsiia*, No. 10, 1922, pp. 473–4. The dispute derived from the overlapping jurisdictional authority of three Moscow party organizations, the city, district, and regional. See *Moskva v dvukh revoliutsiiakh* (Moscow, 1958), p. 394.

14. The Bureau included other prominent leaders at various times in 1917, among them Andrei Bubnov (1883) and Sokolnikov (1888). These seven, however, constituted its inner leadership. See Lomov's autobiography in *Deiateli*, I, p. 339; his memoirs in *Proletarskaia revoliutsiia*, No. 10, 1927, pp. 166–8; Stukov's memoirs in *Oktiabr'skoe vosstanie v Moskve*, pp. 40–5; and Iakovleva's in *Proletarskaia revoliutsiia*, No. 10, 1922, pp. 302–6. Among Moscow Committee leaders, not all of them moderates, were (with birth dates): Nogin (1878), Mikhail Olminskii (1863), Ivan Skvortsov-Stepanov (1870), Petr Smidovich (1874), Ivan Teodorovich (1875), N. L. Meshcheriakov (1865), M. F. Vladimirskii (1874), and Pokrovskii (1868). For biographical sketches of some of them, see *Geroi oktiabria: kniga ob uchastnikakh velikoi oktiabr'skoi sotsialisticheskoi revoliutsii v Moskve* (Moscow, 1967).

15. Smidovich quoted in *Voprosy istorii KPSS*, No. 12, 1967, p. 49.

16. Iakovleva in *Proletarskaia revoliutsiia*, No. 10, 1922, p. 304; and quoted in *Istorik marksist*, No. 5–6, 1935, p. 16. Similarly, see *Proletarskaia revoliutsiia*, No. 10, 1922, pp. 471–6; and No. 10, 1927, pp. 166–8.

17. *Deiateli*, II, p. 96. Similarly, see Lomov's remarks in *Proletarskaia revoliutsiia*, No. 10, 1927, pp. 167–8.

18. Simon Liberman, *Building Lenin's Russia* (Chicago, 1945), p. 172. For Iakovleva and her brother, see *Deiateli*, III, pp. 274–80. Bukharin dedicated the Russian edition of his *Historical Materialism* to the memory of Nikolai, who was killed in the civil war.

19. See Lenin, *Soch.*, XXVII, p. 592; *Shestoi s"ezd*, p. 451; and *Shestoi s"ezd* (1934 ed.), pp. 331–2.

20. *Oktiabr' v Moskve*, p. 143; *Voprosy istorii KPSS*, No. 8, 1967, p. 63.

21. *Put' k oktiabriu*, I, p. 241; E. Iaroslavskii, *Istoriia VKP(b)*. Vol. IV (Moscow and Leningrad, 1929), p. 223. See also *Proletarskaia revoliutsiia*, No. 4, 1924, p. 137; Bukharin, "Avtobiografiia," p. 55; and Maretskii, "Bukharin," p. 273. Their takeover remained a source of friction inside the party throughout the year.

22. Bukharin, "Avtobiografiia," p. 55; Maretskii, "Bukharin," p. 273; Lenin, *Soch.*, XXII, p. 517, n. 45; and *1917 god v Moskve (khronika revoliutsii)* (Moscow, 1934), p. 66.

23. *Protokoly tsentral'nogo komiteta RSDRP(b): avgust 1917–fevral' 1918 g.* (Moscow, 1958), p. 6.

24. For a collection of his 1917 speeches, see Bukharin, *Na podstupakh k oktiabriu: stat'i i rechi mai—dekabr' 1917 g.* (Moscow and Leningrad, 1926). His many activities in 1917 are documented in the various memoirs, documents, and histories cited above in this chapter. See also Vera Vladimirova *et al.*, *Revoliutsiia 1917 goda (khronika sobytii)* (6 vols; Moscow and Leningrad, 1927–1929?), III, pp. 59, 65, 169, 233; IV, pp. 127, 251, 265, 291; V, p. 173; and VI, p. 89.

25. Max Eastman, *Love and Revolution* (New York, 1964), p. 353; *Oktiabr'skoe vosstanie v Moskve*, pp. 56–7; John Reed, *Ten Days That Shook the World* (New York, 1935), p. 253.

26. Neither *Sotsial Demokrat* nor *Spartak* have been available. Several of his articles are collected in his *Na podstupakh*. He wrote frequently in 1917 under the name K. Tverdovskii.

27. *Economic Theory of the Leisure Class*, pp. 9–10.

28. Bukharin, *Klassovaia bor'ba i revoliutsiia v Rossii* (Moscow, 1917). A sequel appeared in early 1918. Both were then published together as *Ot krusheniia tsarizma do padeniia burzhuazii* (Kharkov, 1923). For the reviewer, see *Proletarskaia revoliutsiia*, No. 10, 1922, p. 496.

29. See *Voprosy istorii KPSS*, No. 9, 1967, p. 93; Trotsky, *Russian Revolution*, III, pp. 145–6; and Daniels, *Red October*, pp. 56, 65, 90.

30. In addition to material on Moscow cited above, see *Moskovskii voenno-revoliutsionnyi komitet: oktiabr'–noiabr' 1917 goda* (Moscow, 1968); and S. Mel'gunov, *Kak bol'sheviki zakhvatili vlast'* (Paris, 1953), pp. 277–373.

31. Maretskii, "Bukharin," pp. 273–4; *Proletarskaia revoliutsiia*, No. 10, 1922, pp. 165, 313; Bukharin in *Pravda*, October 25, 1928, p. 5; Vladimirova, *Revoliutsiia 1917 goda*, V, p. 173; *Oktiabr'skoe vosstanie v Moskve*, pp. 23, 39, 237; Mel'gunov, *Kak bol'sheviki zakhvatili vlast'*, p. 281.

32. Vladimirova, *Revoliutsiia 1917 goda*, VI, p. 89; *Oktiabr'skoe vosstanie v Moskve*, pp. 44–5; Bukharin, *Na podstupakh*, pp. 170–3.

33. The young Muscovites apparently developed, for example, the habit of meeting informally outside regular party channels, see *Proletarskaia revoliutsiia*, No. 10, 1922, pp. 304–5, 320, and No. 10, 1927, p. 168.

34. Though Bukharin seems to have been resented less, he, too, would feel the backlash later. See, for example, Olminskii's bitter attack on him in *Krasnaia nov'*, No. 1, 1921, pp. 247–51, which will be discussed in Chapter III.

35. See, for example, Lenin's April Theses and his "K peresmotru partiinoi programmy," written less than three weeks before the coup, *Soch.*, XX, p. 89; and XXI, p. 312. The party's program in 1917 was really no more than Lenin's April Theses. See Bukharin, "Programma oktiabria," *Pravda*, March 23, 1929, p. 2.

36. See, for example, Osinskii quoted on the ambiguities of workers' control, in E. H. Carr, *The Bolshevik Revolution* (3 vols; New York, 1951–3), II, p. 60.

37. Sukhanov, *Russian Revolution*, I, p. 284, and II, pp. 420–1, 554–5.

38. *Soch.*, XXVII, p. 401; similarly, see XXI, p. 312, where he warns Bukharin and Smirnov, only weeks before the coup, not to "*boast on the way to battle*."

39. Gankin and Fisher, *Bolsheviks*, pp. 230, 231, 398.

40. See his remarks in *Imperialism and World Economy*, pp. 69, 137; *Novyi mir* (New York), March 27, 1917, p. 4; and *Na podstupakh*, pp. 144–7. Compared to Western cities, he later recalled: "Moscow impressed me as being a shabby hamlet." *Pravda*, January 15, 1927, p. 3.

41. *Novyi mir* (New York), March 27, 1917, p. 4.

42. *Na podstupakh*, p. 146; *The Class Struggle* (New York), No. 1, 1917, p. 21; and his *Ot krusheniia tsarizma*, p. 7.

43. *Shestoi s"ezd*, pp. 104–5.

44. Revolutionary war, called for by Lenin in his April Theses, was written into the party's resolutions at the Sixth Congress in July. Only one Bolshevik, Stalin, questioned its feasibility and implications for Russia. *Ibid.*, p. 250.

45. As is evident from his *Spartak* articles on modern capitalism in May–September 1917. *Spartak* has not been available, but his articles were widely discussed and quoted. See, for example, *Bol'shevik*, No. 18, 1929, pp. 27–9, 37.

46. *Shestoi s"ezd*, p. 103. Similarly, see Bukharin quoted in N. Leman and S. Pokrovskii, *Ideinye istoki pravogo uklona: ob oshibkakh i uklonakh tov. Bukharina* (2nd ed.; Leningrad, 1930), p. 12.

47. *Shestoi s"ezd*, pp. 102–3, 138.

48. Reed, *Ten Days That Shook the World*, p. 248; see also Mel'gunov, *Kak bol'sheviki zakhvatili vlast'*, p. 316.

49. Their differences were reconciled when a new program was finally written and adopted in 1919. Bukharin's proposals were set out in *Spartak*, No. 4, 1917, which has not been available. For Lenin's views and a discussion of rival suggestions, see *Soch.*, XXI, pp. 297–318. For the 1917–19 program discussions, see also *Leninskii sbornik*, XIII, pp. 35–40.

50. *Shestoi s"ezd*, pp. 103, 137, 202.

51. *Proletarskaia revoliutsiia*, No. 10, 1922, p. 319.

52. *Na podstupakh*, pp. 144–7. Bukharin's compromise proposal regarding the forthcoming Constituent Assembly should also be noted. On November 29 (December 12), he suggested that rather than prevent the Assembly from convening, the Constitutional Democrats should be expelled and the left parties sit as a "revolutionary Convention." He hoped that Bolsheviks and left Socialist Revolutionaries together would have a majority, and that this would satisfy the widespread support for the Assembly among the population. *Protokoly tsentral'nogo komiteta*, pp. 149–50.

53. Daniels, *Red October*, p. 207; *Voprosy istorii KPSS*, No. 6, 1967, p. 21.

54. *Oktriabr'skoe vosstanie v Moskve*, p. 45.

CHAPTER III

1. Osinskii in *Deviatyi s"ezd RKP(b). Mart–aprel' 1920 goda: protokoly* (Moscow, 1960), p. 115.

2. Daniels, *Conscience*, pp. 63–9.

3. *Protokoly tsentral'nogo komiteta*, pp. 160–1. See also *Proletarskaia revoliutsiia*, No. 10, 1922, pp. 476, 485.

4. *Vserossiiskoe uchreditel'noe sobranie* (Moscow and Leningrad, 1930), pp. 25, 29.

5. *Dekrety oktiabr'skoi revoliutsii* (2 vols; Moscow, 1933), I, p. 226; E. N. Gorodetskii, *Rozhdenie sovetskogo gosudarstva: 1917–1918 gg.* (Moscow, 1965), pp. 242–3. The document was co-authored by Mikhail Savelev. See also Carr, *Bolshevik Revolution*, II, pp. 73–4.

6. Lenin, *Soch.*, XXII, p. 289; Carr, *Bolshevik Revolution*, II, pp. 74–5, 86; *Deiateli*, I, p. 339, and II, p. 96; M. P. Iroshnikov, *Sozdanie sovetskogo tsentral'nogo gosudarstvennogo apparata* (Moscow and Leningrad, 1966), p. 49.

7. See, for example, Lenin, *Soch.*, XXII, p. 596 n. 80; and N. K. Krupskaya, *Reminiscences of Lenin* (Moscow, 1959), p. 435.

8. Lenin, *PSS*, LIV, pp. 383, 691, n. 612; *Protokoly tsentral'nogo komiteta*, pp. 152–3; Lenin, *Soch.*, XXII, p. 588, n. 49; and *Pravda*, May 5, 1922, p. 7.

9. Iroshnikov, *Sozdanie sovetskogo tsentral'nogo gosudarstvennogo apparata*, p. 207.

10. For the history of Left Communism, see Schapiro, *Communist Autocracy*, Chapters vi, viii; and Daniels, *Conscience*, Chapter iii.

11. *Sed'moi ekstrennyi s"ezd RKP(b). Mart 1918 goda: stenograficheskii otchet* (Moscow, 1962), pp. 24–40. Bukharin, his contemporaries, and Soviet and Western historians agree on his leading role.

12. Schapiro, *Communist Autocracy*, pp. 100–1, 130; Daniels, *Conscience*, pp. 75–7; Iaroslavskii, *Istoriia VKP*, IV, p. 299; Trotsky, *My Life*, p. 383; Geogory Zinoviev, *Lenin* (London, 1966), p. 44.

13. Leon Trotsky, *Lenin* (New York, 1959), p. 108.

14. L. Stupochenko, "V brestskie dni," *Proletarskaia revoliutsiia*, No. 4, 1923, p. 97.

15. See, for example, his ambiguous remarks in *Sed'moi ekstrenny s"ezd*, pp. 247–8. That his position changed somewhat between early January and mid-February is also suggested by Lenin's remark on February 18: "Bukharin did not notice that he has gone over to the position of revolutionary war." Quoted in Gaisinskii, *Bor'ba s uklonami*, p. 21.

16. *Sed'moi ekstrenny s"ezd*, pp. 34, 299.

17. Andrei Bubnov, *VKP(b)* (Moscow and Leningrad, 1931), p. 651.

18. *Kommunist* began publication in Petrograd, where eleven issues appeared between March 5 and 19 under the editorship of Bukharin, Uritskii, and Radek. It was re-established in Moscow as the "Organ of the Moscow Region Bureau," where four issues appeared between April 20 and early June.

19. *The Case of the Anti-Soviet "Bloc of Rights and Trotskyites": Report of Court Proceedings* (Moscow, 1938), p. 482; Lenin, *Soch.*, XXII, p. 609, n. 128; Schapiro, *Communist Autocracy*, p. 135; *Leninskii sbornik*, XI, p. 46.

20. *Leninskii sbornik*, XI, pp. 47, 48; and Bukharin in *Pravda*, January 21, 1925, p. 1. When Lenin called the Left Communists "premature Left Socialist Revolutionaries," Bukharin replied: "Then Lenin is our papa." *Leninskii sbornik*, XI, p. 85.

21. For this murky episode, see the various accounts in *Pravda*, January 3, 1924; and Schapiro, *Communist Autocracy*, pp. 117, 142–4.

22. Quoted in Voline, *Nineteen Seventeen: The Russian Revolution Betrayed* (New York, 1954), pp. 97–8.

23. See, for example, Osinskii's objections to Bukharin in *Shestoi s"ezd*, pp. 107–8. In addition, Bukharin clearly did not share Lomov's willingness to exclude Lenin from power nor Uritskii's desire to tie the dispute to past controversies. See their remarks in *Sed'moi ekstrennyi s"ezd*, pp. 243, 249, 267. Finally, see the remarks of Bukharin and Zinoviev in *Sed'moi ekstrennyi s"ezd*, pp. 44–5, 248.

24. Trotsky, *Russian Revolution*, III, pp. 392–3. See also Bukharin in *Sed'moi ekstrennyi s"ezd*, p. 31.

25. *Sed'moi ekstrennyi s"ezd*, pp. 32–3; also, pp. 25–6, 104.

26. *Ibid.*, pp. 24, 31.

27. *Ibid.*, pp. 27–9; also pp. 258–9, 261, 263.

28. Trotsky, *Russian Revolution*, III, p. 392; Liberman, *Building Lenin's Russia*, pp. 24, 69; Reed, *Ten Days That Shook the World*, p. 125.

29. *Sed'moi ekstrennyi s"ezd*, pp. 26, 31–2, 35, 106, 243, 248, 292, 321.

30. *Ibid.*, pp. 263–4; Trotsky, *My Life*, pp. 389–90.

31. *Sed'moi ekstrennyi s"ezd*, pp. 24, 29.

32. "Mezhdunarodnoe khoziaistvo i bor'ba gosudarstv," *Novyi mir* (New York), August 17, 1917, p. 4. This had been and was to remain a regular theme in Bukharin's writings. See, for example, his "Krizis burzhuaznoi kul'tury," *Pravda*, November 7, 1922, p. 7.

33. *Sed'moi ekstrennyi s"ezd*, p. 109; also see his speech to this congress, pp. 7–24.

34. Quoted in V. Sorin, *Partiia i oppozitsii: iz istorii oppozitsionnykh techenii (fraktsiia levykh kommunistov)* (Moscow, 1925), p. 72.

35. *Sed'moi ekstrennyi s"ezd*, pp. 26, 29–31, 34–5, 104–5, 266.

36. *Ibid.*, pp. 26, 33–5, 105, 107–9, 261.

37. Both points are made in John Erickson, *The Soviet High Command* (New York, 1962), pp. 27, 676 n. 11. See also Deutscher, *Prophet Armed*, p. 388. Probably for political reasons, Bukharin later said Lenin had been right about the benefits of a "breathing spell." *Pravda*, October 11, 1918, p. 3.

38. Carr, *Bolshevik Revolution*, II, pp. 35, 55–88; Maurice Dobb, *Russian Economic Development Since the Revolution* (London, 1928), Chapter ii.

39. See his article in *Soch.*, XXII, pp. 435–68, which elaborated on proposals originally made on April 4, and, for his answer to his critics, pp. 469–98, 505–28.

40. *Ibid.*, pp. 482, 483.

41. Drafted on April 4, the Left's theses appeared as "Tezisy o tekushchem momente" in *Kommunist* (Moscow), No. 1, 1918. They are reprinted in Lenin, *Soch.*, XXII, pp. 561–71.

42. See, for example, Bukharin, *V zashchitu proletarskoi diktatury: sbornik* (Moscow and Leningrad, 1928), pp. 133–4; and his remarks in *Inprecor*, VIII (1928), p. 988.

43. "Nekotorye osnovnye poniatiia sovremennoi ekonomiki," *Kommunist* (Moscow), No. 3, 1918. This issue has not been available; but Bukharin's article was widely quoted and will be discussed below.

44. *Programma kommunistov (bol'shevikov)* (Petrograd, 1918); and Sidney Heitman, "Between Lenin and Stalin: Nikolai Bukharin," in *Revisionism*, p. 80.

45. This interpretation is contrary to that of most Soviet and Western historians, who portray Bukharin as the leader of the economic opposition. It is, however, confirmed, if only inadvertently, by the basic Soviet source. See A. Sidorov, "Ekonomicheskaia programma oktiabria i diskussiia s 'levymi kommunistami' o zadachakh sotsialisticheskogo stroitel'stva," *Proletarskaia revoliutsiia*, No. 6 (89), 1929, pp. 26–75, and No. 11 (94), 1929, pp. 26–64.

46. See *ibid.*, No. 6 (89), 1929, pp. 57–8; Osinskii's autobiography in *Deiateli*, II, p. 96; *Case of the Anti-Soviet Bloc*, pp. 465–6. See also N. Osinskii, *Stroitel'stvo sotsializma* (Moscow, 1918); his speech in *Trudy I vserossiiskogo s"ezda sovetov narodnogo khoziaistva: stenograficheskii otchet* (Moscow, 1918), pp. 56–64; and his "Priamye otvety," *Kommunist* (Moscow), No. 2, 1918, pp. 16–18.

47. See, for example, N. Bucharin (*sic*), *The Communist Program* (New York, 1920), pp. 20–1, 50–1; "Anarchizm i nauchnyi kommunizm," *Kommunist*, No. 2, 1918, p. 11; *Na podstupakh*, p. 145; "Sindikalizm i kommunizm," *Pravda*, January 25, 1918, p. 1; and Bukharin quoted in Lenin, *Soch.*, XXII, pp. 494, 519.

48. *Soch.*, XXII, p. 492.

49. The theses appeared over the signature of *Kommunist's* "editorial board," that is, Bukharin, Osinskii, Smirnov, and Radek.

50. *Leninskii sbornik*, XI, p. 54; *Trudy I vserossiiskogo sovetov narodnogo khoziaistva*, p. 7.

51. Their dispute over a new party program, for example, flared up again, but was resolved through mutual compromise. See *Sed'moi ekstrennyi s"ezd*, pp. 148–53, 160–1, 163.

52. *The Communist Program*, pp. 36–7, 40–5; *Na podstupakh*, pp. 145–6; *Protokoly zasedanii vserossiiskogo tsentral'nogo isponitel'nogo komiteta. 4-go sozyva* (Moscow, 1920), p. 233; *Trudy I vserossiiskogo s"ezda sovetov narodnogo khoziaistva*, p. 7.

53. *The Communist Program*, p. 43; *Kommunist*, No. 1, 1918, p. 20; and Bukharin quoted in Osinskii, *Stroitel'stvo sotsializma*, p. 25.

54. *The Communist Program*, p. 43.

55. Carr, *Bolshevik Revolution*, II, p. 396.

56. See *ibid.*, pp. 59–60; *Na podstupakh*, pp. 145–6; and *The Communist Program*, pp. 49–56.

57. *Protokoly zasedanii vserossiiskogo tsentral'nogo ispolnitel'nogo komiteta*, pp. 233–4; and Lenin, *Soch.*, XXII, p. 494.

58. See Bukharin's review of *State and Revolution* in *Kommunist*, No. 1, 1918, p. 19; and Lenin, *Soch.*, XXI, pp. 446, 451. See also Lenin's reaffirmation of the vision in *Sed'moi ekstrennyi s"ezd*, pp. 143–4.

59. Bukharin, *The Communist Program*, p. 26; and Daniels, *Conscience*, p. 86.

60. *Protokoly zasedanii vserossiiskogo tsentral'nogo ispolnitel'nogo komiteta*, p. 234.

61. See, for example, his remarks in *Vserossiiskoe uchreditel'noe sobranie*, p. 26.

62. Quoted in Bukharin, *Ekonomika perekhodnogo perioda*, p. 106; and *Proletarskaia revoliutsiia*, No. 11 (94), 1929, pp. 46–7. See also above, note 43.

63. *Ekonomika perekhodnogo perioda*, p. 107. As Bukharin later acknowledged, he and Lenin were never able to agree on the concept of state capitalism. See *Krasnaia nov'*, No. 4, 1925, p. 265.

64. *Proletarskaia revoliutsiia*, No. 11 (94), 1929, p. 49; see also Leman and Pokrovskii, *Ideinye istoki pravogo uklona*, pp. 62–3.

65. Lenin, *Soch.*, XXII, p. 513.

66. *Ataka*, pp. 259–60.

67. See, for example, Lenin's remarks in *Soch.*, XXIII, p. 40.

68. *Pravda*, October 25, 1928, p. 3.

69. *Voprosy istorii KPSS*, No. 1, 1967, p. 60.

70. Carr, *Bolshevik Revolution*, II, pp. 51, 53, 98–9; Dobb, *Russian Economic Development*, pp. 58, 59; Leonard Schapiro, *The Communist Party of the Soviet Union* (New York, 1960), p. 188.

71. Serge, *Memoirs*, p. 117. See also Carr, *Bolshevik Revolution*, II, pp. 147–268.

72. Schapiro, *Communist Party*, p. 191.

73. N. Buharin (*sic*) and E. Preobrazhensky, *The ABC of Communism* (London, 1922), pp. 196–7. See also his speech in *Vos'maia konferentsiia RKP(b): protokoly* (Moscow, 1961), p. 165; and *Deviatyi s"ezd*, pp. 137–8.

74. "The International Bourgeoisie and Karl Kautsky, Its Apostle," *Inprecor*, V (1925), p. 921.

75. Bukharin, *Historical Materialism*, p. 260; and *Pravda*, March 23, 1929, p. 3. The best Soviet study of these years, published shortly afterward, is Kritsman's *The Heroic Period of the Great Russian Revolution*.

76. See Daniels, *Conscience*, pp. 93, 104–15; Schapiro, *Communist Autocracy*, Chapter xiii; and *Iz istorii bor'by leninskoi partii protiv opportunizma* (Moscow, 1966), pp. 388–420.

77. *Deviatyi s"ezd*, pp. 135–9.

78. For Bukharin's resignation, see *Sed'moi ekstrennyi s"ezd*, pp. 265, 269.

79. *Pravda*, October 11, 1918, p. 5. See also *XV konferentsiia vsesoiuznoi kommunisticheskoi partii(b) 26 oktiabria–3 noiabria 1926 g.: stenograficheskii otchet* (Moscow and Leningrad, 1927), pp. 594–5.

80. *Pravda*, October 11, 1918, p. 5.

81. They were debated at the party congress in March 1919. See *Vos'moi s"ezd RKP(b): protokoly* (Moscow, 1959), particularly pp. 45–8, 107–10. For the compromises involving preparation of the party program, see *Leninskii sbornik*, III, pp. 458–9, 481–7, and XIII, pp. 56–8.

82. See Adam Ulam, *The Bolsheviks* (New York, 1965), p. 360; and Fischer, *Lenin*, p. 222. There is some evidence that Bukharin was the Bolshevik leader closest to the Lenin family at this time. See M. I. Ul'ianova, *O Lenine* (Moscow, 1964), p. 86. He was especially close to Lenin's sister, Mariia. Their relationship will be discussed in Chapter VII.

83. *PSS*, L, pp. 87–8.

84. L. D. Trotskii, *O Lenine* (Moscow, 1924), p. 106. According to Trotsky, his quotation later provoked a storm in the post-Lenin leadership: "Stalin, Zinoviev, and Kamenev . . . felt terribly offended by it. . . . But the fact remains that Lenin only mentioned Sverdlov and Bukharin." *My Life*, p. 338.

85. Schapiro, *Communist Autocracy*, p. 367; *Vos'moi s"ezd*, p. 341; *Vos'maia konferentsiia*, p. 221; Lenin, *Soch.*, XXV, p. 604, n. 63.

86. See, for example, *Pravda*, May 5, 1927, p. 2; and Lenin's correspondence in *PSS*, L, p. 291, LI, pp. 203, 225, 251, 272, and LIV, p. 291.

87. *Pamiati Karla Libknekhta i Rozy Liuksemburg: sbornik statei* (Petrograd, 1919), p. 26; Maretskii, "Bukharin," p. 274.

88. Lenin, *PSS*, L, p. 229; also Bukharin's discussion of the document in *Pervyi kongress Kominterna. Mart 1919* (Moscow, 1933), pp. 75–85.

89. "Rasskaz 'tovarishcha Tomasa,'" *Sotsialisticheskii vestnik: sbornik No. 1* (April 1964), pp. 132, 141 n. 16; *Kommunisticheskii internatsional: kratkii istoricheskii ocherk* (Moscow, 1969), p. 98; Franz Borkenau, *World Communism* (Ann Arbor, Mich., 1962), pp. 163–5.

90. Iuri P. Denike, Interview No. 17 (unpublished manuscript, The Menshevik Project, Columbia University, October 25, 1963).

91. See, for example, *Soviet Russia*, II (1920), p. 46; Lenin, *PSS*, LI, pp. 47, 385; Nicolaevsky, *Power and the Soviet Elite*, p. 18; and *Deviatyi s"ezd*, pp. 70, 223, 247, 558–61.

92. *Desiatyi s"ezd*, pp. 293–4; Denike, Interview No. 17; Isaac McBride, *"Barbarous Soviet Russia"* (New York, 1920), p. 108.

93. *Leninskii sbornik*, XIII, p. 31; *Ataka*, p. 203.

94. Bukharin in *Tretii vserossiiskii s"ezd RKSM 2–10 oktiabria 1920 goda: stenograficheskii otchet* (Moscow and Leningrad, 1926), p. 126.

95. *Vos'moi s"ezd*, p. 49.

96. *Sotsialisticheskii vestnik*, No. 9, 1925, p. 10; and *The Militant*, October 15, 1929, p. 6.

97. *The ABC*, p. 13, and Chapter xiv.

98. *Ibid.*, p. 23.

99. See Bukharin's "Po povodu poriadka dnia partiinogo s"ezda," *Pravda*, January 25, 1923, p. 1; Sidney Heitman's introduction to a reprint of *The ABC* (Ann Arbor, Mich., 1966), not paged; Isaac Deutscher, *Stalin: A Political Biography* (2nd ed.; New York, 1967), p. 299; and Löwy, *Die Weltgeschichte*, p. 115.

100. Maretskii, "Bukharin," p. 282; F. A. Mackenzie, *Russia Before the Dawn* (London, 1923), p. 35.

101. See Olminskii's remarks about the "obligatory character" of *The ABC* in *Krasnaia nov'*, No. 1, 1921, p. 247; and the cartoon testifying to its biblical status in *Prozhektor*, No. 8, 1923, p. 26.

102. See Zev Katz, "Party-Political Education in Soviet Russia" (unpublished Ph.D. dissertation, University of London), pp. 94, 232, 347, 440, 448, 568; Denike, Interview No. 17; and Bukharin's foreword to I. Podvolotskii, *Marksistskaia teoriia prava: ocherk* (Moscow, 1923). See also his report on the training of new party cadres in *Vos'maia konferentsiia*, pp. 156–68.

103. See B. Nikolaevskii, "Vneshniaia politika Moskvy," *Novyi zhurnal*, No. 1, 1942, pp. 238–9; and Bukharin's remarks in *Pravda*, March 23, 1929, p. 3.

104. See, for example, Stanley W. Page, *Lenin and World Revolution* (New York, 1959), p. 128; *Ataka*, p. 99; *Pervyi kongress Kominterna*, p. 84; and Bukharin's speech reprinted in *The Second Congress of the Communist International as Reported and Interpreted by the Official Newspapers of Soviet Russia* (Washington, D.C., 1920), pp. 133–4.

105. *Vos'moi s"ezd*, pp. 36, 40.

106. *Ataka*, pp. 95, 111; similarly, *The ABC*, p. 81.

107. *Ataka*, p. 111; and, similarly, *Deviatyi s"ezd*, pp. 217, 418.

108. *Deviatyi s"ezd*, pp. 215–16, 260–1; *Ataka*, pp. 89–114.

109. See, for example, his "Ekonomika diktatury proletariata," *Pravda*, December 19, 1918, p. 1; *Ataka*, p. 112; and "S"ezd sovkhozov," *Pravda*, January 22, 1920, p. 1.

110. *Vos'moi s"ezd*, pp. 44, 114; *Pervyi kongress Kominterna*, p. 82; "Sel'kokhoziaistvennye kommuny ili khlebnye fabriki?," *Pravda*, December 20, 1918, p. 1; *The ABC*, p. 323; "S"ezd zemotdelov, kommun, kombedov," *Pravda*, December 22, 1918, p. 1; and *Deviatyi s"ezd*, p. 215.

111. See Dobb, *Russian Economic Development*, p. 61.

112. *Soch.*, XXIV, p. 536. See also his later admission that the leadership as a whole had believed in the efficacy of the policies. *Ibid.*, XXVII, p. 29. For a collection of party views during war communism, see *Oktiabr'skii perevorot i diktatura proletariata: sbornik* (Moscow, 1919).

113. *Ataka*, p. 104.

114. See *Ekonomika perekhodnogo perioda*, pp. 5–6, 123 n. 1; and Bukharin's and Piatakov's joint answer to its critics, "Kavaleriiskii reid i tiazhelaia artilleriia," *Krasnaia nov'*, No. 1, 1921, pp. 256–74.

115. *VKA*, XXVI (1928), pp. 12–14. The other two were Lenin's *State and Revolution* and Kritsman's *The Heroic Period of the Great Russian Revolution*. For the influence of *The Economics*, see Adam Kaufman, "The Origin of 'The Political Economy of Socialism': An Essay on Soviet Economic Thought," *Soviet Studies*, No. 3, 1953, pp. 244–5, 248.

116. See Chapters i–iii, vii, and xi.

117. See, for example, Lenin's "The Proletarian Revolution and the Renegade Kautsky," *Soch.*, XXIII, pp. 331–412; and Trotsky's *Terrorism and Communism: A Reply to Karl Kautsky* (Ann Arbor, Mich., 1961).

118. "Diktatura proletariata v Rossii i mirovaia revoliutsiia," *Kommunisticheskii internatsional*, No. 4, 1919, pp. 487–8; *Historical Materialism*, p. 266.

119. *Ekonomika perekhodnogo perioda*, Chapters iii, vi, and pp. 63–4.

120. *Ibid.*, pp. 48, 97–8.

121. For Hilferding, see *ibid.*, p. 47; and *VKA*, XXVI (1928), p. 13. Bukharin described the prevailing social democratic views as follows: "The proletariat . . . removes the commanding 'heads,' whom it dismisses more or less gently, and then assumes control of the social apparatus of production, which has been developed to a splendid and uninjured maturity in the bowels of the capitalist Abraham. The proletariat installs its own 'heads' and the thing is done." *Historical Materialism*, pp. 259–60.

122. See the unnamed person mentioned in Ne-revizionist, "O knige tov. N. Bukharina (otvet tov. M. Ol'minskomu)," *Krasnaia nov'*, No. 1. 1921, pp. 254–5.

123. See the remarks of Bukharin and Piatakov in *Krasnaia nov'*, No. 1, 1921, pp. 257, 272; Pokrovskii's comment that it represented a turning point in political economy, *VKA*, XXVI (1928), pp. 13–14; Kritsman, *Geroicheskii period*, pp. 19, n. 2, 167, n. 144; *Krasnaia nov'*, No. 1, 1921, p. 254; and Maretskii, "Bukharin," pp. 280, 282.

124. *Ekonomika perekhodnogo perioda*, pp. 52–6.

125. *Ibid.*, p. 60; also p. 58.

126. The concept of equilibrium was implicit in Volume II of *Capital*, where Marx had employed static and dynamic models to explain capitalist accumulation, and explicit in Chapter xvi of Hilferding's *Finance Capital*. The importance of the concept in Bukharin's economic thinking over the years is discussed in Knirsch, *Bucharins*.

127. *Ekonomika perekhodnogo perioda*, pp. 127–8; also pp. 129–30, n. 1.

128. *Ibid.*, pp. 56, 113; for the process of "statization" and militarization, see especially Chapters vi–viii.

129. *Ibid.*, pp. 108–9. This argument appears throughout. See pp. 63–4, 71–2, 83–4.

130. *Ibid.*, pp. 84, 138–9.

131. As did his party critics. See Olminskii's attack in *Krasnaia nov'*, No. 1, 1921, pp. 247–51.

132. *Ekonomika perekhodnogo perioda*, pp. 7–8.

133. See Oskar Lange, *Political Economy*, I (New York, 1963), p. 84, n. 46; and Kaufman, "The Origin of 'The Political Economy of Socialism,'" p. 248. For confirmation that it was the majority Bolshevik view, see *Proletarskaia revoliutsiia*, No. 12, 1929, p. 178. See also the debate of the question in *VKA*, XI (1925), pp. 257–346.

134. *Ekonomika perekhodnogo perioda*, pp. 124–5, 134–5.

135. Both charges were leveled by Olminskii in *Krasnaia nov'*, No. 1, 1921, pp. 247–51; and partly also by Lenin's elder sister A. I. Elizarova. See the discussion of an archive copy of her 1921 review, *Voprosy istorii KPSS*, No. 1, 1972, pp. 118–22.

136. See, for example, *Ekonomika perekhodnogo perioda*, pp. 138–9, and his comment on the role of coercion in creating a Communist man, p. 146.

137. *Ibid.*, pp. 62–3, 101–3, 110, 132–3, and Chapter viii *passim*.

138. *Ibid.*, pp. 132–3. Later, when Bukharin's thinking had changed, his critics would cite this passage as evidence that he had once understood that equilibrium did not apply to the transition period. See A. Leont'ev, *Ekonomicheskaia teoriia pravogo uklona* (Moscow and Leningrad, 1929), p. 41.

139. *Ekonomika perekhodnogo perioda*, pp. 82–5, 146, and Chapter v *passim*.

140. *Ibid.*, pp. 85–7.

141. *Ibid.*, p. 151.

142. L. Trotskii, *Sochineniia*, XII (Moscow and Leningrad, 1925), p. 413, n. 19. For evidence that parts of the book influenced non-Bolsheviks as well, see A. V. Chayanov, *The Theory of Peasant Economy* (Homewood, Ill., 1966), pp. xliii–iv; and Chayanov quoted by Bukharin and Piatakov in *Krasnaia nov'*, No. 1, 1921, pp. 272–3.

143. For Olminskii's attack and defenses by Bukharin and a pseudonymous author, see *Krasnaia nov'*, No. 1, 1921, pp. 247–51, 252–74. Olminskii apparently first planned to voice his objections in a letter to the Central Committee, but decided instead on a public review. It was dated April 1921, and written just after the introduction of NEP. He was especially worried about the book's influence on the young. He was supported by Lenin's elder sister. See *Voprosy istorii*, No. 5, 1964, pp. 23–4; and above, note 135.

144. *Leninskii sbornik*, XI, pp. 347–403.

145. *Ibid.*, pp. 355, 356, 359, 360, 361, 369, 371, 372, 385, 387, 400–1.

146. Early in his career, Lenin, too, had used "sociological" language. See, for example, *Soch.*, I, pp. 55–115. But his bitter philosophical (and political) dispute with Bogdanov in 1909 and after seems to have made him distrustful of contemporary Western social thought and particularly any effort to enrich Marxism with it. Their different intellectual orientations underlay the recurring clashes between Lenin and Bukharin over Bogdanov's work. In September 1920, for example, Bukharin protested a bad-tempered article on Bogdanov by V. Nevskii, which Lenin liked and sponsored. Bukharin complained that the issue was not whether Bogdanov's ideas were correct, but rather to understand them, and "this minimum Nevskii does not have." *Leninskii sbornik*, XII, pp. 384–5.

147. *Leninskii sbornik*, XI, pp. 396, 402.

148. *Pravda*, October 25, 1928, p. 3.

149. Eric Hoffer, *The True Believer* (New York, 1960), p. 20.

150. As would be at least tacitly admitted in some later official accounts. See, for example, A. Aikhenval'd, *Sovetskaia ekonomika* (Moscow and Leningrad, 1927), p. 31; and A. Slepkov, *Kronshtadtskii miatezh* (Moscow and Leningrad, 1928), p. 15.

151. Bukharin, "S"ezd sovkhozov," *Pravda*, January 22, 1920, p. 1.

152. For this period, see Paul Avrich, *Kronstadt 1921* (Princeton, N.J., 1970), Chapter i.

153. See Leon Trotsky, *The New Course* (London, 1956), pp. 60–1; and Deutscher, *Prophet Armed*, pp. 496–8.

154. For Osinskii's proposals, see his *Gosudarstvennoe regulirovanie krest'-ianskogo khoziaistva* (Moscow, 1920); and *Deiateli*, II, p. 93. For Politburo discussion and Lenin, see Carr, *Bolshevik Revolution*, II, pp. 280–1; and *Istoriia kommunisticheskoi partii sovetskogo soiuza*, IV (Moscow, 1970), Book 1, pp. 47, 49.

155. Bukharin, "O likvidatorstve nashikh dnei," *Bol'shevik*, No. 2, 1924, p. 4.

156. See Bukharin's remarks on Heine in *Inprecor*, VIII (1928), p. 158.

157. Arthur Ransome, *Russia in 1919* (London, 1920), pp. 82–3.

158. B. Dvinov, *Moskovskii sovet rabochikh deputatov 1917–1922: vospominaniia* (New York, 1961), p. 181; and Bukharin in *The Communist Review*, No. 6, 1921, p. 73.

159. For these events, see Denike, Interview No. 17; Nicolaevsky, *Power and the Soviet Elite*, p. 18; Liberman, *Building Lenin's Russia*, p. 70. For Bukharin at the Cheka, see also Lenin, *PSS*, LI, p. 47.

160. *Vzryv 25 sentiabria 1919 g.* (Moscow, 1920), pp. 19–20.

161. *Ekonomika perekhodnogo perioda*, p. 147; see, for example, his discussion in Chapter iv of how the technical intelligentsia is drawn into socialist construction.

162. *Ibid.*, p. 42.

163. *The ABC*, p. 195.

164. "Rabochaia aristokratiia ili splochenie rabochikh mass?", *Pravda*, September 14, 1919, p. 2. For other examples of his remarks on Soviet bureaucracy, see *Pravda*, December 19, 1918, p. 1, and November 21, 1919, p. 1.

165. *Sed'moi ekstrennyi s"ezd*, p. 25.

166. *Ekonomika perekhodnogo perioda*, pp. 52, 58, 64, 142–3; see also *Vos'moi s"ezd*, p. 43.

167. *Desiatyi s"ezd*, pp. 221, 224, 225.

168. *Pravda*, January 22, 1920, p. 1; *Pravda*, February 18, 1920, p. 1; *Tretii vserossiiskii s"ezd professional'nykh soiuzov: stenograficheskii otchet* (Moscow, 1921), pp. 5–6; *Pravda*, May 30, 1920, p. 2; *Tretii vserossiiskii s"ezd RKSM*, pp. 38–44, 50–2, 57.

169. *Proizvodstvennaia propaganda* (Moscow, 1920), pp. 7, 11–12; and Michael Farbman, *Bolshevism in Retreat* (London, 1923), p. 266.

170. *Tretii vserossiiskii s"ezd RKSM*, 52; *Proizvodstvennaia propaganda*, p. 7, 11–12.

171. Quoted in *Proletarskaia revoliutsiia*, No. 12, 1929, p. 16.

172. See Schapiro, *Communist Autocracy*, Chapters xiv–xvii; and Daniels, *Conscience*, Chapter v.

173. The main platforms are reprinted in Lenin, *Soch.*, XXVI, pp. 540–78.

174. "K vyboram po moskovskuiu konferentsiiu," *Pravda*, November 15, 1920, p. 1.

175. *XIV s"ezd vsesoiuznoi kommunisticheskoi partii(b) 18–31 dekabria 1925 g.: stenograficheskii otchet* (Moscow and Leningrad, 1926), p. 398.

176. *Diskussiia o profsoiuzakh: materialy i dokumenty 1920–1921* (Moscow and Leningrad, 1927), pp. 78–80; Lenin, *Soch.*, XXVI, p. 132.

177. Lenin, *Soch.*, XXVI, pp. 114, 569–73; *Diskussiia o profsoiuzakh*, pp. 78–81; and Bukharin quoted in Iaroslavskii, *Istoriia VKP*, IV, p. 438, and in *Proletarskaia revoliutsiia*, No. 12, 1929, p. 14.

178. *Soch.*, XXVI, pp. 63–81, 92–3, 113–45.

179. *Selected Works*, III, p. 793.

180. *Soch.*, XXVI, p. 93; see also *Deviatyi s"ezd*, p. 380.

181. Bukharin, "Sindikalizm i kommunizm," *Pravda*, January 25, 1921, p. 1. For their joint platform, see Lenin, *Soch.*, XXVI, pp. 551–62. It was signed by many people, including eight Central Committee members.

182. Lenin, *Soch.*, XXVI, p. 558; and Bukharin quoted in *Proletarskaia revoliutsiia*, No. 12, 1929, p. 34.

183. "Grom ne grianet, muzhik ne perekrestitsia," *Pravda*, February 15, 1921, p. 1.

184. Slepkov, *Kronshtadtskii miatezh*, p. 15.

185. For these events and the rebellion, see Avrich, *Kronstadt 1917*.

186. *Desiatyi s"ezd*, pp. 403–15.

187. Elizaveta Drabkina, "Zimnii pereval," *Novyi mir*, No. 10, 1968, p. 39.

188. *Desiatyi s"ezd*, p. 328.

CHAPTER IV

1. *Bol'shevik*, No. 2, 1924, pp. 3–4.

2. *Desiatyi s"ezd*, p. 230.

3. The major Western statement is Raymond A. Bauer, *The New Man in Soviet Psychology* (Cambridge, Mass., 1952), Chapter ii. Similarly, see Gustav A. Wetter, *Dialectical Materialism* (New York, 1958), pp. 143–9. For examples of the Soviet argument, see I. Luppol, "K voprosu o teoreticheskikh korniakh pravogo uklona," *Bol'shevik*, No. 18, 1929, pp. 11–25; and B. Gessen and I. Podvolotskii, "Filosofskie korni pravogo opportunizma," *PZM*, No. 9, 1929, pp. 1–29.

4. *Teoriia istoricheskogo materializma: populiarnyi uchebnik marksistskoi sotsiologii* (Moscow, 1921). Unless otherwise indicated, all references are to the English translation, *Historical Materialism*.

5. David Joravsky, *Soviet Marxism and Natural Science: 1917–1932* (New York, 1961), pp. 48, 54, 56, and Chapter iii.

6. See V. Sarabianov's review in *PZM*, No. 3, 1922, pp. 62–76; and Bukharin, "Po skuchnoi doroge (otvet moim kritikam)," *Krasnaia nov'*, No. 1, 1923, pp. 275–89.

7. For Trotsky, see Joravsky, *Soviet Marxism*, pp. 97–100; for Preobrazhenskii, see his "Problema khoziaistvennogo ravnovesiia pri konkretnom kapitalizme i v sovetskoi sisteme," *VKA*, XVII (1926), pp. 35–76, and XVIII (1926), pp. 63–84.

8. Rykov quoted in Joravsky, *Soviet Marxism*, p. 40.

9. *Teoriia istoricheskogo materializma* (Moscow and Petrograd, 1923), pp. 5–6; Bukharin, "K postanovke problem teorii istoricheskogo materializma (beglye zametki)," *Ataka*, pp. 115–16.

10. See Pitirim Sorokin's review in *Ekonomist*, No. 3, 1922, p. 148.

11. *Historical Materialism*, Chapters i–ii, vi, and pp. 76–9, 226, 268.

12. *Ibid.*, pp. 207–8, 264; also *Krasnaia nov'*, No. 1, 1923, pp. 287–8.

13. *Historical Materialism*, pp. 169, 227, 228, 256; also *Ekonomika perekhodnogo perioda*, p. 62.

14. *Historical Materialism*, Chapter viii. Bukharin enumerated what he thought were his successful innovations in *Ataka*, pp. 115–27.

15. See, for example, the treatment of Bukharin as a theorist in V. Polonskii, *Ocherkii literaturnogo dvizheniia revoliutsionnoi epokhi* (2nd ed.; Moscow and Leningrad, 1929), Chapter viii.

16. Quoted in Hughes, *Consciousness and Society*, p. 79. In addition to Hughes (Chapters iii, viii), for the impact of Marxism on early sociological thought, see T. B. Bottomore and Maximilien Rubel, *Karl Marx: Selected Writings in Sociology and Social Philosophy* (New York, 1964), pp. 29–48.

17. In addition to note 16, see T. B. Bottomore, "Karl Marx, Sociologist or Marxist?", *Science and Society*, XXX (1966), pp. 11–24; Ralf Dahrendorf, *Class and Class Conflict in Industrial Society* (Stanford, Calif., 1966), Part I; and Raymond Aron, *Main Currents in Sociological Thought*, I (Garden City, N.Y., 1968), pp. 145–236.

18. In *Consciousness and Society*, p. 74.

19. In the English translation, *Historical Materialism: A System of Marxist Sociology*.

20. *Ibid.*, pp. xii–xv.

21. *Ibid.*, pp. x–xii; see, for example, his effort to answer the élite theories of Michels and Pareto, pp. 309–11.

22. Bottomore and Rubel, *Karl Marx*, pp. 39–45; George Lichtheim, *Marxism: An Historical and Critical Survey* (New York, 1962), p. 305.

23. The history of Russian and Soviet sociological ideas remains to be written. Among the existing, largely fragmentary studies are Pitirim Sorokin, "Russian Sociology in the Twentieth Century," *American Sociological Society: Papers and Proceedings*, XXI (1926), pp. 57–69; and *Soviet Sociology: Historical Antecedents and Current Appraisals*, edited by Alex Simirenko (Chicago, 1966).

24. *Soch.*, I, p. 62.

25. *PSS*, XLIX, p. 294.

26. *Soviet Sociology*, p. 19; see also the discussion in *Istorik marksist*, II (1929), pp. 189–213.

27. See, for example, *PZM*, No. 3, 1922, pp. 62–3, and No. 11–12, 1922, pp. 172–3. Bukharin complained of people who "imagine that the theory of historical materialism should under no circumstances be considered a Marxian sociology." *Historical Materialism*, pp. xiv–xv.

28. *Kommunisticheskaia revoliutsiia*, No. 2, 1930, p. 20.

29. Polonskii, *Ocherki literaturnogo dvizheniia*, p. 178. For Sorokin, see *Ekonomist*, No. 3, 1922, p. 148.

30. See Seymour Martin Lipset's introduction to Robert Michels, *Political Parties* (New York, 1962), p. 27, n. 22.

31. For the differences between Marx and Engels, see Z. A. Jordan, *The Evolution of Dialectical Materialism* (New York, 1967); for Lenin, see his *Filosofskie tetradi* (Moscow, 1933); and for Deborin, see René Ahlberg, "The Forgotten Philosopher: Abram Deborin," in *Revisionism*, Chapter ix.

32. *Ataka*, pp. 116, 118; *Historical Materialism*, p. 75.

33. *Historical Materialism*, pp. 217, 276; *Ataka*, pp. 118, 121.

34. The general argument is spread throughout several chapters, especially iii, v, vi, and vii.

35. *Historical Materialism*, pp. 64, 72–5; *Ataka*, pp. 117–18.

36. *Historical Materialism*, pp. 74, 78–9, 239–41.

37. *Ibid.*, Chapters v–vi; *Ataka*, p. 119.

38. *Historical Materialism*, pp. 242–9, 261–2.

39. *Ibid.*, pp. 79–83.

40. *Ekonomika perekhodnogo perioda*, pp. 36, 44, 87–9, and Chapter x.

41. See, for example, M. Z. Selektor, *Dialekticheskii materializm i teoriia ravnovesiia* (Moscow and Leningrad, 1934). After 1917, Bukharin regularly assailed Bogdanov's theories and policies, which he thought were of a piece. In one famous theoretical dispute involving the possibility of a proletarian culture, he agreed with Bogdanov and disagreed with Lenin. Nonetheless, he supported the subordination of Bogdanov's recalcitrant *Proletkult* organization to the party. And when a few dissident young Bolsheviks inspired by Bogdanov's ideas emerged in 1921, Lenin put Bukharin in charge of the ideological counterattack. See Bukharin,

"K s"ezdu Proletkul'ta," *Pravda*, November 22, 1921, pp. 1–2; and Lenin, *PSS*, XLIV, p. 266. While admiring him, Bukharin had come to regard Bogdanov as a "semi-Marxist" whose "divergence from orthodox Marxism and from Bolshevism became . . . for Bogdanov a personal tragedy." *Pravda*, April 8, 1928, p. 3.

42. *Ataka*, p. 120.

43. *Ekonomist*, No. 3, 1922, p. 146.

44. Bogdanov quoted in Kendall E. Bailes, "Philosophy and Politics in Russian Social Democracy: Bogdanov, Lunacharsky and the Crisis of Bolshevism, 1908–1909" (unpublished Russian Institute essay, Columbia University, 1966), p. 86; and Bukharin, *Teoriia istoricheskogo materializma* (1923 ed.), p. 6.

45. Sorokin in *Ekonomist*, No. 3, 1922, p. 146.

46. See *Historical Materialism*, pp. 86–7, 99, 104, 151, 209, 219, 255.

47. See his "Zametki ekonomista," *Pravda*, September 30, 1928, pp. 2–3.

48. See, for example, Gil'ferding, *Finansovyi kapital*, Chapter xvi; and Selektor, *Dialekticheskii materializm*, Chapter ix, especially pp. 169–70.

49. *Historical Materialism*, p. 75; see also *Ekonomika perekhodnogo perioda*, pp. 129–30, n. 1.

50. *Historical Materialism*, pp. 69, 70; on page 233, however, he insists that "there is no such thing as society 'in general.'"

51. *Ibid.*, p. 115; *Pravda*, July 3, 1926, p. 2.

52. See, for example, Ralf Dahrendorf, "Out of Utopia: Toward a Reorientation of Sociological Analysis," *American Journal of Sociology*, LXIV (1958), pp. 115–27; Bottomore, "Karl Marx, Sociologist or Marxist?"; and Lewis A. Coser, *The Functions of Social Conflict* (Glencoe, Ill., 1956), Chapter i. The conclusion is by Cynthia Eagle Russett, *The Concept of Equilibrium in American Social Thought* (New Haven, Conn., 1966), p. 53.

53. See, for example, V. S. Bruikov, *Marksizm i teoriia ravnovesiia* (Moscow, 1965).

54. *Ekonomika perekhodnogo perioda*, p. 130; *Historical Materialism*, p. 240.

55. *Historical Materialism*, pp. 87–8; *Ataka*, p. 150.

56. *Historical Materialism*, p. 219.

CHAPTER V

1. Kritsman, quoted in Avrich, *Kronstadt 1921*, p. 8.

2. See Carr, *Bolshevik Revolution*, Chapters xviii–xix; and Bukharin's remarks in *Bol'shevik*, No. 8, 1925, pp. 4–5.

3. As of 1923. See Alexander Baykov, *The Development of the Soviet Economic System* (New York, 1947), p. 107.

4. The definitive study of peasant society during the NEP years is M. Lewin, *Russian Peasants and Soviet Power: A Study of Collectivization* (Evanston, Ill., 1968).

5. For the resolutions, see *Desiatyi s"ezd*, pp. 571–6; and Daniels, *Conscience*, pp. 146–53.

6. Leon Trotsky, *Whither Russia: Towards Capitalism or Socialism?* (New York, 1926).

7. Trotsky, *The New Course*, p. 53.

8. E. H. Carr, *Socialism in One Country* (3 vols; New York, 1958–64), I, p. 9.

9. Bukharin, *O rabkore i sel'kore: stat'i i rechi* (Moscow, 1926), p. 77; and his "The Epoch of Great Tasks," *Soviet Russia*, IV (1921), p. 190.

10. *Desiatyi s"ezd*, p. 324.

11. *Selected Works*, III, p. 653.

12. "Nashi zadachi," *Bol'shevik*, No. 1, 1924, p. 3; for those more skeptical, see Bukharin's account of the views of Kamenev and Zinoviev in 1925. *XIV s"ezd*, pp. 135–6.

13. Quoted in N. Valentinov, "Ot NEPa k stalinskoi kollektivizatsii," *Novyi zhurnal*, No. 72, 1963, p. 242.

14. *Desiatyi s"ezd*, pp. 230–1; see also his remarks in *Pravda*, August 28, 1921, p. 3.

15. *Pravda*, January 25, 1923, p. 1.

16. See, for example, Lenin, *Selected Works*, III, pp. 703–4; and Bukharin, *Ataka*, pp. 254, 263.

17. The first two terms are Lenin's, *Soch.*, XXVII, pp. 58, 137; for the other see, N. Ustrialov, *Pod znakom revoliutsii* (2nd ed.; Harbin, 1927), p. 107.

18. See Bauer, *New Man in Soviet Psychology*, pp. 14–15.

19. For Trotsky as revolutionary hero, see the three-volume biography by Isaac Deutscher, and the sketch in Carr, *Socialism*, I, pp. 139–52. For the quotations here, see Deutscher, *Prophet Unarmed*, pp. 24, 44; and Leon Trotsky, *Literature and Revolution* (New York, 1970), pp. 190–1. See also his "Uroki oktiabria," in *Za leninizm: sbornik statei* (Moscow and Leningrad, 1925), pp. 433–86; and *The New Course*.

20. See his theses in Lenin, *Soch.*, XXVII, pp. 440–6; E. Preobrazhensky, *The New Economics* (London, 1965), p. 39; and Alexander Erlich, *The Soviet Industrialization Debate, 1924–1928* (Cambridge, Mass., 1960), p. 37.

21. N. Valentinov, "Sut' bol'shevizma v izobrazhenii Iu. Piatakova," *Novyi zhurnal*, LII (1958), pp. 140–61. I am quoting here from a longer version of this memoir in N. N. Vol'skii (Valentinov), Memoirs (unpublished manuscript, Russian and East European Archive, Columbia University, 1956).

22. A. Yugow, *Russia's Economic Front for War and Peace* (New York, 1942), pp. 5–6; and *Kommunisticheskaia revoliutsiia*, No. 10–11, 1929, p. 96.

23. David Thomson, *Democracy in France* (London, 1960), p. 19; Alan Bullock, *Hitler* (New York, 1964), pp. 28–30.

24. It was mainly associated with Larin. For his and other versions, see Bukharin's remarks in *Ataka*, p. 276; *Bol'shevik*, No. 9–10, 1925, pp. 7, 13; and *Chetyrnadtsataia konferentsiia rossiiskoi kommunisticheskoi partii (bol'shevikov): stenograficheskii otchet* (Moscow, 1925), pp. 185–6.

25. Bukharin, *Proletarskii iakovinets: pamiati F. E. Dzerzhinskogo* (Moscow, 1926); Pitirim Sorokin, *Leaves From a Russian Diary* (New York, 1924), p. 93; and Mathiez's 1920 article translated in *Dissent* (Winter 1955), pp. 77–86.

26. Schapiro, *Communist Party*, p. 290.

27. Michael Farbman, *After Lenin* (London, 1924), p. 3; Ustrialov, *Pod znakom revoliutsii*, pp. 41–6; and Bukharin's remarks on the Menshevik Martov in *Puti mirovoi revoliutsii*. *Sed'moi rasshirennyi plenum ispolnitel'nogo komiteta kommunisticheskogo internatsionala: stenograficheskii otchet* (2 vols; Moscow and Leningrad, 1927), I, pp. 80–1, and II, p. 118.

28. Leon Trotsky, *The Stalin School of Falsification* (New York, 1962), p. 146; see also *My Life*, p. 513. The Zinovievist was Petr Zalutskii. See *XIV s"ezd*, p. 358; and *Novaia oppozitsiia: sbornik materialov o diskussii 1925 goda* (Leningrad, 1926), p. 45.

29. See, for example, V. I. Lenin, *Selected Works*, IX (New York, 1937), pp. 149, 212–14, 221, 286; Bukharin, "Novyi kurs ekonomicheskoi politiki," reprinted in Bukharin and Preobrazhenskii, *Azbuka kommunizma* (Kharkov, 1925), p. 309; Bukharin's remarks in *Piatyi vserossiiskii s"ezd RKSM: stenograficheskii otchet* (Moscow and Leningrad, 1927), pp. 109–10, 112–14; and Liberman, *Building Lenin's Russia*, pp. 94–5.

30. It was Beso Lominadze. See *Novaia oppozitsiia*, p. 163.

31. *Soch.*, XXVI, pp. 305–6, 321–52, 408, and XXVII, pp. 50–1, 65, 342–5, 525; *Odinnadtsatyi s"ezd RKP(b). Mart-aprel' 1922 goda: stenograficheskii otchet* (Moscow, 1961), pp. 23–7.

32. *Soch.*, XXVII, pp. 79, 80, 323. For Lenin's reformist legacy, see also Valentinov, *Doktrina*, pp. 14–15.

33. Lenin, *Soch.*, XXVII, pp. 308, 400; Bukharin, *Politicheskoe zaveshchanie Lenina* (2nd ed.; Moscow, 1929), pp. 7–8. The concept actually originated with Marx. See Karl Marx and Frederick Engels, *Selected Works* (2 vols; Moscow, 1955), II, p. 454.

34. Bukharin in *Za leninizm*, p. 373; and his *Nekotorye voprosy ekonomicheskoi politiki: sbornik statei* (Moscow, 1925), p. 48.

35. For example, *Pravda*, August 24, 1929, quoted in *Iz istorii bor'by leninskoi partii protiv opportunizma*, p. 512. Indeed, Stalinist critics would later equate Bukharinism with social democratic reformism. See, for example, D. Petrovskii, *Bor'ba kompartii s reformizmom* (Leningrad, 1929).

36. Christian Gneuss, "The Precursor: Eduard Bernstein," in *Revisionism*, pp. 33–6.

37. *Pravda*, January 21, 1925, p. 2. Bukharin described them as such regularly, including in a famous speech entitled *Lenin's Political Testament*. For Lenin's articles, see *Soch.*, XXVII, pp. 387–418.

38. See, for example, Preobrazhenskii, *New Economics*, pp. 230–1, 234; Leon Trotsky, *The Third International After Lenin* (New York, 1957), pp. 31–2; Valentinov's testimony in *Novyi zhurnal*, LII (1958), p. 149; and Bukharin, "Ekonomicheskie perspektivy v derevne," *Pravda*, November 5, 1927, p. 5.

39. *Soch.*, XXVI, pp. 321–52, and XXVII, p. 395.

40. As he acknowledged, *ibid.*, XXVII, p. 62. See also *Voprosy istorii KPSS*, No. 1, 1967, pp. 61–2.

41. *Odinnadtsatyi s"ezd*, pp. 139–41; *Krasnaia nov'*, No. 4, 1925, p. 265.

42. See *Leninskii sbornik*, IV, pp. 384–5, and III, p. 21.

43. *Soch.*, XXVI, pp. 388, 391, 393–4, and XXVII, pp. 29–30, 44–6, 83; and *Odinnadtsatyi s"ezd*, pp. 13–21, 32.

44. *Soch.*, XXVI, p. 336, and XXVII, pp. 303–4, 348–9. For the cooperatives, see Carr, *Bolshevik Revolution*, II, pp. 120–5.

45. *Soch.*, XXVII, p. 366; L. A. Fotieva, *Iz vospominanii o V. I. Lenine* (Moscow, 1964), p. 18.

46. *Soch.*, XXVII, pp. 387–90, 398, 401, 405.

47. *Ibid.*, pp. 392–4.

48. *Ibid.*, XXVI, p. 336, and XXVII, pp. 391, 396. For an interesting attempt to reconcile Lenin's two views, see *Voprosy istorii KPSS*, No. 12, 1966, pp. 44–55.

49. *Soch.*, XXVII, pp. 396–7, 414, 417–18. For the last months of Lenin's life, see Moshe Lewin, *Lenin's Last Struggle* (New York, 1968).

50. See, for example, *Pravda*, August 28, 1921, p. 3. Also Sidney Heitman's introduction to N. I. Bukharin, *Put' k sotsializmu v Rossii* (New York, 1967), pp. 36–7.

51. *Bol'shevik*, No. 2, 1924, p. 3.

52. See *Leninskii sbornik*, IV, pp. 380–5; and *Vserossiiskaia konferentsiia RKP(b): biulleten'*, No. 2 (December 20, 1921), p. 50.

53. *Protokoly desiatoi vserossiiskoi konferentsii RKP(b)* (Moscow, 1933), p. 100. The article appeared in *Pravda*, August 6, 1921, and was reprinted in the 1925 edition of *Azbuka kommunizma*, pp. 301–9.

54. *Desiatyi s"ezd*, pp. 224–5; *The New Policies of Soviet Russia* (Chicago, 1921?), pp. 43–61; *Tretii vsemirnyi kongress kommunisticheskogo internatsionala*, pp. 264–8, 379–82; *Azbuka kommunizma* (1925 ed.), pp. 301–9.

55. *Krasnaia nov'*, No. 1, 1921, p. 269; *Azbuka kommunizma* (1925 ed.), pp. 306–7.

56. *Azbuka kommunizma* (1925 ed.), pp. 301, 307.

57. *IV vsemirnyi kongress kommunisticheskogo internatsionala 5 noiabria—3 dekabria 1922 g.* (Moscow and Leningrad, 1923), p. 192; and *Vserossiiskaia konferentsiia RKP(b): biulleten'*, No. 2 (December 20, 1921), pp. 49, 51.

58. *Ataka*, pp. 216–41; Maretskii, "Bukharin," p. 283.

59. *Ataka*, pp. 219–32. See also his *Proletarskaia revoliutsiia i kul'tura* (Petrograd, 1923), pp. 17–22; and "Problema kul'tury v epokhu proletarskoi revoliutsii," *Izvestiia*, October 15, 1922, p. 3.

60. *Ataka*, pp. 222, 227, 232–6; *Proletarskaia revoliutsiia i kul'tura*, p. 33; *Historical Materialism*, pp. 305–8; *Pravda*, August 28, 1921, p. 3.

61. As he later pointed out. See his *Tri rechi (k voprosu o nashikh raznoglasiiakh)* (Moscow and Leningrad, 1926), p. 35.

62. *Ataka*, pp. 237–40; *Proletarskaia revoliutsiia i kul'tura*, pp. 46–7; *Historical Materialism*, pp. 310–11.

63. See, for example, his *A Short Course of Economic Science* (London, 1927), pp. 35–41, 70, 179, 452, 463–6. Also N. Karev, "O gruppe 'rabochaia pravda,'" *Bol'shevik*, No. 7–8, 1924, pp. 32–4.

64. *Ataka*, p. 227; *Proletarskaia revoliutsiia i kul'tura*, p. 23; *Pravda*, November 23, 1921, p. 2.

65. *Historical Materialism*, pp. 309–10; *Ataka*, pp. 239–40. See also *Izvestiia*, October 15, 1922, p. 3.

66. See, for example, his remarks in *Puti mirovoi revoliutsii*, II, pp. 117–18.

67. See, for example, *O rabkore i sel'kore*, pp. 75–7; *Za leninizm*, p. 292; *XIV s"ezd*, p. 824; and his *Put' k sotsializmu i raboche-krest'ianskii soiuz* (Moscow and Leningrad, 1925), p. 71. For his skepticism about the Thermidor analogy, see "Na poroge desiatogo goda," *Pravda*, November 7, 1926, p. 2.

68. While denouncing the political forces he claimed were involved, Bukharin's few public remarks on the Kronstadt revolt reflected more sorrow than malice. See *Desiatyi s"ezd*, pp. 224–5; and the unsigned editorials in *Pravda*, March 25, 1921, p. 1, and May 22, 1921, p. 1 (his authorship is identified in Lenin, *Soch.*, XXVI, pp. 661, 671). He is quoted as having told delegates to the Third Comin-

tern Congress later in 1921: "Who says that the Kronstadt rising was White? No. For the sake of the idea, for the sake of our task, we were forced to suppress the revolt of our erring brothers. We cannot look upon the Kronstadt sailors as our enemies. We love them as our true brothers, our flesh and blood. . . ." Raphael Abramovitch, *The Soviet Revolution 1917-1939* (New York, 1962), p. 203.

69. *Desiatyi s"ezd*, pp. 322-3; *Tretii vsemirnyi kongress kommunisticheskogo internatsionala*, p. 382; "Iz rechi t. Bukharina na vechere vospominanii v 1921 g.," *Proletarskaia revoliutsiia*, No. 10, 1922, pp. 321-2.

70. For an early example, see *Pravda*, August 28, 1921, p. 3.

71. *Zapiski kommunisticheskogo universiteta imeni Ia. M. Sverdlova*, II (Moscow, 1924), pp. 255-9; *O rabkore i sel'kore*, pp. 36-7. Organizations of worker and peasant newspaper correspondents became his favorite example.

72. "Vliianie NEPa i 'uklony' v rabochem dvizhenii," *Pravda*, March 25, 1923, p. 3; *The Communist International*, No. 25, 1923, p. 13; "Krest'ianstvo i rabochii klass v blizhaishii istoricheskii period," *Pravda*, September 28, 1923, p. 1. This judgment is based on Bukharin's speeches to the Twelfth Party Congress in April 1923, where he discussed the major issues of the day—industrial policy, nationality policy, and the international movement. His position on each reflected what was becoming known as the "pro-peasant orientation." See *Dvenadtsatyi s"ezd rossiiskoi kommunisticheskoi partii (bol'shevikov): stenograficheskii otchet* (Moscow, 1923), pp. 169-76, 561-5; and his *Krizis kapitalizma i kommunisticheskoe dvizhenie* (Moscow, 1923).

73. *Zapiski kommunisticheskogo universiteta*, II, pp. 254-5.

74. *Pravda*, September 28, 1923, p. 1; *Ataka*, p. 279. See also *Pravda*, January 25, 1923, p. 1, and March 25, 1923, p. 2.

75. *IV vsemirnyi kongress kommunisticheskogo internatsionala*, pp. 192-3; similarly, "R.S.F.S.R.," *Pravda*, December 3, 1922, p. 3.

76. *Pravda*, January 25, 1922, p. 3; *Zapiski kommunisticheskogo universiteta*, II, p. 264.

77. See *Pravda*, December 3, 1922, p. 3; *Ataka*, p. 240; and *IV vsemirnyi kongress kommunisticheskogo internatsionala*, p. 190.

78. "Kritika i kritika," *Pravda*, June 30, 1923, p. 1; *Pravda*, September 28, 1923, p. 1.

79. I. V. Stalin, *Voprosy leninizma* (4th ed.; Moscow and Leningrad, 1928), pp. 169-203.

80. *IV vsemirnyi kongress kommunisticheskogo internatsionala*, p. 191.

81. *Doklad na XXIII chrezvychainoi leningradskoi gubernskoi konferentsii VKP(b)* (Moscow and Leningrad, 1926), p. 37.

82. *Bol'shevik*, No. 2, 1924, p. 6. Indeed, the whole controversy over the novelty of "socialism in one country" was in some respects a misleading one. Bukharin and the party leadership had thought of war communism as leading to socialism quite separate from the prospects of European revolution. Even before Stalin, in June 1924, one Petrov had referred to Lenin against Bogdanov's contention that socialism could not begin in a single country. *Bol'shevik*, No. 5-6, 1924, pp. 99-100. And finally, Preobrazhenskii, economist of the Left which opposed the idea, formulated his "law of primitive socialist accumulation" tacitly as a way to build socialism in an isolated, backward country.

83. Iu. L. Molchanov, *Komintern: u istokov politiki edinogo proletarskogo fronta* (Moscow, 1969), pp. 115-19; Bukharin's remarks in *Piatyi vsemirnyi kon-*

gress kommunisticheskogo internatsionala. 17 iiunia–8 iiulia 1924 g.: stenografi- cheskii otchet (2 vols; Moscow and Leningrad, 1925), I, p. 257; *Pravda*, November 7, 1922, p. 7; and *Proletarskaia revoliutsiia i kul'tura*, p. 3.

84. *IV vsemirnyi kongress kommunisticheskogo internatsionala*, p. 196.

85. *Dvenadtsatyi s"ezd*, p. 169; *Pravda*, May 13, 1923, p. 3; *Rasshirennyi plenum ispolnitel'nogo komiteta kommunisticheskogo internatsionala: otchet* (Moscow, 1923), p. 246; *Krizis kapitalizma*, p. 24.

86. *Krizis kapitalizma*, pp. 25, 81–2; see also *The Communist International*, No. 25, 1923, p. 16; and *Pravda*, September 28, 1923, p. 1.

87. *The Communist International*, No. 25, 1923, p. 16.

88. See the remarks of Petrovskii in *XIV s"ezd*, p. 168; and Trotsky, *New Course*, p. 51.

89. For the history of the triumvirate, see Daniels, *Conscience*, Chapters viii–ix; and Deutscher, *Prophet Unarmed*, Chapter ii.

90. G. Zinov'ev, *Sochineniia*, XI (Moscow and Leningrad, 1929), p. 390; Lenin, *PSS*, XLV, p. 345.

91. André Morizet, *Chez Lénine et Trotski: Moscou 1921* (Paris, 1922), p. 63. See also *Sotsialisticheskii vestnik*, September 8, 1922, p. 4. Until Lenin's death, the full Politburo members were himself, Trotsky, Zinoviev, Kamenev, Stalin, Rykov, and Tomskii, the last two being secondary figures. In his "testament," Lenin mentioned only Trotsky, Stalin, Zinoviev, Kamenev, Bukharin, and Piatakov, who became a regular oppositionist. *PSS*, XLV, pp. 344–5.

92. See Max Eastman, *Since Lenin Died* (New York, 1925), p. 30; Lenin, *PSS*, XLV, p. 345; Sarabianov's remarks in *PZM*, No. 3, 1922, p. 63; V. Astrov, *Krucha (roman)* (Moscow, 1969), p. 55; and Roy A. Medvedev, *Let History Judge: The Origins and Consequences of Stalinism* (New York, 1971), p. 64.

93. A. Ia. Viatkin, *Razgrom kommunisticheskoi partiei trotskizma i drugikh antileninskikh grupp*, I (Leningrad, 1966), p. 115.

94. See Lenin, *Soch.*, XXVII, pp. 277–80, 537–8; and Nicolaevsky, *Power and the Soviet Elite*, p. 50.

95. Lenin, *Soch.*, XXVII, pp. 379–82; *Vsesoiuznoe soveshchanie o merakh uluchsheniia podgotovki nauchno-pedagogicheskikh kadrov po istoricheskim naukam: 18–21 dekabria 1962 g.* (Moscow, 1964), p. 290.

96. *PSS*, XLV, p. 345.

97. *Leninskii sbornik*, XX, p. 353; see also XXIII, p. 33, and *PSS*, XLV, p. 524. The latter quote is from Denike, Interview No. 17. The story was also related to me by Boris I. Nicolaevsky, who reported having heard it from Krestinskii.

98. See, for example, Lenin, *PSS*, XLV, pp. 145–6, and LIV, pp. 141, 524.

99. See Bukharin's account of these meetings related in Nicolaevsky, *Power and the Soviet Elite*, pp. 12–13. Supporting evidence that Bukharin visited Lenin regularly during the last year or so of his life may be found in Denike, Interview No. 17; Serge, *Memoirs*, p. 176; Bukharin, "Il'ich," *Pravda*, September 24, 1922, p. 4; Fotieva, *Iz vospominanii*, p. 42; and Lenin, *PSS*, XLV, pp. 682, 686, 693, 716. According to the Soviet historian Roy Medvedev, Lenin felt a "great love" toward Bukharin at this time. See his *K sudu istorii* (samizdat ed.; Moscow, 1968), p. 153. See also M. N. Roy, *Memoirs* (Bombay, 1964), p. 498, who says Lenin viewed Bukharin "as his spiritual son." Bukharin doubtless believed that Lenin considered him "the one most able to convey his thoughts. He spoke with him so that Bukharin would write what he himself had left unsaid." See Nicolaevsky, *Power and the Soviet Elite*, p. 13. On the other hand, some of Lenin's last writings also supported Trotsky's call for more industrial planning.

100. For the Georgian affair, see Lewin, *Lenin's Last Struggle;* S. V. Kharmandarian, *Lenin i stanovlenie zakavkazskoi federatsii, 1921–1923* (Erevan, 1969); and Lenin, *PSS,* XLV, pp. 346, 356–62, and LIV, pp. 329–30. For Trotsky, see also Deutscher, *Prophet Unarmed,* pp. 91–3.

101. See Kharmandarian, *Lenin i stanovlenie zakavkazskoi federatsii,* pp. 348, 351–6, 369. At the congress, he was jokingly referred to as an "honorary Georgian." *Dvenadtsatyi s"ezd,* p. 564.

102. *Dvenadtsatyi s"ezd,* pp. 561–5; *Krizis kapitalizma,* pp. 33, 63.

103. *The Communist International,* No. 25, 1923, p. 16. For a later example, see *Pravda,* February 2, 1927, p. 4.

104. Quoted in Trotsky, *Stalin School,* p. xiv. See also Bukharin's remarks on party norms in *Desiatyi s"ezd,* pp. 217–33, and his theses, pp. 644–51.

105. Quoted by Trotsky in *Trinadtsatyi s"ezd RKP(b). Mai 1924 goda: stenograficheskii otchet* (Moscow, 1963), pp. 147–8.

106. Trotsky's account of Bukharin's sobbing dependence on him, however, is clearly apocryphal. *My Life,* pp. 470–2. See also Deutscher, *Prophet Unarmed,* pp. 82–3.

107. Denike, Interview No. 17.

108. *XIV s"ezd,* pp. 398–9, 455–6.

109. See, for example, *Moskovskie bol'sheviki v bor'be s pravym i "levym" opportunizmom, 1921–1929* (Moscow, 1969), p. 67.

110. Deutscher, *Prophet Unarmed,* pp. 35–7; and Stalin quoted in V. M. Ivanov and A. N. Shmelev, *Leninizm i ideino-politicheskii razgrom trotskizma* (Leningrad, 1970), p. 349.

111. Known as the "Platform of the Forty-Six," it is reprinted in E. H. Carr, *The Interregnum, 1923–1924* (New York, 1954), pp. 367–73.

112. *Pravda,* January 3, 1924, p. 5.

113. See Carr, *Interregnum,* Chapters iii–iv; and Deutscher, *Prophet Unarmed,* pp. 99–104.

114. He had for months been trying to counter the "psychological demoralization" and "pessimism" generated by NEP, sentiments to which the opposition responded and appealed. See *Piatyi vserossiiskii s"ezd RKSM,* p. 112; *Zapiski kommunisticheskogo universiteta,* II, p. 263; *Pravda,* March 25, 1923, p. 2, and June 30, 1923, p. 1.

115. "Doloi fraktsionnost'!," in his *K voprosu o trotskizme,* pp. 10–11, 20, 31, 43.

116. *Ibid.,* pp. 7–43. It appeared originally in *Pravda,* December 28 through 30, 1923, and January 1 and 4, 1924.

117. *Za leninizm,* p. 333; *K voprosu o trotskizme,* p. 9; A. I. Rykov and N. I. Bukharin, *Partiia i oppozitsionnyi blok* (2nd ed.; Moscow and Leningrad, 1926), p. 85.

118. Bukharin, *K itogam XIV s"ezda VKP(b)* (Moscow, 1926), pp. 4–5; his speech in *Leningradskaia organizatsiia i chetyrnadtsatyi s"ezd: sbornik materialov i dokumentov* (Moscow and Leningrad, 1926), pp. 86–8; Trotsky's letter to Bukharin, January 9, 1926 (T2976); and Astrov, *Krucha,* pp. 294–5. Stalin seems also to have objected to their demand.

119. For a somewhat misleading account, see Deutscher, *Prophet Unarmed,* pp. 257–8. This will be discussed in Chapter VII.

120. N. Valentinov (Vol'skii), *Novaia ekonomicheskaia politika i krizis partii posle smerti Lenina: vospominaniia* (Stanford, 1971), p. 91.

121. *Ataka,* pp. 242–84. The most famous example is Stalin's *Foundations of Leninism,* which originated as lectures at Sverdlov University in early April 1924.

122. Compare, for example, *ibid.,* p. 271, to Stalin, *Voprosy leninizma, p.* 115.

123. *Ataka,* pp. 274–5, 278–9; *Za leninizm,* p. 287.

124. *Ataka,* pp. 275–6.

CHAPTER VI

1. See, for example, *Za leninizm;* and *KPSS v rezoliutsiiakh,* II, pp. 163–72.

2. *Za leninizm,* p. 285. Preobrazhenskii's law first appeared in his "Osnovnoi zakon sotsialisticheskogo nakopleniia," *VKA,* VIII (1924), pp. 47–116; and then as the second chapter of his *The New Economics.*

3. *KPSS v rezoliutsiiakh,* II, pp. 116–26; Carr, *Socialism,* I, pp. 249–75.

4. Daniels, *Conscience,* Chapter ii.

5. Bukharin's politics in the middle twenties will be discussed in Chapter VII.

6. The fullest statement of his thinking appeared in his *Put' k sotsializmu i raboche-krest'ianskii soiuz* (Moscow and Leningrad, 1925). It was, however, a popularized account, lacking the theoretical depth of his major works. Later, he began, but never completed, a theoretical treatment. See *Pravda,* July 1, 3, and 7, 1926.

7. *New Economics,* pp. 77–146. The fullest treatment of Preobrazhenskii's ideas is Erlich, *Soviet Industrialization,* on which I have relied heavily.

8. *New Economics,* pp. 84, 88–9, 124.

9. *Ibid.,* pp. 85–8. See also Karl Marx, *Capital,* I (Moscow, 1958), Part 3.

10. *VKA,* VII (1924), p. 79; *New Economics,* pp. 110–11.

11. *New Economics,* pp. 136–46, and Chapters i and iii.

12. Between November 1924 and January 1925, Bukharin published three of his major statements on economic policy: "Khoziaistvennyi rost i problema raboche-krest'ianskogo bloka," *Bol'shevik,* No. 14, 1924, pp. 25–36, reprinted in his *Nekotorye voprosy;* "Novoe otkrovenie o sovetskoi ekonomike, ili kak mozhno pogubit' raboche-krest'ianskii blok," *Pravda,* December 12, 1924, reprinted in *Za leninizm;* and "K kritike ekonomicheskoi platformy oppozitsii (uroki oktiabria 1923 g.)," *Bol'shevik,* No. 1, 1925, also reprinted in his *Nekotorye voprosy.* All were attacks on Preobrazhenskii, though he was not mentioned by name in the first.

13. *Partiia i oppozitsionnyi blok,* p. 52.

14. *XV konferentsiia,* p. 593; *Nekotorye voprosy,* p. 53; *Doklad,* p. 18; *Za leninizm,* pp. 311–12.

15. "Teoriia permanentnoi revoliutsii," in *Za leninism,* pp. 347–8, 359; "Revoliutsiia 1905 goda," *Vestnik truda,* No. 12, 1925, p. 8; *Politicheskoe zaveshchanie Lenina,* pp. 7–8; "Znachenie agrarno-krest'ianskoi problemy," *Bol'shevik,* No. 3–4, 1925, pp. 5, 16.

16. See, for example, *Tri rechi,* p. 26; *K itogam XIV s"ezda,* p. 47; *Za leninizm,* pp. 298–9, 341–9; and *Put' k sotsializmu,* pp. 18–19.

17. See, for example, *Za leninizm,* p. 298; *Put' k sotsializmu,* p. 28; and *Krasnaia nov',* No. 4, 1925, pp. 263, 267.

18. Deutscher, *Prophet Unarmed,* p. 234.

19. Marx and Engels, *Selected Works*, II, pp. 24–5. For a discussion, see Robert C. Tucker, *Philosophy and Myth in Karl Marx* (Cambridge, England, 1961), especially pp. 11–27.

20. *Economic Theory of the Leisure Class*, pp. 158, 168; see also *Ataka*, p. 69.

21. *Protsess eserov: rechi zashchitnikov i obviniaemykh* (Moscow, 1922), pp. 139, 144; *Ataka*, p. 215; *Put' k sotsializmu*, p. 92.

22. *Za leninizm*, pp. 292, 297; Bukharin quoted in *KPSS v rezoliutsiiakh*, II, p. 558; and Preobrazhenskii, *New Economics*, pp. 228–9.

23. *Za leninizm*, pp. 351, 352; Bukharin, *Imperializm i nakoplenie kapitala (teoreticheskii etiud)* (4th ed.; Moscow and Leningrad, 1929), pp. 121, 131; *Bol'shevik*, No. 3–4, 1925, pp. 6–8, 16–17; *Rasshirennyi plenum ispolkoma* (1925), pp. 305–6, 528.

24. *Bol'shevik*, No. 3–4, 1925, p. 17; *Za leninizm*, pp. 351, 353; *Building Up Socialism* (London, 1926), pp. 64–5.

25. *Za leninizm*, pp. 287, 351; *Bol'shevik*, No. 3–4, 1925, p. 8.

26. *Put' k sotsializmu*, pp. 13–14; *O rabkore i sel'kore*, p. 60; *Rasshirennyi plenum ispolkoma* (1925), p. 312; "Mezhdunarodnoe polozhenie i zadachi Komsomola," *Pravda*, March 26, 1925, p. 3.

27. *Za leninizm*, p. 296; *K itogam XIV s"ezda*, p. 45; *Inprecor*, VIII (1928), pp. 1270–1; *Put' k sotsializmu*, pp. 5–6.

28. Marx, *Capital*, I, pp. 713–14, 760; Bukharin, *Imperializm i nakoplenie kapitala*, p. 106; Bukharin, "Na temy dnia," *Pravda*, May 27, 1928, p. 2. See also his remarks in *Pravda*, July 7, 1926, p. 2.

29. *Pravda*, May 27, 1928, p. 2; *Put' k sotsializmu*, pp. 12, 89; "Uchitel'stvo i Komsomol," *Pravda*, February 4, 1925, p. 5.

30. "Zametki ekonomista," *Pravda*, September 30, 1928, p. 2. Similarly, see *Za leninizm*, pp. 288–92; and *Nekotorye voprosy*, pp. 8–9.

31. *Pravda*, September 30, 1928, p. 2; *Pravda*, February 4, 1925, p. 5.

32. *Doklad*, p. 23; "Sud'by russkoi intelligentsii," *Pechat' i revoliutsiia*, No. 3, 1925, p. 8. See also *Tri rechi*, p. 26.

33. *Proletarskaia revoliutsiia i kul'tura*, p. 47; *Krasnaia nov'*, No. 4, 1925, p. 268; *Bol'shevik*, No. 9–10, 1925, p. 6.

34. *Za leninizm*, pp. 290–2, 315–17. Similarly, see *Nekotorye voprosy*, pp. 8–9.

35. *Pravda*, September 30, 1928, pp. 2–3; *Nekotorye voprosy*, p. 6.

36. *Vestnik truda*, No. 12, 1925, pp. 5–6; *Inprecor*, VII (1927), pp. 423, 431; *Pravda*, September 30, 1928, pp. 2–3.

37. Though he did refer obliquely to it as a matter of "principle," *Nekotorye voprosy*, p. 8.

38. *Pravda*, September 30, 1928, p. 2; "Organizovannyi kapitalizm," pp. 184, 197; *Inprecor*, VII (1927), p. 199. He developed this argument at length in *Nekotorye voprosy*, pp. 3–13, 45–85.

39. Bukharin, *Tekushchii moment i osnovy nashei politiki* (Moscow, 1925), p. 17.

40. Also like Preobrazhenskii, Bukharin welcomed foreign credits while doubting that more than "a drop in the sea" would be forthcoming. See his "O partiinom rukovodstve rabsel'korami," *Pravda*, May 28, 1926, p. 3; and *Bol'shevik*, No. 8, 1925, p. 4.

41. *Partiia i oppozitsionnyi blok*, pp. 61–2. See also *Za leninizm*, p. 280; and *Pravda*, July 7, 1926, p. 2.

42. *Imperializm i nakoplenie kapitala*, pp. 66, 78, and Chapter iii *passim*. The articles making up this book appeared originally in late 1924 and early 1925. Their main target was Rosa Luxemburg's theory of capitalist crises. For Tugan-Baranovskii, see Paul M. Sweezy, *The Theory of Capitalist Development: Principles of Marxian Political Economy* (New York, 1942), pp. 158–72.

43. *Kommunisticheskii internatsional*, No. 31–2, 1928, p. 35. For a critical discussion of Bukharin's treatment of Tugan-Baranovskii, see Erlich, *Soviet Industrialization*, pp. 18–21.

44. *Nekotorye voprosy*, pp. 5–6, 60. See also *Pravda*, July 7, 1926, p. 3; and *Pravda*, September 30, 1928, pp. 2–3.

45. *Put' k sotsializmu*, p. 41; *Nekotorye voprosy*, p. 5.

46. *Nekotorye voprosy*, p. 52; *Bol'shevik*, No. 9–10, 1925, p. 3; *Za leninizm*, pp. 303, 371; *Put' k sotsializmu*, pp. 3, 41.

47. *Nekotorye voprosy*, p. 6; *Leningradskaia organizatsiia*, p. 105; *Bol'shevik*, No. 8, 1925, p. 7; *Tekushchii moment i osnovy*, p. 13.

48. *Nekotorye voprosy*, pp. 51–4, 76.

49. *Bol'shevik*, No. 9–10, 1925, p. 3; *Put' k sotsializmu*, pp. 31, 41–2; *Leningradskaia organizatsiia*, p. 99.

50. *Leningradskaia organizatsiia*, p. 98; *Tri rechi*, pp. 16–18, 20.

51. See, for example, his "O novoi ekonomicheskoi politike i nashikh zadachakh," *Bol'shevik*, No. 8, 1925, pp. 3–14, and No. 9–10, 1925, pp. 3–15.

52. *Nekotorye voprosy*, pp. 4, 6, 12, 76; *Tekushchii moment i osnovy*, pp. 20–2; *Bol'shevik*, No. 9–10, 1925, pp. 5, 14.

53. *Bol'shevik*, No. 9–10, 1925, pp. 4–5.

54. Bukharin, *V zashchitu proletarskoi diktatury: sbornik* (Moscow and Leningrad, 1928), p. 147; *Tekushchii moment i osnovy*, p. 35. He was obliged to retract the slogan on two other occasions in 1925 as well. See *Novaia oppozitsiia: sbornik materialov o diskussii 1925 goda* (Leningrad, 1926), p. 47; and "Zaiavlenie tov. Bukharina," *Pravda*, December 13, 1925, p. 3.

55. *Tekushchii moment i osnovy*, pp. 13, 16; *Put' k sotsializmu*, p. 45.

56. *Bol'shevik*, No. 9–10, 1925, p. 4; *Tekushchii moment i osnovy*, p. 13; *Nekotorye voprosy*, pp. 9–10. See also Erlich, *Soviet Industrialization*, pp. 13–14.

57. *Nekotorye voprosy*, pp. 54, 66.

58. *Ibid.*, pp. 63–71, 77–85; *Za leninizm*, pp. 299–305; *Put' k sotsializmu*, pp. 44–5; *Partiia i oppozitsionnyi blok*, p. 57.

59. *Za leninizm*, pp. 308–9; *Nekotorye voprosy*, p. 77.

60. *Partiia i oppozitsionnyi blok*, pp. 57–8; see also *Za leninizm*, pp. 306–10.

61. *Za leninizm*, p. 307; *Inprecor*, VII (1927), p. 199; "*Organizovannyi kapitalizm*," p. 191; *Pravda*, June 12, 1929, p. 3.

62. See, for example, *Za leninizm*, p. 305; *Nekotorye voprosy*, pp. 77–84; *Doklad*, pp. 32–3; and *Partiia i oppozitsionnyi blok*, pp. 62–4

63. *VII s"ezd vsesoiuznogo leninskogo kommunisticheskogo soiuza molodezhi: 11–12 marta 1926 goda* (Moscow and Leningrad, 1926), p. 255.

64. Preobrazhenskii quoted in Deutscher, *Prophet Unarmed*, p. 415.

65. *Leningradskaia organizatsiia*, p. 103.

66. See, for example, *ibid.*, p. 102; and *Tekushchii moment i osnovy*, p. 15.

67. *Leningradskaia organizatsiia*, p. 91.

68. See, for example, *Inprecor*, V (1925), pp. 987, 1025; *Tekushchii moment i osnovy*, p. 15; and *Za leninizm*, p. 371.

69. *Tekushchii moment i osnovy*, p. 16.

70. *Put' k sotsializmu*, pp. 54, 66; *Bol'shevik*, No. 8, 1925, pp. 8–9, 14.

71. See Bukharin's remarks in *Nekotorye voprosy*, p. 57; and Carr, *Bolshevik Revolution*, II, Chapter xx, and his *Socialism*, I, Chapter x.

72. *Bol'shevik*, No. 2, 1924, pp. 4–5; *Nekotorye voprosy*, pp. 60–2; *Put' k sotsializmu*, p. 30; *Za leninizm*, pp. 337–8; *Rasshirennyi plenum ispolkoma* (1925), pp. 372–4.

73. *Bol'shevik*, No. 2, 1925, p. 5, and No. 8, 1925, p. 9; N. Bukharin and A. Thalheimer, *Report on the Program Question* (Moscow, 1924), p. 24; *Nekotorye voprosy*, p. 3; *Rasshirennyi plenum ispolkoma* (1925), p. 374; *Partiia i oppozitsionnyi blok*, p. 47; *Pravda*, July 3, 1926, pp. 2–3.

74. *Za leninizm*, p. 310; *Pravda*, July 7, 1926, p. 3.

75. *Tekushchii moment i osnovy*, pp. 4, 17–18. See also *Pravda*, October 24, 1924, p. 5.

76. *Bol'shevik*, No. 8, 1925, p. 14; *Ataka*, p. 205.

77. *Bol'shevik*, No. 8, 1925, pp. 3–4; *Tekushchii moment i osnovy*, pp. 12–13.

78. *K voprosu o trotskizme*, p. 20; *Za leninizm*, p. 287; *Tri rechi*, p. 27.

79. *XIV s"ezd*, p. 135. Elsewhere Bukharin argued that the idea of building socialism by "slow snail's paces" could be found in Lenin's last articles of 1923. *K itogam XIV s"ezda*, p. 22. For a different interpretation of his use of the metaphor, see Erlich, *Soviet Industrialization*, pp. 78–9.

80. *Partiia i oppozitsionnyi blok*, p. 64; *Put' k sotsializmu*, pp. 42, 45.

81. See Bukharin's remarks in *Ataka*, p. 128; and *Trinadtsatyi s"ezd*, p. 316.

82. The examples are Bukharin's. See *Pravda*, May 28, 1926, p. 3; *Tekushchii moment i osnovy*, pp. 39–40; *Chetyrnadtsataia konferentsiia*, p. 189; and *Piatyi vserossiiskoi s"ezd RKSM*, p. 113.

83. *Politicheskoe zaveshchanie Lenina*, p. 10.

84. *Trinadtsatyi s"ezd*, p. 526. See also his "Enchmeniada," in *Ataka*, pp. 128–70.

85. Leon Trotsky, *The Revolution Betrayed* (New York, 1945), p. 29.

86. *Bol'shevik*, No. 8, 1925, p. 8.

87. *Doklad*, p. 21; *Pravda*, July 7, 1926, p. 2. See also *Puti mirovoi revoliutsii*, II, p. 116; and *Nekotorye voprosy*, p. 47.

88. See, for example, *Rasshirennyi plenum ispolkoma* (1925), p. 364; *Doklad*, pp. 10–11, 34; and *K itogam XIV s"ezda*, p. 31.

89. Ustrialov quoted in Bukharin, *V zashchitu*, p. 148. Bukharin actually had the Bolshevik Left in mind. See *Inprecor*, VII (1927), p. 1603.

90. Quoted in Farbman, *Bolshevism in Retreat*, p. 304.

91. *Piatyi vserossiiskii s"ezd RKSM*, pp. 113–14.

92. Zinoviev in *XIV s"ezd*, pp. 101, 103; and Bukharin in *Leningradskaia organizatsiia*, p. 110.

93. *Tri rechi*, p. 34; *Bol'shevik*, No. 2, 1924, p. 8.

94. "Chem my pobezhdaem," *Dvadtsat' piat' RKP (bol'shevikov): 1893–1923* (Moscow, 1923), p. 137.

95. See Zinoviev and Kamenev quoted in *Voprosy istorii KPSS*, No. 8, 1967, p. 78; and Bukharin's account of their views in *XIV s"ezd*, pp. 135–6.

96. See, for example, Bukharin's remarks in *Doklad*, p. 36.

97. See Valentinov, *Doktrina*, pp. 52–3, 60; and Deutscher, *Stalin*, p. 299. Formal paternity of the idea was not always clear to participants in the debates, oppositionists attributing it sometimes to Stalin, sometimes to Bukharin, or to them jointly. See, for example, the oppositionists quoted in Carr, *Socialism*, II, p. 43, n. 3; and *A Documentary History of Communism*, edited by Robert V. Daniels (2 vols; New York, 1962), II, p. 13.

98. *Tekushchii moment i osnovy*, pp. 4–6, 9–12.

99. As Trotsky documented thoroughly. See his *Russian Revolution*, III, pp. 398–9; and *The Third International After Lenin* (New York, 1957), pp. 37–9.

100. *Tekushchii moment i osnovy*, p. 9.

101. *XIV s"ezd*, pp. 135–6. For his other major statements on "socialism in one country" in 1925–6, see *Tekushchii moment i osnovy*, pp. 4–6, 9–12; *Put' k sotsializmu*, pp. 100–6; *K itogam XIV s"ezda*, pp. 16–24; *Building Up Socialism*, pp. 49–63; and *Puti mirovoi revoliutsii*, II, pp. 110–17.

102. *K itogam XIV s"ezda*, p. 22; *Building Up Socialism*, pp. 50–2, 62; *Puti mirovoi revoliutsii*, II, p. 111.

103. *Rasshirennyi plenum ispolkoma* (1925), p. 378; *K itogam XIV s"ezda*, p. 24.

104. *Tekushchii moment i osnovy*, pp. 5–6.

105. *Doklad*, pp. 16–17, 46; *Inprecor*, *VII (1927)*, p. 1423; *Tekushchii moment i osnovy*, pp. 5–6. See also *Put' k sotsializmu*, pp. 39, 82, 103–4.

106. See Lenin, *Soch.*, XXVII, p. 405; and Carr, *Socialism*, I, Chapter iii.

107. For the problems of computing peasant strata and its policy implications, see M. Lewin, "Who Was the Soviet Kulak?", *Soviet Studies* (October 1966), pp. 189–212; Lewin, *Russian Peasants*, Chapters ii–iii; and Carr, *Socialism*, I, Chapters iii, v. For the view that the old kulak had disappeared, see V. Bogushevskii, "O derevenskom kulake ili o roli traditsii v terminologii," *Bol'shevik*, No. 9–10, 1925, pp. 63–4. The figure of 14 per cent was Kamenev's. See Popov, *Outline History*, II, p. 244.

108. See, for example, Maizlin (V. Smirnov) in *Bol'shevik*, No. 18, 1926, pp. 108–11; and *The Platform of the Left Opposition (1927)* (London, 1963), pp. 25–34.

109. See, for example, *Zapiski kommunisticheskogo universiteta*, II, pp. 254–5; *O rabkore i sel'kore*, pp. 61–2, 66; and *Partiia i oppozitsionnyi blok*, pp. 48–50.

110. *K itogam XIV s"ezda*, p. 53.

111. As Bukharin pointed out in *Politicheskoe zaveshchanie Lenina*, p. 22. For Lenin's remarks in 1918, see *Soch.*, XXIII, pp. 207–8.

112. See, for example, *XIV s"ezd*, p. 151.

113. See, for example, *Bol'shevik*, No. 9–10, 1925, p. 5; *Chetyrnadtsataia konferentsiia*, pp. 182–3; *Pravda*, December 13, 1925, p. 5; *Leningradskaia organizatsiia*, p. 107; and *Tri rechi*, pp. 3, 23.

114. *Put' k sotsializmu*, p. 13; *Bol'shevik*, No. 9–10, 1925, p. 4; and Bukharin quoted in Fischer, *Stalin and German Communism*, pp. 543–4. For the argument he failed to develop, see *Tekushchii moment i osnovy*, pp. 25–6.

115. *Bol'shevik*, No. 8, 1925, pp. 13–14; *Put' k sotsializmu*, pp. 49–50.

116. *Nekotorye voprosy*, p. 11; *Tri rechi*, pp. 20–1; *K itogam XIV s"ezda*, pp. 48–9; *Doklad*, pp. 29–30; *Leningradskaia organizatsiia*, p. 111.

117. *Put' k sotsializmu*, p. 27.

118. *Ibid.*, p. 48; *Tekushchii moment i osnovy*, p. 24. For opposition charges, see *Leningradskaia organizatsiia*, p. 111; and Bukharin, *K itogam XIV s"ezda*, p. 47.

119. See, for example, *O rabkore i sel'kore*, p. 61; *Put' k sotsializmu*, pp. 47–8; *Tri rechi*, pp. 3, 25–6; *XIV s"ezd*, pp. 148–9; and *K itogam XIV s"ezda*, pp. 47–8.

120. *K itogam XIV s"ezda*, pp. 43–5; *Leningradskaia organizatsiia*, p. 112; *Doklad*, pp. 18–23; *Partiia i oppozitsionnyi blok*, pp. 42, 60; *Pravda*, November 6–7, 1927, p. 3.

121. *Put' k sotsializmu*, p. 99; *Pravda*, November 6–7, 1927, p. 3.

122. *Put' k sotsializmu*, pp. 70, 99.

123. *Ataka*, p. 279; *Za leninizm*, pp. 290, 312; *Pravda*, July 7, 1926, p. 3. See also *Nekotorye voprosy*, pp. 4, 46–51, where he argues that the theory was adumbrated by Lenin.

124. *Doklad*, pp. 14–15. For a later attack on the two-class theory, see I. Sol'ts, "O 'teorii dvukhklassovogo obshchestva' i raboche-krest'ianskom soiuze," *Pravda*, November 28, 1929, p. 3.

125. See *Novaia oppozitsiia*, pp. 144–93.

126. See *Tri rechi*, pp. 28–32; *K itogam XIV s"ezda*, pp. 32–42.

127. *V zashchitu*, p. 129.

128. Carr, *Socialism*, I, pp. 216–22; and Bukharin's remarks in *Chetyrnadtsataia konferentsiia*, pp. 181–9.

129. *Pravda*, August 28, 1929, p. 4.

130. *Rasshirennyi plenum ispolkoma* (1925), p. 319; *Put' k sotsializmu*, p. 47.

131. *Pravda*, March 6, 1925, p. 3.

132. *Marksizm i s.-kh. kooperatsiia* (Moscow, 1928), p. 222. For his restatements, see *Bol'shevik*, No. 9–10, 1925, p. 12; *Chetyrnadtsataia konferentsiia*, p. 188; and *Tekushchii moment i osnovy*, p. 29.

133. *Marksizm i s.-kh. kooperatsiia*, pp. 220–1. Similarly, see *Za leninizm*, p. 294; and *Bol'shevik*, No. 9–10, 1925, p. 13.

134. *Tri rechi*, p. 33. For his remarks on Lenin's "cooperative plan," see also *Za leninizm*, pp. 287, 293, 371; and *Bol'shevik*, No. 9–10, 1925, p. 9.

135. *Tekushchii moment i osnovy*, p. 36; *Pravda*, June 19, 1925, p. 5. For a full statement of his views on the cooperatives, see *Put' k sotsializmu*, Chapters vi–ix.

136. *Bol'shevik*, No. 9–10, 1925, p. 12; *Tri rechi*, p. 27. See also *Put' k sotsializmu*, pp. 31–3.

137. *Inprecor*, V (1925), p. 1025; *Doklad*, p. 23; *Put' k sotsializmu*, p. 58; *Tri rechi*, p. 27.

138. *Chetyrnadtsataia konferentsiia*, p. 187; *Put' k sotsializmu*, p. 58.

139. *Za leninizm*, pp. 294, 299; and I. Vermenichev, "O kooperativnom plane tov. Bukharina," *Pravda*, October 12, 1929, p. 2.

140. See, for example, *Za leninizm*, pp. 293–6; *Bol'shevik*, No. 9–10, 1925, pp. 8–13; *Chetyrnadtsataia konferentsiia*, pp. 182–7; *Tekushchii moment i osnovy*, pp. 30–5; and *Put' k sotsializmu*, pp. 34–8.

141. Quoted in Selektor, *Dialekticheskii materializm*, p. 265.

142. *Pravda*, July 1, 1926, p. 3; *Inprecor*, VIII (1928), p. 986; *Tekushchii moment i osnovy*, pp. 34–5; *Bol'shevik*, No. 9–10, 1925, p. 8; *Chetyrnadtsataia konferentsiia*, pp. 182–3.

143. *Tekushchii moment i osnovy*, p. 23; *Put' k sotsializmu*, p. 57; *Doklad*, pp. 22–3; *V zashchitu*, p. 124.

144. *Inprecor*, V (1925), p. 998. See also *Pravda*, March 6, 1925, p. 3.

145. *Put' k sotsializmu*, p. 49. For his earlier statements, see *Chetyrnadtsataia konferentsiia*, p. 187; and *Tekushchii moment i osnovy*, p. 35.

146. *Nekotorye voprosy*, p. 47.

147. *Pravda*, July 7, 1926, p. 3; *Nekotorye voprosy*, pp. 46–51.

148. See *Nekotorye voprosy*, pp. 48–9; *Bol'shevik*, No. 2, 1924, pp. 5–6, and No. 8, 1925, pp. 9, 14; *Krasnaia nov'*, No. 4, 1925, pp. 266–8; *Chetyrnadtsataia konferentsiia*, pp. 186–8; and *Put' k sotsializmu*, passim.

149. *Doklad*, pp. 11–12; *Nekotorye voprosy*, p. 48; *Put' k sotsializmu*, p. 54.

150. *Krasnaia nov'*, No. 4, 1925, p. 266; *Chetyrnadtsataia konferentsiia*, p. 187; and Bukharin quoted in Carr, *Socialism*, I, p. 261.

151. Quoted in Leont'ev, *Ekonomicheskaia teoriia*, p. 68.

152. *Put' k sotsializmu*, pp. 64–5, 70; *Inprecor*, V (1925), p. 1025.

153. *Partiia i oppozitsionnyi blok*, pp. 49–51; *Inprecor*, V (1925), p. 990.

154. *Bol'shevik*, No. 8, 1925, p. 9; *Za leninizm*, pp. 308–9.

155. "Kakoi dolzhna byt' molodezh?", *Molodaia gvardiia*, No. 2, 1926, pp. 83–4; *Put' k sotsializmu*, p. 64.

156. *Doklad*, p. 8. For his civil peace theme, see also *Nekotorye voprosy*, pp. 47–8; and *Put' k sotsializmu*, pp. 51–2.

157. *Pravda*, May 28, 1926, p. 3.

158. *Krasnaia nov'*, No. 4, 1925, p. 267; *Put' k sotsializmu*, pp. 18, 70–1; *Rasshirennyi plenum ispolkoma* (1925), p. 371.

159. *Tekushchii moment i osnovy*, p. 38; William Reswick, *I Dreamt Revolution* (Chicago, 1952), pp. 77, 96.

160. See, for example, his *O rabkore i sel'kore, passim;* and "The Russian Revolution and Social Democracy," *Inprecor*, VII (1927), p. 1528.

161. *Nekotorye voprosy*, p. 48; *Put' k sotsializmu*, p. 68; *Inprecor*, V (1925), p. 921.

162. *Pechat' i revoliutsiia*, No. 3, 1925, p. 8; *Inprecor*, V (1925), p. 923; *Sed'moi s"ezd professional'nykh soiuzov SSSR: stenograficheskii otchet* (Moscow, 1927), p. 21. His latter point seems to have been true. See Merle Fainsod, *Smolensk Under Soviet Rule* (Cambridge, 1958), p. 177.

163. *Put' k sotsializmu*, pp. 53–4; *O rabkore i sel'kore*, pp. 65–6.

164. *Nekotorye voprosy*, p. 12.

165. *Pravda*, October 24, 1924, p. 5, and February 4, 1925, p. 5; *Put' k sotsializmu*, p. 79; *XIV s'ezd*, p. 824.

166. *Nekotorye voprosy*, p. 12.

167. *Put' k sotsializmu*, pp. 80–1; *O rabkore i sel'kore*, p. 69. Emphasis on persuasion became one of his recurrent themes. For his characterization of the party's war communist régime, see *Put' k sotsializmu*, p. 78.

168. *Pravda*, February 4, 1925, p. 5. See also *XIV s"ezd*, pp. 820–1.

169. *Partiia i oppozitsionnyi blok*, pp. 71–2.

170. *Put' k sotsializmu*, p. 78; *Nekotorye voprosy*, p. 13; *Rasshirennyi plenum ispolkoma* (1925), p. 370.

171. *Partiia i oppozitsionnyi blok*, p. 75. For the "revitalization" campaign, see Carr, *Socialism*, II, Chapter xxii.

172. See Carr, *Socialism*, II, Chapter xiv; Edward J. Brown, *The Proletarian Episode in Russian Literature 1928–1932* (New York, 1953), Chapter iii, and for the resolution, pp. 235–40. Bukharin's role is also discussed in Polonskii, *Ocherki literaturnogo dvizheniia*, Chapter viii. The resolution's language and reasoning were very similar to those of Bukharin in the debate. See *K voprosu o politike RKP(b) v khudozhestvennoi literature* (Moscow, 1924), pp. 35–9; and *Krasnaia nov'*, No. 4, 1925, pp. 263–72.

173. See, for example, his "Pervaia lastochka," *Pravda*, January 12, 1923, p. 1; " 'Rychi Kitai!' v teatre Meierkhol'da," *Pravda*, February 2, 1926, p. 3; and his remarks in *K voprosu o politike*, p. 36, and *Krasnaia nov'*, No. 4, 1925, pp. 263–5. He had been less tolerant during the civil war, when arguing for proletarian culture he exclaimed: "The old theater must be broken. Anyone who does not understand this, understands nothing." *Pravda*, December 16, 1929, p. 1. By the twenties, however, he was quoting the saying, *De gustibus non est disputandum*. See his introduction to Ilya Ehrenburg's very nonproletarian novel, *Neobychainye pokhozhdeniia Khulio Khurenito* (3rd ed.; Moscow and Leningrad, 1927), p. 5. As we shall see, he was also a protector of disfavored writers and poets, such as Osip Mandelstam and Boris Pasternak.

174. *K voprosu o politike*, pp. 36–8; *Krasnaia nov'*, No. 4, 1925, pp. 263–5.

175. *Krasnaia nov'*, No. 4, 1925, pp. 263, 269, 272; *K voprosu o politike*, p. 36–8.

176. *Leningradskaia organizatsiia*, pp. 101–2; *XIV s"ezd*, p. 824; Bukharin quoted in Valentinov, *Doktrina*, p. 23; *Put' k sotsializmu*, p. 79.

177. Bukharin regularly protested official Soviet *proizvol*. See, for example, *Put' k sotsializmu*, pp. 78–81; *Nekotorye voprosy*, pp. 12–13; *XIV s"ezd*, p. 151; and above, note 165. For its presence in nineteenth-century Russian thought, see, for example, the discussion of official lawlessness in Alexander Herzen, *From the Other Shore, and The Russian People and Socialism* (New York, 1956), pp. 181–3; and G. A. Dzhanshiev, *Epokha velikikh reform* (St. Petersburg, 1907), p. 328.

178. *VII s"ezd vsesoiuznogo leninskogo kommunisticheskogo soiuza molodezhi*, pp. 256–7; *Krasnaia nov'*, No. 4, 1925, p. 270. See also *Pravda*, February 4, 1925, p. 5.

179. *XIV s"ezd*, p. 824.

180. See, for example, *Zapiski kommunisticheskogo universiteta*, II, pp. 256–7; *O rabkore i sel'kore*, pp. 8–9, 12, 16–25, 34–40, 68, 75–7; and *Pravda*, May 29, 1926, p. 3.

181. Or as he put it: "the growth of what I . . . conditionally call *sovetskaia obshchestvennost'*." The expression may be translated as Soviet social structure, community, or simply as Sovietism. *Zapiski kommunisticheskogo universiteta*, II, pp. 256–9. See also *Bol'shevik*, No. 7–8, 1924, pp. 22–4.

182. *O rabkore i sel'kore*, pp. 74–7. See also, for example, *Tekushchii moment i osnovy*, p. 38; *Pravda*, June 19, 1925, p. 5; and *Molodaia gvardiia*, No. 2, 1926, p. 89.

183. See his *O rabkore i sel'kore*, especially pp. 8–9, 18–25, 34–40, 51–7, 61–3; *Pravda*, May 28, 1926, p. 3, and May 29, 1926, p. 3. For the worker-peasant correspondents, see Carr, *Socialism*, I, pp. 195–8.

184. For the charge, see *Za marksistsko-leninskoe uchenie o pechati* (Moscow, 1932), pp. 81–5, 108–10; and "Protiv opportunizma v rabsel'korovskom dvizhenii," *Pravda*, December 11, 1929, p. 4. For Bukharin's response, see *Politicheskoe zaveshchanie Lenina*, p. 25; and his angry denunciation of bureaucratization in *Pravda*, December 2, 1928, pp. 3–4.

185. See, for example, *O rabkore i sel'kore*, pp. 15–16, 56.

186. *Tekushchii moment i osnovy*, p. 37.

187. The expression is Demian Bedny's, quoted in Carr, *Socialism*, II, p. 79.

188. *Za leninizm*, pp. 294, 296, 317.

189. See Bukharin's remarks in *Bol'shevik*, No. 9–10, 1925, p. 5; and *XIV s"ezd*, p. 824.

190. Preobrazhensky, *New Economics*, p. 303.

191. The term is Ivan Smilga's. See *VKA*, XVII (1926), p. 199.

192. This account of the Left's critique is based on Erlich, *Soviet Industrialization*, pp. 30–59.

193. *Doklad*, p. 3; *Tri rechi*, p. 17; *Nekotorye voprosy*, p. 7. For the industrial figures, see Popov, *Outline History*, II, p. 261.

194. *VII s"ezd vsesoiuznogo leninskogo kommunistcheskogo soiuza molodezhi*, p. 255; *Leningradskaia organizatsiia*, p. 114. In December 1915, he observed that industry was producing "an insufficient quantity of goods," but did not treat it seriously. *Tri rechi*, p. 19.

195. Erlich, *Soviet Industrialization*, p. 38. For Bukharin, see *Rasshirennyi plenum ispolkoma* (1925), pp. 369–70; and *Bol'shevik*, No. 9–10, 1925, p. 4.

196. During the debates, Bolsheviks were mindful of the czarist agrarian reforms conducted by Stolypin, who had described them as a "wager not on the drunken and the weak but on the sober and the strong—on the sturdy individual proprietor." Quoted in Richard Charques, *The Twilight of Imperial Russia* (London, 1965), pp. 177–8. Hence Bukharin's regular denial that his policies constituted a "wager on the kulak."

197. This is a major theme of Lewin, *Russian Peasants*.

198. See Lewin's discussion in *Soviet Studies* (October 1965), pp. 163–4; and Erlich, *Soviet Industrialization*, pp. 34–6. There is a dispute among scholars over the level of marketed grain surplus in the twenties. Some tend to support official figures used by Stalin, which put marketed produce in 1926–7 at 13.3 per cent of the harvest, compared to 26 per cent in 1913. Some argue that these figures were inaccurate and the discrepancy between 1913 and 1926–7 considerably smaller. See Jerzy F. Karcz, "Thoughts on the Grain Problem," *Soviet Studies* (April 1967), pp. 399–434; and R. W. Davies, "A Note on Grain Statistics," *Soviet Studies* (January 1970), pp. 314–29. Even assuming the more favorable figures, it remained a very serious problem.

199. Carr, *Socialism*, I, pp. 290–7.

200. See Lewin's discussion in *Soviet Studies* (October 1965), pp. 162–97.

201. *Tekushchii moment i osnovy*, p. 11.

202. *Partiia i oppozitsionnyi blok*, p. 58.

203. See Erlich, *Soviet Industrialization*, Chapter iv.

CHAPTER VII

1. For the end of the triumvirate, see Daniels, *Conscience*, pp. 253–7; and Carr, *Socialism*, II, Chapter xiii. For evidence of a gradual emergence of the Stalin-Bukharin alliance in late 1924 and early 1925, see *XIV s"ezd*, pp. 136, 397–8, 459–60, 502; and Carr, *Socialism*, II, pp. 43–5. Though no formal leadership posts existed, the position of Stalin and Bukharin as co-leaders in 1925–7 was tacitly and officially acknowledged in various ways. See, for example, their positioning in the official picture of the Central Committee elected in December 1927. *Ogonek*, January 1, 1928, not paged.

2. *K itogam XIV s"ezda*, p. 4.

3. The term "groupings" is Bukharin's, *ibid.* See also Lashevich's observation that the Politburo was not really a collectivity of leaders but a number of "combinations," *XIV s"ezd*, p. 181.

4. For Stalin's growing organizational power, see Carr, *Socialism*, II, pp. 196–214; and Daniels, *Conscience*, pp. 165–71, 193–8. The term "principality" was used regularly and critically in this connection in the twenties. See, for example, Bukharin, *Doklad*, p. 53; and *Shestnadtsataia konferentsiia VKP(b) aprel' 1929 goda: stenograficheskii otchet* (Moscow, 1962), p. 749.

5. Boris Souvarine, *Stalin: A Critical Survey of Bolshevism* (New York, 1939), p. 476. In 1929, Bukharin would call it a "secretarial régime." Quoted in Gaisinskii, *Bor'ba s uklonami*, p. 196.

6. Serge, *Memoirs*, p. 211; *XIV s"ezd*, p. 524; V. M. Ivanov, *Iz istorii bor'by partii protiv "levogo opportunizma"* (Leningrad, 1965), pp. 155–200.

7. See *XIV s"ezd*, p. 149; *Pravda*, December 13, 1925, p. 5; *Tri rechi*, pp. 3–4. See also Maretskii, "Bukharin," p. 278; Carr, *Socialism*, I, p. 269; and Valentinov, *Doktrina*, passim.

8. Indeed, this was the gravamen of Zinoviev's complaint at the Fourteenth Party Congress. See *XIV s"ezd*, especially pp. 101–9.

9. *Rasshirennyi plenum ispolkoma* (1925), pp. 528–44. They appeared originally under Bukharin's name in *Pravda*, April 1, 1925, and contained virtually every one of his theoretical innovations on building socialism in a peasant society. They became controversial later when Stalinists tried to deny that Bukharinism had ever been official policy. See, for example, E. Iaroslavskii, "Ob odnoi fal'shivoi ssylke," *Pravda*, November 17, 1929, p. 2. Bukharin's updated views on international revolution and Comintern policy will be discussed in Chapter VIII.

10. Robert V. Daniels has written about Stalin's alliance with the Bukharinists: "In matters of policy and doctrine their line was his guide; in matters of organization, his power was their support." See "Stalin's Rise to Dictatorship, 1922–1929," in *Politics in the Soviet Union: Seven Cases*, edited by Alexander Dallin and Alan F. Westin (New York, 1966), p. 27.

11. See, for example, *XIV s"ezd*, pp. 494, 503–4.

12. For a discussion, see Alexander Erlich, "Stalin's Views on Soviet Economic Development," in *Continuity and Change in Russian and Soviet Thought*, edited by Ernest J. Simmons (Cambridge, Mass., 1955), pp. 81–99; and Valentinov, *Doktrina*, pp. 81–5. For a different view, see Rudolf Schlesinger, "A Note on the Context of Early Soviet Planning," *Soviet Studies* (July 1964), pp. 22–44.

13. *XIV s"ezd*, pp. 254, 494. For similar opposition statements, see the remarks of Smilga and Radek in *VKA*, XVII (1926), pp. 199, 247; and of Kamenev in *XIV s"ezd*, pp. 255–6, 269–70.

14. *Bol'shevik*, No. 1, 1924, p. 3.

15. See Carr, *Socialism*, II, p. 55; and *Vestnik leningradskogo universiteta* (Istoriia-iazyk-literatura), No. 2, 1971, p. 26.

16. *Partiinaia i sovetskaia pechat' v bor'be za postroenie sotsializma i kommunizma, Part I* (Moscow, 1961), p. 76; *Krasnaia pechat'*, No. 4, 1926, p. 7. See also *Vestnik leningradskogo universiteta* (Istoriia-iazyk-literatura), No. 2, 1968, p. 26.

17. *XIV s"ezd*, p. 254. See also Zinoviev's complaint, *ibid.*, pp. 113–17.

18. *Kommunisticheskii internatsional: kratkii istoricheskii ocherk*, pp. 261–2; *Vlast' sovetov za desiat' let: 1917–1927* (Leningrad, 1927), p. xxxvii.

19. Among others, Aleksandr Slepkov, Valentin Astrov, Aleksandr Aikhenvald, and E. Goldenberg, all prominent young Bukharinists in the Soviet party, worked occasionally in the Comintern apparatus after 1925. Bukharin brought Slepkov, for example, into its Political Secretariat, recommending him as "an excellent organizer." Jules Humbert-Droz, *De Lénine à Staline, 1921–1931* (Neuchatel, 1971), p. 285. Two lesser-known Soviet Bukharinists, Grolman and Idelson, apparently ran the Soviet party cell in the Executive Committee. See *Pravda*, November 22, 1929, p. 3, and December 16, 1929, p. 3. Humbert-Droz, the Swiss delegate and a leading figure in the Comintern apparatus, was especially close to Bukharin. He and others will be discussed in Chapter IX.

20. See Pokrovskii's remarks in *VKA*, XI (1925), p. 320; and Volfson's in *Literaturnaia entsiklopediia*, I (Moscow, 1929), p. 634. See also Eastman, *Love and Revolution*, pp. 353–4; and *The New York Times*, November 4, 1926, p. 12.

21. For his attack on Zinoviev, see *XIV s"ezd*, pp. 136–51; for his Leningrad speeches, see *Leningradskaia organizatsiia* and *Doklad*. Preobrazhenskii described Bukharin as his "most learned" and "principal opponent," *New Economics*, pp. 8, 295.

22. The attacks began in Leningrad in early 1925, reaching a crescendo at the congress in December. See *Novaia oppozitsiia*, pp. 11, 64–5, 176; and *XIV s"ezd*. See also Safarov quoted in Ustrialov, *Pod znakom revoliutsii*, p. 225; and Preobrazhensky, *New Economics*, p. 280.

23. *XIV s"ezd*, pp. 109, 165, 254, 274.

24. See, for example, Trotsky in *Biulleten' oppozitsii*, No. 12–13, 1929, p. 18; and I. Smilga, "Platforma pravogo kruga VKP(b)," (T2825), p. 3. For the Stalinist attack, see *Pravda*, September 18, 1929, p. 3, and October 20, 1929, p. 3.

25. *PZM*, No. 3, 1922, p. 85. And as Bukharin later pointed out, they had actually begun to form in 1919–20. *Case of the Anti-Soviet Bloc*, p. 385.

26. Bukharin-Kamenev memorandum (T1897); and *Case of the Anti-Soviet Bloc*, p. 387. For Tseitlin's (sometimes spelled Tsetlin) Komsomol career, see his memoir in *Iunosheskoe dvizhenie v Rossii*, edited by A. Kirov and V. Dalin (2nd ed.; Moscow and Leningrad, 1925), pp. 235–6; and *VLKSM v rezoliutsiiakh ego s"ezdov i konferentsii: 1918–1928* (Moscow and Leningrad, 1929), p. 7.

27. First Zinoviev and then Stalin, for example, tried to recruit the best young Bukharinists for their own secretariats. See *Pravda*, July 24, 1927, p. 5; *Bol'shevik*, No. 11–12, 1927, pp. 38–9; and Astrov, *Krucha*, p. 318. For Stalin, see *Memoirs of a Bolshevik-Leninist* (to be published by Pathfinder Press, New York).

28. Avtorkhanov, *Stalin*, p. 24. See, for example, Maretskii's "Bukharin."

29. *Zapiski kommunisticheskogo universiteta*, II, p. 259.

30. *Za povorot na filosofskom fronte: sbornik statei*, I (Moscow and Leningrad, 1931), p. 101. See also above, Chapter V, note 92.

31. For the Institute, see Katz, "Party-Political Education in Soviet Russia," *passim*; A. Alymov, "Desiat' let IKP," *VKA*, No. 12, 1931, pp. 13–18; *Istoricheskii arkhiv*, No. 6, 1958, pp. 73–90; Avtorkhanov, *Stalin*, Chapters i, iii–v, x; and A. I. Gukovskii, "Kak ia stal istorikom," *Istoriia SSSR*, No. 6, 1965, pp. 76–99.

32. See, for example, Meshcheriakov, "Bukharin," *MSE*, I (Moscow, 1929), p. 914; Serge, *Memoirs*, p. 163; Futrell, *Northern Underground*, p. 142; and the memoirs quoted throughout in Löwy, *Die Weltgeschichte*. For Trotsky's remark, see *Writings of Leon Trotsky (1937–38)* (New York, 1970), p. 166.

33. Lenin, *Soch.*, XXVI, p. 121. See, for example, *Desiatyi s"ezd*, p. 293; and *XIV s"ezd*, pp. 223, 461.

34. *Works*, XII, p. 25.

35. Meshcheriakov in *MSE*, I (Moscow, 1929), p. 914.

36. Bernhard Reichenbach, "Moscow 1921," *Survey*, No. 53 (1964), p. 17; Margaret McCarthy, *Generation in Revolt* (London, 1953), p. 112. For *Pravda*, see the memoirs in *M. I. Ul'ianova—sekretar' Pravdy* (Moscow, 1965), p. 186.

37. See the dedication to Bukharin in V. Astrov and A. Slepkov, *Sotsialdemokratiia i revoliutsiia* (Moscow and Leningrad, 1928).

38. See below, Epilogue, note 2.

39. *Sotsialisticheskii vestnik*, July 18, 1927, p. 14. For Petrovskii, see below, Chapter X, note 86. For Stetskii, see *Geroi oktiabria*, II (Leningrad, 1967), pp. 444–5; and *Shestoi s"ezd*, p. 466. Astrov later wrote two thinly disguised novels about himself and the young Bukharinists. See his *Ogni vperedi* (Moscow, 1967); and *Krucha*.

40. See *Rul'*, November 7, 1929, p. 3; and *Pravda*, November 18, 1929, p. 3. For Goldenberg, see *Pravda*, July 21, 1929, p. 4.

41. See Slepkov's *Klassovye protivorechiia v 1-i dume* (Moscow, 1923); Astrov's *"Ekonomisty" predtechi men'shevikov: ekonomizm i rabochee dvizhenie v Rossii na poroge XX veka* (Moscow, 1923); and Maretskii's study of Austrian marginalism in *Trudy instituta krasnoi professury*, edited by M. N. Pokrovskii, I (Moscow, 1923), pp. 247–75. Astrov and Slepkov continued to publish as historians in the twenties. Aikhenvald and Goldenberg were regular contributors to economic journals. The former's major work was *Sovetskaia ekonomika* (Moscow and Leningrad, 1927).

42. Zinoviev complained that the young Bukharinists "fill our central organs with their articles," *XIV s"ezd*, p. 117. A bibliography of their writings would fill many pages. Suffice it to say that few issues of *Pravda* or *Bol'shevik* appeared in 1925–7 without articles by one or more of them. For examples, see the following collections: *Novaia oppozitsiia; Ob ekonomicheskoi platforme oppozitsii: sbornik statei* (Moscow and Leningrad, 1926); and *Partiia protiv oppozitsii: sbornik statei i dokumentov*, edited by L. Robinskii and A. Slepkov (Moscow and Leningrad, 1927). For examples of their Bukharinist monographs, see Slepkov's *O propagande leninizma v rabochei partiinoi shkole* (Moscow, 1925), and *Proletariat i krest'ianstvo v revoliutsii* (2nd ed.; Kharkov, 1926); D. Maretskii, *Tak nazyvaemyi 'termidor'* (Moscow, 1927); and A. Zaitsev, *Ob Ustrialove, "neonepe" i zhertvakh ustrialovshchiny* (Moscow and Leningrad, 1928). For examples of their public appearances, see *VKA*, XI (1925), pp. 322–7, 332–4, and XVII (1926), pp. 236–41, 246–7, 249–54, 261–5.

43. See, for example, Zaitsev in *PZM*, No. 6–7, 1924, pp. 280–91; Maretskii in *Bol'shevik*, No. 5–6, 1925, pp. 106–10; and Maretskii's "Bukharin."

44. *Pravda*, September 18, 1929, p. 3, and October 20, 1929, p. 3.

45. Iaroslavskii in *Pravda*, July 24, 1927, p. 5. For Bukharin's denials, see *Tri rechi*, p. 3; and *XIV s"ezd*, p. 823.

46. F. M. Vaganov, *Pravyi uklon v VKP(b) i ego razgrom (1928–1930)* (Moscow, 1970), p. 143.

47. See *XIV s"ezd*, p. 504; *Voprosy istorii KPSS*, No. 6, 1967, p. 58; and *Vsia Moskva 1927* (3 vols; Moscow, 1927), II, p. 358.

48. See V. Dubrovin, *Povest' o plamennom publitsiste (S. M. Kirov i pechat')* (Leningrad, 1969), pp. 201, 204; and Astrov, *Krucha*, pp. 392–3, 399, 419, 473.

49. See above, note 19. Slepkov played a major role in the correspondent movement, see *Pravda*, May 25, 1926, p. 3.

50. See, for example, *Pravda*, November 13, 1929, p. 3, and November 18, 1929, p. 3; Abramov, *O pravoi oppozitsii*, pp. 252–3; and Vaganov, *Pravyi uklon*, Chap-

ters iv–v. Aikhenvald's *Sovetskaia ekonomika*, a Bukharinist textbook published in 1927, had gone through five editions totaling 100,000 copies in Russian and Ukrainian by 1929. See *Bol'shevik*, No. 18, 1929, pp. 131–6; and *Sotsialisticheskii vestnik*, March 8, 1929, p. 13.

51. *Pravda*, July 21, 1929, p. 4.

52. *XIV s"ezd*, p. 1003; *Ocherki istorii leningradskoi organizatsii KPSS*, II (Leningrad, 1968), pp. 316–21; *XV konferentsiia*, p. 838; and *Piatnadtsatyi s"ezd VKP(b) dekabr' 1927 goda: stenograficheskii otchet* (2 vols; Moscow, 1961–2), II, p. 1534.

53. *VKA*, XI (1925), p. 326.

54. *Bol'shevik*, No. 9–10, 1925, pp. 59–64.

55. See Bukharin's remarks in *Leningradskaia organizatsiia*, p. 89; the discussion in *XIV s"ezd*, pp. 187, 204, 408, 417; and *Bol'shevik*, No. 7–8, 1930, pp. 104–5. Despite the scandal, Bogushevskii himself went on to have an extraordinary career, becoming a leading figure among Stalinist industrializers, and an editor and author of the official Stalinist history of the first five-year plan. See V. Bogushevskii, "Kanun piatiletki," in *God vosemnadtsatyi: al'manakh vos'moi*, edited by M. Gor'kii (Moscow, 1935), pp. 461–537. Who sponsored him is unclear, though it was probably Valerian Kuibyshev. See G. V. Kuibysheva, *et al.*, *Valerian Vladimirovich Kuibyshev: biografiia* (Moscow, 1966), p. 313.

56. *XIV s"ezd*, p. 335. See also Anastas Mikoian, "Iz vospominanii o Lenine," *Iunost'*, No. 4, 1970, p. 46. That Lenin is understood best as a kind of charismatic leader is argued persuasively in Robert C. Tucker's *Stalin as Revolutionary: A Study in History and Personality* (New York, 1973).

57. "Tovarishch," in *Vladimir Il'ich Lenin: sbornik* (Ivanovo-Voznesensk, 1924), p. 15; *Pravda*, February 27, 1929, p. 3. Though he did not mention Stalin by name, like Sokolnikov quoted above, Bukharin was contrasting Lenin's authority to that of the general secretary.

58. Delegate quoted in Carr, *Socialism*, II, p. 226; and Bukharin, *Tri rechi*, p. 40.

59. The expression is Zinoviev's, *XIV s"ezd*, p. 460.

60. See, for example, *Sotsialisticheskii vestnik*, November 14, 1928, p. 14.

61. Bukharin-Kamenev memorandum (T1897). For tactical reasons, Stalin had argued otherwise in 1925, see *XIV s"ezd*, p. 506.

62. The term "authoritative leader" or "authoritative representative of the party" was so used regularly in the twenties. See, for example, Meshcheriakov's biography of Bukharin in *MSE*, I (Moscow, 1929), p. 913; and *VKA*, XVII (1926), p. 247.

63. Bukharin-Kamenev memorandum (T1897). See also Deutscher, *Stalin*, p. 290.

64. Trotsky, *My Life*, p. 521.

65. No one, for example, would have considered soliciting Stalin's views during the discussion of literature in 1924–5. For the area of foreign affairs, see Leon Trotsky, *Problems of the Chinese Revolution* (Ann Arbor, Mich., 1967), p. 169.

66. Ypsilon, *Pattern for World Revolution*, p. 102.

67. Nikita S. Khrushchev, *The Crimes of the Stalin Era* (New York, 1956), pp. 10–11. See also Lenin, *PSS*, XLV, p. 346, and LIV, pp. 329–30.

68. For Ulianova, see *M. I. Ul'ianova—sekretar' Pravdy*. She and Bukharin seem to have become friends in Moscow before 1910. That they were close in 1918 is indicated in M. I. Ul'ianova, *O Lenine* (Moscow, 1964), p. 86. In 1919, she,

along with Bukharin, was ousted from *Pravda* by Stalin, *M. I. Ul'ianova—sekretar' Pravdy*, p. 259. On this whole question, see also *Trotsky's Diary in Exile: 1935* (New York, 1963), p. 33.

69. *XIV s"ezd*, pp. 158–66, 299.

70. *The Communist International*, No. 4, 1926, p. 14.

71. I. P. Razumovskii, *Kurs teorii istoricheskogo materializma* (2nd ed.; Moscow and Leningrad, 1927), pp. 511–12.

72. Loren R. Graham, *The Soviet Academy of Sciences and the Communist Party* (Princeton, N.J., 1967), pp. 92, 95, 114.

73. *Stalin: sbornik statei k piatidesiatiletiiu so dnia rozhdeniia* (Moscow and Leningrad, 1929), p. 48.

74. For official biographies of Rykov, see *Deiateli*, II, pp. 223–30; Iu. Vereshchagin, *Predsedatel' soveta narodnykh kommissarov* (3rd ed.; Moscow and Leningrad, 1925); and Boris Fradkin, *12 biografii* (Moscow, 1924), pp. 34–9. For Tomskii, see *Deiateli*, III, pp. 146–50; and B. Kozelov, *Mikhail Pavlovich Tomskii* (Moscow, 1927).

75. Private communication from Boris Nicolaevsky, Rykov's brother-in-law. For this period, see A. I. Rykov, *Stat'i i rechi* (Moscow and Leningrad, 1927–8).

76. Vereshchagin, *Predsedatel'*, pp. 22–3.

77. Quoted in Valentinov, *Doktrina*, p. 21. Rykov is a central figure in Valentinov's (Vol'skii) memoirs, *Novaia ekonomicheskaia politika;* and Reswick's *I Dreamt Revolution*. For his antipathy to Trotsky, see also his introduction to *Za leninizm*, pp. 3–8.

78. For his views, see *Trinadtsataia konferentsiia rossiiskoi kommunisticheskoi partii (bol'shevikov): stenograficheskii otchet* (Moscow, 1924), pp. 6–20; his *Derevnia, novaia ekonomicheskaia politika i kooperatsiia* (Moscow and Leningrad, 1925); *XIV konferentsiia*, pp. 143–4; and *XIV s"ezd*, pp. 408–17.

79. Jay Bertram Sorenson, "The Dilemma of Soviet Trade Unions During the First Period of Industrial Transformation" (unpublished Ph.D. dissertation, Columbia University, 1962), p. 90. Similarly, see *XV konferentsiia*, p. 669; and *Platform of the Left Opposition*, p. 65.

80. Tomskii in *Inprecor*, X (1930), p. 687; and Gaisinskii, *Bor'ba s uklonami*, pp. 209–10. For the unions and Tomskii's leadership in the twenties, see Jay B. Sorenson, *The Life and Death of Soviet Trade Unionism* (New York, 1969); Isaac Deutscher, *Soviet Trade Unions* (London, 1950); and *Vsia Moskva*, II, pp. 201–2.

81. Carr, *Bolshevik Revolution*, II, pp. 190–1, 221–3; Kozelev, *Tomskii*, pp. 81–4.

82. Quoted in Gaisinskii, *Bor'ba s uklonami*, p. 202.

83. See Deutscher, *Soviet Trade Unions*, pp. 76–9; and Kozelev's remarks in *Vestnik truda*, No. 11, 1925, p. 35. Tomskii's views will be discussed further in Chapter IX.

84. B. Nikolaevskii, "Sorok let tomu nazad," *Sotsialisticheskii vestnik* (February–March 1961), p. 27; and his "Revoliutsiia v Kitae, Iaponiia i Stalina," *Novyi zhurnal*, VI (1943), pp. 241–4.

85. See Carr, *Socialism*, III, Chapter xxxvi; M. Tomskii, *Stat'i i rechi*, VI (Moscow, 1928); B. Freidlin, *Soiuzy SSSR v bor'be za edinstvo professional'nogo dvizheniia* (Moscow, 1925); and David E. Langsam, "Pressure Group Politics in NEP Russia: The Case of the Trade Unions" (unpublished Ph.D. dissertation, Princeton University, 1973), Chapter iv.

86. *XIV s"ezd*, pp. 277–9; *XV konferentsiia*, p. 294. The official trade union journal, *Vestnik truda*, also suddenly began to give Bukharin special prominence. See the review of his book in No. 11, 1925, pp. 216–18, and his article in No. 12, 1925, pp. 5–8.

87. Reswick's *I Dreamt Revolution* suggests that they were a group as early as 1924–5.

88. *XIV s"ezd*, pp. 18, 289, 418. Their remarks were particularly significant because of Kamenev's warning to the congress that Stalin's rise signified "the theory of a 'leader' . . . the creation of a leader." *Ibid.*, pp. 274–5. For Stalin's promoters, see the remarks of Voroshilov and Kuibyshev, *ibid.*, pp. 397, 628.

89. Reswick, *I Dreamt Revolution*, pp. 116–20, 150. In a 1921 letter, Stalin sneered at "the philistine 'realism' . . . of Rykov, who . . . is immersed to his ears in routine. . . ." *Works*, V, pp. 50–1.

90. Stalin, *Works*, XI, p. 229; Gaisinskii, *Bor'ba s uklonami*, pp. 209–10.

91. Carr, *Socialism*, III, pp. 500, 585–8, 592–3; *Sotsialisticheskii vestnik*, January 16, 1925, pp. 8–10, 15.

92. *Sotsialisticheskii vestnik*, January 15, 1927, p. 15, and July 8, 1927, p. 14.

93. See, for example, *Sed'moi s"ezd professional'nykh soiuzov*, pp. 19–23; and *Pravda*, December 2, 1928, p. 3.

94. All sides of course claimed to represent the authentic "Left," regarding the designation "Right" as anathema. The terms "Left," "Right," and "center" do not have their customary meanings in the context of Bolshevism, and are used here cnly relatively to designate respective areas of the overall spectrum of opinion and politics within the left-wing Bolshevik Party. On Stalin's cultivation of the center, see Deutscher, *Stalin*, pp. 295–7. Piatakov is quoted in Valentinov, *Novaia ekonomicheskaia politika*, p. 164.

95. Quoted in Bukharin-Kamenev memorandum (T1897).

96. Walter Kolarz, *Russia and Her Colonies* (New York, 1955), pp. 9–10, 18. Some people worried, on the other hand, that the victory of the Right would bring a "Russian supra-state chauvinism." Avtorkhanov, *Stalin*, p. 71. According to Boris Nicolaevsky in a private communication to the author, Bukharin, Rykov, and Tomskii were known as the "Ivanoviches," a reference to their Russianness, despite the fact that Tomskii's patronymic was Pavlovich.

97. Valentinov in *Novyi zhurnal*, No. 75 (1964), p. 174; Michael Kitaeff, *Communist Party Officials* (New York, 1954), p. 49; Reswick, *I Dreamt Revolution*, pp. 84–96.

98. Kitaeff, *Communist Party Officials*, p. 49.

99. See below, Chapter IX, note 3.

100. For the Mensheviks, see Valentinov, *Novaia ekonomicheskaia politika;* and Naum Jasny, *Soviet Economists of the Twenties* (New York, 1972). Both writers also discuss the Socialist Revolutionaries, who were drawn to Bukharin's agrarian policies while the Mensheviks were attracted to his planning views. For Rykov, see also Liberman, *Building Lenin's Russia*, pp. 64–8.

101. F. E. Dzerzhinskii, *Izbrannye proizvedeniia* (2 vols; Moscow, 1957), II, p. 349; see also, pp. 83–4. His headship of the Council forms the bulk of Valentinov's memoirs, *Novaia ekonomicheskaia politika*.

102. See Valentinov-Volskii's memoirs in *Novyi zhurnal*, No. 74 (1963), pp. 197, 202, and No. 75 (1964), pp. 170–1; and A. F. Khavin, *U rulia industrii* (Moscow, 1968), pp. 48–9.

103. See his autobiography in *Deiateli*, III, pp. 165-76; his biography in *Izvestiia*, November 30, 1928, p. 3; and Voroshilov's remarks in *XIV s"ezd*, p. 394.

104. For the Moscow leadership, see *Pravda*, December 15, 1925, p. 7; and *Vsia Moskva*, II, pp. 196-8. It was slightly different in 1928. Riutin, Penkov, Kulikov, and Iakovlev were district secretaries, Moroz was secretary of the Moscow Control Commission, and Mandelshtam was head of the committee's agitprop. All were members of the inner Bureau headed by Uglanov and Kotov. Their role will be discussed further in Chapter IX.

105. Ivanov, *Iz istorii bor'by partii*, pp. 36, 75; Carr, *Socialism*, I, p. 154, and II, pp. 52-9.

106. *Ocherki istorii moskovskoi organizatsii*, pp. 395, 429-30, 439; Carr, *Socialism*, I, pp. 344-5, 376.

107. E. Iaroslavskii, *Istoriia VKP(b)*, II (Moscow, 1933), p. 296.

108. *Deiateli*, III, pp. 165-76.

109. Gaisinskii, *Bor'ba s uklonami*, p. 209.

110. *Odinnadtsatyi s"ezd*, p. 837; *Pravda*, December 15, 1925, p. 7; *Deiateli*, II, pp. 27-32; Carr, *Socialism*, II, pp. 56-7.

111. *Proletarskaia revoliutsiia*, No. 10, 1922, p. 320. For places named after Bukharin, see, for example, *Vsia Moskva*, II, pp. 116, 278, 308, 488, and III, p. 611. For the Moscow Soviet, see *Pravda*, May 13, 1923, and March 17, 1929, p. 3.

112. The count is based on the speeches collected in Stalin's *Works;* see also Vol. IX, p. 159.

113. *Tri rechi*, pp. 15-40.

114. The documents appear in *Novaia oppozitsiia*, pp. 36-40, 44-50. They echoed Bukharin in many other ways as well. Young Bukharinists were probably especially active in propaganda departments of the Moscow party, either through *Pravda* and *Bolshevik* or through the Institute of Red Professors, which worked closely with the Moscow party. For this latter relationship, see V. Zeimal' and P. Pospelov, "IKP v bor'be za general'nuiu liniiu partii," *Pravda*, December 1, 1931, p. 3; and Astrov, *Krucha*, pp. 77, 194, 220. The link between Bukharin and Moscow has also been pointed out by Rudolf Schlesinger in *Soviet Studies* (April 1960), p. 406.

115. See Uglanov's remarks in *XIV s"ezd*, p. 193. In addition to himself, Kotov, Kulikov, Mikhailov, and K. V. Ukhanov were full members of the Central Committee elected in December 1925. By December 1927, Riutin and another Muscovite, V. I. Polonskii, were also Central Committee members.

116. Uglanov in *XV konferentsiia*, p. 633. See also Riutin's praise for Bukharin in *XIV s"ezd*, pp. 154-6.

117. *Molodaia gvardiia*, No. 2, 1926, p. 86; *Inprecor*, VII (1927), p. 200; "Leninizm i problema kul'turnoi revoliutsii," *Pravda*, January 27, 1928, p. 5.

118. *Trinadtsatyi s"ezd*, p. 526.

119. See, for example, *VKA*, XI (1925), p. 292. Objecting to such tendencies, he wrote in a letter in 1927: "Discussion may and should be conducted, but not by methods such as these, which in essence correspond little to reality and are clearly harmful politically. This is my *personal* opinion." Quoted in *Pravda*, August 24, 1930, p. 5.

120. On his continuing role as a protector or "intercessor," see below, Chapter X, note 90.

121. "Zlye zametki," in his *Etiudy* (Moscow and Leningrad, 1932), pp. 204, 207-8. It appeared originally in *Pravda*, January 12, 1927.

122. Quoted in a letter from Trotsky to Bukharin dated January 6, 1926 (T2976).

123. *XIV s"ezd*, pp. 149–50; *VI s"ezd vsesoiuznogo leninskogo kommunisticheskogo soiuza molodezhi*, p. 243; and Bukharin quoted in Trotsky's letter (T2976).

124. For his private memoranda on this matter, see Astrov, *Krucha*, pp. 294–5, 310–12, 317.

125. *Leningradskaia organizatsiia*, p. 108; and *K itogam XIV s"ezda*, pp. 4–5.

126. The only record of the correspondence, on which this account is based, are copies of three of Trotsky's letters to Bukharin dated January 8, March 4, and March 19, 1926, preserved in the Trotsky Archives (T2976, 868, 869).

127. Trotsky's later assumption that "Stalin most categorically forbade him to do so" is wholly incompatible with the evidence. For Bukharin's various attacks on Soviet anti-Semitism, see *Pravda*, February 2, 1927, p. 4, and November 24, 1927, p. 3; and *VIII vsesoiuznyi s"ezd VLKSM 5–16 maia 1928 goda: stenograficheskii otchet* (Moscow, 1928), p. 24.

128. Trotsky, *Problems of the Chinese Revolution*, p. 169; Bukharin, *Ob itogakh ob"edinennogo plenuma TSK i TSKK VKP(b)* (Moscow and Leningrad, 1927), p. 23. For an example of their dialogue in late 1927, see *Partiia i oppozitsiia nakanune XV s"ezda VKP(b): sbornik diskussionnykh materialov*, I (Moscow and Leningrad, 1928), pp. 67–9.

129. *Partiia i oppozitsionnyi blok*, pp. 79, 89; *XV konferentsiia*, p. 42; *K itogam XIV s"ezda*, p. 63.

130. *XV konferentsiia*, pp. 599, 601. Eleven months earlier he had said: "We have never demanded that Zinoviev publicly renounce his error"—*XIV s"ezd*, p. 150. Deutscher has described this as "Bukharin's strange, almost macabre performance," *Prophet Unarmed*, p. 305.

131. See Bukharin's remarks in *Pravda*, January 15, 1927, p. 3. There is some evidence that Stalin tried and failed to expel the Left from the party in the summer or fall of 1927, meeting resistance from the Politburo Right. See Schapiro, *Communist Party*, p. 304; and Deutscher, *Prophet Unarmed*, pp. 355–6. See also Stalin's curious letter of October 8, 1926, criticizing Slepkov for being too easy on Trotsky in a recent polemic. *Works*, VIII, pp. 217–19.

132. Information about such a plan was given to me by the late Boris Nicolaevsky in 1965. He obtained it from a foreign Communist who lived in the Soviet Union in the twenties. Equally elliptical and no less inconclusive evidence has appeared more recently, see Astrov, *Krucha*, p. 217; and Medvedev, *Let History Judge*, p. 50. Astrov was an important Bukharinist and in a position to know; but his testimony is weakened by the fact that it appears in a novel which is unreliable about actual events in many ways. Medvedev is very reliable, but here is citing only "some reports." Neither mentions Bukharin in this connection; but if such a move had been under way, he would undoubtedly have been a central participant.

133. See *XIV s"ezd*, pp. 503–4; and *Works*, VII, pp. 155–7.

134. *XIV s"ezd*, pp. 47–8, 504–5.

135. *VII s"ezd vsesoiuznogo leninskogo kommunisticheskogo soiuza molodezhi*, p. 257.

136. Quoted in Trotsky, *My Life*, pp. 433, 450. For the other opinions, see *ibid.*, p. 512, and Trotsky, *Stalin*, p. 393. Privately, Stalin was already hinting that he thought of himself as "one man standing at the head of the state." Quoted in Medvedev, *Let History Judge*, p. 325.

137. Bukharin-Kamenev memorandum (T1987).

138. *K voprosu o trotskizme*, p. 3; *XIV s"ezd*, pp. 133, 134; *V zashchitu*, p. 241.

139. *XIV konferentsiia*, p. 181.

140. *Sotsialisticheskii vestnik* (July–August 1962), p. 119. See also Sourvarine, *Stalin*, p. 426.

CHAPTER VIII

1. See, for example, Bukharin's remarks in *Pravda*, May 28, 1926, p. 3; and the resolution in *KPSS v rezoliutsiiakh*, II, pp. 258–67.

2. See, for example, *Leningradskaia organizatsiia*, p. 114; and *XV konferentsiia*, pp. 12, 19–20. He repeated this argument against Stalin in 1928. See *Pravda*, September 30, 1928, pp. 2–3.

3. *Building Up Socialism*, pp. 2–4; *Inprecor*, VII (1927), p. 195. Henceforth, he regularly emphasized the difficulties ahead.

4. *V zashchitu*, p. 225; see also pp. 223–4. For his warning against tying up resources, see also *Pravda*, November 24, 1927, p. 4; and Erlich, *Soviet Industrialization*, pp. 80–3.

5. For small manufacturing, see Bukharin quoted in *XV s"ezd*, II, p. 1370; and Erlich, *Soviet Industrialization*, pp. 84–5.

6. See, for example, his "Leninizm i stroitel'nyi period proletarskoi revoliutsii," *Pravda*, January 21, 1927, p. 2.

7. *XV konferentsiia*, pp. 471, 585, 775.

8. *Building Up Socialism*, pp. 63–4.

9. See, for example, *Pravda*, January 15, 1927, p. 3, June 18, 1927, p. 3, July 5, 1927, p. 3; and *Ob itogakh ob"edinennogo plenuma*, pp. 4–5.

10. *Building Up Socialism*, p. 62.

11. *Inprecor*, VII (1927), p. 1421; *V zashchitu*, pp. 224–5.

12. As he termed Stalin's policies in 1928. *Pravda*, December 2, 1928, p. 3.

13. *Pravda*, November 24, 1927, p. 3. See also *Building Up Socialism*, p. 2, where he called it a "hard nut to crack."

14. See, for example, *Pravda*, May 28, 1926, pp. 3–4, February 2, 1927, p. 3, and November 24, 1927, p. 3; *Partiia i oppozitsiia nakanune XV s"ezda*, pp. 62–3; and *V zashchitu*, pp. 224, 226–8.

15. See *Pravda*, January 15, 1927, p. 3, and February 2, 1927, pp. 3–4.

16. For the first, see his "Na poroge desiatogo goda," *Pravda*, November 7, 1927, p. 2; *V zashchitu*, pp. 210–11, 215, 229; and *Pravda*, November 23, 1927, p. 4. For the second, see *VII s"ezd vsesoiuznogo leninskogo kommunisticheskogo soiuza molodezhi*, p. 255; *V zashchitu*, p. 224; and Erlich, *Soviet Industrialization*, p. 86.

17. See, for example, *Pravda*, May 28, 1926, pp. 3–4; and *Inprecor*, VII (1927), p. 1421.

18. *Pravda*, November 24, 1927, p. 3.

19. As he would characterize Stalinist planners in 1928. See *Pravda*, September 30, 1928, pp. 2–3.

20. *Inprecor*, VII (1927), pp. 1369, 1421; *V zashchitu*, pp. 219–25; *Pravda*, November 24, 1927, p. 3. The goal of "more or less crisis-free development" was adopted by the Fifteenth Party Congress and defended by Bukharin in 1928. See, for example, *Pravda*, September 30, 1928, pp. 2–3, where he also expands on the meaning of "basic economic proportions."

21. See his *New Economics*.

22. *Pravda*, July 3, 1926, pp. 2–3. For the development of this idea in Bukharin's thought, see above, Chapter IV, and *Za leninizm*, p. 310. It was derived from a passage in a letter by Marx. See Marx and Engels, *Selected Works*, II, p. 461. Its importance in Bukharinism may be judged by the treatment in Aikhenval'd, *Sovetskaia ekonomika*, Chapter xxii.

23. *Pravda*, September 30, 1928, p. 2.

24. Speech to the July 1928 plenum (T1901).

25. See, for example, *XV konferentsiia*, p. 604; *Inprecor*, VII (1927), pp. 197–200, 1420; and *V zashchitu*, p. 213.

26. He issued the slogan in a speech on October 12. *Inprecor*, VII (1927), p. 1422. He elaborated on it two weeks later, see *V zashchitu*, pp. 202–11, 215, 228–31. Though it apparently represented a collective leadership decision, Bukharin's formulation seems to have been his own, and to have caught some leaders by surprise. See Kalinin's remarks in *XV s"ezd*, II, pp. 1229–31.

27. Leon Trotsky, *The Real Situation in Russia* (New York, 1928), p. 11.

28. See Bukharin's explanations cited above, note 26.

29. *Ibid.* See also *Pravda*, November 6–7, 1927, p. 3; and Bukharin, *Uroki khlebozagotovok, shakhtinskogo dela i zadachi partii* (Leningrad, 1928), p. 84, from which these quotes are taken.

30. *V zashchitu*, pp. 224–5; *Pravda*, January 27, 1928, p. 5. See also Erlich, *Soviet Industrialization*, p. 84.

31. See, for example, *Inprecor*, VII (1927), p. 1423; *V zashchitu*, pp. 201, 229; and *Pravda*, November 5, 1927, pp. 4–5, November 6–7, 1927, p. 3, and November 23, 1927, p. 3.

32. For a discussion and evaluation, see Erlich, *Soviet Industrialization*, pp. 87–9.

33. See, for example, *V zashchitu*, pp. 226–8; his "O starinnykh traditsiiakh i sovremennom kul'turnom stroitel'stve," *Revoliutsiia i kul'tura*, No. 1, 1927, pp. 17–22; and his article on "Leninism and the Problem of Cultural Revolution" in *Pravda*, January 27, 1928, pp. 5–6.

34. An insight of Professor Alexander Erlich.

35. *Puti mirovoi revoliutsii*, I, p. 7.

36. See, for example, *Ataka*, pp. 185–95; *Za leninizm*, p. 368; *Pravda*, June 19, 1925, p. 5; and *Inprecor*, VII (1927), pp. 194, 1348–50.

37. For his major statements of this view, see *Bol'shevik*, No. 3–4, 1925, pp. 3–17; and *Rasshirennyi plenum ispolkoma* (1925), pp. 304–28, 528–44. See also *Pravda*, October 24, 1924, p. 5, June 19, 1925, p. 5; and *Inprecor*, V (1925), p. 863, from which the final quote comes.

38. For his earlier drafts, see *Ataka*, pp. 285–303; and "Program of the Communist International" (copy of Bertram Wolfe, New York Public Library).

39. See, in particular, his long reports in *Puti mirovoi revoliutsii*, I, pp. 30–112; and *XV s"ezd*, I, pp. 623–93, 819–42.

40. His first explicit remarks appeared in *XV s"ezd*, I, pp. 626–33, 823–30. For his earlier, tacit understanding, see *XV konferentsiia*, pp. 16–17, 93.

41. The quotes are from Bukharin's two articles, published in the summer of 1929, summarizing his views on modern capitalism. They are reprinted in *"Organizovannyi kapitalizm,"* pp. 168–99. He argued similarly, though less explicitly, in 1926–8.

42. *Ibid.*, pp. 183–4; *XV s"ezd*, I, pp. 630–2, 823–8; *Inprecor*, VIII (1928), pp. 727, 730.

43. *"Organizovannyi kapitalizm,"* pp. 168, 183.

44. *Inprecor*, VIII (1928), p. 1035.

45. *"Organizovannyi kapitalizm,"* p. 185.

46. *Ibid.*, pp. 176–7, 195–6; *XV s"ezd*, I, pp. 632–3.

47. Quoted in Leont'ev, *Ekonomicheskaia teoriia pravogo uklona*, p. 125. See also Bukharin's remarks in *Politicheskoe zaveshchanie Lenina*, p. 12.

48. See, for example, *XV s"ezd*, I, pp. 832, 834; and *Inprecor*, VIII (1928), pp. 728, 865, 874.

49. *XV konferentsiia*, p. 29; *Puti mirovoi revoliutsii*, I, p. 48.

50. See his remarks, largely about events in China, in N. Bukharin, *Problems of the Chinese Revolution* (London, 1927); *Puti mirovoi revoliutsii*, I, pp. 48–9, 83–91; *XV konferentsiia*, pp. 23–9; *Inprecor*, VII (1927), pp. 874–6, 897–9; *Ob itogakh ob"edinennogo plenuma*, pp. 36–53; and *XV s"ezd*, I, pp. 659–74.

51. *Puti mirovoi revoliutsii*, I, p. 30; *Ob itogakh ob"edinennogo plenuma*, p. 46; *Politicheskoe zaveshchanie Lenina*, p. 12. Nicolaevsky has pointed out that nationalist revolution became for Bukharin not only a battering ram against imperialism, but also a "thing in itself." *Novyi zhurnal*, III (1942), p. 190.

52. *Problems of the Chinese Revolution*, p. 6; *Ob itogakh ob"edinennogo plenuma*, pp. 39–46; *Inprecor*, VII (1927), p. 1370.

53. *Inprecor*, VIII (1928), p. 1269.

54. Lin Piao, *Long Live the Victory of People's War!* (Peking, 1966), pp. 47–9.

55. See his remarks on "super-profits" at the Sixth Comintern Congress. *VI kongress Kominterna: stenograficheskii otchet* (6 vols; Moscow and Leningrad, 1929), I, p. 41, and III, pp. 139–43.

56. See, for example, his remarks in *ibid.*, I, pp. 601–4.

57. See above, note 50; and *Pravda*, March 26, 1925, p. 3.

58. See, for example, his remarks on British unions in *Inprecor*, VI (1926), pp. 830–4, 850–2; his *O mezhdunarodnom polozhenii* (Leningrad, 1926), pp. 15–18; *Shestoi rasshirennyi plenum ispolkoma Kominterna (17 fevralia—15 marta 1926 g.): stenograficheskii otchet* (Moscow and Leningrad, 1927), pp. 203, 206, 208; and *XV konferentsiia*, pp. 37–9, 89–93. And his remarks on their European counterparts in *Kommunisticheskii internatsional*, No. 3, 1926, pp. 92–3; *Puti mirovoi revoliutsii*, I, pp. 102–3; and *XV s"ezd*, I, pp. 653–8, 676, 679.

59. *Inprecor*, VIII (1928), p. 1275. For this "tragedy of the working class" which "Jack London . . . perfectly understood," see *IV vsemirnyi kongress kommunisticheskogo internatsionala: izbrannye doklady, rechi i rezoliutsii* (Moscow and Petrograd, 1923), pp. 181–2. Similarly, see *Pravda*, April 28, 1927, p. 3; and *VI kongress Kominterna*, III, p. 142.

60. This subject is examined at length in Theodore Draper, "The Strange Case of the Comintern," *Survey* (Summer 1972), pp. 91–137.

61. *Inprecor*, VIII (1928), p. 1269; *Pravda*, June 12, 1927, p. 1.

62. *Krizis kapitalizma*, p. 29; *Puti mirovoi revoliutsii*, I, p. 48; *O mezhdunarodnom polozhenii*, pp. 47–8.

63. *Pravda*, February 2, 1927, p. 3.

64. *XV s"ezd*, I, p. 670. For his statements during these events, see *Problems of the Chinese Revolution*, pp. 45–50; *Pravda*, June 18, 1927, pp. 3–5; *Inprecor*, VII (1927), pp. 874–6, 897–9, 927–30; and *Ob itogakh ob"edinennogo plenuma*, pp.

36–53. For Comintern policy in China, see Benjamin I. Schwartz, *Chinese Communism and the Rise of Mao* (New York, 1967); and Conrad Brandt, *Stalin's Failure in China* (New York, 1966).

65. *Ob itogakh ob"edinennogo plenuma*, pp. 47, 51.

66. *Inprecor*, VI (1926), pp. 831–4; *O mezhdunarodnom polozhenii*, pp. 15–19; and his "Velikaia bor'ba," *Pravda*, May 1, 1927, p. 1.

67. *XV s"ezd*, I, pp. 656, 658.

68. See, for example, Trotsky, *Problems of the Chinese Revolution;* his *Stalin School of Falsification*, pp. 161–77; and *Platform of the Left Opposition*, pp. 77–96.

69. Compare his remarks in *Put' k sotsializmu*, p. 41, and *Ob itogakh ob"edinennogo plenuma*, pp. 5–6.

70. Bukharin, *Uroki khlebozagotovok*, pp. 24–5; and Mikoyan in *XV s"ezd*, II, p. 1094. See also Lewin, *Russian Peasants*, pp. 178–86.

71. Rykov quoted in Trotsky, *Third International After Lenin*, p. 282.

72. William Henry Chamberlin, *Russia's Iron Age* (Boston, 1934), p. 355.

73. For these events, see Daniels, *Conscience*, Chapter xii; and Souvarine, *Stalin*, pp. 440–72.

74. The expression belongs to the left oppositionist Zorin. See his letter to Bukharin in *Sotsialisticheskii vestnik*, January 12, 1928, p. 14. For such reports, see above, Chapter VII, note 131.

75. *V zashchitu*, p. 260; *Partiia i oppozitsiia nakanune XV s"ezda*, p. 259.

76. Quoted in Deutscher, *Prophet Unarmed*, p. 428.

77. Quoted in P. J. D. Wiles, *The Political Economy of Communism* (Cambridge, 1962), p. 47. See also E. H. Carr and R. W. Davies, *Foundations of a Planned Economy* (2 vols; New York, 1969–71), I, pp. 865–74.

78. See the elliptical evidence in *Voprosy istorii KPSS*, No. 12, 1967, pp. 75–6; and *Istoriia KPSS*, IV, pp. 524–5. See also Popov, *Outline History*, II, p. 354; and Voroshilov's remarks in *XVI s"ezd vsesoiuznoi kommunisticheskoi partii: stenograficheskii otchet* (2 vols; Moscow, 1935), I, p. 516.

79. *XV s"ezd*, II, pp. 1441–68.

80. See Lewin, *Russian Peasants*, Chapter viii.

81. *XV s"ezd*, I, pp. 51, 63.

82. Bukharin did not speak on domestic affairs at the congress. See Rykov's remarks there, especially *XV s"ezd*, II, pp. 870–1, 1423.

83. *Ibid.*, I, pp. 693–705, 722–31.

84. Other subtle moves by Stalin against the Right, notably Rykov, may have been under way. See Trotsky, *Stalin School of Falsification*, pp. 20–1. At the same time, the Politburo Right evidently tried a ploy of its own at the congress, Rykov moving to have Lenin's last, anti-Stalin writings appended to the congressional stenograph. See *XV s"ezd*, I, p. 623. The motion carried, but the writings were published only in the weekly bulletins. See Medvedev, *Let History Judge*, p. 29.

85. Bukharin used the expression to describe his own treatment in 1928–9. Quoted in Stalin, *Works*, XII, p. 109.

86. See his remarks in *Inprecor*, VIII (1928), p. 218; *V zashchitu*, p. 3; and Bukharin quoted in Serge, *Memoirs*, p. 232.

87. Said Bukharin in January 1926: "Where is it written that in the Bolshevik Party mouths can never be silenced?" *K itogam XIV s"ezda*, p. 62.

88. *Partiia i oppozitsiia nakanune XV s"ezda*, p. 259.

89. Letter to Bukharin dated January 8, 1926 (T2976).

90. Bukharin-Kamenev memorandum (T1897); and Trotsky quoted in Deutscher, *Prophet Unarmed*, p. 315. Bukharin's overture was directed to Zinoviev and Kamenev, but was clearly meant to include Trotsky as well, and was so interpreted.

91. Letter from Zorin published in *Sotsialisticheskii vestnik*, January 12, 1928, p. 14.

CHAPTER IX

1. As the official Stalinist history pointed out, *History of the Communist Party of the Soviet Union (Bolsheviks): Short Course* (New York, 1939), p. 305.

2. The figures for artisan production refer to the Russian Republic for 1928-9. See *Voprosy istorii KPSS*, No. 7, 1971, pp. 83-4; and Carr and Davies, *Planned Economy*, I, p. 390.

3. *Shestnadtsataia konferentsiia*, p. 458. As we have seen, the Commissariat of Agriculture was dominated by former Socialist Revolutionaries, and the Supreme Economic Council by former Mensheviks. At Gosplan, of 527 employees in 1924, only 49 were party members. And 88 per cent of the staff of the central cooperative institutions, and most department heads, were non-Communists in 1924. See *Voprosy istorii KPSS*, No. 3, 1967, p. 55, and No. 10, 1970, pp. 81-2. A similar situation prevailed in other large ministries at the end of the NEP years. See *XV s"ezd*, I, pp. 446-7.

4. Samuel Northrup Harper, *Civic Training in Soviet Russia* (Chicago, 1929), p. 263. Similarly, of all engineers working in state industry in 1928, only 139 were party members. *Leningradskie rabochie v bor'be za sotsializm* (Leningrad, 1965), p. 49.

5. Of 152 staff members of the Leningrad party's central organ, for example, only 28 were party members in 1926. *Vestnik leningradskogo universiteta* (Istoriia-iazyk-literatura), No. 2, 1971, p. 31.

6. These figures are for the Russian Republic in 1926-7, Bernstein, "Leadership and Mobilization," p. 213. The national percentage of Bolshevik chairmen rose to 37.7 by 1928-9, D. J. Male, *Russian Peasant Organization Before Collectivization: A Study of Commune and Gathering 1925-1930* (New York, 1971), p. 128.

7. Schapiro, *Communist Party*, p. 343. For aspects of party thought in the twenties, see Joravsky, *Soviet Marxism and Natural Science;* Bauer, *The New Man in Soviet Psychology;* and Fitzpatrick, *The Commissariat of Enlightenment.* Among the party's most interesting journals were *Vestnik kommunisticheskoi akademii* and *Pod znamenem marksizma.*

8. The commissar responsible for overseeing cultural affairs in the twenties, Anatoly Lunacharskii, was famous for his liberal attitudes and gentle direction. See Fitzpatrick, *Commissariat of Enlightenment.* A sense of the excitement and ferment of NEP culture is conveyed in the early chapters of Ehrenburg's *Memoirs.* To give one example of the competing sponsorship of writers: in 1927, private publishers accounted for 6 per cent of the total number of books, but 25 per cent of all titles. *The Soviet Union: Facts, Descriptions, Statistics* (Washington, D.C., 1929), p. 196.

9. For various aspects of NEP culture, see Robert A. Maguire, *Red Virgin Soil: Soviet Literature in the 1920's* (Princeton, N.J., 1968); Marc Slonim, *Russian Theater from the Empire to the Soviets* (Cleveland, 1961), Chapters viii-ix;

Anatole Kopp, *Town and Revolution: Soviet Architecture and City Planning, 1917–1935* (New York, 1970); Dwight MacDonald, *On Movies* (New York, 1971), Part IV; Joseph Freeman, *et al., Voices of October* (New York, 1930), and *Art in Revolution: Soviet Art and Design Since 1917* (London, 1971).

10. Such occurrences were sometimes reported and denounced in the official press. One writer who had a difficult. though not intolerable, time in the twenties was the great poet Osip Mandelstam. See Nadezhda Mandelstam, *Hope Against Hope,* pp. 35, 138, 173.

11. Beginning in 1929, the Stalinist régime conducted a fierce attack against "rotten liberalism," sometimes called "bourgeois liberalism," which it defined as "an attitude of conciliation, of toleration, not only toward opportunist, but also toward directly hostile ideas" and "the result of a relaxed or lost sense of party vigilance." Popov, *Outline History,* II, pp. 433–4. Also see "Glashataiam liberalizma net mesta v bol'shevistkoi partii," *Pravda,* November 21, 1929, p. 3; and *Protiv burzhuaznogo liberalizma v khudozhestvennoi literature: diskussiia o "perevale" (aprel' 1930)* (Moscow, 1931).

12. I have borrowed this insight from Max Hayward's discussion of Soviet literary dissent. Patricia Blake and Max Hayward, eds., *Dissonant Voices in Soviet Literature* (New York, 1962), p. xvii. It is confirmed by an anecdote in Ehrenburg, *Memoirs,* p. 76.

13. See, for example, Rudolf Schlesinger, *The Family in the U.S.S.R.* (London, 1949), Parts I and II.

14. Nicholas DeWitt, *Education and Professional Employment in the U.S.S.R.* (Washington, D.C., 1961), p. 577; *The Soviet Union,* p. 197; N. A. Semashko, *Health Protection in the U.S.S.R.* (London, 1934). Literacy among those over nine years was 24 per cent in 1897 and 51.1 per cent in 1926. What part of the increase was due to Soviet efforts is impossible to judge.

15. Male, *Russian Peasant Organization;* and Yuzuru Taniuchi, *The Village Gathering in Russia in the Mid-1920's* (Birmingham, England, 1968). For village life during NEP, also see Lewin, *Russian Peasants,* Chapter i. In 1927, there were 319 party members for every 10,000 urban dwellers, and only 25 for every 10,000 peasants. Three-fourths of the villages experienced no organized party activity. *The Communist International: Between the Fifth and Sixth Congresses* (London, 1928), pp. 499, 504.

16. Karl Borders, *Village Life Under the Soviets* (New York, 1929), pp. 132–3, 183, 191; Male, *Russian Peasant Organization,* pp. 129, 209, 212; and Fainsod, *Smolensk,* pp. 138–41.

17. Schapiro, *Communist Party,* p. 332; *The Soviet Union,* pp. 184–5; Carr and Davies, *Planned Economy,* I, Chapters xxii and xxvii; and Sorenson, *Soviet Trade Unionism,* Chapters ix, xi. Poor factory conditions were regularly documented and deplored in the official press. Wartime destruction, population growth, and lagging housing construction had reduced the average urban dweller's floor space from 7 square meters in 1913 to 5.8 in 1928. Arvid Brodersen, *The Soviet Worker* (New York, 1966), p. 113.

18. I have borrowed this concept of "revolution of status" from David Schoenbaum, *Hitler's Social Revolution* (Garden City, N.Y., 1967), Chapters viii–ix.

19. Soviet defectors, probably an unrepresentative group, would later recall NEP as "a kind of golden era of Soviet development." See Raymond A. Bauer, Alex Inkeles, and Clyde Kluckhohn, *How the Soviet System Works* (New York, 1960), p. 138. If nothing else, per capita food consumption in the countryside was to drop drastically between 1928 and 1932. See Iu. A. Moshkov, *Zernovaia*

problema v gody sploshnoi kollektivizatsii sel'skogo khoziaistva SSSR (1929–1932 gg.) (Moscow, 1966), p. 136.

20. The population of Moscow, for example, increased by 204,000 in two years, 156,000 of whom were migrants. *Inprecor,* IX (1929), p. 153.

21. Rykov hoped that as a result the problems of rural overpopulation and unemployment could be solved in five years. *XV s"ezd,* II, p. 874.

22. For a vivid impression of Soviet Russia in the twenties, view Dziga Vertov's famous documentary film *Man with a Movie Camera* (1929) and his earlier newsreel series *Kino Pravda.* Also useful is Stuart Chase, Robert Dunn, and Rexford Guy Tugwell, eds., *Soviet Russia in the Second Decade* (New York, 1928).

23. See Bukharin's remarks on this still "powerful prejudice" in 1928, *VIII vsesoiuznyi s"ezd VLKSM,* p. 31. The spirit was frequently expressed in novels of the period. For a famous example, see Feodor Gladkov, *Cement* (New York, 1929), pp. 189, 251.

24. For first-hand accounts, see Serge, *Memoirs, pp. 196–9;* Ehrenburg. *Memoirs,* pp. 66–70; Reswick, *I Dreamt Revolution,* pp. 53–4, 56, 231; and Walter Duranty, *I Write as I Please* (New York, 1935), pp. 145–9. The novelist Iurii Libedinskii spoke of the "violent zealots" among party writers, which provided the title for S. Sheskulov, *Neistovye revniteli: iz istorii literaturnoi bor'by 20-kh godov* (Moscow, 1970), pp. 3–4.

25. See, for example, Leon Trotsky, *On Literature and Art* (New York, 1970), pp. 63–82.

26. Indeed, two years after NEP's abolition, the Stalinist régime was still officially proclaiming its existence. "NEP eshche ne zakonchen," *Pravda,* March 21, 1931, p. 1.

27. Caricatures of leaders appeared regularly in the magazines *Prozhektor* and *Ogonek.* Also see, for an example, Boris Efimov, *Karikatury* (Moscow, 1924), p. 153. With Stalin's victory in 1929, such "friendly caricatures" were no longer permissible. See *M. I. Ul'ianova—sekretar' Pravdy,* pp. 199–201.

28. For explicit references to the Aesopian debate, see Leont'ev *Ekonomicheskaia teoriia,* p. 52; "Ob oshibkakh i uklone tov. Bukharina," *Pravda,* August 24, 1929; p. 1; and *KPSS v rezoliutsiiakh,* II p. 563. The leaders had, of course, argued by "symbols" earlier in the twenties before disputes became public. See Bukharin's admission, *XIV s"ezd,* p. 133.

29. As Voroshilov pointed out. Quoted in Vaganov, *Pravyi uklon,* p. 175. For examples of how rank-and-file members perceived the struggle in mid-1928, see the reports in *Informatsionnaia spravka,* July 21, 1928 (T2021).

30. *Shestnadtsataia konferentsiia,* p. 523.

31. Article 107 had been passed in 1926 but not previously used. G. Koniukhov, *KPSS v bor'be s khlebnymi zatrudneniiami v strane (1928–1929)* (Moscow, 1960), pp. 98–9. Statements by Rykov and Iosif Vareikis suggest that the original decision had been unanimous and that the Right had not foreseen its consequences. See Rykov's remarks at the July 1928 plenum (T1835); and Vaganov, *Pravyi uklon,* p. 149.

32. Lewin, *Russian Peasants,* Chapter x; Koniukhov, *KPSS v bor'be,* p. 119; and V. P. Danilov, "K kharakteristike obshchestvenno-politicheskoi obstanovki v sovetskoi derevne nakanune kollektivizatsii," *Istoricheskie zapiski,* No. 79 (1966), p. 42. Stalin's special role in the campaign was later applauded as the start of a "great strategic plan conceived by Stalin." Bogushevskii, "Kanun piatiletki," p. 463.

33. For a sample of Stalin's direct remarks to local officials, see *Works,* XI, pp. 3–11, 18. Also Lewin, *Russian Peasants,* p. 217; and "Pervye itogi khlebozago-

tovitel'noi kampanii i zadachi partii," *Pravda*, February 15, 1928, p. 1, which discusses the directive of January 6.

34. Koniukhov, *KPSS v bor'be*, p. 119; L. Kaganovich, *Tseli i zadachi politicheskikh otdelov MTS i sovkhozov* (Moscow, 1933), p. 13. Apparently the only rightist to take part was Uglanov, and he only briefly. V. Molotov, "Na dva fronta," *Bol'shevik*, No. 2 (January 31), 1930, p. 21.

35. Fragments of Stalin's remarks in Siberia were published twenty years later in his *Works*, XI, pp. 3–11; for his itinerary, see pp. 389–90. Also see N. I. Nemakov, *Kommunisticheskaia partiia—organizator massovogo kolkhoznogo dvizheniia (1929–1932 gg.)* (Moscow, 1966), p. 25.

36. For the Politburo meeting, see Daniels, *Conscience*, p. 325. As early as January 31, Uglanov had hinted at Stalin's complicity in the excesses. See *Pravda*, February 4, 1928, p. 2. And compare A. I. Rykov, *Khoziaistvennoe polozhenie SSSR* (Moscow-Leningrad, 1928) and Bukharin, *Uroki khlebozagotovok*, pp. 5–41, to Stalin's remarks in *Works*, XI, pp. 3–11, 52–3.

37. Lewin, *Russian Peasants*, p. 231; Stalin, *Works*, XI, pp. 12–22. Even the stridently anti-kulak editorial in *Pravda*, February 15, 1928, p. 1, condemned the "excesses."

38. Carr and Davies, *Planned Economy*, I, p. 58. Smirnov's replacement, N. A. Kubiak, soon clashed with Stalin over the future of private farming. Stalin, *Works*, XI, p. 278.

39. Danilov, "*K kharakteristike . . . ,*" p. 42; *Shestnadtsataia konferentsiia*, p. 387.

40. The Politburo usually met once a week, on Thursday, for five hours. Ivanov and Shmelev, *Leninizm i ideino-politicheskii pazgrom trotskizma*, p. 362. "The other six days," said one Communist, Stalin "has control of the party through the apparatus." Reswick, *I Dreamt Revolution*, p. 58.

41. Kuibyshev quoted in V. I. Kuzmin, *Istoricheskii opyt sovetskoi industrializatsii* (Moscow, 1969), p. 40. For Uglanov, see *Ocherki istorii moskovskoi organizatsii*, p. 445. Other Moscow leaders spoke similarly. See Gaisinskii, *Bor'ba s uklonami*, pp. 187–8.

42. Bukharin, "Leninizm i problema kul'turnoi revoliutsii," *Pravda*, January 27, 1928, pp. 5–6; V. Astrov, "Lenin—khranitel' ortodoksii," *Pravda*, January 21, 1928, p. 3; A. Slepkov, "Lenin i problemy kul'turnoi revoliutsii," *Pravda*, January 21, 1928, p. 2.

43. For the Moscow incident, see Stalin, *Works*, XI, p. 247; and *Ocherki istorii moskovskoi organizatsii*, p. 445. A garbled account of the Institute episode appeared in V. Zeimal' and P. Pospelov, "Iacheika IKP v bor'be za general'nuiu liniiu partii," *Pravda*, December 1, 1931, p. 3. In February, Bukharin sharply criticized as putschism the abortive Canton uprising of December 1927, which Lominadze and Heinz Neumann had instigated (some believed on Stalin's orders). See *VI kongress Kominterna*, IV, pp. 319–24. The challenge to Tomskii's Western policies came at the Fourth Profintern Congress, which opened on March 17. See Trotsky, "Dorogoi drug," June 1928 (T1588); and *XVI s"ezd*, II, pp. 781–7, 1167.

44. For Rykov's proposal, see Vaganov, *Pravyi uklon*, pp. 113–14; and *Istoriia kommunisticheskoi partii sovetskogo soiuza*, IV, Book I (Moscow, 1970), p. 551. Rumors now related a struggle between Rykov and Stalin. *Sotsialisticheskii vestnik*, March 21, 1928, p. 14.

45. *Ogonek*, May 6, 1928, not paged; *Pravda*, May 13, 1928, p. 7.

46. For Stalin's use of the Shakhty affair, see *Works*, XI, pp. 57–67, and XII, pp. 11–20; Avtorkhanov, *Stalin*, pp. 28–30; *Sotsialisticheskii vestnik*, May 18, 1928, p. 12; and Reswick, *I Dreamt Revolution*, p. 246.

47. One was Kuibyshev. See Kuibysheva, *V. V. Kuibyshev*, pp. 290–1; Carr and Davies, *Planned Economy*, I, pp. 585–6. For Stalin's reputation, see Iu. N. Flakserman, *Gleb Maksimilianovich Krzhizhanovskii* (Moscow, 1964), pp. 171–2.

48. Vaganov, *Pravyi uklon*, p. 102; *XVI s"ezd*, I, p. 568.

49. See, for example, Bukharin, *Uroki khlebozagotovok*, pp. 42–53; Rykov, *Khoziaistvennoe polozhenie SSSR*, pp. 40–51; and E. F. Tsetlin, "Po belomu bolotu," *Pravda*, March 27, 1928, p. 3.

50. Bogushevskii, "Kanun piatiletki," pp. 499–500.

51. *Ibid.*, p. 507; Stalin, *Works*, XI, pp. 31–42, 102–3, 133–44; and *KPSS v rezoliutsiiakh* (8th ed.) Vol. IV (Moscow, 1970), pp. 94–8.

52. See, for example, the remarks of Astrov, Uglanov, and Slepkov in *Pravda*, April 20, 1928, p. 3; April 26, 1928, p. 2; and June 17, 1928, p. 3; and "Tezisy tov. A. Slepkova o samokritike," *Komsomol'skaia pravda*, April 19, 1929, p. 2.

53. *KPSS v rezoliutsiiakh*, II, pp. 492–510; Lewin, *Russian Peasant*, pp. 296–7. For evidence that speeches at the plenum may have differed markedly, see Vaganov, *Pravyi uklon*, pp. 125, 139–40.

54. Trotsky, "Dorogoi drug," June 1928 (T1588). Trotsky's report appears to be confirmed by Vaganov, *Pravyi uklon*, p. 102; *Bol'shevik*, No. 21 (November 15), 1930, p. 35; and Stalin, *Works, XIII*, p. 14.

55. *Works*, XI, pp. 30–68. About the same time, Stalin tried and failed to revise the land code to the detriment of private farming. Schapiro, *Communist Party*, p. 363.

56. *Uroki khlebozagotovok*, pp. 32–3. That Bukharin was referring to Stalin and people around him was later confirmed by Astrov in *Pravda*, July 3, 1929, p. 3.

57. Carr and Davies, *Planned Economy*, I, pp. 63–6. Also see Koniukhov, *KPSS v bor'be*, p. 129.

58. This was a central theme of Bukharin's report on the April plenum *(Uroki khlebozagotovok)* and one he repeated throughout the year. See, for example, "Zametki ekonomista"; and Vaganov, *Pravyi uklon*, pp. 139–40.

59. See, for example, Stalin, *Works*, XI, pp. 85–101, 105–20; and Stalin's subsequent account of his early differences with Bukharinists, *Works*, XII, pp. 11–20.

60. *Ibid.*; Bogushevskii, "Kanun piatiletki," p. 479. Also see the Bukharinist attacks on Stalinist thinking cited below, note 66.

61. See Chapter 7, note 173; Bogushevskii, "Kanun piatiletki," pp. 476–82; and Carr and Davies, *Planned Economy*, I, pp. 876–9.

62. Tomskii at *XVII s"ezd vsesoiuznoi kommunisticheskoi partii(b). 26 ianvaria–10 fevralia 1934 g.: stenograficheskii otchet* (Moscow, 1934), p. 249.

63. See, for example, Bukharin, *Uroki khlebozagotovok*, pp. 29–31; V. Astrov, "K tekushchemu momentu," *Pravda*, July 1, 1928, p. 2; and the editor's note to Kritsman's article in *Pravda*, July 7, 1928, p. 2.

64. From Bukharin's notes to the Politburo and a letter to Stalin in May–June 1928, quoted in Vaganov, *Pravyi uklon*, pp. 112, 140.

65. *VIII vsesoiuzny s"ezd VLKSM*, pp. 13–14, 21–6, 30; and *Pravda*, May 27, 1928, p. 2.

66. D. Maretskii, "Fal'shivaia nota," *Pravda*, June 30, 1928, p. 2; Astrov in *Pravda*, July 1, 1928, p. 2, and July 3, p. 3.

67. Compare, for example, their speeches at the Eighth Komsomol Congress

in May. *VIII vsesoiuznyi s"ezd VLKSM*, pp. 13–16, 18–41; and Stalin, *Works*, XI, pp. 70–82.

68. A partial record of Stalin's talk appears in *Works*, XI, pp. 85–101. For a firsthand account, see Avtorkhanov, *Stalin*, Chapter 1. Also see Daniels, *Conscience*, p. 328. Its programmatic importance was contained in Stalin's unprecedented reversal of the party's official formula on agriculture. Instead of placing the improvement of private farming before the creation of collective and state farms, as was the custom, he gave it the lowest priority. Under political pressure, he subsequently reverted to the prevailing formula; but in April 1929, after his victory over Bukharin, he again reversed the order. Finally, on December 27, 1929, he abandoned the dual formula altogether, announcing that collectivization was the only "way out." *Works*, XI, pp. 217–18, 272, and XII, pp. 62, 151–2.

69. Vaganov, *Pravyi uklon*, pp. 112, 140–1, 144–5; Bukharin-Kamenev memorandum (T1897); Stalin, *Works*, XI, p. 334; and Istituto Giangiacomo Feltrinelli, *Annali*. Anno Ottavo (Milano, 1966), p. 902.

70. For these events, see Vaganov, *Pravyi uklon*, pp. 141–2, 144–5; Stalin, *Works*, XI, pp. 121–32; and Bukharin-Kamenev memorandum (T1897).

71. Xenia Joukoff Eudin and Robert M. Slusser, eds., *Soviet Foreign Policy 1928–1934: Documents and Materials* (2 vols; University Park and London, 1966–7), Vol. I, p. 175.

72. The Uglanov leadership appears to have begun its pro-Right activity early in 1928. See Penkov's testimony, *XVI s"ezd*, I, pp. 644–6; *Moskovskie bol'sheviki v bor'be s pravym i "levym" opportunizmom, 1921–1929 gg.* (Moscow, 1969), pp. 244–58; Vaganov, *Pravyi uklon*, pp. 153–6; and Trotsky, "Dorogoi tovarishch," September 1928 (T2442).

73. The trade unionist Kozelev quoted in G. K. Ordzhonikidze, *Stat'i i rechi*, Vol. II (Moscow, 1957), p. 245. Also see "Zaiavlenie V. Kozeleva," *Pravda*, July 6, 1930, p. 4; *Komsomol'skaia pravda*, April 19, 1929, p. 2; *XVI s"ezd*, II, pp. 1134–5; *Pravda*, December 1, 1931, p. 3; and Trotsky, "Dorogoi drug," June 1928 (T1588).

74. See above, note 72. That Bukharin also lobbied provincial delegates is clear from the bizarre testimony in *Case of the Anti-Soviet Bloc*, pp. 118, 128.

75. Trotsky, "Dorogoi drug," June 1928 (T1588). For Stetskii and Petrovskii, see *Ocherki istorii leningradskoi organizatsii*, II, 316.

76. Bukharin-Kamenev memorandum (T1897); Kozelev in *Pravda*, July 6, 1930, p. 4; Uglanov at *XVI s"ezd*, II, p. 1299; and Gaisinskii, *Bor'ba s uklonami*, p. 198. Said Uglanov: "Stalin is sitting on the party's neck, and we've got to remove him." Quoted in Daniels, *Conscience*, p. 333.

77. Bukharin-Kamenev memorandum (T1897).

78. That the Right counted on the pro-peasant Kalinin is understandable. The military chief, Voroshilov, was a long-time crony of Stalin; but he was said to fear the impact of Stalin's rural policies on the overwhelmingly peasant Red army. As for Kuibyshev and Rudzutak, Bukharin's reference to the Politburo "septemvirate" suggests that for some reason they either abstained or did not participate regularly in the voting at this time. See *ibid.* For Voroshilov and Kalinin, see also Carr and Davies, *Planned Economy*, I, p. 57; *Sotsialisticheskii vestnik*, October 10, 1929, p. 14; and Istituto Giangiacomo Feltrinelli, *Annali*, p. 903.

79. Bukharin reported in July: "The Orgburo is ours"—Bukharin-Kamenev memorandum (T1897). It is confirmed by Vaganov, *Pravyi uklon*, p. 144. The full members of the Secretariat were Stalin, Molotov, Kosior, Uglanov, and Aleksandr Smirnov. The last two supported the Right.

80. The firm bloc of approximately 15 votes with which Bukharin began included the Moscow and trade union delegates, the Politburo trio, plus Stetskii, Osinskii, and Sokolnikov. The figure does not include Voroshilov and Kalinin, who shortly went over to Stalin, or Krupskaya and Kubiak, who eventually supported the Right. Central Committee voting was not published.

81. Vaganov, *Pravyi uklon*, p. 144.

82. Bukharin-Kamenev memorandum (T1897). In addition, Bukharin revealed at the July plenum (T1901) that Iagoda had provided him with data on peasant uprisings which he had been unable to obtain through normal channels. Also see Menzhinskii's remarks at the plenum (T1901) and the testimony of Bukharin and Iagoda in *Case of the Anti-Soviet Bloc*, pp. 385–6, 568, 692. OGPU officials, who had to cope with civil disturbances, were reportedly worried about the rising tide of peasant unrest. Personal friendships with the Right may have also played a role. See Simon Wolin and Robert M. Slusser, *The Soviet Secret Police* (New York, 1957), pp. 43–6. While Trilisser was removed from the OGPU in 1929 (*Izvestiia*, October 30, 1929, p. 4), Iagoda went on to serve as Stalin's police chief and then to stand trial and perish with Bukharin and Rykov in 1938.

83. Vaganov, *Pravyi uklon*, p. 144; *Sotsialisticheskii vestnik* (July–August 1962), p. 119.

84. Of the eight nonvoting Politburo members, only Uglanov supported the Right.

85. See, for example, Avtorkhanov, *Stalin*, pp. 48, 54; and Penkov's reference to "two Moscow committees"—Uglanov's official committee and another loyal to Stalin. *XVI s"ezd*, I, p. 646. Also Lewin, *Russian Peasants*, p. 278.

86. To Iagoda, for example, "it was clear that the Right was heading for power." *Case of the Anti-Soviet Bloc*, p. 692. This was also Trotsky's impression in the early summer of 1928. Deutscher, *Prophet Unarmed*, pp. 412, 428.

87. Deutscher, *Prophet Unarmed*, p. 428. For the resolutions see *KPSS rezoliutsiiakh*, II, pp. 511–24.

88. A partial stenograph of the proceedings is in the Trotsky Archive under numbers T1832–6, 1900–1. Supplementary material appears in Trotsky's, "Dorogoi tovarishch," September 1928 (T2442). Only Stalin's speeches were ever published. *Works*, XI, pp. 147–205.

89. Bukharin-Kamenev memorandum (T1897).

90. *Ibid*. Even those who eventually supported Stalin were worried about the situation in the countryside. See, for example, the remarks of Andreev and the Ukrainians Kosior and Chubar (T1835, T2442). Voroshilov demonstrated his allegiance by interrupting and heckling Bukharin's speech (T1901).

91. According to Rykov (T1835). Molotov (T1833) objected to the Bukharinist press attacks on the emergency measures. See above, note 66; and the editorial note affixed to Kritsman's article in *Pravda*, July 7, 1929, p. 2.

92. Bukharin's speech (T1901).

93. Stalin, *Works*, XI, pp. 165–205; Bukharin-Kamenev memorandum (T1897).

94. Bukharin-Kamenev memorandoum (T1897).

95. *Ibid*. Sokolnikov, who accompanied Bukharin, had arranged the meeting on July 9, the day of Stalin's "tribute" speech to the plenum. Bukharin and his secretary Tseitlin, who himself had informal contacts with the left camp, later insisted that Kamenev's notes were misleading and one-sided. But they did not deny their basic authenticity. Istituto Giangiacomo Feltrinelli, *Annali*, pp. 889, 893–4, 897–8.

96. For their subsequent meetings, see "Vnutri pravo-tsentristskogo bloka," *Biulleten' oppozitsii*, No. 1-2, 1929, pp. 15-17.

97. See above, note 43. The Executive Committee plenum had announced a "class against class" policy and ordered leftward turns in the British and French parties, but cautioned against extremes. See Bukharin's address, "The Opposition in the C.P.S.U. and in the Comintern," *Inprecor*, VIII (1928), pp. 213-18. For the contradictory and ambiguous resolutions of the Profintern congress, see *Rezoliutsii i postanovleniia IV kongressa Profinterna* (Moscow, 1928).

98. Bukharin-Kamenev memorandum (T1897).

99. Stalin and his supporters had first adumbrated their new line in December 1927. They developed it in closed meetings before and during the Comintern congress. See Stalin's later account in *Works*, XII, pp. 21-9; and O. V. Kuusinen, "Novyi period i povorot v politike Kominterna (pod rukovodstvom tov. Stalina)," *Kommunisticheskii internatsional*, No. 2 (January 24), 1930, pp. 3-19.

100. E. Gol'denberg, "Germanskaia problema," *Bol'shevik*, No. 5 (March 15), 1928, p. 35. The author was a well-known Bukharinist. An editorial note indicated that his article was treating disputed questions.

101. In this connection, Bukharin's views were unchanged. Despite his compromises, he restated them at the Sixth Comintern Congress. For his major speeches, see *VI kongress Kominterna*, I, pp. 26-64, 587-615; III, pp. 7-32, 122-55.

102. *Works*, VI, p. 294. For the origins and history of the concept of social fascism, see Theodore Draper, "The Ghost of Social-Fascism," *Commentary* (February 1969), pp. 29-42. According to Draper, Zinoviev floated and then dropped the idea in 1924. Stalin later made it his own.

103. His speeches at the Comintern congress indicate that a heated debate was under way in closed sessions. See *VI kongress Kominterna*, III, pp. 30-1, 137-8, 143-5, and V, p. 130.

104. *Ibid.*, III, pp. 144-5. Similarly, in December 1927, he had insisted that the leftward turn "does not exclude proposing a united front and voting in separate instances for socialist candidates when a reactionary candidate might win." *XV s"ezd*, I, p. 656. Equally significant is the major study of social democracy published by two leading young Bukharinists in 1928. While politically hostile to its subject, the book contained nothing akin to the concept of social fascism. See Astrov and Slepkov, *Sotsial-demokratiia i revoliutsiia*.

105. For these events, see Stalin, *Works*, XIII, pp. 21-2; Draper, *American Communism and Soviet Russia*, Chapter xiv; Istituto Giangiacomo Feltrinelli, *Annali*, p. 900; *Revolutionary Age*, November 1, 1929, p. 15; and *KPSS v rezoliutsiiakh*, II, pp. 558-9.

106. Draper, *American Communism and Soviet Russia*, Chapters xi-xiv; Paolo Spriano, *Storia del Partito communista italiano*, Vol. II (Turin, 1969), p. 175. Though the official leader of the German party was the Stalinist Ernst Thälmann, an "enormous majority" of its Central Committee was closer to Bukharin's position. See *XVI s"ezd*, II, p. 779. For another example, see L. J. Macfarlane, *The British Communist Party* (London, 1966), Chapters ix-x.

107. For the key resolutions and program, see *VI kongress Kominterna*, II, pp. 7-161, 192-3, and particularly the sections on the "third period," fascism and social democracy, trade union tactics, and the "right deviation." For references to compromises behind the scenes, see Istituto Giangiacomo Feltrinelli, *Annali*, p. 495; and, obliquely, Popov, *Outline History*, II, p. 366.

108. See, for example, Bertram D. Wolfe's remarks in *Revolutionary Age*, November 15, 1929, pp. 3-4; and *The Crisis in the Communist Party, U.S.A.:*

Statement of Principles of the Communist Party (Majority Group) (New York, 1930).

109. Humbert-Droz, *De Lénine à Staline*, pp. 348–9. According to Humbert-Droz (p. 340), Bukharin never returned to the Comintern offices after the congress.

110. Daniels, *Conscience*, pp. 336–7. For Bukharin's remarks and the pertinent resolution, see *VI kongress Kominterna*, I, pp. 58–60, 610–14, and II, p. 80.

111. See above, Chapter VIII, note 4.

112. Daniels, *Documentary History*, I, pp. 309–13.

113. *Works*, XI, pp. 256–8.

114. "Zametki ekonomista (k nachalu novogo khoziaistvennogo goda)," *Pravda*, September 30, 1928, pp. 2–3.

115. Vaganov, *Pravyi uklon*, pp. 161–3, 174–5.

116. See, for example, Khavin, *U rulia industrii*, p. 65; *Ocherki istorii kommunisticheskoi partii Turkmenistana* (2nd ed.; Ashkhabad. 1965), pp. 361–3; I. V. Stalin, *Sochineniia*, Vol. XI (Moscow, 1949), p. 220; and Carr and Davies, *Planned Economy*, I, p. 554. Rumors of Stalin's desire to oust Tomskii apparently were already circulating. See Kozelev's remarks in *Pravda*, July 6, 1930, p. 4.

117. As is evident from the one-sided accounts in Vaganov, *Pravyi uklon*, pp. 153–73; and *Moskovskie bol'sheviki v bor'be*, pp. 258–98.

118. Trotsky, "Dorogoi tovarishch," September 1928 (T2442); Avtorkhanov, *Stalin*, Chapters iv–vi. For Comintern events, see *Pravda*, November 22, 1929, p. 3; Jules Humbert-Droz, "*L'oeil de Moscou*" à Paris (Paris, 1964), pp. 256–9; and Vaganov, *Pravyi uklon*, pp. 197–8.

119. Istituto Giangiacomo Feltrinelli, *Annali*, p. 898.

120. Vaganov, *Pravyi uklon*, pp. 143–4; also Trotsky, "Dorogoi tovarishch," September 1928 (T2442). *Bolshevik*'s new editors were announced in the issue of August 15, 1928. Though Bukharin reportedly was able to influence or compose a *Pravda* editorial as late as September 23 (see Tetiushev, p. 10), the real editors were now Iaroslavskii, Maksimilian Savelev, and Garald Krumin.

121. See, for example, the editorials on the July plenum in *Pravda*, July 13 and 14, 1928, p. 1, whose authorship is attributed to Bukharin. Tetiushev, p. 10.

122. The public anti-Right campaign was initiated in *Pravda* editorials on September 15 and 18, 1928, p. 1. For the covert attack on Bukharin, see his remarks in Istituto Giangiacomo Feltrinelli, *Annali*, pp. 899, 901; and Vaganov, *Pravyi uklon*, p. 175.

123. See, for example, Mandelshtam in *Pravda*, August 11, 1928, p. 5; Uglanov in *Pravda*, September 21, 1928, pp. 3–4; and Riutin's veiled criticism of Stalin in "Rukovodiashchie kadry VKP(b)," *Bol'shevik*, No. 15 (August 15), 1928, pp. 18–29.

124. *Biulleten' oppozitsii*, No. 1–2, 1929, p. 15.

125. For these events, see Daniels, *Conscience*, pp. 337–44; *Moskovskie bol'sheviki v bor'be*, pp. 279–98; Vaganov, *Pravyi uklon*, pp. 160–73; and Stalin, *Works*, XI, pp. 231–48.

126. *Pravda*, November 28, 1928, p. 3; L. Kozlova, *Moskovskie kommunisty v bor'be za pobedu kolkhoznogo stroia* (Moscow, 1960), pp. 46–7. Uglanov lost his majority on the Bureau and control of the Moscow Control Commission and Agitprop Department when Moroz and Mandelshtam were dismissed on October 19. *Pravda*, October 20, 1928, p. 4.

127. S. Krylov and A. Zykov, *O pravoi opasnosti* (2nd ed.; Moscow-Leningrad, 1929), pp. 53–4, 159–61; E. Levi, ed., *Bol'sheviki Moskvy 1905* (Moscow-Leningrad, 1925), pp. 16–17.

128. Iu. V. Voskresenskii, *Kommunisty vo glave politicheskogo i trudovogo pod"ema (1926–1929 gg.)* (Tula, 1958), p. 26; and, for an example, *Ocherki istorii kommunistichskoi partii Turkmenistana*, p. 362.

129. *Biulleten' oppozitsii*, No. 1–2, 1929, pp. 15–16. The approximate date of his return is indicated by a speech in *Pravda*, November 10, 1928, p. 3; and Istituto Giangiacomo Feltrinelli, *Annali*, p. 542.

130. For these events, see *Biulleten' oppozitsii*, No. 1–2, 1929, pp. 15–16; Vaganov, *Pravyi uklon*, pp. 115, 176–8; *KPSS v rezoliutsiiakh*, II, p. 566; and Istituto Giangiacomo Feltrinelli, *Annali*, p. 542. Among other things, Bukharin demanded the removal of two Stalinists, Krumin from *Pravda* and Neumann from the German party. See also Stalin, *Works*, XII, pp. 27–8.

131. The capital investment figure adopted was 1,650 million rubles against 1,330 million in 1927–8, two thirds earmarked for heavy industry. Vaganov, *Pravyi uklon*, p. 178. Bukharin, Rykov, and Tomskii presumably urged a figure closer to that of 1927–8.

132. The appointment was made on November 29, 1928, two days after Uglanov's dismissal as secretary of the Moscow party. *Izvestiia*, November 30, 1928, p. 3. That it was a last-minute decision is suggested by the public celebration of Shmidt's ten-year "jubilee" as Commissar of Labor only twelve days earlier. *Izvestiia*, November 17, 1928, p. 2. Shmidt had been named one of Rykov's deputy premiers in August, a post he apparently retained for the time. *Izvestiia*, August 14, 1928, p. 2.

133. Vaganov, *Pravyi uklon*, pp. 180–8.

134. Stalin, *Works*, XI, pp. 255–302; *KPSS v rezoliutsiiakh*, II, pp. 525–48.

135. Vaganov, *Pravyi uklon*, p. 184. Rykov and Tomskii reportedly attended infrequently.

136. *Works*, XI, pp. 307–24.

137. *The Communist International, 1919–1943: Documents*, edited by Jane Degras, Vol. III (London, 1965), p. 27; Draper, *American Communism and Soviet Russia*, Chapter xvii. For Bukharin's protests, see Vaganov, "Razgrom pravogo uklona," p. 75; Stalin, *Works*, XII, pp. 27–8; and Humbert-Droz, *De Lénine à Staline*, p. 340.

138. Iaglom quoted in *XVI s"ezd*, II, p. 1194. For the outside attack, spearheaded by the Komsomol newspaper, see *Shestnadtsataia konferentsiia*, p. 783, n. 78. For Tomskii's fall, see also Daniels, *Conscience*, pp. 344–8.

139. Gaisinskii, *Bor'ba s uklonami*, p. 210; David E. Langsam, "Pressure Group Politics in NEP Russia: The Case of the Trade Unions" (unpublished Ph.D. doctoral thesis, Princeton University, 1973).

140. *Vos'moi s"ezd professional'nykh soiuzov SSSR (10–24 dekabria 1928 g.): polnyi stenograficheskii otchet* (Moscow, 1929). In addition to Tomskii's speeches (pp. 3–6, 24–5, 186–207), see the remarks of Rykov, Shmidt, Ugarov, Kozelev, and Iaglom. See also Gaisinskii, *Bor'ba s uklonami*, p. 203; L. Nedachin, "Apolitichnost' v profrabote nedopustim," *Pravda*, December 12, 1928, p. 4; and *XVI s"ezd*, II, p. 1134.

141. Daniels, *Conscience*, pp. 347–8; Gaisinskii, *Bor'ba s uklonami*, pp. 175–6; Vaganov, "Razgrom pravogo uklona," p. 71; *Pravda*, July 6, 1930, p. 4; and Vaganov, *Pravyi uklon*, p. 193.

142. *XVI s"ezd*, I, p. 122.

143. Popov, *Outline History*, II, p. 377; *KPSS v rezoliutsiiakh*, II, pp. 557–8.

144. Bukharin-Kamenev memorandum (T1897).

145. "Tekushchii moment i zadachi nashei pechati," *Pravda*, December 2, 1928, pp. 3–4.

146. "Lenin i zadachi nauki v sotsialisticheskom stroitel'stve," *Pravda*, January 20, 1929, pp. 2–3.

147. It appeared in both *Pravda* and *Izvestiia* on January 24, 1929. All references are to the pamphlet edition, *Politicheskoe zaveshchanie Lenina* (2nd ed.; Moscow, 1929).

148. Postyshev quoted in Vaganov, *Pravyi uklon*, p. 198; Leont'ev, *Ekonomicheskaia teoriia pravogo uklona*, p. 85. For an example of later attacks, see I. Cherniak, *Politicheskoe zaveschanie Lenina v izobrazhenii tov. Bukharina* (Moscow, 1930).

149. *Politicheskoe zaveshchanie Lenina*, p. 27.

150. Deutscher, *Prophet Armed*, pp. 469–71; Istituto Giangiacomo Feltrinelli, *Annali*, p. 648.

151. "O perevyborakh sovetov," *Pravda*, January 1, 1929, p. 1; Vaganov, *Pravyi uklon*, pp. 127–8; Carr and Davies, *Planned Economy*, I, pp. 100–5.

152. A very fragmentary stenograph of the proceedings, obtained by Tasca probably from Bukharin's secretary Tseitlin, is in Istituto Giangiacomo Feltrinelli, *Annali*, pp. 889–905. Only Stalin's remarks were subsequently published, and in an abridged form twenty years later. *Works*, XI, pp. 332–40. Also see *KPSS v rezoliutsiiakh*, II, pp. 556–65.

153. For these events, see *Biulleten' oppozitsii*, No. 1–2, 1929, p. 17; Istituto Giangiacomo Feltrinelli, *Annali*, pp. 897–8; Vaganov, *Pravyi uklon*, pp. 199–202; and *XVI s"ezd*, I, pp. 578–80. According to Vaganov, the commission members were Bukharin, Kirov, Korotkova, Rudzutak, Stalin, Molotov, Voroshilov, Ordzhonikidze, and Iaroslavskii. The last four were almost certainly reliable Stalinists.

154. Reconstructed from quotes in *KPSS v rezoliutsiiakh*, II, p. 560; *Biulleten' oppozitsii*, No. 1–2, 1929, p. 17; and *XVI s"ezd*, I, pp. 157, 363, 578.

155. Reconstructed from quotes in Istituto Giangiacomo Feltrinelli, *Annali*, pp. 899, 901; *KPSS v rezoliutsiiakh*, II, pp. 562–3; and Vaganov, *Pravyi uklon*, pp. 115, 198.

156. Quoted in *XVI s"ezd*, I, pp. 577–8.

157. Reconstructed from quotes in *ibid.*, p. 363; and Vaganov, *Pravyi uklon*, pp. 105, 118, 200, 202–3.

158. Quoted in Molotov, "Na dva fronta," *Bol'shevik*, No. 2 (January 31), 1930, p. 14. Also see *KPSS v rezoliutsiiakh*, II, pp. 558–9.

159. *KPSS v rezoliutsiiakh*, II, pp. 556–67.

160. Reports circulated that Stalin was now determined to oust them at the forthcoming April plenum. See *Biulleten' oppozitsii*, No. 1–2, 1929, p. 15; and *Sotsialisticheskii vestnik*, May 4, 1929, p. 3.

161. *Works*, XI, p. 340.

162. Istituto Giangiacomo Feltrinelli, *Annali*, p. 903. This kind of concern may have been behind the abortive compromise of February 7. See Ordzhonikidze's apologetic assurance a year later that "we did everything possible to keep comrades Rykov, Bukharin, Tomskii, and Uglanov at leading posts in the party." This in response to unnamed party members who worried that "they kicked out Zinoviev, Kamenev, and Trotsky, and now they plan to kick out Rykov, Bukharin, and Tomskii." *Otchety TSK TSKK i delegatsii VKP(b) v IKKI XVI s"ezd VKP(b)* (Moscow-Leningrad, 1930), p. 291.

163. *Ogonek*, February 24, 1929, not paged; *Pravda*, March 8, 1929, p. 7, and March 17, 1929, p. 4; Graham, *Soviet Academy of Sciences*, pp. 92, 95, 103.

164. The expression is Lewin's, *Russian Peasants*, p. 325. For Bukharin's complaint that they "were being hauled over the coals" and subjected to "civil execution," see Stalin, *Works*, XII, p. 109.

165. For Rykov, see Stalin, *Works*, XI, p. 337; and Voroshilov's remarks at *XVI s"ezd*, I, p. 516. His retreat was reflected in the resolution of February 9, which censured him in terms far less harsh than those applied to Bukharin or Tomskii. For Stetskii, see *Pravda*, March 8, 1929, p. 7; and his article in *Pravda*, March 17, 1929, p. 1.

166. *Biulleten' oppozitsii*, No. 1-2, 1929, p. 15. Bukharin spoke out against Stalin and his policies on four occasions in February and March, but more obliquely each time. See *Pravda*, February 27, 1929, p. 3; March 12, 1929, p. 3; March 17, 1929, p. 4; and March 23, 1929, pp. 2-3.

167. Carr and Davies, *Planned Economy*, I, Chapter xxxvii.

168. *Shestnadtsataia konferentsiia*, pp. viii-ix, xiii, 794, n. 135; *Istoriia KPSS*, IV, Book I, p. 563; Vaganov, *Pravyi uklon*, pp. 209-10; Stalin, *Works*, XII, pp. 86-7.

169. Lenin, *PSS*, XLV, p. 346.

170. Humbert-Droz, *De Lénine à Staline*, p. 356, and the frontispiece facsimile. Two weeks later, in a clear reference to Stalin, Bukharin reminded the party that Lenin had prevailed in the party because he was loved and respected, and not by "simple 'commanding' or 'administrative fiat.'" *Pravda*, February 27, 1929, p. 3.

171. Stalin, *Works*, XII, p. 1.

172. The resolution censuring the Bukharinists is said to have passed with 10 negative votes and 3 abstentions. *Shestnadtsataia konferentsiia*, p. ix. In addition to the Politburo trio, the thirteen dissenters would have included Uglanov, Kotov, Kulikov, Shmidt, the Leningrad trade union leader Ugarov, and Rozit, a Bukharinist member of the Central Control Commission. Krupskaya may have been one of the other four. In January, she had defended Bukharin's position that Lenin's famous article on peasant cooperatives had envisaged market associations, not collective farms. "Il'ich o kolkhoznom stroitel'stve," *Pravda*, January 20, 1929, p. 4.

173. Stalin, *Works*, XII, pp. 1-113.

174. Rykov's more moderate tone is suggested by quotes from his speech. Also see Avtorkhanov, *Stalin*, pp. 128-9; and Stalin, *Works*, XII, p. 3. For Uglanov, see *Bol'shevik*, No. 2 (January 31), 1930, p. 19.

175. See Stalin's references to "accusations of a personal nature." *Works*, XII, p. 2.

176. Bukharin's remarks are reconstructed from quotes in *ibid.*, pp. 83, 103; *XVI s"ezd*, I, p. 327; *Shestnadtsataia konferentsiia*, pp. 803, n. 215, 806, n. 236; Vaganov, *Pravyi uklon*, p. 217; and *Bol'shevik*, No. 2 (January 31), 1930, p. 18. For Tomskii's remark, see *Shestnadtsataia konferentsiia*, p. 803, n. 215.

177. *KPSS v rezoliutsiiakh*, II, pp. 549-67.

178. In addition, Uglanov was removed from the Politburo and Secretariat following the party conference. A month later, Rykov was replaced by Sergei Syrtsov as premier of the Russian Republic, a post he had held jointly with the all-Union premiership. The announcement, however, implied no disgrace; it said only that the duties of the two positions together had become too burdensome for one person. *Izvestiia*, May 19, 1929, p. 2. It should be noted that the plenum's removal of Bukharin and Tomskii from their posts meant little more than a formalizing of their intractable resignations. Stalin's tone and charges at the plenum implied

much stronger sanctions. What purports to be, but probably is not, the "verbatim report" of his speech was published twenty years later. It records Stalin disagreeing with "some comrades" who demanded that Bukharin and Tomskii be expelled from the Politburo. These "comrades" were almost certainly his personal supporters, and his demurral, oddly placed at the very end of the speech, apparently represented his diplomatic bowing to the resistance to "such an extreme measure." *Works*, XII, p. 113. See also above, note 160; and Lewin, *Russian Peasants*, p. 325.

179. *KPSS v rezoliutsiiakh*, II, pp. 569–89; Lewin, *Russian Peasants*, pp. 350–8. The share of socialized agricultural production was to increase from 2 per cent in 1927 to 21.9 per cent in 1932–3. Carr and Davies, *Planned Economy*, I, p. 253.

180. See above, note 68; and *Works*, XII, pp. 91–7.

181. Avtorkhanov, *Stalin*, pp. 133–6.

182. *Shestnadtsataia konferentsiia*, pp. 3, 5–24, 666.

183. *Ibid.*, p. 440.

184. Istituto Giangiacomo Feltrinelli, *Annali*, p. 900. Similarly, see Uglanov quoted in *Bol'shevik*, No. 2 (January 31), 1929, p. 19.

185. For Stalin's civil war motif, see *Works*, XI, pp. 13, 62, 72–3, 81, 85, 226–7, 233; and XII, pp. 41, 221–2. For the "vernalization front," see Lysenko, quoted in Zhores A. Medvedev, *The Rise and Fall of T. D. Lysenko* (New York, 1969), p. 17.

186. Voroshilov at *XVI s"ezd*, I, p. 513.

187. A. Kosarev, *Komsomol v rekonstruktivnyi period* (Moscow, 1931), p. 58; *Kommunisticheskaia revoliutsiia*, No. 22–3 (December), 1929, p. 66.

188. See Robert C. Tucker, *The Soviet Political Mind* (revised ed.; New York, 1971), pp. 40–1; and his *Stalin as Revolutionary: A Study in History and Personality* (New York, 1973).

189. Stalin introduced his theory at the July 1928 plenum. *Works*, XI, pp. 179–80. A qualified version was officially endorsed in April 1929. *KPSS v rezoliutsiiakh*, II, p. 552. Bukharin restated his view most fully in *Politicheskoe zaveshchanie Lenina*, pp. 9–10, 20–3. It was shared by Rykov. *XVII s"ezd*, p. 209. As Stalin rightly insisted, the class struggle issue was at "the root" of the dispute. *Works*, XII, pp. 11–20, 30–41.

190. See Tucker's introduction to Robert C. Tucker and Stephen F. Cohen, eds., *The Great Purge Trial* (New York, 1965), pp. xv–xvi.

191. Bukharin-Kamenev memorandum (T1897).

192. Central Committee plenum, July 1928 (T1901). Bukharin went on to warn against an "artificial implanting of communism in the countryside." Quoted in Z. I. Kliucheva, *Ideinoe i organizatsionnoe ukreplenie kommunisticheskoi partii v usloviiakh bor'by za postroenie sotsializma v SSSR* (Moscow, 1970), p. 256. For "vulgar realism," see Carr and Davies, *Planned Economy*, I, p. 323; and the statement that Bukharin's planning arguments, while "mathematically" correct, were irrelevant, as the victory of the Red army proved. *Inprecor*, IX (1929), p. 972.

193. For his war communism charge, see his unsigned editorial in *Pravda*, July 14, 1928, p. 1. The others have been cited above.

194. *Pravda*, April 24, 1929, p. 1; *Izvestiia*, April 23, 1929, p. 1; Postyshev quoted in *Istoricheskii arkhiv*, No. 2, 1962, p. 193; and *Pravda*, October 4, 1929, p. 2. Kaganovich accused Bukharinists of seeking to "demobilize the party." Central Committee plenum, July 1928 (T1835).

195. As he indicated to Kamenev in July 1928. Bukharin-Kamenev memorandum (T1897).

196. See, for example, his speech to the July 1928 plenum (T1901); his unsigned editorial in *Pravda*, July 14, 1928, p. 1; and *Pravda*, September 30, 1928, p. 2. Indeed, he argued that noncoercive methods were to be used in dealing with passive opponents of the régime generally. *Pravda*, November 10, 1928, p. 3.

197. *Politicheskoe zaveshchanie Lenina*, pp. 12–16; also see *VI kongress Kominterna*, III, pp. 150–2. He had made this point earlier against the Left. See *Ob itogakh ob"edinennogo plenuma*, pp. 30–1.

198. Compare, for example, his remarks in *Works*, XI, pp. 3–11, 85–101.

199. *Pravda*, September 30, 1928, pp. 2–3; unsigned editorial in *Pravda*, September 23, 1928, p. 1, whose authorship is attributed to Bukharin in Tetiushev, p. 10; his remarks at the July 1928 plenum (T1901); *Uroki khlebozagotovok*, pp. 12–16; and *Pravda*, January 27, 1928, pp. 5–6.

200. For Bukharin's remarks, see *Pravda*, September 30, 1928, pp. 2–3; Vaganov, *Pravyi uklon*, pp. 112, 115; *VIII vsesoiuznyi s"ezd VLKSM*, pp. 29–32; *XVI s"ezd*, II, p. 1015; *VI kongress Kominterna*, III, pp. 27–9; and *Pravda*, March 17, 1929, p. 4. Also see the editorial in *Pravda*, May 24, 1928, p. 1. Rykov is quoted in Carr and Davies, *Planned Economy*, I, pp. 215–16.

201. See Vaganov, *Pravyi uklon*, pp. 127–8; and Maretskii in *Pravda*, June 30, 1928, p. 2.

202. *Pravda*, September 30, 1928, p. 3. Similarly, see *Uroki khlebozagotovok*, pp. 29–31; Bukharin's speech to the July 1928 plenum (T1901); *Pravda*, December 2, 1928, p. 3; and *Pravda*, March 12, 1929, p. 2.

203. See, for example, his premonition of a "slave" economy in the summer of 1928. *Kommunisticheskii internatsional*, No. 31–2, 1928, p. 35. Despite his predictions of "collapse," the possible success of "applied Tuganism" was also implied in his "Zametki ekonomista," *Pravda*, September 30, 1928, pp. 2–3.

204. Rykov in *XV s"ezd*, II, p. 870; Erlich, *Soviet Industrialization*, Chapter iv.

205. The fullest statement of his revised views on industrial policy and his objections to Stalin's is "Zametki ekonomista," *Pravda*, September 30, 1928, pp. 2–3. See also *Uroki khlebozagotovok*, pp. 37–8; his speech to the July 1928 plenum (T1901); *Pravda*, December 2, 1928, pp. 3–4, and January 20, 1929, pp. 2–3; and, for the rewards of technological and organizational science, "Organizovannyi kapitalizm," pp. 168–99.

206. V. A. Pisarev quoted in *Pravda*, August 29, 1929, p. 3.

207. The fullest statement of Bukharin's views on planning is "Zametki ekonomista," *Pravda*, September 30, 1928, pp. 2–3. Also see *Uroki khlebozagotovok*, pp. 7–14; his speech to the July 1928 plenum (T1901); and *Kommunisticheskii internatsional*, No. 31–2 (August 13), 1928, pp. 32–40. For the dangers of "overcentralization" and "taking on too much," see also *Inprecor*, VIII (1928), p. 1272; *Pravda*, January 20, 1929, pp. 2–3; and "Organizovannyi kapitalizm," pp. 183–99.

208. *Pravda*, September 30, 1928, pp. 2–3. Similarly, see *Pravda*, November 10, 1928, p. 3; and *Pravda*, December 2, 1928, pp. 3–4. For Rykov, see Vaganov, *Pravyi uklon*, pp. 98, 215. In his Politburo declaration of January 30, 1929, Bukharin warned: "We can fasten the most enormous resources onto industrialization, but one fine day we shall see with astonishment that it is necessary to cut back at a vital place, curtail, shut down, etc." Quoted in Vaganov, *Pravyi uklon*, p. 118.

209. *Pravda*, September 30, 1928, pp. 2–3; "Organizovannyi kapitalizm," pp. 184, 197. Also see *Pravda*, May 27, 1928, p. 2.

210. *Pravda*, September 30, 1928, p. 2. In Bukharin's Aesopian language, his charge was against " 'super-industrialists' of the Trotskyist type."

211. See, for example, P. Miliukov, *Ocherki po istorii russkoi kul'tury*, Part I (5th ed.; St. Petersburg, 1904), pp. 141–3; G. V. Plekhanov, *Istoriia russkoi obshchestvennoi mysli*, Vol. I (2nd ed.; Moscow-Leningrad, 1925), pp. 51–5; and A. L. Sidorov, "V. I. Lenin o russkom voenno-feodal'nom imperializme," *Istoriia SSSR*, No. 3 (May–June, 1961), pp. 47–70.

212. These expressions are attributed to young Bukharinists. *Pravda*, November 21, 1929, p. 3. Another is quoted as saying, "as a result of the policy of military-feudal exploitation of the peasantry, the USSR may be renamed the Golden Horde," an allusion to the Mongol suzerainty in Russia. Ark. Abramov, *O pravoi oppozitsii v partii* (Moscow, 1929), pp. 114–15.

213. The charge rankled. For the immediate Stalinist response, see Stalin, *Works*, XII, pp. 52–9; P. Boiarskii, "Legenda o 'voenno-feodal'noi eksploatatsii krest'-ianstva,'" *Sputnik kommunista*, No. 8 (April 1929), pp. 8–16; and Kaganovich in *Komsomol'skaia pravda*, November 28, 1929, p. 2. It is still held against Bukharin in official Soviet literature.

214. See, for example, his plea in *Pravda*, December 2, 1928, pp. 3–4.

215. See Bukharin's unsigned editorial in *Pravda*, July 14, 1928, p. 1; Astrov's account of the requisitioning process in *Pravda*, July 3, 1928, p. 3; and Stalin, *Sochineniia*, Vol. XII (Moscow, 1949), p. 61.

216. *Pravda*, December 2, 1928, pp. 3–4; *Pravda*, June 12, 1929, p. 3.

217. Bukharin-Kamenev memorandum (T1897); *Pravda*, December 2, 1928, p. 3.

218. *Politicheskoe zaveshchanie Lenina*, p. 27; "*Organizovannyi kapitalizm*," p. 191; *Pravda*, June 12, 1929, p. 3. Also see *Pravda*, September 30, 1928, p. 3.

219. Stalinists ritualistically stigmatized the Right as "the kulak agent" in the party. In more lucid moments, however, it was said that Bukharinists represented the country's "petty bourgeois elements," meaning the peasantry. See, for example, Vareikis at *XVI s"ezd*, I, pp. 244–5; and similarly, *Partiinoe stroitel'stvo*, No. 2 (December 1929), p. 3. For the judgments of Bukharinists and noncombatants, see below, notes 228 and 225.

220. See, for example, *Kommunisticheskaia revoliutsiia*, No. 18 (September 1929), pp. 27–39; *Partiinoe stroitel'stvo*, No. 1 (November 1929), pp. 39–51; *Bol'shevik*, No. 9 (May 15), 1930, pp. 18, 22–3; and *Pravda* and *Izvestiia* regularly during the second half of 1929. For the purge of the state apparatus, for which there are no complete figures, see S. N. Ikonnikov, *Sozdanie i deiatel'nost' ob"edinennykh organov TSKK-RKI v 1923–1934 gg.* (Moscow, 1971), pp. 284–93.

221. S. P. Trapeznikov, *Kommunisticheskaia partiia v period nastupleniia sotsializma po vsemu frontu: pobeda kolkhoznogo stroia v derevne (1929–1932 gg.)* (2nd ed.; Moscow, 1961), pp. 40–1. For evidence of persistent rightist sentiment in the factories, see *Partiinoe stroitel'stvo*, No. 1 (November 1929), pp. 39–41; *Pravda*, December 11, 1929, p. 4; and *Biulleten' tret'ei leningradskoi oblastnoi konferentsii VKP(b)*. No. 9 (Leningrad, 1930), pp. 5–8. The Stalinist Shvernik, who replaced Tomskii as trade union chief, complained in November 1928: "workers still insufficiently perceive the full danger resulting from the right deviation." Quoted in Vaganov, *Pravyi uklon*, p. 187.

222. Frumkin is quoted in Gaisinskii, *Bor'ba s uklonami*, p. 179. Evidence of widespread rightist sentiment in the party was provided regularly by Stalinists themselves. See, for example, *Partiinoe stroitel'stvo*, No. 1 (November 1929), pp. 39–51; *Bol'shevik*, No. 16 (August 31), 1929, pp. 39–62; *Shestnadtsataia konferentsiia*, pp. 300–1, 384; and *Pravda* regularly in 1929. Soviet historians have been reluctant to document its extent, though it is tacitly acknowledged in many provincial party histories published since Stalin's death. See, for example, K. V. Nekrasov, *Bor'ba kommunisticheskoi partii za edinstvo svoikh riadov v period*

mezhdu XV i XVI s"ezdami VKP(b) (Vologda, 1959), pp. 35, 41–42; P. N. Sharova, *Kollektivizatsiia sel'skogo khoziaistva v tsentral'no-chernozemnoi oblasti 1928–1932 gg.* (Moscow, 1963), p. 80; *Ocherki istorii kommunisticheskoi partii Turkmenistana*, pp. 361–3; *Ocherki istorii kommunisticheskoi partii Gruzii*, Part II (Tbilisi, 1963), pp. 85–6. Also see Fainsod, *Smolensk*, pp. 54–5, 211–12.

223. T. H. Rigby, *Communist Party Membership in the USSR, 1917–1967* (Princeton, N.J., 1968), pp. 176–81; and Thomas Paul Bernstein, "Leadership and Mobilization in the Collectivization of Agriculture in China and Russia" (unpublished Ph.D. Thesis, Columbia University, 1970), pp. 246–7. A frequent Stalinist complaint was that "a significant part of the Communists in the countryside" opposed the new policies, and that they were "sub-kulaks with a party card." Krylov and Zykov, *O pravoi opasnosti*, p. 202; Gaisinskii, *Bor'ba s uklonami*, p. 230.

224. For commentary on this phenomenon, see Kosarev, *Komsomol v rekonstruktivnyi period*, p. 17; *XVI s"ezd*, I, p. 207; and Bukharin quoted in Abramov, *O pravoi oppozitsii*, p. 132.

225. Eugene Lyons, *Assignment in Utopia* (New York, 1937), p. 152; Serge, *Memoirs*, p. 253. Similarly, see Theodor Seibert, *Red Russia* (London, 1932), pp. 129, 348.

226. For the specter of a "third force," see Bukharin's retrospective remarks at *XVII s"ezd*, pp. 124–5; and Tomskii's at *XVI s"ezd*, I, p. 264. Though frequently violated, the stricture against discussing party disputes at nonparty gatherings had become a "tradition." See Bukharin's remarks to a delegation of German workers on November 9, 1927 (unpublished stenograph preserved at the International Institut voor sociale Geschiedenis, Amsterdam).

227. Serge, *Memoirs*, p. 245.

228. See Astrov in *Pravda*, July 1, 1928, p. 2; his editorial note in *Pravda*, July 7, 1928, p. 2; Rykov's and Bukharin's remarks at the July 1928 plenum (T1835, 1901); Bukharin in *Pravda*, September 30, 1928, p. 2; and Stalin, *Works*, XII, p. 96.

229. Nikolai Ustrialov quoted in Leont'ev, *Ekonomicheskaia teoriia pravogo uklona*, p. 5.

230. *Biulleten' oppozitsii*, No. 1–2, 1929, p. 16. Earlier, it will be recalled, he had endorsed the Comintern resolution against "the right deviation." At that same congress, however, he made an attempt to argue that the question was not whether policy was left or right, "but whether it is correct or incorrect, whether it corresponds or does not correspond to the objective situation." *VI kongress Kominterna*, I, p. 46.

231. For an official complaint about political illiteracy among Komsomol members, equally applicable to the party, see Kosarev, *Komsomol v rekonstruktivnyi period*, p. 41. An anecdote related in an official history makes the same point. A Komsomol member is asked about deviations in the party. He replies that there are three: right, left, and central. The Right, he explains, is for slow industrial development, the Left for rapid, and the central for a middle course. "And who is in the central deviation?" he is asked. "Our party, the Central Committee." Abramov, *O pravoi oppozitsii*, pp. 210–11. Bukharin's analysis of party officialdom in 1928–9 was, of course, very similar to that of Trotskyists. Even a disillusioned Stalinist concluded that party officials were a "political quagmire" of "philistines." See L. Shatskin, "Doloi partiinogo obyvatelia!," *Komsomol'skaia pravda*, June 18, 1929, p. 2.

232. Quoted in *Biulleten' oppozitsii*, No. 1–2, 1929, p. 17. Also see N. Tiushevskii, *Vnutripartiinyi rezhim i pravyi uklon* (Leningrad, 1929). The other right leaders were caught in the same contradiction between their past intolerance and present

espousal of freedom for loyal dissent. For Tomskii and the Moscow leaders, for example, see Gaisinskii, *Bor'ba s uklonami,* pp. 197-8, 209; and Vaganov, *Pravyi uklon,* pp. 157-8.

233. Bukharin-Kamenev memorandum (T1897).

234. Popov, *Outline History,* II, p. 369. He was similarly constrained with his Comintern supporters. See Löwy, *Die Weltgeschichte,* pp. 327, 365. And by 1929 his meetings with them were as "conspiratorial" and ineffectual as those with Kamenev. For one such meeting, see Istituto Giangiacomo Feltrinelli, *Annali,* pp. 653-9. Tomskii later commented movingly on the Right's predicament and the constraints imposed by "party unity and party discipline." *XVII s"ezd,* p. 250; also *XVI s"ezd,* I, p. 260.

235. Smilga quoted in Deutscher, *Prophet Unarmed,* p. 541.

236. The following, for example, were among ranking provincial party secretaries in 1928-9 who earlier had worked in Stalin's central bureaucracy: Bauman (Moscow), Kaganovich (the Ukraine), Iosif Vareikis (Central Black Earth Region), Sergei Syrtsov (Siberia), Boris Sheboldaev (Lower Volga), Nikolai Shvernik (the Urals), Mendel Khataevich (Middle Volga), and Stanislav Kosior (the Ukraine).

237. Schapiro, *Communist Party,* pp. 444-5.

238. Or as Stalin threatened the pro-Bukharinist leadership of the American party in May 1929: "At present you still have a formal majority. But tomorrow there will be no majority at all and you will turn out to be completely isolated. . . ." Eudin and Slusser, *Soviet Foreign Policy,* I, p. 177.

239. Bukharin-Kamenev memorandum (T1897). Also see *Ocherki istorii kommunisticheskoi partii Ukrainy* (2nd ed.; Kiev, 1964), pp. 376-7; and G. Mariagin, *Postyshev* (Moscow, 1965), p. 79.

240. *Shestnadtsataia konferentsiia,* p. 214. For the Ukrainians and Leningraders, see Khavin, *U rulia industrii,* pp. 67-8; V. Drobizhev and N. Dumova, *V. Ia. Chubar'* (Moscow, 1963), pp. 48-50; and Stetskii in *Pravda,* March 17, 1929, p. 1.

241. The latter consideration may have been the "special hold" Bukharin believed that Stalin had over Voroshilov and Kalinin. See *Writings of Leon Trotsky (1937-38)* (New York, 1970), pp. 167-8; and Daniels, *Conscience,* p. 329. For Stalin's investigatory powers, see Kaganovich's remarks at *XVI s"ezd,* I, p. 153.

242. A Georgian Bolshevik in 1921, quoted in S. V. Kharmandarian, *Lenin i stanovlenie zakavkazskoi federatsii, 1921-1923* (Erevan, 1969), p. 218.

243. Bukharin quoted in Höglund, *Moskva tur och retur,* p. 208. While doubtless an exaggeration, Bukharin does appear to have neglected badly his own organizational bailiwicks. See, for example, Humbert-Droz's complaints that Bukharin had little time for Comintern affairs. "*L'oeil de Moscou*" *à Paris,* pp. 242.

244. Lazar Shatskin quoted in *The Revolutionary Age* (New York), No. 1 (November 1), 1929, p. 16. That senior members saw the Central Committee as a differentiated assembly is clear from Bukharin's remarks in Bukharin-Kamenev memorandum (T1897).

245. That these were the key party organizations is indicated in "Podchinit'sia partii ili kapitulirovat' pered melkoburzhuaznoi stikhiei," *Pravda,* April 23, 1929, p. 3, a Stalinist article applauding them for officially renouncing the Right. In addition to the Muscovites, it will be recalled, Bukharin had hoped for the support of the Leningraders and the Ukrainians. He also listed Andreev, secretary of the North Caucasus, as a possible ally. Bukharin-Kamenev memorandum (T1897). Syrtsov, party chief of Siberia where Stalin had unveiled his "extraordinary measures" in January 1928, replaced Rykov as premier of the Russian Republic in May

1929. See above, note 178. The only formal gathering of this unofficial oligarchy seems to have been the enlarged Politburo meeting in January–February 1929, which censured the opposition.

246. See, for example, the characterization of Kirov as a "military-political figure" in *Poslantsy partii: vospominaniia* (Moscow, 1967), p. 181; and Molotov's statement that "the overwhelming majority of us are not theoreticians but practical politicians (*praktiki*)," *Bol'shevik*, No. 3 (February 15), 1931, p. 20. A large number of them were, like Stalin, Transcaucasians, rough, burly, mustachioed men for whom the civil war had been an especially harsh experience. For their political personality and ethos, see A. I. Mikoian, *Dorogoi bor'by*, Vol. I (Moscow, 1971). A number of others, including Kirov, had made their careers in the Transcaucasus and were so identified.

247. Because of his political role and subsequent assassination in the thirties, Kirov is an important example. Previously secretary of the Azerbaidzhan party, and with close ties to Stalin's Transcaucasian supporters, he took over the Leningrad party after Zinoviev's defeat in 1926. He is usually regarded as a faithful Stalinist proconsul, and his Leningrad organization as firmly loyal to the general secretary in the late twenties. That this was not the case is suggested by evidence that Kirov resisted the Secretariat's efforts to dictate appointments in Leningrad in 1926 (see *Vestnik leningradskogo universiteta*, No. 8, 1968, pp. 82–3); by Bukharin's expectation of Leningrad support in 1928 and the prominence of his local supporters, notably Stetskii, Petrovskii, and the trade union leader Fedor Ugarov; and by the striking lack of evidence that Kirov himself played any role in the anti-Bukharin struggle until April 1929, when the outcome was already certain. (I have not, however, had access to the Leningrad press.) Instead, Kirov seems to have stood aside from the conflict during its crucial months. Though his views in 1928 are unclear, his initial response to Stalin's industrial plan was that it was "unrealistic." *Istoricheskii arkhiv*, No. 5, 1961, p. 109. Stalin's displeasure was probably behind two unusual attacks on the Leningrad party (and thus implicitly on Kirov), one on its newspaper and the other on its Control Commission, in 1928 and 1929. See Kuibyshev's speech in *Pravda*, September 25, 1929, p. 3; S. V. Krasnikov, *S. M. Kirov v Leningrade* (Leningrad, 1966), pp. 49–56; and *Pravda*, September 4, 1929, p. 3.

248. Astrov, *Krucha*, p. 220. Stalinists, not unreasonably, regularly portrayed Bukharin as "the chief leader and inspirer" of the opposition. *Pravda*, November 18, 1929, p. 1. The contention that the Right "tried to make Comrade Bukharin the leader of our party" is less persuasive. *Biulleten' tret'ei leningradskoi oblastnoi konferentsii VKP(b)*. No. 3 (Leningrad, 1930), p. 14. Despite his pre-eminence, Bukharin made no effort to assert himself over Rykov and Tomskii, themselves "practical politicians." As evidenced by his overtures to Kamenev and Zinoviev, he still thought in terms of a collective leadership.

249. For the "continuous concessions" charge, see Krylov and Zykov, *O pravoi opasnosti*, pp. 159–70. The Bukharin-Rykov proposal to import grain to alleviate the crisis was especially unpopular and criticized as "the greatest attack on our tempo of industrialization." Vaganov, *Pravyi uklon*, p. 106; *Voprosy istorii KPSS*, No. 5 (May 1969), p. 30.

250. Bukharin at *VI kongress Kominterna*, I, p. 33. Or, as the Bukharinist Aikhenvald put it: "it is better to be a right deviationist than a hopeless idiot." Quoted in *Pravda*, November 3, 1929, p. 3. Elsewhere Bukharin countered by calling for an "earthly optimism." *Pravda*, June 12, 1929, p. 3.

251. The alliance between Stalin and younger party-Komsomol leaders was epitomized by a group of radical anti-Bukharinists sometimes called the "Young Stalinist Left." Serge, *Memoirs*, p. 259. Protégés of Stalin since the early twenties,

their best-known representatives were Lominadze, Shatskin, and Ian Sten, and also included foreign Comintern allies such as Heinz Neumann. Several were shortly to grow disillusioned and break with Stalin. See *Pravda*, December 1, 1931, p. 3; and Margarete Buber-Neumann, *Kriegsschauplätze der Weltrevolution* (Stuttgart, 1967), pp. 282–4 and *passim*.

252. Kuibyshev quoted in *Voprosy istorii KPSS*, No. 10, 1967, p. 76; S. M. Kirov, *Izbrannye stat'i i rechi (1912–1934)*, Vol. II (Moscow, 1957), p. 539; G. K. Ordzhonikidze, *Stat'i i rechi*, Vol. II (Moscow, 1957), p. 174.

253. Stalin's accusation that the Right preached a philosophy of pessimism was probably his most effective. See above, notes 194 and 250. It was also leveled against Bukharin's Comintern views, particularly his argument that European revolution was unlikely without a general war. See, for example, *Komsomol'skaia pravda*, November 17, 1929, p. 2.

254. For the party oligarchs, the central issue in the struggle was industrial growth and planning. Collectivization, which they (like Bukharin) still viewed as a gradual, voluntary undertaking, was a supplementary concern, while Comintern controversies seem to have concerned them very little. That they had not repudiated NEP was emphasized by an official editorial on the Right's defeat: "NEP is the only correct policy of socialist construction." *Pravda*, April 28, 1929, p. 1. Indeed, some of Stalin's supporters were still worried by aspects of his advocacy, including his notion of an intensifying class struggle and enthusiasm for "extraordinary measures." See, for example, the editorial concern expressed in *Izvestiia*, April 23, 1929, p. 1; and Eikhe's remarks at *Shestnadtsataia konferentsiia*, p. 91.

255. See, for example, *Works*, XI, pp. 217, 257, 290–3.

256. See, for example, A. I. Mikoian, *Mysli i vospominaniia o Lenine* (Moscow, 1970), pp. 145, 196, 233; and *Khrushchev Remembers* (Boston, 1970), pp. 27, 50.

257. For the plenum's proceedings, see *Inprecor*, IX (1929), Nos. 35, 40–1, 44–9, 51, 53, 55, 57, 59. The new line was spelled out by Molotov, Kuusinen, and Manuilskii. Stalin did not address the plenum; but he had signaled the new course in two speeches in May. I. Stalin, *O pravykh fraktsionerakh v amerikanskoi Kompartii* (Moscow, 1930).

258. For these developments, see Lewin, *Russian Peasants*, pp. 375, 453.

259. Kozlova, *Moskovskie kommunisty*, p. 43. Soviet statistics on rural disturbances, characterized as "kulak terrorist acts," are elliptical and contradictory. It is particularly difficult to obtain comparative figures for 1928 and 1929. It is reported, for example, only that "kulak terrorist acts" in the Ukraine were four times greater in 1929 than in 1927. *Voprosy istorii KPSS*, No. 2, 1966, p. 101.

260. The major study of rural policy and events in the countryside in 1929 is Lewin, *Russian Peasants*, Chapters XIV–XVIII.

261. *Inprecor*, IX (1929), p. 745.

262. *Sovetskii entsiklopedicheskii slovar'*, Vol. I (Moscow, 1931), p. 221. The post was held previously by Kamenev. *Politicheskii slovar'* (Leningrad, 1929), p. 660.

263. *Pravda*, June 12, 1929, p. 3.

264. "Nekotorye problemy sovremennogo kapitalizma u teoretikov burzhuazii," *Pravda*, May 26, 1929, pp. 2–3; and "Teoriia 'organizovannoi beskhoziaistvennosti,' " *Pravda*, June 3, 1929, pp. 3, 5.

265. The three reportedly had complained of their "unequal position" and had sought "legalization" of their status. See *KPSS v rezoliutsiiakh*, II, p. 662.

266. *Biulleten' oppozitsii*, No. 1–2, 1929, p. 14.

267. In June and July, two leaders of the "Young Stalinist Left," Shatskin and Sten (see above, note 251), protested demands for uncritical party obedience in much the same terms used by Bukharin earlier in June. See *Komsomol'skaia pravda*, June 18, 1929, p. 2, and July 26, 1929, p. 2. Their complaints probably reflected a growing anxiety among Stalin's followers over his social policies. Both recanted under pressure—see *Pravda*, November 2, 1929, p. 4; and November 12, 1929, p. 6—but participated in the more serious rebellion of Syrtsov and Lominadze in 1930. For other evidence of alarm in the police, Central Committee, and Politburo, see *Sotsialisticheskii vestnik*, June 14, 1929, p. 14, and October 10, 1929, p. 14; and Lewin, *Russian Peasants*, pp. 460–1.

268. See above, note 248.

269. Avtorkhanov, *Stalin*, Chapter vi.

270. It would be pointless to list even a few of the hundreds of anti-Bukharin articles. They appeared regularly in *Pravda, Bolshevik, Komsomolskaia pravda, Kommunisticheskaia revoliutsiia, Propagandist,* and elsewhere from late August onward. More substantial attacks on his career and theoretical writings appeared regularly in *VKA, PZM,* and *Proletarskaia revoliutsiia*. For examples of pamphlets and books, see V. Sorin, *O raznoglasiiakh Bukharina s Leninym* (Moscow, 1930); Leman and Pokrovskii, *Ideinye istoki pravogo uklona;* Abramov, *O pravoi oppozitsii;* and Bukhartsev, *Teoreticheskie oruzhenostsy opportunizma.*

271. As his Stalinist critics complained. See *Za povorot na filosofskom fronte: sbornik statei* (Moscow, 1931), pp. 91, 101, where one pointed out that compared to Bukharin, Trotsky was a "quantité négligeable" in theoretical matters. Also see Stetskii's remarks, *XVI s"ezd*, I, p. 488.

272. Ulianova was dismissed from *Pravda*. Krupskaya, while formally remaining Deputy Commissar of Education, was deprived of her responsibilities and authority. *M. I. Ul'ianova—sekretar' Pravdy*, p. 259; and *Pravda*, February 26, 1964, p. 4. For Krupskaya's support for Bukharin in 1929, see above, note 172.

273. A point now emphasized by Soviet historians of collectivization. See M. L. Bogdenko, "Kolkhoznoe stroitel'stvo vesnoi i letom 1930 g.", *Istoricheskie zapiski*, No. 76 (1965), p. 21; Danilov, "K kharakteristike . . . ," p. 42; and Nemakov, *Kommunisticheskaia partiia*, p. 194. The campaign had the same impact on advocates of industrial balance. See G. Sorokin in *Pravda*, December 1, 1963, p. 4. For admissions that the "anti-collective farm mood" was still widespread in the party, see *Pravda*, August 28, 1929, p. 4; and Krylov and Zykov, *O pravoi opasnosti*, p. 142.

274. See above, note 11; and Abramov, *O pravoi oppozitsii*, p. 249.

275. See Joravsky, *Soviet Marxism*, Part IV; Sheila Fitzpatrick, "The Emergence of Glaviskusstvo: Class War on the Cultural Front, Moscow, 1928–29," *Soviet Studies* (October 1971), pp. 236–53; and Brown, *Proletarian Episode*.

276. This point is now emphasized by several Soviet historians in connection with mass collectivization. See, for example, N. A. Ivnitskii, "O kriticheskom analize istochnikov po istorii nachal'nogo etapa sploshnoi kollektivizatsii (osen' 1929–vesna 1930 g.)," *Istoricheskii arkhiv*, No. 2, 1962, pp. 193–8; Bogdenko, "Kolkhoznoe dvizhenie nakanune sploshnoi kollektivizatsii (1927 g.–pervaia polovina 1929 g.)," *Istoricheskie zapiski*, No. 80 (1967), pp. 78–9. Ivnitskii refers to the Stalin group in power as "a narrow circle of people" (p. 196). See also Lewin, *Russian Peasants*, Chapters XV–XVII.

277. I. Stalin, *Sochineniia*, Vol. XII (Moscow, 1949), pp. 130–2.

278. Lewin, *Russian Peasants*, pp. 460–1.

279. Vaganov, *Pravyi uklon*, pp. 246–9; *Bol'shevik*, No. 2, 1930, pp. 7–26; *KPSS v rezoliutsiiakh*, II, pp. 662–3.

280. Harsh attacks on Bukharin during closed and unpublished proceedings are usually quoted extensively from archive sources by Soviet historians. Apart from those of Stalin and his inner circle, I have found none originating at this plenum.

281. Lewin, *Russian Peasants*, pp. 458–65; *KPSS v rezoliutsiiakh*, II, pp. 620–32, 642–56. Lewin states that the plenary resolutions fully reflected the Stalin-Molotov line; his excellent pioneering study, however, contains persuasive evidence for the contrary view, which I have taken. Other evidence, including the recommendations of the subsequent collectivization commission, suggests that when the plenum adjourned, its leading members did not regard 1930 as the official target date.

282. See the statements of Kotov, Mikhailov, Uglanov, and Kulikov in *Itogi noiabr'skogo plenuma TSK VKP(b)* (Leningrad, 1929), pp. 187–92.

283. *Ibid.*, p. 193.

284. *Ibid.*, p. 196. Their last Central Committee supporter, the Leningrader Fedor Ugarov, capitulated the same day.

285. Avtorkhanov, *Stalin*, pp. 155–6.

286. Bukharin explained his concern for them to Boris I. Nicolaevsky, *Power and the Soviet Elite*, p. 19. Menacing attacks on the young Bukharinists appeared regularly in *Pravda* in October and November. Aikhenvald, for example, was linked ominously with exiles in Berlin, and expelled from the party. *Pravda*, November 18, 1929, p. 3; and November 20, 1929, p. 5. They continued, however, to insist that "Comrade Bukharin is not a right deviationist but a revolutionary Bolshevik." *Pravda*, November 10, 1929, p. 5. After Bukharin's surrender, most then signed similar recantations. See *Pravda*, November 25, 1929, p. 3; November 28, 1929, p. 3; December 3, 1929, p. 3; and December 6, 1929, p. 4.

287. *Stalin: sbornik statei k piatidesiatiletiiu so dnia rozhdeniia*, pp. 22, 52. Also see *Pravda* for December 21; and K. Popov, "Partiia i rol' vozhdia," *Partiinoe stroitel'stvo* (January 1930), pp. 5–9.

288. For these events, see Lewin, *Russian Peasants*, pp. 465–519; and M. A. Vyltsan, N. A. Ivnitskii, Iu. A. Poliakov, "Nekotorye problemy istorii kollektivizatsii v SSSR," *Voprosy istorii*, No. 3, 1965, pp. 3–25.

CHAPTER X

1. *Sovetskaia istoricheskaia entsiklopediia*. Vol. VI (Moscow, 1965), pp. 25–34; Nove, *Economic History*, Chapters viii–ix.

2. Lyons, *Assignment in Utopia*, p. 196; Iurii Zhukov, *Liudi 30-kh godov* (Moscow, 1966).

3. Moshkov, *Zernovaia problema*, p. 136; Nove, *Economic History*, pp. 209, 249–51, 260.

4. For the story of collectivization, see Lewin, *Russian Peasants*, pp. 482–519; Nove, *Economic History*, Chapter vii; and Fainsod, *Smolensk*, Chapter xii.

5. Lewin, *Russian Peasants*, Chapter xvii; M. L. Bogdenko, "Kolkhoznoe stroitel'stvo vesnoi i letom 1930 g.," *Istoricheskie zapiski*, No. 76 (1965), p. 31.

6. Nove, *Economic History*, p. 186; Nemakov, *Kommunisticheskaia partiia*, pp. 257–9; *Ocherki istorii kommunisticheskoi partii Ukrainy*, p. 401.

7. According to an official circular quoted in Fainsod, *Smolensk*, pp. 185–6.

8. See, for example, William Henry Chamberlin, *Russia's Iron Age* (New York, 1935), pp. 82–8, 367–9; Arthur Koestler, *The Yogi and the Commissar* (New York, 1965), p. 128; Reswick, *I Dreamt Revolution*, Chapter xxv; and Medvedev, *Let History Judge*, pp. 94–6.

9. Estimates vary from slightly less than 10 million to considerably more. Stalin later confided the figure 10 million to Winston Churchill. See *The Hinge of Fate* (New York, 1950), p. 498.

10. As Preobrazhenskii pointed out: *XVII s"ezd*, p. 238.

11. Nove, *Economic History*, pp. 180, 186. A comparison of all agricultural products and state procurements between 1926–9 and 1930–9 reveals a similar pattern. See Medvedev, *Let History Judge*, pp. 90–2.

12. Quoted in Tucker, *Soviet Political Mind*, p. 124.

13. For these developments, see Nicholas S. Timasheff, *The Great Retreat* (New York, 1946); and Robert V. Daniels, "Soviet Thought in the Nineteen-Thirties: An Interpretative Sketch," in *Indiana Slavic Studies*, edited by Michael Ginsburg and Joseph Thomas Shaw, Vol. I (Bloomington, Ind., 1956), pp. 97–135.

14. The definitive account of the terror is Robert Conquest, *The Great Terror: Stalin's Purge of the Thirties* (New York, 1968), His statistics are necessarily approximate, but the most reliable we have.

15. *Ibid.*, Chapters viii, xiii; Robert Conquest, "The Great Terror Revised," *Survey*, No. 78 (1971), pp. 92–3; and Medvedev, *Let History Judge*, Chapter vi.

16. As has been acknowledged by the Soviet government since Stalin's death. For the charges against Bukharin, see *Vsesoiuznoe soveshchanie*, p. 298.

17. Conquest, *Great Terror*, p. 251.

18. *Ibid.*, p. 471; *Istoriia kommunisticheskoi partii sovetskogo soiuza*, Vol. I, Book 1 (Moscow, 1970), p. 7.

19. For an analysis, see Tucker, *Soviet Political Mind*, Chapter i. The end of party government between 1939 and 1953 is tacitly acknowledged by some Soviet historians. See *Materialy k lektsiiam po kursu istorii KPSS: temy 11–13*, edited by P. P. Andreev (Moscow, 1964), pp. 43–4.

20. The first substantial evidence of this covert struggle was the document known as *Letter of an Old Bolshevik: The Key to the Moscow Trials* (New York, 1937). For the origins and authorship of the *Letter*, see below, note 143. Using the *Letter*, and other materials, Boris Nicolaevsky developed a historical analysis of the struggle in various articles, two of which are collected in his *Power and the Soviet Elite*. Soviet sources published since 1953 have largely confirmed, and significantly expanded, the *Letter*'s account. Many of them are cited in Conquest, *Great Terror*, Chapters i–ii and *passim*, which provides the fullest account now available.

21. Kalinin, though apparently not a regular member of the moderate group, also opposed the purge of 1936–9. When he objected to the arrest of party officials, Stalin replied: "You, Mikhail Ivanovich, always were a liberal. . . ." A. Tolmachev, *Kalinin* (Moscow, 1963), pp. 226–7.

22. *Ocherki istorii kommunisticheskoi partii Gruzii*, Part II (Tbilisi, 1963), p. 105. One who objected was the Ukrainian party chief Kosior. *Kratkaia istoriia SSSR*, Part II (Moscow-Leningrad, 1964), pp. 251–2. Kalinin and Ordzhonikidze criticized *Pravda*, Stalin's mouthpiece, for inciting excesses. *Vsesoiuznoe soveshchanie*, pp. 299–300. For Stalin's article calling the halt and blaming local officials,

see *Works*, XII, pp. 197–205, and for its origins, p. 218. Stalin and his personal supporters continued to place the full blame on local officials. See, for example, K. Voroshilov, *Na istoricheskom perevale* (Moscow-Leningrad, 1930), p. 85.

23. Gaisinskii, *Bor'ba s uklonami*, pp. 272–88; *Bol'shevik*, No. 21, 1931, pp. 22–47; Medvedev, *Let History Judge*, p. 142.

24. It seems clear, for example, that Lominadze spoke for a majority of Transcaucasian party secretaries, Syrtsov for many government administrators at the center, and that they were supported by several Komsomol leaders. See *Pravda*, December 2, 1930, p. 6; and above, note 23. By 1932: "The predominant view in party circles was that Stalin had led the country into an impasse," *Letter of an Old Bolshevik*, p. 12. It also seems clear, however, that Stalin's charge of a conspiratorial "bloc" between the two men was untrue.

25. Medvedev, *Let History Judge*, pp. 152–3. For the perception of a threat to the régime's existence, see below, note 66.

26. Medvedev, *Let History Judge*, p. 138; Khavin, *U rulia industrii*, pp. 101, 112–15; *Novyi mir*, No. 1, 1967, pp. 40, 66.

27. See, for example, the case of Amaiak Nazaretian related in *Pravda*, November 17, 1964, p. 4.

28. *Letter of an Old Bolshevik*, p. 13.

29. Paul M. Cocks, "Politics of Party Control" (unpublished Ph.D. dissertation, Harvard University, 1968), pp. 173–4, 493–4, 517–23.

30. Conquest, *Great Terror*, pp. 28–9; Medvedev, *Let History Judge*, pp. 142–3. They were probably supported also by a majority of the candidate Politburo members, including Grigorii Petrovskii whose son, Petr, was implicated in the Riutin affair. *Pravda*, October 11, 1932, p. 5.

31. On September 25, 1936, in a secret directive in effect inaugurating the great purge, Stalin referred back to the Riutin affair by declaring that the secret police were "four years behind" in "unmasking enemies." Quoted in Nikita S. Khrushchev, *The Crimes of the Stalin Era* (New York, 1962), p. 23.

32. *Letter of an Old Bolshevik*, p. 35; Medvedev, *Let History Judge*, pp. 155–6; L. Shaumian, "Cult of An Individual," *Soviet Studies in Philosophy* (Summer 1966), p. 32. According to Medvedev, 270 of the 1,966 delegates to the Seventeenth Party Congress voted against Stalin and only 3 against Kirov. The anti-Stalin voters are not known, but one appears to have been the Ukrainian leader and candidate Politburo member Petrovskii. See F. Bega and V. Aleksandrov, *Petrovskii* (Moscow, 1963), p. 303; and above, note 30.

33. *Letter of an Old Bolshevik*; Nicolaevsky, *Power and the Soviet Elite*, pp. 69–97.

34. Fainsod, *Smolensk*, pp. 185–6; Nicolaevsky, *Power and the Soviet Elite*, pp. 90–1, 95–6; *Letter of an Old Bolshevik*, p. 54.

35. *Letter of an Old Bolshevik*, pp. 21–2; *XVII s"ezd*, pp. 8–36, 251–9.

36. According to the edited stenograph, Bukharin received "applause." *XVII s"ezd*, p. 129. According to *Pravda*, January 31, 1934, p. 2, he received "prolonged applause."

37. It is even possible that Stalin lost the title of general secretary at this plenum. Nicolaevsky, *Power and the Soviet Elite*, p. 92.

38. *Ibid.*, p. 135.

39. *Letter of an Old Bolshevik*, p. 21. For his remarks on the continuing menace of internal enemies, see, for example, his speeches to the Central Committee in

January 1933 and to the Seventeenth Party Congress. *From the First to the Second Five-Year Plan* (New York, 1933), pp. 54–6, 76–8; and *Works*, XIII, pp. 356–8.

40. Conquest, *Great Terror*, pp. 38–40, which I am quoting; and Medvedev, *Let History Judge*, p. 156.

41. *Letter of an Old Bolshevik*, p. 35.

42. Conquest, *Great Terror*, Chapter ii; Medvedev, *Let History Judge*, Chapter v.

43. Evgenia S. Ginzburg, *Into the Whirlwind* (London, 1967), p. 11.

44. Conquest, *Great Terror*, pp. 82–4, 98–9, 185–91; Medvedev, *Let History Judge*, pp. 193–7.

45. As indicated, for example, by the symbolic role and abolition of the Society of Old Bolsheviks in May 1935.

46. Avtorkhanov, *Stalin*, p. 171. Similarly, see G. A. Tokaev, *Comrade X* (London, 1956), p. 62. This seems also to have been true for foreign Communists. H. M. Wicks, *Eclipse of October* (Chicago, 1957), p. 261.

47. Thus even during his defamation in 1929–33, his attackers were obliged to acknowledge his former "services" and popularity. See, for example, *Partiinoe stroitel'stvo*, No. 2, 1929, pp. 9–10; *VKA*, Book 34 (1929), p. 20; and *XVI s"ezd*, I, pp. 420, 515.

48. *XVI s"ezd*, I, p. 488, and similarly p. 441; and *Voprosy prepodavaniia leninizma, istorii VKP(b), i Kominterna* (Moscow, 1930), p. 71. Also see above, Chapter ix, note 271.

49. *Pravda*, May 27, 1930, p. 1; *XVI s"ezd*, I, pp. 244–5.

50. Gaisinskii, *Bor'ba s uklonami*, pp. 177, 247–9. For the Smirnov group, see *KPSS v rezoliutsiiakh*, III, p. 199. A content analysis of *Pravda*'s attacks on oppositionist manifestations in May–June 1930 revealed that approximately 85 per cent of the offenses were "rightist" in one fashion or another. *Biulleten' oppozitsii*, No. 14, 1930, pp. 5–6. As Stalin pointed out, even the Left's economic opposition had become substantially "rightist." *Works*, XIII, p. 370.

51. *XVI s"ezd*, I, p. 324, and similarly pp. 207, 248. For similar admissions of widespread rightist sentiment in 1930–3, see *Bol'shevik*, No. 21, 1930, p. 46; and *From the First to the Second Five-Year Plan*, p. 129. It was particularly strong in Moscow. See *Pravda* for May 26, 29, and 31, 1930. Also see *Sotsialisticheskii vestnik*, June 14, 1930, p. 15; and *Biulleten' oppozitsii*, No. 34, 1933, p. 32.

52. *Biulleten' oppozitsii*, No. 19, 1930, p. 18.

53. *Letter of an Old Bolshevik*, p. 15.

54. A point suggested by T. Szamuely, "The Elimination of Opposition Between the Sixteenth and Seventeenth Congresses of the CPSU," *Soviet Studies* (January 1966), p. 321.

55. "Velikaia rekonstruktsiia," *Pravda*, February 19, 1930, pp. 2–4. His remarks were promptly attacked. *Bol'shevik*, No. 7–8, 1930, pp. 153–7.

56. Bukharin, *Etiudy*, pp. 341–5. The article, "Finansovyi kapital v mantii papy," appeared originally in *Pravda*, March 7, 1930, pp. 2–4. Bukharin's Jesuit-Stalinist analogy was obvious, but he also included a telltale clue—an oblique reference to Stalin's "withered" arm. *Etiudy*, p. 338. Bertram Wolfe was the first scholar to note the article's importance. *Three Who Made a Revolution*, pp. 36–7.

57. Gaisinskii, *Bor'ba s uklonami*, p. 253.

58. See Nicolaevsky, *Power and the Soviet Elite*, p. 24; and *Biulleten' oppozitsii*, No. 19, 1931, p. 18, where the date is unclear.

59. *XVI s"ezd*, I, pp. 246, 367, and *passim*. Bukharin was rumored to have been ill during the congress; but, as Stalinists pointed out, this did not preclude a written statement.

60. "Zaiavlenie N. Bukharina v TSK VKP(b)," *Pravda*, November 20, 1930, p. 5. The nature of the negotiations may be surmised from Molotov's account in *Bol'shevik*, No. 3, 1931, pp. 17–22; Kaganovich's in *Pravda*, December 30, 1930, p. 4; and Gaisinskii, *Bor'ba s uklonami*, pp. 302–6.

61. *Bol'shevik*, No. 3, 1931, p. 18.

62. The Riutin group, for example, criticized Bukharin in this connection. See *Biulleten' oppozitsii*, No. 31, 1932, p. 23; and *Case of the Anti-Soviet Bloc*, p. 163.

63. Future Politburo moderates took an active part in the disgracing of Syrtsov and Lominadze. See, for example, Kirov's speech in *Pravda*, December 2, 1930, p. 6.

64. The press was now threatening Bukharin with expulsion. *Pravda*, November 4, 1930, p. 3. Equally ominous, Bukharin's views were being linked with those of the defendants at the 1930 trial of former specialists. See *Pravda*, October 9 and 10, 1930, p. 5; and *Propagandist*, No. 3–4, 1930, pp. 1–9.

65. See his remarks in *Case of the Anti-Soviet Bloc*, p. 381; and Nicolaevsky, *Power and the Soviet Elite*, p. 18.

66. *Case of the Anti-Soviet Bloc*, pp. 380, 776; *XVII s"ezd*, pp. 124–5; Joseph Berger, *Nothing But the Truth* (New York, 1971), p. 99. One Soviet historian has concluded that Stalin's policies of 1929–33 created "a threat to the very existence of the dictatorship of the proletariat." See *Ocherki istorii kollektivizatsii*, p. 45.

67. *Etiudy*, p. 151.

68. See his retrospective remarks in "Rech' tov. Bukharina na ob"edinennom plenume TSK i TSKK VKP(b)," *Pravda*, January 14, 1933, p. 3.

69. An interesting example of Bukharin's public conduct was his refusal to join in the ritual of praising Stalin lavishly and acknowledging him as the leader and architect of the country's achievements. Indeed, he rarely mentioned Stalin in 1930–2, referring instead to "the leadership of our party . . . and its Central Committee." When he did acknowledge Stalin's role, he chose a modest formula: "the Central Committee headed by Stalin." See, for example, *Etiudy*, p. 304, and *XVII konferentsiia vsesoiuznoi kommunisticheskoi partii(b): stenograficheskii otchet* (Moscow, 1932), pp. 76, 80. For his warning to specialists, see *Etiudy*, pp. 242, 290; and for a different interpretation of this speech, Graham, *Soviet Academy*, pp. 186–7.

70. He was head of the Academy's Institute of the History of Natural Sciences and Technology. *V.O.K.S.*, Vol. V (1933), p. 18. His role there is discussed in Graham, *Soviet Academy*. For the London congress and his visit, see his report in *Science at the Cross Roads* (London, 1931), pp. 1–23; and his "Science and Politics in the Soviet Union," *New Statesman and Nation*, July 11, 1931, pp. 37–8. Also see the accounts in J. G. Crowther, *Fifty Years with Science* (London, 1970), pp. 76–80; *Science at the Cross Roads* (2nd ed.; 1971), pp. xi–xxix; *VKA*, No. 8–9, 1931, pp. 93–100; and Colin Holmes, "Bukharin in England," *Soviet Studies* (July 1972), pp. 86–90. For his hosting of foreign scientists in the U.S.S.R., see Crowther, p. 86; and Julian Huxley, *A Scientist Among the Soviets* (New York, 1932), p. 64. For a collection of his essays, see *Etiudy*. His journal, *Sotsialisticheskaia rekonstruktsiia i nauka*, known also as *Sorena*, began publication in 1931. It was later attacked as "a captive of bourgeois ideology." *Pravda*, February 8, 1937, p. 3.

71. Two of his paintings were exhibited in 1931. Alexander Weissberg, *The Accused* (New York, 1951), p. 185. A fragment of his work on Marx was published in 1933: "Uchenie Marksa i ego istoricheskoe znachenie."

72. Pieced together from the following: Orlov, *Stalin's Crimes,* p. 280; Löwy, *Die Weltgeschichte ist das Weltgericht,* pp. 279–80, 388–9; Alliluyeva, *Twenty Letters,* p. 30; "Memuary P. Iakira," *Russkaia mysl',* October 28, 1971; and *Posev* (June 1969), p. 59.

73. See *Etiudy* and his "Nekotorye mysli o sovetskoi zhivopisi," *Izvestiia,* July 11, 1933, p. 3.

74. "Uchenie Marksa i ego istoricheskoe znachenie," p. 79; and the attack by E. V. Pashukanis in *VKA,* No. 5, 1933, pp. 40–56.

75. Graham, *Soviet Academy,* pp. 45, 56–67; and his "Bukharin and the Planning of Science," *The Russian Review* (April 1964), pp. 135–48. In particular, see Bukharin's reports in *Etiudy,* pp. 236–305; and "Tekhnicheskaia rekonstruktsiia i tekushchie problemy nauchno-issledovatel'skoi paboty," *Sotsialisticheskaia rekonstruktsiia i nauka,* No. 1, 1933, pp. 5–35.

76. *Etiudy,* p. 276. He argued the necessity of a "technological revolution" regularly. See *Pravda,* December 15, 1929, p. 3; *Pravda,* February 19, 1930, pp. 2–4; "Tekhnika i ekonomika v planovom khoziaistve," *Za industrializatsiiu,* March 20, 1930, pp. 2–4; *Etiudy,* pp. 9–34, 64–107, 211–305; *XVII konferentsiia,* pp. 76–80; "Mirovoi krizis, SSSR i tekhnika," *Sotsialisticheskaia rekonstruktsiia i nauka,* No. 1, 1933, pp. 5–35; and "Perestroika upravleniia i problemy nauchno-tekhnicheskogo obsluzhivaniia promyshlennosti," *Pravda,* August 4, 1933, pp. 2–3.

77. *Etiudy,* pp. 291–8.

78. *Sotsialisticheskaia rekonstruktsiia i nauka,* No. 9–10, 1932, p. 3. He spoke at the Seventeenth Party Conference in 1932 as a representative of the Commissariat. *XVII konferentsiia,* pp. 75–80.

79. N. Popov, *Ocherki istorii vsesoiuznoi kommunisticheskoi partii (bol'shevikov),* Vol. II (15th ed.; Moscow, 1932), p. 304; *XVII konferentsiia,* p. 138.

80. *Pravda,* January 14, 1933, p. 3.

81. Slepkov, Maretskii, and Petrovskii. *Pravda,* October 11, 1932, p. 5.

82. Nicolaevsky, *Power and the Soviet Elite,* pp. 74–5. The published proceedings of the plenum only hinted at the actual controversies that occurred. Compare, for example, the speeches of Stalin and Ordzhonikidze in *From the First to the Second Five-Year Plan.*

83. *Pravda,* August 4, 1933, pp. 2–3; and his "Gody pobed," *Plannovoe khoziaistvo,* No. 7–8, 1933, pp. 117–23. A major sign of his new status was his May Day article, "Znamia nauki v rukakh proletarskoi diktatury," *Izvestiia,* May 1, 1933, p. 3.

84. For Kirov, see above, Chapter IX, note 247.

85. Nor, however, did they go unnoticed. At the Seventeenth Party Congress, Stalin observed that the views of "a section of party members," who were urging a general relaxation, "are exactly like the well-known views of the right deviators," *Works,* XIII, pp. 357–8.

86. *Pravda,* October 11, 1932, p. 5; A. Mil'chakov, *Pervoe desiatiletie: zapiski veterana Komsomola* (2nd ed.; Moscow, 1965), p. 227; F. Bega and V. Aleksandrov, *Petrovskii* (Moscow, 1963), p. 303.

87. See above, note 36.

88. *Letter of an Old Bolshevik,* p. 37. His appointment, dated February 21, was announced in *Izvestiia,* February 22, 1934, p. 2.

89. *Mikhail Kol'tsov, kakim on byl* (Moscow, 1965), p. 97.

90. The best-documented instance of his helping mistreated writers involves the ill-fated poet Osip Mandelstam. See Mandelstam, *Hope Against Hope*, pp. 22–3, 112–18, 136, 145. He also helped the writers Ehrenburg and Panteleimon Romanov. Ehrenburg, *Memoirs*, p. 235; Vyacheslav Zavalishin, *Early Soviet Writers* (New York, 1958), p. 281.

91. *Pervyi vsesoiuznyi s"ezd sovetskikh pisatelei: stenograficheskii otchet* (Moscow, 1934), pp. 479–503, 573–7, 671.

92. Gleb Glinka, "Na putiakh v nebytie," *Novyi zhurnal*, XXXV (1953), p. 136; Gustav Regler, *The Owl of Minerva* (New York, 1960), p. 208; Berger, *Nothing But the Truth*, pp. 106–7. Bukharin answered "fierce attacks" on his speech in his concluding remarks and again in a separate statement issued later in the congress. *Pervyi vsesoiuznyi s"ezd sovetskikh pisatelei*, pp. 573–7, 671. For the congress and his role, also see Mikhail Koriakov, "Pervyi s"ezd," *Novoe russkoe slovo*, June 10, 13, and 17, 1971.

93. *Pravda*, May 17, 1937, p. 4. Even at the time, the Stalinist attitude toward the congress was notably unlike Bukharin's. See the editorial in *Pravda*, August 1, 1934, p. 1.

94. *Izvestiia*, February 8, 1935, p. 1; Nicolaevsky, *Power and the Soviet Elite*, p. 22.

95. Nicolaevsky, *Power and the Soviet Elite*, p. 22; G. A. Tokaev, *Betrayal of an Ideal* (London, 1954), p. 3. Bukharin himself emphasized the importance of these provisions. See his "Konstitutsiia sotsialisticheskogo gosudarstva," *Izvestiia*, June 14, 1936, p. 2, and June 15, 1936, pp. 2–3. There is, in addition, fragmentary evidence that Bukharin was thinking of evolution toward some kind of two-party or at least two-slate elections. See Nicolaevsky, *Power and the Soviet Elite*, pp. 15–16; and Tokaev, *Comrade X*, p. 43.

96. *Letter of an Old Bolshevik*, pp. 9, 57–8; and Bukharin quoted in Nicolaevsky, *Power and the Soviet Elite*, p. 22.

97. For first-hand accounts of Bukharin's editorship, see the anonymous memoir published in the Soviet *samizdat* journal *Politicheskii dnevnik*, No. 55 (April 1969), p. 40a; and Crowther, *Fifty Years with Science*, p. 143. For the paper's reputation, see Berger, *Nothing But the Truth*, p. 105; and *The Times* (London), March 16, 1938, p. 16.

98. *Vsesoiuznoe soveshchanie*, 270.

99. See the discussion of this problem in *Letter of an Old Bolshevik*, pp. 48–50, of which Bukharin was either the author or main source.

100. *Ibid.*, p. 55. At the Seventeenth Party Congress, he called Stalin "the glorious fieldmarshal of the proletarian forces," an odd appellation in the Bolshevik context, as Bukharin himself implied when, two months later, he praised Soviet President Kalinin as "no fieldmarshal Hindenburg." *XVII s"ezd*, p. 129; " 'Kalinych,' " *Izvestiia*, March 30, 1934, p. 2. On some important occasions, he did not mention Stalin at all, an unusual omission. See, for example, his May Day article, "Pochemu my pobedim?", *Izvestiia*, May 1, 1934, p. 3. Elsewhere he pointedly described Lenin in terms now reserved for Stalin. See his "Our Leader, Our Teacher, Our Father," *Izvestiia*, January 21, 1936, p. 2. His least restrained contribution of the Stalin cult came late, when the danger to him was very great. See his "Piramida velikikh del," *Izvestiia*, May 15, 1936, p. 3.

101. *Vtoroi vsesoiuznyi s"ezd kolkhoznikov-udarnikov 11–17 fevralia 1935 goda: stenograficheskii otchet* (Moscow, 1935), pp. 145–53; Bukharin, "Nuzhna li nam marksistskaia istoricheskaia nauka?", *Izvestiia*, January 27, 1936, pp. 3–4.

102. This despite his presence on official commissions appointed in early 1936 to oversee the rewriting of textbooks on Russian and Soviet history. *Na fronte istoricheskoi nauki* (Moscow, 1936), pp. 5, 11; *Pravda*, March 4, 1936, p. 1. Indeed, in January of that year, he restated the traditional, negative Bolshevik view of czarist Russia as "a nation of Oblomovs." The remark was sharply attacked by *Pravda*, and Bukharin compelled to retract it. See *Izvestiia*, January 21, 1936, p. 2; and his "Otvet na vopros," *Izvestiia*, February 14, 1936, p. 1. Equally faithful to the old Bolshevik outlook was his unsigned editorial eulogizing not the czarist but the "revolutionary traditions" of nineteenth-century Russia. "Velikie traditsii," *Izvestiia*, February 5, 1936, p. 1, whose authorship Bukharin claimed in *Izvestiia*, February 14, 1936, p. 1.

103. Conquest, *Great Terror*, p. 111.

104. During his talks with Nicolaevsky in Paris in 1936, Bukharin explained that, in addition to his articles, he had composed a series of unsigned *Izvestiia* editorials, set in an identifiable type, on the current struggle over policy. Tucker and Cohen, eds., *Great Purge Trial*, p. xxxvii. My treatment of his thinking in 1934–6 does not make reference to these editorials because, first, their identification is problematic; and, second, his ideas are sufficiently clear from his many signed articles.

105. For another example, see Chimen Abransky, "Kamenev's Last Essay," *New Left Review*, No. 15 (1962), pp. 32–8.

106. Leo Strauss, *Persecution and the Art of Writing* (Glencoe, Ill., 1952), Chapter 11; and S. G. F. Brandon, *Jesus and the Zealots* (New York, 1967).

107. *Soch.*, IV, p. 373. For a discussion of Aesopian language in Russia, see Sidney I. Ploss, ed., *The Soviet Political Process* (Waltham, Mass., 1971), pp. 73–7.

108. In addition to above, note 83, and *Pravda*, January 14, 1933, p. 3, see his "Mir, kak on budet," *Izvestiia*, November 7, 1934, pp. 4–5. Also *XVII s"ezd*, pp. 124–9; "Ekonomika sovetskoi strany," *Izvestiia*, May 12, 1934, p. 3; "Surovye slova," *Izvestiia*, December 22, 1934, p. 2; and "Novyi etap v razvitii sovetskoi ekonomiki," *Izvestiia*, October 12, 1935, p. 3.

109. Ernst Genri, "Otkrytoe pis'mo pisateliu I. Erenburgu," *Grani*, No. 63 (1967), p. 198; Heinz Brandt, *The Search for a Third Way* (Garden City, N.Y., 1970), pp. 70–1, 80. For examples of Communist pressure for a new policy, see *Iz istorii Kominterna* (Moscow, 1970), pp. 104–36.

110. See Robert M. Slusser, "The Role of the Foreign Ministry," *Russian Foreign Policy*, edited by I. J. Lederer (New Haven, Conn., 1962), pp. 217–30; Nicolaevsky, *Power and the Soviet Elite*, pp. 79–90; and George F. Kennan, *Russia and the West Under Lenin and Stalin* (Boston, 1960), Chapters xix–xxi.

111. Reprinted in *Soviet Documents on Foreign Policy*, edited by Jane Degras, Vol. III (London, 1953), p. 184. This speech, which confirms the high-level controversy over Nazi Germany, was brought to my attention by Robert M. Slusser.

112. *XVII s"ezd*, p. 13.

113. See above, note 110; Tucker's introduction to Tucker and Cohen, eds., *Great Purge Trial*, pp. xxxiii–xl; and Louis Fischer, *Russia's Road From Peace to War* (New York, 1969), Chapter xxii.

114. "Uchenie Marksa i ego istoricheskoe znachenie," p. 99; also see *Izvestiia*, May 1, 1933, p. 3.

115. *XVII s"ezd*, pp. 127–9.

116. See *Culture in Two Worlds* (New York, 1934); "Vystrel printsipa," *Izvestiia*, June 28, 1934, p. 1; *Izvestiia*, November 7, 1934, pp. 4–5; *Vtoroi vsesoiuznyi s"ezd kolkhoznikov-udarnikov*, pp. 151–2; "Mysli v godovshchinu fevral'skoi

revoliutsii," *Izvestiia*, March 12, 1935, p. 2; "Problema mira," *Izvestiia*, March 30, 1935, p. 2; "Vtoroe rozhdenie chelovechestva," *Izvestiia*, May 1, 1935, p. 3; "Fashizm i voina,'" *Izvestiia*, August 1, 1935, pp. 3–4; "Filosofiia kul'turnogo filistera," *Izvestiia*, December 8, 1935, p. 2, and December 10, 1935, p. 3; "O geopoliticheskom voiazhe," *Izvestiia*, February 15, 1936, p. 6; *Les Problèmes fondamentaux de la Culture contemporaine* (Paris, 1936); "Rasshirenie sovetskoi demokratii," *Izvestiia*, May 1, 1936, p. 4 (for his contrasting of "bourgeois democracy" with fascism); and "Marshruty istorii: mysli vslukh," *Izvestiia*, July 6, 1936, pp. 3–4. Also see the garbled account of his private remarks in *Case of the Anti-Soviet Bloc*, pp. 230, 361, 422–3.

117. *Izvestiia*, March 30, 1935, p. 2. Also see *Izvestiia*, June 28, 1934, p. 1; *Izvestiia*, February 15, 1936, p. 6; and his "Imperialism and Communism," *Foreign Affairs* (July 1936), reprinted in *The Soviet Union, 1922–1962: A Foreign Affairs Reader*, edited by Philip E. Mosley (New York, 1963), pp. 138–52.

118. *Case of the Anti-Soviet Bloc*, pp. 230–1.

119. *XVII s"ezd*, p. 127; "Vsia strana," *Izvestiia*, June 20, 1934, p. 2; *Izvestiia*, December 22, 1934, p. 2 (where he speaks explicitly of "reforms"); *Vtoroi vsesoiuznyi s"ezd kolkhoznikov-udarnikov*, pp. 145–53; "Nekotorye itogi revoliutsionnogo goda i nashi vragi," *Izvestiia*, November 7, 1935, p. 5; "Oprokinutye normy (vnutrennee obozrenie)," *Izvestiia*, January 1, 1936, p. 3; *Izvestiia*, May 1, 1936, p. 4; and *Izvestiia*, July 6, 1936, pp. 3–4. In this connection, he told Nicolaevsky that Communist alliances with socialists abroad had "enormous positive significance . . . for relations inside the USSR." B. Nikolaevskii, "Chetvert' veka nazad," *Novoe russkoe slovo*, December 6, 1959, p. 2.

120. *Culture in Two Worlds*, p. 4; *Les Problèmes fondamentaux*, p. 8; *Izvestiia*, June 14, 1936, p. 2; and Bukharin quoted in Nicolaevsky, *Power and the Soviet Elite*, p. 19.

121. *Izvestiia*, December 8, 1935, p. 2, and December 10, 1935, p. 3; *Les Problèmes fondamentaux*, p. 23. The importance of his article on Berdiaev's *The Fate of Man in the Modern World* (New York, 1935) has been noted by Mikhail Koriakov in *Novoe russkoe slovo*, July 29, 1971, p. 3.

122. Bukharin quoted in Nicolaevsky, *Power and the Soviet Elite*, pp. 16–17; and his articles in *Izvestiia*, May 1, 1936, p. 4; and *Izvestiia*, July 6, 1936, pp. 3–4. Similarly, in addition to the items cited above, notes 120 and 121, see *Izvestiia*, November 7, 1934, pp. 4–5; *Izvestiia*, May 1, 1935, p. 3; and *Izvestiia*, January 1, 1936, p. 3.

123. *Les Problèmes fondamentaux*, p. 22. On leadership cults, see also his subtle juxtaposition in "Proizvodstvennyi konvent velikoi proletarskoi revoliutsii," *Izvestiia*, November 15, 1935, p. 4.

124. Quoted in Edward J. Brown, *Russian Literature Since the Revolution* (New York, 1969), p. 208. Also see *Protiv burzhuaznogo liberalizma v khudozhestvennoi literature* (Moscow, 1931), especially pp. 25–7, 102–3.

125. The idea apparently began to form in his mind as early as 1929. See his discussion of the alienation theme in Marx's early manuscripts, *Pravda*, December 15, 1929, p. 3; his Aesopian attack on collectivization in *Etiudy*, pp. 335–53; and his allusion to Gorky's "humanism" in "Novoe chelovechestvo," *Pravda*, October 17, 1932, p. 3.

126. *Izvestiia*, December 10, 1935, p. 3; *Izvestiia*, January 1, 1936, p. 3. Also see *Culture in Two Worlds*, pp. 25–8; *Izvestiia*, May 12, 1934, p. 3; *Pervyi vsesoiuznyi s"ezd sovetskikh pisatelei*, pp. 499–501; *Izvestiia*, November 7, 1935, p. 5; *Izvestiia*, December 8, 1935, p. 2; and *Les Problèmes fondamentaux*, pp. 12–25.

127. *Izvestiia*, November 7, 1935, p. 5; and Bukharin quoted in Nicolaevsky, *Power and the Soviet Elite*, pp. 16–17. For his contrasting of socialism and fascism, also see *Culture in Two Worlds; Izvestiia*, May 1, 1935, p. 3; *Izvestiia*, December 8, 1935, p. 2, and December 10, 1935, p. 3; and *Les Problèmes fondamentaux*.

128. See, for example, *Culture in Two Worlds; Les Problèmes fondamentaux;* and *Izvestiia*, December 10, 1935, p. 3.

129. *XVII s"ezd*, p. 129; *Culture in Two Worlds*, p. 10.

130. *Izvestiia*, December 8, 1935, p. 2.

131. Quoted in Nicolaevsky, *Power and the Soviet Elite*, pp. 15, 18–19.

132. *Izvestiia*, January 1, 1936, p. 3. Similarly, see *Izvestiia*, May 12, 1934, p. 3; *Izvestiia*, October 12, 1935, p. 3; *Izvestiia*, November 7, 1935, p. 5; and *Izvestiia*, November 15, 1935, p. 4.

133. Ehrenburg, *Memoirs*, p. 289. Bukharin published three articles on Kirov's assassination in *Izvestiia*, December 2, 6, and 22, 1934. The last was especially interesting. Though obliged to suggest a connection between party oppositionists and the crime, he concluded in a strikingly different vein. The purpose of the murder, he wrote, was to disrupt the "reforms," to *"wreck the internal course."* The question, he pointed out, was "whose interests" had it served? It is possible that Bukharin learned the true story from the police chief Iagoda, one of the few people who knew the facts and with whom he was apparently still friendly. See Mandelstam, *Hope Against Hope*, pp. 22–3, 82.

134. Conquest, *Great Terror*, pp. 57–8, 85–9.

135. Nicolaevsky, *Power and the Soviet Elite*, p. 14.

136. Alliluyeva, *Twenty Letters*, pp. 115, 140; and her *Only One Year* (New York, 1969), pp. 147, 166.

137. L. Dan, "Bukharin o Staline," *Novyi zhurnal*, 75 (1964), p. 181. He reportedly said, for example, that the great ovation he received at the writers' congress in 1934 "signed my death warrant." Berger, *Nothing But the Truth*, p. 107.

138. Quoted in Medvedev, *Let History Judge*, p. 333.

139. Jules Humbert-Droz, "Mes relations avec le groupe des droitiers et des 'Versöhnler'" (unpublished document from 1935 in the possession of A. G. Löwy); and *Pravda*, February 10, 1936, p. 3.

140. Dan, "Bukharin o Staline," *Novyi zhurnal*, 75 (1964), p. 182.

141. Nicolaevsky, *Power and the Soviet Elite*, p. 9.

142. Dan, "Bukharin o Staline," *Novyi zhurnal*, 75 (1964), p. 182; André Malraux, *Fallen Oaks: Conversations with De Gaulle* (London, 1972), p. 103. Also see Reswick, *I Dreamt Revolution*, p. 325.

143. Although its reliability has been confirmed, the *Letter's* exact authorship remains unclear. It appeared originally in the émigré Menshevik journal *Sotsialisticheskii vestnik* (December 22, 1936, pp. 20–33 and January 17, 1937, pp. 17–24) over the initials "Y.Z." In 1959, Nicolaevsky confirmed rumors that he had written the *Letter* on the basis of his talks with Bukharin in March–April 1936 and supplementary information from other informants. He drafted it initially, he explained, as a dialogue, but on his editor's urging reworked it into a narrative account. See *Novoe russkoe slovo*, December 6, 1959, p. 2; and *Sotsialisticheskii vestnik* (December 1959), p. 246. Nicolaevsky later elaborated on this explanation in his *Power and the Soviet Elite*, pp. 3–25. As Robert M. Slusser has pointed out, however, this explanation is difficult to reconcile with either the editorial note that accompanied the *Letter's* original publication or internal evidence in the *Letter* itself, which deals with secret events in the Soviet leadership as late as September 1936. See Slusser's discussion in *Russian Foreign Policy*, edited by I. J.

Lederer (New Haven, Conn., 1962), pp. 221–2; and *Slavic Review* (September 1966), pp. 530–1. Only Bukharin or Rykov presumably knew, for example, that the investigation against them was dropped in September 1936 "without an examination of the accused." *Letter*, p. 60. Various hypotheses could reconcile these discrepancies, one (suggested by Slusser) being that Bukharin (or, it might be added, Rykov) smuggled the actual text of the *Letter* or supplementary material to Nicolaevsky in late 1936. This gains some credence from the striking reference—perhaps Bukharin's internal signature—to the street urchins of the author's childhood, which appears both in the *Letter*, p. 40, and in Bukharin's autobiography, "Avtobiografiia," p. 53. Whatever the case, there is no doubt that, in one form or another, Bukharin was the source of the *Letter*.

144. Dan, "Bukharin o Staline," *Novyi zhurnal*, 75 (1964), p. 182; Nicolaevsky, *Power and the Soviet Elite*, p. 6. There was another consideration. Though his wife was with him, Bukharin had left behind, in effect as hostages, his elderly father, his first wife, and his former companion Esfir Gurvich and their young daughter.

145. *Izvestiia*, May 1, 1936, p. 4.

146. "Pevets razuma," *Izvestiia*, June 20, 1936, p. 2; "Gor'kii: poslednee 'prosti,'" *Izvestiia*, June 23, 1936, p. 2.

147. *Izvestiia*, July 6, 1936, pp. 3–4. Its importance has been noted by other writers. See, for example, Tucker's introduction to Tucker and Cohen, eds., *Great Purge Trial*, pp. xxxvi–viii; and Katkov, *Trial of Bukharin*, pp. 94–6.

148. *Case of the Anti-Soviet Bloc*, pp. 360–1, 422–3.

149. *Izvestiia*, July 6, 1936, pp. 3–4; Nicolaevsky, *Power and the Soviet Elite*, p. 25.

150. *The Case of the Trotskyite-Zinovievite Terrorist Centre: Report of Court Proceedings* (Moscow, 1936), pp. 55–6, 68, 73, 115–16; and *Pravda*, August 22, 1936, p. 4.

151. *Pravda*, August 23, 1936, p. 2; Victor Serge, *Twenty Years After* (New York, 1937), p. 226.

152. See *Pravda* for August 22, 23, and 26, 1936.

153. Conquest, *Great Terror*, pp. 151–3.

154. Scholars differ as to whether there was a full Central Committee plenum in September, a series of Politburo meetings, or some variation. See the discussion in *ibid.*, p. 153; and *Slavic Review* (December 1967), pp. 665–77. For the decision on Spain, see Slusser cited above, note 110.

155. Introduction to Andrei Platonov, *The Fierce and Beautiful World* (New York, 1970), p. 8. Also, *Letter of an Old Bolshevik*, pp. 60–2. Bukharin traveled to Tashkent in August. *Case of the Anti-Soviet Bloc*, p. 228.

156. His last signed article appeared on July 6. The paper's editorial tone changed markedly with the Zinoviev trial in mid-August, though as Slusser points out (see above, note 110), Bukharin or his associates may have been able to compose a discreet editorial or two opposing Stalin's foreign policy until late September. Nominally at least, Bukharin still had *Izvestiia* press credentials as late as November 7. Medvedev, *Let History Judge*, p. 171.

157. For these events, see Conquest, *Great Terror*, pp. 154–6.

158. Orlov, *Stalin's Crimes*, p. 280.

159. Quoted in Medvedev, *Let History Judge*, p. 171.

160. *Pravda*, December 2, 1936, p. 2; *Pravda*, December 12 and 15, 1936.

161. *The Case of the Anti-Soviet Trotskyite Centre: Report of Court Proceedings* (Moscow, 1937); also see Conquest, *Great Terror*, pp. 164–85.

162. Medvedev, *Let History Judge*, p. 174. For an apparent reference to Bukharin's virtual house arrest, see Mandelstam, *Hope Against Hope*, p. 276. The term "last stand" is Conquest's. *Great Terror*, Chapter vi.

163. Conquest, *Great Terror*, pp. 185–92.

164. Medvedev, *Let History Judge*, p. 174; *O perestroike partiino-politicheskoi raboty: k itogam plenuma TSK VKP(b) 1937 g.* (Moscow, 1937), p. 55; and Stalin, *Sochineniia*, edited by Robert H. McNeal, Vol. I (Stanford, Calif., 1967), p. 194.

165. Reprinted in Medvedev, *Let History Judge*, pp. 182–4. The circumstances of its composition are related in a letter by Bukharin's wife, Larina, written in 1961 or 1962. Dr. Peter Reddaway provided me with a copy of her letter from the collection of the Alexander Herzen Foundation.

166. Alexander Uralov (Abdurakhman Avtorkhanov), *The Reign of Stalin* (London, 1953), pp. 45–6. Uralov's account has been questioned because he apparently misdates the plenum, placing it in the fall of 1936. (See above, note 154.) His version of Bukharin's statement, however, is substantiated in important respects by other sources. See Medvedev, *Let History Judge*, p. 174; *Writings of Leon Trotsky (1937–38)* (New York, 1970), pp. 128–9; and Conquest, *Great Terror*, p. 195. It is also very similar in spirit and tone to Bukharin's last letter quoted above. Finally, Bukharin's defiance at the plenum was officially reported at the time. See Khrushchev's report in *Pravda*, March 17, 1937, p. 2.

167. Quoted in Medvedev, *Let History Judge*, p. 174.

168. Conquest, *Great Terror*, pp. 193–5; and *ibid*.

169. Medvedev, *Let History Judge*, p. 174. For the date of their arrest, see Larina's letter, above, note 165; and *Case of the Anti-Soviet Bloc*, p. 185.

170. It was the inspiration, in 1947, for Maurice Merleau-Ponty's celebrated philosophical treatise *Humanisme et Terreur*, and reappeared as late as 1967 in Jean Luc Godard's film *La Chinoise*. Koestler has said that Rubashov was an amalgam, "his manner of thinking modeled on Nikolai Bukharin's, his personality and physical appearance a synthesis of Leon Trotsky and Karl Radek"—*The Invisible Writing* (Boston, 1955), p. 394. In fact, Rubashov's "manner of thinking" and "personality" are inseparable.

171. Some Western and Soviet scholars have since argued that he did not confess. See, for example, Avtorkhanov, *Stalin*, Chapter xxviii; Tucker's introduction to Tucker and Cohen, eds., *Great Purge Trial*, pp. xl–xlviii; Katkov, *Trial of Bukharin*, Part II; and Medvedev, *Let History Judge*, pp. 176–8. Among those who understood at the time were the British eyewitness Fitzroy MacLean, *Escape to Adventure* (Boston, 1950), pp. 67–75; and, from afar, Manès Sperber. See *Survey* (Summer 1969), p. 101.

172. *Case of the Anti-Soviet Bloc*. For eyewitness accounts, see MacLean, *Escape to Adventure*, pp. 61–83; and Walter Duranty, *The Kremlin and the People* (New York, 1941), pp. 76–81.

173. MacLean, *Escape to Adventure*, p. 82; Duranty, *Kremlin*, p. 78.

174. See, for example, *Case of the Anti-Soviet Bloc*, pp. 675–6. For the problem of reading the trial transcript on various levels, see Nathan Leites and Elsa Bernaut, *Ritual of Liquidation* (Glencoe, Ill., 1954).

175. *Case of the Anti-Soviet Bloc*, pp. 626–31.

176. Orlov, *Stalin's Crimes*, p. 277.

177. MacLean, *Escape to Adventure*, p. 68; *Case of the Anti-Soviet Bloc*, pp. 656–7.

178. Medvedev, *Let History Judge*, Chapter viii. Similarly, Conquest, *Great Terror*, Chapters v and ix.

179. Aleksander Wat, "The Death of an Old Bolshevik," in *Kultura Essays*, edited by Leopold Tyrmand (New York, 1970), p. 72.

180. Medvedev, *Let History Judge*, p. 187; Orlov, *Stalin's Crimes*, pp. 280–2; *Case of the Anti-Soviet Bloc*, pp. 648, 777. Mikoyan later told an American journalist that Bukharin was not tortured. Conquest, *Great Terror*, p. 391.

181. Conquest, *Great Terror*, pp. 142, 330–2; "Memuary P. Iakira," *Russkaia mysl'*, October 28, 1971. Unlike prisoners with wives who had shared their revolutionary past and would expect to share their political fate, those with younger wives were at a special disadvantage. And they, of course, would have had younger children as well.

182. As Bukharin's last letter and trial testimony made clear. *Case of the Anti-Soviet Bloc*, pp. 474, 768, 777.

183. *Ibid.*, p. 777.

184. *Ibid.*, pp. 372, 768.

185. Tucker's introduction to Tucker and Cohen, eds., *Great Purge Trial*, pp. xliv–viii.

186. *Case of the Anti-Soviet Bloc*, p. 778.

187. Tucker's introduction to Tucker and Cohen, eds., *Great Purge Trial*, p. xlv.

188. Orlov, *Stalin's Crimes*, p. 282; *Case of the Anti-Soviet Bloc*, pp. 129, 767, 778; Katkov, *Trial of Bukharin*, pp. 125–6. A Soviet edition of Feuchtwanger's apologia for the trial, *Moscow 1937*, appeared in November 1937. During the trial, Vyshinsky tried to intimidate Bukharin by implying that his wife had been present at a conspiratorial meeting. Bukharin firmly denied it. *Case of the Anti-Soviet Bloc*, pp. 350–2.

189. *Case of the Anti-Soviet Bloc*, p. 777. According to one account, while in prison Bukharin was writing a book on "the nature of man." Berger, *Nothing but the Truth*, p. 110. It is not known whether the manuscript survived.

190. MacLean, *Escape to Adventure*, p. 68.

191. *Case of the Anti-Soviet Bloc*, pp. 370, 778.

192. *Ibid.*, pp. 348–9, 378, 396, 413, 424, 504, 771. Other examples could be given.

193. *Ibid.*, pp. 125–7, 383, 496–7, 769, 771. For Karelin and other witnesses, see MacLean, *Escape to Adventure*, p. 66.

194. *Case of the Anti-Soviet Bloc*, pp. 767, 776–9. Many anti-Stalinists and anti-Communists abroad, it should be remembered, agreed.

195. See, for example, *ibid.*, pp. 128–36, 184, 380. Also Tucker's introduction to Tucker and Cohen, eds., *Great Purge Trial*, p. xxxi; and Katkov, *Trial of Bukharin*, pp. 128–30.

196. *Case of the Anti-Soviet Bloc*, p. 778.

197. *Ibid.*, pp. 168, 369–70, 381.

198. *Ibid.*, pp. 379, 381–2.

199. *Ibid.*, pp. 423, 667; also pp. 397, 400, 435, 650. And *Izvestiia*, March 9, 1938, quoted in Medvedev, *Let History Judge*, p. 178.

200. *Case of the Anti-Soviet Bloc*, pp. 423, 667.

201. *New York Times*, March 8, 1938, pp. 1, 8; MacLean, *Escape to Adventure*, pp. 62–3. There was one notable exception, the American ambassador Joseph Davies. After "sifting the wheat from the chaff—the truth from the false," he reported that the charges and confessions were true "beyond a reasonable doubt."

When the war began, Ambassador Davies liked to say that the trials "destroyed Hitler's Fifth Column in Russia." Joseph E. Davies, *Mission to Moscow* (New York, 1941), pp. 269, 272.

202. *New York Times*, March 8, 1938, p. 8, and March 13, 1938, p. 30; *Case of the Anti-Soviet Bloc*, p. 685; MacLean, *Escape to Adventure*, p. 74.

203. *New York Times*, March 13, 1938, p. 30. It should be noted, though it cannot be explained, that this same correspondent, Harold Denny, then wrote of the trials: "in the broad sense they are not fakes." *New York Times*, March 14, 1938, p. 4.

204. Anonymous reviewer of Katkov's *The Trial of Bukharin*, in *The Times Literary Supplement*, January 29, 1970.

205. *Case of the Anti-Soviet Bloc*, p. 696; *Pravda*, March 10, 1938, p. 1.

206. *Case of the Anti-Soviet Bloc*, pp. 791, 799; *New York Times*, March 16, 1938, p. 4. Trotsky saw a "tragic symbolism" in the coincidence of the trial and Hitler's *Anschluss—Writings of Leon Trotsky (1937-38)* (New York, 1970), p. 146. Also see Katkov, *Trial of Bukharin*, p. 183.

207. Victor Kravchenko, *I Chose Freedom* (New York, 1946), p. 283; Margaret McCarthy, *Generation in Protest* (London, 1953), p. 112.

EPILOGUE

1. *History of the Communist Party of the Soviet Union (Bolsheviks): Short Course* (New York, 1939), p. 346.

2. When the German invasion began, the NKVD summarily executed thousands of camp inmates sentenced as Bukharinists and Trotskyists in the thirties. Joseph Scholmar, *Vorkuta* (London, 1954), p. 169. Bukharin's protégé of the twenties, Valentin Astrov, spent most of the Stalin years in camps. See W. Cladius, "In a Soviet Isolator," *St. Antony's Papers: Soviet Affairs*. No. 1 (London, 1956), pp. 143-5. Astrov returned to Moscow in the fifties and published two historical novels, *Ogni vperedi* (Moscow, 1958) and *Krucha* (Moscow, 1966). The latter, a fictionalized account of party political life in the twenties, has been criticized by contemporary Soviet dissidents because of Astrov's "slandering of his former comrades," the Bukharinists. See *Novoe russkoe slovo*, February 2, 1971, p. 3.

3. It should be recorded that two Soviet poets, Boris Pasternak and Pavel Vasiliev, courageously refused to sign demands for Bukharin's execution in 1937. Vasiliev was arrested and shot soon after. See Vasily Grossman, *Forever Flowing* (New York, 1972), p. 33; and Wolin and Slusser, *Soviet Secret Police*, p. 186, where Vasiliev's act of defiance is misdated.

4. *History of the Communist Party of the Soviet Union*, p. 346.

5. Khrushchev, *Crimes of the Stalin Era*.

6. Quoted in Medvedev, *Let History Judge*, pp. 184-5.

7. B. Nikolaevskii, "Problema destalinizatsii i delo Bukharina," *Sotsialisticheskii vestnik*, Collection No. 4 (December 1965), pp. 22-38; Michael Tatu, *Power in the Kremlin from Khrushchev to Kosygin* (New York, 1969), p. 245. Reports of his impending legal rehabilitation circulated widely in October 1962. See *Politika* (Belgrade), October 16, 1962, p. 4; and *New York Times*, October 19, 1962.

8. *Vsesoiuznoe soveshchanie*, p. 298. The speaker was Petr Pospelov, who as

a rising young Stalinist in 1937 had eagerly assailed Bukharin, Rykov, and their "spying, wrecking, and terrorist organization." *Pravda*, November 6, 1937, p. 3.

9. See, for example, *Voprosy istorii KPSS*, No. 8, 1967, p. 63, and No. 10, 1970, p. 105; and *Novyi mir*, No. 2, 1969, p. 192.

10. Vaganov's *Pravyi uklon* (1970) reflects the prevailing official attitude toward Bukharin and Bukharinism. See the laudatory review in *Kommunist*, No. 18, 1970, pp. 115–19.

11. See, for example, Imre Nagy, *On Communism: In Defense of the New Course* (New York, 1957); Ota Sik, *Plan and Market Under Socialism* (White Plains, N.Y., 1967); and the essays by East European Marxists in Erich Fromm, ed., *Socialist Humanism* (Garden City, N.Y., 1966).

12. See the comparison of the Polish and Soviet treatment in Warren Lerner, "The Unperson in Communist Historiography," *The South Atlantic Quarterly* (Autumn 1966), pp. 444–6; and the treatment of Bukharin in Predrag Vranicki, *Istorija Marksizma* (Zagreb, 1961).

13. An interesting example is Nagy's *On Communism*, where NEP is cited in defense of his own "new course."

14. *Materialy k lektsiiam po kursu istorii KPSS: temy 11-13* (Moscow, 1964), p. 44; and Daniel Tarschys. *Beyond the State: The Future Polity in Classical and Soviet Marxism* (Stockholm, 1971), pp. 161, 191.

15. See Moshe Lewin's forthcoming study, *Political Ideas in Soviet Economic Debates: From Bukharin to Modern Reformers* (Princeton University Press).

16. See, for example, A. Rumiantsev, "Partiia i intelligentsiia," *Pravda*, February 21, 1965, pp. 2–3.

17. For the range of post-Stalin writing on collectivization, see M. A. Bogdenko and I. E. Zelinin, "Istoriia kollektivizatsii sel'skogo khoziaistva v sovremennoi sovetskoi istoriko-ekonomicheskoi literature," *Istoriia SSSR*, No. 4, 1962, pp. 133–51; *Istoriia sovetskogo krest'ianstva i kolkhoznogo stroitel'stva SSSR* (Moscow, 1963); and *Ocherki po istoriografii sovetskogo obshchestva* (Moscow, 1965), Chapter viii. Lewin (above, note 15) discusses the critique of Stalin's industrial policies. Criticism of Stalin's Comintern line is only beginning to take shape. See, for example, V. M. Leibzon and K. K. Shirinia, *Povorot v politike Kominterna* (Moscow, 1965), pp. 125, 177; and *Ocherki istorii istoricheskoi nauki v SSSR*, Vol. IV (Moscow, 1966), pp. 692, 712–15.

18. Or as Bertram D. Wolfe wrote very early, throughout the process of destalinization Bukharin has been "the ghost at the banquet," a specter who "does not keep to his grave though the stake is driven into his corpse again and again." *Khrushchev and Stalin's Ghost* (New York, 1957), pp. 135, 139.

19. A significant part of recent Western scholarship on collectivization and related issues, though by no means all of it, now tends to support, with some qualifications, the merits of Bukharin's economic arguments and policies. For the range of this scholarly opinion, see the continuous discussion of collectivization that appeared in *Soviet Studies* in 1965–71; Herbert J. Ellison, "The Decision to Collectivize Agriculture," *American Slavic and East European Review* (April 1966), pp. 189–202; Alec Nove, "Was Stalin Really Necessary?," *Encounter* (April 1962), pp. 86–92; E. H. Carr, *The October Revolution* (New York, 1969), Chapters vi and vii; Erlich, *Soviet Industrialization*, Part II; Lewin, *Russian Peasants;* and Isaac Deutscher, *The Unfinished Revolution* (New York, 1967). Like opinion on the French revolution, Soviet historical opinion will probably divide eventually into rival schools of interpretation associated with major revolutionary figures and programs—Bukharinist, Trotskyist, neo-Stalinist, and so forth. Such a division is already adumbrated in Soviet writings and in heated discussions among Soviet

historians published unofficially. See, for example, "Obsuzhdenie maneta 3-go toma *Istorii KPSS*," *Grani*, No. 65 (1967), pp. 129–56.

20. Prominent among them is the young historian Leonid Petrovskii, the son of the purged Bukharinist Petr Petrovskii. See below, note 22. In 1967, children of old Bolsheviks sent a letter to the Central Committee protesting Stalin's official rehabilitation. Among the signers were Bukharin's son and the sons of three executed Bukharinists—Petrovskii, Aikhenvald, and Shmidt. *Posev* (June 1969), p. 59. Historical information about Bukharin, including his last letter, has circulated in *samizdat*. An interesting indication of his status in the dissident imagination comes from Solzhenitsyn: "Stalin was wary of people committed to staying poor, like Bukharin. He did not understand their motives." Aleksandr I. Solzhenitsyn, *The First Circle* (New York, 1969), p. 121.

21. Medvedev, *Let History Judge*, p. 65. While reporting this as the opinion of "some historians," Medvedev adds that he personally "would not like to take such a stand." His critique of Stalin's economic policies, however, is distinctly Bukharinist. See his Chapter iii.

22. From Leonid Petrovskii's open letter to the Central Committee, translated in the Washington *Post*, April 27, 1969, pp. c1, c5.

SELECTED BIBLIOGRAPHY

This is a selected bibliography in that it does not include all the materials used in preparing this book, nor even all the items cited in the notes. To keep it manageable, I have listed only those which have been most helpful or cited most frequently. In particular, not all of Bukharin's separate periodical publications (notably those appearing in *Pravda* and *Izvestiia*), which number several hundreds, have been listed. The reader wishing a comprehensive and annotated bibliography of Bukharin's publications between 1912 and 1929 should consult Sidney Heitman's *Nikolai I. Bukharin: A Bibliography* (Stanford, Calif., 1969). Heitman's otherwise excellent work is less complete on Bukharin's writings and speeches of 1930–6, and for this period should be used in conjunction with my notes to Chapter X of the present work.

I. BUKHARIN'S WRITINGS AND SPEECHES

A. Books and Pamphlets:

The ABC of Communism. With co-author E. Preobrazhensky. London, 1924.

Ataka: sbornik teoreticheskikh statei. Moscow, 1924.

Azbuka kommunizma. With E. Preobrazhenskii. Kharkov, 1925.

Building Up Socialism. London, 1926.

The Communist Program: An Analysis of the Principles of the Russian Communist Party. New York, 1920.

Culture in Two Worlds. New York, 1934.

Doklad na XXIII chrezvychainoi leningradskoi gubernskoi konferentsii VKP(b). Moscow and Leningrad, 1926.

The Economic Theory of the Leisure Class. New York, 1927.

Ekonomika perekhodnogo perioda. Chast' I: obshchaia teoriia transformatsionnogo protsessa. Moscow, 1920.

Etiudy. Moscow and Leningrad, 1932.

Historical Materialism: A System of Sociology. New York, 1925.

Imperialism and World Economy. New York, 1929.

Imperializm i nakoplenie kapitala (teoreticheskii etiud). 4th ed. Moscow and Leningrad, 1929.

K itogam XIV s"ezda VKP(b). Moscow and Leningrad, 1926.

K voprosu o trotskizme. Moscow and Leningrad, 1925.

Krizis kapitalizma i kommunisticheskoe dvizhenie. Moscow, 1923.

Les Problèmes fondamentaux de la Culture contemporaine. Paris, 1936.

Na podstupakh k oktiabriu: stat'i i rechi mai–dekabr' 1917 g. Moscow and Leningrad, 1926.

Nekotorye voprosy ekonomicheskoi politiki: sbornik statei. Moscow, 1925.

The New Policies of Soviet Russia. With others. Chicago, 1921.

O mezhdunarodnom polozhenii. Leningrad, 1926.

O rabkore i sel'kore: stat'i i rechi. 2nd ed. Moscow, 1926.

Ob itogakh ob"edinennogo plenuma TSK i TSKK VKP(b). Moscow and Leningrad, 1927.

Ot krusheniia tsarizma do padeniia burzhuazii. Kharkov, 1923.

Partiia i oppozitsionnyi blok. With A. I. Rykov. 2nd ed. Moscow and Leningrad, 1926.

Politicheskoe zaveshchanie Lenina. 2nd ed. Moscow, 1929.

Problems of the Chinese Revolution. London, 1927.

Proizvodstvennaia propaganda. Moscow, 1920.

Proletarskaia revoliutsiia i kul'tura. Petrograd, 1923.

Put' k sotsializmu i raboche-krest'ianskii soiuz. Moscow and Leningrad, 1925.

Put' k sotsializmu v Rossii: izbrannye proizvedeniia. Edited by Sidney Heitman. New York, 1967.

Report on the Program Question. With A. Thalheimer. Moscow, 1924.

Tekushchii moment i osnovy nashei politiki. Moscow, 1925.

Teoriia istoricheskogo materializma: populiarnyi uchebnik marksistskoi sotsiologii. Moscow and Petrograd, 1923.

Tri rechi (k voprosu o nashikh raznoglasiiakh). Moscow and Leningrad, 1926.

Uroki khlebozagotovok, shakhtinskogo dela i zadachi partii. Leningrad, 1928.

V zashchitu proletarskoi diktatury: sbornik. Moscow and Leningrad, 1928.

B. Periodical Articles:

"An Abrupt Turn in the Chinese Revolution," *Inprecor*, Vol. VII (1927), pp. 897–9, 927–30.

"Aggressive Tactics," *The Communist Review* (October 1921), pp. 72–4.

"The Austrian Social-Democrats' New Programme," *The Communist International*, No. 1, 1926, pp. 2–6.

"Avtobiografiia," *Deiateli*, Vol. I (1925), pp. 52–6.

"Chem my pobezhdaem," *Dvadtsat' piat' let RKP (bol'shevikov): 1898–1923*. Moscow, 1923, pp. 130–7.

"Diktatura proletariata v Rossii i mirovaia revoliutsiia," *Kommunisticheskii internatsional*, No. 4, 1919, pp. 487–94.

"Doklad na IX chrezvychainoi partkonferentsii vyborskogo raiona," *Leningrad-skaia organizatsiia i chetyrnadtsatyi s"ezd: sbornik materialov i dokumentov.* Moscow and Leningrad, 1926, pp. 84–115.

"Gody pobed," *Plannovoe khoziaistvo,* No. 7–8, 1933, pp. 117–23.

"The Imperialist Pirate State," Olga Hess Gankin and H. H. Fisher. *The Bolsheviks and the World War: The Origin of the Third International.* Stanford, California, 1940, pp. 236–9.

"The International Bourgeoisie and Its Apostle, Karl Kautsky," *Inprecor,* Vol. V (1925), Nos. 62, 64–5, 67–9.

"The International Situation and the Internal Situation in the Soviet Union," *Inprecor,* Vol. VII (1927), pp. 189–200.

"Iz rechi t. Bukharina na vechere vospominanii v 1921 g.," *Proletarskaia revoliutsiia,* No. 10, 1922, pp. 216–23.

"K teorii imperialisticheskogo gosudarstva," *Revoliutsiia prava: sbornik pervyi.* Moscow, 1925, pp. 5–32.

"Kak ne nuzhno pisat' istoriiu oktiabria: po povodu knigi t. Trotskogo *1917,*" *Za leninizm: sbornik statei.* Moscow and Leningrad, pp. 9–25.

"Kakoi dolzhna byt' molodezh?," *Molodaia gvardiia,* No. 2, 1926, pp. 73–92.

(With Iurii Piatakov), "Kavaleriiskii reid i tiazhelaia artilleriia," *Krasnaia nov',* No. 1, 1921, pp. 256–74.

"Kul'turnye zadachi i bor'ba s biurokratizmom," *Revoliutsiia i kul'tura,* No. 2, 1927, pp. 5–12.

"Lozung sovetov v venskom vosstanii," *Kommunisticheskii internatsional,* No. 43, 1927, pp. 11–14.

"Nastoiashchaia potekha i nastoiashchee muchenie," *Krasnaia nov',* No. 2, 1921, pp. 313–20.

"Nekotorye problemy sovremennogo kapitalizma u teoretikov burzhuazii," *"Organizovannyi kapitalizm": diskussiia v Komakademii.* 2nd ed. Moscow, 1930, pp. 168–82.

"Novoe otkrovenie o sovetskoi ekonomike, ili kak mozhno pogubit' rabochekrest'ianskii blok (k voprosu ob ekonomicheskom obosnovanii trotskizma)," *Za leninizm: sbornik statei.* Moscow and Leningrad, 1925, pp. 285–317.

"O formal'nom metode v iskusstve," *Krasnaia nov',* No. 3, 1925, pp. 248–57.

"O likvidatorstve nashikh dnei," *Bol'shevik,* No. 2, 1924, pp. 3–9.

"O nekotorykh voprosakh iz pervoi chasti proekta programmy K.I.," *Kommunisticheskii internatsional,* No. 31–2, 1928, pp. 32–40.

"O nekotorykh zadachakh nashei raboty v derevne," *Bol'shevik,* No. 7–8, 1924, pp. 21–6.

"O novoi ekonomicheskoi politike i nashikh zadachakh," *Bol'shevik,* No. 8 and No. 9–10, 1925, pp. 3–14, pp. 3–15.

"O politike partii v khudozhestvennoi literature," *K voprosu o politike RKP(b) v khudozhestvennoi literature.* Moscow, 1924, pp. 35–9.

"O starinnykh traditsiiakh i sovremennom kul'turnom stroitel'stve (mysli vslukh)," *Revoliutsiia i kul'tura,* No. 1, 1927, pp. 17–22.

"O teorii permanentnoi revoliutsii," *Za leninizm: sbornik statei.* Moscow and Leningrad, 1925, pp. 332–73.

"The Opposition in the C.P.S.U. and in the Comintern," *Inprecor,* Vol. VIII (1928), pp. 213–28.

"Po skuchnoi doroge: otvet moim kritikam," *Krasnaia nov'*, No. 1, 1923, pp. 275-89.

"The Position of the Chinese Revolution," *Inprecor*, Vol. VII (1927), pp. 874-6.

"Program of the Communist International: Draft Submitted as a Basis for Discussion at the Fifth Congress of the Communist International." Copy of Bertram D. Wolfe, Delegate from Mexico, New York Public Library.

"Proletariat i voprosy khudozhestvennoi politiki," *Krasnaia nov'*, No. 4, 1925, pp. 263-72.

"Questions of the International Revolutionary Struggle," *Inprecor*, Vol. VI (1926), pp. 830-4, 850-4.

"Rech' na oktiabr'skom plenume TSK i TSKK VKP(b)," *Partiia i oppozitsiia nakanune XV s"ezda VKP(b): sbornik diskussionnykh materialov*. Vol. I. Moscow and Leningrad, 1928, pp. 59-71.

"Rech' tov. Bukharina v germanskoi komissii," *Kommunisticheskii internatsional*, No. 3, 1926, pp. 92-103.

"The Results of the VI World Congress of the C.I.," *Inprecor*, Vol. VIII (1928), pp. 1267-77.

"Revoliutsiia 1905 goda," *Vestnik truda*, No. 12, 1925, pp. 5-8.

"The Russian Revolution and Its Significance," *The Class Struggle*, No. 1, 1917, pp. 14-21.

"The Russian Revolution and Social Democracy," *Inprecor*, Vol. VII (1927), pp. 1527-30.

"Ten Years of Victorious Proletarian Revolution," *Inprecor*, Vol. VII (1927), pp. 1347-55, 1418-23.

"The Tenth Anniversary of the February Revolution," *Inprecor*, Vol. VII (1927), pp. 421-3, 454-7.

"Teoriia 'organizovannoi beskhoziaistvennosti,' " *"Organizovannyi kapitalizm": diskussiia v Komakademii*. 2nd ed. Moscow, 1930, pp. 183-99.

"Theory and Practice from the Standpoint of Dialectical Materialism," *Science at the Cross Roads*. London, 1931, pp. 1-23.

"Twelfth Congress of the Russian C.P.," *The Communist International*, No. 25, 1923, pp. 10-17.

"Sud'by russkoi intelligentsii," *Pechat' i revoliutsiia*, No. 3, 1925, pp. 1-10.

"Uchenie Marksa i ego istoricheskoe znachenie," *Pamiati Karla Marksa: sbornik statei k piatidesiatiletiiu so dnia smerti, 1883-1933*. Moscow, 1933, pp. 9-99.

"Vtoroi internatsional pod flagom 'levogo kommunizma,' " *Bol'shevik*, No. 5-6, 1924, pp. 16-25.

"Za uporiadochenie byta molodezhi," *Byt i molodezh': sbornik statei*. Edited by A. Slepkov. Moscow, 1926, pp. 6-9.

"Znachenie agrarno-krest'ianskoi problemy," *Bol'shevik*, No. 3-4, 1925, pp. 3-17.

II. OFFICIAL PROCEEDINGS

IV vsemirnyi kongress kommunisticheskogo internatsionala. 5 noiabria-3 dekabria 1922 g.: izbrannye doklady, rechi i rezoliutsii. Moscow and Petrograd, 1923.

Chetvertyi vserossiiskii s"ezd professional'nykh soiuzov: stenograficheskii otchet. Moscow, 1922.

Chetyrnadtsataia konferentsiia rossiiskoi kommunisticheskoi partii (bol'shevikov): stenograficheskii otchet. Moscow, 1925.

XIV s"ezd vsesoiuznoi kommunisticheskoi partii(b). 18–31 dekabria 1925 g.: stenograficheskii otchet. Moscow and Leningrad, 1926.

Desiatyi s"ezd RKP(b). Mart 1921 goda: stenograficheskii otchet. Moscow, 1963.

Desiatyi s"ezd RKP(b). Mart–aprel' 1920 goda: protokoly. Moscow, 1960.

IX vsesoiuznyi s"ezd VLKSM: stenograficheskii otchet. Moscow, 1931.

Dvenadtsatyi s"ezd rossiiskoi kommunisticheskoi partii (bol'shevikov): stenograficheskii otchet. Moscow, 1923.

Odinnadtsatyi s"ezd RKP(b). Mart–aprel' 1922 goda: stenograficheskii otchet. Moscow, 1961.

Pervyi kongress Kominterna. Mart 1919. Moscow, 1933.

Pervyi vsesoiuznyi s"ezd sovetskikh pisatelei: stenograficheskii otchet. Moscow, 1934.

XV konferentsiia vsesoiuznoi kommunisticheskoi partii (b) 26 oktiabria–3 noiabria 1926 g.: stenograficheskii otchet. Moscow and Leningrad, 1927.

Piatnadtsatyi s"ezd VKP(b). Dekabr' 1927 goda: stenograficheskii otchet. 2 vols. Moscow, 1961.

Piatyi vsemirnyi kongress kommunisticheskogo internatsionala. 17 iiunia–8 iiulia 1924 g.: stenograficheskii otchet. 2 vols. Moscow and Leningrad, 1925.

Piatyi vserossiiskii s"ezd RKSM: stenograficheskii otchet. Moscow and Leningrad, 1927.

Protokoly tsentral'nogo komiteta RSDRP(b): avgust 1917–fevral' 1918. Moscow, 1958.

Protokoly zasedanii vserossiiskogo tsentral'nogo ispolnitel'nogo komiteta. 4-go sozyva. Moscow, 1920.

Protsess eserov: rechi zashchitnikov i obviniaemykh. 2 vols. Moscow, 1922.

Puti mirovoi revoliutsii. Sed'moi rasshirennyi plenum ispolnitel'nogo komiteta kommunisticheskogo internatsionala: stenograficheskii otchet. 2 vols. Moscow and Leningrad, 1927.

Rasshirennyi plenum ispolkoma kommunisticheskogo internatsionala (21 marta–6 aprelia 1925 g.): stenograficheskii otchet. Moscow and Leningrad, 1925.

Rasshirennyi plenum ispolnitel'nogo komiteta kommunisticheskogo internatsionala (12–23 iiunia 1923 goda): otchet. Moscow, 1923.

Sed'moi ekstrennyi s"ezd RKP(b). Mart 1918 goda: stenograficheskii otchet. Moscow, 1962.

Sed'moi s"ezd professional'nykh soiuzov SSSR: stenograficheskii otchet. Moscow, 1927.

VII s"ezd vsesoiuznogo leninskogo kommunisticheskogo soiuza molodezhi: 11–12 marta 1926 goda. Moscow and Leningrad, 1926.

XVII konferentsiia vsesoiuznoi kommunisticheskoi partii (b): stenograficheskii otchet. Moscow, 1932.

XVII s"ezd vsesoiuznoi kommunisticheskoi partii (b). 26 ianvaria–10 fevralia 1934 g.: stenograficheskii otchet. Moscow, 1934.

Shestnadtsataia konferentsiia VKP(b) aprel' 1929 goda: stenograficheskii otchet. Moscow, 1962.

XVI s"ezd vsesoiuznoi kommunisticheskoi partii: stenograficheskii otchet. 2 vols. Moscow, 1935.

484 · SELECTED BIBLIOGRAPHY

VI kongress Kominterna: stenograficheskii otchet. 6 vols. Moscow and Leningrad, 1929.

Shestoi rasshirennyi plenum ispolkoma Kominterna (17 fevralia–15 marta 1926 g.): stenograficheskii otchet. Moscow and Leningrad, 1927.

Shestoi s"ezd rossiiskogo leninskogo kommunisticheskogo soiuza molodezhi: stenograficheskii otchet. Moscow and Leningrad, 1924.

Shestoi s"ezd RSDRP (bol'shevikov). Avgust 1917 goda: protokoly. Moscow, 1958.

III kongress krasnogo internatsionala profsoiuzov. 8–22 iiulia 1924 g.: otchet. Moscow, 1924.

Tretii vserossiiskii s"ezd professional'nykh soiuzov. 16–13 aprelia 1920 goda: stenograficheskii otchet. Moscow, 1921.

Tretii vserossiiskii s"ezd RKSM 2–10 oktiabria 1920 goda: stenograficheskii otchet. Moscow and Leningrad, 1926.

Trinadtsataia konferentsiia rossiiskoi kommunisticheskoi partii (bol'shevikov): stenograficheskii otchet. Moscow, 1924.

Trinadtsatyi s"ezd RKP(b). Mai 1924 goda: stenograficheskii otchet. Moscow, 1963.

Trudy I vserossiiskogo s"ezda sovetov narodnogo khoziaistva 26-go maia–4 iiunia 1918 g.: stenograficheskii otchet. Moscow, 1918.

Voprosy prepodavaniia leninizma, istorii VKP(b) i Kominterna: stenogrammy soveshchaniia, sozvannogo obshchestvom istorikov—marksistov 9 fevral' 1930 g. Moscow, 1930.

Vos'maia konferentsiia RKP(b). Dekabr' 1919 goda: protokoly. Moscow, 1961.

Vos'moi s"ezd professional'nykh soiuzov SSSR (10–21 dekabria 1928 g.): polnyi stenograficheskii otchet. Moscow, 1929.

Vos'moi s"ezd RKP(b): protokoly. Moscow, 1959.

VIII vsesoiuznyi s"ezd VLKSM. 5–16 maia 1928 goda: stenograficheskii otchet. Moscow, 1928.

Vserossiiskaia konferentsiia RKP(bol'shevikov): biulleten'. No. 1–5. Moscow, 1921.

Vserossiiskoe uchreditel'noe sobranie. Moscow and Leningrad, 1930.

Vtoroi kongress kommunisticheskogo internatsionala: stenograficheskii otchet. Moscow, 1920.

Vtoroi vsesoiuznyi s"ezd kolkhoznikov-udarnikov: stenograficheskii otchet. Moscow, 1935.

III. CONTEMPORARY SOVIET AND OTHER WORKS

Abramov, A. *O pravoi oppozitsii v partii.* Moscow, 1929.

Aikhenval'd, A. *Sovetskaia ekonomika.* Moscow and Leningrad, 1927.

Astrov, V., and A. Slepkov. *Sotsial-demokratiia i revoliutsiia.* Moscow and Leningrad, 1928.

Baevskii, D. "Bol'sheviki v bor'be za III internatsional," *Istorik marksist,* No. 11, 1929, pp. 12–48.

———. "Bor'ba Lenina protiv bukharinskikh 'shatanii mysli,'" *Proletarskaia revoliutsiia,* No. 1(96), 1930, pp. 18–46.

——. "Partiia v gody imperialisticheskoi voiny," *Ocherkii po istorii oktiabr'skoi revoliutsii: raboty istoricheskogo seminariia instituta krasnoi professury.* Edited by M. N. Pokrovskii. Vol. I. Moscow and Leningrad, 1927, pp. 333–518.

Bogdanov, Aleksandr. *Filosofia zhivogo opyta.* Moscow, 1920.

——. *Tektologiia: vseobshchaia organizatsionnaia nauka.* Berlin and Petrograd, 1922.

Bogushevskii, V. "Kanun piatiletki," *God vosemnadtsatyi: al'manakh vos'moi.* Edited by M. Gor'kii. Moscow, 1935, pp. 461–537.

Bol'sheviki: dokumenty po istorii bol'shevizma s 1903 po 1916 god byvsh. moskovsk. okhrannogo otdeleniia. Moscow, 1918.

Bubnov, A. *VKP(b).* Moscow and Leningrad, 1931.

Bukhartsev, D. *Teoreticheskie oruzhenostsy opportunizma: oshibki pravykh v mezhdunarodnykh voprosakh.* Moscow and Leningrad, 1930.

The Case of the Anti-Soviet "Bloc of Rights and Trotskyites": Report of Court Proceedings. Moscow, 1938.

The Case of the Anti-Soviet Trotskyite Centre: Report of Court Proceedings. Moscow, 1937.

The Case of the Trotskyite-Zinovievite Terrorist Centre: Report of Court Proceedings. Moscow, 1936.

Cherniak, I. *Politicheskoe zaveshchanie Lenina v izobrazhenii tov. Bukharina.* Moscow, 1930.

The Crisis in the Communist Party, U.S.A.: Statement of Principles of the Communist Party (Majority Group). New York, 1930.

Deiateli soiuza sovetskikh sotsialisticheskikh respublik: oktiabr'skoi revoliutsii (avtobiografii i biografii): 3 parts. Moscow, 1925–8.

Diskussiia o profsoiuzakh: materialy i dokumenty 1920–1921. Moscow and Leningrad, 1927.

Dunaev, B. A. "V iunosheskie gody," *Piatyi god: sbornik vtoroi.* Edited by M. Miliutina. Moscow and Leningrad, 1926, pp. 16–63.

Dvadtsat' piat' let RKP(b): 1898–1923. Moscow, 1923.

Dzerzhinskii, F. E. *Izbrannye proizvedeniia.* Vol. 2. Moscow, 1957.

Fradkin, Boris. *12 biografii.* Moscow, 1924.

From the First to the Second Five-Year Plan. New York, 1933.

Gaisinskii, M. *Bor'ba s uklonami ot general'noi linii partii: istoricheskii ocherk vnutripartiinoi bor'by posleoktiabr'skogo perioda.* 2nd ed. Moscow and Leningrad, 1931.

Hilferding, Rudolf. *Böhm-Bawerk's Criticism of Marx.* Edited by Paul M. Sweezy. New York, 1949.

——. *Finansovyi kapital: noveishaia faza v razvitii kapitalizma.* 3rd ed. Petersburg, 1918.

History of the Communist Party of the Soviet Union (Bolsheviks): Short Course. New York, 1939.

Hobson, J. A. *Imperialism: A Study.* Ann Arbor, Mich., 1965.

Iaroslavskii, E. *Istoriia VKP(b).* Vol. 4. Moscow and Leningrad, 1929.

Istituto Giangiacomo Feltrinelli. *Annali.* Anno Ottavo. Milano, 1966.

Itogi noiabr'skogo plenuma TSK VKP(b). Leningrad, 1929.

K voprosu o politike RKP(b) v khudozhestvennoi literature. Moscow, 1924.

Kalendar' kommunista na 1929 god. Moscow and Leningrad, 1929.

Kirov, S. M. *Izbrannye stat'i i rechi.* Vol. II. Moscow, 1957.

———. *Stat'i i rechi 1934.* Moscow, 1934.

Kommunist. Geneva, 1915.

Kosarev, A. *Komsomol v rekonstruktivnyi period.* Moscow, 1931.

Kozelev, B. *Mikhail Pavlovich Tomskii: biograficheskii ocherk.* Moscow, 1927.

———. "Slavnyi iubilei (k 20-letiiu revoliutsionnoi deiatel'nosti M. P. Tomskogo)," *Vestnik truda,* No. 1, 1925, pp. 18–39.

KPSS v rezoliutsiiakh i resheniiakh s"ezdov, konferentsii i plenumov TSK. Parts II–III. Moscow, 1954.

Kritsman, L. *Geroicheskii period velikoi russkoi revoliutsii (opyt analiza t.n. 'voennogo kommunizma').* 2nd ed. Moscow and Leningrad, 1926.

Krupskaya, Nadezhda K. *Memories of Lenin.* 2 vols. New York, n.d.

Krylov, S., and A. Zykov. *O pravoi opasnosti.* 2nd ed. Moscow and Leningrad, 1929.

Leman, N., and S. Pokrovskii. *Ideinye istoki pravogo uklona: ob oshibkakh i uklonakh tov. Bukharina.* 2nd ed. Leningrad, 1930.

Lenin, V. I. *Polnoe sobranie sochinenii.* 5th ed.; 55 vols. Moscow, 1958– .

———. *Selected Works.* 3 vols. Moscow, 1960.

———. *Sochineniia.* 3rd ed.; 30 vols. Moscow, 1928–37.

Leningradskaia organizatsiia i chetyrnadtsatyi s"ezd: sbornik materialov i dokumentov. Moscow and Leningrad, 1926.

Leninskii sbornik. 33 vols. Moscow, 1924–40.

Lentsner, N. *O pravoi opasnosti v Kominterne.* 2nd ed. Moscow and Leningrad, 1929.

Leont'ev, A. *Ekonomicheskaia teoriia pravogo uklona.* Moscow and Leningrad, 1929.

Letter of an Old Bolshevik: The Kev to the Moscow Trials. New York, 1937.

London, Jack. *The Iron Heel.* New York, 1957.

Lyons, Eugene. *Assignment in Utopia.* New York, 1937.

Maretskii, D. "Nikolai Ivanovich Bukharin," *Bol'shaia sovetskaia entsiklopediia.* 1st ed. Vol. VIII. Moscow, 1926, pp. 271–84.

Marksizm i s.-kh. kooperatsiia: sbornik osnovnykh materialov po voprosam s.-kh. kooperatsii ot Marksa do nashikh dnei. Moscow, 1928.

Meshcheriakov, N. "Nikolai Ivanovich Bukharin," *Malaia sovetskaia entsiklopediia.* Vol. I. Moscow, 1929, pp. 912–15.

Miliutin, V. *Agrarnaia politika SSSR.* Moscow and Leningrad, 1926.

Na fronte istoricheskoi nauki. Moscow, 1936.

Novaia oppozitsiia: sbornik materialov o diskussii 1925 goda. Leningrad, 1926.

O perestroike partiino-politicheskoi raboty: k itogam plenuma TSK VKP(b) 1937 g. Moscow, 1937.

Ob ekonomicheskoi platforme oppozitsii: sbornik statei. Moscow and Leningrad, 1926.

Oktiabr'skoe vosstanie v Moskve. Edited by N. Ovsiannikov. Moscow, 1922.

Ordzhonikidze, G. K. *Stat'i i rechi.* Vol. II. Moscow, 1957.

Osinskii, N. *Stroitel'stvo sotsializma.* Moscow, 1918.

Pamiati V. I. Lenina: sbornik statei k desiatiletiiu so dnia smerti 1924–1934. Moscow and Leningrad, 1934.

Platform of the Left Opposition. London, 1963.

Politbiuro TS.K. V.K.P.(b): biografii. Moscow, 1928.

Polonskii, Viacheslav. *Ocherki literaturnogo dvizheniia revoliutsionnoi epokhi*. 2nd ed. Moscow and Leningrad, 1929.

Popov, K. *Diskussiia 1923 goda: materialy i dokumenty*. Moscow and Leningrad, 1927.

Popov, N. *Ocherki istorii vsesoiuznoi kommunisticheskoi partii*. Moscow and Leningrad, 1927.

———. *Outline History of the Communist Party of the Soviet Union*. 2 vols. New York, 1934.

Preobrazhensky, E. *The New Economics*. London, 1965.

Put' k oktiabriu: sbornik statei, vospominanii i dokumentov. 5 vols; Moscow, 1923–26.

Reed, John. *Ten Days That Shook the World*. New York, 1935.

Rykov, A. I. *Derevnia, novaia ekonomicheskaia politika i kooperatsiia*. Moscow and Leningrad, 1925.

———. *Khoziaistvennoe polozhenie SSSR*. Moscow and Leningrad, 1928.

———. *Na perelome*. Moscow, 1925.

———. *Stat'i i rechi*. 2 vols. Moscow and Leningrad, 1927–8.

Selektor, M. E. *Dialekticheskii materializm i teoriia ravnovesiia*. Moscow, 1934.

Shatskin, L. "VLKSM," *Bol'shaia sovetskaia entsiklopediia*. 1st ed. Vol. XI. Moscow, 1930, pp. 618–48.

Sidorov, A. "Ekonomicheskaia programma oktiabria i diskussiia s 'levymi kommunistami' o zadachakh sotsialisticheskogo stroitel'stva," *Proletarskaia revoliutsiia*, No. 6(89) and No. 11(94), 1929, pp. 26–75, 26–64.

Slepkov, A. *Kronshtadtskii miatezh (k sed'moi godovshchine)*. Moscow and Leningrad, 1928.

Sorin, V. *Bor'ba Bukharina i Rykova protiv partii Lenina-Stalina*. Moscow, 1937.

———. *Partiia i oppozitsiia: iz istorii oppozitsionnykh techenii (fraktsiia levykh kommunistov)*. Moscow, 1925.

Stalin, I. V. *Voprosy leninizma*. 4th ed. Moscow and Leningrad, 1928.

———. *Works*. 13 Vols. Moscow, 1952–5.

Stalin: sbornik statei k piatidesiatiletiiu so dnia rozhdeniia. Moscow and Leningrad, 1929.

Sukhanov, N. N. *The Russian Revolution 1917: Eyewitness Account*. 2 vols. New York, 1962.

1917 god v Moskve (khronika revoliutsii). Moscow, 1934.

Tiushevskii, N. *Vnutripartiinyi rezhim i pravyi uklon: na trotskistskikh pozitsiiakh v orgvoprosakh*. Leningrad, 1929.

Trotsky, Leon. *My Life*. New York, 1960.

———. *The History of the Russian Revolution*. 3 vols. New York, 1937.

———. *The New Course*. London, 1956.

———. *O Lenine*. Moscow, 1924.

———. *Problems of the Chinese Revolution*. Ann Arbor, Mich., 1967.

——. *The Real Situation in Russia*. New York, 1928.

——. *Stalin*. New York, 1941.

——. *The Stalin School of Falsification*. New York, 1962.

——. *The Third International After Lenin*. New York, 1957.

——. *Whither Russia: Towards Capitalism or Socialism?* New York, 1926.

Trudy instituta krasnoi professury. Edited by M. N. Pokrovskii. Vol. I. Moscow and Petrograd, 1923.

Ul'ianova, M. *O Lenine*. Moscow, 1964.

Ustrialov, N. *Pod znakom revoliutsii*. 2nd ed. Harbin, 1927.

Vereshchagin, Iv. *Predsedatel' soveta narodnykh kommissarov: Aleksei Ivanovich Rykov*. 3rd ed. Moscow and Leningrad, 1925.

Vladimirova, Vera, *et al. Revoliutsiia 1917 goda (khronika sobytii)*. 6 vols. Moscow and Leningrad, 1927–29?.

Vol'fson, S. "Nikolai Ivanovich Bukharin," *Literaturnaia entsiklopediia*. Vol. I. Moscow, 1929, pp. 631–4.

Vsia Moskva 1927. 3 vols. Moscow, 1927.

Za leninizm: sbornik statei. Moscow and Leningrad, 1925.

Za marksistsko-leninskoe uchenie o pechati. Moscow, 1932.

Za povorot na filosofskom fronte: sbornik statei. Vol. I. Moscow and Leningrad, 1931.

Zaitsev, A. *Ob Ustrialove, "neonepe" i zhertvakh ustrialovshchiny*. Moscow and Leningrad, 1928.

Zalezhskii, V. "Nikolai Ivanovich Bukharin," *Malaia sovetskaia entsiklopediia*. 2nd ed. Vol. II. Moscow, 1934, pp. 173–6.

Zapiski kommunisticheskogo universiteta imeni Ia. M. Sverdlova. Vol. II. Moscow, 1924.

IV. SCHOLARLY AND OTHER WORKS

Abramovitch, Raphael. *The Soviet Revolution 1917–1939*. New York, 1962.

Aleksandrov [pseudo]. *Kto upravliaet Rossiei?* Berlin, 1933.

Alliluyeva, Svetlana. *Twenty Letters to a Friend*. New York, 1967.

Astrov, Valentin. *Krucha (roman)*. Moscow, 1969.

——. *Ogni vperedi*. Moscow, 1967.

Avrich, Paul. *Kronstadt 1921*. Princeton, N.J., 1970.

Avtorkhanov, Abdurakhman. *Stalin and the Soviet Communist Party: A Study in the Technology of Power*. New York, 1959.

Bauer, Raymond A. *The New Man in Soviet Psychology*. Cambridge, Mass., 1952.

Berger, Joseph. *Nothing But the Truth*. New York, 1971.

Bernstein, Eduard. *Evolutionary Socialism*. New York, 1965.

Bogdenko, M. L. "Kolkhoznoe stroitel'stvo vesnoi i letom 1930 g.," *Istoricheskie zapiski*, No. 76 (1965), pp. 17–41.

Borkenau, Franz. *World Communism: A History of the Communist International*. Ann Arbor, Mich., 1962.

Bottomore, T. B. "Karl Marx, Sociologist or Marxist?," *Science and Society* (Winter 1966), pp. 11–24.

———, and Maximilian Rubel. *Karl Marx: Selected Writings in Sociology and Social Philosophy.* New York, 1964.

Brown, Edward J. *The Proletarian Episode in Russian Literature.* New York, 1953.

Bunyan, John, and H. H. Fisher. *The Bolshevik Revolution 1917–1918: Documents and Materials.* Stanford, Calif., 1934.

Carr, E. H. *The Bolshevik Revolution.* 3 vols. New York, 1951–3.

———, and R. W. Davies. *Foundations of a Planned Economy.* 2 vols. New York, 1969–71.

———. *The Interregnum: 1923–1924.* New York, 1954.

———. *Socialism in One Country.* 3 vols. New York, 1958–64.

Chamberlin, William Henry. *The Russian Revolution: 1917–1921.* 2 vols. New York, 1960.

Chigrinov, G. A. *Razgrom partiei pravykh kapituliantov.* Moscow, 1969.

Conquest, Robert. *The Great Terror: Stalin's Purge of the Thirties.* New York, 1968.

Dahrendorf, Ralf. *Class and Class Conflict in Industrial Society.* Stanford, Calif., 1966.

———. "Out of Utopia: Toward a Reorientation of Sociological Analysis," *The American Journal of Sociology,* LXIV (September 1958), pp. 115–27.

Dan, L. "Bukharin o Staline," *Novyi zhurnal,* No. 75 (1964), pp. 176–84.

Daniels, Robert V. *The Conscience of the Revolution: Communist Opposition in Soviet Russia.* Cambridge, 1960.

———, ed. *A Documentary History of Communism.* 2 vols. New York, 1962.

———. *Red October: The Bolshevik Revolution of 1917.* New York, 1967.

———. "The 'Withering Away of the State' in Theory and Practice," *Soviet Society: A Book of Readings.* Edited by Alex Inkles and Kent Geiger. Boston, 1961, pp. 22–43.

Danilov, V. P. "K kharakteristike obshchestvenno-politicheskoi obstanovki v sovetskoi derevne nakanune kollektivizatsii," *Istoricheskie zapiski,* No. 79 (1966), pp. 3–49.

———. "Kolkhoznoe dvizhenie nakanune sploshnoi kollektivizatsii (1927 g.–pervaia polovina 1929 g.)," *Istoricheskie zapiski,* No. 80 (1967), pp. 28–81.

———, ed. *Ocherki istorii kollektivizatsii sel'skogo khoziaistva v soiuznykh respublikakh.* Moscow, 1963.

Deutscher, Isaac. *The Prophet Armed: Trotsky, 1879–1921.* New York and London, 1954.

———. *The Prophet Outcast: Trotsky, 1929–1940.* London and New York, 1963.

———. *The Prophet Unarmed: Trotsky, 1921–1929.* London and New York, 1959.

———. *Soviet Trade Unions.* London, 1950.

———. *Stalin: A Political Biography.* 2nd ed. New York, 1967.

Dobb, Maurice. *Russian Economic Development Since the Revolution.* London, 1928.

———. *Soviet Economic Development Since 1917.* New York, 1966.

Drachkovitch, Milorad M., and Branko Lazitch. *The Comintern: Historical Highlights.* New York, 1966.

Draper, Theodore. *American Communism and Soviet Russia: The Formative Period.* New York, 1960.

———. "The Ghost of Social-Fascism," *Commentary* (February 1969), pp. 29–42.

———. *The Roots of American Communism.* New York, 1957.

———. "The Strange Case of the Comintern," *Survey* (Summer 1972), pp. 91–137.

Drobizhev, V. Z. *Glavnyi shtab sotsialisticheskoi promyshlennosti: ocherk istorii VSNKH 1917–1932 gg.* Moscow, 1966.

Dvinov, B. *Moskovskoi sovet rabochikh deputatov 1917–1922: vospominaniia.* New York, 1961.

Eastman, Max. *Love and Revolution: My Journey Through an Epoch.* New York, 1964.

Ehrenburg, Ilya. *Memoirs: 1921–1941.* Cleveland and New York, 1964.

———. *People and Life: 1891–1923.* Moscow, 1962.

Erlich, Alexander. *The Soviet Industrialization Debate, 1924–1928.* Cambridge, 1960.

———. "Stalin's Views on Soviet Economic Development," *Continuity and Change in Russian and Soviet Thought.* Edited by Ernest J. Simmons. Cambridge, 1955, pp. 81–99.

Ermolaev, Herman. *Soviet Literary Theories 1917–1934: The Genesis of Socialist Realism.* Berkeley, Calif., 1963.

Fainsod, Merle. *Smolensk Under Soviet Rule.* Cambridge, 1958.

Fischer, Louis. *The Life of Lenin.* New York, 1964.

Fischer, Markoosha. *My Lives in Russia.* New York, 1944.

Fisher, Ruth. *Stalin and German Communism.* Cambridge, 1948.

Fitzpatrick, Sheila. *The Commissariat of Enlightenment: Soviet Organization of Education and the Arts Under Lunacharsky.* Cambridge, England, 1970.

Fotieva, L. A. *Iz vospominanii o V. I. Lenine.* Moscow, 1964.

Futrell, Michael. *Northern Underground.* New York, 1963.

Gankin, Olga Hess, and H. H. Fisher. *The Bolsheviks and the World War: The Origin of the Third International.* Stanford, Calif., 1940.

Gay, Peter. *The Dilemma of Democratic Socialism: Eduard Bernstein's Challenge to Marx.* New York, 1962.

Graham, Loren R. *The Soviet Academy of Sciences and the Communist Party: 1927–1932.* Princeton, N.J., 1967.

Gramsci, Antonio. *The Modern Prince and Other Writings.* New York, 1959.

The Great Purge Trial. Edited by Robert C. Tucker and Stephen F. Cohen. New York, 1965.

Heitman, Sidney. "Between Lenin and Stalin: Nikolai Bukharin," *Revisionism: Essays on the History of Marxist Ideas.* Edited by Leopold Labedz. New York, 1962, pp. 77–90.

———. "The Myth of Bukharin's Anarchism," *The Rocky Mountain Social Science Journal* (April 1963), pp. 39–53.

Hilferding, Rudolf. "State Capitalism or Totalitarian State Economy?" *Verdict of Three Decades.* Edited by Julian Steinberg. New York, 1950, pp. 445–53.

Höglund, Gunhild. *Moskva tur och retur: En dramatisk period i Zeth Höglunds liv.* Stockholm, 1960.

Hughes, H. Stuart. *Consciousness and Society: The Reorientation of European Social Thought, 1890–1930.* New York, 1961.

Humbert-Droz, Jules. *De Lénine à Staline: dix ans service de l'internationale communiste, 1921–1931.* Neuchâtel, 1971.

———. *"L'oeil de Moscou" à Paris.* Paris, 1964.

Iroshnikov, M. P. *Sozdanie sovetskogo tsentral'nogo gosudarstvennogo apparata.* Moscow and Leningrad, 1966.

Istoriia kommunisticheskoi partii sovetskogo soiuza. Vol. IV. Moscow, 1970.

Istoriia sovetskogo krest'ianstva i kolkhoznogo stroitel'stva SSSR. Moscow, 1963.

Ivanov, V. M. *Iz istorii bor'by partii protiv 'levogo opportunizma': leningradskaia partiinaia organizatsiia v bor'be protiv trotskistsko-zinov'evskoi oppozitsii v 1925–1926 gg.* Leningrad, 1965.

———, and A. N. Shmelev. *Leninizm i ideino-politicheskii razgrom trotskizma.* Leningrad, 1970.

Iz istorii bor'by leninskoi partii protiv opportunizma. Moscow, 1966.

Jackson, George D., Jr. *Comintern and Peasant in East Europe 1919–1930.* New York and London, 1966.

Jasny, Naum. *Soviet Economists of the Twenties.* New York, 1972.

———. *Soviet Industrialization: 1928–1952.* Chicago, 1961.

Joravsky, David. *Soviet Marxism and Natural Science: 1917–1932.* New York, 1961.

Jordan, Z. A. *The Evolution of Dialectical Materialism.* New York, 1967.

Katkov, George. *The Trial of Bukharin.* New York, 1969.

Kaufman, Adam. "The Origin of 'The Political Economy of Socialism': An Essay on Soviet Economic Thought," *Soviet Studies,* No. 3, 1953, pp. 243–72.

Keep, J. L. H. *The Rise of Social Democracy in Russia.* London, 1963.

Kharmandarian, S. V. *Lenin i stanovlenie zakavkazskoi federatsii, 1921–1923.* Erevan, 1969.

Khavin, A. F. *U rulia industrii.* Moscow, 1968.

Khrushchev, Nikita S. *The Crimes of the Stalin Era.* New York, 1956.

Kitaeff, Michael. *Communist Party Officials: A Group of Portraits.* New York, 1954.

Knirsch, Peter. *Die ökonomischen Anschauungen Nikolaj I. Bucharins.* Berlin, 1959.

Koestler, Arthur. *Darkness at Noon.* New York, 1961.

Kommunisticheskii internatsional: kratkii istoricheskii ocherk. Moscow, 1969.

Koniukhov, G. *KPSS v bor'be s khlebnymi zatrudneniiami v strane (1928–1929).* Moscow, 1960.

Kuibysheva, G. V., et al. *Valerian Vladimirovich Kuibyshev: biografiia.* Moscow, 1966.

Leites, Nathan, and Elsa Bernaut. *Ritual of Liquidation.* Glencoe, Ill., 1954.

Lerner, Warren. *Karl Radek: The Last Internationalist.* Stanford, Calif., 1970.

Lewin, Moshe. *Lenin's Last Struggle.* New York, 1968.

———. *Russian Peasants and Soviet Power: A Study of Collectivization.* Evanston, Ill., 1968.

Liberman, Simon. *Building Lenin's Russia.* Chicago, 1945.

Lichtheim, George. *Marxism: An Historical and Critical Study.* New York, 1962.

Löwy, A. G. *Die Weltgeschichte ist das Weltgericht. Bucharin: Vision des Kommunismus.* Vienna, 1969.

M. I. Ul'ianov—sekretar' Pravdy. Moscow, 1965.

MacLean, Fitzroy. *Escape to Adventure.* Boston, 1950.

Maguire, Robert. *Red Virgin Soil: Soviet Literature in the 1920's.* Princeton, N.J., 1968.

Mandelstam, Nadezhda. *Hope Against Hope: A Memoir.* New York, 1970.

Marx, Karl. *Capital.* 2 vols. Moscow, 1958–61.

———, and Frederick Engels. *Selected Works.* 2 vols. Moscow, 1955.

McKenzie, Kermit E. *Comintern and World Revolution 1928–1943: The Shaping of Doctrine.* New York, 1964.

Medvedev, Roy A. *Let History Judge: The Origins and Consequences of Stalinism.* New York, 1971.

Mel'gunov, S. *Kak bol'sheviki zakhvatili vlast': oktiabr'skii perevorot 1917 goda.* Paris, 1953.

Mil'chakov, A. *Pervoe desiatiletie: zapiski veterana Komsomola.* 2nd ed. Moscow, 1965.

Mints, I. I. *Istoriia velikogo oktiabria.* Vol. I. Moscow, 1967.

Moshkov, Iu. A. *Zernovaia problema v gody sploshnoi kollektivizatsii sel'skogo khoziaistva SSSR (1929–1932 gg.).* Moscow, 1966.

Moskovskie bol'sheviki v bor'be s pravym i "levym" opportunizmom: 1921–1929 gg. Moscow, 1969.

Narkiewicz, Olga A. *The Making of the Soviet State Apparatus.* Manchester, England, 1970.

Nemakov, N. I. *Kommunisticheskaia partiia—organizator massovogo kolkhoznogo dvizheniia (1929–1932 gg.).* Moscow, 1966.

Nicolaevsky, Boris I. *Power and the Soviet Elite: "The Letter of an Old Bolshevik" and Other Essays.* New York, 1965.

———. "Problema destalinizatsii i delo Bukharina," *Sotsialisticheskii vestnik.* Collection No. 4 (December 1965), pp. 22–38.

Nove, Alec. *An Economic History of the U.S.S.R.* London and Baltimore, 1969.

———. "Was Stalin Really Necessary?," *Encounter* (April 1962), pp. 86–92.

Ocherki istorii kommunisticheskoi partii Ukrainy. 2nd ed. Kiev, 1964.

Ocherki istorii leningradskoi organizatsii KPSS. Vol. II. Leningrad, 1968.

Ocherki istorii moskovskoi organizatsii KPSS: 1883–1965. Moscow, 1966.

Orlov, Alexander. *Secret History of Stalin's Crimes.* New York, 1953.

Pipes, Richard. *The Formation of the Soviet Union: Communism and Nationalism, 1917–1923.* Cambridge, 1954.

Pollack, Frederick. "State Capitalism: Its Possibilities and Limitations," *Studies in Philosophy and Social Science,* No. 2, 1941, pp. 200–25.

Reswick, William. *I Dreamt Revolution.* Chicago, 1952.

Revisionism: Essays on the History of Marxist Ideas. Edited by Leopold Labedz. New York, 1962.

Rosmer, Alfred. *Moscou sous Lénine: les Origines du Communisme.* Paris, 1953.

Schapiro, Leonard. *The Communist Party of the Soviet Union.* New York, 1960.

———. *The Origin of the Communist Autocracy.* Cambridge, 1956.

Schwartz, Benjamin I. *Chinese Communism and the Rise of Mao.* New York, 1967.

Serge, Victor. *Memoirs of a Revolutionary: 1901–1941.* London, 1963.

Shub, David. *Lenin.* Garden City, N.J., 1949.

Slusser, Robert M. "The Role of the Foreign Ministry," *Russian Foreign Policy.* Edited by Ivo J. Lededer. New Haven, Conn., 1962., pp. 197–239.

Sorenson, Jay B. *The Life and Death of Soviet Trade Unionism: 1917–1928.* New York, 1969.

Sorokin, Pitirim. "Russian Sociology in the Twentieth Century," *American Sociological Society: Papers and Proceedings,* XXI (1926), pp. 57–69.

Souvarine, Boris. *Stalin: A Critical Survey of Bolshevism.* New York, 1939.

Soviet Sociology: Historical Antecedents and Current Appraisals. Edited by Alex Simirenko. Chicago, 1966.

Spulber, Nicolas. *Soviet Strategy for Economic Growth.* Bloomington, Ind., 1964.

Sweezy, Paul M. *The Theory of Capitalist Development: Principles of Marxian Political Economy.* New York, 1942.

Tetiushev, V. I. "Bor'ba partii za general'nuiu liniiu protiv pravogo uklona v VKP(b) v period mezhdu XV i XVI s"ezdami," *Vestnik moskovskogo universiteta.* Series IX. No. 3, 1961, pp. 3–25.

Thompson, J. M. *Leaders of the French Revolution.* New York, 1967.

Trukan, G. A. *Oktiabr' v tsentral'noi Rossii.* Moscow, 1967.

Tucker, Robert C. *The Marxian Revolutionary Idea.* New York, 1969.

———. *The Soviet Political Mind.* Revised edition. New York, 1971.

———. *Stalin as Revolutionary: A Study in History and Personality.* New York, 1973.

Ulam, Adam. *The Bolsheviks: The Intellectual and Political History of the Triumph of Communism in Russia.* New York, 1965.

Uralov, Alexander. *The Reign of Stalin.* London, 1953.

Vaganov, F. M. *Pravyi uklon v VKP(b) i ego razgrom (1928–1930).* Moscow, 1970.

———. "Razgrom pravogo uklona v VKP(b) (1928–1930 gg.)," *Voprosy istorii KPSS,* No. 4, 1960, pp. 62–80.

Valentinov (Vol'skii), N. *Doktrina pravogo kommunizma.* Munich, 1960.

———. *Novaia ekonomicheskaia politika i krizis partii posle smerti Lenina: vospominaniia.* Stanford, Calif., 1971.

Viatkin, A. Ia. *Razgrom kommunisticheskoi partiei trotskizma i drugikh antileninskikh grupp.* Part I. Leningrad, 1966.

Vsesoiuznoe soveshchanie o merakh uluchsheniia podgotovki nauchno—pedagogicheskikh kadrov po istoricheskim naukam: 18–21 dekabria 1962 g. Moscow, 1964.

Weissberg, Alexander. *The Accused.* New York, 1951.

Wetter, Gustav A. *Dialectical Materialism.* New York, 1958.

Wolfe, Bertram D. *Khrushchev and Stalin's Ghost.* New York, 1957.

———. *Three Who Made a Revolution.* Boston, 1955.

Wolin, Simon, and Robert M. Slusser. *The Soviet Secret Police.* New York, 1957.

Ypsilon. *Pattern for World Revolution.* Chicago, 1947.

V. UNPUBLISHED MATERIALS

Denike, Iurii P. Interview No. 16–17. Unpublished manuscript, The Menshevik Project, Columbia University, June 11 and October 25, 1963.

Flaherty, John E. "The Political Career of Nicolas Bukharin to 1929." Unpublished Ph.D. dissertation, New York University, 1954.

Heitman, Sidney. "Bukharin's Conception of the Transition to Communism in Soviet Russia: An Analysis of His Basic Views, 1923–1928." Unpublished Ph.D. dissertation, Columbia University, 1963.

Katz, Zev. "Party-Political Education in Soviet Russia." Unpublished Ph.D. dissertation, University of London.

Nikolaevsky, Boris I. Private communications with author, 1963–5.

Sorenson, Jay Bertram. "The Dilemma of Soviet Trade Unions During the First Period of Industrial Transformation: 1917–1928." Unpublished Ph.D. dissertation, Columbia University, 1962.

Trotsky, Leon. The Trotsky Archives. Unpublished materials, Houghton Library, Harvard University.

Vol'skii, N. N. "Memoirs." Unpublished manuscript, Russian and East European Archives, Columbia University, 1956.

VI. PERIODICALS

Biulleten' oppozitsii

Bol'shevik

The Communist International

The Communist Review

International Press Correspondence

Istoricheskie zapiski

Istoricheskii arkhiv

Istorik marksist

Izvestiia

Kommunist (Moscow, 1918)

Kommunisticheskaia revoliutsiia

Kommunisticheskii internatsional

Krasnaia nov'

Krasnaia pechat'

Molodaia gvardiia

Novyi mir (New York)

Novyi zhurnal

Pechat' i revoliutsiia

Pod znamenem marksizma

Pravda

Proletarskaia revoliutsiia

Prozhektor

Sotsialisticheskaia rekonstruktsiia i nauka

Sotsialisticheskii vestnik

Soviet Russia

Soviet Studies

Survey

Vestnik kommunisticheskoi akademii

Voprosy istorii

Voprosy istorii KPSS

Za industrializatsiiu

INDEX

INDEX

A Note About the Author

Stephen F. Cohen was born in Indiana in 1938 and grew up in Kentucky. He received his B.S. and M.A. degrees from Indiana University and, in 1969, his Ph.D. and Russian Institute Certificate from Columbia University. From 1965 to 1968 Professor Cohen taught at Columbia College, and since 1968 he has been in the Department of Politics of Princeton University, where he is now an associate professor. Professor Cohen was co-editor with Robert C. Tucker of *The Great Purge Trial*, published in 1965. He lives with his wife and two children in New York City.